The Copyright Wars

The Copyright Wars

THREE CENTURIES OF TRANS-ATLANTIC BATTLE

Peter Baldwin

PRINCETON UNIVERSITY PRESS

PRINCETON AND OXFORD

Published by Princeton University Press, 41 William Street, Princeton, New Jersey 08540
In the United Kingdom: Princeton University Press, 6 Oxford Street, Woodstock,
Oxfordshire OX20 1TW

press.princeton.edu

Jacket design by Leslie Flis

Library of Congress Cataloging-in-Publication Data

Baldwin, Peter, 1956– author.
   The copyright wars : three centuries of trans-Atlantic battle / Peter Baldwin.
     pages cm
   Includes bibliographical references and index.
   ISBN 978-0-691-16182-2 (alk. paper)
   1. Copyright—Europe—History. 2. Copyright—United States—History. I. Title.
   K1420.5.B359 2014
   346.404′82–dc23   2013049603

British Library Cataloging-in-Publication Data is available

This book has been composed in Sabon Next LT Pro and Scala Sans OT display

Printed on acid-free paper. ∞

Printed in the United States of America

10 9 8 7 6 5 4 3 2 1

For

Tom
Jemima
Daniel
Sam
Sigi
Lucy
Ben

the next generation of my unexpected family

Contents

Introduction: The Agon of Author and Audience   1

1. The Battle between Anglo-American Copyright and European
Authors' Rights   14

2. From Royal Privilege to Literary Property: A Common Start to
Copyright in the Eighteenth Century   53

3. The Ways Part: Copyright and Authors' Rights in
the Nineteenth Century   82

4. Continental Drift: Europe Moves from Property to Personality
at the Turn of the Century   126

5. The Strange Birth of Moral Rights in Fascist Europe   163

6. The Postwar Apotheosis of Authors' Rights   199

7. America Turns European: The Battle of the Booksellers Redux
in the 1990s   262

8. The Rise of the Digital Public: The Copyright Wars Continue
in the New Millennium   318

Conclusion: Reclaiming the Spirit of Copyright   383

Acknowledgments   411

Notes   413

Index   513

The Copyright Wars

Introduction

In 1948 several Soviet composers, including Dmitri Shostakovich, objected to the use of their music in an American spy film, *The Iron Curtain*, that was distinctly anti-Communist. These Soviet composers understandably feared the gulag for appearing in Hollywood's first Cold War effort.[1] Though their music was unchanged, they protested its political use. When Shostakovich sued in the United States, he failed. The works were in the public domain, thus freely available for anyone's use, the composer had been credited, the film did not claim that he agreed with its views, and the music had not been distorted. How, the court asked, had the artist's rights been violated? "Is the standard to be good taste, artistic worth, political beliefs, moral concepts, or what is it to be?"[2] But in France a court ascertained "moral damage." The film was banned and the composers were awarded damages.

In 1988 the director John Huston sued to prevent the *Asphalt Jungle*, which he had filmed in 1950 in black and white, from being shown on television in a colorized version. In the United States, according to the work-for-hire doctrine, the film studio—and not the director it employs—is the author. But in France, after Huston's death that year, his children and his screenwriter invoked the continuing aesthetic claims, or "moral rights," that remain with authors in French law even after they have sold their works. Over the next six years, five different French courts first prevented screening, then allowed the film to be broadcast only if the director's objections were publicized, and finally levied hefty fines on Turner Entertainment, the errant colorizers.[3]

Prince Michael of Greece, related through his mother to a family that still pretends to the long-abolished French throne, writes histories and historical novels. *La nuit du sérail* (1982) was ghostwritten with Anne Bragance, who signed a work-for-hire contract under New York law, renouncing her moral rights, including that of being named as a coauthor.[4] When sales of the book took off, however, Bragance sought not only a more generous slice of the proceeds but also to be named as coauthor—and in typeface larger than the putative author. Since in French law the author's moral rights cannot be alienated, a French court set aside her contractual obligations. She won a place next to the prince on the title page of French editions, though not more of the royalties, nor any font-size favoritism.[5]

Samuel Beckett gave famously precise stage directions. He objected, for example, when directors performed his plays with women, non-white casts, or incidental music.[6] He sued the American Repertory Theater in Cambridge for playing *Endgame* in an abandoned Boston subway station and the Comedie Française for doing so on a set bathed in pink light.[7] Female Vladimirs and Estragons were pursued in Paris, Holland, Nashville, and Pontedera. Beckett also quibbled about stagings of *Godot* in Dublin, London, Salzburg, Berlin, and Miami.[8] In Avignon in 1991, *Godot* was allowed a female cast—as long as the estate's letter of objection was read aloud at each performance.[9] "Women don't have prostates," Beckett insisted, alluding to Vladimir's constant urination.[10] In Nashville, Avignon, and Pontedera, the theaters cravenly argued that, though played by women, the characters remained male.[11] In Australia, with the use of music at issue, the director pushed back more robustly, complaining that "in coming here with its narrow prescriptions, its dead controlling hand, the Beckett estate seems to me to be the enemy of art."[12]

None of these events was earth shattering. Yet each speaks to a view of the position of authors in society—their rights in their works, their relationship to their interpreters, performers, and audiences, and their power to enforce their claims. As Congress considered giving American authors similar claims in 1987, Sydney Pollack, director of *Tootsie*, *Out of Africa*, and other popular movies, testified that "this is a debate about the dignity with which society regards artists and the value society places on the integrity of artistic endeavors."[13]

More generally, such disputes pose the basic dilemma of intellectual property. Intellectual works are both the property of their creators and society's cultural patrimony. How to resolve this inherent tension? The author seeks fame, recognition, and reward. The audience wants easy, cheap, and quick access to a cultural cornucopia worth treasuring. Too little reward and authors are discouraged. Kept from its culture by too high prices or overly narrow access, the audience is stunted. The *pas de trois* among author, audience, and the disseminators who mediate between the two is delicate. How to strike the right balance between rewarding authors to stay productive yet also letting in the audience, whose cultural engagement is, after all, the authors' presumed goal? The interests have to be weighed against each other. But whether the angle has tilted in the authors' or the audience's favor has varied, both over the course of copyright's development and among nations.

These anecdotes illustrate two broader points. First, seen historically, from the eighteenth century to the present, rights holders—whether authors or disseminators—have won an ever-stronger stake in their works. In certain nations some claims remain with the author and his estate perpetually. But in all countries rights have been continually extended on their owners' behalf. The first British (1710) and American (1790) copyright laws gave authors rights over verbatim copies of their writings for fourteen years after publication. As of 1993 in the European Union and 1998 in the United States, that had expanded to seventy years after the author's death, not only for the primary work but also for all manner of other works derived from it. Assuming that authors live the same seventy-nine years as the average American, they, their heirs and—most often—their assignees now generally own works for well over a century.

Over the past three centuries the single most common complaint voiced by authors in defense of their prerogatives has been the alleged contrast between how conventional property belongs to its owners forever while works of the mind are the author's and his heirs' for only a limited time before they join the public domain, free for all to use. Why, countless authors have demanded to know, do we not own our works perpetually, able to pass them to our descendants, just as others can with their houses, factories, or farms?[14] But this is authorial bellyaching. Intellectual property has in fact come to be treated *more* favorably than its conventional cousins, especially real property. First and foremost, unlike real estate the value of a copyright is not taxed.[15] California (to take just one example) assesses annual property taxes at 1 percent of sales prices. The state thus takes your house, or at least its cash value, once every century.[16] In the European Union and the United States, the author's estate loses the work to the public domain seventy years after death. Excepting the occasional modern Mozart, dead at thirty-five, authors thus "own" their works for longer than they do their houses. In the nineteenth century it was, in fact, suggested as a reasonable trade-off that, if literary property were granted perpetual protection, as many demanded, it should also be taxed.[17] But since it is not, it is hard to spot why its truncated protection is unfair. By contrast, it is certainly easy to see the social benefits of open access and an expansive public domain.

Not only does copyright today last a very long time, it is now also granted much more easily, indeed automatically. The first copyright laws required authors to jump burdensome bureaucratic hoops to assert their claims: application, registration, deposit, and the like. Yet, as of 1908, all member states of the first international copyright union, the Berne Convention, were obliged to grant copyright without any formalities whatsoever. Every scribble, doodle, and bathtub aria was thus a protected work as of its creation. The shopping list on the fridge is as copyrighted as Dan Brown's latest blockbuster. Previously, all works used to be born into the public domain, except for those few someone considered worth the trouble of protecting. Today every possible creation—however trivial—is legally protected as its creator's private property.

Nor are we talking only of money. For the last three centuries authors have increasingly been given control over all conceivable forms of their works. In the eighteenth century neither translations nor abridgments, nor most other derivative uses of works, infringed. A translation, for example, was not seen as the same work, nor—thanks to the language difference—as competing in the same market. Therefore, it was of no concern to the author. Abridgments were considered socially beneficial, able to enlighten more efficiently than lengthy originals. Authors were not thought harmed when others shortened their works.

In the meantime authors have gained control over the broadest possible panoply of different works, as well as largely all derivative uses thereof. In the words of one witness before the Royal Copyright Commission in 1878, authors were now given "every advantage which can possibly be derived from that work of art, even indirectly and by independent exercise of ability."[18] Throughout the nineteenth century German composers could freely set poems to music.[19] In 1965, however, the poets' lobby prevailed, ending the composers' right to accompany their verse musically as they pleased, reprinting their texts along with the music.[20] That alone is perhaps not to blame for the decline of *Lieder*, the once archetypical German musical art form. But today any would-be Schubert has to fight with all the other composers who already have rights to Goethe's *Erlkönig* and negotiate with Wilhelm Müller, author of *Die schöne Müllerin* and *Die Winterreise*.

In aesthetic terms, too, American and especially European authors have received ever-greater powers over the past two centuries. They may decide how their works appear, whether others may make use of them for derivative creations, and if so, under what circumstances. They can prevent changes they do not like, and in some nations they can withdraw works they no longer agree with. In certain cases such powers of aesthetic control last perpetually. Whether forever or only seventy years postmortem, authors and their estates have not been shy in locking down what was permissible. Beckett and his heirs prevent women from playing *Godot*. The Gershwin estate specifies that *Porgy and Bess* be played only by blacks. Meanwhile, in 1954 the French banned *Carmen Jones*, the Otto Preminger filming of *Carmen*, since Bizet's heirs found its setting among black Americans unworthy of the master.[21] And a century and a half after its publication in 1862, Victor Hugo's great-great-grandchildren for years kept the French justice system in knots all the way up to the Supreme Court, pondering whether sequels to *Les Misérables* were permissible.

The 1913 statue of the Little Mermaid by Edward Eriksen is among Copenhagen's biggest tourist attractions. It prettily embodies the main character of Hans Christian Andersen's fairy tale and is helped too by its picturesque location in the harbor. That has not tempered the sculptor's heirs' pursuit of their interests. They have brought or threatened suit against cities that presumed to erect their own variants. Not coincidentally they offer authorized replicas ($101,741 for the five-foot version).[22] And they have kept their great-grandfather's statue under firm aesthetic control. In 2008 they objected to the Scandinavian artist duo Elmgreen and Dragset's *When a Country Falls in Love with Itself*, which placed a mirror in front of the mermaid. Rather than staring wistfully out to sea after her lost prince, she now posed before the tourist hordes, admiring her own reflection.[23]

Perhaps the most remarkable aspect of this vast expansion of authors' and rights holders' claims to their intellectual property is that it reversed the course followed at much the same time for conventional forms of property. Regarded suspiciously as the outcome of humanity's fall from grace by medieval theologians, property was elevated to the status of a human right during the Enlightenment.[24] The right of property was defined in 1765 by the great British jurist William Blackstone as "that sole and despotic dominion" exerted by owners over their belongings "in total exclusion of the right of any other individual in the universe."[25] In 1804 the Napoleonic Code embodied this view in statute, describing property as "the right of enjoying and disposing of things in the most absolute manner."[26]

Despite such bravado, over the following two centuries European, British, and American law leached away at the pretentions to absolute dominion entertained by the owners of conventional property. Everywhere property has been ever more subjected to restrictions imposed by the state as the ultimate regulator. From nuisance laws to rent regulation, from zoning codes to health-and-safety rules, from taxation to outright takings, conventional property—the state has made clear—is possessed on society's premises and only insofar as private ownership is compatible with broader social objectives. The social determinants of private property became ever more prominent.

For intellectual property, in contrast, developments went in the opposite direction. Owners—whether authors themselves or their assignees—gained ever-firmer control over their works. Their ownership not only approximated that of conventional property, in many respects it exceeded it. In part, such unleashing of the claims staked by owners of intangibles followed developments in the history of property more generally. Land was the ultimate source of power and prestige in the Middle Ages. But the French Revolution's expropriations demonstrated that, as immovable, it had nowhere to hide and was vulnerable to changing political circumstances. For a while urban property supplanted it in importance as growing cities concentrated wealth in the hands of a new landlord bourgeoisie. But as new democratic governments—facing housing shortages early in the twentieth century—responded to their voters and imposed rent moratoria and controls and otherwise restricted rights, urban property owners too discovered the limits of their free control.[27]

Instead, intangible forms of property became the preferred investment. Because he appreciated their flexibility, John Wemmick, the bill collector in Dickens' *Great Expectations*, was obsessed with "portable property," small objects of value easily convertible to cash. Intangible property took such advantages further. Government debt has been marketed since the late thirteenth century, nor are bonds, stocks, securities, and other financial instruments recent inventions. Yet their importance has mushroomed in recent centuries compared to real property. Both more liquid and fungible—"more fluid than water and less steady than the air," as the German poet Heinrich Heine said—they were also harder for governments to clamp down on.[28] In our own day, with the globalization of financial markets, capital's transnational mobility and its outmaneuvering of the taxman has become a leitmotif.

The growing heft of intellectual property is thus part of a larger secular shift from ownership of immovables to movables and from tangibles to intangibles. Intellectual and other immaterial property has become an increasingly dominant element of modern economies. Already in 1863 the Scottish economist Henry Dunning Macleod classified most wealth as incorporeal: the franchises of ferry, railway, telegraph and telephone companies, as well as patents, trademarks, goodwill, and annuities.[29] In one Pennsylvania county intangible assets in probated estates grew from 10 percent in the colonial period to over two-thirds by the end of the nineteenth century.[30] In tandem, the concept of property expanded enormously from land and movables to encompass almost everything under the sun, including such entirely dematerialized "things" as business goodwill, trade secrets, and personality.[31] Property is "everything which has exchangeable value," Supreme Court Justice Noah H. Swayne declared already in 1873.[32] Today, over 40 percent of the market value of American companies is intellectual capital.[33]

However much some may still strike the pose of misunderstood Romantic artists in their garrets, authors have become economically and socially more powerful than ever before. What used to be a calling, pursued only by those motivated by more than material reward, has become a profession like any other. Most authors are today salaried employees, not the independent intellectual entrepreneurs for whom the copyright and patent systems were first designed. Their rights are usually surrendered to corporate employers in return for wages, health insurance, vacation time, and pensions. Nonetheless, there are more of them than ever before, and their output underpins modern economies.

Yet that is only half the story. The second point our starting anecdotes illustrate is that, while intellectual property has become ever more economically important across the globe, it has also been treated differently among nations. Sticking to those aspects of intellectual property dealt with by copyright, authors' rights over their works have—quite simply—been stronger in some nations than in others. In particular, authors have enjoyed a stronger legal position in continental Europe than in the Anglophone world. Britain and America's copyright systems draw clear distinctions between authors and rights owners. The two may overlap. But once the author has assigned rights to his work, they usually diverge. When Anglophone authors sell rights to publishers, producers, and other disseminators, they lose almost all control, while the new owners are largely free to do as they please. Work-for-hire, a core doctrine of Anglo-American copyright, transforms the employer into not only the owner but also the legal author of his employees' work.

Continental Europe, in contrast, has respected the personal connection between author and work even after economic rights were alienated. What are known as authors' "moral rights" continue their control over works even after sale, ensuring that they are not altered against their wishes. In Europe, more than in the Anglophone world, authors have thus retained aesthetic control even as they surrender economic rights. Though they may no longer be rights holders, they retain sway as authors. Two quite different approaches—Anglo-American copyright and continental European authors' rights—thus have voiced divergent views of intellectual property. Copyright was intended to give authors sufficient encouragement to remain fruitful, thus enriching the public domain and serving useful social functions—to enlighten, entertain, and educate. In authors' rights systems, in contrast, the creator was the focus, not the public domain nor the audience. Thanks to his investment of labor and creativity, the author owned his works like other forms of property. To guarantee his just desserts when he sold them in the marketplace was the point of the Continental approach.

How have the owners of intellectual property massively enhanced their rights over the past three centuries? And how did trans-Atlantic differences arise over the claims that authors could stake to their works and the access that audiences could demand to their patrimony? Those are the questions this book asks. As we will see, the basic dispute between these two approaches to intellectual property—one giving priority to authors, the other to their audience—has been with us for almost three centuries and continues into the digital age. Positions first adopted already in the eighteenth century remain surprisingly unchanged today.

When authors were first granted statutory rights to their works three centuries ago, both the civil law nations of France and Germany and the Anglophone common law world sought to balance between the new powers thus granted creators and the public's demand for access. Starting in the eighteenth century, authors were made only the interim masters of their works. After these rights expired, their creations were quickly added to the public domain, society's store of common knowledge. During the nineteenth century, authors' rights expanded both in Europe and in the Anglophone world: to new works beyond books, plays, and engravings and to ever-lengthier terms of authorial control. Additionally, in Europe a novel ideology of authors' rights emerged that went well beyond the limited scope of mere copyright. At first it founded creators' claims on the allegedly natural right to property, extended now to include also literary property. In the nineteenth century, however, it expanded further to embrace the idea that, since works inherently expressed the personalities of their authors, they could never be wholly separated from them.

Both tacks of the European authors' rights ideology—natural rights of property and of personality—strengthened the creators' sway. Their purchase over works was won at the expense of disseminators, of other authors, and of the audience. Disseminators no longer owned works outright, able to do as they pleased. Authors of derivative works, as well as performers and interpreters, found their own artistic freedom curtailed by primary creators. And the panoply of culture otherwise available to audiences was circumscribed as authors asserted their control over the uses that works could be put to.

In late nineteenth-century France and Germany authors were thus given expansive new powers, including moral rights of aesthetic control that lasted even after they had sold their works. Unexpectedly for a reform that so favored authors, moral rights were strengthened by the fascist regimes of the interwar years, claiming to venerate authors even as they brutally subordinated them to the alleged will of the people. But the high point of the Continental ideology of authors' rights came with the legislative incarnation of moral rights during the 1950s and '60s. France and Germany sought to distinguish their nascent postwar democracies both from their totalitarian predecessors and from what they and their fascist forebears alike saw as the Anglophone world's crass commercialization of culture.

In contrast, during the nineteenth century Britain and especially America maintained the Enlightenment ideal of an expansive public domain. Authors were to be empowered not—as in Europe—because they were owners of their works and therefore deserved reward but because—and only insofar as—productive creators enriched the public domain. The social utility of enhancing the common store of culture, not natural rights to property and certainly not personality rights to works, spoke for protecting authors. Anglophone authors received few of the perks of creatorship granted their colleagues on the European continent. Terms were extended only grudgingly. Rights of aesthetic control were shunned as fanciful and needless concessions to foppish artistes. Employers retained the upper hand over their employees' creativity.

In 1886, after decades of lobbying by writers and other authors, supported by France and other major European powers, the Berne Union was founded to coordinate authors' rights internationally. With it, the Continental ideology of long and strong protection for authors began its global march. Fearing isolation, Britain joined from the outset but then defended its own approach to copyright from within. The United States, however, refused to recognize copyright for foreign authors until 1891, and then for the next hundred years it kept a wary distance from Berne. Only when its policymakers switched camps did America finally join Berne, in 1989. Once a culture importer and therefore a copyright pirate, the United States had since become the world's largest exporter of content. Impelled by its content industries—emblematically represented by Hollywood—America now crept to the cross of the Berne ideology. While it never gave up work-for-hire and refused to implement moral rights in any but a pro forma fashion, it abandoned its traditional view of copyright as a temporary monopoly to encourage authors. Instead, it adopted the European view of works as a form of property, entitled by natural right to long and strong protection. Even in the United States, the author and his assignees came to reign supreme over the public.

The massive expansion of literary and artistic property rights of the late twentieth century is often blamed on Hollywood alone—and especially everyone's favorite whipping boy, Disney. Doubtless, the American content industries stood to gain from strong authorial rights, assigned by creators to their corporate masters. But seen in a longer, transnational accounting, Hollywood had merely discovered that its interests, as a content exporter, now coincided with what had all along been the position of the European *Kulturnationen*. Where Europe led, Hollywood eagerly followed.

In our own era, however, the digital revolution has derailed what recently seemed to be a developing international consensus on the Berne principles of strong rights for authors and their assignees. Digital technologies have both promised universal accessibility to intellectual property and threatened across-the-board lockdown of it. They sparked new versions of the copyright battles fought during the eighteenth and nineteenth centuries. In the United States proponents of the Anglo-American copyright tradition, concerned for the public, have sought to reassert old verities against fifth columnists from the now Europeanized content industries. During the 1990s film and music corporations fought consumers over open access, peer-to-peer downloading, and digital rights management, sounding themes familiar from earlier debates. Meanwhile, consumer electronics, internet, and new media enterprises have developed a stake in the free flow of web content, adding economic muscle to the formerly marginal hacker and open access communities. Together, they have begun to stand up to the demands for digital control advanced by the content industries. When, in January 2012, Congress sought to pass new laws forcing internet providers to police infringing content on their networks, Wikipedia shut down in solidarity for a day, disrupting homework worldwide.

Even in Europe, where strongly protecting authors has been dogma since the nineteenth century, the digital age upended inherited assumptions. Authors and rights holders have so far retained their ascendancy in legislation. But, for the first time in almost two centuries, Continental skeptics asked whether authorial privileges had not reached, and possibly breached, the necessary maximum. Early in the new millennium anarchistic pirate parties in Sweden and Germany challenged the authorities' authorphilia. They found soul mates among the citizens of the former East Bloc, who were also impatient with the inherited pieties of the Western European high cultural establishment.

History books sensibly shy away from predictions. How this most recent formulation of long-standing battles will eventually end is unforeseeable. But we can note that today's struggles are fought in terms that would have been eminently comprehensible to those nineteenth-century reformers who battled over how broadly to extend rights and powers to authors and even to the disputants of the eighteenth century. The copyright wars of our own era are only the latest iteration of a long-fought struggle. They can therefore not be grasped without understanding its history. Chronologically blinkered as we all are, the digital generation thinks it is fighting for the first time a battle that, in fact, stretches back three centuries.

1

The Battle between Anglo-American Copyright and European Authors' Rights

Works are created by their authors, reproduced and distributed by their disseminators, and enjoyed by the audience. These three actors, each with their own concerns, negotiate a delicate dance. Most generally, all must be kept content: the author productive, the disseminator profitable, and the audience enlightened. Get the balance wrong and things fall out of kilter. If authors become too exacting, the audience suffers. If the disseminators are greedy or the audience miserly, culture and eventually the public domain dessicate. But within these extremes there is much room for adjustment. Will copyright laws take as their first task protecting authors? Or will they consider the audience and the public domain also as important? Seen historically, that has been the fundamental choice faced as copyright developed in the Anglo-American world and in the major continental European nations, France and Germany. Each position has much to recommend it: public enlightenment for one, nurturing high-quality culture for the other. Neither can exist alone. The choice between them has never been either/or but always a question of emphasis, a positioning along a spectrum. And yet the battle between these views has also been what the Germans call a *Kulturkampf*, a clash of ideologies and fundamental assumptions, that has stretched back well over two centuries.

The laws governing how artists, writers, musicians, choreographers, directors, and other authors relate to their works are usually called "copyright" in English. But this one word covers two different approaches. The very terms used to designate the European "authors' rights" alternative—*Urheberrecht* in German and *droit d'auteur* in French—voice a more encompassing approach. To capture it as we examine how these two approaches arose and evolved, this book will attempt consistently to call the Anglo-American approach "copyright" and the continental European view "authors' rights."[1]

Copyright and authors' rights take very different approaches to authors and their social role. Seen historically over its long development, copyright has focused on the audience and its hopes for an expansive public domain. Authors' rights, in contrast, have targeted creators and their claims to ensure the authenticity of their works. Copyright's defenders see it as imbued with the spirit of the common good. Copyright promotes authors' creativity to benefit the public domain, allowing rights owners to exploit works efficiently. For its detractors copyright is philistine and commercial, treating noble creation as a mere commodity. It regards the creator as an entrepreneur and the work as a product.[2]

The authors' rights tradition, in turn, valiantly protects the creator's vision from commercialization and exploitation. It claims to rest on the eternal verities of natural rights and regards copyright as a utilitarian, man-made creature of statute.[3] For its detractors the authors' rights approach indulges seemingly whimsical *artistes* at the expense of the public.[4] Its culturally conservative insistence that the creator retain the final say on a work's form hinders collective and collaborative efforts, let alone acknowledgment of the audience's role in determining a work's meaning. From this vantage the authors' rights approach embodies in statute an outmoded Romantic notion of the individual *artiste*, alone in a garret, dictating how his genius should be venerated. Copyright encourages innovation and promotes dissemination. Authors' rights restrain distribution, inhibiting experimentation and public exposure. Authors' rights speak for creators, while copyright favors disseminators and interpreters and ultimately the audience.[5]

Copyright sees culture as a commodity. Its products can be sold and changed, largely like other property. But the authors' rights, especially their "moral rights," run counter to the market. Inalienable claims, they remain with the creators or their representatives even if they conflict with the commercial ambitions of the rights owners. The authors' rights ideology sees itself speaking for high culture. It is elitist and exclusive, while copyright is democratic and egalitarian.[6] Copyright gives authors a limited economic monopoly over their work to stimulate their creativity, eventually enrich the public domain, and thereby serve the public interest. Private interests are thus subordinated to the public good. Authors' rights, in contrast, make no attempt to serve the public good as such, except tangentially insofar as happy authors better society.

The Continental ideology assumes that the author's and the audience's interests do not contradict each other directly. The public eventually benefits when authors are treated well. But copyright's adherents see a tense negotiation between author and audience. In their utilitarian calculation the public domain is served by protecting authors only as necessary to keep them contented and productive. Rewarding authors is not the goal but only the means to further their productivity. Social goals are preeminent, and the author's and the audience's claims do not always reconcile. "It is somehow typical of the American reasoning regarding copyright," says a French observer, "to oppose the interests of consumers to those of authors and performers."[7]

Authors' rights, in contrast, derive from natural rights. The Continental approach defends creators and their work. In a sense it seeks no other interest—public or otherwise. Authors' rights, says a distinguished French jurist, seek to protect the author, not society.[8] Because it sets the author before all, writes a French law professor, balancing interests, on the model of the copyright systems, is foreign to the French tradition.[9] The author, in the words of a standard French legal textbook, "owes society nothing. He has no more obligations in this respect than the mason who builds or the farmer who ploughs. Quite the contrary, society owes him."[10]

This contrast between copyright and authors' rights has often escalated into a "clash of civilizations" between the Anglophone world and the Continent.[11] As one observer has recently ventured, the European position, represented especially by France, is directly antithetical in almost all respects to that of the United States.[12] Copyright is but the regulation of the entertainment industry's affairs, as a Continental jurist put it in 1990. It ignores the author's personality, on whose protection the essence of civilization rests. "An intimate and mysterious tie binds the work to its author. It is this connection which French law strives to protect. American law is not even aware of its existence."[13]

As the battle between copyright and authors' rights has been fought across the channel and especially across the Atlantic from the late eighteenth century on, such vague cultural confrontations have been increasingly anchored in statute. That copyright speaks mainly for the content industries is a European commonplace. One German observer calls Anglo-American copyright the "producer's copyright," an instrument of industrial policy corresponding to the Americans' fondness for competition.[14] Europeans protect the author's "basic human property rights," another German insists, while the Anglo-Americans aim only at a "simple protection of commercial and technical interests."[15] In the United States and the United Kingdom it is inconceivable that business should be disturbed by an author's scruples.[16] French law, as a legal textbook puts it, specifically repudiates the idea that protecting intellectual property serves to stimulate creativity. Rather, it is a mark of respect to works of the spirit and their creators.[17]

Europeans often insist that copyright is primitive and archaic compared to their refined approach.[18] Recognition of creativity and "establishment of authors' rights is one of the essential features of European culture."[19] The danger, French commentators warn, is letting the Anglo-Saxons gain the upper hand. That way lies the "slow decline of the authors' rights to mere copyright" and the rise of a "mercantilistic Europe" built on the "ruins of humanistic Europe."[20]

When in 1957 the French passed their first comprehensive law on the subject since the 1789 revolution, they invoked the author's moral rights to distinguish themselves from the mercantile Anglo-Saxons.[21] Down to our own day, the French battle for their "cultural exceptionalism." In 2004 a French government report praised the nation for having formulated the principle of the author's personal rights, while the Anglo-Saxons protected merely business investors.[22] As of this writing in 2014, trade negotiations between the European Union and the United States hinge on whether an exception to free trade will be permitted to the French cultural industries. On such issues all French agree, left and right. During recent parliamentary debates Communist and Socialist senators vied with each other in support of France's tradition of moral rights, railing against the "facile logic of copyright *à l'américaine*."[23]

Such clashes pit against each other not just two legal systems but diametrically opposed philosophies.[24] The French take for granted that there is a contrast, indeed a debate and an antagonism across the Atlantic.[25] A standard French legal textbook from 2005 insists that the individualistic French approach radically differs from the more communitarian line—guided by the public's interest, not the author's—taken by the Communists, Nazis, and Americans (together at last!).[26]

THE STAKES

Why should we care about woolly-headed disputes over authorial rights and the social role of creativity? More is at stake than the amour propre of the creative classes. Fought in a recognizably modern sense for over two centuries, such debates have recently flared up again as intellectual property has become increasingly important to modern economies. The human mind, claims the internet visionary John Perry Barlow, "is replacing sunlight and mineral deposits as the principal source of new wealth."[27] The cost of manufacturing a pair of Nike shoes is 4 percent of its retail price. The rest consists of intangibles: patents, trademarks, brand image, know-how, and the like.[28] In 2010 industries heavily based on intellectual property provided 27 percent of US jobs.[29]

Issues of ownership and its enforcement have extended beyond obvious industries like film, music, publishing, and software also to manufacturers—computers, pharmaceuticals, agricultural chemicals, car parts, and fire alarms. Pirating digital products is far more lucrative than counterfeiting physical items. A knock-off Gucci handbag costs roughly the same in materials as the original, though spared the investment of whatever design genius lies behind it. To develop a semiconductor chip can cost $100 million, to copy it a thousandth of that.[30] With software the disparity is even starker. Digitization has steered the marginal cost of a pirated software program, song, or film toward zero. The laws originally formulated for writers, artists, composers, and publishers have become serious business. Modern economies demand legally clear and enforceable intellectual property rights across a global economy.

International trade too has become more focused on intellectual property. During the 1990s the United States, Europe, and Japan faced the developing world and the rising Asian nations in disputes over copyrights and patents. Threatened with being cut-off from access to first-world markets for their—mainly agricultural and commodity—export goods, poor countries now had to impose regulations against counterfeiting and infringement formulated in Washington and Brussels.[31] Arguably, this strict global enforcement of intellectual property rights introduced late in the twentieth century prevented emerging nations from following the same low road of piracy that the currently industrialized ones—none more shamelessly than the United States—had themselves travelled during the previous two centuries.[32] Today, the US shakes its fist at China's pirates, as Europe did at America's a century ago. But China is already the third largest patentor in the world, trailing only the United States and Japan, and it joined the Berne Convention (the first international copyright union) in 1992, only three years after the Americans.[33] At some point soon, if it has not already happened, China too—like the US in the 1980s and '90s—will switch from pirate to policeman.

THE BATTLE IS JOINED

Inherent in the clash between copyright and authors' rights are strikingly divergent attitudes toward the creation and dissemination of culture, the reciprocal obligations and interests of creators and society, and the nature and social function of art, literature, and music. While authors' rights have many defenders in the English-speaking world, few Europeans believe in the Anglo-Saxon system. European criticism of copyright as sacrificing culture on the altar of commodity is therefore commonly known on both sides of the Atlantic. But defenders of copyright are scarce on the Continent. Europeans are unfamiliar with the idea that the copyright ideology could be something more than support of the content industries' self-interest. The traditional copyright approach's defense of the public interest and of a balance between the competing claims of audience and author are rarely heard there. But in the English-speaking world, copyright's social purpose was widely debated up until the late twentieth century, when the United States changed course and largely adopted the Continental position of strong intellectual property rights.

The dichotomy between the two ideologies has not always been equally pronounced. Early in the eighteenth century both Anglo-Saxon and Continental nations deprived booksellers of their royal publishing privileges, instead giving authors property rights in their works, based on natural rights. But during the nineteenth century the seas parted. In Britain and America the fiction of a natural right to works was largely abandoned, replaced instead with claims founded merely on statute. On the Continent, however, the idea of authors' strong property claims, anchored in natural rights, continued. Late in the nineteenth century it was reinforced by an allegedly equally natural claim based no longer on property, but on personality. The work was not just the author's possession. It was part of his very being. The Anglosphere received such ideas skeptically.

Formed in 1886, the Berne Union was long the foremost international venue for propagating the authors' rights ideology. Britain joined from the start, but grudgingly. To this day its allegiance to crucial Berne tenets has been partial at best. As the most radical interpreter of the copyright tradition, the United States long resisted Berne, joining only in 1989. But during the 1990s the US swung around, and the erstwhile copyright outlaw became intellectual property's international policeman. Spurred on by its now powerful content exporters, it began championing strong property rights for authors and their assignees. For other aspects of the Continental ideology, especially the pesky nuisance of the author's moral rights, the United States and Britain were eventually compelled to don legal fig leaves just big enough to render modesty its due.

The digital era's debates over intellectual property echo these battles of the past two centuries. Will the internet be a free and open forum? Or will it be a turbo-charged but traditional form of dissemination, restrained by inherited property rights? In the 1990s public opinion was whipped to a froth as the recording industry sued its downloading customers for seven-figure sums, while lawmakers were deluged by e-mails from irate music fans. Shadowy bands of digital hackers shut down corporate websites. Current disputes are heavily colored by inherited positions. The digital millennialists, so prominent in the United States, dream of a dramatically expanded public domain. They formulate what is arguably a modern version of the now-embattled US copyright tradition. In Europe, in contrast, inherited concepts of intellectual property continue to dominate. The internet is seen more as a threat to authors than a promise for the public. Until recently, digital visionaries have been marginalized. Shunned by the establishment, their views have been advocated mainly by a radical fringe of pirate parties in nations like Sweden and Germany.

The dichotomy between copyright and authors' rights has thus fluctuated. Moderate during the eighteenth century, it became pronounced in the nineteenth. The postwar American conversion to strong intellectual property rights tempered it again, but in recent years the tension has flared up anew. Polemical accounts supporting authorial rights often emphasize the distinction between the two approaches as they attack Anglo-Saxon cultural mercantilism. Since they survey the long sweep, historical accounts have done so too. But legal scholars, writing for today's practitioners, sometimes downplay the distinction.[34] Some differences remain stark: the role of work-for-hire (where the employer receives the author's rights) and the importance of fair use (exceptions to the author's exclusive rights) are greater in the copyright systems than on the Continent. But other differences have been effaced as intellectual property regulation globalized. As Berne members most nations now downplay the once-important role of certain formalities that used to be required for staking authorial claims. Today, the United States and the European Union both set the length of protection at seventy years postmortem. Given the internationalization of intellectual property legislation, the differences between the two approaches can best be identified through historical analysis. Seen over the *longue durée*, for example, terms have invariably been longer, and they have been extended earlier on the Continent than in the Anglosphere.

Though waxing and waning, the distinction between the two systems persists to this day. In 2006 the French conducted an extended debate over whether author or audience should take priority. They now located the origins of the divergence between European-style authors' rights and Anglophone copyright not with the world's first modern copyright law, the British Statute of Anne of 1710. Instead they regarded the first American national copyright law of 1790 as the more dangerous precedent.[35] The immediate enemy had shifted westward within the Anglosphere, but the fundamental antagonism remained. The trans-Atlantic spat over authors' rights is thus part of a broader quarrel that has long pitted the Continent against the Anglo-Saxon world, or more narrowly, the French against the Americans.

PARSING THE DIFFERENCES BETWEEN COPYRIGHT AND AUTHORS' RIGHTS

Differences between copyright and authors' rights are clear at a general and philosophical level. But in the hurly-burly of implementation and administration, they are frequently obscured by everyday practical considerations. Outcomes are often dictated by functional necessity, not philosophical disagreement.[36] Courts on both sides of the Atlantic have sometimes reached similar conclusions, but for different reasons.[37] Let us therefore clarify the specific distinctions between these two systems. How have the ideological differences been expressed in law and jurisprudence?

Among the concrete ways in which copyright and authors' rights have differed are these:

1. *Duration of term.* The Continental systems have historically had longer terms of protection for authors. Indeed, over three centuries terms have always been shorter in the United States than in France or Germany, and only as of 1998 have they been largely the same.[38]

That holds for the United Kingdom too, except between 1911 and 1934 when Britain adopted the Berne fifty-year postmortem term before Germany did, and the two years of 1995–1997 until the French got around to implementing the EU requirement of seventy years. Anglophone term extensions have almost invariably followed Continental precedents. Natural rights ideology instinctively dictated perpetual rights, using the analogy of conventional property.[39] Perpetual rights made it into statute in Venice in 1780, in 1814 in Holland, at the end of the nineteenth century in Mexico, Venezuela, and Guatemala, and in Portugal in 1927. But on the whole they have not proven realizable. Yet to this day perpetuity remains a constant ideal of the Continental rhetoric of strong authorial rights. Recent standard French legal textbooks advocate perpetual rights in ways that are inconceivable in their Anglophone equivalents.[40] In contrast, the American Constitution prohibits perpetuity, specifically restricting copyright protection to limited times. Perpetual Anglophone copyrights have existed only as a few rare anomalies: the British Crown for the King James translation of the Bible; Oxford and Cambridge universities for works given them by their authors; and the Great Ormond Street Hospital for Children for J. M. Barrie's *Peter Pan*.[41]

European opinion has almost unanimously seen long terms as an unmitigated good. Only the maximum possible protection, as one observer put it, can enhance the full development of culture.[42] In contrast, the Anglophones have more often worried that the public domain would thus be curbed. *Eldred v. Ashcroft* (2003) challenged the constitutionality of extending terms for existing works after the United States had stretched them from fifty years postmortem to the EU norm of seventy.[43] The Supreme Court, however, ruled that yet another retrospective extension of term did not render it unlimited and thus unconstitutional. Despite the plaintiffs' failure, *Eldred* highlighted a basic trans-Atlantic difference. Their lawyer, Lawrence Lessig, questioned whether there was a constitutional limit on America's ability to imitate the Europeans "as they continually expand the term in light of their own vision of what copyright is about."[44] Europe had nothing like the American outpouring of legal opinion criticizing the relentless lengthening of copyright's duration.[45]

The globalization of intellectual property regulation has erased many of the actual differences between copyright and authors' rights. Most nations now have largely the same lengthy term durations. But their national preferences have been revealed by whether they have actively espoused long terms or have reformed only under pressure, with dispute and foot dragging. Seen historically, authors' right countries have favored longer terms, while copyright nations resisted them.

2. *Formalities of protection*. Based on authors' inherent claims to their work, the Continental approach has discounted the formalities traditionally required to protect works—registering, affixing notice to and depositing the work, renewing rights, and the like. Protection is triggered by the sheer fact of creation. Why should authors lose their claims for having overlooked some paperwork? The work is often covered even without being fixed—as for lectures, improvisations, and the like.[46] On the few occasions where the Continental systems require formalities, neglect of them generally merely delays or curtails protection.[47]

In the Continental view formalities are artificial obstacles to the author's natural property rights. But from copyright's vantage the point of formalities was to ensure that only those works worth jumping hoops for were kept in private hands and out of the public domain. A 1975 US Senate report's first reason to support formalities was that they placed in the public domain the large body of published material that no one bothered to copyright.[48] The opposition between the two systems can be summed up thus: in authors' rights works were born as private property. But in copyright they belonged automatically to the public domain unless the author took pains to register them. "No registration, no right."[49] Formalities thus underlined the copyright thesis that intellectual property was not based on natural rights but was an artificial creation of statute.

On this point, too, the two approaches have come to approximate each other. And yet the antagonism has not wholly vanished. The UK followed Berne's dictate to eliminate formalities in 1911, but it now also requires that authors formally assert their moral rights—a true muddle. Though the US eliminated formalities starting in 1976 as it edged toward joining Berne, American critics to this day still lament the sacrifice and have attempted to challenge its constitutionality, arguing that automatically protecting most works impedes the progress of science and the useful arts.[50]

3. *Alienability*. Eighteenth-century reforms aimed to give authors property rights in their works to sell on the market. Unless the works were entirely theirs to alienate, they would receive less than full value.[51] In this respect, copyright regarded the work as akin to other forms of property. After alienation the creator and creation had parted. In authors' rights systems, in contrast, works can never be wholly divorced from their creators. They retain significant control, even after having assigned economic rights. As a free man cannot sell himself into slavery, so the author cannot alienate his work. In German law authors quite simply cannot assign or transfer the work as such but only limited use rights. In France today moral rights (to which we come shortly) are inherently inalienable. As shown in the case of Prince Michael of Greece, discussed in the introduction, even if alienated by contract, moral rights remain with the author. By contrast, in the Anglophone world rights (including those moral rights recognized in statute) are largely assignable. Indeed, as we will see with the work-for-hire doctrine, in legal terms owners are regarded as authors.

4. *Contracts*. Since copyright allows fuller alienability of works, contracts in the Anglosphere have usually been freer than in authors' rights countries.[52] Continental nations often regulate how authors can transfer rights to future works.[53] The French law of 1957, for example, forbade all blanket transfers of future works and then specified allowable transfers in numbing detail. Only five future works in any given genre within five years were legal. The publisher had to decide to accept each work within three months after submission. The author was able to revoke the agreement if the publisher rejected two successive works in one genre, and so forth. The author was assumed to be the weaker party, in need of protection against rapacious disseminators.[54] We want to defend the author against himself, explained Jean Zay, minister of education in the French Popular Front government of the late 1930s.[55] Authors were helpless,

unworldly *Luftmenschen*, unable to defend themselves—or so the French argued during their campaign to insert strong authorial rights into the U.N. Declaration of Human Rights in 1948.[56]

Copyright nations, on the other hand, have generally considered authors able to manage their own affairs. Authors are seen as free agents in the marketplace, knowing the value of their works and selling them only for a fair price. But even market-driven systems have sometimes cosseted them. The 1976 US Copyright Act allowed authors a second bite of the apple. After thirty-five years they could renegotiate terms (termination of transfer) since the "unequal bargaining position of authors" meant they could not know the value of their work until it had been exploited.[57] But only rarely did US law allow copyright law to trump contract.

5. Identity of the Author and Work-for-Hire. Work for an employer (work-for-hire) or by corporate or collective entities has been closely connected to alienability. The Continental systems have recognized mainly flesh-and-blood creators, not legal entities nor anyone other than the actual author. There are exceptions to this generalization. For collective works with many individual contributors, authorship is sometimes vested in corporate entities.[58] In 1985 France vested rights for software in the corporate employer of the programmers. But, as a rule, even work done for hire in the French and German systems entitles employee authors to similar rights in their creations as their self-employed peers.

In contrast, copyright systems have routinely vested authorship in corporate entities, attributed work-for-hire to the sponsoring entity, and resolved issues surrounding collective, collaborative, and corporate works by contract.[59] Not only is the corporate entity behind the work the first owner of copyright, it is often regarded as the author too.[60] Who was the author of *Citizen Kane*, Milos Forman asked rhetorically in 1994? And who is it today? RKO Pictures in 1941 and now Turner Broadcasting were the—in his eyes—ludicrous answers.[61] The 1909 US Copyright Act founded corporate authorship by including employers as authors of work-for-hire. The 1911 UK Copyright Act introduced work-for-hire too and vested authorship of photographs and musical recordings in the corporate owner. The 1976 US Copyright Act deemed the employer of the creator not only the owner of "all of the rights comprised in the copyright" but also the author of the work.[62] Work-for-hire demonstrated how copyright resisted Romantic ideas of individual authorship even as the Continent remained indebted to them.[63] It remains perhaps the most important divergence between the two systems, especially considering the large fraction of all content that is produced as work-for-hire in the Anglo-Saxon nations.

6. *Exceptions to the author's exclusive rights.* As we would expect, the Anglophone nations have generally accepted broader exceptions to authorial rights, allowing other authors, interpreters, and the audience to make use of works without the permission of rights holders. The US "fair use" doctrine has allowed use of protected works without permission or compensation for broad, socially beneficial purposes. American practices have been more expansive than the "fair dealing" of other Anglophone nations. That in turn has tended to be more inclusive than the Continental counterparts, with their specific excepted uses enumerated in statute. Here too, international standardization has scrubbed away stark differences. But, as we will see, the issue has reappeared in recent years as France and Germany were pushed to expand their otherwise miserly exceptions to authorial rights.

7. *Compulsory licensing.* Compulsory licensing (sometimes known as equitable remuneration) allows works to be reproduced without the author's permission so long as certain criteria—usually royalty payment—are met. It has been used to bring works efficiently to the public without much regard for the author's rights, other than that of being paid. It has meshed more naturally with copyright practices than the Continental approach and was adopted earlier and with less fuss in the Anglophone world.[64] Licensing violated the core Continental principle of the author's exclusive rights since, in effect, it legalized infringement in return for automatically paid fines. Licensing destroyed his power of bargaining, George Bernard Shaw complained to a parliamentary committee in 1909. If competitors could issue their own editions at rates determined by law, the first publisher would offer less than for exclusive rights.[65] Compulsory licensing thus spoke to the interests of the public and disseminators. Some advocates have seen it as a way to overcome the perennial con-

flict between authors' property rights and society's insistence on access. Squaring the circle, compulsory licensing granted authors their (pecuniary) due, perhaps even perpetually, while throwing open the doors to any royalty-paying disseminator. Both Mark Twain and Ezra Pound proposed systems of perpetual authorial rights, tempered by compulsory licensing to reprint.[66]

Compulsory licensing has also been used to override authors' attempts to suppress works altogether. Most nations allow new editions, even against the rights holder's will. The British 1842 Copyright Act permitted the Privy Council to grant compulsory licenses. Early in the twentieth century American and British composers were forced to accept compulsory licensing in return for being granted rights to sound recordings of their works. More recently, developing nations have favored compulsory licensing to gain better terms than those allowed by a classic regime of exclusive rights. And some open access advocates support licensing to break the "cyberlords' information monopolies."[67]

8. *Originality.* We might have expected that the Continental nations, with their emphasis on the personal connection between author and work, would demand a higher standard of originality than the copyright countries. In fact, the contrast has not been dramatic. The Anglophone nations imposed a doctrine of "sweat of the brow," demanding effort but not necessarily creativity. The United States, however, also required a minimum level of originality. This was reaffirmed in 1991, when the Supreme Court refused protection to a telephone directory that had merely been copied from another.[68] In the meantime the Continental originality bar has never been high, though it is defined more stringently in Germany than in France. In 1991, for example, the EU Software Directive broadly harmonized the standard of originality for computer programs at the Anglo-Saxon level. Such works had to be the author's own intellectual creation, but nothing more.[69]

9. *Moral rights.* The fundamental premise of the European authors' rights ideology is to consider works as a form of property, sanctified by natural rights. During the nineteenth century this was expanded to include also a personal connection that—equally based on nature—reinforced the tie between authors and their works. Moral

rights seek to protect in law that investment of authorial personality. By granting authors powers to control works even after they have sold their exploitation rights, moral rights privilege creators at the expense of disseminators, interpreters, and the audience. In Anglo-American copyright, in contrast, moral rights have played a much smaller role, protected—if at all—only incidentally or outside the copyright statutes.

THE IDEOLOGY OF MORAL RIGHTS

Moral rights allow the author to determine when and how his work is released (disclosure). They ensure that he is recognized as its au-thor (attribution). And they prevent his work from being changed without approval (integrity). In addition to these three primary moral rights has also come the author's right to withdraw his work from dissemination should he change his mind. And finally, the re-sale right, usually called the *droit de suite*, is an ordinary economic right that guarantees artists a bite of the apple each time their art-works are resold. Evidently not a moral right, the droit de suite has nonetheless often been invoked to demonstrate the author's strong position in the Continental nations. It was a further enrichment of the artist's legal position, one Italian commentator celebrated dur-ing the Fascist era.[70] France was the first to institute the resale right in 1920, followed by the Belgians in 1921, and the Italians in 1941.[71]

The term "moral rights" is a translation from the French (*droit moral*). Effectively a misnomer, it has nothing to do with morality but serves to distinguish such rights from the economic rights of exploitation. Usually attributed to the French legal writer André Morillot around 1870, in fact the term had been used in France al-ready during the 1840s.[72] As a bulwark against the market, moral rights are the anti-copyright. They subordinate private law—con-tracts, property, divorce, inheritance, bankruptcy—to the author's aesthetic interests.[73] But what the author gains from the law he may lose from his pocket as disseminators discount works in proportion to the control the author continues to exert.[74] From the Continental vantage such objections miss the point. The exercise of moral rights defends authors' idealistic aspirations, even if it undermines their economic ambitions.

From copyright's view, the more incisive argument against moral rights has been not economic but social and aesthetic. Moral rights not only curb the disseminator's sway, they also deprive the public. By strengthening the control of authors and their descendants—sometimes perpetually—moral rights in effect prevent the work from ever falling wholly into the public domain.[75] More broadly, moral rights restrict artistic possibilities, not just for disseminators and the audience, but also for interpreters and performers. They give authors an aesthetic veto.[76]

Copyright is freely alienable. Moral rights are not. In copyright, authors assign rights to their works, retaining little if any interest. Indeed, the aim of copyright was to give the creator something to take to the marketplace. As first legislated during the eighteenth century in all the nations examined here, the point of depriving booksellers of their privileges in favor of authors was to allow writers to sell their works. As personal rights, moral rights, in contrast, remain the author's whatever happens to the work. At any time, authors can change their minds. Even after signing away a right to integrity or attribution, they have prevailed in Continental courts to enforce them. As we have seen, ghostwriters—whom the French call "Negroes"—have come in from the self-imposed obscurity of their contracts to be named on their books.[77]

Moral rights cover a broad field, and no one definition in the voluminous European literature is canonical. Least controversially, they include three main ones: disclosure, attribution, and integrity.

Disclosure (or divulgation) is the authors' right to decide when and how their work appears. The most self-evident of the moral rights, it is similar to the fundamental premise of copyright, the right of publication.[78] After having cut up and thrown away some paintings in 1914, the French painter Charles Camoin discovered that they had been retrieved, repaired, and sold to collectors. When they were put up for auction, he sued for their return and for damages. By discarding them he may have renounced his physical claims, the court ruled, but the moral right to decide whether his works should appear remained.[79]

Other cases have been morally less clear-cut. In 1843 the Heidelberg theologian Heinrich Paulus published his notes on lectures by the philosopher Friedrich Schelling, adding a critical commentary four times as long. When Schelling sued to block publication, he lost on appeal. A lower court had supported the philosopher's right to determine when and how his work appeared. But a higher instance judged that the length of the commentary made the published work more than just Schelling's. The public had a legitimate interest in Paulus's views.[80] Paulus accused Schelling of summoning "the police to make himself irrefutable."[81]

Whatever its intrinsic virtues, the disclosure right has consequences for the audience and for culture more generally. If we took seriously the claims of authors—and their families and estates—to decide whether, when, and how works appear, we would have lost Virgil's *Aeneid*, possibly Ovid's *Metamorphoses*, most of Kafka, all of Foucault's posthumous works, some of Philip Larkin, Sainte-Beuve, T. S. Eliot, Anatole France, George Sand, Maurice Barrès, Antonin Artaud, Thomas Hardy, and much of Katherine Mansfield.[82] Emily Dickinson's poems would be known only in her family's heavily edited version.[83]

Attribution (or paternity) gives authors the right to be recognized as the creator of their work (even under a pseudonym) and conversely not to be falsely identified as the author of works not theirs. This too has been largely uncontroversial. Variants exist in copyright systems, though an attribution right is nowhere spelled out in US copyright law.[84] Copyright's major exception to attribution is that work-for-hire vests both owner- and authorship of commissioned works with the employer. In the Continental systems, whatever the details of their contracts, employee authors fully retain their moral rights, and corporate authorship is broadly ruled out of court.

Can an author refuse to be acknowledged as the creator of a work? Edward S. Ellis, author of many novels, including the *Deerfoot* series, failed to prevent a publisher from cashing in on his fame by reissuing in his birth name novels that had originally appeared under a nom de plume.[85] Conversely, the painter de Chirico denied authorship of a painting that bore his signature and that was shown to be his. Since his disavowal lowered its value, he had to pay damages.[86] Hollywood has elegantly sidestepped the need to withdraw works while still sparing authors the pain of being associated with something they detest. From 1969 directors horrified by their film's editing could ask to have their name replaced with "Allen Smithee," who thus joined Anonymous as among our most versatile and protean authors.[87]

Integrity (sometimes called the "right of respect") protects the work from changes unapproved by its author. Even though they may already have assigned economic rights, authors can still veto uses or changes of works. Arguably the core moral right, integrity has had the least counterpart in the Anglophone systems. It is also the trickiest of these claims. It varies depending on the art form. Singular works—paintings or sculptures, say—are protected against physical change or defacement. In the performing arts, however, author and performer or interpreter more equally rely on each other: playwright and director, composer and conductor, screenwriter and director, choreographer and dancer. Staging Mozart's *Seraglio* in a brothel is not the same as adorning the *Mona Lisa* with a moustache.

Integrity comes in at least two variants. A strong version, found in French and Belgian law, forbids any alteration the author has not explicitly approved. As early as 1932, French courts decided that "it is up to the author to ensure that his work is not altered or deformed in either its form or its spirit."[88] In its most extreme interpretations even restoring an artwork might violate integrity as it substitutes a new work for the original and imposes an unwanted collaboration on the original author.[89] Other nations, like Germany, Denmark, and Italy, protect the author only against changes that demonstrably injure his reputation or honor. The author cannot object, for example, to changes not shown in public, nor to changes that might improve the work. In this interpretation of integrity, the author does not decide whether a modification is actionable. To judge how a change affects his reputation or honor requires knowledge of his social position, society's sense of what counts as a violation, and evidence that harm has been done—ultimately matters the author alone cannot evaluate.

Moral rights are commonly portrayed as the opposite of exploitation rights. But, in fact, the moral and the mercenary blur. Personality rights are also economic rights.[90] Some observers have even argued that moral rights are a new form of property since an author's control over his work has economic value, much as a lease on a rent-controlled apartment is a form of ownership.[91] Insofar as an author's reputation and the work's authenticity affect his market value, he has an economic stake in his attribution and integrity rights. "By protecting the authorship and authenticity of a work, moral rights also serve consumer interests," a 1996 EU report concluded unflinchingly.[92] Seen thus, moral rights are akin to trademark protection, the guarantee of a brand.[93]

Yet impairing a work's integrity does not invariably damage the author's reputation. Indeed, it may improve it. A painter was not harmed by having his work photographed or engraved, Lord Fermoy argued during discussion leading to the British Fine Art Copyright Act of 1862. The more it happened, the higher the artist's reputation.[94] "Editors have been known, on occasion, actually to improve an article," the *New Republic*'s editors waspishly opined a century later in 1988.[95] Against the artist's objections, the prominent art critic Clement Greenberg (one of Tom Wolfe's kings of Cultureburg), stripped the paint off several of David Smith's metal sculptures, claiming to enhance them both aesthetically and economically. They did eventually command higher prices, though whether thanks to any inherent improvement or Greenberg's influential opinions is hard to say.[96]

If authors could forbid changes to their work, should they not also be allowed to prevent its destruction? This seemed a logical corollary of integrity and arguably the ultimate moral right. But it has rarely been legislated.[97] In the early 1920s the French Assembly pondered allowing artists to buy back works from owners who intended to destroy them.[98] The Swiss law of 1992 permitted authors to repurchase art that owners were going to destroy, though mercifully this did not apply to architecture.[99] French cases have punished the neglect and destruction of public fountains.[100] But on the whole, the owner's property rights have trumped the author's claims. While alterations might threaten an author's honor or reputation, complete destruction of the work did not.[101] A perversely logical consequence came in the 1981 case of a German artist, Otto Herbert Hajek. He had decorated a corporate building with sculptures, strips of color, textured areas, and paintings. When the building was remodeled, parts of these adornments were removed, and Hajek sued for violation of the work's integrity. The Munich court returned a Solomonic judgment: the owner could restore the work to its original state or he could end the violation of its integrity by removing it altogether.[102] Destruction trumped integrity.

Contemporary artists who work with the detritus of everyday life have run an especially high risk of inadvertent destruction. Gustav Metzger's plastic bag of trash was discarded, even though proudly part of his *Recreation of First Public Demonstration of Auto-Destructive Art* in 2004. The beige paint stain under Martin Klippenberger's 2011 *When It Starts Dripping from the Ceiling* was mistakenly scrubbed away. The photographer Alfred Stieglitz is thought to have tossed out the original of Duchamp's *Fountain* with the trash.[103] Not surprisingly Joseph Beuys, whose favorite materials were felt and fat, suffered this indignity twice: a child's bathtub full of junk was mistakenly cleaned out in the 1970s (and then—injury to insult—used by the Social Democratic Party of Leverkusen in West Germany to cool beer). A museum janitor mopped up an artistic grease stain by Beuys in 1986.[104] And what if the work cried out to be defiled? What integrity rights did Duchamp's Ready-mades demand when one of their points, as everyday objects, was to undermine the remaining craft aspects of art? And what of the claims made by the five artists who took up what they considered Duchamp's challenge and urinated in one of the eight copies of his *Fountain*?

Beyond this classic trinity of moral rights (disclosure, attribution, integrity), some nations have also extended others.

Repenting (or withdrawal) is the most controversial and least applied of these additional moral rights. It allows authors to withdraw a work from circulation should it no longer express their meaning. Their ideal interests trump their contractual obligations. From copyright's vantage that is the least of the withdrawal right's offenses. Subtracting from the common store of knowledge by withdrawing a work violates the primacy of the public domain. In the foundational copyright case *Millar v. Taylor* (1769), Justice Yates made this point forcefully: "But when an author prints and publishes his work, he lays it entirely open to the public. . . . Neither the book, nor the sentiments it contains, can be afterwards recalled by the author."[105]

A limited repenting right, proposed in Nazi Germany, came to nothing.[106] Yet in the midst of the Second World War, Fascist Italy introduced a proper one, allowing authors to withdraw their work if they could no longer stand by it.[107] In France withdrawal rights were introduced in 1957, and Germany gained them in 1965.[108] As the most extreme moral right, repenting has also been the least invoked. Authors have to compensate assignees for losses, and in practical terms their repenting is unlikely to have much effect on an already published work.[109] Yet, however inconsequential in practice, withdrawal lay at the heart of the central conundrum of moral rights—how a personal right survives the person. Other moral rights are assignable and inheritable. Spouses, descendants, heirs, representatives, and sometimes the state itself were expected to safeguard what they understood to be the author's intentions. The withdrawal right, in contrast, almost by its nature dies with the author. It can generally not be exercised by anyone else.[110]

By assuming the fiction of a coherent lifelong authorial personality, the withdrawal right implicitly allows an author to rewrite his own history. The author should be able to withdraw a work that embarrassed him in old age, one delegate insisted at the International Literary Congress in Paris in 1878, the fountainhead of the author's rights ideology.[111] The French law of 2012 on digitizing out-of-print works specifically permits authors to block the reappearance of works that harm their honor or reputation. A work written during the occupation of the Second World War, but now regretted, was offered as the disconcertingly frank example of what authors could quietly bury.[112] Withdrawal gave the old writer purchase over his youthful enthusiasms and indiscretions.

Should Céline have been allowed to expunge his anti-Semitic writings, as his widow tried to? Wagner the political radicalism of his youth? Saint Augustine the paganism of his early years? Manzoni his atheism, and Hugo or Lamennais their early Catholicism? Having criticized the kings of Poland and Sweden in his *Anti-Machiavel* shortly before ascending the Prussian throne in 1740, Frederick the Great vainly implored Voltaire to convince his Dutch publisher to make it disappear.[113] Voltaire in turn regretted his youthful satire of Joan of Arc, *La Pucelle d'Orleans*, and published a heavily edited version thirty years later, in 1762.

Though an ardent champion of authors' rights, Victor Hugo proposed a moderated version of withdrawal. The work was intimately tied to the author's personality but only at the moment of creation. An author could thus correct the style of an earlier work, but no longer suppress his meaning. Why? "Because now another person, the public, has taken possession of the work."[114] Even the author, Hugo argued, should not be allowed to rewrite his works. Imagine what might happen. The elderly Racine disliked his mature tragedies.[115] Goethe distanced himself from his *Werther*. Though Mahler's First Symphony originally had five movements, the composer removed one (only to have it reintroduced by Seiji Ozawa's recording).[116] Having fled Berlin for exile in Stockholm, Nelly Sachs refused to reprint her prewar German works.[117]

But if the work was part of the author's personality only at its birth, why have a withdrawal right at all? In effect, the author's withdrawal right contradicts the work's integrity right. Arguably the work has to be protected even against its own author. In defending their right to stage *Godot* with female actors, a French theater troupe argued that "a formal respect for the author's wishes could be contrary to the interests of his work."[118]

In the Anglo-Saxon world the fear has been that withdrawal would allow authors to rewrite their histories. Before the Royal Copyright Commission in 1878, Thomas Farrer, permanent secretary of the Board of Trade, argued that lengthening copyright terms allowed authors to suppress their earlier opinions by vetoing new editions. "I do not think that copyright exists or ought to exist in order to enable an author to recall that which he has once given to the public."[119] Farrer cut to the heart of the matter. The withdrawal right potentially contradicted integrity. Did integrity protect the inviolability of the work as such or of the author's personality? If the work expressed the author's personality, then he determined integrity and could do what he pleased. But if the work itself was protected, then its creator might have no more right than anyone else to violate it. The Austrian expressionist writer Hermann Bahr took the latter line, seeking a form of habeas corpus protecting works against later mutilations, even by the author.[120]

Who said an author's intentions were always pure? What if the author used withdrawal for greed or revenge, to stiff creditors or an ex-spouse? Or, for that matter, to foil pirates? Rudyard Kipling rewrote the end of *The Light That Failed* in hopes of spoiling pirate editions, as did Gabrièl Garcia Marquez with his *Memories of My Melancholy Whores*.[121] Was that an aesthetically valid motive?

What if authors insist on new and revised editions mainly to prolong their economic rights?[122] That was a venerable strategy. In the early eighteenth century Jacob Tonson thus extended his hold over Shakespeare.[123] Late in life Walter Scott warded off creditors by bringing out new editions of his works.[124] Much as modern textbook authors issue ever-new editions, Stravinsky revised his compositions to extend his claims. He sold the copyrights of at least three versions of the *Firebird*—in pre- and post-revolutionary Russia and in American exile. When the Leeds Music Corporation, owner of the third version, released a fox-trot rendition, Stravinsky was incensed. But usually he was less picky. In Hollywood during the war, he allowed Disney drastically to prune the *Rite of Spring* for *Fantasia*.[125] Is the author always the best steward of his works?

MORAL RIGHTS IN THE LONG RUN

Moral rights link author and work by insisting that works mean only what the author intended. Since the work expresses its author's personality, his control must continue even after alienation.[126] But what happens at his death? Many personal rights expire with the person. In the Anglophone nations defamation and libel law protect only the living. But the Continental nations have had to grapple with the paradox of personal rights outliving the person.

Though moral rights generally last only as long as economic claims, in some nations, like France, they continue forever. That has raised the question of whom to entrust as caretaker of the author's wishes. However devoted the author's family and however specific his instructions, in the long run the work slips into posterity's hands. When moral rights are inherited, on what terms? Are their recipients caretakers of the author's intent or actors in their own right? Are the authors' families, as the likely successors, the best safeguards of their interests?

The Marquis de Sade's family burned his unpublished manuscripts, though they were spared further effort when his published works were outlawed after his death in 1814. Samuel Richardson's grandson strongly disliked fiction, including *Pamela* and *Clarissa*. Boswell's eldest son thought his father's *Life of Johnson* "a blot in the escutcheon of the family."[127] As a good Christian, Baudelaire's mother, Madame Aupick, sought to pull one of the poems from the posthumous edition of *Les Fleurs du Mal*.[128] Rimbaud's sister, Isabelle, tried to prevent publication of his work after his death in 1891.[129]

And even if the author has a sympathetic postmortem representative, are they obliged to follow the deceased's intentions? Jules Verne's five posthumous novels were heavily altered by his son, then restored by his grandson.[130] Nietzsche's posthumous *Will to Power* was a concoction of snippets from his unpublished writings by his sister, Elisabeth Förster-Nietzsche, which she tailored to make him sound like Hitler's court philosopher. In 1964 the first edition of Hemingway's memoirs appeared, titled *A Moveable Feast*. Unfinished at his suicide in 1961, the manuscript was edited and introduced by his fourth wife, Mary, and harshly portrayed his second wife, Pauline Pfeiffer. In 2009 his son Seán released a new edition, which softened the portrait of his mother, Pauline.[131] Where does it end? A right may be personal and die with the person, or be perpetual and inheritable. Can it be both?[132]

As many examples from the copyright world attest, obstructive heirs or representatives are not empowered by moral rights alone. Conventional exploitation rights have often been used to assert personal control too. But in those countries where they are enforced, like France and Germany, moral rights give descendants especially powerful tools. The secretary of Maurice Utrillo's widow inherited the painter's right of attribution and thus the right to authenticate or challenge the provenance of paintings said to be his. He used this to good effect in the Paris and London art markets.[133] In 1984 the children of Albert Camus successfully invoked the writer's moral rights against his British publisher, Hamish Hamilton, maintaining that it had damaged the writer's reputation with a critical biography by Patrick MacCarthy.[134]

Heirs have invoked aesthetic motives to achieve their own economic goals. The Gershwin heirs—mostly nephews and grandnephews of George and Ira—have been keenly commercial. "Our responsibilities are to not have *Porgy and Bess* stuck in an attic, to open up the property to younger generations," said Jonathan Keidan, a digital-media executive, whose grandmother was George and Ira's sister, "and to make money for the families."[135] Who says that heirs are concerned mainly with upholding the artistic vision of their ancestor author? Picasso's offspring has chased the unauthorized use of his name and images on coffee mugs, T-shirts, plates, and makeup, the better to license them for eyewear, clocks, textiles, stationery, posters, shopping bags, scarves, wallpaper, and even a Citroën car.[136]

Even without money as a motive, heirs have exerted an onerous tutelage. Stephen Joyce's control of his grandfather's estate was notorious. Like most writers, Joyce himself believed in a natural right to intellectual property, and the ethos seems to have permeated the family.[137] New print and digital editions of his works were denied until copyright finally lapsed in 2011; exorbitant fees were charged for public readings, translations, and anthologies; musical adaptations were forbidden altogether.[138] Bertolt Brecht sought to determine the precise staging of his plays, and his daughter continued this after his death.[139] John Cage's publishers have collected royalties on his silent piece *4'33"* and threatened performers of other soundless compositions for infringing on his silence.[140]

Richard Wagner illustrates the dilemma of achieving suitable balance between giving primary authors and their heirs full control of works and the concern of other authors, and their audience, to make free use of them. The Nazis worried lest his music be trivialized in light comedies.[141] In the meantime we have gone to the opposite extreme. Many films use his music—usually the "Ride of the Valkyries"—to suggest Nazism or more general evil. In D. W. Griffith's

Birth of a Nation, it accompanied the KKK's ride against liberated slaves. In Francis Ford Coppola's *Apocalypse Now*, it undergirded a helicopter attack on a Vietnamese village (as it had accompanied Nazi newsreels reporting Luftwaffe airstrikes). It appeared in Chaplin's *Great Dictator*, Kubrick's *Full Metal Jacket*, Nicholas Ray's *Rebel without a Cause*, and Fellini's *8½*.[142] Had moral rights on the French model given Wagner's heirs the ability to forbid using his music, as Shostakovich could, little of this would have been possible. But would we wish such powers for the Wagner estate?

For every author legitimately concerned about vulgarizing exploiters, others have eagerly sought to enforce their personal control. Alexander Calder rightfully complained that a massive mobile, bought and donated to the Pittsburgh airport, had been repainted from black and white to the splendid colors of Allegheny County, green and gold, and its elements soldered in place to make it a stabile.[143] In 1981 Michael Snow successfully objected when his sculpture of flying geese, *Flightstop*, commissioned for the atrium of the Eaton Centre in Toronto, was festooned with Christmas ribbons around their necks.[144]

But, on the other hand, authorial vanity is legion. Miffed at the cutting of a scene of an opera for which he was set and costume designer, Fernand Léger sought to have the program indicate the absence of his "Crossing of the Andes."[145] The widow of Georges Dwelshauvers, the Belgian psychologist and philosopher, felt denigrated when a new edition of one of his books failed to list all his positions and other publications.[146] The cellist Mstislav Rostropovich objected to the use of his recording of *Boris Godunov* as soundtrack for the filmed version of the opera by Andrzej Żuławski because at certain moments cinematic noise (expectoration, urination, gasps) interfered with the perfect enjoyment of his work.[147] One could go on. Artistic skin is thin.

THE DEAD HAND OF THE PAST

Authors and their heirs have often hoped to preserve works in aspic. In nations like France and Germany, they have enlisted their moral rights to that end. But performers and interpreters want to use them for their own purpose. Difficult choices are unavoidable, especially if moral rights are perpetual and heirs active. No *West Side Story*? No Manet redoing Titian? No Warhol *Mona Lisas*? Why is it fair that the passing of Johann Sebastian's heirs allows Wendy Carlos to switch on Bach, while Gustav Holst's estate hinders Tomita's electronic version of the *Planets*? What if the Grimm brothers had not wanted to be a Disney cartoon or if Rodgers and Hammerstein spurned John Coltrane? Are we condemned in all eternity to Bach played on original instruments?

When decisions pass to descendants and representatives, who polices the policemen? In France and Italy moral rights are perpetual. And forever is a long time. The consequences of enforcing the author's moral rights for decades, sometimes centuries, after his death have often been peculiar. In 1988 the sole lineal descendant of the painter Achille Deveria (died 1857) secured a court decision against the French magazine *L'Express* for printing a portrait of Franz Liszt from 1832, removing its bottom part and adding some color.[148] Should Sophocles's heirs hold integrity rights to his works? A facetious example, perhaps. But consider the 1989 case of the Danish director Jens Jørgen Thorsen. His early 1970s film on the life of Christ spiced it up—in the tediously predictable way of would-be provocateurs—with brothels and orgies, Mao and Uncle Sam. The Danish parliament and public asked whether the project was blasphemous and if it violated the moral rights of the authors of the gospels of Matthew, Mark, Luke, and John (whoever they were). When the Danish Film Institute withdrew its financial support, Thorsen sued. The court took expert testimony from Lars Trier, the future *auteur* of the Danish 1990s Dogme school of filmmaking (who then did not yet affect his faux aristocratic "von"). The Film Institute was wrong to recall its support, it ruled. But it was no longer obliged to finance the project.[149] Echoing Louis Vaunois, one of the few Frenchmen to criticize moral rights, we might well ask: who are the heirs of King David, author of the Psalms?[150]

If moral rights are perpetual, it follows that eventually they have to be entrusted to an institution, presumably some sort of government authority. Moral rights are then transformed into a caretaking of cultural patrimony—something like the preservation codes that uncontroversially guard buildings, monuments, and landscapes.[151] In

1913 Wagner's copyrights were set to expire. With them Wagner's insistence on limiting *Parsifal* performances to his purpose-built theater in Bayreuth would go too. Wagner's family and followers suggested a compromise, permitting stagings elsewhere, but only if closely supervised by a government authority—in effect a *Reichsparsifalkommissar*.[152] Later, the collectivist-minded Nazis drew the ultimate conclusion from the inevitable passing of the author's work into government hands. Since the author, in their view, was the mouthpiece of the people, the collectivity could prevent him or his heirs from mutilating or desecrating his works.[153] The work, not the author, was the focus of protection.

In the long run, as the protection of the authors' rights turned against the creator himself, the ultimate contradiction of perpetual personal rights emerged in those nations with such legislation. At the outset of any work's trajectory, moral rights were highly individualistic. They undergirded the author's claim to enforce the singularity of his vision even after death. But the passage of time gnawed away at this personal tie. His descendants and heirs allegedly did his bidding. But their motives weakened as his presence receded. Ultimately, the collectivity necessarily stepped in to preserve what by now—if he remained of interest—had become the author's position in a canon. By this point cultural bureaucrats safeguarded not his individual vision, but a socialized understanding of where he fit in the pantheon.[154]

Such control could take the innocent form of preventing destruction of valuable works. One of the first instances of the state using moral rights, introduced by the Italian Fascists in 1925, came four years later at the death of Marco Praga, a popular playwright. His will ordered his manuscripts destroyed, but the minister of education decreed otherwise. To this day Praga's works and letters remain in the Brera Academy of Milan.[155]

But what happens when the motives are more personal? Even the French—fervent moral rightists—recognized the problem. In 1959 the Société des Gens de Lettres sought an injunction against use of *Les liaisons dangereuses* as the title of a film based on the eighteenth-century novel by Pierre Choderlos de Laclos. The film was by Roger Vadim, he who launched Brigitte Bardot and turned Jane Fonda into Barbarella. Though perhaps no more erotic than the original book, the film was set in the contemporary underworld, not a rococo court. The lower court injunctions against the film were criticized for accepting the Société's pretensions to speak for Choderlos's moral interests. The society had not even existed during his lifetime! Choderlos's own intentions were not mentioned since it was difficult to say whether a writer who died in 1803 would have welcomed a filming of his novel. Ultimately, reason prevailed and the Society did not. The Court of Appeals dismissed the Société's claim to represent the author as a task it had arrogated, not one anchored in law.[156]

In 1964 the French National Literary Fund, created in 1946 to defend the integrity of public domain works, similarly sought to suppress an abridgment of Victor Hugo's *Les Misérables* (1862). The court refused, reasoning that Hugo's living heirs—two great-grandchildren, Jean and Marguerite Hugo—were the ones to safeguard his moral rights.[157] When, thirty-seven years later in 2001, a writer was commissioned to write two sequels to *Les Misérables*, a great-great-grandchild, Pierre Hugo, a goldsmith from Aix-en-Provence, went to court to enforce respect for his ancestor's œuvre. In the first instance the courts proved themselves more sensible stewards of the French cultural legacy than the legislators. Since he had lived long before moral rights had been legislated, the court divined Hugo's intentions by analyzing his writings and speeches. At the 1878 International Literary Congress, he had adamantly opposed heirs controlling their ancestors' works. The court concluded that Hugo's wishes should be respected in this instance too.[158]

On appeal in 2004, however, the great-great-grandchild was granted standing and indeed won his claim that the sequels violated Hugo's moral rights. But the law on moral rights was upheld only by emasculating it. The court symbolically fined the publisher two euros, while not blocking sales of the sequels.[159] For good measure, the highest court then overturned this ruling in 2007, declaring that, although they could not violate the moral rights of the original, sequels were among the adaptation rights allowable once the work was in the public domain.[160]

Disappointed, Pierre Hugo lashed out at those who would cash in on the genius of famous authors. "I am not just fighting for myself, my family and for Victor Hugo," he claimed, "but for the descendants of all writers, painters and composers who should be protected from people who want to use a famous name and work just for money."[161] Alas for the conviction his complaint carries, this is the same descendant who invokes his ancestor to hawk his luxury fountain pens on the web. These he describes as "truly works of art," which have been "launched at Bergdorf Goodman." The most "prestigious" of the entirely hand-engraved Bois d'Epave line (also available in ballpoint technology) is "dedicated to his great-great-grandfather Victor Hugo."[162]

THE BATTLE LINES

Moral rights are a political issue swaddled in culture. They encompass more than the legal leverage they give the author in dealing with disseminators, assignees, interpreters, performers, and the public. Speaking to the implicit social compact between author and society, they testify to the priorities of a culture. Is the author or the audience primary? Should this unique individual, the author, stand inviolate? Or are even authors citizens, owing the public domain in return for their legally protected claims and the social recognition of their talent?

Moral rights have thus epitomized the broader cultural clash between Anglo-American copyright and European authors' rights. Each system sees the author's role differently. The Continental system has hoped to insulate culture from the market and protect authors from disseminators, interpreters, and the audience. Moral rights are a "fundamental human right," while copyright is merely a "socially useful right," granted to encourage authors and benefit society.[163] At their most elevated authors' rights—and especially moral rights—have been considered human rights, a legacy of the Enlightenment and the French Revolution.[164]

So universal have the French regarded moral rights that foreigners can assert their claims in French courts regardless of their standing at home.[165] In the case of Bragance's authorial credit for the novel she had ghostwritten with Prince Michael, French law trumped a contract signed according to New York law.[166] With the colorization of Huston's *Asphalt Jungle*, French courts took up a case where the American plaintiffs had received no satisfaction at home.[167] In an act of what the French approvingly hailed as French legal imperialism, countering American economic hegemony, Huston's moral rights in French law trumped those of the California jurisdiction where he had signed the contracts and undertaken the work.[168] French courts assumed that for moral rights foreign local law violated the principles of international law to which French statute corresponded.[169] This was, as one observer of the Bragance case put it, "to slide towards recognizing a universal principle or a natural right."[170] It was certainly a heady dose of cultural and legal hubris.

In the most heroic formulations of the Continental ideology, authors' rights go beyond even property claims to become human rights. The inalienability of moral rights demonstrate the affinity most clearly. "You can no more sell your authors' rights in what you create than you can (legally) sell your soul," one observer has claimed.[171] The French jurist Bernard Edelman voiced the Continental ideology at its most messianic in 1987. Since the work embodies the author's personality, harming it also attacks its creator, he insisted. Just as a worker cannot rent out his labor permanently without becoming a slave, so the author cannot alienate his work without alienating himself. Juridically, the work is equivalent to the person, except that it is perpetual. It is thus quasi-divine.[172] The author cannot alienate his moral rights, another French observer agreed. Renouncing the defense of his personality would be a form of "moral suicide."[173] Moral rights are absolute, yet another French commentator wrote in the 1930s. As natural rights they live forever. They are beyond relativity (*hors de la relativité*).[174] When law professors and jurists, ostensibly discussing a topic as pedestrian as copyright, are moved to speak of slavery, soul-selling, the absolute, quasidivinity, and moral suicide, something odd is afoot.

Until recently, authors' rights have been the received orthodoxy in continental Europe, with little if any dissent. In the Anglosphere, however, there have long been two sides to the issue. Many have favored the Continental approach, agreeing with its criticism of copyright. Others, in contrast, have argued that the Anglo-American copyright approach does not just represent the narrow self-interest of the content industries but also embodies principles of public access, broad dissemination, flexible use of works, and efficient stimulus of creativity. From this vantage copyright is as consistent, as socially motivated, and in that sense, as ideological as the Continental defense of authors' rights. The difference comes down to the broader social values that are defended in each system: artistic quality and authorial authenticity in one, public enlightenment and democratic access in the other.

Moral rights privilege the author's intended meaning at the time of creation. Other possible interpretations are restricted by his rights—meanings that are inadvertent, revealed only in new contexts, plumbed by interpreters and other creators, or otherwise outside the author's expressed aim. "The work remains and perpetuates the person after his death," writes the author of a standard French textbook on intellectual property. "[T]hose responsible for ensuring its respect do not exercise it in their own interest but . . . should seek, as it were, to put themselves in his shoes or adopt his viewpoint."[175] In practical terms supporters of the authors' rights ideology have listed examples of the consequences: No shortening of Shakespeare, Molière, or Balzac. No translating Rabelais into modern usage. No modern-dress versions of classic plays. No playing Mozart's *Ave Verum* in coffeehouses. No jazz versions of Strauss waltzes. No performing Chopin's funeral march on a theater organ.[176]

Prompted by the Grieg Fund, the Norwegian Academy of Music, upholder of cultural standards *à la française*, once expressed its considered opinion that Duke Ellington's version of the *Peer Gynt* suites infringed moral rights. Because the offending records were voluntarily withdrawn from the Norwegian market, no legal action was required.[177] Norwegian commentators condemned the *Song of Norway* (1944), the operetta based on Grieg's life and music, for its American "lack of piety," as an "act of vandalism towards the music of the Master," and as "commercial prostitution."[178] In 1987 US congressman Richard Gephardt introduced a bill to ban film colorization. As illustrative of the artistic desecration he sought to spare the nation, he offered Louis Armstrong's music set to a disco beat.[179] How difficult to know—much less uphold—the supposed purity of the original author's intent! At no moment do we more date ourselves than when we draw the line between culture and barbarism. Your artistic abuses are your children's classics.

The defenders of moral rights have typically portrayed themselves as progressives, defending the artist against the Moloch of the market. But others see such cementing of the author's power as culturally conservative, stifling experimentation and transformation.[180] Consider how the Wagner family squabbled with the opera-going public as his copyrights expired in 1913. The immediate issue was only the end of his copyright. But the broader concern was the sort of aesthetic control that moral rights were intended to secure for authors and their heirs. Wagner regarded *Parsifal* as a religious expression and insisted that it would be degraded by performance at any theater other than the one built in Bayreuth as a shrine to his own œuvre. His followers agreed.[181] *Parsifal* on another stage would be like hearing "Ave Maria" from the lipsticked mouth of a harlot, warned Hans Richter, first conductor of the Bayreuth festival. As 1913 neared, his supporters sought to extend Wagner's terms or at least restrict *Parsifal* to Bayreuth. They failed. Rarely has the liberation into the public domain been as spectacularly demonstrated as with the outpouring of pent-up *Parsifal* stagings outside Bayreuth at the close of 1913. In Barcelona the curtain rose a few seconds after midnight on 1 January 1914. Later that same day a performance struck up in Berlin, the next day in Frankfurt and Mainz; St. Petersburg followed on January 3, with a new series in Berlin again on January 5, and the following day in Dresden. In all, *Parsifal* was staged in more than fifty European cities between January and August 1914—a climax of European high culture before the trenches were dug.[182]

COLOR AS A SIN

More recently the dispute over film colorization has exemplified the mutual incomprehension of copyright and authors' rights. Today, colorization is no longer contentious. But in the late 1980s fierce battles were fought both in the United States and across the Atlantic as American directors sought to assert their moral right to spare pristinely black-and-white works from chromatic manipulation.

When are changes to an older incarnation of a work a technical improvement? When are they an aesthetic alteration? Few recording artists have railed against remastering mono renditions in stereo. But some writers resisted replacing Fraktur (Blackletter) with Antiqua as the dominant typeface in German publishing late in the nineteenth century. Opinions differ about playing Scarlatti on the piano rather than the harpsichord. Whether silent films could be given voice-overs has prompted discussion.[183] Whether conventional films can be remade in 3-D is perhaps a question that awaits us. Now the issue was whether colorization was an improvement or vandalism.

Colorization was easier in the Anglo-Saxon world than on the Continent because the film copyright owner tended to be the corporation that made it, not the director. A few directors (Orson Welles for *Citizen Kane*, Warren Beatty for *Reds*, and Woody Allen for most of his work) deliberately retained rights. But generally the producer owns the adaptation rights, including that of colorizing. A black-and-white film might earn $100,000 in ten years, the colorized version a million dollars annually.[184] No wonder the media mogul Ted Turner aimed to colorize several thousand films. As we have seen, the dispute culminated with the French case over a colorized version of Huston's *Asphalt Jungle*. In 1991 Huston posthumously won: in France colorized films could not be broadcast if authors objected.

The United States responded with a half-hearted attempt to emulate European standards while also protecting the owners' economic exploitation rights. In 1987 Representative Richard Gephardt introduced a film integrity bill to give a movie's "artistic authors" (the principal director and screenwriter) the right to prohibit colorization or other "material alteration" of the work, regardless of copyright ownership. The outcome was the National Film Preservation Act of 1988, which drew up a list of culturally significant films and outlawed screening a listed work that had been colorized or otherwise altered without disclosing the fact.[185]

Interestingly, only Americans debated colorization. Europeans seem to have simply assumed that colorization was indefensible. Some Americans in favor of authorial rights, and thus against colorization, were as vociferous as any European. Sydney Pollack, the well-known director, was shocked. American film masterpieces, he testified before Congress, "are being altered and then exhibited or sold to mass markets." But rank commercialism was not the only charge leveled by this consummate Hollywood insider. The colorizers were trying to rewrite history too. "In Orwellian fashion, the machines revise film history, trampling upon the honor and reputation of the great directors who created those works."[186] Woody Allen remained firmly in character as an American auteur, leading the charge against the vulgarians, even though he had colorized a newsreel snippet in *Bullets over Broadway* and inserted himself into old news footage in *Zelig*—not to mention chopping, rearranging, and redubbing two Japanese spy movies in his 1966 directorial debut, *What's Up, Tiger Lily?*

The auteur's opposition to colorization was predictable. More interesting was how others defended it. Business interests donned the vestments of populism and democracy. "The choice lies with the public," argued an executive at one of the colorizing companies. "The public loudly and clearly indicates a preference for color."[187] The expressed wishes of the viewing public, hypocritically trumpeted by the companies with most to gain, clashed with the Hollywood masters' unabashed elitism.[188] "The creation of art is not a democratic process," Steven Spielberg pontificated before Congress. "The public has no right to vote on whether a black-and-white film is to be colored any more than it has the right to vote on how the scenes should be written."[189]

Why the fuss, others asked? As long as the monochromatic originals remained, "let a thousand skunk weeds bloom."[190] Ideological pro-colorizers had no economic interest in the dispute and did not necessarily think colorization was a worthy enterprise. Instead they asked what was best for the public domain and for cultural innovation. How did colorization differ from other changes to works intended to broaden their audience: modern-dress versions of historic plays, Baroque music played with Romantic instrumentation, or translations of novels? What concept of authenticity held once a work's performance differed from that at its first release?[191] Filmmakers were often the first to appropriate, change, and even mutilate others' works. Why this sudden persnickety emphasis on authorial authenticity in cinema?[192]

In Europe no controversy spoiled the consensus. All united behind the author. This was true not only of colorization but also of most disputes over authors' rights during the digital revolution of the 1980s and '90s. To the Europeans the Anglo-Saxons seemed incomprehensible. American courts, one French jurist insisted, simply failed to understand the essence of moral rights.[193] That there might be another side to the story rarely occurred to Continental observers. Only once before the digital age had the Europeans seriously debated the preeminent role of the author and his relationship to the public good. That, as we shall see, was during the fascist era. The 1920s and '30s brought the first sustained challenge to the author's supremacy on the Continent, though it was mixed with a great deal of cultural posturing on behalf of strong creative personalities. After 1945, however, the European position reverted to its mean. The perverted collectivist vision of interwar Europe made any later challenges to authorial preeminence impossible. The authors' rights ideology enjoyed its apotheosis during the Cold War as a riposte to the mass culture of both Babelsberg and Hollywood. As in so many other respects, postwar Europe abjured its own past demons, avoiding anything even remotely tainted by totalitarianism.

WHAT IS THE PUBLIC INTEREST?

Seen historically, copyright has aimed to serve the public interest directly. The Continental ideology claims to do so too, but only insofar as protecting authors also benefits their audience. The European Commission betrayed its order of priorities when it noted in 1991 that a high level of protection helped to stimulate creativity "in the interests of authors, the cultural industries, consumers, and ultimately of society as a whole."[194] Both systems appealed to the public good; both believed themselves to take account of the interests of authors, disseminators, and the audience. But much hinged on how the public interest was defined. Did adhering faithfully to the author's wishes and vision produce high-quality culture? Or was the goal a great variety of culture, cheaply and universally available?

The public interest has not been a given. One might cynically say that every interest group—authors, disseminators, public—has its own definition. Do we want to stimulate new creativity or distribute existing content? Was the goal the best, the most, or the cheapest cultural production? Pirates dreamed of cheap, ready, and fast access to works. In its 2010 election platform, the Swedish Pirate Party advocated open digital access to works after five years.[195] But what if incentives were insufficient? A short-term boon for the public might prove a cultural catastrophe in the longer run. A widely opened public domain could dampen creativity and eventually shrink to a size smaller than one restricted by copyright.

The public interest could also mean an emphasis not just on availability but on the richness, multiplicity, and quality of cultural creation. Moral rights, a French observer insists, serve the public interest.[196] Stronger protection encourages authenticity and quality, even as it restricts audience access. That is the golden-goose problem: poor nesting conditions mean the laying ceases. The public interest, in other words, is not necessarily the same as the interest of the public.[197] Consumer wants might contradict citizens' higher aims. That is the democracy problem: what the public thinks it wants is not necessarily what (others conclude) is best for it.[198]

Take John Ruskin, advocate of traditional craftsmanship and self-professed friend of the laboring classes. As was customary in nineteenth-century Britain, his works appeared in editions too expensive for the poor. In America, where publishers pirated foreign works and paid no royalties, cheap editions made Ruskin almost as popular as Dickens. Perhaps British publishers would have issued affordable editions for the US market, one American commentator ventured. But why would the English publisher "see his interest in selling a large edition at a low price, when the sale of a small costly edition would afford an equal pecuniary return"?[199] The jurist and statistician Leone Levi thought that British publishers had "yet to learn the first lessons of political economy respecting supply and demand." As they ignored the "wonders of the penny newspapers" and kept editions small and prices high, only subscription libraries and retail competition allowed books to "pass beyond the upper classes of society."[200] Market logic could not settle the issue. The same profit was attainable one way or the other. Other reasons were needed to prompt authors and publishers to choose whether to be known among a select few for sumptuous editions or to cut a broad swath across the reading public with cheap and cheerful ones.

Authors deserved protection, but how much? Nineteenth-century French observers advocated authors' perpetual property rights to their works. The sight of great writers' heirs living off their ancestors' works was a public good, they insisted, that stimulated others to exercise their talents.[201] During the British debates of the 1830s over lengthening copyright terms, the poet Wordsworth argued that extensive protection most helped quality literature, which, being less popular, took longer to catch on. Not only did authors gain, but society benefited too through better literature.[202] But in the copyright systems authors' rewards were justified only insofar as they stimulated creativity and enriched the public domain. Wordsworth's nemesis, the historian Thomas Babington Macaulay, argued that copyright "ought not to last a day longer than is necessary for the purpose of securing the good" of encouraging authors.[203] Any expansion of authors' deserts had to be justified by higher social goals.

Such battles have been fought continuously for almost three centuries within Britain, France, Germany, and the United States. And each of these nations belonged to larger groupings of legislative affinity. No country purely exemplified either copyright or authors' rights. Today all are hybrid and ever more similar. Yet fundamental differences over whether to focus primarily on authors or on the audience remain embodied in legislation and given voice in debates. Through distinctions in degree and emphasis, these disputes persist even today. Both the Continental and copyright systems have sought to balance the interests of authors and audience, but they did so at different angles. It is to how that divergence of emphasis, and its profound cultural implications, arose historically that we now turn.

2

From Royal Privilege to Literary Property

A COMMON START TO COPYRIGHT IN THE EIGHTEENTH CENTURY

By the mid-nineteenth century, copyright and authors' rights had begun to diverge. But in the eighteenth century Britain, the United States, France, and Germany (which passed laws in that order) shared much the same goals. Everywhere, legislators sought to curb publishers' privileges and vest rights to works instead in their authors. All regarded works as property justified by natural rights because of the authors' labor. Authors, all agreed, were entitled to benefit when they sold their works to publishers. To stave off the expropriation of their royal privileges that this threatened, publishers advanced the same logic of natural rights. Since authors owned their works, they could also fully assign them to publishers. As the booksellers saw it, they were therefore the absolute masters of the manuscripts they bought, owning them perpetually. But this was an illusion. Unlike conventional, tangible property—the exclusive domain of one owner—literary property was inherently promiscuous. By its nature, it yearned to be used by many. When published, works were, in effect, given away. Only society's copyright laws—not natural rights—prevented them from being copied *ad libitum* thereafter. By demanding perpetual rights to works they bought from authors, publishers were therefore overreaching. Since their only enforceable powers of control derived from statute, the law also decided the terms on which they possessed their literary property.

The point of the new copyright laws was twofold. First, by granting ownership rights, they would stimulate authors to further productivity. But just as importantly, they aimed to ensure the swift and efficient transfer of works into the public domain. As a result the rights given authors—and thus also those they could in turn assign publishers—were limited: to fourteen years after publication in Britain and the United States and to five and ten years postmortem in France. Publishers, however, hoped to invoke either natural rights or common law to substantiate their own everlasting stake. Though writers and booksellers both claimed to believe in works as a form of property, in fact they were at cross-purposes. This antagonism was fought out in the so-called Battle of the Booksellers. By the early nineteenth century courts in Britain and America had settled the issue there. Copyright was declared a merely statutory right, founded immediately on man-made law and only abstractly on natural rights or on the common law. Whether held by an author or a publisher, ownership therefore lasted only as long as the copyright laws decreed. In Europe, in contrast, the idea endured much longer that works were property founded directly on natural rights (as formulated in statute) and thus—in theory at least—owned in perpetuity. That helped push France and Germany along a path that soon diverged from Anglo-American copyright.

The invention of printing with moveable type in fifteenth-century Germany made writings easily reproducible for the first time. By reducing the physical toil of copying by hand, printing also allowed anyone—not just their legitimate owners—to reproduce printed materials. At the very moment that mass reproduction promised authors a market, it also threatened to snatch it from them and their authorized booksellers (as publishers were called in the eighteenth century). Earlier, authors had often been clerics, expecting no tangible reward, or they were supported by patrons, courts, or the church. Who owned works and captured their benefit was not pressing. But when the printing press created new markets for works, ownership became an issue. Did the work belong to the author, the bookseller he allowed to disseminate it, or to a pirate publisher? These were the questions that copyright sought to answer.

Before copyright there was privilege. Privileges originated in the fifteenth century, in Venice, Germany, and elsewhere. They were royal grants of exclusive, but time-limited, dissemination and exploitation rights for publishers and sometimes guilds, like the London Stationers' Company. Publishers were allowed to make and sell particular books, images, or pamphlets as monopolies. But privileges could be enforced locally at best. In fragmented early modern Europe popular tracts were reprinted elsewhere and smuggled across borders. The southwestern German principalities and, most notoriously, Austria were the print pirates of their time.[1] In more centralized nations like England and France, the battle of the privileges pitted the publishers of Paris and London, printing with royal assent, against provincial competitors, with their cheap knock offs. Scottish reprint publishers dogged the London booksellers. In France the booksellers in the provinces, Lyon for example, fought their Parisian colleagues.[2] Swiss publishers escaped both the French monarchy's censorship and its grants of privileges.[3]

Publishers and their authors fought too. Privileges were generally given to publishers, who usually paid authors for manuscripts. But they were for short periods only and thus subject to renewal. During the late seventeenth century, authors and their heirs began to insist that renewal of publishers' privileges depended on their say-so. They argued that transfer to the bookseller of the physical manuscript and his right to publish a first edition should not include future editions as well. Both booksellers and authors began claiming that their rights to works derived not from royal favor, but from nature itself.

THE BATTLE OF THE BOOKSELLERS

The natural rights concept of property was revived by both authors and publishers in the eighteenth century. John Locke's theory of property was pressed into service. His *Second Treatise on Government* (1690) portrayed property as wrested from nature by the owner's labor. It was thus an innate right, not a social convention, and it existed naturally, prior to and independent of society and its laws.[4] Locke himself did not think that property in things could be simply extended to intellectual works. He favored a limited copyright term, believing that a perpetual property right in books threatened to harm the spread of learning.⁵ He scoffed at the booksellers' "absurd and ridiculous" pretensions to own the works of classical antiquity, whose authors were centuries dead.⁶ But other thinkers sought to elide the difference between natural rights in physical property and authors' claims to their works. Concepts of property inherited from Roman law had relied on occupancy—not labor—as validating ownership and were anchored in the materiality of property. They shed little light on the emerging concept of immaterial literary property. Locke's justification of property by labor filled this vacuum.⁷

The "Battle of the Booksellers" refers to the struggle fought during the eighteenth century over property in literary works. Ultimately the dispute pitted booksellers against authors. But proximately it was pitched between the booksellers of the capitals, who were favored with royal privileges, and their provincial rivals, who were not. Booksellers were the first to recognize the advantages of the labor theory of property for their cause. They employed a concept of law—understood as common law in Britain and natural rights on the Continent—that preceded and transcended mere statute. With it, they hoped to claim perpetual ownership for what earlier had been granted them only provisionally by royal decree as privileges. Authors, they argued, had a common law or natural rights claim to their works in perpetuity. Independent of any rights granted them in statute, they could dispose of such property as they pleased. The booksellers claimed to be supporting authors' just and natural right to property. But in fact their aim was to take for themselves what nature had supposedly granted their clients.

This was a cuckoo defense of property rights—publishers invoking authors' rights on their own behalf, slipping their eggs into others' nests. One of the earliest instances of such tactics had come already in 1586, with arguments advanced by the jurist Simon Marion. Marion made his case before the highest court of Old Regime France, the Parlement of Paris, on behalf of an annotator of Seneca, Marc Antoine de Muret. Muret's edition had originally been published without any restrictions in Rome. Two Parisian publishers were now quarrelling over a privilege granted one of them for a new edition. Marion argued the author's right to decide the conditions under which he released his work, including that of asking nothing in return. By "common instinct," the jurist insisted, men recognize others to be the master of what they create. Just as God is master of the world, so is the author of his book.[8] Marion won his case, the privileges of the defendant bookseller were revoked, and the volume—per the author's wishes—was left in the public domain, freely reprintable by anyone. Marion's rhetoric was seemingly selfless. But he had not, in fact, been arguing on the author's behalf. Quite the contrary. Muret was long dead and the case had been brought by one bookseller against another, aiming to publish a competing edition. Authors' rights were being invoked on behalf of the disseminators, not the creators.

While they might dispute who had rights to the work, at least authors and their chosen publishers were united in advancing natural rights arguments against competitors with pirated editions. The author and his legitimate publisher had a common interest in the emerging theory of intellectual property based on natural rights. The Battle of the Booksellers was thus fought on two fronts. It set the publishers with privileges against provincial competitors. But in the longer run it also set authors, whom nature favored with these new rights, against their publishers, who gained such rights only derivatively. Privileges still had to be renewed and still depended on royal whim. If publishers could convince the courts that privileges were not the source but merely a reflection of their underlying natural property rights, they could secure a monopoly for their lists. This appeal to natural rights cut two ways. Publishers' rights derived from authors' prior claims to their works. Their act of creation was natural and primary compared to the formality of alienation (or selling rights) and the contractual relations by which publishers secured their rights from authors. The more convincing the publishers' claims were, the stronger the author's rights became.

In the eighteenth century natural rights theories of literary property were brandished in Britain and France as the authorized booksellers sought to assert claims to their books. An anonymous brief stated the Parisian publishers' position in 1690, the year of Locke's *Second Treatise*. It argued that, since booksellers risked resources and invested energy, their claims were just. Their privileges acknowledged this, and they ought to be—so went the cheeky suggestion—perpetual.[9] Louis d'Héricourt agreed a few decades later in 1725. The Parisian booksellers, he insisted, owned their books not through privileges from the king but through the property rights their authors granted them. The rights in the manuscripts bought from authors were genuine possessions (*véritables possessions*) of the same sort as land, houses, or chattels. When selling his manuscript, the author transferred all rights. Publishers and their descendants therefore owned the manuscript in perpetuity, to dispose of as they pleased.[10]

But authors too appealed to natural rights. When publishers' privileges came up for renewal, authors advanced their property rights to overcome their publishers' demands for extensions. In 1761 La Fontaine's granddaughters wrested back his *Fables* from his Parisian publisher after almost a century. Their argument was the same as the publishers', but the goal was the opposite. Both invoked the right of property.[11]

THE AMBIGUITIES OF LITERARY PROPERTY

The natural rights argument was simple and intuitive. It promised to give authors a stake and to free literary works from royal privilege, with its arbitrary assignments and durations and its whiff of censorship. Authors sought to become intellectual entrepreneurs—freed from patrons, emoluments, and charity. A lively debate ensued: who owned literary property? Could it be fully assigned to others? And, above all, was intellectual property like conventional, physical property?

Authors and booksellers both advanced natural rights to property but in fundamentally asymmetrical ways. As authors saw it, their rights were supposedly born of nature herself. Publishers, whose claims derived via contract or statutory law, could never hope to emulate the authors' relationship to their works, except insofar as the author's rights were fully assignable to them. Since natural rights to property derived from the fruits of labor, literary property was not only equal to other kinds of property, it was arguably property's primary form. Physical laborers needed tools, land, raw materials, and at times, helpmates. But spiritual work was an inherently personal and solitary effort. Diderot put the argument powerfully in 1763. What could belong to man more than the products of his mind? The purest property was intellectual, not physical. Nature offered all humans a field, tree, or vine. But authors' ideas sprang from their very core, from their souls.[12]

The French revolutionary, Isaac le Chapelier, is best remembered for the law of 14 June 1791, bearing his name, which abolished many of the Old Regime's intermediary institutions between citizen and the state. It swept away the foundations of corporatist society, especially guilds and workingmen's fraternities, thus leaving the individual naked and unmediated vis-à-vis an ever more powerful state.[13] In a less world-historical role, le Chapelier was the National Assembly's spokesman on authors' rights and in 1791 the sponsor of a decree on the subject. Explaining why a play belonged to its author, not to the owner of the theater staging it, he claimed in an oft-quoted phrase that the work, the fruit of a writer's thoughts, was "the most sacred, legitimate, unquestionable and most personal of all properties."[14] When presenting the second of the revolutionary laws on authors' rights in 1793, his colleague at the National Convention, Joseph Lakanal, argued equally forcefully that literary property, precisely because it sprang from the individual alone, was unlike other forms of ownership and thus did not run counter to revolutionary ambitions to equality or liberty.[15] What the individual himself produced was his alone and no concern of society's.

In Britain an anonymous pamphlet of 1735 had claimed that literary property was more obviously rooted in nature than any other. "A Father cannot more justly call his Child, than an Author can his Work, his own."[16] In 1769 Justice Aston said that, "I do not know, nor can I comprehend any property more emphatically a man's own, nay, more incapable of being mistaken, than his literary works."[17] The American states agreed. The preamble to the Massachusetts Copyright Act of 1783, copied or paraphrased in other states, stated that the author had a right to his works since there was no property "more peculiarly a man's own that that which is produced by the labour of his mind."[18] From the start the personal connection between author and work was a leitmotif and the foundation of the new idea of property rights in intellectual works.

Authors argued for property rights founded in nature since they secured them not only against pirates but also against their own, authorized publishers. The booksellers agreed for their own reasons. The author could bindingly sell only that which he undisputedly owned. As Diderot put it in 1763, "The right of the owner is the true measure of the right of the buyer."[19] But publishers' claims depended on how much authors could assign. Were all their rights transferable or only some? How could publishers own this supposedly personalist property as absolutely as authors?

Unsurprisingly, publishers argued that they assumed the entirety of the author's stake. That is why Héricourt had called them *véritables possessions*. Hence the publishers claimed to own in perpetuity the manuscripts they had bought, just like other forms of real or moveable property. With hindsight authors' and publishers' insistence that claims to literary works were more natural and more intrinsic than to other forms of property seems a foreshadowing of the nineteenth-century personality-based theories of authors' rights.[20] But the opposite is true. The thrust of the eighteenth-century publishers' argument was that authors had the right to alienate their creations fully, breaking both their economic and their personal connections to their works—not as creators but as owners.

The publishers' first rhetorical move was thus to argue that author and work were inherently connected. "If there is any property that is sacred, obvious, indisputable," the French lawyer Cochu argued on behalf of the Parisian booksellers in 1778, "it is that of authors in their works." Literary productions, he continued, are the "children of their talents." Authors therefore had greater claims to their works than did others to property acquired by normal means.[21] Booksellers conceded that this did not hold for every form of intellectual property. Claims to inventions remained a privilege, not a natural right. Because inventions were assembled out of elements available to anyone, inventors' claims could not be perpetual.[22] But authors, as the bookseller Leclerc argued in 1778, were not asking for rights to their ideas but only to their expression. Ideas were common goods, but expression was individual and unique.[23] Inventions were by their nature communal. Because future inventors tinkered and improved, rights for the current inventor could be only temporary, argued Simon Linguet, a lawyer and spokesmen for the Parisian booksellers, in 1777.[24] Literary works, in contrast, sprang from the author's mind fully and perfectly formed. Possibly they could be improved but only by their author. In his letters of 1778, the abbé Pluquet, a theologian and philosopher, denied categorically that two authors could ever write exactly the same book. A writing is "always and exclusively mine," and therefore the author deserved unconditional property rights.[25]

The point of the eighteenth century's personalist view of the author's works was thus to sever, and not to cement, an indissoluble bond of ownership between creator and creation. Yes, the work was the personal creation of its author. But precisely that intimate claim to the work also allowed the author to alienate it fully. The work was entirely his to do with as he pleased. The abbé Pluquet, who supported the Parisian booksellers' hopes of winning perpetual rights to works, argued that if the author could not transmit his property rights to others, then he did not own his work. In selling his work, the author put the bookseller "in his own place" ("il le met à son lieu et place").[26] "If the author is not master of his work," Diderot agreed, "no one in society owns his possessions. The bookseller owns the work in the same way as the author did." Diderot admonished his own children not to follow the bad example of La Fontaine's granddaughters who had reclaimed the *Fables*. He, Diderot, had freely parted with the rights to his works. His children retained no more claim to them than to a piece of land he might have sold to pay for their educations.[27]

Natural rights promised publishers a firmer grasp on their books than royal privilege. When they argued for a Lockean personal relationship between author and work, they hoped to assert that literary property was true property and thus as alienable. But precisely this personalism of the author's tie to his work threatened to undermine publishers' claims to fully possess it. Given the special nature of the connection between author and work, could he assign it fully? He was, after all, invested in his sonnet or sonata more intrinsically than the turner in his table leg, the farmer in his turnip, the shepherd in his wool. A personal aspect crept into the themes of labor-based property from the start, though the booksellers still thought they could steer this argument toward their own purposes. They had not yet grasped that, even though the author's rights might be alienable, assignees could never pretend to the same ineffably personal connection with the work.

A second ambiguity of nature-based property rights concerned the parallels drawn between conventional and literary property. In 1791 le Chapelier famously argued for an inherent bond between creator and creation. That was a commonplace of the era. In a less remembered passage, where he actually shed doubt on natural rights, he went on to highlight the distinctions between literary and conventional property. Having agreed that plays belonged by nature to their writers, not theater owners, he cautioned that literary property was not like other forms of property. Once the work was public, the author had in effect given it away. It was only fair that authors (and for a few years their heirs) controlled their works. Thereafter, however, the works belonged to the public domain, free to all.[28] Le Chapelier noted how natural rights of authorship were inevitably limited.[29] Nature might intrinsically bond the author with his work. But once his work was public, the author controlled it only through positive, man-made law.

As we have seen, natural rights were first advanced by publishers with royal privileges, who hoped to secure perpetual monopolies of their lists, and then by authors, demanding better terms from publishers. In Britain common law served much the same purpose as natural rights on the Continent. It too allowed an appeal to intuitive principles of justice as the basis of rights to literary property much like those to conventional ownership. But what about publishers who did not enjoy privileges? The editions issued by these pirate publishers spread learning and pleasure on the cheap. The authorized publishers viewed the pirates as thieves. The pirates returned the favor, regarding them, in turn, as monopolists. As reprinting publishers saw it, authors' rights derived from society, not nature. Whether authors and publishers were due a monopoly was a political dispute like all others; it was not a matter of teasing out the inscrutable intentions of the universe. In *Tonson v. Collins* (1762) lawyers for the defendants, who had reprinted Addison and Steele's periodical, the *Spectator*, argued in this vein. There was no common law perpetual property in literary works, only what the state had granted in statute. Once published, and then in the public domain, a work was "thrown into a state of universal communion." The work had become "like land thrown into the highway, it is become a gift to the public."[30] Copyrights were like patents, temporary monopolies granted authors and inventors to stimulate their activities.[31]

The Enlightenment philosopher Condorcet took up cudgels against Diderot in 1776 over such issues. Diderot, as we have seen, spoke for the Parisian publishers' allegedly natural and thus perpetual rights to their books. Condorcet instead provided ammunition for the reforming ambitions of Turgot, the French minister of finance, who sought to suppress guild monopolies, allowing also provincial publishers to compete on the Parisian book market. Condorcet argued against the pretensions of authors and their authorized publishers to own works forever. Ideas were not the product of an individual mind, he insisted. Their formulator could not own them. At most a creator could hope to own the expression of his ideas, not their substance. Claims to literary works thus relied on society's protection; they were conventional, not natural.[32] The provincial booksellers' case was also supported by the jurist Jean-François Gaultier de Biauzat in 1776. Seeking to defeat the privileged Parisian booksellers, he argued that literary works were like inventions. Once made public, anyone could copy them. If such copying were restricted, however, it was only by government authority, as embodied in copyright statute, not by transcendent natural rights.[33]

In this view literary property was not as firmly grounded as conventional property. The landowner's wealth was recognized by all who passed. The inventor or poet, however, remained a pauper until, paradoxically, he disseminated his patrimony. As Justice Aston put it in the foundational British copyright case, *Millar v. Taylor* (1769), "property, without the power of use and disposal, is an empty sound."[34] An author wrote only in order to publish, the abbé Pluquet insisted in 1777. So long as his work remained in his briefcase, it was of no use.[35] The point of literary works was not—as it was with conventional property—exclusive possession, but the opposite. As a commission set up under France's Bourbon Restoration in 1825 pointed out, works were "essentially destined" for an audience. So how, then, could an author reclaim a property right in something that he had published and thus effectively given to society?[36]

Moreover, once a work was public, its creator lost nothing more, however widely it was now distributed. Even if he were not paid royalties by pirate publishers, who flogged unauthorized copies of his work, the author's renown grew. Most tangible property could be used by only one person at a time. Ignoring inherently singular objects, like paintings, literary property could be enjoyed by many simultaneously. It was, as economists say, nonrivalrous. So why restrict the audience at all? As Thomas Jefferson put it, an idea has the quality that "no one possess the less, because every other possess the whole of it."[37]

Even claims to tangible property were ultimately socially created, not the outcome of transcendent natural rights. Without the law, courts, and police, even the highest-walled estate belonged to the wielder of the biggest club. The dependence of literary property on statute's man-made protection was, of course, even more obvious. Once disseminated, literary works belonged to all, able to be copied *ad libitum* except as the law gave the author control over them. Spiritual creations were not, in that sense, property except—obviously and trivially—when the author kept them to himself. Abel-François Villemain, minister of education during France's July Monarchy, later put his finger on the issue. Works of the spirit, he pointed out in 1841, might at first glance seem to be the most personal sort of property. But actually they required special protection because they existed only in the act of being communicated—which also partly alienated them.[38]

While nature might believe in individual property rights for tangible objects, she seemed a socialist when it came to fruits of the mind. Was the very idea of literary property therefore a contradiction in terms? The fundamental dispute that was to run throughout the copyright wars for the following three centuries emerged early. Was there something natural and inherent in authors' claims to their works? Could authors, and by assignment their publishers, therefore demand perpetual rights or extensive protection, much as homeowners could over their houses? Or were literary property rights a mere grant of a temporary monopoly, resting on society's judgment of what authors deserved?

THE UTILITARIAN ORIGINS OF ANGLO-AMERICAN COPYRIGHT

Starting in the eighteenth century, the Anglophone nations provided one possible approach to literary property. Britain was the first country to shift publishing from privileges and royal favor to ownership rights traded in the market and regulated by law. Its example was followed closely in the North American colonies during their unification. To understand the disputes in both the UK and the US, a basic distinction is required. *Common law* copyright, or the right an author retained in an unpublished manuscript, was based on ideas of property founded on natural rights. Until he had made it public, the creator retained a natural and perpetual right to his work. *Statutory copyright*, in contrast, was the legal monopoly that gave the author a limited control of his work after it had been published. But did common law copyright persist also after publication? Natural rights advocates claimed for the author a perpetual post-publication right to works based on common law and merely recognized—but not created—by copyright statute. Their opponents regarded publication as a voluntary gift of the work to the audience that ended its common law protection and initiated the limited coverage and duration of copyright statute. How this conflict was resolved would be crucial for the Anglophone copyright tradition.

Copyright law was formulated first in Britain in 1710 in the Statute of Anne, named for the reigning monarch. Some eighty years later came the first state laws in the United States and then the federal Copyright Act of 1790. The first British and American statutes gave authors a temporary monopoly, but they also transferred rights promptly to the public domain, fourteen (renewable to twenty-eight) years after publication. Indeed, by limiting the duration of exploitation rights, the Statute of Anne in effect first created the public domain.[39] In both nations copyright granted the creator rights. But ultimately its purpose was to further the public good.

The Statute of Anne was to encourage "learned men to compose and write useful books," just as the Constitution sought to promote "the progress of science and useful arts."

In London the Stationers' Company, incorporated in 1557, represented the book trade—binders, printers, sellers—but not authors. It issued stationers' copyrights to its members and imposed the government's religious censorship. The 1662 Licensing Act lapsed in 1695, and the Stationers lost both their censorship function and their monopoly on publishing. When the Statute of Anne took effect in 1710, the Stationers hoped to regain their powers. But the government sought to keep the market open to publishers outside the guild.[40]

Two main differences distinguished the Statute of Anne from the old system of royal privileges. First, protection had a clearly defined duration. Locke had suggested fifty or perhaps seventy years after either publication or death as the proper length of copyright.[41] But Parliament gave authors and their assignees (generally publishers) the right to print and reprint works for one term of fourteen years only. The author—if alive—could renew this term once. The Statute of Anne thus abandoned the common law fiction of copyright as perpetual property right. Second, anyone could register a copyright, thus breaking the Stationers' monopoly.

The Statute of Anne was not primarily about authors' rights. But compared to what had gone before and what held true elsewhere, it did safeguard some of their interests. They could own copyright in their works, and they alone could renew that right. Otherwise, the statute conferred no exclusive advantages on authors. It merely granted limited property rights in literary works that could be owned by authors—but equally (except for renewal) by anyone they sold their claims to. The statute was based on a Lockean concept that authors derived their rights from having created the work. But they did not own it like conventional property and certainly not forever.

The Stationers did not come away empty-handed from the Statute of Anne. Existing rights continued for a transitional twenty-one years. During that time publishers hoped to persuade Parliament or the courts that common law copyright, the British version of an argument from natural rights with its presumption of perpetuity, had not been supplanted by the new statutory right in the Statute of Anne. Their arguments presented publishers as harmoniously aligned with authors. Authors had a perpetual copyright deriving from common law. This claim was theirs to assign, independent of copyright as formulated in mere statute. When publishers acquired copyright in a work from an author, it therefore was also forever.[42] If the courts accepted the continued existence of common law copyright even after publication, the booksellers would thus have restored their monopoly through legal legerdemain.

In 1769 the booksellers won a brief victory. In *Millar v. Taylor* they persuaded the Court of King's Bench to recognize the author's perpetual common law copyright as continuing despite the Statute of Anne and its short copyright terms.[43] Notably, even though the author's common law copyright was the issue, no author was involved. The plaintiff bookseller owned the copyright to a work that had been reprinted by another publisher after the Statute of Anne's fourteen-year term had expired. The plaintiff argued that the author's perpetual common law right continued nonetheless and, with it, his own. Though *Millar* was soon overturned, it nailed fast the idea that copyright was an author's right.[44] But what started as an author's right quickly passed, by assignment, to other rights holders, usually publishers, once the creator sold his copyright. The Statute of Anne vested rights "in the authors or purchasers of such copies," that is, in the publishers as rights holders. At stake here, then, was whether the author's perpetual common law copyright continued after publication, and if so, whether the publisher received it by assignment along with the limited statutory copyright.

Five years later, the House of Lords ended the publishers' claims to the author's perpetual common law copyright. In 1774 *Donaldson v. Beckett* imposed a Solomonic partitioning. Common law copyright was acknowledged as the author's natural right—but only until that moment when, by publication, he released his work into the world. After that, it was protected by statutory copyright alone. An Edenic paradise of everlasting natural rights was truncated by an abrupt expulsion into a postlapsarian world of printers, publishers, sellers, and the public. And the delights taken from authors were equally snatched from publishers. The Lords now ended the book-sellers' pretensions to have acquired perpetual property rights to their works. They were left with the Statute of Anne's fourteen-year terms.

At stake for the Lords was the social benefit of diffusing knowl-edge. Although the judges who advised the House appear to have backed perpetual common law copyright, the Lords voted other-wise, demonstrating their concern to allow the public easy access to works whose statutory protection had lapsed. Few have so heartily praised the public domain as Charles Pratt, first Earl Camden, a fer-vent advocate of other civil rights too and one of the most robust denouncers of a common law right to literary property. Science and learning were by their nature public, he insisted, and they ought to be as free and general as air or water. Society's goal was to enlighten minds and improve the common welfare. Providence intended ge-niuses to share their learning with all. Knowledge—of no value to the solitary owner—had to be communicated to be enjoyed. Great minds worked for glory, not the bookseller's pittance. Knowledge should not remain locked up in the hands of the publishers, two of whom he contemptuously immortalized as "the Tonsons and the Lintons of the age."[45]

After some wobbles, copyright in Britain was thus nailed down by 1774 as a creation of statute. Once works were published, the au-thor was protected only by man-made law. Authors had certain nat-ural rights in their work by virtue of having created it, but not claims like those to conventional property, least of all perpetual owner-ship.[46] Copyright merely protected them and their assignees for lim-ited times against verbatim copies, giving them exclusive right to publish and sell. The authorities' power to define copyright inde-pendently of nature was demonstrated with aplomb the year after *Donaldson*. Passed in record time, the Universities Act of 1775 granted Oxford and Cambridge perpetual copyright in all works that au-thors gave them.[47] What had been denied the booksellers was given to the universities. But the universities' perpetual ownership—the holy grail of the booksellers' arguments from natural rights—was founded on parliamentary power, as was the limited copyright in the Statute of Anne. What Parliament could take, it could also give.[48]

With both *Donaldson* and the Universities Act, Parliament aimed neither to help booksellers nor authors. It strove for the public good.[49] Copyright in Britain, and later in America, stemmed from a utilitarian vision of promoting the common good of learning and enlightenment by rewarding the creator justly, but temporarily.[50]

THE STATUTE OF ANNE IN AMERICA

At a time when privileges and monopolies for well-connected booksellers remained common on the Continent, British law granted authors substantial property rights in their works. After the 1776 revolution this novelty was avidly emulated in the fledgling United States. Except Delaware, all the original states passed copyright statutes modeled broadly on the Statute of Anne, with short terms. As in Britain, this was thought to promote knowledge and the public good. In 1787 the Constitution empowered the federal government to legislate on patents and copyright. Thomas Jefferson thought that justice between generations prevented one from incurring debts to be met by the next. Based on the "law of nature" and Buffon's mortality statistics, he concluded that generations stood in the same relation to each other as independent nations do and that no debt should extend beyond nineteen years. That, therefore, was to be the duration of copyrights and patents.[51] The same sort of reasoning from nature's alleged first principles that in Europe had been advanced for perpetual rights to works served the opposite conclusion in the New World. The Constitution followed Jefferson and rejected unlimited ownership rights. It gave Congress power to promote the progress of science and useful arts by securing authors and inventors the exclusive right to their writings and inventions "for limited times."[52]

The federal Copyright Act was passed three years later in 1790 and drew the consequences of such reasoning. The various state copyright laws had been based on a natural rights belief that authors possessed certain innate claims to their works. Their underlying premise was that individual and public interests neatly coincided. The more rights authors received, the more the public benefited. The New Jersey statute of 1783 justified the rights it granted authors with the self-evident public advantages that would flow to learning, the nation's honor, and mankind's greater good.[53] But in 1790 the federal act elevated the progress of science and useful arts to first place and turned authors' rights into a means of achieving that.[54] As we will see in the following chapter, in nineteenth-century America authors and their rights took a backseat to the goal of broad, accessible, and cheap public enlightenment.

Modeled closely on the Statute of Anne, the 1790 act dispensed with any appeal to natural rights. It presented copyright as the creation of statute and as a grant made by government, not an inherent right.[55] The constitutional copyright clause united authors and inventors, promising them both exclusive rights to their writings and discoveries. The first draft bills of the Copyright Act also treated patents and copyrights together, though the two were separated in the final law.[56] Both the British and Americans took for granted that inventors' patent rights were a limited monopoly granted by statute, not something that existed in common law or as a natural right. Even those who argued fervently for a natural rights basis of copyright agreed that patents were different. That the Americans lumped them together suggests they saw both patents and copyrights as the creation of statute.

The Constitution gave Congress power to promote science and art by "securing" the exclusive right of authors and inventors to their writings and discoveries. Did that mean that these rights were preexisting natural ones, merely recognized by statute? Or that they were now created by positive law? The word "securing" is inherently ambiguous.[57] Some have argued that the founding fathers sought to enforce with statute what already existed by nature. But most historians agree that they intended to create a new statutory right.[58] If perpetual rights already existed in common law and the federal act now limited their duration, then clearly statute and natural rights were diverging.[59] And if rights came from the natural link between author and work, why was the federal act limited to US citizens and residents?[60] Indeed, the battle fought throughout the nineteenth century over whether to extend copyright to foreign authors—to which we will come—demonstrated how little credence the supposedly natural basis of these rights enjoyed in the United States.

All forms of property, especially literary, were artificial social creations, not absolute natural claims: that was the American position. The founding fathers, Senator James Beck argued later in the nineteenth century, assumed that neither the author nor the inventor was the "absolute owner" of his works "for all time." Once he had sold them, the new owners could do what they wanted, "and but for the protection the Constitution authorized Congress to throw around him, his title was gone the moment he made his sale."[61] Henry Charles Lea, the publisher and historian, put it even more strongly in 1888 to the Senate Committee on Patents: "Society recognizes no absolute and unlimited ownership in any species of property. All that the individual makes, earns, or inherits is held under such limitations as society sees fit to impose in return for the protection which is afforded by the social compact and the value which is imparted to ownership by the aggregation of individuals in communities." That held doubly for "so purely an artificial creation as copyright."[62]

When Noah Webster, the dictionary author and a tireless advocate of perpetual copyright, argued that the author's claims to his work were as natural as those of the farmer to his produce, Daniel Webster, the politician and his cousin, replied: "But, after all, property, in the social state, must be the creature of law; and it is a question of expediency . . . how and how far the rights of authorship should be protected."[63] Daniel, not Noah, formulated the essence of the American approach to copyright. "Stable ownership," as Jefferson put it in 1813, "is the gift of social law, and is given late in the progress of society."[64] American political culture is often thought to embrace property as a foundational and absolute right. But it was a commonplace in the nineteenth century that property ultimately rests on what society agrees, not on what nature decrees.[65]

The implications of this approach were spelled out in *Wheaton v. Peters* (1834)—the American equivalent to the British case of *Donaldson* sixty years earlier, which had ended common law perpetual copyright for published works. Could a Supreme Court reporter, Richard Peters, publish cases condensed from the accounts by an earlier reporter, Henry Wheaton? What should prevail, the author's right to control his work or the public's interest in a wide and efficient spread of information? In a sense, the outcome of *Wheaton* was more heavily foreordained than *Donaldson*. Donaldson had claimed perpetual property in a work of literature; no pressing issue of public interest was in play. The court reporter Wheaton, in contrast, arguably claimed a private stake in public documents, rights to the decisions of the Supreme Court justices.[66] Neither Britain nor America had yet fully developed the modern distinction between public and private records. Courts still relied heavily on oral opinions delivered by justices and transcribed by attendees.[67] Wheaton claimed that no public documents issued from the Supreme Court and its hearings. Peters insisted that the reports of the court's sessions were the dissemination of the judicial determinations themselves, thus the very law of the land.[68] As such, they were inherently public. Two separate issues were intertwined in *Wheaton*: the public nature of government documents in which private copyright was claimed and the persistence of perpetual common law copyright even after publication.

One issue informed the other in the court's decision. The majority of the justices easily decided that Wheaton did not have perpetual rights to his volumes since the property he claimed was so obviously public.[69] But was copyright in the court reporter's own annotations and other apparatus secured by common law or statute? The court's conclusion echoed Daniel Webster's formulation to Noah. A man is entitled to the fruits of his labors, the court admitted. But he could "enjoy them only, except by statutory provision, under the rules of property which regulate society, and which define the rights of things in general."[70] The philosophical justification for an author's rights to his work might be nature or the common law. But after *Wheaton* copyright was judged to be a creature of statute.[71]

Anglo-American copyright was founded in an abstract sense on natural rights ideas of an inherent relationship between the creator and his work. But it restricted these rights to what was determined by statute. Literary property's duration was circumscribed by the general social interest of enlarging the public domain. Yet literary property was like other forms of property in being fully alienable. Authors' economic rights of selling and publishing works could be wholly assigned. Except for the personal right of extending renewal terms—given by the Statute of Anne to authors alone, not to their assignees—all copyright holders, authors or not, enjoyed identical legal positions.

Copyright thus started by accepting the intuitive plausibility of the natural rights argument that author and work were united. But it then immediately violated that premise by making the author's rights fully assignable. This was possible because the only rights in question were narrowly economic: printing, reprinting, and selling. Any creative interests the author might have—in maintaining the work's integrity, say, or protecting his reputation—were not integral parts of copyright. They did not remain wholly ignored in the common law nations. But to the extent they were protected it was in case law and other statute.

The main concern of Anglo-American copyright was to promote the public good by stimulating the production of works and moving them efficiently into the public domain. Samuel Johnson put the argument thus in 1773: authors might have a perpetual claim to their works, a "metaphysical right." But reason and learning spoke against it. Were rights forever, no book could be disseminated broadly if the author gainsaid it. No book could be improved by others' annotation and editing. Though the author deserved reward, once his work was published "it should be understood as no longer in his power, but as belonging to the publick."[72]

THE FRENCH REVOLUTIONARIES BRING UP THE REAR

The Continent and the Anglo-American world would later diverge. But in the eighteenth century the French and Germans also dealt with the author's natural rights to his literary property. Continent and Anglosphere both appealed to natural rights, but—despite the fulminations of booksellers and authors—neither thought that literary property was cut from the same cloth as conventional property. Both traditions started out more alike than different.[73] Self-consciously remaking the world, the French revolutionaries nonetheless also worried about publishers, as had the Old Regime's enlightened reformers. Were monopoly rights to be taken from publishers? If so, should they be transferred to authors? Or was that simply shifting the evil of monopoly from one set of profiteers to another?

On 30 August 1777 several decrees belatedly reformed the Old Regime's royal publishing privileges.[74] Bowing to natural rights of property, authors were given perpetual and inheritable ownership of their writings—but only if they themselves published their works. If—as was common—authors sold them to publishers, then they received only limited rights. The author's rights were thus either perpetual or assignable but not both. Despite howls of protest from the publishers that what belonged to the author and his heirs perpetually could not, when assigned to them, be shorter, nonetheless their claims lasted only as long as the author lived, or ten years, whichever was longer.[75]

By thus distinguishing among various allegedly natural property rights, the authorities strongly implied that statute, not nature, ruled. Their aims were to help provincial publishers and break the Parisian booksellers' monopoly. Once a privilege had expired, any and all booksellers could publish the work. Rights to a work could be renewed only if a significantly expanded edition was forthcoming and then only to that new edition. The old one entered the public domain. The author's rights were thus enshrined in law. But his claims in practice were strictly limited—as were those of the publishers—by the reforming administration's hopes to encourage multiple editions and lower prices.

The revolutionaries followed in the same spirit. After abortive attempts to legislate on the issue, two laws of 1791 and 1793 came to govern authors' rights in France down to the twentieth century. Once the publishers' guilds had been abolished in 1791, privileges had few defenders, and the strongest spokesmen for natural rights in works had been weakened. The outcome resembled the solution achieved in Britain in 1774 with *Donaldson* and followed the example of the 1777 decrees. Authors received rights, but compared to other forms of property, these were strictly limited. During their lifetimes writers (at first only playwrights) were given powers to determine how and when their works were staged. After death this passed to their heirs for five years.

The bill was presented by le Chapelier, the revolutionary who presided over the Constituent Assembly on the night of 4 August 1789, when the Old Regime had been largely dismantled in one session. He placed the issues firmly within the revolution's ambition—inherited from the Old Regime's reformers—of breaking monopolies and freeing talent. Playwrights were public spirited, he was convinced, and they did not seek to control their works long after death. Allowed to sell their works during their lifetimes, they were happy to see them fall quickly into the public domain thereafter. The authorities aimed to break the monopoly granted the Comédie Française and two other official Parisian theaters in staging the classics—Racine, Molière, Beaumarchais, Legrand, and the like. Why should the theater not be as open to talent and ambition as any other profession? England was held up as the model to follow in terms of authors' rights.[76] Two years later, in 1793, a follow-up law protected creators other than playwrights—writers, composers, painters—and lengthened the heirs' control to ten years after death.[77]

These French revolutionary laws were part of the era's discussions of circumscribed natural rights on both sides of the channel and the Atlantic. Britain, America, and France alike all still concerned themselves as much with the public domain as with authors.[78] The point of the French revolutionary laws, as with the Statute of Anne, was to give authors something that they could transfer, making them equal contractual partners with the publishers and theater owners and removing the taint of privilege, monopoly, and servility inherent in patronage.[79] Half a century later, in 1842, the French attorney general André Dupin put it thus: the point of the 1793 law was not to give art a soul. That it already had. It was to give art a body, to make it material, to allow it to be brought to market.[80] What had earlier been given the publishers by royal fiat they now had to bargain for with authors.

As le Chapelier explained to the National Assembly in 1791, literary property was fully alienable. Anyone could take the author's place as its rightful owner.[81] A century later Victor Hugo marked the significance of the revolutionary laws. By giving only privileges, the Old Regime kept authors subservient. But literary property freed them. "L'écrivain propriétaire, c'est l'écrivain libre."[82] A century after that, in 2008, both a Socialist senator and the minister of culture of a center-right French government agreed that property rights were the foundation of the author's social position as a full citizen, no longer a lackey or courtesan.[83] Property made the author an equal citizen with all the other independent owners who, in the French social imagination, constituted society's backbone. As in England and America, the only rights yet up for discussion were the economic ones of publishing, selling, and distributing. Rights of aesthetic control would come later.

GERMANY FORESHADOWS AUTHORS' RIGHTS

Especially in French accounts, Germany is often portrayed as a copyright laggard. True, the fragmented and decentralized state of the future German empire prevented unified legislation across wide swaths of territory, amplifying the problem of piracy. Privileges for publishers were not abolished until well into the nineteenth century.[84] Nonetheless, German thinkers were breaking new ground compared to the French, British, and Americans. By the early nineteenth century German laws were in some respects more sophisticated than those elsewhere.

During the late seventeenth and early eighteenth centuries many German legal theorists argued from similar principles of natural rights as their French and English colleagues.[85] At the same time the continuing influence of Roman law, with its focus on tangible property and its absolute and perpetual nature, threw up hurdles to any easy conceptual elision between physical and literary forms of property. The looser, conceptually less stringent Lockean notion of property came late to Germany, at a time when the influence of the natural rights doctrine was declining.[86] Locke had seen property as the basis of individual autonomy: the primary property was the individual's ownership and thus sovereignty over himself.[87] In contrast, the great jurist Friedrich Savigny rejected this idea as leading to immoral consequences: property in oneself implied that suicide was a legitimate exercise of ownership.[88] Two of the most important German thinkers to consider authors' rights, Immanuel Kant and Johann Gottlieb Fichte, rejected the analogy between conventional and literary property altogether. Though their influence on legislation was limited at first, their day would come.[89]

Kant viewed the text as less important than its ideas and its ideas as something that could not be taken from their thinker. This prepared the way for a conception of authors' rights based on a foundation other than property. The printed work, he argued in his 1785 essay, "On the Illegality of Unauthorized Editions," was important not as a thing but an act.[90] A book was in essence a speech, the printed page merely its medium of delivery. Since the publisher only facilitated this act, his claims depended on the author's permission. Pirating was illegitimate not because it violated property rights but because the pirate falsely claimed to be acting on behalf of the author.

Though heavily influenced by natural rights, Kant did not extend such ideas to property. He accepted the Roman idea of property as absolute control over tangible things. Artworks were property in this sense. Because they were works (*Werk* or *opus*), thus things and not acts (*Handlung* or *opera*), an owner might do with them what he wanted, including reproducing and selling them, even under his own name. But as materialized speech the book was an act and not a thing. By its nature it could not be delivered by anyone else. The author had a personal right (*jus personalissimum*) for his speech to be given in his name and as he intended. The publisher was a mere mediator. Had the work been a thing, then it could be fully alienated by its creator. But since the work was an act, the author could only concede (*verwilligen*) but not fully alienate it.[91]

Many scholars have argued that Kant did not foreshadow authors' rights formulated as a right of personality and that the personal right he mentioned was the publisher's right to disseminate the author's speech to his audience.[92] True, Kant spoke also of the publisher's personal right.[93] But most important, he argued that the author had the right to address his audience in his name and as he chose. Because the publisher acted only at the author's behest, and not as the work's owner, he could not do as he pleased. He had to speak for the author. Kant here granted the author a control over his work, even after having alienated it, that was not yet foreseen in the Anglophone or French discussion.

At the risk of anachronism, we might say that Kant foreshadowed what would later be known as the moral rights of attribution and integrity—the right of the author to be acknowledged as the creator and to control changes to the work. But he formulated these rights very restrictively. Only a writer spoke to his audience. Artists produced merely things, which did not convey meaning. Also indicative of Kant's narrow-gauge approach was his conclusion that, if a text had been so altered as to become effectively a new work, then the original author lost his claims. Nor could the author prevent translations since they were no longer the same speech, even though the ideas remained as in the original.[94] Limited as these authors' rights might be, however, Kant had broached the most contentious future issue, one then barely noticed elsewhere: artistic control. If the work was a property, then alienation gave the new owner full rights, including aesthetic control. If not, then the alienation was conditional, and the transferred property right was truncated. By rejecting the property analogy altogether and defining works as acts, Kant sidestepped the problem that would bedevil those theorists, jurists, and lawmakers who remained beholden to the idea of works as property.

The Idealist philosopher Fichte followed Kant closely. But he was able to retain property as the conceptual base for authors' rights because his idea of property was less demanding. Kant's understanding of property remained absolute. He saw it as fully alienable and thus an unsuitable foundation for the author's claims. Fichte instead restricted what the author could claim. The creator, he argued, retained control over neither the physical object of the work nor the ideas contained therein but merely the form in which those ideas were expressed. Thus Fichte identified two main rights for creators: their authorship must be recognized and the form of their ideas could not be stolen (presumably forbidding both piracy and plagiarism).[95]

The work's integrity seems to have concerned Fichte less than Kant. Instead he emphasized the purchaser's absolute rights over the physical work. He also argued that the reader, in his mind, appropriated and understood a work by reformulating its ideas in his own language and concepts. Both notions played up the audience's claims over the creator's. Since the author controlled only the particular form he gave his ideas, and since that form changed as his audience received and made the ideas their own, the work was inherently malleable and integrity was accordingly unimportant.

Fichte limited the publishers' claims even more than Kant did. They received no property whatsoever but at most a usufruct or use right (*Nießbrauch*).[96] Indeed, the publisher acquired only the right to sell the chance for readers to make the author's ideas their own. He was acting not in his own name but in that of the author. Fichte conceded that the publisher might own this use right. Pirates broke the law, after all, by stealing it.[97] His argument was thus based on natural rights. But he pushed beyond the purely economic rights granted authors in Anglo-American and French law. The author had a property right—not to the ideas as such but to the form he had given them. He had the right to control and protect that form. This implied that, even though he may have sold the use right, the author retained the power to dictate how his work appeared.[98]

Neither Kant nor Fichte immediately influenced German legislation of the late eighteenth century. Nonetheless, early German laws intriguingly differed from those of other countries. Though the Prussian Civil Code of 1794, the *Allgemeines Landrecht*, followed on the heels of the French revolutionary laws, it struck out in novel directions. First, the publisher's right was distinguished from a simple, or full, property right and was identified as a separate publication right (*Verlagsrecht*). Allowing the author to issue and market works, it derived from a contract negotiated with him.[99] The work was not treated as a form of literary property. Carl Gottlieb Svarez, one of the Landrecht's two main drafters, insisted that ownership of the work itself was not transferred to the publisher, who acquired only the sales right (*Verkaufsrecht*), the right to reproduce and disseminate.[100] Unless otherwise specified, the right to assign the *Verlagsrecht* belonged to the author for life. It did not pass to his heirs, except that a publisher bringing out a new edition of a work in the public domain had to compensate the author's children.[101] In this sense the

Prussian Code recognized the author's intellectual rights as something distinct from his exploitation rights, which were assigned to his publisher.

On the other hand, though he had alienated only the publication right, the author did not retain much control—perhaps because the publisher Friedrich Nicolai helped draft the Prussian Code.[102] Unless otherwise specified in the contract, the publisher could issue any number of impressions (*Auflagen*), and thus copies. Until they had been sold, or the author had bought back remaining copies, the author could not bring out a new edition.[103] Works thus reverted to the author or fell into the public domain only after the original publishing house no longer existed and the author had no heirs with contractual rights over new editions. On the other hand, unlike legislation elsewhere, the author was given limited rights of control over his work even after its alienation. A new edition, one with changes and emendations, required a renewed contract with the author.[104] The Badenese Civil Code of 1809 also forbade altering a text, though publishers could print as many copies of the original edition as they liked.[105]

Such ideas broke with a strictly property-based approach. But, on the whole, German legislation of the early nineteenth century did not differ markedly from laws elsewhere. Duration lasted somewhat longer. In 1829 the Grand Duchy of Hesse protected authors, or their assignees, from unauthorized editions for up to ten years postmortem.[106] The more elaborate Prussian Copyright Act of 1837 was often cited abroad as a model. In this the author, not the publisher, was key. He or his assignee had to consent to any publication or republication of his work. He could alienate all or part of his right to publish and sell. But these economic rights were all that was at stake. Protection lasted for thirty years postmortem.[107]

Legislation in France, Germany, Britain, and the United States thus developed similarly during the late eighteenth and early nineteenth centuries.[108] Royal privilege was replaced by a system of limited property rights in literary works. These were demanded first by publishers in their own interests. But authors soon recognized the advantages for themselves. Natural rights undergirded the author's claims, which he could—and usually did—assign his publisher. But at the same moment that both authors and publishers gained firm footing for their ownership, statute replaced nature as the ultimate guarantor of property. And statutory claims were limited to certain, usually short, periods. As Édouard Laboulaye (jurist, poet, antislavery agitator, and spiritual father of the Statue of Liberty) observed in 1858, the French revolutionary edicts may have insisted that literary works were property's most sacred form. Yet what they actually granted authors was a modest stake for a short time, founded on positive, not natural, law. Rather than a royal privilege, authors had been given a social privilege.[109] As an ardent defender of absolute rights to works, Balzac was more blunt in 1841: the French revolutionary laws had confiscated the author's property.[110]

British and American law made the statutory basis of literary property most explicit. But France and Germany's refusal to implement perpetual property rights indicated that there, too, limits were set on natural rights. Concerned as they were to protect authors, Continental authorities also sought to accommodate publishers as well as the public's appetite for cheap and accessible editions. Authorial property rights were a temporary way station on the road to the public domain. The author was enshrined as bearer of rights to his own work, but only the economic claims of publishing and selling were at stake.

The French Revolution did not mark a major break in authors' rights. Old Regime reforms had foreshadowed the revolutionary edicts that, in any case, largely mirrored what had long been the case in Britain and was already being implemented in the United States and across the Rhine. The German situation was anomalous only in that some imaginative thinkers hinted at what was to come.

3

The Ways Part

COPYRIGHT AND AUTHORS' RIGHTS IN
THE NINETEENTH CENTURY

Are literary rights a form of property—like a house or a farm—to be
enjoyed in perpetuity? That was certainly the argument that
nineteenth-century authors and publishers put about. Authors' property rights in their works were partly embodied in laws passed by the
early nineteenth century, first in Britain and then in the United
States, France, and Germany. Authors insisted that literary and conventional property were analogous. Rights to their works should
thus last forever. Most lawmakers, however, were unconvinced by
such special pleading. Their mandate included society as a whole,
not just rights holders. The first laws therefore instituted (at most) a
conditional natural rights understanding of literary property. Authors owned their works and could sell them in the literary marketplace like the producers of other goods. But they were owners only
on the terms that society considered just and that statute extended to
them.

Britain, America, France, and Germany thus started from a common premise: works were a form of property to which authors had
an inherent claim. But, to protect the public domain, neither authors
nor disseminators owned works for more than a limited time. From
this shared eighteenth-century position, however, things began to
diverge. In all nations authors and their assignees were given increasingly broad claims to an expanding palette of works. But with works
treated as property, an inherent contradiction was gradually revealed.
Conventional property could be fully alienated, and its new owner

then possessed it absolutely, free to do as he pleased. Works, however, were commonly recognized as different. A publisher could not just change a manuscript as he saw fit, editing or altering it, giving it a new title and so forth.

Works could in fact not be fully alienated. Even if just in custom and understanding, authors retained some say over works as they passed to their assignees. To a limited extent such continued aesthetic rights were elaborated in the early copyright laws of Britain and America. Yet Anglo-American copyright broadly allowed works to be alienated with only few enduring claims. Indeed, the nineteenth-century Anglophone world firmly emphasized the passing of works in their entirety to disseminators and then their eventual assumption into the public domain. In the late 1830s a vehement debate in Britain pitted authors seeking longer copyright terms against the reading public. The outcome, though a compromise, clearly clipped the wings of authorial ambitions. In nineteenth-century America, copyright was altogether a hard sell. Strong rights for authors and publishers were regarded as Old World monopolies, thwarting the educational aspirations of a fledgling democracy. Since the United States shared the language of British literature's riches, pirating UK books became official American policy. Not until 1891 were foreign authors grudgingly granted copyright protection in America.

In nineteenth-century France and Germany, however, both long terms and the authors' continued aesthetic control, even after they had assigned their economic rights, were taken more seriously. During an intense debate in 1841, French parlamentarians began to discover the contradictions of treating works as conventional property. If works expressed the author's personality, then they could not be wholly alienated. Authors inherently retained an aesthetic say. Pondering the difficulties of applying Napoleonic property law to literary works at divorce, death, and bankruptcy, deputies of the July Monarchy's Chamber of Deputies began formulating what would eventually be codified as the author's moral rights.

Copyright was a legislative snowball. The first laws covered mainly book writers, protecting them from verbatim reprinting in unauthorized editions. But what about engravings, paintings, music, or architecture? And what of abridging, excerpting, translating, performing, or altering works? How much control should authors have over how others might appropriate, use, allude to, quote, and change their works? Nineteenth-century Britain and America dealt with copyright's broadening focus by strengthening statutory property rights. Meanwhile, France and Germany insisted that authors' rights were natural rights. They now began adding personal or moral rights, aiming to preserve the inherent tie between author and work. These two paths of development—copyright and authors' rights—would not, however, emerge as distinct until the end of the nineteenth century.

Perhaps the parting of the ways can be dated to the 1878 International Literary Congress in Paris. Here, the Continental delegates argued the fine points of a natural right to literary property. Was it perpetual? How far could the public domain encroach on authorial rights? Whatever the specific conclusions, nearly all delegates enthusiastically endorsed a resolution claiming that authors' rights to their work were not a concession of law but a form of property given by nature. Only the British delegate stood apart, pleading his inability to participate at all in such discussions. Their very premise, he apologized, violated the fundamental assumption of British legislation, that literary property was protected by positive, man-made law, not by natural rights.[1] That the same held true for the United States will become evident below.

The British Copyright Commission's report of the same year also marked the distance between Anglophone copyright and the Continental approach. Thomas Farrer, permanent secretary to the Board of Trade, found the "absolute and indefensible" rights of authors too robustly propounded. The proposals advanced were outrageous. Having designed a house, an architect should be able to ban others from building a similar one! Or "still more extravagant": having sold their pictures, artists should be able to prevent subsequent owners from copying, engraving, or photographing them. Proposed rights of this ilk irritated the British commissioners and "embittered the discussion of the subject of copyright with Canada and with the United States."[2] In France and Germany, by contrast, such claims were beginning to be seen as worthy goals.

When the publisher Alexander Macmillan blithely tried to convince the commission of perpetual copyright, claiming to see no harm in his firm's owning Shakespeare's works forever, he faced skeptical questioning.[3] The commission considered the high price of British books an outcome of publishers and lending libraries plotting to issue expensive first editions. The book industry demanded copyright for British authors and publishers in the United States. But what result, the commission asked, might that have? Perhaps cheap American editions would merely continue while British books remained dear. The commissioners' tone was searching, and they clearly aimed at public benefit.[4]

INCORPOREAL PROPERTY

As authorial rights expanded, the need to parse what, exactly, authors were laying claim to followed. What was the essence of the work: its physical embodiment, the ideas advanced, the way they were expressed? Property could be both tangible and evanescently incorporeal. The intangibility of literary works made authors' claims less easily graspable, yet also more personal and unique to their creator.

Incorporeal property rights developed early in Britain. The Roman law view of property as something primarily physical remained strong on the Continent. But Anglo-Saxon common law had a wider array of property concepts at its disposal.[5] Options, advowsons, commons, rights-of-way, tithes, offices, franchises, rents, pensions, and other "incorporeal hereditaments": all were intangible property rights that it recognized.[6] Incorporeal property as a general concept soon became accepted in Britain. Between *Millar* (1769) and the debate twenty years later, in 1787, over protecting designs on calico, the idea of property in intangibles ceased being questioned.[7]

For copyright's development the distinction between tangible and intangible property was crucial. Only by fundamentally separating the work as an object from its intellectual content could the author retain rights to something that, in its physical incarnation, he had evidently released—first to his publisher and then, by publication, to the world. Though they had bought the physical book, pirate publishers neither had rights over its content nor permission to issue their editions. By the early nineteenth century a literary work was commonly considered more than the physical book that embodied it. Laws soon enforced the distinction. In 1809, for example, the civil code of Baden neatly distinguished between the manuscript and its content. Depending on his agreement with the publisher, the content remained with the author. In that case its ownership founded his claims both against unauthorized reprinting and against changes or additions to the work.[8]

The distinction between the work's physicality and its immaterial content was elaborated in *Pope v. Curl* (1741). The bookseller Edmund Curl had published letters to and from Alexander Pope without permission. Curl argued that, once sent, the letters had left Pope's possession and control. Owning the physical letter meant controlling its intellectual content. Pope countered that he remained the author of the letters and thus was entitled to decide on publication. The court sided with Pope, distinguishing ownership of the paper on which the letters were written from the "license ... to publish them to the world," which remained with the writer. The substance of literary property was abstracted from its physical medium.[9]

But what exactly did the author then claim, if not the physical manifestation of his work? Could he have property in his ideas? If so, how to distinguish among thinkers to whom the same concept had occurred independently? Were ideas discoveries, waiting to be plucked from nature? Then how could they belong to anyone? Such difficulties had led to patent law being regarded as without any basis in natural rights. Patents did grant ownership in ideas, and therefore such ownership was only a temporary monopoly created by statute. What authors of literary works could own came into focus only gradually. The outcome gave them rights, not to their ideas but to the most personal and unique aspect of the work, their expression.

Engravers were among the first to distinguish between what, for written works, would become ideas and their expression. Led by the great engraver William Hogarth, a group petitioned the House of Commons to protect their reproductions. The resulting Engravers' Act of 1735 was tailored to Hogarth's needs. Unusual among engravers, he created his own pictures rather than copying those of others. The law gave engravers exclusive rights to engravings of their own invention and design.[10] The engravers conceded that, while a direct copy of another engraving was theft, a new study of the same subject was not. "Every one has undoubtedly an equal right to every subject." Instead, the act protected the engravers' approach, "the manner" that "will so apparently be his own."[11]

In 1774 the lawyer Francis Hargrave scoffed at authors retaining rights in their ideas as "absurd and impracticable." That was the realm of patents. Writers claimed only the right of printing their works. But he added, "every man has a mode of combining and expressing his ideas peculiar to himself." Two works might resemble each other, but still display the "infinite variety in modes of thinking and writing." A work, "like the human face, will always have some singularities, some lines, some features, to characterize it."[12] Such individuality founded authors' claims to the expression of ideas found in their works.

The Continent's booksellers also rested their claims to works on this distinction. The privilege granted Voltaire's *Henriade* (1723), the abbé Pluquet pointed out, did not forbid others from writing about Henry of Navarre's siege of Paris. But it did prevent them from stealing Voltaire's version.[13] Authors claimed rights not to ideas but their expression. In 1793 the German poet Fichte came close to the modern formulation of the distinction. He separated the intellectual content of the physical book into its ideas and their expression. Any reader could come to own the thoughts. But their formulation remained the author's.[14] "The wells of literature are open to all," as a British lawyer put it in 1828, "but no one has a right to use the bucket of another."[15]

At the core of the natural rights argument thus lay a personalist vision of the nature of each work, its tie to its creator. Ideas were common to all, but the author owned their particular and unique formulation. In 1839, during France's July Monarchy, Count Portalis took this argument to its limit. Man's most intimate property is his intelligence. The products of his mind are internal and remain part of him, even once released. Literary property is property "by nature, by its essence, by the inability to separate [author and work], by the indivisibility of its object and its subject."[16] When booksellers argued this line, however, the point was to allow authors to alienate their efforts. That which was most personal was also a fully assignable chattel. But how could the work be both uniquely personal and fully alienable? Thanks to this irresolvable contradiction, the natural rights argument, which had both personalist and property-based elements, was gradually supplemented over the course of the nineteenth century by a new philosophy where creator related to his work as it expressed his personality. To that development we will come shortly.

"NOT ONLY ROBBED, BUT MURDERED": OWNERSHIP AND CONTROL IN COPYRIGHT

From the outset literary work differed from other property in being owned only temporarily. But it resembled other property in being assignable in economic terms. A chair, sold to a new owner, is at his mercy. He can paint it any color, use it as a ladder, stick it in the corner, or break it up for kindling. The purchaser of a book too can do what he wants with his physical copy. But what about the work itself? Pirates clearly violated the law. But what about the copyright owner who was not also the author? Could he change the book's title, rewrite it, publish it as he saw fit (or not at all), or even issue it under his own name? The earliest laws governed mainly economic rights—to publish and sell. They protected the author and his legitimate publisher against pirating. The unexpressed assumption was that publishing would occur broadly in the form the author intended. But what about distortions, edits, abbreviations, or other alterations?

Sebastian Brant, the unpaid author of a pre-Reformation critique of the church, *Das Narrenschiff* (1494), had no economic interests at stake. But he objected to pirate editions because they omitted or changed his sentences and inserted new ones.[17] Martin Luther obviously wrote for God, not Mammon. In 1541 he lashed out against his many unauthorized editions. Not only did his legitimate publishers lose money, but the pirate editions, riddled with errors, distorted his work.[18] Negotiating before enactment of the Statute of Anne in 1710, British authors and publishers implicitly assumed that writers retained the right to alter and revise their works.[19] In 1695 Daniel Defoe considered no one but a book's "proprietor" entitled to abridge the work. Proprietor meant the author *or* his assignees. But Defoe considered the author best qualified.[20] Though he might not have a legally exclusive right to be the only abridger, entrusting him made sense.

The Statute of Anne in 1710 allowed authors to transfer their economic rights of publishing and selling to booksellers. But the law was not entirely oblivious to broader authorial control. While it allowed authors to alienate rights, it also specified that those acquiring such rights did so "in order to print or reprint the same." That does not sound as though changes were permitted.

In case law authors sought to enforce control over their works even after selling them. Thomas Burnet's Latin work *Archaeologia Philosophica* (1692) included a facetious conversation between Eve and the serpent. When unauthorized excerpts appeared in English, an embarrassed Burnet sought to prevent translations or unauthorized editions. Shortly after his death in 1715, a group of booksellers planned an English edition. His brother and executor, George Burnet, countered with an injunction. Arguing that Thomas had not wanted an English language edition, Burnet *frère* also claimed that the proposed translation was "erroneous, and the sense and words of the author mistaken, and represented in an absurd and ridiculous manner." Though the court agreed that the Statute of Anne did not prohibit translations, it ruled for Burnet on other grounds. The author had sought to conceal his "strange notions" from the common reader by writing in Latin, the court noted. It forbade a translation—not because it violated the author's statutory rights, but because the court was swayed by the author's hope of managing his reputation.[21]

More control was considered, but rejected, a century later in a case involving youthful indiscretions. In 1794 Robert Southey, age twenty and a political radical, entrusted his publisher with a dramatic poem, *Wat Tyler*, about the leader of the English peasant revolt of 1381. In 1817 Southey was now forty-three, conservative, one of the Lake Poets and—Walter Scott having turned down the position—the poet laureate. The publisher then decided to issue the manuscript with the express intent of embarrassing him.[22] Southey failed to suppress his poem largely because copyright was then not recognized in immoral works. The judge, Lord Eldon, had sympathy with the repenting author. But he also seems to have thought that, by leaving it with the publisher for so long, Southey had forfeited rights over his work.[23]

It was for the graphic arts that British law first protected works for something beyond economic rights. Though the Statute of Anne guarded authors from unauthorized reprinting, it covered only verbatim reproduction and failed to consider works that had been altered—translated or abridged, for example. For engravings a quarter century later, the law's embrace was more supple. As we have seen, the Engravers' Act of 1735 distinguished between the work itself and the ideas it embodied. It outlawed simple reproduction while permitting anyone to use the same motifs. To outsmart cheats, however, it also forbade reproductions that made only minor alterations to an existing engraving.[24] However rudimentarily, the work's integrity was guarded under the law.

The graphic arts in Britain were also the first to receive some protection with respect to the author's aesthetic control—what would later come to be called his moral rights. The 1862 Fine Art Copyright Act dealt with attribution. It forbade signing and selling artworks with other than the actual artist's name.[25] Playwrights also aspired to control their works aesthetically. Before they won performance rights in 1833, they claimed that unauthorized stagings damaged their reputations as well as their income.[26] In 1822 Byron's publisher unsuccessfully sued a theater for putting on an abbreviated version of *Marino Faliero, Doge of Venice*. His lawyer argued economics, claiming that performances would leach away the printed version's market. Byron himself may have been offended that the manager of the Theatre Royal in Drury Lane had openly stated that he would remove certain soliloquies that "however beautiful and interesting in the closet, will frequently tire in public recital."[27] The dramatist Douglas Jerrold put a similar point before a parliamentary select committee in 1832. Unauthorized performances, he complained, hurt authors twice. They were not paid and their works were mutilated. Thus they were "not only robbed but murdered."[28]

Abridged books, too, raised issues of artistic rights that went beyond the purely economic. Did an author control variant publications? Abridged books were common in the flourishing periodical literature of the eighteenth century. Focused on verbatim reprinting, the Statute of Anne did not directly outlaw them. And abridgers argued the public benefit of their work in succinctly enlightening a wide audience. In the mid-eighteenth century, courts weighed the nature and extent of truncation and allowed "fair abridgments" insofar as they were not merely shortened versions. The Statute of Anne had given away the store by forbidding only verbatim reprinting. Case law now clawed back for authors some of what they had surrendered. Yet these cases also continued the statute's emphasis on the general good over authors' claims. Reasonable abridgments were seen as bringing more good to the public than harm to authors and thus they were often permitted. If I were to forbid all abridgments, mused Lord Hardwicke, who judged a pivotal case, *Gyles v. Wilcox* (1741), the mischievous consequence would be to outlaw learned books and journals.[29]

Such concerns for the author's aesthetic interests could be pursued in Britain more readily during the period before *Donaldson* (1774) restricted common law copyright and limited protection to what the Statute of Anne provided. In *Millar* (1769), the case that briefly perpetuated common law copyright beyond the statute's fourteen-year term, Lord Mansfield listed the rights that nature granted authors in their unpublished works—rights he thought should continue also after publication. The author should earn from his efforts, his name should not be used by someone else, and he should choose when and how to publish. The author should decide which publisher could be trusted not to foist additions on the text. If not, Lord Mansfield continued, the author would no longer master his own name. He could not prevent additions, retract errors, or amend or cancel a faulty edition. Anyone might print and perpetuate an imperfect text to the author's disgrace and against his will.[30] In effect, as Mansfield defined the author's common law claims to control works even after publication, he was arguing for what would later be considered the author's moral rights of attribution and integrity.

Mansfield's solicitude for authors did not last in Britain, however. Five years later, in 1774, *Donaldson* severely restricted their common law rights. While the work remained in manuscript, authors had common law property rights. Once published, however, only the protections of the Statute of Anne survived: the right to print, publish, and sell. Mansfield had foreseen an important element of artistic control. The Lords who decided *Donaldson* took a narrower approach. The brief put forth on behalf of Donaldson, the pirate publisher, denied the existence of common law rights in literary property. It rejected the idea that a book consisted of two parts, material and immaterial. It was absurd, it concluded, that the material book was sold and its purchaser could do as he pleased, but meanwhile the doctrine within it remained the author's possession and under his control. That was as silly as arguing that one man could own a horse's carcass and another its color, shape, or speed. Once sold, an author retained as little control over his work as he did over any other chattel.

On the other side, Lord Chief Baron Smythe, continuing in Lord Mansfield's spirit, argued for continued common law rights even after publication. Pirated editions stole both an author's ideas and his name. The work was then passed off as his, even though he no longer could correct errors, "nor cancel any part, which subsequent to the first publication, appears to be improper." Smythe lamented the loss of such common law rights. But his colleague Lord Chief Justice De Grey, speaking for the winning side, feared them. If an author had perpetual property rights, he warned, he could set whatever price he wished for the first edition, refuse a second one altogether, and recall his ideas.[31] The author's published work belonged to society. It could not be clawed back.

The Statute of Anne dealt with reproducible literary works. Singular artworks raised their own problems. Buying a piece of art was long regarded as including the rights of reproduction too. That deprived the artist of both an economic and an aesthetic claim. Engravers, broadly speaking, controlled their own original designs.[32] But what happened when a painter sold his work? Did he retain rights to reproduce it via engraving? The question was important because—in an early foreshadowing of the power of infinite reproducibility—the income from engravings often dwarfed sales of the original artwork. Benjamin West, the most commercially successful British painter of the late eighteenth century, produced at least five replicas of his popular *Death of General Wolfe* (1770), charging between £250 and £400 each. But engravings of the painting earned at least £7000 for the engraver and £15,000 for Wolfe's agent, John Boydell. (How much Wolfe himself took home we do not know.)[33]

When it came to reproducing artworks, in Britain the artist did not prevail. The draft bill of the 1862 Fine Art Copyright Act proposed to keep copyright with the artist of a drawing, painting, or photograph even after sale. Art buyers protested. Allowing an artist to retain copyright in a work he had sold "was about as unreasonable a proposition as had ever been submitted to Parliament" and an unwarranted interference with property rights, one MP complained. Artists would suffer most as the prices they commanded were discounted by the rights they retained.[34] Lawmakers listened and gave the artist copyright after sale only if expressly reserved in writing. But the buyer did not gain copyright either.[35] Absent a written sales contract, copyright was lost altogether.

Another doctrine that became a staple of Anglo-American copyright also undercut the author's right of continued aesthetic control: work-for-hire. This gave rights to the employer and sometimes even regarded him as the legal author. Divorcing creation from control, it deprived the author of rights even before he had created the work. In Britain's 1798 Sculpture Act, the person granted "sole right and property" in the artwork was either the "person who shall make" or the person who shall "cause to be made."[36] The 1862 Fine Art Copyright Act gave copyright to those who commissioned art works, unless otherwise specified in writing.

As always in British life, dogs played a role in copyright too. Who, the Royal Commission on Copyright of 1878 pondered, had rights to a canine portrait?[37] The dog's owner, it decided, should receive both the portrait and its copyright unless agreed otherwise in writing. For collective works like encyclopedias, periodicals, and series, the 1842 Copyright Law Amendment Act gave the publisher "the same rights as if he were the actual author thereof" in his employees' output, except that he could not publish them as stand-alone pieces.[38] As was the concern for film a century later, publishers feared that if each contributor controlled copyright to his own piece, the collective work would fall apart.[39]

The Anglo-American copyright tradition did not wholly ignore authors' aesthetic rights. The eighteenth-century British and Americans who thought that common law still governed literary property even after publication sought to give the author a continued say. Their opponents saw him as having only the economic rights specified by statute. With *Donaldson* in 1774, this latter position triumphed in Britain, as it did in the United States with *Wheaton* in 1834. As the Anglophone nations supplanted common law with statute, artistic control faded as a concern. Protecting the author's economic rights and swiftly transferring works to the public domain were their main ambitions. Did the author alienate all rights when selling copyright? If not, what control did he retain? To such questions the copyright tradition had few clear answers.

THE BIRTH OF AUTHORS' RIGHTS OUT OF THE SPIRIT OF LITERARY PROPERTY IN FRANCE

In Britain and America the debate positioned authors' supporters, who favored perpetual common law rights, against those who recognized no claims to literary property beyond statute's temporary monopoly. The outcome gave authors limited economic rights after publication. It made little mention of artistic control beyond that, except as it specifically deprived them of it. On the Continent legislative outcomes during the late eighteenth and early nineteenth centuries were much the same. Significant divergence would come only later. But during the mid-1800s France and Germany heard the first stirrings of a push beyond a concept of authors' rights that was property based (whether natural rights or merely statute).

Needless to say, Romanticism and its celebration of heroic creators fertilized the soil from which authors' rights sprang (a point we will touch on in the following chapter). But, like natural rights theory, Romanticism was a cultural constant in all our nations without leading to the same results. So something else must also have been at work. In the French parliamentary debates of 1841, when many of the constituent legal elements of moral rights were first recognized, allusions to broad cultural currents—Romantic or otherwise—or to foreign precedents and influences were largely absent. Instead, discussion circled around the intractable problems that Napoleonic law threw up to the transmission of works after death or divorce. Family law drove developments in authors' rights.

The idea of moral rights emerged almost by spontaneous intellectual generation as parliamentary deputies attempted to square the circle of intellectual property's inherent conceptual contradictions. No new actors or interests sprang forth. Authors enjoyed their new-found rights. Disseminators hoped to acquire their authors' claims entirely. Insofar as anyone spoke for it, the public wanted cheap, accessible, well-stocked libraries, bookstores, museums, galleries, and concert halls. But literary property was an unstable concept with a paradox at its core. It was considered especially tied to the author because he had created it by his own efforts. And because it was wholly his, the author could assign it as he pleased. His property was personal *and* alienable. But could it be both? Out of attempts to reconcile this tension in mid-nineteenth century France and Germany came new ideas of authors' rights founded on personality rather than property.

In the eighteenth century all nations under the glass here had concluded that the author enjoyed property claims to his work based on the inherent logic of natural rights. But once it was published—given to the public—in practice only claims granted by statute remained. During the nineteenth century two issues arose repeatedly. The first voiced a natural rights–inspired attempt to fuse conventional and literary property. If literary property was property, why was it not perpetual? A perennial question, it persists even today.

The other, more fruitful question prompted new avenues of inquiry and eventually legislation. Could the author alienate his work fully, as with other property, abandoning all aesthetic control? Conventional property was both perpetual and wholly alienable. But those who insisted that authors should own their works forever usually refused to accept the corollary that an author could also fully part with it. Property ultimately proved an inadequate conceptual tool because authors wanted its perpetuity but not its absolute alienability. One of the first to recognize this was Guillaume de La Landelle, a naval officer and novelist. At the International Literary Congress in 1878, he noted the central paradox: if literary property was perpetual, it had to be alienable. The new owner could therefore freely transform, abuse, or even destroy it. Since that was wrong for works of the spirit, it followed that literary property, if property at all, could neither be fully alienated nor last forever.[40]

Thinking of literary works as conventional property, the French discovered, had undesirable results. Problems arose when works passed from authors to spouses, children, family, or creditors who now were called on to make aesthetic choices. Unexpected consequences led to laws being tested in court. Bills were drafted, and new proposals hashed out in marathon sessions of parliamentary examination and debate. Gradually over the nineteenth century, new ideas forced their roots into the cracks of the property concept, breaking apart the inherited certainties.

In 1777 Simon Linguet, a lawyer and a representative of the Parisian booksellers, had foreshadowed the conceptual problems to come. Authors' works were a "genuine creation" to which they had firm claims. Like others who spoke for publishers' interests, his goal was to give authors rights they could transfer. The only novelty was his argument for something resembling the integrity right. Like Defoe seventy years earlier, Linguet held that, since a literary work sprang perfect from the author's mind, only his hand might change it. But since Linguet sought to justify transferring the work, he also argued that the publisher "completely and continually assumes the author's prerogatives. To dispute the bookseller's property rights is to misunderstand those of the author."[41] Linguet thus granted the author an aesthetic veto over changes, yet also insisted on full alienability to the publisher.[42] He had posed the problem without solving it.

During the Napoleonic era full alienability remained the norm in France. In 1810 it was decreed that authors could cede their rights fully to publishers.[43] But around this time the internal contradictions of the property concept as applied to literary works began to emerge. In 1826, during the Bourbon Restoration, a commission suggested intriguingly that the author deserved an integrity right over published works during his lifetime. The author should be able to prevent changes to his work, editorial cuts in new editions, and commentary by others, thus enforcing the "respect" and "consideration" he was due. A work had never achieved its final form while the author was still living. The commission thus toyed with authorial rights distinct from publishing and selling. But its draft bill retained no traces of integrity. The only right was to publication, granted the author for his lifetime and his heirs for another half century.[44]

In 1834 Balzac took up the author's claims. What riled him most was that novels were turned into theater pieces. A dramatist would steal your story, feeling as little guilt as if he had taken your wife.[45] Even worse, though your adulterous wife was a willing accomplice, your innocent novel had no choice. Yet authors did not write books to see them turned into dramas or vaudeville shows.[46] Despite his gripes, Balzac still argued for artistic control within the conceptual frame of conventional property rights. Dramatists mangled writers' work, he complained: "butchered, drawn, stripped, quartered, grilled on the footlights, and served up to the patrons of the theater." But to judge from where his attention lingered, his main lament was the money that theaters earned. He was irked too that his fellow Frenchmen patronized libraries rather than bookstores. Balzac did not defend authors' rights of aesthetic control so much as attack those who were wringing profit from his work.

During the early nineteenth century France's Restoration and July Monarchy pursued reform in commissions and bills. The eighteenth-century heritage still dominated, and—as in Britain and America—discussions weighed the opposing interests of public and authors. Despite heated rhetoric, the authorities never seriously considered perpetual rights to literary works. If you treat literary works as just another form of property, passing forever like land from family to family, the minister of education warned the Chamber in 1839, they might disappear from public view. More important interests were at stake than the author and his children. Racine's verses could not remain the private property of just one family. They belonged to everyone.[47]

The author could do as he pleased with his manuscript, the Viscount Siméon agreed. But once published, it became a property shared by author and society. No longer a real property claim based on natural rights, the authors' rights were now a fair concession or privilege granted by society.[48] The author was in fact already favored. Once he had sold his work, no natural right prevented the buyer of a copy from making more. "When you sell, you cannot keep anything back," as Joseph Gay-Lussac, the peer and chemist who invented the measure of alcohol by volume, put it in 1839.[49] Only statute prevented authors from losing all control over their works.

THE LAMARTINE DEBATE

But the era when France still balanced rights equally between authors and their audience was drawing to a close. Change began in 1841, shepherded by Alphonse de Lamartine, the politician who was to proclaim the Second Republic in 1848. This was the age when the Napoleonic Code's vision of indivisible and absolute property rights was defended most strongly—as a reaction to the revolution's expropriations and spurred on by the socialists' and anarchists' attacks on the very concept of property.[50] Lamartine hoped to extend a Napoleonic concept of property to the author's claims. While earlier reformers of the July Monarchy had taken a dim view of authors' demands for full natural rights, Lamartine—himself a noted writer—was more sympathetic. In 1841 he reported to the Chamber of Deputies on a literary property bill. While it never passed, the Chamber's long and detailed discussions uncovered the property concept's inherent contradictions and led to a sea change in attitude that would mark all later French jurisprudence and statute.

Until then, the July Monarchy had balanced the rights of authors and the public. It had rejected the authors' demand for perpetuity and trimmed proposals for a fifty-year postmortem term to follow instead the Prussian example of thirty. Lamartine, in contrast, was in thrall to the idea that authors had natural property rights to their works. His draft bill distinguished literary from other forms of property only in limiting term durations, and that only because of practical considerations. In theory, he preferred perpetual rights. The day the law gave authors unlimited protection, he insisted, human intelligence would be emancipated. Opposing the government bill's thirty-year term, Lamartine proposed half a century, with the possibility of further future extensions.[51]

Lamartine's support of a natural rights–based concept of literary property was not unchallenged. Saint-Albin Berville (like Lamartine, a politician and man of letters) viewed property rights in artistic works skeptically. The scant years of exploitation that patents granted inventors compared unfairly with the long decades claimed by authors and artists. Moreover, treating works as property and allowing rights to be inherited meant introducing a new actor, the author's family and heirs. Unhappy families, he warned, might suppress works. Though he rejected authorial property claims, Berville did emphasize the personal connection between creator and work. Our works "are a part of ourselves, a part of our substance." Authors had to be able to change and perfect them. But to avoid granting heirs too many rights, aesthetic control should be given only to living authors, with perhaps a few additional years on behalf of close family.[52] Rights deriving from the intimate bond to the work, Berville concluded, could scarcely be extended beyond the author. A few years earlier, a commentary on the 1837 Prussian law had welcomed families' control of authors' works. Granting thirty-year terms meant that widows, children, and close relations could protect authors' literary and civil honor, and that was evidently a good thing.[53] But this assumption—that family would invariably do the right thing—was now being questioned in the French Chamber.

During discussion of the 1841 Lamartine bill, French deputies slowly came to realize that property and the personal might be antithetical. As the deputy Armand Jacques Lherbette pointed out, if an author was indebted, creditors could seize an existing edition and publish new ones. Creditors might refuse permission to alter a work, fearing the author would devalue their assets. Embarrassing but bestselling juvenilia might come back to haunt an author. "The usurers will become editors," as one deputy put it.[54] The heirs' right, another pointed out, was a mixed property claim, belonging both to author and society. Society's justified claims meant that the heirs, while legitimate owners, could not have absolute rights—to suppress the work, for example.

Lamartine's hope of expanding the scope of literary property met stiff headwinds in the French Chamber. Fearing that creditors might gain control of a work even during the author's life, deputies instructed his commission to rein in the work's full alienability. Lamartine conceded the point, invoking what he called, in one of the first uses of this precise terminology, "considérations morales." The author should have a continued right of control (*tutelle*) over his work and a right to repent of thoughtlessly published work. The commission proposed limiting the full alienability of literary property by making it unattachable, thus unable to fall into the hands of creditors.

Still, some deputies remained unhappy to see the government backtrack on making literary property fully alienable. The minister of education responded by pivoting the argument. Until now, the claim that works were an especially personal form of property had been advanced to allow authors to alienate them. But now he described the author's exercise of will in creating his work as so personal an act that it became inalienable. Though a creditor might seize what remained of an existing edition, he could not substitute for the author to bring out a new one.[55] In other words, the author retained artistic control even when the work's economic value had passed to his creditors.

In one respect, however, the Chamber's incipient concept of moral rights in 1841 differed from later formulations. Unattachability—preventing others from bringing out new editions—was a personal right. Thus, Lamartine reasoned, it adhered only to the author and neither to heirs nor to creditors. But what about the widow? A Napoleonic decree of 1810 had given widows full rights over their spouses' literary property for their lifetimes, after which it passed to the children for twenty years. The decree spoke of the *droit de propriété*—publishing and selling—and not artistic control.[56]

In the same spirit they had denied creditors control over works, the deputies in 1841 now also insisted that unpublished manuscripts were not part of community property, thereby not falling into the hands of an author's widow and heirs at death. Imagine a politically charged memoir. Might they not suppress or bowdlerize it? The author should be able to will it to someone else.[57] By exempting literary property from normal Napoleonic inheritance rules, the deputies attempted in effect to hedge its full alienability. The bill was changed to specify that only literary property's monetary outcome became community property. But the bill's final wording was so unclear that no one knew whether it dealt with the economic fruits alone or also the author's right of control.[58]

Matters grew trickier with posthumous works, not yet published at death. Under Napoleonic law inheritance was strictly governed by a prescribed order of heirs. The spouse, her family, and the children all had claims that restricted the deceased's right to will his estate freely. A fierce debate in the 1841 Chamber probed the distinctions being drawn between conventional and literary property. Lamartine's commission sought to treat unpublished works as a normal part of the estate. To exempt some of an author's estate from the usual rules of inheritance might unfairly favor one child with a (possibly) valuable asset. Having sacrificed herself and her dowry for the husband's work, his wife could find herself a pauper. Other deputies disagreed. An unpublished work was an intimate and personal form of property, one argued. It *was* the author, another agreed. "Mon manuscrit, ce n'est pas mon bien, c'est moi-même." The living author could refuse to publish and could even destroy his work. In death he should be granted the right to dispose of it. An amendment was added, giving the author free rein over his unpublished works. The author, deputies agreed, should command his work like an absolute monarch, not merely a constitutional one.[59]

After endless debate, Lamartine's bill failed to pass. The anarchist Pierre-Joseph Proudhon celebrated its demise as the "abolition of capitalistic property—property incomprehensible, contradictory, impossible and absurd."[60] Major legislative reform had to wait for a century. But it came eventually, and capitalist property thrived in the interim. Yet the Lamartine deliberations revealed the issues at stake already here.

The July Monarchy's deputies came up against an impasse created by conflicts among their intuitions about creativity, their sentimentally familialist view of authorship, and the Napoleonic system of inheritance. The personal tie between author and work was by now a venerable theme. But the author was not—Romantic individualism be damned—just the creator by himself. To be fully owned, property demanded to be transmittable. Allowing authors to treat works like other chattels, passing rights to heirs, had been a constantly pressed ambition among supporters of robust intellectual property rights from the very beginning. Family ownership was almost inherent in the concept of property. What was the point of owning without the right to bequeath? As the 1841 deputies saw it, the moral entity of the author was the creator, spouse, and children. The spouse was portrayed as a helpmate and the children as having natural claims. But there lay the rub. What the author created bore a personal stamp. Yet, when his widow too died, the Napoleonic system gave half the married couple's joint holdings to her legally designated heirs: siblings, parents, children from a former marriage, and so forth. The author was thus legally obligated to impart much of his work to distant relatives by marriage—sometimes people whose very existence he did not suspect.

A later case illustrates the issue. In 1895 the painter Pierre Bonnard began living with his model. She had claimed to be an Italian aristocrat, Marthe de Méligny. Only when they formally married in 1925 did he learn that she was French and her name was Maria Boursin. When he was widowed in 1942, he should have advertised to identify heirs among her family—relatives he had never known. But he had been horrified to discover that, when Matisse's wife had died, the painter had lost his canvases to her heirs. Aghast at surrendering half his works to total strangers, Bonnard now forged his wife's will, leaving him her sole successor. When he died five years later in 1947, a genealogist tracked down her heirs, who then claimed their part of his estate.[61]

Divorce raised similar problems. Allowing the estranged spouse's claims violated the work's personal nature. Not allowing them undermined the (possibly wronged) spouse's role as helpmate. "On the one hand, iniquity; on the other, blatant despoilment," as one deputy put it during the 1841 debates.[62] The solution then proposed called Solomon's bluff, neatly bisecting the baby. The economic rights remained part of communal property, divided as the Civil Code dictated. The moral rights were part of the author's personal claims, to be disposed of as he saw fit. The logic of literary property's personal nature had been stood on its head.

During the French Revolution, Lakanal's argument, that literary property is property's most personal form, had served to allow the author to alienate his works fully. Now, half a century later, this very same personal connection bolstered the opposite claim, that works could never completely be turned over to others. During the Lamartine debate many deputies came to believe that the author should retain artistic control even after selling his work, even after his death, and even in the face of creditors' and heirs' legitimate claims. During the debate of 1841, the logic of literary property's basis in natural rights and its personal nature had reversed. From the deputies' wrestling with the inherent contradictions of natural rights property had sprung the notion of moral rights.

In the Lamartine debate the deputies seem to have been largely ignorant of the German theorists who had advanced early ideas on authors' rights. Once or twice someone mentioned Kant or the Prussian copyright law and English developments too. But on the whole the discussion was hermetically sealed off from foreign influences. Romanticism, with its celebration of the author, may have lurked in the background, but it too was not a palpable influence on the debates among the Chamber's members, many of them writers and literary figures. Apparently spontaneous objections arose from deputies as they realized the implications of Lamartine's proposals. Their first and most important insight was that personal property was either personal or it was property. It could not fully be both. From there, moral rights eventually emerged in the parliamentary sausage factory out of deliberations over the unanticipated consequences of death, divorce, bankruptcy, and inheritance in the Napoleonic system. From lowly origins great things rise.

FROM PARLIAMENT TO CASE LAW

The creator's control of his work after alienation was broached, but not legislatively incarnated, in France during the 1840s. But it began to emerge in case law. In 1864 a journalist, Delprat, sued his editor for having cut and changed an article. The Seine court instructed the editor to publish a letter explaining the issue. The Paris court overturned this, finding that the editorial changes had been minor, neither changing the article's meaning nor hurting the author's reputation.[63] This judgment, in turn, was rejected in 1867 on appeal to the Cour de Cassation, France's Supreme Court. In the note that usually accompanies French cases, the jurist Henri Thiercelin rejected the idea of literary property altogether, retreating instead to the idea of privileges. Literary works were protected, not as property but by a privilege granted by society. Though seemingly a step backwards, Thiercelin's conceptual framing opened up issues that would soon be resolved altogether differently.

Thiercelin agreed with the Paris court that Delprat had not been harmed, not even in reputation. Using the property concept, there could be no compensation without damage.[64] But imagine, he continued, that authors' rights were not property but a privilege to "ensure respect for his thoughts and thus his works." Then the author could claim compensation even if not damaged in the conventional sense. The author was the sole judge of his work, Thiercelin argued. Its mutilation affected not a thing but his thought and his self. Changes made to a literary work might inflict damages only the author could recognize. Thus, what was misleadingly termed intellectual property was in fact not governed by the rules of conventional property. The author's rights instead protected "the essentially elusive and unattachable [*insaisissable*] thought of the author." Thiercelin used archaic terminology when he called this a "privilege." But he aimed to found the author's rights not on property and its pesky requirement of measurable damage (even if only to the social good of the author's reputation) but instead on the author's purely subjective evaluation of harm.

The court did not entirely follow Thiercelin here. Violated property rights were the basis for its decision that Delprat was entitled to a published declaration that his article had been changed without permission. Nonetheless, it did agree that the author was the "absolute master of his work," a nod toward Thiercelin's view that the author himself evaluated how he was harmed, regardless of his reputation or any damage to property.[65] Personality was not yet the basis of the author's rights. But the limits of the property concept as applied to literary work were approaching.

In the early 1870s jurisprudence began to chisel out moral rights from the surrounding marble of the property concept. As in 1841 seemingly tangential claims—this time of creditors—prompted the conceptual heavy lifting. Could creditors republish works or publish manuscripts for the first time? The issue had been left unresolved by the law of 14 July 1866, which otherwise extended and specified the rights of authors' heirs.[66] To answer, André Morillot, a lawyer at the Paris Court of Appeals and an expert on German law, drew on the Napoleonic Code's implicit distinction between those claims a creditor could exercise and those "exclusively attached to the person" of the debtor.[67] The latter rights included disciplining children and consenting to their marriage, pursuing wives' adultery in court, and demanding a "séparation de corps" (then the practical equivalent of divorce). Among these personal rights Morillot wanted to include the author's right to publish or republish his work. Since he did not discuss further rights of artistic control, in effect he advocated only an already broadly accepted claim. Nor did he make a strictly personality-based argument. Rather, he worried that an author's reputation would suffer if he were unable to decide when to publish or reprint.

Though closely related, reputation and personality were not the same. Reputation was as much an aspect of property as of personality. Its monetary value could be damaged or destroyed. The author had good reasons—fully comprehensible in the parlance of property—to protect it. Morillot now moved away from harm to reputation as the triggering event and came close to asserting a personality basis for the author's claim to control his work. Not just his reputation, but indeed his person's inviolability, was breached were he forced to (re)publish ideas he had renounced. The fear of scandal—a preoccupation of French debates—resurfaced here. Having penned a scabrous work in his reckless youth, the repenting author should be able to ban his ill-fated juvenilia.[68]

Six years later, in 1878, having written a book on authors' rights in Germany, Morillot continued developing the moral rights concept.[69] Preventing an author from controlling his work's publication did not violate his property rights. Rather, it was moral damage and an attack on his personality. Disclosure, attribution, and integrity: all these claims remained the author's, even after death. These new moral rights Morillot founded on a distinction between the work as such (its conception in the author's mind), which Morillot thought could never be alienated, and the work's expression, which was the subject of conventional authors' rights. Though nothing practical was to emerge in law for another three-quarters of a century, Morillot here gave moral rights their most explicit formulation yet. Moral rights, in his vision, ascended to the position formerly held by property. They, not property, now rested on the universal logic of natural rights. The usual authorial economic rights were, by contrast, the creation of mere statute. Moral rights in Morillot's scheme were probably inalienable (he was vague whether such intensely personal rights could be assigned to others). In any event, moral rights remained the author's even after he had alienated his economic claims.[70]

BETWEEN PROPERTY AND PERSONALITY IN GERMANY

Early nineteenth-century German laws were not based as exclusively on property as was legislation elsewhere. A commentary on the 1810 Badenese Civil Code emphasized that the work represented the author's personality.[71] The 1794 Prussian Allgemeines Landrecht gave publishers only a "publishing right," not a full property right. But the 1837 Prussian law dealt only with economic rights. Kant and Fichte had sketched out a way of sidestepping the property question entirely. Then, in the nineteenth century, German jurists formulated theories that based authors' claims on their personal connection to the work. Nonetheless, some of the most interesting and influential work also sought to marry aesthetic control to property rights. German-speaking jurists thus developed flexible and differentiated views of property—and how extending it beyond the tangible promised authors extensive powers over their works.

In 1827 the jurist Wilhelm August Kramer formulated a view that granted authors significant aesthetic control while still invoking their property rights. Ownership of the original work conveyed the right to change and disseminate it. Purchasers of copies thus received only a limited right that excluded any reprinting. The author had an attribution right. Though he flirted with a repenting right, Kramer also conceded that, once alienated, authors could not reclaim the right to disseminate "at the expense of the legal owner." More interesting was Kramer's corollary that, even after dissemination, the author's work "continues to remain subject to his control."[72] Extended control was to become the core of moral rights. Kramer spelled it out, much as Fichte had: the author alienated not the property rights as such, but a use right (*Gebrauchsrecht*). And yet, just as he toyed with inalienable rights, Kramer pulled back from the brink. His dependence on the property concept forced him to accept that even the right of changing the work could be transferred to others.

Property remained central to Kramer's view. Other German legal theorists left it behind. In 1824 Leopold Joseph Neustetel based authors' claims instead on the Roman concept of *injuria*.[73] Injuria was a portmanteau concept covering a wide variety of harm to others, from hitting, raping, and poisoning to insults and slander.[74] Unauthorized editions violated authors' claims, not by reproducing the work but by disseminating it. Since the author decided who would publish, reprinting violated his personality. This was the sort of brazen impertinence against which injuria protected. In 1877 the jurist Carl Gareis went so far as to herald the death of property-based authors' rights altogether.[75]

But if down, property concepts were not yet out. At the end of the nineteenth century, Josef Kohler gave them their most sophisticated and persuasive formulation yet. Kohler was an exhaustingly polymathic German professor of law with a limitless supply of illustrative examples at his fingertips and an irredeemably picaresque style. From the 1880s on, he valiantly attempted to generalize ideas of intellectual property (*geistiges Eigentum*) into a broader theory of intangible goods (*Immaterialgüter*). To break the stranglehold of Roman law over the German legal imagination, he loosened up the concept of property, deemphasizing its material and perpetual nature.

Even conventional property, Kohler emphasized, remained under society's control. Because real property—whether forests, factories, or mines—had an impact on others, society regulated the owner's free disposition.[76] Intangible property was equally overseen by society. Beyond economic, alienable claims, personality rights were inseparable from the creator. Among the rights that we today recognize as moral, Kohler rejected the withdrawal of a work. But personality rights protected works against being changed (integrity), and nothing should be disseminated under the author's name that was not his (a variant on attribution).

Yet Kohler was still hobbled by the property concept. Discussing work-for-hire, he revealed how indistinct his concept of personality rights remained. When authors worked for hire, the economic rights belonged to the employer. But what about the personal rights? Contractually the author assigned the employer not only the future result of his creation but also "the work itself (and thus all rights associated with it)." On the other hand, a painter working on commission promised his client the "painting" but not the "composition," as Kohler phrased the distinction he aimed at between the actual work and its artistic essence. Yet he made exceptions for portraits. The commissioner or the person portrayed owned the portrait absolutely, including its authorship (Urheberrecht). That held true too for depictions of private life—a painting of a woman's boudoir, say, or her husband's study.[77] Kohler thus subordinated authorship to work-for-hire as well as to the commissioner's privacy right. Founding personality rights on property made such slippage hard to avoid. Kohler's nimble attempts to sustain a property-based account of authors' rights found few acolytes toward the end of the nineteenth century as the rationale shifted increasingly to personality.

The most elaborated account of personality-based ideas was formulated at the turn of the century by the German legal historian Otto von Gierke. To Gierke, authors' rights were protected as part of his "sphere of personality."[78] Following Kant, he rooted such rights in the spiritual realm. Economic claims derived from the ideal ones. The usual economic rights were limited in time, transferable, inheritable, and otherwise fully alienable. More important for Gierke were the author's ideal rights. He did not formulate these in absolute terms, as a pure emanation of the author's personality. The point of authorial control remained the venerable one of preserving reputation and honor. But Gierke also added another aim—closer to the moral rights concept—of ensuring that the author could freely attain his scientific and artistic intentions. Implicit here were attribution (claim to reputation) and integrity (achievement of goal). More clearly aiming at integrity, Gierke also reserved for the author the right to ensure that no changes were made to his work and that he alone retained sway over his work's inner substance (*inneren Bestand*).[79]

As personality rights these ideal elements of the author's claims could not be fully alienated. Exploitation rights could be assigned. But the work's *Substanz* remained with the author. Yet Gierke was contradictory. He also claimed that the author could, in fact, alienate all his rights, including control of the work's *inneren Bestand*.[80] Unlike others who shared his basic approach, Gierke firmly grasped the central tension between personality and property: property rights implied absolute but also wholly alienable claims. Personality claims, however, were inherently inalienable. The tie between creator and work was unbreakable. But since the creator was mortal, so was the tie. After death his family or others might continue the author's wishes. But eventually the personal tie would dissolve. It should end, Gierke thought, as the economic rights expired.[81]

MACAULAY BESTS TALFOURD IN BRITAIN

During the mid-nineteenth century the French and Germans formulated the first personality-based authorial rights in theory and case law, though not yet in statute. Meanwhile, the British and Americans were conducting a very different debate over the government's duty to ensure popular access to knowledge. The public domain had been a primary concern of the French revolutionary decrees and throughout the July Monarchy. But by the 1840s authors' claims began to take precedence on the Continent. Not so in the Anglophone world.

In both Britain and America, supporters of natural rights property faced down those who believed that authors owed their claims only to society's rulemaking. Britain debated whether copyright should be short, long, or even perpetual. Whether exclusive authorial rights should be replaced with automatic royalty payments was also discussed. Less interested in copyright duration, the Americans questioned whether foreign authors should enjoy copyright at all. Domestic writers and their concerns—the focus of the British debates—were largely sacrificed to the public's appetite for cheap editions of foreign authors. British publishers and authors, understandably weary of US pirates, were keen on protection in what was rapidly becoming their largest market. But authors' demands for increased rights—beginning to be fulfilled on the Continent—were largely rejected in the Anglosphere.

From 1837 to 1842, the British debated the designs of British judge and MP Thomas Noon Talfourd to strengthen and lengthen copyright. The story has been often and well told of Talfourd's battle on behalf of authors and the vigorous opposition that forced him to compromise. In both Parliament and the press the debate assembled a cast of unparalleled literary eminence, ranging from the historian Thomas Babington Macaulay (against) to the poet William Wordsworth (for).[82] Was literary property a natural right with perpetual or at least lengthy terms? Or had the public a claim to quick access once creators had been reasonably compensated? Fought out in parallel to the Corn Law debates and similar struggles over stamped paper (taxes collected on official documents), the copyright debate too was framed in terms of free trade and monopolies.[83] In this instance as well, the British favored laissez-faire more than the Continentals. Radicals portrayed authors as would-be monopolists hoping to impose a "tax on readers for the purpose of giving a bounty to writers" (in Macaulay's immortal phrase).[84] A parallel dispute over abolishing patents was also part of this larger debate between free trade and permissible monopolies.[85] Publishers specializing in cheap reprints of public domain works, like Thomas Tegg, argued that long copyrights were akin to monopolies and should instead be crafted like patents, with an eye to public utility.[86] Thirty thousand signatures were gathered for petitions opposing longer copyright terms.[87]

Talfourd sought to extend the copyright term beyond the current twenty-eight years or the author's lifetime, whichever was longer. He would have liked to give authors perpetual rights, but he accepted life plus sixty as a compromise. Five years and eleven drafts of his bill later, in 1841, Macaulay's brilliant oratorical skills in Parliament forced Talfourd's followers to settle for life plus seven, or forty-two years in total. Talfourd thought that lengthened terms would give authors greater powers to preserve "the purity of their works," preventing changes that would "emasculate, or pervert, or pollute them."[88] His opponents saw long terms as a sop to authors at the audience's expense.

The newly lengthened copyright dropped a windfall on some authors and their publishers. When the act came into effect on 1 July 1842, Walter Scott's *Waverly* had been published six days short of twenty-eight years. Scott's son, son-in-law, and his publisher, all owners of the copyright, were the first in line when the Stationers' Company opened its doors that morning, registering it and much of Scott's prose for additional protection.[89] But the Talfourd debate's overall outcome was a compromise that spoke as much to the interests of the public as to those of authors.[90] Beyond length of term, the debate's core had been whether literary works were property based on natural rights or merely insofar as society recognized them as such. Talfourd had argued a classic natural rights position.[91] Macaulay pointed out that, even if property was founded on natural rights, its inheritance and succession could not be, given the variety of approaches taken in other nations.[92]

The free-trade and antimonopoly themes of the Talfourd debates then continued before the Copyright Commission in the late 1870s. Again, the British concern with the consuming public and its distrust of publishers was without compare in Europe. Several commissioners and many witnesses lamented the publishers' hammerlock and the high prices that the British reading public endured. Since publishers typically first exhausted the market for expensive editions, compulsory licensing was proposed to satisfy the public's need for cheap and quickly published books. Authors and publishers would be paid royalties for all copies sold. But anyone could reprint works after an initial short period of exclusivity. The author of the proposal, Louis Mallet, the permanent under-secretary of state for India, doubted the need for copyright at all. America's lack of copyright for foreign authors did not seriously harm British writers, he noted, and had the great merit of ensuring an affordable and abundant supply of books. The existing British system failed to satisfy the popular craving for literature. New books were a luxury, restricted to the wealthy. Were prices brought within reach of the masses, demand would mushroom.[93]

Others who testified before the commission were similarly radical. Charles Trevelyan, the colonial administrator and civil service reformer (and not coincidentally Macaulay's brother-in-law and literary heir), railed against the "monstrous evil" of publishers milking the market for luxury editions for years before issuing cheaper ones. He saw affordable books as the publishing pendant of universal suffrage and national education. The working classes deserved books too. If books were as cheap in the UK as America, the character of the stolid working classes would dramatically improve.[94] Thomas Farrer, a civil servant and eager free trader, supplied concrete figures demonstrating that the market alone was no solution. British publishers refused to produce and price books cheaply. After all, they made the same profit by selling fewer expensive ones. He shared the worldwide Anglophone reading public's desire that British publishers' high monopoly prices not extend abroad. Meanwhile, at the center of the empire, the British public could ill afford publishers' domestic markups.[95]

In retrospect we see that by 1878, when the Copyright Commission rejected radical reform, deciding instead to reaffirm copyright as based on exclusive authorial rights, Britain was poised to be drawn into the maw of Continental developments. Scarcely a decade later, in 1886, the Berne Union was born. Upon joining, Britain could then do little except prevaricate and foot drag to defend its inherited copyright tradition and the public's interest against the European authors' rights maximalists. Defense of the Anglo-Saxon tradition of protecting the public domain and democratizing access to knowledge passed to the Americans.

THE SUNSHINE OF HEAVEN: COPYRIGHT AND POPULIST DEMOCRACY IN THE UNITED STATES

Even compared to the Talfourd debates in Britain, the American copyright discussion in the nineteenth century was vehement. After mid-century the US remained the only major nation (other than Russia, China, and the Ottoman Empire) still outside the spreading web of bilateral agreements that mutually protected other nations' works. The United States deliberately stayed outside international copyright to benefit from its outlaw status. Keen to encourage the former colonies' economic development in the eighteenth and nineteenth centuries, the American authorities had taken a cavalier approach also to patent rights. Ambitions to diminish dependence on British imports, while producing American substitute goods instead, meant a flagrant disregard of British inventors' rights. Patents were granted, for example, for merely introducing new techniques, regardless of who had invented them. The first federal patent statute in 1790 seemingly reversed course to protect only original inventions. But in practice this was often ignored. And since foreigners could not hold US patents, foreign inventions were in effect declared common property within the new republic's borders.[96]

A similar disregard for property claims held for copyright too. In limiting the 1790 Copyright Act's benefits to US citizens, Congress consciously chose the advantages of counterfeiting and piracy for the fledgling nation. Reprinting foreign works was not only permitted but encouraged.[97] Almost constitutionally, America was a copyright rogue. With the spread of cheap print, mass education, and universal literacy, America developed the world's largest reading audience. As massive American demand met lavish British supply, a symbiosis emerged—"monopoly tempered by piracy."[98] "It seems to be their opinion," complained Arthur Sullivan (the composer of Gilbert-and-Sullivan fame), "that a free and independent American citizen ought not to be robbed of his right of robbing somebody else."[99] Though American publishers sometimes offered royalties voluntarily, British authors were told to be content with the knock-on effects for home sales of their New World popularity. American writers, in turn, struggled with the premium that copyright imposed on their writings, driving up the cost of publishing domestic books compared to the free British imports that American publishers could choose from.

The United States was not the only pirate nation. Belgium had long reprinted French books. In the eighteenth century the Austrians had blazed a shortcut to enlightenment by encouraging reprinting of German works.[100] But by the mid-nineteenth century the Americans were the largest copyright offender. Moreover, they gussied up mercenary advantage in the vestments of high principle.

Senator Justin Morrill's 1873 report on copyright simply dismissed claims to authors' absolute property as incompatible with the Constitution. Its protection "for limited times" prohibited authors' claims to perpetual property, a goal that remained remarkably persistent on the Continent. The founding fathers had rejected demands "so extensive on the part of authors." The Constitution's concern was with the "interest of science" and to that "the rights and interests of authors are subordinated." Copyright could not promote science if it allowed claims "so partial and engrossing."[101] Rarely had authorial pretension been so summarily punctured.

American piracy and the cheap-print revolution of the nineteenth century were fostered by conscious government policy.[102] The deliberate embrace of piracy as national policy was not, as observers often imagined, a willful, barbaric neglect of civilization's imperatives—which should have led to greater protection of the nation's creative classes. Rather, piracy was part of a purposeful attempt to jumpstart a new, more enlightened and democratic polity. Piracy was a useful arrow in the policy quiver.[103]

The absence of international copyright not only benefited publishers, or at least those reprinting British books, but also helped educate America's new citizens. Just as Macaulay had attacked Talfourd's lengthy copyright terms in 1841 as a tax on readers, now forty years later Gardiner Hubbard, founder of Bell Telephone and an opponent of intellectual property rights in all forms, called international copyright "a tax on knowledge."[104] American democracy required "the diffusion of knowledge and instruction over the whole mass." The country's ill-educated immigrants—"a mighty deluge of superstition and ignorance"—could vote and run for office. Low-cost books were the best hope of educating and assimilating these newcomers.[105] American authors could not yet compete in quality; for now, the task was to make knowledge as "free and universal as the sunshine of heaven."[106] Universal national education, a major plank of domestic policy, was founded on affordable and easily available literature. Ever more mechanized presses, improvements in paper manufacturing, and a good-enough attitude toward the end result made for affordable newspapers and books. Expensive editions for the libraries of the rich reeked of Old World inequality. Since the vast American book

market was the outcome of a massive investment in public school-
ing, the British publishing strategy of small and expensive editions
contradicted both ideology and policy.[107]

The US postal system too was drawn into the project of public
enlightenment. Government subsidies promoted the vigorous circulation of information. Rates for newspapers were heavily discounted
compared to letters, so that "the information, contained in any one
paper within the United States, might immediately spread from one
extremity of the continent to the other."[108] To encourage exchange
and borrowing among papers, editors could send copies gratis to
their colleagues. Scissors in hand, they cut and pasted content into
their own periodicals, which in turn became the sources for yet others.[109] Except for being conducted on paper via post, their activities
resembled nothing so much as today's blogs.

During the early 1800s Jacksonian populist democrats encouraged
widespread access to knowledge. The British and Americans alike
placed copyright in the broader framework of monopoly and economic reform. In Britain free trade and short copyright terms lined
up neatly. But in America protectionism and free trade were positions held in a more haphazard fashion. Henry Clay, the senator and
representative from Kentucky, supported both the American System
of protectionism for domestic industrial products and international
copyright (which would have extended copyright to foreign authors).
His opponents gleefully skewered him for slapping tariffs on British
industrial goods, yet seeking to protect their literary imports.[110] Other
protectionists, like Henry Carey, heir to the Philadelphia publishing
house that did a brisk business in British reprints, tended to oppose
international copyright.[111]

American publishers helped defeat international copyright during the nineteenth century and then worked to keep the United
States out of the Berne Union during the twentieth. But publishing
interests were not uniform.[112] Publishers who also printed and bound
books mostly opposed copyright. Those not involved in production
favored international copyright.[113] Houses specializing in British reprints naturally had no interest in protecting foreign writers. Those
that issued mainly American works did. Reprinters made up only
about a quarter of all publishers. But they were vocal and insistent,

punching above their weight among lawmakers.[114] So influential were they that, in 1873, a Senate report judged the majority of American publishing interests to be against international copyright.[115] That the reprinters managed for so long to mold national policy to their will suggests that they spoke not just for their own profit but also for broader aspects of cultural ideology.

Slavery too intersected ambiguously with copyright. Polemicists in favor of international copyright drew a strained analogy between slaves and unprotected foreign authors, both deprived of their natural rights. "An English writer is treated by America," a satirist in the English magazine *Punch* complained in 1847, "as America treats her negroes: he is turned into ready money for the benefit of the smart dealer who robs him. . . . America sells the bodies of blacks, and steals the brains of the whites."[116]

This was dangerous rhetorical territory, however, veined with logical pitfalls. Those in favor of international copyright argued that both were natural rights positions—the natural rights of slaves to property in themselves, and thus to their freedom, and the natural right of authors to property in their works. Only barbaric nations refused to recognize them.[117] But there were other ways to approach the problem. The abolitionists argued that something hitherto regarded as a natural form of property was not just immoral but also illegitimate. There could be no natural right to ownership of other humans.[118] If analogies were to be drawn, why not between authors and slaveholders? The alternative vision was for liberation—of slaves and of literature. That was the argument made by Carey, the Philadelphia reprint publisher. The aristocratic Southerner and the East Coast publisher of American authors were united behind copyright and monopoly prices. Midwesterners and enfranchised blacks, in contrast, wanted cheap books.[119]

The inherent political affinities were incarnated in legislation when the Confederacy made international copyright an issue. Charles Dickens was an abolitionist and wrote of his feeling of the uncanny when encountering his first slave, serving him dinner at his hotel in Baltimore in 1842.[120] Yet, when senators from the slave states assured him of their support for international copyright, he warmed up. His intense dislike of the Northern publishers, who chiseled him out of his royalties, encouraged his eventual support for the Southern cause during the Civil War.[121] One might have thought that the Southern states had more pressing concerns in 1861 than copyright (just as one might have thought this about the French revolutionaries in 1791). But the political implications of copyright were significant enough to justify such an investment by the rebel politicians. With few publishing interests the South stood to lose little to copyright. To distinguish itself from the North, cultivate an aristocratic and nonmercantile national identity, and appeal to the British, the Confederacy passed an international copyright law, protecting foreign authors whose governments extended reciprocal protection to Americans. Southern gentlemen, one Confederate journalist claimed, would rather pay quintuple the price for a British edition than buy a pirated Yankee one.[122]

Throughout the nineteenth century British authors and publishers (and their American allies) sought to persuade the US government to protect foreign works. Congress was petitioned over a hundred times (from both sides) in the years up to 1875.[123] The debate also spilled over into Canada and then—thanks to Macaulay's 1835 reforms making English the language of higher education—into the Indian market.[124] No natural language barriers insulated British authors, and their works were siphoned off into the former colonies. By the late nineteenth century the American market—the world's largest—was twice the British, with the disproportion further enhanced by America's higher literacy rates.[125] Already in 1820, when the United States had only half the British population, initial print runs of American editions were the same or longer than the British ones.[126] British and other European authors were to be found everywhere in the States. Even in 1775 almost as many copies of Blackstone's *Commentaries* had been sold in America as England. Every major American city issued its own edition of Byron. Macaulay's *History of England*, for sale even in small Colorado towns, had been bought ten or twenty times as often as in Britain by the 1890s. François Guizot's *History of France* could be had in every American state. Dickens was serialized on the back of railroad time tables.[127]

Despite the buccaneering some American publishers paid some British authors through "trade courtesy," an informal system of recognizing rights. Charles Darwin was among them, and Herbert Spencer declared himself satisfied by his treatment.[128] But generally British writers did not realize the profits of full copyright protection. Both their property and reputations, British authors complained, were injured by cheap knock offs. Though read throughout America, Walter Scott derived no gain from his fame. His renown did not help cushion the debts and travails of his later life. And American editions, British authors complained, were often rushed and full of misprints.[129]

The formidable American publishing industry was, however, not to be trifled with. The United States issued three or four books to every British one, Senator William Preston calculated in 1837.[130] With its ancillary trades, publishing sustained some two hundred thousand jobs. "Here are interests too extensive and important to be overlooked," the Senate Committee on Patents concluded in 1838. Providing copyright protection for foreign writers and lowering tariffs on imported books would shift book production from America to Europe.[131]

American publishers who focused on the reprint trade (Carey of Philadelphia and Harper of New York were the biggest names) aligned themselves with the interests of the reading public.[132] All Americans could afford cheap editions of foreign works, Senator Buchanan argued in 1837. British authors' hopes of copyright protection threatened this.[133] In Boston Tennyson's works cost less than half the London price. German immigrants in the Midwest enjoyed cheaper editions of Goethe and Schiller than Germans in Germany—or so Reichstag deputies lamented in the fatherland.[134] Books were so inexpensive, the publisher George Putnam noted, that they were often bought for a railroad journey, then thrown away.[135] The country was flooded with the best of English literature, Mark Twain complained on behalf of American authors who had to face the competition, "at prices which make a package of water closet paper seem an 'edition de luxe' in comparison."[136]

American periodicals like the *New World* and *Brother Jonathan* cheaply serialized foreign novels. Special editions often printed novels in their entirety. *New World*'s 1841 Christmas issue measured over six by four feet.[137] When these periodicals extended their reach to the

Old World, British publishers feared the competition. A year's sub-scription cost about the same as a novel in a London bookstore.[138] In 1838 the Senate Patent Committee offered examples of how cheap US books were compared to British editions. Half the price was, by far, the most expensive. As a rule of thumb, American print runs were four times the size of the British, and each volume cost a quarter of its British counterpart.[139] High prices in the UK were to some extent offset by its many libraries. America's sparse settlement across vast distances, on the other hand, meant that books had to be bought.[140] "The multiplication of cheap editions of useful books, brought within the reach of all classes," the Senate Patent Committee noted in 1838, "serves to promote the general diffusion of knowledge and intelligence, on which depends so essentially the preservation and support of our free institutions."[141]

Sentimental portraits of snowed-in Vermont villages waiting for the stagecoach to deliver books did service as Americans explained to the British why the nation resisted international copyright. Wal-ter Scott's novels made their way from homestead to homestead, their cheapness compensating for the absence of lending libraries. With fewer wealthy book buyers than Britain, American publishers aimed immediately at the mass market.[142] Ultimately, the United States focused on the reader, not the author. "The Americans were courteous," the *Edinburgh Review* reported of their response in 1878 to British demands for protection, "but they had a fair answer, that their first duty was to their own public."[143] Copyright for foreign authors, the publisher Roger Sherman thundered in 1886, was "the clamor of two hundred authors against the interests of fifty-five mil-lions of people."[144]

Those who favored copyright protection for foreign authors ar-gued from common decency. They included American authors, who hailed mainly from the Northeast and were organized in the Copy-right Association, and those publishers who issued original domestic works. George Palmer Putnam and his son George Haven were em-blematic: founders of a publishing dynasty and tireless spokesmen for authors' natural rights to property, for international copyright, and later for American membership of the Berne Union.[145] The United States, they argued, was civilized enough for its legal system to recognize foreign authors' rights. Better than a cheap book, said the poet James Russell Lowell in 1886, "is a book honestly come by."[146] American writers were outgunned by the mass of freely available British literature. To compete, they needed a level playing field. "While other forms of industry are protected in this country by an almost prohibitory tariff," Edward Eggleston, novelist and historian charged, "it marks the lowness and materialistic character of our civilization that the highest kind of production is discouraged by being subjected to direct competition with stolen wares."[147]

He had not read an American manuscript in two years, one publisher admitted to the Senate in 1886. Given royalty-less British works of proven mettle, why take chances on an unknown local author?[148] Washington Irving struggled to help a young colleague get published. "The country is drugged from one end to the other with foreign literature which pays no tax," he complained.[149] American writers competed against "substantially all the European authors, in editions sold at the price of stolen fruit."[150] By the century's end, with the onset of the Berne Union and reciprocal agreements among most nations, the US stood alone and proponents' arguments took on an insistent edge. If America did not extend copyright to foreign authors, a House report warned, it would become "the literary Ishmael of the civilized world."[151] Senator Jonathan Chace, sponsor of the bill that finally introduced international copyright in 1891, portrayed the United States as the "Barbary coast of literature" and Americans as "buccaneers among books."[152]

Besides the humiliation of remaining the only "corsairs on the great ocean of literature," as Chace put it, proponents of international copyright also argued that the nation was moving beyond the need merely for cheap and easy access to European works. What about America's own culture? Faced with unbridled foreign competition, American authors needed help.[153] No longer a colony, America should not depend on British culture. Without international copyright, Samuel Morse wrote in 1842, America's national character was still Britain's and not truly independent.[154] British bilge of the worst popular taste was washing over the country, Senator Chace complained, while good domestic literature was discouraged by the absence of international copyright.[155] The vulgar British fare flooding across the Atlantic, reformers warned, fostered bad instincts, hampered domestic creativity, and retarded local culture. America's own literature, "in its diction, opinion, and illustrations, even in its treatment of scenes and manners" was more like that of a British province than "a great Republic in the New World." Popular American fiction was imitative, with more larks and nightingales than robins and mockingbirds.[156] Bad British culture "sweeps the land, and puts at nought all petty distinctions of district and neighborhood, and settles down, at its leisure, into a dark, slimy, universal pond."[157]

At mid-century the opponents of international copyright still held the upper hand. When Dickens toured America in 1842, he soured his otherwise ecstatic welcome by supporting what his audiences considered a selfish ploy by British authors to milk their American popularity for profit.[158] Dickens saw himself as "the greatest loser . . . alive" of America's lack of international copyright. His American fans thought their adulation so burnished his reputation that it compensated for his lack of royalties. Some argued that he was so popular precisely because his writings were unprotected and therefore cheap and widely read. Dickens himself could think of little but the monies foregone. His second American tour in 1868 was therefore one of public readings, a moneymaker that sent him home a wealthy man.[159]

During the first half of the nineteenth century, reprint publishers and the reading public alike ignored the plight of American authors. But when American authors began holding their own against foreign competition, the tide gradually turned. Harriet Beecher Stowe's *Uncle Tom's Cabin* (1852) was the most successful book of its era on both sides of the Atlantic. Huge pirated editions in Britain gave the Americans a taste of their own medicine, highlighting the advantages of international agreements. John Camden Hotten notoriously pirated American authors he thought would sell in Britain, including Mark Twain and Walt Whitman.[160] Unsurprisingly, Twain published a petition for international copyright in 1886, signed by 144 American men of letters.[161] Bills for international copyright were presented repeatedly during the latter decades of the century.[162] American authors, who sought international copyright for obvious reasons, and the book manufacturing trades, which feared international competition, eventually agreed on a horse trade. Thanks to a manufacturing clause requiring that protected foreign works be produced in the United States, copyright was finally extended to foreign authors in 1891.[163] By now the Berne Union, founded in 1886 without the Americans, with its ever-increasing focus on authors was beginning to have an influence too. Even in the US the balance of power was shifting from the public to authors and their rights or—more precisely—to publishers and their profits. And in the twentieth century, as the United States turned from an eager importer of European content to the world's largest exporter, it shifted from copyright rogue to strict enforcer. But that story is to come.

FAINT ECHOES IN EUROPE?

Until the United States introduced international copyright in 1891, European literati were aghast at the Americans' trampling of authors' rights.[164] And yet, Europe too had debates between authors and the reading public, though not as vigorously as in the Anglophone world. In France a few jurists and reformers took up the public's cause: Augustin-Charles Renouard, Edouard Calmels, Louis Wolowski, and Léonce de Lavergne.[165] Proudhon, the anarchist who famously declared all property theft, saw no reason to change his mind when it came to its intellectual variant. Lamartine took his aphorism as a provocation to highlight the urgency of giving intellectual property a foundation in law. Not only was property property, but literary property was property too.[166] Proudhon attacked Lamartine and his proposals to strengthen literary property rights. He disagreed with their fundamental premise: that authors created something de novo which they therefore owned. Authors were like laborers or craftsmen, he thought, who joined their skill and labor with materials provided by nature and society. Ultimately, they did not create their ideas. They received them. They did not fashion the truth but discovered it. They did not bring forth beauty but recognized it. Society and creators jointly produced works. But all the rewards went to the individual, none to society. Perpetual rights would impoverish the public domain.[167]

In Germany, too, a few voices were raised for the public. The socialist Eugen Dühring was influenced by the American publisher Carey to argue against overly extensive protection for authors. In the 1860s Albert Schäffle applied economic logic for perhaps the first time to authors' rights, concluding that terms should be shortened and entirely abolished when authors were rewarded by other means, like salaries or prizes. Yet his colleague Constantin von Wrangell, who also favored shortening terms, still felt obliged to tilt his arguments against what remained the reigning Continental paradigm, perpetual literary property.[168]

In the Continent's parliaments and decision-making fora, debate was scarce and anemic. Only rarely did deputies or reformers formulate the arguments voiced insistently and often in the Anglo-American world. We have seen how the revolution's concern with the public domain lasted in France down to the 1830s, then to be superseded by a new attention to the author's personality rights. French reformers who opposed perpetual rights feared that heirs would withdraw works from circulation.[169] By contrast, in the UK perpetual rights were never seriously considered, and in the US they were ruled out by the Constitution itself. In the newly unified Germany, during debates over the 1870 copyright law, the parliamentarian Karl Braun, a National Liberal and free trader, argued against a thirty-year term in favor of a decade of protection with royalties paid thereafter—an abbreviated version of the compulsory licensing adopted for books in the UK in 1911, as we will see in the next chapter. This reform, Braun argued, would spread cheap editions to the common people. In the United States pirates already gave German-Americans cheaper editions of Goethe and Schiller than at home. If German authors and publishers were less protected, prices might fall in Germany too.[170]

Amid a thunderous chorus in support of perpetual literary property at the International Literary Congress in 1878, only a few voices dared argue on behalf of short terms. Eugene Marie Dognée, an archeologist, spoke for the poor and their right to accessible and cheap editions.[171] Even Victor Hugo swam against the tide, insisting that if he had to choose between authors' claims and those of the public, he would side with the public.[172] Carlo del Balzo, republican politician and Neapolitan man of letters, agreed and attacked perpetuity. Since literary property was created by the author's personal labor, it could not be transmitted to heirs like a house. Once the author was dead, he argued, the work belonged to society, to humanity. His eloquent rhetoric was rebuffed by others, who repeatedly lamented the scandal that the children of famous authors languished in poverty. It was as unjust to deprive authors of their property as it was to dispossess the Rothschilds. Gustave de Molinari, the radically laissez-faire economist, agreed that the public domain was a communist concept.[173]

Perhaps the closest Continental approximations to Britain's Talfourd debates of the 1830s and 1840s and the prolonged American discussions over international copyright were fought in the German Reichstag leading up to its 1901 and 1907 copyright laws. As we will see in chapter 4, these laws introduced some of the first legal embodiments of moral rights. But as a counterweight the government also sought to emphasize public access. Among the issues debated was whether music could be performed and literary works anthologized under fair use exemptions without the author's permission. Many who welcomed the new forms of authors' rights also resisted a liberal interpretation of fair use. Others argued for the public's interests and the government's ambition to promote popular education.[174]

Similar themes continued early in the twentieth century as Germany debated whether to retain its thirty-year term or to follow the Berne recommendation of fifty. Richard Wagner's heirs, struggling to maintain their monopoly on the performance of some of his works at Bayreuth, pushed for long terms. But their self-interest was too obvious, and others who also supported fifty-year terms took pains to distance themselves from the avaricious Wagner clan.[175] The shorter period, the German government argued in 1910, fairly reconciled author and society by allowing free access to the best national works after a reasonable time. What if Goethe had entered the public domain only in 1883, as he would have under the proposed new rules?[176] The author's demand for long terms, the Prussian Academy of Science concluded, was trivial compared to the public's interest in cheap and easy access. The writings of Theodor Fontane and the music of Brahms should not be denied the German poor for another twenty years. The German people needed good affordable books and artistic prints, not to mention sheet music for *Hausmusik*.[177]

Surprisingly perhaps, some German publishers also opposed long terms. Imagine the "inexpressible narrowing of the spiritual and artistic life of broad groups of Germans during the 1860s and '70s" had Beethoven and Goethe entered the public domain only a decade or two later.[178] When fifty-year terms were debated during the Berne Union's 1908 Berlin and 1928 Rome conferences, the Germans supported thirty years. The foreign minister Gustav Stresemann, a National Liberal and one of the Weimar Republic's most capable politicians, was decisive. The longer term, he concluded, would undermine general education and enlightenment.[179] It fell to the Nazis to implement the Berne Convention's solicitude for authors, extending protection to half a century postmortem. Then, after the Second World War, Germany shifted its concern even more to authors, becoming the international locomotive for still longer terms. Cutting back authors' rights in favor of the public had begun to be seriously debated in Germany only during the last years of the Weimar Republic. As we will see in chapter 5, this discussion was then enthusiastically pursued during the early Nazi regime. That association, however fleeting, in turn made support for the public an untenable argument in Germany for the rest of the twentieth century.

Thus, on the European continent, the public's advantage was most insistently advocated by an anarchist, Proudhon, and then later by the Nazis. In Britain the same attitude was espoused by moderate and respected reformers like the historian Macaulay and his Whig supporters. In the United States a *bien pensant* consensus of politicians, reformers, and businessmen rejected any form of copyright for foreign authors. Even when international copyright was finally accepted in the US in 1891, its proponents were careful to insist that they would keep the "American system, which is that of cheap literature for the people."[180] This trans-Atlantic and trans-channel divide, sharp as it already was, would become even more stark in the twentieth century as the Europeans embraced moral rights.

4

Continental Drift

EUROPE MOVES FROM PROPERTY TO PERSONALITY
AT THE TURN OF THE CENTURY

The stakes rose in the nineteenth century as authors and their assignees were given increasingly extensive rights to ever more different kinds of works, as well as the derivations shaped by others out of their primary creations. Earlier, authors had controlled only verbatim copies of their writings. Anything else—translations or abridgements, for example—did not infringe. As they gained power also over derivative works, it was no longer just the authors' expression of their ideas that was safeguarded. The work's protected essence now had to be defined also across its incarnation in various media. Authors thus gained rights over something beyond the expression of their ideas, something that approximated the ideas themselves.

As intellectual property thus broadened and deepened, the public domain of unprotected work shrank. To compensate the audience for rights holders' growing sway, legislators reined in some of what was otherwise given them. "Fair use" defined a zone of legal free use of works that rights holders could not forbid. Compulsory licensing developed to allow use of works—even without rights holders' permission—so long as set royalties were paid. Since both techniques limited authors' property rights in favor of the audience's access, unsurprisingly they enjoyed more success in Britain and America than in Europe.

While authorial claims were thus being modestly curtailed, especially in the Anglophone world, on the European continent newly formulated moral rights were expanding them into new realms. In

France and Germany moral rights developed first in jurisprudence and case law during the late nineteenth century. They extended authors' aesthetic control over their works even after they had sold their economic rights. The work could thus not be wholly alienated. In the eighteenth century authors' rights, based on natural rights to property, had been viewed as fully alienable. That had been their attraction for the publishers who thereby expected to own works fully and perpetually. Now in the nineteenth century, authors' rights were based instead, or additionally, on the work's status as an emanation of its creator's personality. They thus became fundamentally inalienable. The author and his highly personal work could never be fully parted. And in those jurisdictions, like France, where moral rights were eventually declared perpetual, the work also never wholly fell into the public domain, open to everyone's free use.

ADDING PERSONALITY TO PROPERTY

By the early nineteenth century authors in Britain, America, France, and many of the German principalities had won property rights in their works, though typically only the ability to assign them for limited times. During the 1800s their rights broadened from books and plays to include letters, paintings, sculpture, lectures, music, opera, photos, and architecture. Their rights also deepened beyond control of exact reproductions to include derivations: translations, abridgements, engravings, dramatizations, and performances. During the early nineteenth century legal and legislative experience had revealed that—beyond ownership—decisions were needed on authors' aesthetic control. Having assigned economic rights, should they retain a say? Were assignees allowed to modify works as they pleased? Did control pass to the author's heirs and, if so, how? Could it be seized by creditors? Such questions—raised above all in the Lamartine debate of 1841—foreshadowed the moral rights that developed later in the nineteenth century.

Derivative works raised similar issues. Were translation, abridgements, or adaptations new works? And what of works related to or inspired by other works—a play based on a novel, an engraving on a sculpture, a photograph on a painting? Who owned the right to reproduce a painting: artist or buyer? Was photography art or a mere technology? Was recording music legally equivalent to reproducing its score? Some of these questions were answered by technical modifications of the law. Others were central to the expansion of authors' rights.

What had been free grew increasingly regulated and legalized. Literary property expanded dramatically into realms never previously ownable. In the late nineteenth century, at the same time that conventional property became ever more regulated (labor laws, rent control, factory legislation, health and safety, consumer and environmental protection, etc.) and society's interests took precedence over those of owners, intellectual property rights, in contrast, increasingly benefited authors and their assignees over the public.[1] So vast was this expansion of right holders' prerogatives that it, in turn, prompted the need for exceptions—what in the UK became known as fair dealing and in the US as fair use.

By the cusp of the twentieth century, then, all nations had significantly expanded authors' rights but in increasingly different ways. In 1907 the prominent German jurist Josef Kohler, whom we met in the previous chapter, wrote that, by puncturing the fiction of natural rights, *Donaldson v. Beckett* (1774) had ended the concept of immaterial property in Britain, thereby making a stepchild of authors' rights in the common law nations.[2] He was right. Anglo-American authors' claims were now limited to what society was willing to concede. The Continent, in contrast, slowly added one concept of natural rights to another. Property was joined by the (supposedly equally) natural right of the author's inviolable expression of personality.

At their most messianic, authors' rights based on property and on personality both presumed a basis in nature: by virtue of the author's labor or because of the unbreakable connection between personality and work. André Morillot, the French jurist who first formulated the concept in 1878, explicitly derived moral rights from natural rights. "It is a principle of law, higher than any statute," he declared, that every person's liberty be protected. This obliged the authorities to safeguard the author's moral rights to his work.[3] In a belt-and-suspenders argument, Alcide Darras wrote in 1887 that the author's claims rested on both the recompense he was due for his labor and the respect due his personality. A claim based on either one of these was unavoidably a natural right.[4] Such ideas multiplied on the other side of the century's cusp.[5] By the interwar years authors' rights were justified also by this new natural right of personality. Moral rights, one observer celebrated in 1926, were absolute. They stood outside time; the law did not create them but simply recognized their prior existence. They were natural rights.[6]

This Continental drift from property to personality was nebulous, meandering, and incomplete. Both concepts remained current in tandem, moving in and out of use. Personality supplemented but never supplanted property. Early in the nineteenth century the Germans did not develop the concept of property rights in works as enthusiastically as the French. Kant and Fichte had instead emphasized the author's personal stake in his works. When Germany unified in 1871 and began codifying national law, it could have followed the French example. But by then German thought rested more on personality-based authorial claims.[7] In the late nineteenth century Kohler shifted the discussion from intellectual property (*geistiges Eigentum*), founded on natural rights, to intangible property (*Immaterialgüterrecht*), based instead on statute. The property concept thus having been unmoored from its origins in natural rights, the next step was to personality-based authors' rights (*Urheberrecht*).[8]

The Prussian law of 1837 had dealt with literary property. But in 1865 Bavarian law used the term *Urheberrecht* to indicate authors' rights that went beyond claims based merely on property. So did the all-German law of 1870. In 1885, when the French proposed that the Berne Convention protect "literary and artistic property" rather than authors' rights, the Germans protested vehemently.[9] Even the French feared the problems we have examined in the previous chapter of conceptually assimilating literary to conventional property. They avoided using the term "property" in draft bills put forth under the July Monarchy.[10]

Although the property concept was increasingly supplemented by that of personality starting in the late nineteenth century, it remained influential. As a quick glance ahead shows, the French reinstituted it in their first major law on the subject since the revolution, that of 1957 on "literary and artistic property."[11] The postwar Germans continued to view the concept more skeptically than the French. The new Bavarian Constitution of 1946 (art. 162) spoke of intellectual property, but the West German Basic Law of 1949 did not. Yet in 1955 the German Supreme Court resuscitated classic eighteenth-century concepts by vindicating intellectual property as a natural right that was only recognized, not created, by statute.[12] Later case law and statute also enthusiastically employed the intellectual property concept.[13] European law followed suit. In 2001 the EU's Information Society Directive blithely assured its constituents that intellectual property had been recognized "as an integral part of property."[14] The unratified draft EU constitution of 2003 solemnly sought to make protecting intellectual property a plank of the Continent's highest law.[15]

Nonetheless, whether based on property or personality, in their Continental variants both these concepts endowed the author with strong, nature-based claims. They differed mainly in that property—however natural—could be alienated, while personality-based rights, as we will see, remained with the author even after he had assigned his exploitation claims.

ROMANTICISM PLAYS A ROLE

To protect authors because they were personally connected to their work was, of course, part of the late eighteenth-century Romantic worship of the artist. Earlier authors had seen themselves more humbly as giving voice to higher forces and as indebted to forerunners.[16] They viewed themselves as embedded in society and in contact with their public.[17] Indeed, as the Greeks and Romans saw it, authors were discoverers, not creators, uncovering the timeless reality of nature's forms.[18] From the Renaissance on, authors were inspired by classical antiquity to imitate nature and emulate the past masters of ancient Greece and Rome.[19] Romanticism supplanted this mimetic view of art. As he himself saw it, the Romantic author drew on his own original and singular genius. Edward Young's celebration of the artist in his garret, *Conjectures on Original Composition* (1759)—a much bigger hit in Germany than at home in Britain—set the tone. Originality connected the creator with the divine, while imitations were mechanical.[20]

Romanticism thus celebrated the author on a heroic scale. The ideology of authors' rights continued this tradition in a minor key. As one critical observer put it, authors' rights sought to protect Romantic tropes in law: unique creation reflecting the author's personality.[21] The most fundamental form of property, Balzac insisted in 1834, was the work, "that which man creates between heaven and earth, that which has no other roots than in his intelligence."[22] The author owed the public nothing.[23] On the Continent, where such *schöngeisterisch* ideas were strongest, law and cultural idiom agreed. By contrast, the Anglosphere remained less persuaded by the claims of Romantic inspiration. Genius, in the British view, served a broader, social purpose. The sublime spirits "who share that ray of divinity we call genius," Lord Camden insisted during the *Donaldson* case in 1774, were entrusted by Providence to impart to others the knowledge "that heaven meant for universal benefit; they must not be niggards to the world or hoard up for themselves the common stock."[24] A century and a half later, in the lead-up to the British 1911 Copyright Act, the MP George Roberts argued against extending copyright terms, cautioning that authors and inventors were not so much original creative geniuses as "the reservoirs of the past. They have profited by the successes and failures of those who have preceded them."[25]

While the British were skeptical of genius, America spurned the concept altogether. The earliest copyright statutes aimed to encourage literature and genius. The usage, however, was not that of overwrought Romanticism but an etymologically pure derivation from "ingenious."[26] The preamble to the Massachusetts copyright statute of 1783 described the advancement of human happiness as depending on "learned and ingenious persons in the various arts and sciences."[27] As in Britain, genius was harnessed to the social good. We seek to encourage literature, the Senate Committee on Patents insisted, as it rejected copyright protection for British books in 1838. "But literature itself is only valuable as it tends to improve and bless mankind. It should not, therefore, be confined to exclusive channels, but diffused and spread throughout the whole mass ... shedding upon the whole face of society the beams of light and knowledge and intellectual improvement."[28]

BROADENING (AND RESTRICTING) THE CONCEPT OF LITERARY PROPERTY

Starting in the nineteenth century, authors' rights expanded from writings to all manner of other works. Along one axis authorial rights extended to new forms of creative endeavor. Along another protection deepened to cover derivative works as well. Some rights were older: to translations, engravings, and dramatizations. Others followed new media: photographs, sound recordings, and film adaptations. But as rights thus included new derivative works, the protected object had to be defined so as to transcend the original medium. Its core had to be identified.

The 1710 Statute of Anne and other early legislation had protected the work's specific instantiation, outlawing only verbatim reproduction. As authors gained rights also in derivations, however, a broader concept was needed of some element of its substance that justified claims when it was reused, even if not verbatim. Copyrights arguably became more like patents. Authors began claiming control of the idea or some essence of the work and not just its particular expression. This gave them power over the work in other media and formats: translations, abridgments, film versions, and so forth. Early laws had distinguished between expression and idea, protecting only expression. Now this distinction blurred.

Because early laws guarded only against verbatim reproduction, altered works were not protected. Thus a plagiarizing artist in nineteenth-century Württemberg got off scot-free because his copy had different dimensions and colors.[29] How changed did a derivative work have to be to win its own legal standing? In the eighteenth century abridgments were regarded as new works. Indeed, until the mid-nineteenth century "fair" abridgments were considered a public service, making books digestible and available. Periodicals relied heavily on extracts, summaries, and reworkings of recent books.[30] But attitudes toward derivative works changed during the nineteenth century, as translations illustrate. Neither the Statute of Anne nor the French revolutionary laws or the Prussian Allgemeines Landrecht protected the author against translations, which were regarded as independent works. Harriet Beecher Stowe, author of *Uncle Tom's Cabin* (1852), the runaway bestseller of the time, authorized a translation for Pennsylvania's German speakers. When in 1853 an unauthorized one appeared in a Philadelphia newspaper, she sued. The court ruled against her, declaring that, on publication, she had lost all rights other than to print and sell her work.[31]

But the tide was turning. In his standard work on copyright from 1847, the American jurist George Ticknor Curtis now argued that translations infringed on authors' rights. The author owned "the ideas and sentiments themselves," the plan of the work, and the mode of treating the subject. His rights were violated "in whatever form his own property may be reproduced."[32] American authors received the right to authorize translations in 1870; the British had in a limited form in 1851 and then more expansively in 1911. In France the shift was similar. What right did a translation violate, the jurist Augustin-Charles Renouard demanded to know in 1838. The change of language eliminated any rivalry, and the author's reputation stood to gain.[33] But in 1845 the Rouen Court of Appeals condemned the unauthorized publication of a French chemistry book in Spanish, noting the harm of its competition with the original edition.[34] In 1847 the Court of Paris ruled that a translation inherently reproduced the original. Everything but the language was copied: the subject, the arguments, the phrasing. A work's essence, the court argued, was not the written idiom, but the ideas presented, their sequence and development.[35]

Abridgments too became protected. In 1828 Robert Maugham had insisted that they were new works. Though they injured sales of the original, they did not infringe.[36] A decade later abridgments were now seen as skimming the cream. Abridging, Francis Lieber lectured in 1838, is the right of my neighbor to drink my wine if he leaves the cask.[37] In *Gray v. Russell* (1839) Justice Joseph Story decided that whether an abridgment infringed depended less on the amount taken than on its quality and value.[38] In 1841 *Folsom v. Marsh* banned a competing use of George Washington's letters, reining in the then-unbridled fair use doctrine.[39] Derivative uses had to be "fair and bona fide" and must not harm the original's market value.[40] Curtis's standard text concluded that "to the author belongs the exclusive right to take all the profits of publication which the book can, in any form, produce."[41] In 1879 Eaton Drone's survey of Anglophone law was clear and severe: abridgments were an outmoded indulgence and a form of piracy.[42]

Over the nineteenth century copyright thus increasingly came to protect the work's value across all media, not just verbatim copies. The doctrine emerged that there could be "non-literal copying," when another author used a story's plot, incidences, or themes.[43] The photographer James Robinson was thus charged with piracy of Henry Wallis's *Death of Chatterton* (1857) when he photographed a model imitating the original's pose of the dead poet.[44] The protected property was increasingly understood to be the work's essential core, no longer just its expression. As his claim to the work was carried across all media, so the author's stake expanded. Stowe lost her case, though she was vindicated when authors gained translation rights in 1870. But her lawyer's logic illustrated how the concept of the work was expanding. The work remained constant, regardless of its language. A good translation transparently transposed it from one tongue to another, thus appropriating it in the act. "A perfect translation will present the identical creation and mental production."[45] In 1847 Curtis defined the protectable work generously as "whatever is metaphysically part or parcel of the intellectual contents of a book."[46] In 1879, when Drone summed up Anglo-American law, literary property was now the "intellectual creation of which language is but the means of expression." Even formulated in different words, the work remained the same. (How that differed from owning the work's ideas was unclear, though Drone was quick to deny that ideas could be possessed.)[47]

In both Europe and the Anglophone world copyright had expanded by the late nineteenth century to give authors a broad say over their work's market value, regardless of medium.[48] Thanks to that, authors today merrily claim ownership of character, plot, and narrative. Thus the heirs of Margaret Mitchell, author of *Gone with the Wind*, sued Régine Desforges, author of *La bicyclette bleue*, for

having told the story of a woman, an estate, and a war—though set
in France in the 1940s, not the South of the 1860s. A French director
sued the US producer of the Arnold Schwarzenegger movie *The
Running Man* for making a film also featuring television, its influence on the masses, and five-armed killers. In turn, the studio behind *Jaws* sued a French company for a movie involving a shark,
summer, and swimmers.[49]

FAIR USE

Yet, as authors' rights expanded, they also had their wings clipped.
With ever more claims aimed at derivative works, the law began to
define and enforce a zone of use over which authors had no say. Fair
use started in the nineteenth century as the right of authors to use
others' works for their own independent creations. So long as the
new work was not derivative or imitative, fair use acknowledged that
authors inspired each other. As authors won control over derivative
uses that once had been free, however, fair use began guarding the
public as well. Only seen against the vast broadening of their rights
during the nineteenth century did fair use limit authors' prerogatives.[50] Unsurprisingly, since its point was to help the audience, fair
use was more generous in the Anglosphere than on the Continent.
Though originating in the nineteenth century, fair use developed to
full fruition only in the twentieth. For the sake of coherence, we will
follow it to that conclusion here.

Fair use was implemented in its broadest form in America. *Folsom
v. Marsh* (1841) was an early weighing of interests between author and
public. Free use was curtailed if derivative works cut into the original's market value. But fair use was also employed to limit the now-
expanded authorial domain. Though the 1909 US Copyright Act
ended the right of fair abridgment, it included a broad exemption for
nonprofit performances of nondramatic literary works and music.[51]

The 1976 Copyright Act eventually codified the fair use doctrine,
removing some of the specific exemptions, like nonprofit performances, while adding new ones. As we will see in chapter 6, the 1976
act aimed to bring the United States into alignment with European

practices, smoothing the path for membership in the Berne Union. Term durations were extended from a maximum of twenty-eight years after publication to the Berne norm of fifty years postmortem. Works were now automatically protected as of creation, with few of the formalities imposed earlier. Fair use was therefore formalized to compensate the public somewhat for this vast expansion of authors' claims.[52]

Congressman Robert Drinan voiced traditional Anglo-American attitudes during the debates over the act, insisting that "copyright as a monopolistic practice can only be justified to the extent it serves the public good."[53] The act enumerated all manner of fair use exceptions: hymn singing at religious services, band music at agricultural fairs, and music at Elks Club dances.[54] The general principle allowed fair use of copyrighted work for purposes "such as" criticism, comment, news reporting, teaching, and scholarship. Teachers and librarians advocated broad pedagogical exemptions. Their opponents in the publishing industry, however, sought to restrict schools, universities, and libraries to the same limits as the general public. The act nonetheless allowed libraries to make copies for interlibrary loans and to preserve deteriorated copies of out-of-print works, thus granting them rights beyond those of the public.[55] Schools and universities also won an exception for copies made for classroom use. And the pedagogical establishment secured a corporatist exemption from fines if employees of schools, universities, libraries, or archives innocently infringed.

Unlike the equivalent European laws, with their restrictive tallies of permitted uses, the 1976 US Copyright Act's enumeration of fair uses was illustrative, not limiting. The law devised a legal algorithm of fair use: what and how much was copied, and for what purpose, and how it affected the work's market value.[56] It opened up a broad array of possible exceptions by allowing courts a calculus to weigh interests.[57] This principle had already been formulated in 1964 by the New York Court of Appeals when it cautioned that courts "must occasionally subordinate the copyright holder's interest in maximum financial return to the greater public interest in the development of art, science and industry."[58]

The British equivalent, the "fair dealing" clause of the 1911 Copyright Act, was narrower and more like its Continental equivalents.[59] It allowed specific, enumerated uses: private study, criticism, review or newspaper summary, the drawing of public sculptures and buildings, public recitations, accounts of nonreserved public lectures, and limited excerpting in school anthologies. While revised in 1956 and again in 1988, the principle behind fair dealing remained undefined.[60] It applied neither to unpublished works nor to news photography. Nor did it empower courts to find uses fair if they were not listed in the law.[61] In 1992 the American artist Jeff Koons unsuccessfully asserted fair use in the United States against a postcard photographer whose motif he had turned into a sculpture. Such a case would never even have come to trial in Britain, where infringing was specifically defined in the 1988 act to include transpositions from two to three dimensions.[62] Britain's 1988 act even included micromanaged exemptions, such as the permission to rent out computer programs fifty years (!) after their first release. Another section allowed teachers to copy parts of works for instructional purposes, but not via a reprographic process, which apparently ruled out xeroxing to prepare lectures.[63]

On the Continent fair use was an even more limited doctrine. The very idea strained Continental concepts of natural rights property. Authors, for obvious reasons, objected.[64] Fair use allowed the public to violate the author's rights with impunity, one eager proponent of the Continental ideology charged.[65] Nonetheless, even the most author-centric nations, like France, needed some fair use. Rejecting the broad and open-ended American practice, European laws have typically listed specific exemptions. Historically, the Germans have been more generous than the French. Already the Prussian Landrecht of 1794 allowed excerpts of works.[66] The Prussian law of 1837 permitted citation of passages and poems in historical and critical works.[67] It also excepted socially worthy uses, like school books and anthologies. Fair use was enshrined in the German law of 1870 but without invoking the public's interest. The 1901 and 1907 laws allowed further exempted uses. Public speeches and unreserved newspaper articles could be reproduced and quotations and excerpts reprinted in school or church anthologies. Musical works could be performed without payment or permission at charitable, private, and other noncommercial events.[68] In Germany's 1965 law such earlier exceptions were limited. Composers were now entitled to royalties for performances except at wholly free public and charitable concerts. Fair use in educational anthologies was narrowed.[69]

The French were more miserly.[70] With no rationale of the public good, the 1957 law exempted only private copies and press reviews, short quotations for critical, educational, or scientific purposes, and accounts of public talks.[71] Fearing harm to journalists, the legislature deliberately clawed back a proposed exemption for news articles.[72] But the law did specifically exempt parodies, caricatures, and pastiches, which—though protected by case law—were not mentioned in British or American statute.[73] In 2001 the European Union specified a list of precisely twenty allowable exceptions, including educational purposes, uses by the disabled, and parody.[74] EU members were required to exempt temporary copies made in the course of digital transmission (since otherwise the web would grind to a legal halt). But all other exceptions were optional, and no nation could adopt any fair use that was not on the EU's list.[75] In other words, EU member states were free to be stingier than Brussels but banned from being more generous. In 2003, after publishers' protests, the French minister of culture cut even the fair use exception for education or research from a draft bill.[76] After much debate the French finally introduced a restrictive educational exception in 2006. But we will see in chapter 8 just how miserly France and Germany were with exemptions to authors' exclusive rights.

COMPULSORY LICENSING

Compulsory or statutory licensing (sometimes also called equitable remuneration) was another technique used to counterbalance authorial control, thus helping the public (and some disseminators). On payment of royalties, at rates often set by the authorities, statutory licenses allowed anyone to disseminate works after a certain period of exclusive rights for owners. Works were thus freely and efficiently available and authors were rewarded. Compulsory licensing had long been discussed during the nineteenth century, both for patents and copyrights. But little came of it until the invention of sound reproduction.[77] First broadly introduced for musical recordings early in the twentieth century, compulsory licensing was then extended to private copying of audio and video materials, public and cable broadcasts, jukeboxes, performances of musical works, noncommercial broadcasting, and satellite retransmissions. It was also used to allow developing nations to translate and reproduce works on affordable terms.[78] In the most ambitious proposals compulsory licensing promised to resolve the inherent contradictions of authors' persistent demand for perpetual property. Rights forever could be granted without choking off the public domain by counterbalancing them with unrestricted reprinting plus royalty payments.[79]

Compulsory licensing violated both absolute property rights and a central tenet of the authors' rights ideology: the creator's control of the work and its dissemination.[80] Licensing in effect deprived authors of exclusive rights in return for guaranteed royalties. He might be paid, one critic complained in 1939, but the author was treated like an artisan and not an artist.[81] In the hands of sloppy licensees, authors also risked their integrity, unable to ensure that new renditions were accurate and complete.[82] Indeed, in the 1976 US law, though they could not change a musical composition's basic melody, licensees were permitted to arrange it "to conform it to the style or manner of interpretation of the performance involved."[83] Thanks to such tinkering, the turn-of-the-century American composer Victor Herbert flatly denied authorship of the compositions recorded under license without his supervision. His goal was artistic control, not just royalties.[84]

In effect, compulsory licensing partially socialized use rights, emphasizing public access on reasonable terms over authors' exclusive claims.[85] American composers were incensed at the two-cent royalty specified in the 1909 Copyright Act that introduced licensing of sound recordings. Imagine, they fumed, a law that banned writers from drawing up their own terms and contracts with publishers.[86] From a free-market perspective compulsory licensing in effect permitted infringement on payment of damages specified in law.[87] Compulsory licensing thus posed philosophical, not just technical, issues. The nations discussed here responded in ways that accorded broadly with their underlying ideologies of intellectual property. As with fair use, all countries were impelled by technological necessity to accept some variant of licensing. And, as with fair use, since licensing sought to broaden public access, it was a technique more favored in the Anglosphere than on the Continent. The United States and Britain adopted the new technique enthusiastically. Fearing diminution of the author's powers, the Continental nations followed only grudgingly.

In Britain compulsory licensing had been broached as early as 1737 by a London booksellers' bill to allow republishing of out-of-print books.[88] In 1837 Thomas Watts, keeper of printed books at the British Museum, suggested a royalty scheme as an alternative to the first Talfourd bill.[89] A variant was first legislated in the British 1842 Copyright Act.[90] With Talfourd's attempt to extend copyright terms, his opponents feared that authors' families would suppress works they disapproved of. Talfourd therefore agreed to allow the Privy Council to grant compulsory licenses for books whose owners refused new editions after the author's death.[91] As this took effect only postmortem, with copyright still in force, it was not precisely compulsory licensing. But the motives were similar: curbing the author's exclusive rights in favor of public access while ensuring a fair return.

Though it finally rejected the idea, Britain's 1878 Royal Commission on Copyright seriously considered a general system of compulsory licensing that promised to be "expedient in the interest of the public, and possibly not disadvantageous to authors." Such reform would have encouraged quick, cheap editions.[92] In 1909 another report again flirted with such ideas.[93] As we shall see, only two years later, in 1911, the British enthusiastically adopted a variant on a much larger scale. In the United States licensing was proposed in the midnineteenth century.[94] Then, in 1909, after a great deal of legislative soul-searching, the Americans—as detailed below—became the first nation to institute compulsory licensing for sound recordings.

Because statutory licensing directly violated the author's exclusive rights, it was discussed but found little favor in France. Lamartine's abortive 1841 bill would have allowed theaters to perform plays of deceased authors in return for royalties, regardless of whether the heirs agreed.[95] In 1863 a commission under Napoleon III proposed coupling perpetual property rights to compulsory licensing. Half a century of full postmortem rights for the author or his heirs would be followed by perpetual royalty payments from anyone reissuing the work.[96] Nothing came of this, though Victor Hugo enthusiastically advocated compulsory licensing.[97] When the issue was discussed at the 1928 Rome conference of the Berne Union, the French protested that royalty payments were merely a form of compensation. Only exclusive rights properly respected the author's claims.[98] The abortive Zay bill during the Popular Front government in 1936, which we will discuss in chapter 5, foresaw compulsory licensing to prevent heirs from hindering republication.[99] Yet not for another half century did such ideas bear fruit in France.

SOUND RECORDINGS

Eventually, however, new technologies forced a discussion of licensing in the late nineteenth century. Proliferating techniques of mechanical sound reproduction allowed an end run around composers and their rights to sheet music. With the coming of mechanical music boxes, player pianos, and then phonographs, sound recordings became wildly popular. Because they had not been anticipated in copyright law, composers and their publishers were left empty-handed. They found themselves supplying a huge market, while gaining at most fame and the sale of a few more sheets of music. The secondary rights they did not control proved vastly more lucrative than the primary ones.

Already in 1880 the German jurist Kohler had argued that, whether notated on paper or reproduced mechanically, a musical idea was conveyed and thus stolen if unauthorized.[100] But the law did not yet consider mechanical sound reproduction infringing. In one of their few successful acts of cultural imperialism, the Swiss and their music-box industry persuaded the Berne Convention in 1886 to leave composers without mechanical reproduction rights.[101] National legislation, like the Austrian law of 1895, the German of 1901, and the British of 1906, followed suit. In France case law (from 1905) and a statute of 1866 allowed music—but not a song's words—to be mechanically reproduced.[102] At the turn of the century, a series of cases across several nations held that the rolls, cylinders, and other replaceable media used to produce sound were not copies of works, and therefore infringing, but merely components of the mechanical devices.[103]

In 1908, however, the Berne Convention changed tack and finally granted composers mechanical reproduction rights.[104] The Germans were eager to support their music manufacturers. But the French and Italians blocked a licensing provision, leaving each nation free to legislate if and as it wished.[105] As the public increasingly abandoned its instruments and amateur orchestras, voting with its feet for the new low-effort technologies of consumption, matters became dire for composers and sheet-music publishers.[106] Fascinating aesthetic debates roiled congressional committees in America. Composers argued that their rights to music's notation on paper was but an imperfect claim. Music was conveyed through the ear, not the eye. They should own their music whether notated or recorded mechanically.[107] The American military-march composer John Philip Sousa, one of the foremost campaigners, argued that "writings" encompassed the actual music, not merely its notation.[108] Copyright should therefore include recordings.[109] The recording industry countered that composers had rights to the expression of their music, its notation on the page. But the recording, "the sounds themselves," were music's idea, which they did not control.[110] Lawmakers noted in Solomonic fashion that, since composers were staking claims to something that was not currently recognized as theirs, they should be content with less than absolute property rights.

Sousa passionately lamented the detrimental effect of recordings on citizens' music making. Vocal cords would become vestigial, he feared, like the tail. "Music develops from the people, the 'folk songs,' and if you do not make the people executants, you make them depend on the machines." But his opponents argued that music lessons and sheet-music sales were actually increasing. In any case, people derived pleasure from phonographs.[111] As always in American copyright debates, the populist rhetoric was strong and even shameless. Music was the most democratic art form, a pure republican art.

Should it be laden with tariffs before reaching a poor man's ears?[112] Talking machines brought music to people who could not afford concerts. Recordings were thus like cheap books earlier in the century, an efficient means of dissemination. Imposing royalties, a manufacturer insisted, was class legislation on behalf of the few, contradicting the happiness of the masses.[113]

The outcome was twofold. Allowing composers rights to mechanical recordings seemed fair. But that threatened the profits of the now-mighty recording industry and could give composers and music publishers a monopoly of a new, popular medium, turning them into a "mechanical-music trust."[114] On both sides of the Atlantic, devices for musical reproduction multiplied: Orchestrions, Aeolians, Apollos, Angeluses, Aristons, Cecilians, Herophons, Orpheons, Pianophones, Pianolas, Pianistas, and Symphonions, as well as graphophones and phonographs. Sousa famously termed it all "canned music."[115] Imagine, as George Bernard Shaw admonished a parliamentary committee, a law against theft exempting milk cans just because stealing them had become a large and important industry.[116]

To complicate matters further, several of the recording firms had surreptitiously cut deals with composers and publishers, promising them broad control over musical reproduction rights once these had been recognized in law.[117] Faced with a potential monopoly—of composers, publishers, talking-machine manufacturers, or some unholy alliance—legislators carefully extracted concessions for the protection now extended. Statutory licensing promised composers royalties, but it also allowed anyone to reproduce music once composers agreed to record it in the first place. This solution, achieved first in the US in 1909, was shortly followed in the UK in 1911.[118]

The Continental nations hesitated. Bowing to their player-piano manufacturers, the Germans quickly followed the Americans, licensing musical reproductions in 1910.[119] But German composers retained more rights than their Anglophone colleagues. Instead of being given an automatic right of mechanical reproduction at government-imposed royalty rates, the recording industry was allowed only to ask composers to negotiate with them.[120] Reformers like Julius Kopsch and Willy Hoffmann eagerly advocated compulsory licensing during the last years of the Weimar Republic.[121] Alas for the idea, they pursued it as well during the Third Reich, damning it by association for many decades thereafter. In West Germany's 1965 law musical licenses were further restricted by exempting works administered by rights-management organizations, whose contracts took precedence, and works the composer wished to withdraw altogether. Nor were composers required to license their music for use in films.[122]

In France an 1866 law had bowed to Swiss demands that music boxes not be considered infringing.[123] But French legal opinion bridled at the injustice, whatever the geopolitics.[124] In the midst of war in 1917, mechanical music reproduction once again fell under the 1793 law, with a few suspiciously peculiar exceptions for music boxes of precisely specified dimensions.[125] Testifying before a British parliamentary committee in 1909, Georges Maillard, a French lawyer and president of the International Literary and Artistic Association, rejected the American initiative of compulsory licensing as a "fatal precedent."[126] During the Berne negotiations of the interwar years, the French staunchly opposed licensing.[127] Their 1957 law emphasized authorial rights and shunned compulsory licensing. Not until 1985 did the French finally accept a limited form of licensing when they allowed phonograph records to be played in public and on the radio in return for royalties and introduced a system of remuneration for private copying.[128]

COPYRIGHT AND AUTHORS' RIGHTS GO THEIR SEPARATE WAYS

During the nineteenth century authors' rights expanded enormously, even as fair use and compulsory licensing reined in what would otherwise have been an exuberant giveaway. By 1900 authors and assignees everywhere were better positioned than they had been a century earlier. But the new exploitation rights were not equivalent to the personality rights anticipated by Kant and Fichte. The fin-de-siècle authors' rights were still property rights—whether based on natural rights or statute—and thus alienable. In practical terms the newly expansive claims to derivative works gave authors some of the same controls as personality-based rights. But the crucial distinction remained. Property can be assigned, while personality claims largely adhere to the author.

Only in the twentieth century were the moral rights—the cap-stone of the divergence between copyright and authors' rights—im-plemented, and it is to their story that we now turn. Moral rights sprang from two sources: German legal theory and French case law.[129] Kant, Fichte, and other German theorists had first formulated the theory of the author's personal rights. But moral rights were first developed in French case law late in the nineteenth century. By the beginning of the twentieth, they had entered French legal text-books.[130] Not until the early 1900s, and then at first in Germany, did they find legislative embodiment. In 1928 the Italian Fascists placed moral rights on the Berne agenda. But not until the culturally bruised years after the Second World War did they finally achieve full legisla-tive fruition on the Continent.

France and Germany approached moral rights differently. Though Continental legal theorists have parsed the distinctions minutely, suf-fice it here to note the division between dualist (French) and monist (German) approaches. French law recognized a general doctrine of personality rights—to name, reputation, honor, privacy, and the like—that belonged to all citizens, not just authors. Why then treat the author's personality rights separately, as though they were pecu-liar to one profession? Instead, the French bisected authorial rights. Exploitation rights dealt with the creator's economic stake and were fully alienable. Moral rights were treated as an aspect of personality rights and remained inalienably with him.

German law, by contrast, did not recognize a general right of per-sonality until after the Second World War. But earlier, it did acknowl-edge individual personality rights.[131] The personal aspects of authors' rights were thus not seen as one element of a larger set of citizens' personality rights. Instead, they were packed together with the ex-ploitation rights into one unified, monist conception of authors' rights.[132] But if the author's personal rights were part of his overall rights, could they too be alienated like his economic rights? To avoid this undesirable outcome, German doctrine drew an even more radi-cal conclusion than the French: no authors' rights—even of exploita-tion—could ultimately be alienated. Unable to assign their works, to this day German authors can therefore at most grant use rights.[133] A practical consequence of Germany's monist approach was that personal rights expire at the same time as economic rights. In France such synchronization was not required, and moral rights remain perpetual.

Despite such differences the French and the Germans shared a sense that the conventional property concept could not extend to intellectual matters. How could a work be both property and personal, be both alienated and yet remain with the author? Hence the discussion sallied forward to personality.[134] Moral rights pushed beyond even extensive immaterial property rights, of the sort that Kohler had elaborated, defending instead what sprang from the creator's personality. Moral rights thus expanded, altered, and arguably transcended property rights. They introduced to chattels restrictions on the owner similar to those already possible for real estate. Chattels could be sold to the initial buyer with contractual conditions attached. But such reservation of rights could not be continued to subsequent owners, in the way that servitudes or easements could be on real estate. Moral rights aimed to introduce such restrictions for personal property, imposing conditions on future owners of works that enforced the author's continued interests.[135]

Moral rights were concretely formulated first in French legal writing and practice, starting in the 1840s. But curiously, the first instance of the phrase used in conjunction with authors' rights occurred in Britain as early as 1793—and it was wielded to justify the Anglo-Saxon approach. The great British jurist Blackstone relied heavily on Locke's idea that the author's labor justified his ownership.[136] So did one of his commentators, the irascible Edward Christian. A professor of law and brother of the *Bounty* mutineer, Fletcher Christian, he was waspishly immortalized as "having died in the full vigor of his incapacity."[137] Christian called the natural right that Locke formulated and Blackstone accepted a "moral right." Moral rights were those intuitively obvious to reason, which sprang from an inquiry "whether it is such as the reason, the cultivated reason, of mankind must necessarily assent to." Christian agreed with Locke and Blackstone that authors had a natural or "moral" right to their works. But then, in classically Anglo-Saxon manner, he marshaled the logic of natural rights on behalf of the public domain. If any private right was sacred, he concluded, "it is that where the most extensive benefit flows to mankind from the labour by which it is acquired." Literary property was "founded upon the same principle of general utility to society, which is the basis of all other moral rights and obligations."[138]

Used in the Continental sense, however, the concept of moral rights was broached perhaps first by the jurist Renouard in 1838. He sought to undercut the idea of literary property rights, harking back instead to the revolutionary ideals of the public domain. But he also foreshadowed moral rights when he spoke of the author's "moral responsibility" to take back, change, and complete his writings since he was their "absolute arbiter."[139] As we have seen in the previous chapter, fully developed moral rights were formulated first by the French jurist André Morillot in the 1870s. He claimed full "moral sovereignty" for the author over his work, both before and after publication, and described our contempt for plagiarists as based on a "droit tout moral."[140] An expert on the monist German doctrine, he nonetheless advocated a dualistic theory, with property rights alongside a personality or moral right. By 1887 the idea that both moral and economic rights were due the author seems to have been commonplace in France.[141] But the crucible of moral rights was neither the theorists nor the lawmakers, who would later become active. It was the courts. Moral rights began as judge-made law.

Disclosure was among the first moral rights to be litigated. It overlapped with an elemental exploitation right: deciding whether, when, and how to convey the work to the public. Yet a moral dimension also slowly emerged. An early example was the composer Vergne, who is said to have died of regret after his mass failed to win a composition prize. When his widow and child fell on hard times, creditors sought to seize and publish the mass. In 1828 the heirs sued to retain control over the manuscript. Because it had been performed twice in a church, but never published, the court agreed that by natural right it belonged to the composer. It could not be taken in lieu of his debts.[142] In another instance a great orator, the abbé Jean-Baptiste Lacordaire, sought successfully in 1845 to block an unauthorized edition of his speeches based on notes taken at public talks.[143] In neither instance was it clear which spoke loudest: Mammon or morality. The author's exploitation right to determine the work's first appearance and his moral right of disclosure were not entirely identical. Some scholars doubt that the mid-nineteenth-century French courts had identified moral prerogatives independent of authors' and heirs' economic rights. Others conclude that by this point case law had recognized disclosure as a moral right.[144]

The Whistler affair of the 1890s also mixed the mercenary and the moral. James Whistler, the American expat painter, had been commissioned to paint Lady Eden for a fee between 100 and 150 guineas. Upon completion, Lord Eden paid one hundred. Apparently miffed, Whistler returned the check, refused to deliver the portrait, and disfigured the face. Eden sued, winning damages. Whistler's lawyer argued that the artist must himself decide when the work was completed. Otherwise, if paid in advance, a painter might have to deliver an unfinished piece. But was the piece not yet ready? Whistler had not only described his portrait as a masterpiece in a press interview, he had also exhibited it.[145]

The case is often thought of as the jurisprudential cornerstone of the disclosure right. But in technical fact it merely found that Whistler could not be held to specific performance. Because he had not delivered the portrait, he had not yet sold it. Eden did not own it, and Whistler could not be compelled to fulfill their contract. But he could—and was—held liable for the commission and damages. The judgment remained well within existing law.[146] Moral rights were not mentioned, though the case for Whistler pointed out that the rights invoked were ones "closely attached to the person of the artist."[147] Interestingly, Eden was refused possession even of the disfigured portrait. But Whistler retained ownership of the canvas only on condition that he render it unrecognizable and thus no longer a portrait. Having returned Eden's commission and paid damages, Whistler still did not fully own his own painting. In the event, Whistler replaced Lady Eden's face with that of Mrs. Herbert Dudley Hale, wife of a prominent architect. What Mrs. Hale thought of having been, in effect, photoshopped onto Lady Eden's body, history does not record.[148]

The case that pitted Anatole France against the editor Alphonse Lemerre was more purely concerned with aesthetics. In 1882, aged thirty-eight, France had delivered the manuscript of a history of his country—France on France. Only thirty years later, in 1910, did the editor announce plans to issue it. France successfully sued to forestall publication and was required only to return his advance.[149] Sparing his reputation by not allowing the publication of outmoded juvenilia seems to have been France's primary concern. An earthier example of case law on disclosure came in 1962 from the most famous kitchen appliance in legal history, the French painter Bernard Buffet's refrigerator. Invited to decorate a fridge to be auctioned for charity, Buffet painted all six panels. Considering them a whole, he signed only one. Half a year later, when an auction catalogue listed one of the panels as a separate piece, the artist prevailed to prevent its sale.[150]

The attribution right had a less compelling history than disclosure. In 1835 the editor Renault was condemned for publishing a work by Lavenas under another's name. During the 1890s a French case pitted a painter against a publisher who reproduced his work with a monogram rather than his signature.[151] More interesting was the slow emergence of integrity from case law. Both the 1794 Prussian Landrecht and the 1809 Badenese Civil Code foreshadowed integrity in forbidding publishers from issuing new and changed editions without authorial permission. In 1814 the jurist Jean-Marie Pardessus argued that the buyer of a manuscript could not change, enhance, or excerpt it. Nor could he destroy or refuse to publish it. He was, in fact, a usufructuary, someone who enjoyed the use of the property but was not its owner. Having sold his manuscript, the author had not also alienated his hopes of fame and reputation.[152] In 1842 the philosopher Auguste Comte won a case against his publisher for unauthorized changes.[153] The same year another French author won damages for changes to his work by a publisher in a new edition. Even if he had alienated his economic rights, the court ruled, he had not given up the right to correct it. Otherwise, he "put his reputation at the mercy of the buyer."[154]

The hurdle to the emergence of fully fledged moral rights was not money but honor and reputation. Reputation might be a more noble ambition than mere lucre. But it did not seamlessly coincide with the work conceived of as the expression of the author's personality. After all, changes to the work—even carried out by others against the author's will—might enhance, not hurt, his reputation. If reputation was the protected good—not authorial control of the final product, warts and all—then a violation of integrity that enhanced the author's standing might not be actionable.[155]

Because of such ambiguities, cases like Comte's sometimes went against the plaintiffs if the modifications had not harmed their reputations or otherwise damaged them.[156] Since harm (to economic or reputational assets) remained the issue, such cases did not found a new means of protecting the author's subjective sense of his work's inviolability. In France such cases remained based on the Civil Code's requirement of restitution for damages.[157] But slowly, the author's right of control emerged, independent of the implications for his reputation. In 1912 the German painter Arnold Böcklin successfully sued to restore a mural on an interior staircase in a private Berlin home. The house owner had retouched Böcklin's naked sirens in the spirit of modesty. The stairwell was private, and the work was seen only by residents and guests. Yet the court, agreeing with the nymph-painting Böcklin, stepped beyond reputation to grant the artist a right to control his work, regardless of whether his public standing was at stake.[158]

At its outer limit, however, integrity inevitably ran up against traditional property rights. A new owner might not be able to alter a work, but he could destroy it. Though artists are said to have property in their works, one British MP commented in 1861, that is not strictly true. Otherwise, they could oblige buyers to care for them. Yet nothing prevented owners from burning works.[159] Artists attempted in vain legally to compel owners to cherish and care for their artworks. But even on the Continent courts agreed that owners could freely destroy art without harming the artist's reputation.[160] When a congregation in Juvisy complained that its chapel wall paintings were unsuitable, the curé had them painted over. Though the artist sued for harm to his reputation, the Paris Court of Appeals ruled in 1934 that the owner was not obligated to preserve the artwork.[161] The family's destruction of Graham Sutherland's controversial portrait of Winston Churchill bothered British observers. But even Britain's introduction of moral rights in 1988 did not oblige owners to preserve works.[162] The Berlin Wall's graffiti artists were found to have no moral right to prevent the destruction of their concrete canvas.[163] Unexpectedly, the United States alone banned destruction under moral rights legislation, although only of well-known visual artworks.[164]

Moral rights thus emerged slowly during the late nineteenth century from the grinding gears of French and German case law, lubricated by theorists' writings but unsanctioned as yet by much legislation. As in the Lamartine debate of 1841, an odd combination of marriage, divorce, inheritance, and debt prompted outcomes that were eventually hailed as fundamental human rights. Noble aspirations were born of the backstage legal machinery of modern life. Divorce, permitted again in France in 1884 for the first time since the revolution, forced the issue of distinguishing between economic and moral rights.[165] *Cinquin v. Lecocq* (1902) is often cited as the first practical formulation of moral rights. That it represented a major change is clear if we compare it to the 1880 case of Masson and his son. In *Masson*, a widowed writer remarried. The son from the first marriage, his mother's sole heir, sued his father for her share of his literary and dramatic works. The courts agreed, treating these as any other chattel, subject to the usual laws of inheritance, as well as being the mother's due for her contributions to the family.[166]

Twenty-two years later, *Masson*'s assumption, that literary property was like any other, was questioned. Charles Lecocq was a composer of light operas, best remembered for his *La Fille de Madame Angot*. When he married in 1876, he exempted his bachelor compositions from the common marital property that is the default position in the Napoleonic system. But he had said nothing about works he might pen in the future.[167] When the couple then divorced in 1897, did the rights to his later compositions belong to both partners? The income from his works was clearly to be shared with his spouse. But was Lecocq obliged to share creative decisions with his ex-wife—whether to publish or to issue new editions? In 1898 the Seine Tribunal made the wife a full co-owner of Lecocq's works composed during their marriage. An appeal in 1900 to the Paris court reversed the decision. Literary property was not the sort that could be shared, the court now ruled. While fair to divide the revenues, the actual property right still belonged to Lecocq. Otherwise, the author must share with his ex-wife (or her heirs should she die) his "most sacred and most personal" rights just when their relations might be at their worst.

The Supreme Court, however, reversed this decision, or at least tempered it. The Paris appeals court had implicitly recognized authors' rights as personal and inalienable, though it had not detailed their content. The public prosecutor, Manuel Baudouin (who also prosecuted Dreyfus's second trial two years later, when he was acquitted), cautiously sought to restrict the lower instance's more radical approach. He rejected the Paris court's assertion that intellectual property was not property, affirming instead conventional views at length. As an incorporeal chattel, literary property became part of community property. He also argued for personal rights, inseparable from their subjects, that could neither be assigned nor attached and did not enter common marital property. Parental and spousal rights were examples. But authors' rights were not among them. True, the concept in the creator's mind was naturally a personal right—but trivially and undisputedly so. Only when the work took on form through dissemination did it become literary property. But this literary property, which Baudouin then folded back into the matrimonial property, meant only the work's income. Like other forms of property, it could be attached by creditors. However—and here things became interesting—Baudouin qualified literary property. The author retained the right, even after his literary property had been seized, to change his work, so long as he acted in good faith, without intending to defraud his creditors.

The Supreme Court agreed. The monetary aspects of literary property belonged to community property. But the author had a right—inherent in his personality—to change his work, or even suppress it, so long as he did not try to harm his spouse. The court thus retained the principle of literary property as a conventional form of property, subject to the laws of divorce and debt. But additionally it recognized a personal right that the author did not share with former spouses or creditors, although it seems to have been limited to the power to make changes and possibly to destroy or suppress the work. Authors' rights had thus been recognized in two forms: pecuniary and personal. But the limiting clause—that personal rights could not be used to harm the economic interests of spouses or creditors—re-strained the author's freedom of action. What an embittered author considered "improvements" to his œuvre might well detract from the monies anticipated by his former spouse or creditors. What if he took the work out of circulation? At the very least, torn between reputation and revenge, the divorced author's decision was not a foregone conclusion.

In *Masson*, literary property, including its moral aspects, had been conceived of as property tout court. *Lecocq* then split it apart, regard-ing only its economic aspects as a form of property. In 1936 the Canal divorce case took a further step. *Canal* was a mirror image of *Lecocq*. Upon divorcing, the husband of the composer Marguerite Canal claimed rights to her works. With no nuptial contract, their property was communal. The court sided with the wife, finding that the fruits of her works published during marriage were her goods. The right to exploit them remained hers, while their income belonged to com-munity property. It was the author's prerogative to control her works, the court ruled, with the one glaring exception that under French law, married women still had to obtain their husband's permission to publish in the first place.[168] *Canal* took a step beyond *Lecocq* by deciding that the author's rights were a faculty inherent in the per-son, thus remaining with her.

But control over works in divorce remained unresolved legisla-tively. Commentators were gripped by fears that creditors, heirs, wid-ows, and even irate ex-spouses might gain sway over authors' most personal decisions. Even an adulterous wife might have a say over whether her ex-husband reissued or suppressed his works.[169] Though the wife composer's moral rights were affirmed in 1938, *Canal* con-tinued to percolate up through the judicial system. In 1945 France's Supreme Court reversed to favor the ex-husband instead.[170] Partly in response to this refusal to consider literary property as exclusively attached to the author, the 1957 law (to which we come in chapter 6) resolved the problem once and for all. It stated explicitly that, what-ever happened to the economic rights, the moral ones remained with the author or his representatives and did not become part of com-mon marital property.[171]

THE BERNE UNION AND THE ASCENT OF THE AUTHOR

In the Berne Union national divergences once again were articulated and pitted against each other. From its beginning in 1886, Berne had broadly championed the Continental view of authors' rights. France embodied the Continental tradition most emblematically, with Germany running a close second. The United States retained the copyright tradition most faithfully. It remained outside Berne for its first century, joining only in 1989. The British fit uncomfortably between the two extremes. Heavily dependent on the American market and hoping to lure the US into the mutually entangling alliances of international copyright, British authors and publishers feared acting unilaterally vis-à-vis the former colonies.[172] But they also wanted to be part of European and global copyright unions, lest they end up being protected only in their own dominions. They hoped to bring the Americans closer to Berne and were heartened when the United States sent an observer to the formative meetings.[173]

Within Berne, the British fought a rearguard battle. They joined from the onset but then prevaricated so as to delay, dilute, and deflect the full consequences of their membership. As Berne expanded to include more member nations, the cost of remaining outside increased. The American disseminating industries wanted access, first to sell their goods and later to combat piracy. As a fifth-column force at home, the media industries worked against the copyright tradition's emphasis on the public domain. And like the publishers of the eighteenth century, they cleverly managed to present their interests as though they were the same as authors'.

The Berne Union emerged from proposals for reciprocal copyright relations broached at the 1878 International Literary Congress in Paris, a writers' jamboree presided over by Victor Hugo, then an overripe literary figure of enormous renown.[174] Berne aimed to deal with foreign authors' works, the treatment of local authors abroad, and other aspects of international copyright. It standardized the treatment of works in foreign countries and set minimum levels of domestic legislation that member nations were encouraged and sometimes required to meet.

The late nineteenth century was the golden age of international organizations. But the coming together of nations, with their varying traditions, ideologies, and political systems, was not always easy. The 1865 International Telegraph Union, the 1874 Universal Postal Union, and the 1875 Treaty of the Meter were hammered out harmoniously enough. But locating the prime meridian in Greenwich raised nationalist hackles in France.[175] And the International Sanitary Conferences (ten starting in 1859) brought different nations toe-to-toe on how to balance citizens' rights with society's needs in the face of dangerous infectious diseases—a political issue of the first magnitude.[176] So, too, ideological battles were fought within the Berne Union, between authors' rights and copyright.

The initial Berne meetings, in the years up to 1886 and then again in 1896 and 1908, choreographed a pas de deux between the different approaches of France and Britain, the two extremes. Often in alliance with other Mediterranean nations and sometimes with members from Central Europe, France was the most principled defender of authors' interests. The UK, generally backed by the Commonwealth, spoke for copyright's concern for the public. As small countries with an appetite for more culture than they produced at home, the Scandinavian nations were eager to import works and therefore to curb authors' and disseminators' rights. They often supported the Anglophone position. For example, while the French sought to give authors control over translations for the full term of exploitation, the Scandinavians insisted on shorter durations.[177] The British colonies agreed. The colonial authorities in India feared that translation rights would raise the price of local-language editions of British books, hampering their educational mission.[178] The translating nations prevailed at first, with a ten-year limit on translation rights. But with the Berlin revision of 1908, authors were granted translation rights for the full fifty-year term. The British gave up bucking the tide. When they conformed their legislation to Berne in 1911, the full term of translation rights now belonged to the author.[179]

As authors' rights minimalists, the British were also the main proponents of national treatment, the principle that each nation dealt with foreign authors on the same terms as its own. The level of treatment might differ among members. But whatever domestic authors received, foreign ones enjoyed too.[180] Yet Berne membership racheted standards upward. If protection was better abroad, why should domestic authors settle for less? When, in 1908, the union proposed to drop the registration formality as a condition of protection, the British government reluctantly followed suit.[181]

Hampered by the Commonwealth nations, in tactical alliance with the Scandinavians, the French and their supporters failed to make the original 1886 convention as protective of authors as had been hoped. The Swiss music-box industry, for example, successfully hindered composers' claims to mechanical reproduction rights. But over the following decades the maximalist position prevailed. Originally Berne protected periodical articles only if they were expressly reserved, while articles on political and current news were freely available to use. But the Berlin revision of 1908 expanded authorial rights, requiring permission for adaptations, musical arrangements, novelizations, theatricalizations, and films and protecting performances of dramatic or musical works. New forms of intellectual property were pulled under Berne's umbrella: architecture and choreography, pantomimes and films. Composers were eventually given partial control over recorded works. Photographs were protected and translation rights extended. Copyright formalities were eliminated and all works were protected from their conception.

GERMANY IN THE BERNE VANGUARD

Though French case law took the first steps toward moral rights, it was Germany that beat the path to statute. Early German laws—Prussia in 1837 and Saxony-Weimar in 1839—took literary property as their subject. But in 1865 the Bavarian law spoke for the first time of *Urheberrecht*—authors' rights—and that terminology continued into the all-German law of 1870. Nonetheless, despite this new concept the laws of 1870 in the German Confederation and 1876 in the newly founded empire did not take matters much beyond the 1837 Prussian law. Corporate authorship and its work-for-hire implication were questioned in 1870: could a mere publisher of a collective work claim authors' rights? A Reichstag commission supported a flesh-and-blood requirement, concluding that only someone who had actually contributed to a work deserved authorial rights.[182] The final law treated the editor of a collective work as the author but also granted all contributing authors rights to their component parts. Authors received translation rights, with restrictions that betrayed a certain concern for the work's integrity. A contemporary work published in a dead language—Latin, say—could not be translated into German without the author's permission. Otherwise, the commission feared, a work by a German *Gelernter* might appear in faulty and imperfect German, thus threatening to "impair the personality of the learned author."[183] But in the main, the German law of 1870 dealt only with unauthorized editions, reprints, and reproductions.[184]

Once Germany had joined Berne in 1886, however, new laws on literature and music in 1901 and on art and photography in 1907 advanced the state of play.[185] They introduced protections that pushed beyond the economic, accomplishing as much as any nation had for moral rights. Authors were often victimized by changes to their works, one Reichstag deputy complained. Why should poets have to tolerate their verse being read aloud in public or composers the recording of their music? The new legislation promised to guard the author's personality and his spiritual claims.[186]

Broadly speaking, the author's basic moral rights now entered German legislation. Personal rights trumped economic considerations. Even if the author was in debt, his works could no longer be foreclosed on, and creditors could not issue unpublished material without permission.[187] The only exception to integrity were the justified alterations that publication required.[188] Derivative uses of works had to specify the author. The author remained the author, one deputy insisted, even after parting with his work, and he kept certain rights in perpetuity.[189] Artists retained reproduction rights after sale of their works.[190] Nonetheless, clients received the rights to portraits—thus subordinating the painter's moral rights to his sitter's privacy.[191] And owners could exhibit artworks without the artist's permission.[192] Even the term "droit moral" was used in the Reichstag debates for these new rights, as France was held up for praise. The new laws assured "the protection of the author's individuality against arbitrary changes to his work," and they protected works "as his spiritual child."[193] Though such rights were still contested elsewhere, the government proudly announced, Germany now took them for granted.[194]

Yet the authors' rights ideology was still in its infancy here at the turn of the century. Work-for-hire, for example, remained ambiguous. Precociously, the 1870 law had made no provisions to vest authorship in employers or commissioning entities. Only the real author was to be protected.[195] But the new laws were less principled. The draft bill of the 1901 law at first retained rights for the author even when he had worked at a publisher's behest and specifications.[196] In the parliamentary commission a proposal to vest rights in employers was vehemently rejected. Imagine large capitalist corporations hiring talented youngsters and claiming rights to their works! The commission left work-for-hire to be determined case by case. Journalists might normally have rights, industrial draftsmen might not.[197] Technically necessary modifications—changes, say, to employee drawings—were permitted.[198] Generally, the bill argued, rights vested in the employer. But the law was to include no precise stipulation.[199] In the end the 1907 law had no provisions about employee creations.

The new German laws also balanced the author's newly amplified rights with the public's access. Despite authors' and publishers' objections, fair use exemptions were extensive. The 1837 Prussian law had already included quotation, church use, educational anthologies, and translations. The 1870 and 1901 laws allowed the reprinting of individual news articles if rights had not been reserved.[200] The principle, the Reichstag commission explained, was to maximize free use of published work.[201] Composers of *Lieder* could freely use any poem, publishing it along with their music.[202] Musical compositions required no permission when performed for free—at popular festivals, private performances, and for charity.

In sum, the fin-de-siècle German laws significantly elevated authors' rights from case law into statute. Not every moral right was clearly articulated, and work-for-hire remained unresolved. But authors now had clear legal claims beyond their economic ones, and they retained these new moral rights even after their works had been assigned.

A "BASTILLE OF LETTERS" AND "NOT A REPUBLIC": ANGLOPHONE RESISTANCE TO BERNE

By contrast, Britain and the United States continued to emphasize the efficient exploitation of works and their quick transfer to the public domain. The UK did so from within the union, the US from outside.[203] Though Berne members, the British resisted several aspects of the Continental ideology. They retained work-for-hire, rejecting the premise of rights reserved for only actual authors.[204] They had pushed successfully in the initial 1886 Berne convention to keep copyright formalities, like registering and depositing works.[205] But the Berlin revision of Berne in 1908 required signatories to protect the work from its creation onward. The British agreed, abolishing registration formalities in 1911.[206] (They did retain library deposit, though protection was not contingent on it and failure prompted only a minor fine.) But the British fought hard against Berne's attempt to extend terms. The Talfourd debates of the 1830s, as we have seen, led not to an easy lengthening of protection, as on the Continent, but to a painful dispute over the public's claims. In 1908 Berne encouraged members to adopt a protective term of fifty years postmortem. The British obliged in the 1911 Copyright Act but cleverly subverted much of the point of the extension.

In the run-up to Britain's 1911 act, the voices of the Talfourd debates were heard once again. Fifty years postmortem worked against the poor's hope for cheap and ready editions. The common people's enlightenment must take precedence over authors' degenerate descendants.[207] Publishers, angling for monopoly, were considered the real interests behind extended terms.[208] Even those who defended long terms, like Sydney Buxton, president of the Board of Trade (soon to be in hot water for failing to reform shipping regulations that would have ensured lifeboats for everyone on the *Titanic*), insisted that they, too, supported the public domain. Longer protection would stimulate more and cheaper editions.[209] In no Continental country was "the battle of the poor and of freedom and of abundance of cheap literature" taken so seriously.[210] According to a Conservative MP, the debate in 1911 was part of a "perpetual struggle between an attempt on the part of the author to secure perpetual copyright and the right of the public to insist on ... a very early determination of the copyright."[211]

Britain's 1911 Copyright Act accepted Berne's fifty-year term pro forma. But it undermined its intent by introducing what amounted to compulsory licensing. Twenty-five years after the author's death, anyone could republish a work if he paid specified royalties to the copyright owner.[212] The period of exclusive rights for heirs was thus but half of what Berne required, with the rights holder promised only royalty payment after that.[213] In other respects, too, authors had their wings clipped. Would authors and their descendants restrict availability?[214] This concern had stirred debate also during *Donaldson* in 1774, and it troubled Macaulay in the 1830s.[215] The 1911 act followed the 1842 act, empowering the Privy Council to implement licensing when owners refused to republish or perform works.[216] Such exceptions to authors' exclusive rights were thought to counterbalance the new half-century term.[217] Finally, as we have seen, the 1911 act formalized Britain's comparatively extensive fair dealing exceptions.

The United States shunned Berne altogether. But in one major respect Americans did come in from the cold. In 1891 the erstwhile "buccaneers of books" decided to protect foreign authors as they did domestic ones.[218] Once an outlaw nation, the US now bowed to foreign and domestic authors and publishers, recognizing copyright for those countries that protected Americans. The quid pro quo, uniting antagonistic domestic interests in a tough horse trade, was the manufacturing clause. This rankly protectionist measure favored book producers by requiring that works be typeset or readied for print in the United States.[219] Foreign works were protected, so long as they were produced in America.

This one step was considered enough for the time being. Isolated American voices pleaded for full Berne membership, but that came only a century later, in 1989. The US Copyright Act of 1909 arguably underscored differences between copyright and authors' rights. In 1908 Berne abolished formalities of notice, deposit, registration, and the like, and the British largely followed suit. But the United States not only retained the usual formalities, it now also required domestic manufacture. Sweeping away this hard-won compromise was impossible. True, America's 1909 act did lessen some formalities. Failing to deposit works no longer meant forfeiting protection, unless the author persisted despite warnings. Nor was copyright lost if notice was not affixed to every copy. But the manufacturing clause was beefed up: books now had to be typeset, printed, *and* bound in the US.[220] The 1909 law also made work-for-hire explicit and introduced corporate copyright, turning employers into the authors of work created on their dime.[221] The gulf between the United States and the emerging European authors' rights doctrine was as wide as ever.

For most of the nineteenth century, the United States had reprinted foreign authors to enlighten its citizenry without the nuisance of paying royalties. Both the 1790 and 1831 acts had allowed the importing, reprinting, and publishing of works by noncitizens and nonresidents. As late as 1873, the congressional Committee on the Library reported as widespread opinion that international copyright was a "hindrance to the diffusion of knowledge among the people and to the cause of universal education."[222] By the end of the century, however, America gradually turned from importing to exporting intellectual property. Economic interests began to beat out the ideology of the public domain. (We will return to this story.) And as the Berne Union expanded, the costs of remaining outside, not to mention grossly violating its strictures, grew. For the moment, by publishing simultaneously in a member nation—most conveniently Canada—the United States gained Berne protection for some American authors.

In the American debates over international copyright, the arguments for cheap books remained strong. Though common decency and international trade favored reciprocal recognition of copyright, old attitudes died slowly. Narrowly technical issues were phrased as broad ideological questions. By the late nineteenth century the most vocal spokesmen for the public domain hailed from the South and West. They bridled at the East Coast publishers' sacrifice of readers to writers.[223] The nation had been founded on the Bible and the primer, two works not subject to copyright.[224] Why not, Senator James Beck of Kentucky thundered in 1888, "allow our own people to obtain in the cheapest way they can the product of the brains of foreigners?"

International copyright threatened to raise prices. "It is the reading public whom I seek to protect," he insisted.[225]

"Cheap books have become a necessity," the essayist Logan Pearsall Smith warned. International copyright threatened to impose "an embargo on the spread of intelligence, on the diffusion of literature, on the spread of education among our people," Texas Senator Richard Coke admonished in 1891.[226] International copyright, Senator John Daniel from Virginia cautioned, contradicted America's most fundamental political premise. As her public schools and other institutions of learning showed, America allowed all to drink freely of the waters of knowledge. But to help authors, books would now become expensive. "It is a bastile [sic] of letters which is here constructed, and not a republic."[227] Since the public domain was still America's framing narrative, even those in favor of international copyright claimed that readers would remain as well and cheaply supplied as before.[228]

In the late nineteenth century a gulf had opened between the copyright and authors' rights ideologies. Lamartine's bill of 1841 and French jurisprudence during the following decades emphasized authors' inalienable rights. But Macaulay and his even more radical American fellow travelers insisted that the public deserved not just consideration but primacy. All nations in the spotlight here had started out in the eighteenth century following much the same approach. Now their paths diverged. That gulf was about to become a chasm as moral rights finally emerged on the Berne agenda—ushered in, curiously enough, by people now remembered for burning books rather than protecting them.

5

The Strange Birth of Moral Rights in Fascist Europe

The author's moral rights were formulated in case law and jurisprudence during the latter half of the nineteenth century. But only during the years between the two world wars were they embodied in statute. Fascist Italy put them on the books in 1925. At the instigation of Mussolini's government, they became part of the Berne Convention in 1928. The Nazi regime in Germany discussed authors' rights extensively, but its only major reform was extending protection from thirty to fifty years postmortem. The totalitarian regimes of the 1930s were curiously ambivalent. As part of their vitalist political ideologies, the fascists prided themselves on fostering strong creative personalities. That, they were convinced, distinguished them from both the moribund bourgeois societies they had replaced and from their enemies, the communist masses in the east.

But the fascists also played to the audience's interests, and more generally to society (as they saw it). In aesthetic terms they regarded authors (however heroically creative) as the mouthpiece of the community, dependent on and wholly part of society. Authors' claims were ultimately subordinate to society's needs. The solitary Romantic artist died in fascist Europe. More mundanely, as mass-based dictatorships hoping for continued popular legitimacy, the fascists were more interested in broad audience access to creative work than in its authors' fiddly whims. As in so many other realms, the fascists' ideology and their authors' rights practices were contradictory and inconsistent. By crediting the actual inventor (not just the first to file) for patents, the Nazis celebrated the individual creator. But by allowing the growing film industry to concentrate creative decision making in the producer and his company, not with film's flesh-and-blood authors, they bowed to the needs of efficient corporate production and dissemination. The fascists thus trumpeted their support of authors and moral rights while also insisting on their populist bona fides. Small wonder, then, that they produced more smoke than fire.

Yet, despite their ineffectual bluster, the regimes of the 1930s had a profound effect on postwar developments. The Nazis advocated the racial community's right to access its cultural patrimony, even while also claiming to support authors. They thus came closer to articulating a sustained Continental version of the classic Anglo-American copyright tradition's concern for the audience than had been heard in Europe since the French Revolution and the July Monarchy. But that damned by association. Once the war was over, reformers in the rejuvenated French and German democracies pursued the author's moral rights, often working closely from draft bills elaborated by their totalitarian predecessors. But they rejected as tainted communitarianism the fascists' concern for the audience's interests.

Moral rights express legislative concern for the creative classes. They have long been important in Europe but only belatedly and grudgingly so in the Anglophone world. Their supporters, both on the Continent and in the United States and Britain, have often assumed, in a vague and unarticulated sense, that moral rights arise from the Western tradition's most enlightened instincts. Their actual legislative pedigree, however, was less pristine. Moral rights first became part of the Berne Convention at the 1928 conference held in Fascist Rome. They did not just "filter" onto the agenda.[1] The Italian delegation placed them there to showcase the Mussolini regime's cultural credentials and register its ambitions for an honored and legitimate place in Europe's patrimony.

Many things we now value and do not give a second thought to can be traced to Europe's interwar fascist regimes: fast (Porsche) and reliable (VW) cars and the highways to drive them on, antismoking science and legislation, jet propulsion, and much rocket science—not to mention the song "Lili Marleen."[2] Some of post-war Europe's virtues are rooted in a hesitation to look too closely at its totalitarian heritage. The death penalty was outlawed in the German Basic Law in 1949 at the prompting of a far-right party that hoped to spare Nazi war criminals the noose. Only later did humanitarian sympathies emerge.[3] The value that Europeans attach to protecting personal privacy would be less urgent if not for the Continent's totalitarian past and the fear of history repeating itself.[4] Germany's present green and ecological sentiments have their precedents in Nazi ideology.[5] Contemporary German laws protecting individual dignity echo Nazi ideas and legislation on honor.[6] To trace something back to discredited regimes does not necessarily diminish its innate quality. But it bears investigation why moral rights—bourgeois, individualist, and culturally worthy—should have been embraced by anti-intellectual, plebian mass regimes.

MORAL RIGHTS AT THE 1928 BERNE CONFERENCE

Moral rights did not arrive unannounced in Mussolini's Rome. Though little had been codified, such ideas had worked their way through French and German case law for half a century. In 1886 the Berne Convention had foreshadowed the attribution right when it insisted that reprinted periodical articles name their source.[7] Moral rights were legislated in Romania (1923), Poland (1926), Czechoslovakia (1926), Portugal (1927), and Italy itself (1925). The Italian act, which had been passed during the legislative session that approved the fundamental laws of the Fascist regime, served as the template of the Berne Rome conference's reforms in 1928.

Like other fascisms the Italian regime's ideology was largely collectivist.[8] Nonetheless, Mussolini's Italy went furthest of all countries to secure moral rights. The 1925 law was hailed as catapulting Italy into the vanguard of authors' rights and as one of the new regime's signal achievements.[9] Of course the Fascist regime quickly reformed authors' rights, its defenders explained. The new government celebrated the primacy of intellectual values, even as it subordinated the individual to the state.[10] The 1925 law introduced the rights of attribution and integrity, with integrity defined expansively as preventing changes to the work that violated the author's "moral interests." The law also introduced a withdrawal right, allowing authors to repent of works if they compensated rights holders. Even published works thus remained within the author's sphere of personality.[11] After his death the author's family safeguarded his moral interests. If they failed to act, the authorities could step in. Resolving the issues broached as early as the Lamartine debate of 1841, the Italians also limited creditors' claims. For unpublished works the author could designate his own executor, rather than the usual statutory heirs.[12]

The Polish and French delegations to the Berne conference also pressed for moral rights.[13] The Polish proposal ranked moral rights among other universal human rights—to life, bodily integrity, liberty, and honor. The French delegation circulated a pamphlet as it lobbied for the cause.[14] But the main mover was the Italian delegate, Eduardo Piola Caselli—senator, procurator general at the Italian Supreme Court (Cassation) and the conference's *rapporteur général*. Having been instrumental in drafting the Italian law of 1925, Piola Caselli proposed a new Berne article (6*bis*). The author was to determine when and how his work appeared, be acknowledged as its author, and be able to oppose all changes prejudicial to his moral interests. These moral rights were to be perpetual and inalienable.

Piola Caselli was a savvy tactician, seeking to smooth the passage of his far-reaching and controversial proposals. The French motion foresaw reforms enforced uniformly across all nations by international legislation. The Italians, however, cleverly left the details of implementation to each Berne member. But even so, Italian ambitions were lofty. Moral rights promised to be a historic advance, they insisted. Their own 1925 law had demonstrated how Fascism supported intellectual workers.[15]

Still, moral rights faced obstacles in 1928. The Commonwealth nations considered such novelties irreconcilable with their copyright tradition. The distance between Anglo-Saxon and Latin mentalities was nowhere more evident, or so the New Zealand delegate reported back home. While the Continental delegates enthused, the English-speaking nations "coldly received" moral rights.[16] The UK Board of Trade thought they fell outside the scope of copyright law. In any case, libel law sufficed to remedy violations.[17] The Commonwealth nations and the British colonies still made up a sizable chunk of the

Berne Union (though they were down from almost two-thirds of its members in 1906).[18] They were not to be trifled with. Piola Caselli sought to bring the Anglophone nations around by arguing that they already protected moral rights, if not by copyright legislation, then in the common law.[19]

The Australian delegate, Sir William Harrison Moore, agreed and helped broker a compromise between the Anglophone heartland and the Continent. The disclosure right was set aside since Britain and other Anglophone nations allowed rights to be fully assigned, including initial publication, future editions, alterations, and adaptations. In British law an author could waive even his personal rights by contract, and the Commonwealth delegates insisted this remain true.[20] In common law, personal rights like protection against defamation died with the person. Gone, therefore, was also any mention of moral rights to be exercised by others after the author's death. In return the Anglo-Saxon signatories agreed to protect authors against their works being deformed or mutilated, whether this damaged their reputation or what was rather grandly termed the interests of literature, science, and the arts.

Indeed, thanks to British protests, the very term "moral interests" in the Italian proposal was replaced by more familiar concepts. Works of the spirit, the delegates agreed, were both economic properties and reflections of their maker's personality. Yet even Piola Caselli considered authors thin-skinned and thought the law should not always kowtow to their possibly exaggerated sensibilities.[21] The original Italian proposal on authors' "moral interests" was therefore tempered to protect against only those changes that threatened their "honor or reputation."[22] These values were already covered by the Commonwealth nations' laws on defamation and passing off (fraudulent misrepresentation of goods or services). Implicitly, then, the Anglophone nations were not expected to introduce new moral rights legislation. Nor would they have to situate the protection now required within their copyright statutes as such.[23] Since "moral interests" were a more expansive and elastic concept than damage to honor and reputation, the new formulation limited the author's powers. The German fresco case of 1912, mentioned in the last chapter, where Arnold Böcklin won damages when his privately placed nudes were clothed, would likely not have been actionable under the Rome terms.[24] Similarly, an actor could not object if a silent film role was jazzed up with a colleague's voice in a talkie version.[25]

At Rome in 1928, reformers understood that tentative pledges for moral rights were all that could be hoped for.[26] The Commonwealth countries had been startled by such ambitious proposals. By leaving implementation to national law, the Continental delegates managed to persuade them not to scuttle negotiations.[27] As mentioned, the disclosure right disappeared in this compromise between Continental ambitions and Anglo-Saxon resistance. Only in 1967 did that become part of Berne. But attribution remained. So did a narrowed version of integrity, though with no mention of rights after death. These were the minimum rights expected of member nations. Whether any wanted to do more was left to their own choice.

THE IDEOLOGY OF MORAL RIGHTS

Perhaps this first international formulation of moral rights was somehow quintessentially Fascist, as Piola Caselli and others claimed. But one should approach such totalitarian braggadocio skeptically. More likely, it was just a political coincidence that the new Italian regime was on deck at the moment when the slow progress of legal reform finally produced this initial codification of moral rights in international law. As we have seen, moral rights had developed in French and German jurisprudence and case law during the late nineteenth century. By the interwar years reformers across the political spectrum and across Europe were pushing to formalize the doctrine in statute. Privileging the author over the audience and over disseminators, moral rights were in one sense liberal and individualistic, legislatively incarnating the Romantic tradition of the heroic creator. That was how French legal theorists and case law understood them. The Fascists in Italy took them up in this spirit too.

Like the early Soviets Italian Fascists were vibrantly modernist and avant-garde. They saw themselves as rejuvenating moribund Italian culture, with its glorious past, slothful present, and neglected future. The Futurists, who despised the bourgeoisie and what they considered the backward, provincial, and lazy Italian upper classes, were close allies of the early Fascists.[28] Though they later fell out, at first the Fascists brought artists, composers, and writers like Marinetti and D'Annunzio into their camp.[29] Right-wing politics and avant-garde culture were frequently allied in all nations during the interwar years. Think only of the American Ezra Pound, Wyndham Lewis and, arguably, T. S. Eliot in Britain, Ernst Jünger in Germany and Louis-Ferdinand Céline in France. But in Italy the association was broader, more consistent, and more carefully cultivated by both movement and regime. Like fascists everywhere, Mussolini's followers fancied themselves as society's spiritual forces, allied against modernity's materialism, and especially its supposedly Anglo-Saxon and Jewish traits. Piola Caselli portrayed himself as an exemplar of the Fascist New Era and a carrier of eternal Roman traditions. Protecting moral rights, he insisted, struck a blow against economic materialism and for civilized ideals and works of the spirit.[30]

Yet moral rights—an inherently malleable and protean set of ideas—could also be understood in a more collectivist way. There was nothing uniquely Fascist about hoping to protect authors from modern media and mass society. Throughout the 1920s and '30s across Europe, proposals, draft bills, and laws introduced moral rights and in other ways too sought to shield authors from the market: in Social Democratic Norway, authoritarian Poland and Portugal, politically cacophonous Weimar Germany, and in France of the leftist Popular Front. As a defense of authors and cultural creativity, moral rights were uncontroversial across the Continent's many political ideologies.

But seen as a broader cultural reflex, moral rights belonged to the cultural pessimism of the interwar years and the pervasive sense that modern life threatened worthwhile values. As on almost every topic, the First World War's slaughter cast a shadow. Europe's most promising youth had died in the trenches. Prewar civilization was now mauled by mass society. High time, many felt, to defend the rights of intelligence and sensibility against oppressive materialism.[31] Whether of the left or right, cultural pessimists worried especially about modern media. Perhaps cinema, radio, and the popular press were democratic in a plebian sense. They entertained, and possibly even educated, the masses. But mass media also threatened high culture and authors. Film, phonograph, and radio had spawned compulsory licensing, undermining authors' exclusive rights.[32] At the Rome conference Piola Caselli presented moral rights as a quid pro quo. Modern technologies expanded the author's economic rights, yet sapped his control. Business wanted a cut, and the audience was clamoring to enjoy its cultural patrimony. In return for legal innovations, like licensing, that enhanced public access, authors should be granted moral rights to ensure that their works were not corrupted or demeaned by modern mass media or their audiences.[33]

MORAL RIGHTS IN NAZI GERMANY

In Germany the laws on authors' rights dated from 1901 and 1907 and were last updated in 1910. During the Weimar Republic, from 1919 on, many agreed that reforms were urgent. Proposals had been broached, though without result, by the time Hitler seized power in January 1933. A lively debate broke out early in the Third Reich over authors' rights. The Nazis' ideas were not novel and indeed were often prompted by reformers active also during the republic. Few changes were actually implemented. But those discussed indicated the Nazis' intentions, had war and defeat not intervened. The Nazi debates also show that authors' rights were not neutral technical and legal issues. They were proxies in a larger ideological battle over the author's role in society and the demands of the collectivity vis-à-vis the creator. And yet, interestingly, for all the controversy during the Third Reich, in time the postwar West German Federal Republic picked up and completed the reform work begun during the Hitler years.

Compared to their Italian cousins the Nazis were culturally conservative. Early on some Nazis did share the Italian Fascists' fondness for the avant-garde. Propaganda minister Joseph Goebbels at first befriended aesthetically pathbreaking artists. Several, like the Expressionist painter Emil Nolde, joined the party early. But Hitler's tastes were more conventional. Which style of art best officially expressed the regime was debated when the Reich Cultural Chamber was founded in 1933. Goebbels and his clique argued that Expressionist painters like Nolde represented a native Germanic art, resting on Gothic traditions and distinct from Latin classicism.[34] At the party congress of 1934, however, Hitler rejected all modernist art—Dadaists, Futurists, Cubists, and Expressionists. Modernist, abstract, and nonfigurative art was now branded degenerate.[35] In their place the regime officially adopted the figurative historical style of the late nineteenth century. Paintings were duly churned out portraying Germany as a timeless land of valiant leaders, industrious workers, heroic soldiers, fertile maidens, blond tots, and picturesque peasants.[36]

Still, like the Italian Fascists, the Nazis welcomed efforts to grant creators moral rights. But their understanding of the author's role in society was largely collectivistic. Art did not stand separate from society, Goebbels lectured the conductor Wilhelm Furtwängler after he had dared a mild protest against the demotion of his Jewish colleague, Bruno Walter. Art both expressed and shaped society, and artists were indelibly part of their community. There could be no art for art's sake, as in liberal democracies.[37] Nonetheless, the Nazi position was more nuanced than a simple totalitarian collectivism. It sought to balance the contradictory demands of author and audience.[38] Seen in the long history of authors' rights, the Nazis came closer to the Anglophone copyright position than had ever been the case in Germany. The Third Reich, oddly enough, was one of the few moments when the Germans intensely discussed the issues that had occupied the British a century earlier, during the Talfourd debates of the late 1830s and early '40s.

The Nazis themselves thought they occupied a sensible middle ground. The Third Reich's jurists, who engaged in lively reform debates, rightly saw attitudes toward authors' rights as expressing political ideologies. The French, they thought, viewed moral rights as individualistic and liberal and were primarily concerned to protect authors.[39] Insofar as they considered the community's interest, they assumed it to be one with that of the authors.[40] At the other extreme the Soviets wholly subordinated the author to the collectivity.[41] French and Italian reformers often regarded Nazi ideas on these matters as akin to the Soviet position. But the Germans indignantly rejected such parallels.[42] Though they worked with the different heritages of Roman and Germanic law, they insisted that Nazi and Fascist reformers both sought to balance the interests of creator and community.[43] Liberalism subordinated society to the author, while Marxism elevated the mass, undermining the role of strong creative personalities. The Nazis, in contrast, claimed to protect authors as members of society, thus transcending the contradiction between creator and community.[44]

Like other Berne members Germany was held to the minimum standards of moral rights adopted in Rome in 1928. Integrity and attribution were already legislated or recognized in German case law, but better protection was called for to meet the new commitments.[45] After Rome the Germans continued moving away from seeing authors' rights as grounded only in property.[46] Courts began to recognize personal rights, distinct from authors' economic claims. In 1929 the heirs of Wilhelm Busch (writer and illustrator of *Max und Moritz* fame) won claims to radio broadcasts of his work with an affirmation of his inalienable personality rights.[47] Then, from the Nazi takeover in 1933 and for a few years, a wave of reform proposals poured forth. The discussion of authors' rights during the Third Reich was typical of Nazi discourse—turgid, pretentious, gnarled, vague, bombastic, and supremely confident that a new age had dawned. Technical and narrowly legal as the issues might seem, the Nazis regarded them as ideological, to be rejiggered in the new political spirit.

At the core of the Rome discussions in 1928 lay a contradiction: the antithetical goals of broadening access to culture, yet expanding authorial rights. The collective squared off against the individual. Nazi reformers sought to reconcile this tension in two ways. First, they regarded moral rights as a trade-off, protecting creators' artistic interests even as their economic claims were undermined by the new media. The new technologies were inherently collectivist—both as produced and consumed. With radio a government monopoly, even the state had its own interests.[48] Moral rights were thus a sop thrown to authors to reconcile them with a populist age. The less power that creators retained over disseminating their works, the more important was their control over how they were presented.[49]

Second, the Nazis singled out authors from disseminators and bombastically celebrated them as geniuses toiling for the community. Soviet and Marxist ideology was built on the masses, liberal bourgeois society on deracinated anomic individuals. Nazi society, in contrast, venerated strong creative personalities, *Schöpferpersönlichkeiten*, who were essentially connected to their community: thus ran the Third Reich's *Lebenslüge*.[50] The nineteenth century, Hitler proclaimed, was the era of great personalities, liberated by the French Revolution.[51] Standing in this tradition, the Nazi regime brought together the racial community, the *Volksgemeinschaft*, and the individual creator, the *Volksgenosse*. Hitler welcomed the aristocratic principle of seeking out talent.[52] Yes, rewarding creative personalities was individualistic. But it was also collectivistic since their vision nourished society. Hence the author and the Volksgemeinschaft no longer contradicted each other. Enforcing the author's control guaranteed the audience's pure enjoyment of his works.[53]

More important, the author created only within and as part of his community. The genius depended on the materials that society placed at his disposal, giving voice to the ideas and emotions of his racial community.[54] The poet expressed himself in his people's language, the musician by using the common elements of melody, harmony, and rhythm. Granting this inheritance, it was only fair to limit creators' rights.[55] Individuality in the new era meant not cultivating personal differences but celebrating the individual's connection with the community. Protecting not just the creator, authors' rights revealed the *Volk*'s spiritual powers. The Nazi author should cultivate not a walled-off garden for the few but a public park for all. Creator and community were inherently intertwined.[56] In the Nazi vision defending the creator's personality thus also safeguarded his community's honor.[57] The author, rooted in his tribal people, his *Volkstum*, incarnated the eternal creative spirit of his race. By protecting the author, the folk protected itself.[58] In *Mein Kampf* Hitler celebrated inventors as the Nazi ideal.[59] No longer a self-centered, socially irresponsible bohemian, the Nazi creator labored for the Volksgemeinschaft—a worker of the head. The Nazi state promised to protect his work—the expression of his inner nature—against distortion and misrepresentation.[60]

Nazis thus lauded authors as part of their racial community. Disseminators, in contrast, they viewed with distrust. They might benefit from some proposed reforms, like compulsory licensing. But the Nazis distinguished moral rights from assignable economic claims and placed them beyond the disseminators' grasp. The 1928 Rome conference had weakened disseminators, one observer noted in 1934. Germany should too. The revival of the Germanic spirit under Nazism would eradicate capitalism and materialism. The authors' interests, not those of the media corporations, were proclaimed primary.[61] The socialization of the creator's talents proclaimed by Nazi aesthetic theories, his rootedness in his community, prevented him from alienating his works to the media industries to do as they pleased with the nation's patrimony. The Nazi revolution, they insisted, had ended the reign of culture as a commodity.[62]

The Nazi pogroms and terror quickly turned Germany into a cultural desert. Yet the regime was convinced that it had managed to balance the interests of authors and their audience. Richard Strauss, the composer, was perhaps the most talented artist to remain in Germany. His relations to Nazism were a complicated mélange of opportunism, contempt, and otherworldliness. Active in the Third Reich's cultural bureaucracy, he also occasionally protected Jewish composers and musicians, as well as his Jewish daughter-in-law and her family. He pinch hit for conductors like Toscanini and Bruno Walter, who had been declared non grata. He happily met Hitler when conducting *Parsifal* in July 1933, seizing the opportunity to discuss the firings of Jews and authors' rights reforms. He lobbied Goebbels to extend the term of a work's protection to fifty years postmortem. As president of the newly formed Reichsmusikkammer in 1933, he still collaborated with Stefan Zweig, the Jewish librettist of *Die schweigsame Frau*, even after he was attacked by the notoriously anti-Semitic Julius Streicher in his paper, *Der Stürmer*.[63]

Strauss spoke for a traditional veneration of the author. Authors' rights legislation, in thrall to publishers, was an impenetrable legal thicket, he thought. Would that reform restore the creator to his rightful place, simplifying relations between authors and disseminators! Only thus could the new regime reconcile noble individualism with the Volksgemeinschaft.[64] Above all, the author's integrity right deserved perpetual protection, and all commercial borrowing from works should be forbidden.[65]

Despite Strauss's pleas, and despite their own claims to venerate creative personalities, the Nazis were equally concerned to temper extreme authorial claims, emphasizing society's interests instead. They saw the Berne Union's Rome conference as the end of the era of ever-expanding authors' rights. New technologies of dissemination and new legal instruments, like compulsory licensing, rightly limited the author's claims.[66] The author's rights were seen as socially bound (*sozialgebundenes Recht*). This idea of socially bound rights became a Nazi leitmotif. But it had been formulated already during Weimar by jurists like Alexander Elster and Julius Kopsch.[67] Indeed, the claim that property was ultimately subordinated to society's demands was emblazoned in the republic's constitution from 1919.[68]

Kopsch was a composer, conductor, lawyer, and a friend of Strauss. He had argued for the socially bound nature of authors' rights at a congress of authors and composers in 1928. Then, he had been attacked for daring to limit authorial rights. Now, in the Nazi regime, his time had come.[69] Far from inventing a new approach, the Nazis continued a Weimar theme. Willy Hoffmann too had been an active legal reformer during Weimar, and he remained so in the Third Reich. The Nazi conception of authors' rights, he insisted, "puts the Volksgemeinschaft at the center of things, grants the author rights, but also sets out his obligations to the community."[70] Liberal Weimar had overemphasized the author. Now the task was to safeguard the German community. "In the new state," another reformer agreed, "we are all socially grounded."[71]

Alongside moral rights Nazi reformers saw the regulation of radio broadcasts, with its possibility of compulsory licensing, as the core of the Rome conference.[72] The committee formulating a government bill in 1934 discussed how compulsory licensing might aid the new regime's commitment to greater public access.[73] Again, strong continuities of thought stretched from Weimar to the Third Reich. Already in 1928, Willy Hoffmann had railed against French skepticism about compulsory licensing. The work stood "in service to the Volksgemeinschaft," he argued, using a rhetoric even then that we find difficult to separate from Nazi ideology but that in fact was common currency during the republic too.[74] In 1928 his colleague Kopsch startled the Confédération Internationale des Sociétés d'Auteurs et

Compositeurs, as it met in Berlin to prepare for the Berne conference, by demanding that authors' rights be limited by compulsory
licensing on behalf of the community. He sang the praises of licensing: it prevented works from becoming capitalist commodities, it
lowered prices and encouraged multiple editions.[75]

Hoffmann, Kopsch, and other jurists now seamlessly carried such
arguments into the Third Reich's more receptive atmosphere. With
a friendly allusion to the socializing goals of Roosevelt's New Deal,
Ludwig Wertheimer, a Frankfurt lawyer, warmly recommended musical licensing in 1936 so composers could pay society back for its
support and inspiration.[76] Overstated authorial property rights were
considered a Roman legal concept, foreign to Germanic law, which
understood property not as absolute control but as a socially tempered power given by statute.[77] The work existed independently of
its author and should be safeguarded for its own sake. The work, not
its creator, was paramount. If society's economic, military, or racial
interests so required, authors could be expropriated.[78] The work
should be protected against degrading changes, even those sought by
its creator. If nationally significant, it might be published against his
wishes.[79] In a debate in March 1933, Hoffmann agreed that the common good took precedence over authorial self-interest. Others countered that—taken to its logical conclusion—his claim meant the end
of the author's economic and possibly his personal rights. The new
Nazi vision, Hoffmann replied, emphasized the collectivity's claims
and the socially determined nature of authors' rights.[80]

Nazi jurists also collectivized moral rights by focusing on honor
and reputation. At the 1928 Rome conference, the Commonwealth
nations had managed to replace "moral interests" as the right protected with the author's honor and reputation instead. This allowed
them to assert that they already protected authors and so spared
them the need to pass new laws. It also slimmed down the authors'
claims. Community standards, not authors' own subjective sensitivi-
ties, determined when harm was done. Giving a tragedy a happy end
when it was filmed might offend the story's author and his moral
interests but probably did not impair his honor or reputation. The
Nazi focus on the author's honor was not motivated by the same

hope as the Commonwealth nations to weasel out of the new Berne obligations. But in much the same way it socialized the goods to be protected. Moral interests, as determined by authors, were kept in check only by the thickness of their skin. Their honor, their *Urheberehre*, in contrast, was a social concept. It mirrored the community's standards (*ein Spiegel im Auge der Gemeinschaft*).[81] The dog in the fight belonged not to a possibly vain and querulous artist but to the Volksgemeinschaft. And who was to define that, if not Nazi officialdom? A work that set itself against the community could be censured. The state protected only those who served it loyally. The egotistical artist who refused to adapt his work to the community's demands could not expect the state to defend his purely personal interests. The author might be forbidden to withhold his work from publication or required to tolerate changes after publication.[82]

Honor was one of those flexible, sonorous, seemingly traditional, evocative, and ponderous terms the Nazis so favored. Like moral rights, honor was an aristocratic throwback that, at first glance, seemed unlikely to appeal to a populist mass movement. But honor was also a portmanteau concept that allowed Nazis to cram together irreconcilable impulses from their ever-fractious and self-contradictory ideology. Honor fused the movement's aristocratic posturing and its egalitarian appeal. The Nazi obsession with honor capped a century-long development of the concept. Originally an aristocratic conceit, honor became increasingly democratized during the nineteenth century as the aspirational middle classes strove for higher status.[83] The Nazis prided themselves on having rejuvenated the concept as a meritocratic measure of worth. No longer the preserve of caste or class, Nazi honor supposedly recognized the individual's contributions to his Volksgemeinschaft.[84] Applied to authors' rights, Nazi honor neatly slipped individualistic moral rights into a social context. The author's honor demanded that a "correct interpretation of the work was to be protected in the Volksgemeinschaft."[85] When the Nazi Justice Ministry formulated the last version of its reform bill in 1939, what had been the *Urheberpersönlichkeitsrecht*, the German translation of "droit moral," was redubbed as the "Urheberehre," the author's honor.[86]

WHAT THE NAZIS WOULD HAVE DONE

While the party planned for major change once it was in power, the regime delivered little.[87] Already in June 1933, the Nazis shifted the supervision of authors' rights from the Interior Ministry to Goebbels's Ministry of Popular Enlightenment and Propaganda. They ratified the revised Berne Convention in October of that year.[88] A burst of ideological discussion then accompanied a series of reform proposals. Little, however, had been implemented by 1939, when the war the Nazis started ended hopes for reform.[89] In addition to the war, reforms also foundered on the diversity of interests clamoring for attention and the regime's characteristic inability or unwillingness to make clear decisions among them.

In the early years, as the Nazis sought and then consolidated a popular base, they criticized capitalism and big business, playing up their national *socialism*. Once he had become chancellor, Hitler's main political predicament was balancing between the populism that had won the NSDAP its broad membership, represented within the party by the SA and the Strasser brothers, and the necessity of tactically allying with the traditional elites. Until June 1934, when Hitler suppressed the party's popular wing in the Night of the Long Knives, socialist-style slogans and ideology were common. Even after that, the party's anticapitalist and populist rhetoric persisted. But the Nazis had to appeal equally to the establishment, whose backing was crucial during the early years before Hitler had consolidated power. The minor issue of authors' rights interestingly encapsulated a wider ideological challenge. It forced the regime to choose between authors/disseminators and the public. As a Frankfurt lawyer remarked in 1936, no other aspect of civil law posed the contradiction between individual interests and the community so sharply.[90]

The regime balanced two contradictory impulses: to celebrate the heroic, creative artist whose gifts served society, but who still remained a pseudo-aristocratic, elitist figure, and to insist that the community was the ultimate source of his creativity and thus entitled to its fruits. As in much Nazi ideology, elitist, aesthetic, aristocratic principles jostled with egalitarian and populist ambitions. Authorial personality rights, having grown throughout the nineteenth century, were to be fulfilled by the new Berne principles. But at the same time the public was now more the focus of attention than at any time since the eighteenth century. Arguably, it was even more so since it was no longer seen as a passively recipient audience. It was now factored into the same aesthetic algorithm that produced works.

Nazi ideology regarded creativity as possible only within its social setting. It turned society into the author's equal in the creative endeavor, in much the same way as the socially determinist postmodernism of our own day. A century after Carl Spitzweg's famous 1839 painting of the poet writing in his attic bed (said to be the second most popular painting among Germans, after the *Mona Lisa*), the cult of the lonely Romantic genius in his garret ended. The themes struck by Weimar reformers and Nazi ideologues were more akin to those of the Anglo-American realm, where the community of creativity and society's preeminence were commonsense positions. In the miserable transition from the last years of the Weimar Republic to the early Third Reich, German discussions of authors' rights had their Talfourd moment. The rhetoric of balance between authorial claims and audience needs—the staple of Anglo-Saxon discussion— was taken up in Germany as never before.

In the summer of 1932, during Weimar's last days, the Ministry of Justice formulated a draft bill on authors' rights, intended jointly for Germany and Austria.[91] It was published only on 12 July 1933, after Hitler became chancellor. Many reformers found it too favorable to authors, insufficiently mindful of society's demands, and not infused with the Third Reich's spirit.[92] In response, Willy Hoffmann wrote a draft bill in his own name.[93] He and Julius Kopsch, in turn, were instrumental in formulating another bill under the imprimatur of the National Socialist Lawyers' Federation (NS-Juristenbund), which reworked the 1932 Weimar draft bill.[94] The Justice Ministry in turn overhauled its own earlier bill several times from 1933 to 1939.[95]

Since none of these bills was implemented, we need not parse their details. All of them assumed the socially embedded nature of creativity and the author's role within his community. But all equally sought to protect authors' moral rights. The 1934 Justice Ministry bill collected the previous laws' scattered passages on moral rights, harmonizing them with the Rome principles; and all the draft bills granted disclosure, attribution, and integrity.[96] A right of repenting in the 1933 bill allowed the author to forbid publication even after assigning his rights, if his standing or reputation were threatened.[97] For film, every creative participant could demand to be named, and alterations required their permission.[98] The Lawyers' Federation's formulation went beyond the 1928 Berne compromise of safeguarding only honor and reputation by protecting the author's "personal expressive will" (*seines eigenpersönlichen Ausdruckwillens*). But the Justice Ministry's 1939 bill more restrictively allowed authors to veto changes only if they violated standing (*Ansehen*) or reputation. A proviso, allowing the minister of propaganda to compel publication of posthumous works of national importance, restricted the disclosure right. But the 1939 bill also bowed to authorial individualism by agreeing that the state could not force posthumous publication of a work if the author's will banned its appearance.[99]

Excepting movie scripts, the first Nazi bills allowed authors to withdraw from publishing contracts if disseminators failed to issue their works. They granted artists access to works (to copy them, for example) now owned by others.[100] Creditors were restricted from foreclosing on or forcing sales of works. Architects could prevent their buildings being replicated.[101] In sum, however much the Nazi rhetoric played up community claims, their bills would have guaranteed the moral rights specified by Berne and then some.

Who would have been vested with these new rights? In the new post-Rome era, legal entities were no longer entitled to authors' rights.[102] As in inherited German laws, the Nazi bills identified the author as the person who had created the work.[103] Alienability was a closely related issue. Economic rights could, of course, be assigned but not personal rights. The trope of the heroic creator forbade it.[104] Existing law merely prevented works from being published under another name or grossly distorted. Moral rights were now to guarantee the creator artistic control even after he had sold his work. As Kopsch explained in 1938, in existing law rights often passed to a capitalist enterprise. But in the Nazi conception, the author remained forever identified with the work and he alone could change it.[105] Hoffmann's draft bill made moral rights inalienable but allowed case

law to decide whether they should last longer than economic rights.[106]
The Nazi Lawyers' Federation's bill declared authors' rights inalienable and in principle uninheritable, though the creator's family or
another designee would safeguard his moral rights after death.[107]

Existing German law allowed juridical entities to be considered
the authors of works like dictionaries and encyclopedias. Moral
rights posed a dilemma: whose personality did a collective work express?[108] The Nazis' view of creativity as collective suggested an elision
to a communitarian view of the author. The Nazis' emphasis on lead-
ership, their *Führerprinzip*, also encouraged the idea that one person
should take charge of collaborative efforts.[109] Yet, instead of collectivizing rights to collaborative works, both the bill of the Nazi Lawyers'
Federation and that of 1939 vested rights to group works in the participants jointly and individually, not collectively in any one primus
among them.[110] They upheld the principle of flesh-and-blood creators as the bearer of rights, rather than taking a more practical administrative approach to lodge them with one person or entity.[111]
Moreover, the 1936 patent law, to which we return, upended existing
law to vest both economic and attribution rights in the actual inventor, even if he was someone else's employee.[112]

And who should stand watch over moral rights, especially in the
long term? Nazi reformers wanted to prevent works of national importance from being degraded. The 1928 Rome Conference's article
6*bis* on moral rights grappled with the issue. But the Nazis considered
it too individualistic, enlisting only the author, and possibly his heirs,
to watch over his works. This would not suffice for works already in
the public domain, nor guard against profiteering or lazy descendants. Something like the *Reichskulturkammer* was needed to protect
works against heirs or even the author himself. If works expressed the
people's creative powers mediated through the author, then he too
could be prevented from changing them.[113] At the least, compulsory
licensing of posthumous works that heirs failed to publish should be
considered. Ultimately, personality rights could not remain a private
matter, passing to ever more distant heirs. They had to be socialized.[114] The Nazi bills all enlisted state institutions to preserve integrity. Only the Volksgemeinschaft, spoken for by the state, could preserve moral interests.[115]

What about society's more immediate claims to access? The flip side of moral rights was licensing arrangements. At Rome in 1928, delegates had battled over whether radio broadcast rights should be granted to authors as exclusive rights or as licensed claims to royalties. The Norwegians, whose own law of 1930 would have a collectivistic streak, advocated licensing.[116] Australia and New Zealand, cultured but sparsely settled lands and therefore alive to the promises of new media like radio, demanded broadcasting rights even if authors resisted.[117] Britain, also a radio-mad country, agreed. But the French delegates insisted that the public interest should not take precedence over exclusive authorial rights.[118]

The Rome conference left specifics to national legislation. Several nations had already introduced variants of compulsory licensing. The Nazis also eagerly followed Rome's invitation to license.[119] The socially determined nature of works, they insisted, cast licensing in a new light. Earlier, licenses had been seen as exceptions to the general rule of exclusive authorial rights. Now they were considered an inherent limit to those claims.[120] The Nazi draft bills all proposed compulsory licensing, the Justice Ministry version no fewer than six variants. Hoffmann's bill permitted radio stations to use published work against payment of fees. The Lawyers' Federation foresaw licensing so long as moral rights were not violated.

WHAT THE NAZIS DID

To judge from the Nazi draft bills, had authors' rights been reformed in the Third Reich, they would have balanced pampering ideologically observant authors with upholding the regime's ideological populism. Moral rights were promised, but creativity's socially determined nature left authors ultimately beholden to the community. Authors' rights were debated especially in the regime's early years, when its populism was still untempered by the compromises of power. The party platform's petty bourgeois, quasi-socialist radicalism was evident in the lambasting of big media.

Authors' rights shared features with agrarian reforms during the early regime.[121] The law on peasant estates was one of the few Nazi laws that reflected the party's original petty-bourgeois radicalism. Other reforms in this vein, while promised before Hitler came to power, were either ignored or watered down after 1933. To win over shopkeepers the Nazis had pledged to close department stores. But when they realized this would put many out of work and hurt workers by raising prices, they only imposed restrictions on large retailers instead.[122] In contrast, the law on peasant estates (*Reichserbhofgesetz*), passed already in September 1933, really did cater to the independent middle classes who had backed the party from the beginning. It created entailed farms, passed to the eldest son, which could be neither sold nor mortgaged.[123] But such solicitude for the core Nazi constituency did not outlast the party's later need to satisfy broader interest groups—much less the requirements of rearmament and war.

The Nazis' reform ambitions for authors' rights were cut from the same cloth. They too applauded the self-employed, not the salaried classes. Yet they were also collectivistic in granting the creative classes few rights that they could actually cash in. As the peasant proprietor was but a trustee for future generations, so the author only transmitted the community's spiritual powers. The Nazis claimed to root for the heroic creator against big media. Their author was, of course, not a rootless avant-garde bohemian. He grew from the soil of the Volksgemeinschaft. But he served the people, not the corporations. Only creators, never entrepreneurs, should own rights, one reformer noted. Authors should not become employees of publishers nor be contractually obliged to produce a specified number of works. The publisher's custom of pulping or discounting unsuccessful books violated the author's honor, sacrificing his personality on the "altar of publishing capitalism" (*Verlegerkapitalismus*). The media industries were considered likely violators of moral rights, blocking society's interests.[124]

The few measures actually implemented in the Third Reich reflected this Nazi concern for authors. Foremost among them was term extension. Germany entered the Third Reich with thirty years postmortem, inherited from the 1837 law. The Berlin revision of Berne in 1908 had accepted fifty years as the goal in principle. But, as we have seen, a debate ensued during the late Weimar and early Nazi years that faintly echoed the furious arguments in Britain almost a century earlier over Talfourd's proposals. Some argued that other nations had increasingly adopted fifty years and that the longer term favored authors and their families. Opponents noted that, since many authors (Brahms, Schopenhauer, Heine, Feuerbach) had no children, only the publishers profited. The German-speakers of central Europe were cultured, well-educated people thanks in part to cheap, good editions entering the public domain already three decades after the author's death.[125] By contrast, a fifty-year term was liberal and individualistic, neglected the community's interests, and threatened to turn the clock back to the nineteenth century.[126] The committee drafting the 1934 bill supported thirty years as speaking for the Volksgemeinschaft. "The people should not be deprived of important works just because the grand-niece of a departed author is living in hardship."[127]

With Strauss leading the charge, authors predictably agitated for longer terms.[128] Faced with a choice between creators and the public, the regime in fact plumped for authors. In 1934, after Strauss had lobbied Goebbels, one of the few major Nazi changes to authors' rights extended protection to half a century postmortem.[129] The German hand had arguably been forced when Austria introduced a fifty-year term in December 1933. German publishers faced the prospect of authors voting with their feet. Fascist Italy too had adopted a half-century term in 1925.[130] Equally influential, the Justice Ministry's bill from 1932 had already come down in favor of the longer duration, much to the delight of the interested parties.[131]

Music too was controversial, raising Nazi hackles. Infamously, they banned jazz as the mongrelized expression of degenerate Judeo-African America.[132] But the Nazis were also flexible. Homespun popular music, presented as a cultural cousin of folk music, was acceptable. The 1930s and '40s were the golden age of German hits—*Schlager*.[133] Yet cultural decline remained a fearsome prospect. With phonograph recordings and radio broadcasts fewer people played instruments. Cultural pessimists—much like Sousa in the United States—worried that popular melodies, cranked out by the hour in the music industries, were supplanting wholesome folk music and dances. Sounding like Frankfurt School theorists, the Nazis lambasted popular music and its stars.[134] Musical potpourris especially galled them. In theory such medleys were forbidden by the 1901 law that outlawed borrowing recognizable melodies.[135] At the time, this had been widely opposed as restricting musical invention and apparently was not strictly enforced.[136] Berne's new Rome obligations, one reformer now argued, meant that medleys violated composers' rights. While an assortment of popular songs perhaps hurt no one's honor, turning serious music into mere entertainment was intolerable.[137] A reformed law on authors' rights, another mused, must ensure that important works not be degraded by unworthy performances or alterations. His example was Heinrich Berté's use of Schubert's music in his 1916 pastiche operetta about the composer's love life, *Das Dreimäderlhaus* (*Blossom Time* in the US, *Lilac Time* in Britain).[138]

Strauss himself found time to write angry letters demanding prison sentences for such travesties. Even classical melodies already in the public domain should not be performed in popular musical styles like fox-trots or marches.[139] In 1934 the Reichsmusikkammer demanded that musical potpourris no longer be based on the great masters.[140] In Baden local regulations sought to preserve the integrity of musical works by outlawing performances in unsuitable places. The German national anthem and the Horst Wessel song—the anthem of the Nazi Party and co-national anthem after 1933—were not to be sung in cafés, bars, and the like.[141] Ironically, the Horst Wessel song itself had to be defended against charges that it, too, was but a pastiche of older folk melodies.[142]

The Reichskulturkammer never followed up. And some rejected a prohibition of borrowed melodies.[143] Justice Minister Franz Gürtner doubted that such uses could be forbidden for public domain music. Others feared that Strauss's approach might ossify culture.[144] Hoffmann's draft bill from 1933 was explicit that use of others' melodies not be forbidden (a stricture it regarded as derived from French law). Indeed, it favored widespread rights to borrow for new creations.[145] Both the 1934 and 1939 bills allowed fair use among musical compositions.[146] The former worried less about serious music being poached by lighter epigones than about exchanges between compositions of the same caliber. In any case, a rigid protection of melodies hampered artistic creativity and unjustifiably protected only music from borrowing.[147] The Nazis never decided such issues. But they seem to have been skeptical of strictures that narrowly protected composers of attractive melodies.

In other respects, too, the regime sought to loosen restrictions on the use of intellectual property. The draft bills followed existing law in allowing music to be played without permission at free or charitable concerts.[148] But on licensing, the Nazis innovated. After the draft bills made clear their intent to facilitate the easy and automatic use of works in new media, the Law on Musical Performance Rights of 1933 introduced a form of compulsory licensing, framed as a safeguard of society's justified rights of access to works.[149] It established a collection agency for musical royalties, the Stagma, whose formula for apportioning fees favored serious music over mere entertainment.[150]

The Nazis also keenly appreciated the new media's potential for propaganda and indoctrination. The phonograph had replaced *Hausmusik*, movies the theater, and the radio newspapers and concerts. No point in nostalgia! The goal was to channel the new media, with their direct access to the masses, on the state's behalf.[151] Radio and film especially interested a regime with sufficient savvy to enlist the latest technologies in its quest for legitimacy. Every German home should have a radio, making use "at every moment of the biggest and most effective instrument of modern mass influence in the interest of the well-being of the *Volksgemeinsamheit*."[152] As early as 1933, a quarter of all households owned radios. Thanks to the affordable *Volksempfänger*, the people's receiver, radio ownership doubled during the Nazi years, though it still lagged behind the UK and the US.[153]

The Nazis cannily recognized film's charms. Rich and poor, burghers and workers, intellectuals and dunces flocked night after night to the cinemas.[154] Goebbels poured money into film studios. Leni Riefenstahl famously put her pathbreaking cinematic techniques at the party's disposal. Cinema was not another version of theater, Goebbels lectured the International Film Congress in 1935, and could not be governed like the old medium.[155] The Nazis mostly avoided over-obvious messages, preferring to slip their ideological payload into seemingly message-free movies. It has been argued that only some 14 percent of films released during the regime were overtly propagandistic.[156]

FILM UNDER NATIONAL SOCIALISM

Because they were inherently collaborative, the new media posed problems for inherited laws on authors' rights.[157] During the late 1920s American writers became acutely aware of the aesthetic control they sacrificed in Hollywood. George Middleton, a playwright active in professional organizations, reported his insight in 1927 that the issue for the author was: "How is he going to protect himself against the hungriest thing in the world, which is a machine?"[158] The situation in Germany was no different.

In whom were rights vested for a collaboration like film? Statute was ambiguous in the early days of the new medium. The director was often regarded as a film's author, sometimes in conjunction with the editor or cinematographer. Some early case law assigned the producer that role, but other instances regarded only the creative contributors as authors.[159] In the early 1920s Wenzel Goldbaum argued for vesting rights in the scriptwriter. Others divided rights among writers, directors, composers, or combinations thereof.[160] When talkies arrived, the musical score lost importance. Increasingly, film was seen not on the model of opera, with its separable creative parts, but as an entity fusing sound and image. The industry pressed for law to treat cinema as a unified whole, with the producer holding rights. Writers, composers, and others argued, by contrast, that different contributors all had their own separate rights.[161]

Here, too, Nazi discussions fit into long-standing debates. In the 1908 Berlin revision of Berne, film was first protected in its own right.[162] In Rome two decades later, the French delegation unsuccessfully sought to have film recognized as belonging to all its "intellectual creators" and not just the producer—especially not if the producer, as is often true with film, was a legal person.[163] In 1935 a French ordinance declared that a producer who actively shaped the film should count among its authors. In 1939 the Paris Court of Appeals pronounced the producer the sole author of a film, denying scriptwriters rights and provoking outrage.[164] The Weimar Justice Ministry's bill of 1932 took up film in light of similar debates. Moral rights obliged the law to recognize all creative participants. But the film industry, bowing to the new logic of vesting rights only in flesh-and-blood authors, now argued that, in this inherently collaborative art form, the producer was in fact the author. He selected the director, the actors, and the work. The scriptwriter and composer followed his direction.[165]

In the Third Reich the movie industry was large, growing, and ideologically important. By 1936 it employed fifty thousand people.[166] Its representatives argued that film was inherently collaborative. One individual could not be singled out as the creator in the traditional sense. Because of the magnitude of the investment and the need to ensure efficient exploitation, rights should be centralized in one pair of hands—the producer's. He might not be a creator in the old-fashioned sense. But film was an industrial, not just a spiritual, product. The scale and risk of investment undercut sentimental talk of authors' personal rights.[167] Recognizing a multitude of coauthors threatened chaos. Even dressers or hairstylists might insist on creative rights. Deciding among the many participants was impossible; the producer remained the most reasonable choice.[168]

Some reformers were willing to grant producers author status if they were creative participants and shouldered not just technical and financial tasks.[169] On the whole, however, Nazi jurists opposed producers as authors. Entitling producers to creative rights confused capitalist interests with authors' rights, they argued.[170] However important he might be in practice, the producer was no creator. Only the actual creator's claims counted.[171] Even granting producers economic powers was sometimes considered suspect. Their decision to broadcast a film, say, might deprive other contributors of artistic and economic rights. Some Nazis vehemently dismissed the producer-as-author concept as a Jewish attempt to submerge individuality into the masses, unjustifiable even by appeals to the primacy of the collectivity.[172]

But drafters of the regime's bills had to contend with the industry's interests. The Justice Ministry's 1932 bill defined the author as the person who created the work, and it excluded juridical entities. Anticipating protest from the movie industry, use rights (*Werknutzungsrechte*) for films were vested in the company.[173] The bill of the Lawyers' Federation, however, took another tack. Though accepting that the author was usually the person who created the work, for film it anointed the producer (*Hersteller*)—even if that was a juridical person. Hoffmann also bit the bullet with his draft bill. Accepting that so collaborative and costly an enterprise simply had to choose a single author from among many contenders, he nominated the producer. But Hoffmann also maneuvered to fit this decision to the regime's insistence on flesh-and-blood authorship. Foreshadowing the auteur theories of the 1960s (though applied to producers, not directors), he heralded the producer as a film's true author. The producer had the idea, supervised the script, and shaped the work.[174] The 1934 revision of the Justice Ministry bill followed suit by endowing the owner of the production company with authorial rights, though it also hedged its bets by retaining rights in the film's various elements (script, score, novel) for their authors.[175]

In 1936 a Committee on Film Rights, convened at the Academy of German Law, weighed the author's moral rights against the film industry's practical needs.[176] It decided that the film's author had to be its creator. Who that was could not always be determined in advance. But it should not automatically be the producer. Having been cut down in theory, the producer was then welcomed back in practice. He was to receive those rights required to exploit the film. Since he got rights to preserve it from demeaning treatment (such as splicing in pornographic inserts), he was also awarded a variant of the integrity right.[177] Some reformers bridled that true authors thereby received too little control.[178] Others foreshadowed the subtle distinctions drawn in the final draft bill that left actual authors with vague aesthetic rights and the producer with the ones that mattered.[179]

The final bill in 1939 continued to redefine personal and economic rights to the point where the distinction largely evaporated. Once again the producer was granted the economic rights and could also take action if a movie was demeaned. Film was a complicated matter, the bill's exposition lamented. It could not specify in advance who the creator was. The industry's economics required vesting exploitation rights in the producer. Yet, since that violated flesh-and-blood authorship, the producer was instead made a trustee (*Treuhänder*) of the creators, much like a publisher.[180] This last attempt at Nazi reform, on the eve of the war, implicitly recognized the actual author's rights and relegated producers to a theoretically secondary status. French commentators sang its praises for supposedly facing down the film industry.[181] But in fact it walked a judicious line between ideological and economic imperatives, much like the Austrian law of 1936. That gave exploitation rights to the producer or owner of the production company but also required naming all creative authors. Their permission was required for changes, translations, and adaptations, though the producer could sue if those authors had no compelling reasons to withhold consent.[182]

Italy achieved a similar solution in the depths of the war, with the law of 22 April 1941 (which still remains in effect).[183] Italy's 1925 law had apportioned film rights evenly between the writer and the producer, possibly shared with the composer. The 1941 law accomplished what the Nazis shied away from by assigning artistic rights to the creative participants and economic rights to the producer. Piola Caselli insisted on authorship only for creative input, not legal entities.[184] Scriptwriters, directors, composers, and scenographers were all recognized. Their permission was required for adaptations or translations, though the producer could also secure that contractually in advance. But producers could make those changes to underlying works that were necessary for adaptation to the new medium.

Although no bill ever passed during the Third Reich, the regime fought major ideological battles over cinema. Not just an important industry, film was also crucial to Nazi hopes of winning hearts and minds. Yet the film industry lobbied for rights that flatly contradicted principles held sacred by the regime's legal theorists. The Nazis had embraced moral rights even as they diluted them by their dogmatically communitarian view of authorship. Obviously, we cannot take at face value the Nazi claim to have espoused moral rights, given that the Third Reich saw authors as mere mouthpieces of a racial community, favored society's interests in case of conflict, and enforced its views with rigid official patronage and censorship—not to mention burning books and murdering and exiling authors.

Nonetheless, personal rights were not just a cynical sop thrown to authors. Nazi reformers embraced moral rights to distinguish themselves, on paper at least, from the Soviet Union's proletarian dictatorship. The Nazis also interpreted moral rights differently from liberal bourgeois regimes—especially the French—and what they saw as their individualistic veneration of the deracinated author. Like their Italian cousins, the Nazis boiled together personality rights and society's claims into one ideological stew. The defense of the author's personality, Piola Caselli argued, derived from the idea that the citizen is integral to the state's superior personality. As best can be made out through the fog of his Fascist Hegelianism, it followed that defending the author's personality coincided with protecting the state.[185] Individual and society—that persistent trope of fascist ideology—were thought to be harmoniously fused. They were not antagonistic opposites as in the anomic liberal democracies.[186]

The 1939 Nazi bill, an awkward hash of different approaches and fine categorical distinctions, kept moral rights for creators while ensuring the film industry's financial prerogatives. Despite the regime's collectivized ideology, the Nazis never just rode roughshod over authors' expectations. That can be seen by comparing the intent and ambitions of their never-passed authors' rights legislation with their reform of patent law.

HEROIC INVENTORS

The Nazis capitalized on the dissatisfactions of the engineers, technicians, and scientists of Weimar's large corporations, who were denied recognition of their inventions by the inherited German system of awarding patents to the first to file. From its origins in 1877, German patent law had been criticized for favoring corporations over inventors.[187] Once again the new regime piled into an ongoing ideological melee. In 1936 the Nazis introduced a variant of the American and British first-to-invent system, which rewarded the actual inventor, not just his corporate master. Not only was the inventor to be named on the patent, but as with moral rights, he could not assign his claim, thus preventing corporations from requiring blanket transfers in their employment contracts.[188] The reform was couched in the usual Nazi rhetoric of balancing individual and community. It reflected the regime's hopes to protect German creators from capitalist exploitation. But its provisions for compulsory licensing echoed the Nazi rule that the community took precedence over the individual.[189]

The new law appealed to the scientists and engineers whom the regime claimed as its political constituency, and it was opposed by big industry. Patents that emerged from the collective work of an enterprise (*Betriebserfindungen*) had earlier belonged to the employer. Now the company had to identify and credit the actual inventor.[190] The law was based, one study of the day concluded, on the Nazis' meritocratic and personality-based ideology (*das Leistungs- und Persönlichkeitsprinzip*).[191] Enforcing respect for strong and creative personalities should not be confused, another argued, with liberal individualism.[192]

Inventors may not have earned much money from the 1936 patent law, but they gained an unmistakable moral victory, with their names now prominently inscribed on patent documents. As with film the ideological imperatives of celebrating authors jostled with corporate requirements. In principle the new law credited the inventor. But to avoid patent claims bogging down while priority was established, the first to file was granted rights in cases heard before the patent office.[193] In practice, therefore, control did not shift unilaterally from employers to hired inventors. Inventors should not expect unlimited exploitation rights, one Nazi reformer cautioned. But they should be honored.[194] Reform here was thus analogous to the vesting of at least moral rights only in flesh-and-blood authors.

Hans Frank, later infamous as governor of German-occupied Poland, presided over this reform as the president of the Academy for German Law. He celebrated the new patent law as steering a course between the twin evils of Bolshevism and capitalism. After the war, despite corporate opposition, first-to-invent remained the theoretical foundation of West Germany's patent system.[195] In much the same way, Nazi draft bills for authors' rights became the basis for Germany's postwar reform of intellectual property law.[196] That is a story continued in the following chapter.

ARE THERE FASCIST AUTHORS' RIGHTS?

At Fascist initiative, moral rights were put on the international agenda in 1928 and eagerly pursued in Italy throughout Mussolini's reign. The Nazis sympathized but accomplished less. Yet moral rights had also been evolving since the mid-nineteenth century. Other nations implemented them too, some being conservatively authoritarian, some liberal, and some social democratic. The principle of moral rights gains adherents each day, the Italian jurist Francesco Ruffini trumpeted in 1926. It is on the verge of becoming a dogma of international law.[197] So what is the political valence, if any, of moral rights?

Piola Caselli called moral rights an example of the Fascist spirit—but also a triumph of the Italian spirit, not to mention of eternal Roman law.[198] In the eyes of the French, moral rights were the height of enlightened bourgeois individualism. After the Second World War they were seen as testifying to France's and Germany's high-brow resistance to fascist totalitarianism, East Bloc propaganda, *and* the Anglophone entertainment industries. Malleable concepts, moral rights were seen both as individualistic and as collectivistic. They were embraced by regimes of both left and right. How best to make sense of such ideological polymorphosity?

Many who pushed for reform during the Third Reich had also been active during the Weimar Republic: Willy Hoffmann, Julius Kopsch, Alexander Elster, Bruno Marwitz, Hans Otto de Boor, and of course Richard Strauss.[199] Many interwar reformers agreed that existing laws overly favored authors while neglecting the public. Even phraseology that, in retrospect, seems characteristically Nazi had been commonplace in unideological legal periodicals of the late Weimar Republic: that the masses needed a *Führer* and measures to support strong personalities;[200] that the author's rights had to be balanced against the community's claims to the Volksgenosse's works; that German conceptions of property were more socially inflected than Roman law;[201] that property was not a natural and unconditional right, but was created and governed by society;[202] that only the actual creator should be recognized and that moral rights were inalienable;[203] that the state should step in to protect the author's moral interests after his death;[204] that in this anti-individualist era moral rights helped counteract collectivist tendencies;[205] that authors owed the Volksgemeinschaft their inspiration and should repay their debts to society;[206] and that popular culture was barbaric and firm governmental control was needed.[207]

Nor were such components of what would become the Nazi view peculiarly German. During the interwar years German- and Italian-style themes were heard in France too. Many French agreed that existing authors' rights legislation hindered hopes of enlightening the masses and developing culture.[208] Indebted to their community for inspiration, creators were organically tied to it. Authors' rights were not individualistic and absolute but relative and socially intertwined. The community also had a say over works. After death works joined the national patrimony. The collectivity, not only the author's heirs, should ensure its integrity. And so forth.[209]

During the early months of the Popular Front government in 1936, Jean Zay, minister of education, put forth a bill to reform the French system in the spirit of the new age.[210] The Matignon Agreements of the same year had secured manual workers the right to strike and organize. Now "intellectual workers" needed help—the only social group not yet protected in law, as Zay complained.[211] Broadly speaking, Zay's proposals differed only in emphasis from the ideas discussed in Fascist Italy, Nazi Germany or, for that matter, Social Democratic Norway.[212] Authors were to receive moral rights, with integrity defined expansively as violation of the author's subjective moral interests, and the work was also protected against destruction. Formalities were done away with. Rights were attached to the author personally, even for minors, wards of courts (*interdits*), and married women. Had this passed, French women, disenfranchised until 1944, would have received rights as authors earlier than the vote—a kind of literary Bismarckianism.[213] Tackling the Napoleonic code's troublesome inheritance rules, the bill awarded married authors control over the income from their works, which did not become part of the common matrimonial estate.

Discussing the Zay bill, the French, too, grappled with collectivist theories of creativity, as in Nazi Germany and the Soviet Union. Many hoped to abandon the exaggerated individualism of nineteenth-century jurisprudence.[214] Yet the Zay bill hewed more closely to the individualistic French tradition, giving authors extensive claims. Fair and other public uses were limited. Signed periodical articles could not be reproduced without permission, and authors controlled derivative works, including public and mass-media performances. In principle the work was inalienable. Able to assign certain use rights (*concessions*), the author was not permitted to assign his work wholly (*cession*).[215] Moral rights passed to the author's heirs or other designees and, in their absence, to state institutions.

However, in a major break with its otherwise clear focus on authors' rights, the Zay bill also imposed compulsory licensing. The traditional French approach, with exclusive authorial rights, was increasingly seen as opposed to society's needs.[216] Descendants were to receive full economic rights for a decade postmortem. But during the next forty years anyone could publish the work in return for royalties. This would have approximated the British system of 1911, though with a shorter period of exclusive rights and longer licensing. The motivation was partly the same as in the Nazi draft bills, to ensure that descendants could not veto new editions.[217]

In one particular aspect reform proposals across Europe during the collectivist 1930s departed from the nineteenth century's more personalist moral rights ideology. Moral rights survived the author's death thanks to their peculiar status as a hybrid of property and personality. As personal claims they were tied to the author. As property they could be assigned to third parties. This tension had been largely ignored during the nineteenth century. During the interwar years it was forced to prominence by the era's new-found emphasis on the socially determined nature of authorship. Heirs, and even the author's personal choice of a representative, might fail to exercise his moral interests. A higher authority then had to step in.

The Weimar and Nazi reform proposals therefore all entrusted the authorities with the ultimate say over works postmortem. The more lasting the work, the less it could be governed by any individual, as one Nazi jurist explained the intent of the "socially determined" concept of property. "Only the state can guard over the purity of the cultural inheritance."[218] In 1921 and 1925 bills put forth by Marcel Plaisant in the French Assembly went so far as to foresee a form of lynch justice, an "action populaire" that empowered anyone who could justify an interest to protect the author's moral rights after his death.[219] The Belgians proposed something similar in 1928 at the Rome conference: moral rights passed to society as a whole and each citizen could exercise them, even against the author's heirs.[220] The Italian law of 1925 vested powers of oversight in the government authorities, while a Romanian law of 1923 allowed the minister of arts to publish works that heirs or assignees had not issued within three years postmortem.[221] The Norwegian law of 1930 empowered the king, acting in the public interest, to expropriate rights from an author's heirs if necessary to ensure public access.[222] In Denmark the Ministry of Education closely monitored possibly demeaning uses of works by now-dead authors.[223]

What, then, are the political valences of moral rights—if any? It is too easy to dismiss Nazi ideas of authors' rights as simply trampling individual prerogative.[224] True, they reinterpreted moral rights to give the collectivity the ultimate authority. Nor is it doubtful which would have won out in any real collision between individual and collective demands. But the Nazis went to some length to sustain and elaborate the rhetoric of moral rights inherited from the Rome conference. As Berne members they felt obliged to afford authors these protections, which were, in any case, prompted by their ideological allies, the Fascists. Rallying behind moral rights helped the Nazis convince themselves that they, unlike the Soviets, were not mindless collectivists. They venerated the creative personality—as long as he was a good Nazi and an Aryan.

Authors' rights were caught up in the Third Reich's endless infighting, in this case between party radicals and big business. Had the regime managed to legislate, corporate interests would doubtless have left a mark. But more was at stake, as the ideological twists and turns over film rights suggest. Some jurists insisted that Nazi ideology forbade vesting rights in corporations or producers. Would these reformers have prevailed? Already the Weimar film industry had opposed moral rights and other concessions to authors made in Rome.[225] But patent reform revealed that the Third Reich was not simply or automatically beholden to business interests.[226] When in 1936 inventors won attribution, Nazi film rights reformers used this precedent to argue against vesting artistic rights in producers and corporations.[227]

The point of authors' rights was to balance between author and audience, as one jurist who remained active during the Third Reich put it in the title of an article in 1931.[228] This claim would not have surprised the Anglo-American copyright world. But on the Continent it was more of a novelty.[229] The Nazis' idea of authors' rights followed from their general view of property as determined as much by the community's needs as by the owner's claims.[230] The emphasis in Nazi ideology on public access echoed the Anglo-American copyright tradition's populist approach. Since the early nineteenth century British and American law had considered intellectual property to be a temporary monopoly granted to benefit society. Now, Nazi ideologues too rejected the inherited Continental concepts of absolute property rooted in natural rights. Intellectual property was socially bound and subordinated to society's needs.[231]

Despite their collectivism, however, the Nazis' support for moral rights was not just window dressing. They claimed to speak for the culture producers, submerged in modern mass media, and for employees, whose initiative and ideas were swallowed by the corporate Moloch. Reform of patents and authors' rights appealed to the traditional independent middle classes and their white-collar peers, who had been among the party's earliest supporters. Engineers and industrial scientists, small businessmen, the *Mittelstand*, as well as artists, writers, and intellectuals: the Nazis courted them all.[232]

Moral rights were put on the international agenda during the interwar years. Long in the making, they were now legislatively incarnated in several nations, including Italy. Though moral rights were debated in Nazi Germany, implementation had to await the postwar Federal Republic. In France the collaborationist Vichy regime legislated the concept for the first time in 1941, in a statute that established a committee of dramatists, composers, and musical editors to defend their "material and moral interests."[233] The fascists did not invent moral rights. Having emerged during the mid-nineteenth century, they were then discussed and legislated throughout the 1920s and '30s. But nor were the fascists an obstacle to their development. In fact, one might say that fascism was their catalyst.

The Italian Fascists and the Nazis did support moral rights and protect authors. But their understanding of creativity was more socially determined than the inherited concept of Romantic authorship. Their concern to balance the author's claims against the needs of the audience had profound consequences for postwar Europe.

Because the fascists were those who first emphasized the public at least as much as the author, debates over how to balance between these two interests—long a commonplace in the copyright nations—were stillborn on the Continent after 1945.

Europe's interwar regimes thus pursued two partly contradictory aims. They fostered moral rights—formulating proposals that would found postwar reforms. Here, the continuities were strong from the 1920s through the fascist dictatorships and into the postwar period. But the fascist regimes also broached—largely for the first time on the Continent—a sustained debate over what the audience could reasonably claim. That was a Judas kiss: audience interests safeguarded by fascists! It would halt any further pursuit of public rights and solicitude for the audience in Europe for another half century. To atone for the populist flirtations of the totalitarian regimes, postwar Continental reformers turned to an exalted veneration of the author. Not until the end of the twentieth century would the discussion sparked by the fascists flare up again, now prompted by the new digital era.

6

The Postwar Apotheosis of Authors' Rights

Moral rights and their veneration of the author had a long and complex history. Kant and Fichte's concept of a personalist connection between artist and work, not beholden to property, had dovetailed with the Romantic view of the artist. Yet such an individualized approach to authors' rights was legislated only when populist politics turned to totalitarian excess during the interwar years. The Italian Fascists made moral rights part of the Berne Convention. The Nazis, too, folded moral rights into their fluid ideology and opportunistic policies to support the heroic creative personality they considered exemplary of their new regime. Yet—rhetoric aside—they trod carefully, lest actual individual rights interfere with their propagandistic control of the new mass media. They also favored broad access to works, appealing to their popular base, even as this would have limited authors' rights. But, beyond extending terms to fifty years postmortem, the Nazis implemented few reforms.

Turning moral rights from case law into statute therefore largely fell to the European democracies that reemerged after 1945. France and Germany passed highly author-centric laws in 1957 and 1965 respectively, explicitly distancing themselves from Anglo-American copyright. In a few instances there was mutual approximation across the Atlantic and the channel. Work-for-hire, which gave rights to the author's employer, remained sacrosanct for the powerful collaborative cultural industries of the Anglophone world—periodicals, film, and advertising especially—even though it violated the core Berne doctrine of rights vested only in flesh-and-blood authors. But collaborative content enterprises were powerful in Europe too, and their interest in more flexible measures was occasionally acknowledged. Postwar France and Germany adopted an undogmatic approach to vesting authorship for film. In 1985 the French computer industry also managed to win work-for-hire status for software programmers.

Nonetheless, the postwar global rapprochement between copyright and authors' rights was achieved largely through changes to the Anglo-American approach. The centripetal force of Berne's ideology was beginning to work its influence in both Britain (already a member) and America (pondering membership). The Anglophone exporting content industries gradually discovered that, to enjoy global protection under the convention's umbrella, they would have to conform more closely to Berne dictates. Their interests now began to sway American and British government policy. Britain finally introduced a very truncated variant of moral rights in 1988, a mere century after signing up for the convention. In the United States more changes were required to join Berne. In 1976, preparing for membership, the US adopted the extensive Berne term duration of fifty years postmortem and began abolishing formalities as a condition of copyright. In 1989, when it finally joined, the United States also officially accepted the principle of moral rights, though only in so limited a way that no new legislation was actually needed.

Looking back from today, contemporary critics often accuse the American government, led astray by its content industries, of orchestrating the international shift to strong protection of intellectual property. Seen in historical perspective, however, it was in fact the Anglophones who changed their inherited systems most in the postwar period. Whatever the case for other policies during the Cold War, on copyright America followed Europe's lead.

Surprisingly perhaps, strong continuities of authors' rights bridged the chasm of the Second World War. In Western Europe postwar reformers cared little that their proposals rested on fascist policy initiatives. Moral rights were blithely considered self-evidently high-minded and progressive, burnishing the liberal, democratic, and—above all—high-culture credentials of newly liberated continental Europe. In the fearsome postwar world, Western Europe felt culturally overshadowed by the two superpowers. The new East Bloc man bore a terrifying resemblance to his fascist predecessor. The Germans, who compared across their internal border, especially noticed the kinship of Communists and Nazis: the mass rallies, goose-stepping military parades, endless political speeches, puritanical sports and outdoor activities, and railing against Western decadence. Walter Ulbricht's DDR even copied the Nazis' "Strength through Joy" program, taking over the same Baltic resorts and plastering up posters with the same proletarian cruise ships—though the West Germans cleverly grabbed the Volkswagen.[1] But to West European intellectuals Hollywood, Broadway, the West End, Nashville, and Motown were even scarier. Their trashy movies, glitzy musicals, and gyrating pop stars had real appeal.[2] What a relief that both left and right could unite in jointly rejecting the false idols of Anglophonia's spiritual Gomorrah! The mass culture of the capitalist West, the Marxists of the Frankfurt School assured Europe's intelligentsia, was but a softer totalitarianism.[3]

The reformers of the interwar years had also seen themselves as defending culture against barbarism. Remembering the slaughter of the Great War and seeing new mass media like radio and film emerge, they hoped that moral rights would preserve civilization against a mediocre modernity.[4] Now, after another world war, Continental intellectuals again battled mass society. French and German legal reformers used moral rights to assert their nations' continued cultural preeminence. True believers of the Romantic tradition, the Continental intelligentsia asserted the superiority of the authors' rights ideology against Anglophonia's cultural factories. Noting America's insidious influence, a French jurist in 1954 called for reform of authors' rights to show that defending writers "is still the fundamental preoccupation of the idealistic nation that we wish to remain."[5] Protecting the author was a national tradition, the French secretary of state for arts and letters insisted in 1956.[6]

The Continental left and right agreed that the Anglophone nations treated culture as a commodity—mass-produced, licensed, and flogged on the market of lowest common denominators. In 1956 French Communists welcomed government proposals to protect authors as a blow against capitalist disseminators.[7] Across the aisle Continental conservatives, too, trumpeted European culture over the Anglosphere's bilge.[8] Moral rights found their justification in this postwar Kulturkampf between the highbrow continent and Anglophone popular culture. In the sober, austere years following the war, the extravagantly individualistic fin-de-siècle approach to moral rights was brought to legislative culmination. As the now ex-Nazi jurist Hans Otto de Boor noted soon after the war, a united front of authors had once again formed in double time to lobby for enhanced rights (perpetual, no less!), based on natural rights and now catalyzed with moral rights too.[9]

BERNE APRÈS-GUERRE

Moral rights expanded apace within the Berne Convention. In 1948, three years after the war ended, its members (minus occupied and divided Germany) met in Brussels without a mention of Hitler, the war, or fascism. The French, among the strongest supporters of moral rights in Rome in 1928, had not yet legislated at home. Abroad, however, they remained proselytizers. They now sought to make moral rights formally inalienable, underlining the gap between authors' rights and copyright.[10] Other proposals sought to continue moral rights after the author's death. All distortions, mutilations, or other changes to the work that damaged the author's reputation or honor were to be punished. So was any derogatory act that harmed the author in any way. Thus, use of the work in certain contexts (art in advertising, say, or serious music in filmed operettas) could be prejudicial, even if the work itself remained intact.

As before the war, the common law nations (joined now by allies like the Swiss and the Dutch) dug in their heels, resisting reform that required new legislation at home.[11] The British delegate insisted that Berne was about economic rights only. Moral rights should not be mentioned at all. Fire-breathing reforms were also tamped down by hopes of enticing the United States to join Berne. British objections helped defeat the ambitions of the French and their allies (Belgium, Austria, Poland, Spain, and Italy) to extend moral rights. Instead, Berne reaffirmed the Rome compromise of protecting only the author's reputation and honor. The British also insisted on leaving any extension of moral rights postmortem to national legislation. Having won the battle in 1928 to protect only honor and reputation (which in common law could be defended only for the living), they were not about to extend authorial rights into the afterlife.[12] The collaborative cultural industries, especially film, also resisted too much leeway for authors. Nor—despite French attempts—were moral rights made unwaivable. But the French did persuade Berne to adopt a droit de suite—the resale right that paid visual artists a percentage whenever works were resold. Instituting this was left optionally to domestic law. More important, the fifty-year postmortem term of protection was now made obligatory for members.

The 1967 Berne conference in Stockholm then pushed matters along only slightly. Proposals sought to require members to safeguard moral rights postmortem for as long as economic rights. But the usual objections from the common law nations, joined by Scandinavia, excepted those countries that did not already protect moral rights after death.[13] On the other hand, any reference was deleted to the author's "lifetime" as the period when he could assert moral rights. Moral rights thus became a general claim, without defined temporal limits.[14] The right of disclosure, though broadly embodied in most Berne members' domestic legislation, also finally became a clearly enunciated part of the Berne Convention.[15] The Paris conference in 1971, held to bring the Stockholm conference to closure, concluded that moral rights had to be recognized by all member nations during the author's lifetime, though not necessarily thereafter. But the author remained protected in only his honor and reputation, and not—as the French had vainly sought since Rome in 1928—in his subjectively defined moral interests as such.[16] The Paris Act of 1971 also did not define an author, thus theoretically admitting that it need not be a flesh-and-blood creator. But most commentators agreed that only natural persons—not legal entities—were real authors.[17]

The postwar Berne revisions thus did not advance the cause of moral rights much beyond what Rome had achieved in 1928. But what Berne failed to do was now taken up by domestic legislation, especially in France and Germany.

AUTHORS' RIGHTS TRIUMPH IN FRANCE

The French had started planning for reform before the war. The basic ideas for the law that finally passed in 1957 had been foreshadowed during the Popular Front government. But the Zay bill of 1936, while punctiliously protecting authors, also aimed to turn them into salaried workers. Its drastic licensing scheme would, in effect, have replaced authors' exclusive rights with royalties. During the German occupation reform plans proceeded apace in professional associations. One draft by the Commission on Intellectual Property, established in the first months of the postwar provisional government, built on work undertaken in the corporatist government organ responsible for music during the collaborationist Vichy regime.[18] Vichy's reformers had reached back to the Popular Front's collectivism, keeping its emphasis on the "social function" of literary and artistic property. They proposed a *domaine public payant* (in effect a tax levied on publishers of public domain works) to support authors and their descendants. Government authorities were to protect authors' moral rights if heirs abused their prerogatives.[19] Though divested of the *domaine public payant*, many of these Vichy provisions found their way verbatim into the 1957 law.

At the end of hostilities, early legislation failed before the Fourth Republic's Constituent Assembly. Not until a decade later, in the mid-1950s, was progress made. Zay's quasi-socialist attempts to fashion authors into workers were abandoned, as were his collectivist licensing arrangements. Instead, the French reaffirmed tradition to ensure authors' economic and now also moral rights. The law that emerged at the end of the Fourth Republic in 1957 was a curious creature. A "legal ode to the glory of creators," it set the author on his throne.[20] Codifying case law over the previous century and a half, it continued the French tradition of authors' rights based on natural rights and was heralded as embodying French national identity, setting the battered nation apart in the postwar world.[21] Yet the law rooted authors' rights not only in vague appeals to personality and its unique connection to the work but also in an old-fashioned, Lockean, labor-based theory of property rights grounded in nature.[22] By the sole fact of having created the work, the law's first article announced, authors had exclusive rights of immaterial property.[23] None of this nonsense one found in America, a contemporary commentator declaimed, about property rights resting only on statute, as if they were a privilege granted by the king![24]

The discussion thus leaped back over the centuries to France's July Monarchy of the 1830s—of all destinations. Then, reforming ministers had argued that authors could not have absolute claims to literary property based on natural rights but only a concession or privilege granted them by statute. Authors had bitterly resented this attempted expropriation of their nature-given claims.[25] As we saw in chapters 3 and 4, during the nineteenth century they had managed to assert their property rights in case law. Now this debate continued. Any doubts about absolute authorial property rights that might have lingered from the interwar discussions were firmly rejected. Natural rights ideology had not been heard this explicitly for well over a century.[26] The author's rights existed wholly independent of statute, a noted French jurist insisted in 1958. The law's sole mission was to recognize a preexisting right, by nature connected to the act of creation.[27]

France's 1957 law thus overtly linked itself to the decrees of the revolution. It echoed le Chapelier's claim in 1791 that literary property was the most personal of all property.[28] But it went further. The revolutionaries had sought to grant the author something that, by belonging fully to him, was also his to alienate fully. The modern, personalist version of literary property, in contrast, sought to remove property from the author's will. It was now so personal that he could never be wholly rid of it. In the words of the 1957 law, the author's rights were perpetual, inalienable, imprescribable—phrasing taken in turn verbatim from the immediate postwar proposals.[29] So intimately tied to his personality were an author's rights, the draft bill announced in 1954, that he could never give them up.[30]

Unsurprisingly, the disseminating industries objected to making moral rights perpetual and inalienable, thus hampering works' exploitation. But the French legislature was clear: the point of the law was to protect the author against vested money interests.[31] Unlike the Anglophone systems with their corporate authorship, only flesh-and-blood creators could be authors. Even an employee, creating for pay, had all the rights of authorship. This "humanistic" conception distinguished the Continental approach from Anglo-Saxon copyright.[32] The very first article of the 1957 law specified that authors enjoyed all rights, whether or not they worked for someone else.

In the French view literary property had a dual nature: material and immaterial. Material rights could be assigned or transferred, and they lasted fifty years postmortem. Immaterial rights, vaguely formulated as the right to respect for name, reputation (*sa qualité*), and work, were the moral rights. These were perpetual and inalienable. And yet—central mystery of all moral rights—while inalienable, they were also transmissible to heirs or other testamentees. Heirs were to follow—forever—the author's presumed wishes.[33]

While this might hold at first, eternity is a long time. Sooner or later the personal ties between work and author, or relatives and heirs, would fade away. Nonetheless, despite the oddity of legislating a perpetual personal connection, the author was given control over the pathways of his legacy. During the mid-nineteenth century the danger that artistic control might pass to hostile descendants (estranged spouses, distant family, creditors) had prompted the insight that moral rights were distinct from exploitation rights and should not be separated from the author as he assigned his economic interests. Now, the 1957 law reaffirmed that the author, no longer the helpless pawn of Napoleonic inheritance law, alone determined to whom rights passed. The right to publish his work posthumously went to those he designated (later case law added also attribution and integrity).[34] Only after their death, or in the absence of any expressed authorial wishes, did rights pass to descendants, surviving spouses (so long as they had not been separated and were not remarried), nondescendant heirs, and so on down the orderly chain of Napoleonic inheritance.

To strengthen the author's control, the new act went beyond existing case law. Regardless of matrimonial law and contract, the disclosure and integrity rights remained with the author or his designees. They did not—like other chattels—become part of community property.[35] As we have seen, the most recent case had pitted the composer Marguerite Canal against her husband, Maxime Jamin, who claimed rights in her works after divorce. In 1936 and 1938 the first two courts had ruled that, whatever happened to the economic fruits of her work, the rights of control remained with her personally, not entering community property. In 1945, however, the highest court had reversed.[36] To prick this annual blister, the 1957 law now explicitly formulated the inherent French conception: moral rights remained with the author (and his assignees). They were not to be treated like other forms of property in divorce, inheritance, bankruptcy, or other circumstances where the owner might have to forfeit control.

Ultimately, the government was responsible for ensuring moral rights after death.[37] If the author's assignees or heirs flagrantly abused their powers (the cases of Baudelaire and Rimbaud were held up as examples) the courts, instructed by the government, could intervene.[38] And since French law made moral rights perpetual, in the long run their safeguarding had to be entrusted to some equally eternal authority. In the absence of any greater source of continuity (France was approaching its fifth republic, not to mention a few other regimes, over 150 years), this fell perforce to the state. When shortly after the war the French state had first been proposed as the guarantor of last resort for authorial rights, critics were incensed. "We are too close to the era when poets saw their works burned on official pyres," Louis Vaunois spoke out in 1946, "not to protest giving the state control over matters of the spirit and art."[39] A decade later, however, no one remembered. Without fuss the 1957 law established a form of protection for cultural works of national significance like that guarding historically important buildings and monuments.[40]

The work itself was protected from the moment of creation, defined as the time the author had realized his conception, even if it was not yet complete. Protection required no formalities of registration or the like. Once again, the French consciously distinguished their approach from that of the Anglo-Saxons.[41] With singular artworks the owner did not automatically receive the incorporeal rights, which remained with the artist.[42] A new right of repenting was added too. Taking a slightly jaundiced view of authors, withdrawal of a work was not only made conditional on paying damages to the disseminator. The law also prevented authors from taking their work back merely to seek better terms. But otherwise the author's ability to withdraw works was not restricted.

Fair use exceptions to the author's exclusive rights were narrow: family performances, strictly private copies, short citations, and reproduction of public speeches.[43] Still, parody, pastiche, and caricature were specifically permitted. The draft bill had also allowed free reproduction of articles of current news and events unless rights were expressly reserved. But the parliamentary commission yanked this provision, fearing it made second-class citizens of journalists, whose writings would be protected only if they complied with formalities of the sort that otherwise were ruled out.[44] The law also spelled out in detail what rights could be assigned and how. It set out terms for various editions and procedures for royalty payment, among many other specifics. Such precision, the law's formulators explained with paternalist solicitude, served to protect uninformed or careless authors from exploiters' cunning tricks.[45] Authors were allowed to renegotiate contracts, for example, if their work proved to be unexpectedly profitable, though only if they had been paid a lump sum.

AND IN GERMANY

Though the West German Federal Republic reacted in many respects against the Third Reich, on authors' rights it partly followed Nazi policy initiatives. The contingent nature of all property, conventional and intellectual, had been a theme of Nazi legal thinking. Though obviously resonant with the regime's communitarianism, such ideas had also continued concepts formulated in German case law at the turn of the century and codified in the Weimar Constitution.[46] The new German Basic Law of 1949 echoed ideas of the socially bound nature of intellectual property, a leitmotif of both Weimar and Nazi discussions.[47] Property entails obligations, it declared, and must serve the public interest. Though phrased in almost the same language as the Weimar Constitution, the Basic Law insisted that every expropriation also be compensated. Yet suspicion of capitalism and a wish to put authors before business interests were also postwar themes rooted in the earlier regimes. The Christian Socialist ideology of the early Christian Democratic Party deliberately sought to inoculate West German voters against communism in the postwar devastation. It moderated the contrast between left and right, compared to the more market-oriented ideologies of other nations' conservative parties. As one postwar German jurist pointed out, both Christianity and socialism taught that human personality takes precedence over lifeless property.[48]

Despite their ambitions to reform authors' rights, the Nazis had accomplished little besides extending terms to half a century postmortem. The Federal Republic was therefore born with the laws of the late Wilhelmine Empire still on the books. Pondering reform, postwar policymakers started from the Weimar Justice Ministry's last-minute draft bill of 1932 and the Nazi version of 1939. The first expressed the state of the reformers' art on the cusp of the totalitarian regime; the latter was thoroughly steeped in its ideology. Stripped of its obvious Nazi trappings (allusions to the minister of propaganda and the Reichskulturkammer, ritual obeisance to Hitler), the 1939 draft bill now served as the basis of reform discussions.[49] As we have seen, the Nazis had sought both to protect authors with new moral rights and to ensure the community's access to works. West German reformers now fine-tuned the regime's draft bill to fit the postwar spirit, focusing on authors and ignoring the audience. Most of the new ideas in what became the 1965 law—and especially its improved treatment of the author—can be traced back to the 1939 bill.[50] Postwar German reformers blamed the war, not the Nazi regime as such, for having interrupted the course of legal evolution.[51] Some of the Third Reich's most active authors' rights reformers, notably Hans Otto de Boor, remained in harness.[52] When introducing the new bill in the Bundestag, the justice minister noted its roots in the Nazi era without particular comment.[53]

Out of this suspect soil grew what has been widely regarded as a progressive and enlightened law, reaching skyward to ensure authors' economic and spiritual interests.[54] Social policy had been improved for other social classes, reformers argued. The 1957 pension reform had helped workers and employees.[55] Now was the time for the independent creative classes.[56] Moral rights of disclosure, attribution, and integrity were spelled out in the 1965 law.[57] To these came the new right of repenting. The author was allowed to withdraw his work not only (as in the Nazi drafts) if his assignee was tardy in exploiting it but also if he had changed his mind. Oddly, this most intimate of personal rights was extended to his heirs—but only if the author had been demonstrably entitled to repent and prevented from doing so.

Unlike France, Germany protected moral rights, not perpetually but only as long as the economic ones. Integrity was protected more than in Berne, less than in France. The Germans wanted to guard against more than just threats to the author's reputation or standing—the compromise demanded by the Anglophone nations in Rome in 1928. Though first-time or pseudonymous authors had no standing or reputation, they still deserved protection. Even when honor and reputation remained unblemished, the 1965 law allowed the author to defend his work's integrity, though only within the confines of his "justified" spiritual or personal interests. Not every feeling of offended artistic amour propre counted equally. Moreover, though the assignee of a use right could not change the work, its title, or attribution, the author had to permit changes that he could not in good faith (*nach Treu und Glauben*) refuse: this allowed the tweaking that dissemination required.[58]

The 1965 German law opened with moral rights. Their economic analogues followed. With a show of rhetoric echoing the Nazis' tub-thumping anticapitalism, the Interior Ministry insisted on this order of priorities. It made no practical difference which came first. But starting with the economic rights, as in the draft bill, would indicate a materialistic and capitalist way of thinking.[59] Placing spiritual values above modern materialism was also the justice minister's motive when he introduced the bill. The *Kulturländer* France and Germany, he argued, led the world in protecting individual creation against modern collectivization.[60] Germany's reputation as the land of poets and thinkers obliged it to pass a law to protect authors, a composers' representative agreed.[61]

Because Germany took a monist approach, moral and economic rights were regarded as inseparable. As in the bills from the 1930s, the author's rights—though they could be inherited—were not fully alienable or assignable. In the dualist French law moral rights were inalienable and perpetual, but economic rights were fully assignable.

In Germany neither were. Unable to assign their economic rights as such, German authors were instead allowed to sell use rights.[62] More than even the French, the Germans thus tempered market forces—at least before works entered the public domain. Exploitation rights were subordinated to the paradigm of unassignable authors' rights.[63]

One Nazi vestige now scrubbed away was entrusting the authorities to protect works in the public domain. While the French had not balked at state cultural control, the Germans understandably feared it.[64] Also eliminated was the corollary that empowered authorities to compel publication of posthumous works against the heirs' will.[65] Since moral rights were not perpetual, nothing protected the work once it had entered the public domain. Moreover, inheritors of an author's moral rights were not bound to follow his expressed wishes. Indeed, strangely at odds with the author's claims to control his work from the grave, heirs inherited these same rights, including bringing forth unpublished works and changing those that had already seen the light. In contrast, French heirs were presumed to follow the author's expressed wishes.[66]

The German law also followed the classic Continental approach of allowing rights for only flesh-and-blood creators, not juridical entities. Work-for-hire was ruled out-of-bounds. Rights were granted to employees for works created on the job unless—a nebulous and potentially expansive qualification—the nature of their employment dictated otherwise. The French sometimes allowed rights to collective works and films to vest in corporate entities and would later introduce a similar regulation for software. But the Germans were attribution fundamentalists. Only the flesh-and-blood author could be recognized as such.[67] Artists were granted a droit de suite for public sales. They retained exhibition rights but could prevent owners from showing their works only if this was specified at the time of sale. They could demand access to sold works as long as this did not violate the owner's justified interests. To get a second bite of the apple, a "bestseller clause" allowed authors to renegotiate contracts that had proven disproportionately lucrative for their disseminators.[68]

Germany also strengthened the author's position by reining in fair use exceptions—though they remained more generous than in France. The author's interests took precedence over society's, reformers agreed. At a minimum, whenever the public was granted access the author deserved royalties.[69] Earlier, composers had been expected to tolerate gratis use of works at public festivals, charity events, and in clubs and associations. After strenuous protest they now won compensation, except for purely noncommercial, free public performances.[70] Fair use of excerpts from writings was allowed only for school- and church-related books, eliminating the old exemption for song collections and anthologies. (Such exceptions were then further restricted in case law and later by the 1972 and 1985 amendments to the law.) Royalties were now due for works reprinted in school and church textbooks, and the use of compositions in church concerts was restricted.[71] The fundamental rule, formulated by the Federal Supreme Court in 1955, granted the author compensation for all uses of his work, even those without commercial purpose.[72] But composers' interests were sacrificed to poets' complaints that their moral rights were violated when others set their poems to music without permission, as had earlier been allowed. At the same time composers' melodies—alone among all works—remained protected against any use whatsoever by others.[73] Overall, West Germany cut back the Nazi insistence on the author's social obligations, instead reaffirming his rights.

Above all, Germany's new law of 1965 strengthened authors by extending protection from half a century to seventy years postmortem. Authors predictably clamored for perpetual protection, but this went nowhere in committee.[74] A twenty-year term extension nonetheless represented excellent value. It gave Germany a far longer term than any major nation, two decades more than the fifty years decreed by the Nazis in 1934 and made obligatory for Berne members in 1948. Composers and their representatives had hotly agitated for the longer term. Fifty years, they argued, was adequate only for pop hits and folk music, not serious works. By enlarging the repertory of public domain works, short terms priced contemporary composers out of concert programs.[75] The two world wars that Germany had fought also encouraged special term extensions for authors caught up in hostilities (to be discussed later), as in France. Most generally, Germany's extra twenty years of protection emerged from a horse trade. To counter insistent proposals for perpetual protection, reformers suggested a *domaine public payant* that would have taxed public domain works to benefit authors. This, however, was judged outside the central authorities' competence, since the new constitution assigned culture to the federal states. German reformers then decided to serve authors more directly by an across-the-board term extension.[76] That authors should be favored was not at issue, only how.

In sum, the Germans subordinated most rights to the author's control. They remained with him for the entire term, and he was permitted to alienate only his use rights. Yet, while the French moved into uncharted and arguably unnavigable territory by making moral rights perpetual, in Germany they expired along with the economic rights. Though not nearly as emphatically as the Nazis, the postwar Germans did emphasize the socially bound nature of the author's rights. He could act against changes only insofar as they damaged his justifiable interests. He had to accept technically necessary alterations by rights holders. And he had to have good reason for withdrawing his work.[77] However faint such hedging about seems from the vantage of the copyright tradition, compared to the more extensively author-centric French approach, these were still concessions to society.

THE ANGLOSPHERE IN A BERNE WORLD

Never was the gap between the authors' rights and copyright systems as wide as in the 1950s and '60s. On the Continent moral rights were articulated in theory and codified in statute. In the Anglo-Saxon world, by contrast, little reform was astir. Within the Berne Union the Commonwealth nations continued their rearguard action to limit reform. The American rejection of Berne principles remained even starker. Of course, some Americans wanted to harmonize with the Europeans. The publishers and authors who had finally achieved international copyright in 1891 now proposed membership in Berne. During the early 1920s bills sought to have the United States join Berne and make domestic legislation conform more closely to European standards—abolishing the manufacturing clause, for example, and removing other copyright formalities.[78] The chances of joining had brightened in 1930 when the labor movement agreed to a bill that would exempt books by foreign nationals from having to be manufactured in the United States.[79]

But the Depression was an inauspicious moment to threaten the jobs created by the manufacturing requirement. Printers, facing high unemployment, were unwilling to give more ground.[80] University presidents, the secretary of state, and even President Roosevelt favored Berne membership.[81] But their well-meaning internationalism—hoping for parity of protection for American authors abroad—was no match for the opposition. Nor were those who opposed Berne motivated just by self-interest. In 1934 Senator Clarence Dill from Washington mounted a spirited defense of the autonomous American copyright tradition. The Berne Convention spoke for Europeans, who regarded copyright as a natural monopoly of the creator or a natural property right. In contrast, the American tradition, built on the Constitution, held copyright to be a limited monopoly, founded only in statute. The Europeans favored the author, he concluded, the Americans the public.[82]

The world was divided into two camps, so said Louis Caldwell, spokesman for the National Association of Broadcasters, in 1931. The French system saw authors' rights as an absolute property claim based on natural rights. The copyright tradition balanced between the interests of author and audience, "between the right of the individual to his work, and the right of the public to have knowledge of that work." Joining Berne meant bowing to the French.[83] Berne's long and strong protection for works undermined research and the spread of knowledge, argued Robert C. Binkley, a historian and apostle for disseminating information through the new technology of microfilming. In the 1930s he planned a forerunner of the Google Books project: a universal library of the world's cultural treasures, accessible via microfilm.[84]

Berne's pieties about the creator's vaunted moral rights also sounded ever more hollow during the 1930s, given how Germany and Italy's fascist regimes treated many authors.[85] As one critic pointed out in 1934, works by Jewish authors—popular songs, for example—were not protected in Germany. Why ask America to enter an international agreement from which many of its citizens were excluded?[86] As E. C. Mills, general manager of ASCAP, the composers' and songwriters' licensing organization, testified in 1936, "The high spokesmen of Germany say that they do not want dumped in Germany ... the intellectual excrement of the non-Aryan."[87] When American authors and their allied publishers smugly portrayed the Berne Union as the quintessence of advanced thought ("the European method, supported by the most enlightened opinion in this country"), they were easy prey for skeptics.[88] Disgracefully, not a single member of the Berne Union had sought to prevent Germany's violation of its principles in the anti-Semitic Nuremberg laws of 1935 and its many other discriminatory measures against Jews. Even writers and their representative bodies, like the Authors League, who had earlier favored Berne membership, no longer saw any point to joining with an ever more fascist Europe.[89]

As a dismayed world watched Germany rearm, the 1930s were obviously a poor time for any international agreements. But longer-term factors also vexed trans-Atlantic rapprochement. American printers and book producers hoped to avoid Berne's lack of formalities and instead keep the manufacturing clause. But their power was waning, and their narrow self-interest was too obvious to win broad support. More important were the growing collaborative and derivative cultural industries. Entrepreneurially marshaling the talents of many contributors and actively using others' works for new ones, magazines and periodicals, music, radio, incipiently television, and above all the film industry viewed Berne suspiciously.[90] Already early in the nineteenth century, the American periodical press was a powerful force. It was over three times the size of its British counterpart during the 1840s. In the 1880s Henry James received fifteen dollars per page from the *Atlantic Monthly*, after which his never-short works appeared in book form.[91] American periodicals, the French marveled half a century later, numbered in the thousands and were often the first publishers even of serious fiction. With massive circulations—up to three million—their advertising budgets were ample, and they paid well.[92] Mechanical sound reproduction also took hold early and fast in the United States. And Hollywood's success was staggering. By the 1930s film was the nation's fourth largest industry and the single greatest source of revenue for American authors and composers.[93]

These collaborative cultural industries wanted a free market to contract with authors for full control of their product. Because they were derivative culture producers—reworking and adapting both new works and older public domain ones—they were allergic to moral rights or indeed any claims by authors to control what they had sold.[94] "We do not get anything for nothing," Gabriel Hess, attorney for the Motion Picture Producers and Distributors of America, insisted in 1935. "Whatever we get we pay for. And having paid for it we seek the protection of a copyright law as copyright owners for that which we produce from the material which we buy."[95] His colleague Louis Swarts was disarmingly candid in 1931. Of course the author had moral claims, he admitted. But that was precisely what the motion picture industry feared. "Therefore it becomes important that we be the author," he insisted on behalf of film producers, "so that we control the moral right where things are gathered together from many sources." The idea was anathema "that each individual in the group should control the showing and demand recognition for the particular contribution that he makes."[96]

America's collaborative cultural industries fiercely resisted the reforms that Berne membership would have required. US periodicals paid authors well, but registered copyright in their own name, rejecting the European practice of protecting writers from the moment of creation.[97] Magazine publishers feared that, with automatic copyright, the innocent publication of a protected work—a poem, say—might trigger an injunction against an entire issue.[98] Automatic copyright also worried the film industry. Formalities, however cumbersome, at least clarified who owned what, allowing users to make binding agreements with owners. As a magpie art form, film depended on a tangle of appropriated works—literary, musical, visual. The more rights each first-line author claimed, the greater the headaches. Copyright without formalities threatened to worsen already intricate legal predicaments.[99]

The power that moral rights gave authors to prevent changes threatened the periodical industry, where scarcely a piece appeared without editing. Radio broadcasters worried lest moral rights prevent them from cutting, condensing, and altering works to fit their medium.[100] And, of course, Hollywood opposed a broad interpretation of moral rights. If plots, scenes, sequences, and characters in literary works could not be changed, it insisted, motion pictures could not be made.[101] Moral rights threatened to prevent alterations "at the whim of the author." Censorship law and local regulations also required tailoring films for different markets.[102] Today, Hollywood has made common cause with authors on both sides of the Atlantic, clamoring for ever-lengthening copyright. But in the 1930s it worried that Berne membership would require longer American terms, thus forcing back into copyright the public domain works it freely pilfered.[103]

WORK-FOR-HIRE

The US collaborative cultural industries also feared Berne's threat to a sacrosanct Anglo-American tradition, work-for-hire. This doctrine violated the principal European rule of crediting only flesh-and-blood authors. But their collaborative nature and high up-front costs impelled the American media industries to insist on centralizing artistic authority in one hand.

The inherent contradictions of work-for-hire were present from the start. In 1690 Locke had justified property by the labor invested. Yet he also promptly qualified his own fundamental axiom. What a man had labored over belonged to him. But so did "the grass my horse has bit, the turfs my servant has cut." Apparently Locke meant that labor could also be alienated so that it and its fruits belonged to someone else.[104] We thus have it on Locke's authority that the labor expended by one person on another's behalf gives that commissioner ownership of the resulting product. Whether Locke would have agreed that this held for a screenplay as much as for turf is another matter.[105]

Work-for-hire emerged early in British law. In the 1798 act on sculpture, both artist and commissioner were granted rights in the work. Confusingly, both were referred to as proprietors.[106] But who owned and who authored collective and collaborative works? The 1842 Copyright Act gave ownership of an article commissioned for an encyclopedia, review, or periodical to the publisher "as if he were the actual author thereof."[107] Expanding this, the 1911 Copyright Act

vested copyright in the employer of contractually employed or ap-
prenticed authors.[108]

The American 1909 Copyright Act went further, defining the employer of those creating works on his dime as the author and not just
the copyright owner. Up to about 1860 American case law had presumed that rights to works belonged to the employee. After the Civil
War, however, courts began to recognize employers' rights in works.
This became jurisprudence and then law after the turn of the century.[109] Arguably work-for-hire violated the Constitution, which empowered Congress to protect only authors' own writings.[110] Perhaps
Congress hoped to make copyright renewal easier for collective
works.[111] During the 1960s court cases stressed that the commissioner
was the author, creating a strong presumption that anyone paying
another was the statutory author of the outcome.[112] The 1976 Copyright Act tempered this extreme interpretation. The employer of an
author or the commissioner of a work was its author, but this could
be modified if both parties agreed in writing.[113]

Even Europe, where authorial authenticity was generally favored,
knew the work-for-hire doctrine in the nineteenth century.[114] Most
nations imposed some variant of it for portraits, with the commissioner and/or the person portrayed owning the work and the right
to reproduce it. German publishers hired writers to churn out would-
be bestsellers. One had a dozen scribbling at a long table in his home
for their daily wage.[115] Publishers had influenced the 1794 Prussian
General Code, receiving rights to collaborative works.[116] Baden's 1809
Civil Code made the commissioner of a work its owner, as did the
1846 Austrian law on literary property.[117] Even France responded to
practical necessity. Its 1957 law recognized authorship for collective
works in the physical or legal entity that published them. For aficio-
nados of fine distinctions, the French law said that the legal entity
was "invested with the author's rights." The American work-for-hire
doctrine said more directly that it was "considered the author." The
significance of this distinction is left to the beholder's eye.[118]

Still, work-for-hire contradicted foundational tenets of the authors' rights ideology. In Europe it was tolerated only to streamline
collective projects like encyclopedias or to protect the privacy of portrait sitters. In the copyright systems, by contrast, work-for-hire followed in principle from the author's ability to wholly alienate his

work. But it also went beyond the author's free decision to sell his work, specifying a default presumption that, in the eyes of the law, the employer took his place. Curiously, the United States refused to assign copyrights to employed authors even though it had insisted from the start on the first-to-invent principle for patents, which vested claims in the actual inventor, not his corporate boss.[119]

The powerful American collaborative cultural industries were not about to sacrifice work-for-hire to Berne membership. The movement in the United States during the 1920s and '30s to join Berne thus foundered on both interwar geopolitics and domestic economic interests. The well-intentioned hopes of authors, librarians, professors, and university presidents to gain international copyright meant little. During the first postwar decades, the Atlantic divide remained. The major postwar copyright reform in the US, the 1976 act, approximated European norms in some respects, but other changes emphasized the divergence. Overall, the trans-Atlantic gap remained wide.

America's 1976 Copyright Act followed the Continent by dating protection from the death of the author, not from publication. Copyright protection of unpublished works, previously covered by the common law of the individual states, was now governed by federal statute as for any other works. The United States thus moved closer to the European position of protecting works from the moment of creation, not just publication.[120] While protection was decoupled from publication, however, formalities remained. True, failure to affix notice of copyright no longer meant automatic loss of protection. And the manufacturing clause, now supported only by a narrow coalition of the printing trade unions, was weakened in 1976. When it was finally removed in 1986, the single greatest obstacle to Berne membership fell. But in other respects formalities remained. The 1976 act specified in painstaking detail the mechanisms of asserting and registering copyright for published works, though it no longer required that copies be deposited in the Library of Congress. Unpublished works had to be registered with the Copyright Office, and registration was needed for action against infringement.

The Continental nations reaffirmed natural rights as the ultimate basis of authors' rights in their postwar reforms. Meanwhile, the Anglophone systems were busy clearing out the last remnants of natural rights founded on common law. The remaining copyright protections based on common law had been largely abolished in Britain in the 1911 act. Unpublished works were now dealt with by statute, on similar terms as publications. Works unpublished at the author's death were covered until publication and then fifty years.[121] That left one final common law loophole: so long as a work remained unpublished, it enjoyed a theoretically indefinite term of protection. Only in the 1988 Copyright Act was this last vestige of common law finally extinguished. Unpublished works were now protected for fifty years from the law's starting date.[122] A similar spring cleaning followed in the United States. The decision taken already in 1834 in *Wheaton v. Peters*—that copyright rested exclusively on statute—was codified in 1976, when almost all traces of the common law were removed.[123] Only unfixed works (improvisations, unrecorded choreographic pieces, performances, broadcasts, and the like) remained governed by common law copyright. It followed that unpublished works were no longer perpetually protected but only for the usual term. The clock now started counting down from the moment of their creation. The aim was to flush unpublished works out of perpetual protection, putting them in the public domain at the same time as all others.[124]

As a final nail in the coffin of US common law copyright, fair use was extended to unpublished works. In principle the 1976 act did not limit fair use to published works. By being protected by statute rather than common law, unpublished works were now also implicitly subject to the fair use doctrine. Nevertheless, several court cases failed to recognize fair use of unpublished material. In 1987 the reclusive writer J. D. Salinger won an appeal preventing publication of Ian Hamilton's unauthorized biography because it quoted from and paraphrased his unpublished letters, held in university archives.[125] After similar cases were brought by L. Ron Hubbard, the founder of Scientology, and the writer Richard Wright, Congress clarified the status of unpublished works and fair use in 1992.[126] Being unpublished no longer exempted a work per se from fair use.

FILM BRINGS EUROPE AND THE ANGLOSPHERE CLOSER

The Continental authors' rights approach had been conceived essentially for an individual creator working alone in a medium controlled by a traditional disseminator. A solo writer producing manuscripts for a publisher was the implicit model. Collective works required a more flexible approach, and exceptions had been carved out for encyclopedias, dictionaries, periodicals, and the like, where authorship and control lay in several different hands. Film too gnawed away at the paradigm of the individual author and his exclusive rights. Its inherently collaborative nature, and the need for a rapid return on a large investment, limited the prerogatives of its many creators. Film might be an art, agreed David Brown, a spokesman for US producers, in 1988. But it was not the work of one or two people. "It is not the same as a Monet. It is not the same as a symphony by Strauss. It represents the fusion of many talents," including those of the producers.[127] Starting in the 1930s, as we have seen, even the French and the Germans debated exceptions to individual authorship and moral rights for cinema.

In the Anglo-American realm, cinema posed few copyright problems. Work-for-hire meant that someone other than the author often controlled rights. Full alienability allowed authors to assign claims to others. Studios and producers were accepted as corporate authors. Film, like other collaborative efforts, relied on contract to decide the details of authorship, attribution, and exploitation. Both the British and American legislatures understood that authors' demands took a back seat to the need for clear lines of decision in all collaborative endeavors. "You will eventually get the situation where the taxi driver who actually drives the typographer to the printing works will ask for a royalty because he played some part in the creation of the thing," Lord Willis, otherwise a spokesman for authors, cautioned in 1987 in the House of Lords.[128] "If every individual obtained a copyright every time he put pen to paper," Lord Hardinge agreed, "anarchy would prevail."[129]

In the UK the 1956 Copyright Act gave a distinct right in films to their "maker"—the person who arranged for them to be made—but not to directors or other creators.[130] Makers could be corporate entities. In the 1988 act, the maker—usually the producer—retained status as the initial copyright owner and was now also designated the film's author. But as a bow to creativity, the director was granted the moral right of being named whenever the film was disseminated.[131] In 1996 the UK designated the director as coauthor, along with the producer.[132] In the US work-for-hire solved the issue by designating the employer as author.[133] But for both the French and the Germans, film was an anomaly in the creative world. Motion pictures aggravated the tension between the inherently individualistic idea of moral rights and the needs of new collective and corporate media. The Continent would have liked to identify only flesh-and-blood authors. But cinema's economic imperatives pushed toward vesting rights in a single person or legal entity.

The French law of 1957 recognized only flesh-and-blood authors of film: the director, composer, and writers of the script, the adaptation, and the dialogue. Cinematic auteur theory had not yet influenced legislation. The director was soon to be proclaimed the film's main author. In the 1950s, however, the talkies remained the big news, and the scriptwriter was the most important creator.[134] The producer (who could be a physical person or, in an exception to the usual assumptions, a legal entity) might be included but only if he (or it) helped create the film.[135] The French bill also frankly admitted that the film industry would be hamstrung were authors given powers to block producers. Authors might misuse moral rights to blackmail a film's makers.[136] An author who refused to complete his part was therefore banned from withdrawing his contribution to the project. Nor could authors invoke moral rights until after a film had been finished, although—as a further complication—the moment of completion had to be determined by common consent among the coauthors.[137]

Though French law eventually took a clear-eyed and unsentimental view of moral rights for film, getting there was difficult. A successful amendment in the Assembly was introduced by Roland Dumas (newly elected moderate Socialist deputy, spokesman for the press commission, and later foreign minister under François Mitterrand). It allowed film authors to object if they felt their moral rights were violated.[138] In the upper house this was criticized as likely to gum up the cinematic machinery, putting many out of work. Violations of moral rights should be restituted by damages, rather than halting production. Those who favored film authors' moral rights worried, for instance, lest pious Catholics take umbrage when directors included spicy (*croustillante*) scenes. In the end pragmatism prevailed, and authors were limited to objecting once the film was in the can.[139] The producer was understood to have contractual relations with his authors, giving him exclusive exploitation rights to their contributions, except to the musical score. While film authors could invoke the moral rights of attribution and integrity, disclosure was subordinated to their contract with the producer. As moral rights were extended to cinema, the industry's needs were thus acknowledged, and producers were given power to market their works.

The Germans, too, grappled with corporate and collective rights. The 1939 Nazi draft bill had nebulously insisted that the actual creators be counted among the film's authors while it also granted the producer the most important rights. The first draft of the postwar law defined a film's authors as the scriptwriter, the composer, and the producer (*Spielleiter*), unless the last had had no creative input.[140] In the 1954 Justice Ministry draft, however, the producer was reenthroned as the movie's primary author—with familiar arguments concerning the film industry's need to unite decision making in one person. As a partial compromise authorship of the movie's components (script, score, and the like) remained with their creators. Yet so many objected to this violation of authorship's basic premise—only flesh-and-blood creators—that it was dropped. Authorship once again was assigned exclusively to the film's creators. Introducing the bill, the justice minister emphasized this as a fine example of how to resist the modern collectivization of culture.[141]

In the final law of 1965, the rights to the components—novel, script, score—remained with their authors. Authorship was thus vested only in creators. But the authors, in turn, had their wings clipped. They had to grant the producer (*Filmhersteller*) the full exploitation rights. And they forfeited their rights to repent and to renegotiate terms under the bestseller clause, as well as their integrity right, unless it had been grossly violated. Even then, they were specifically required to take account of the producer's interests.[142] The same sort of compromise between authorial and executive interests in the complex algorithm of cinematic creativity that the Nazis had struggled with reappeared here in the postwar years.

Computer programs posed similar problems. The artist-in-his-garret paradigm clearly did not fit the corporate gestation of much

software. In 1985 a new French law pragmatically moved in two directions at once.[143] In the arts traditional authors' rights were reaffirmed:
performing artists received moral rights, film producers were removed as authors, and changes to a finished film were forbidden
without its authors' permission. But the law also tightened the producer's control by presuming that authors had signed away all exploitation rights, not just the narrowly cinematographic ones.[144] For
software, however, an abrupt novelty was introduced by accepting
work-for-hire. In 1985 the French software industry was the world's
third largest, and legislators sought to spare it outmoded restrictions.[145] The employer now received all authors' rights to software
created by his employees. Programmers were deprived of their moral
rights—except possibly attribution, which the law did not mention.
They could not object to alterations nor repent. Predictable outcries
followed. France had succumbed to the Anglo-Saxon Moloch and its
mercantile approach to culture![146] The distinction between copyright
and authors' rights had been steamrollered, one observer complained.[147] But in fact, France's traditional approach remained broadly
intact, except for software and, to some extent, film.[148]

Six years later, in 1991, the EU accommodated the French deviation
by declaring the author of software to be the natural persons who
had written it, except as domestic legislation allowed legal entities to
hold rights. In any case, the economic rights to employee works
vested in the employer.[149] Similarly, in 1996 the EU decided that moral
rights were outside the scope of protection for databases. If local
legislation agreed, employers were allowed the rights to such works.[150]
In implementing the 1991 EU software directive, the French then
backpedalled from their 1985 law, extending a faint version of moral
rights to software programmers. Though bereft of the right to repent,
they could complain of changes to their work that violated reputation or honor. This was a weak, Berne-style version of moral rights.
But it did hold out the possibility that programmers could object to
egregious alterations—whatever that might mean for software.[151]

In the 1980s and '90s Europe thus shifted slightly in the direction
of copyright. Early in the twentieth century, as we have seen, the
sound-recording industry had spurred some European nations to impose compulsory licensing on composers' rights to negotiate terms

with disseminators. With film and software the loss of authorial control went beyond licensing to a limited recognition of work-for-hire. The copyright nations had faced the new media with little fuss, armed with a flexible approach to collaborative and corporate creativity and a willingness to alienate rights. The French and Germans, in contrast, had to trim their sails to shifting winds. During the early postwar years France and Germany had enshrined moral rights in law. As the world modernized, they could not entirely sustain tradition. The new collaborative and computerized media required centralized decision making and limits to their many creators' moral rights. Yet, just as the authors' rights ideology slowly adjusted, taking on some aspects of copyright, the time had come for the Anglophones to creep to the Berne cross, now explicitly introducing moral rights.

MORAL RIGHTS IN THE ANGLOPHONE WORLD

The imperatives of collaborative media forced the Continental nations to adopt some features of copyright. But the copyright systems adjusted as much—and arguably more—to the Continental ideology's requirements. Eventually both Britain and America would pay homage, at least pro forma, to its holy grail, moral rights.

To understand why, we must consider the state of moral rights in the copyright world before it officially adopted the doctrine. Although the Anglophone nations (except Canada to a limited extent) had not enshrined moral rights in copyright law, they did protect some authorial interests in other ways.[152] When Britain assented to moral rights at Rome in 1928, and when the United States joined Berne in 1989, it was with the understanding that existing laws other than copyright already protected authors and that no new legislation was required.[153] Though Berne members, the British cheekily denied that their laws were inadequate, even as they formally pledged their allegiance to moral rights. In 1952 the Gregory Committee, established to ponder Britain's obligations under the 1928 Rome act, dispensed with the issue summarily. International pressures to conform were brushed aside, domestic alternatives to dedicated moral rights statutes were pronounced adequate, and the need for further action was dismissed.[154]

Some scholars have argued that the practical protection of moral rights has differed less between the European and Anglo-Saxon nations than the rhetoric.[155] But the notion that moral rights were equivalently protected in the two systems was a polite fiction. Continental authors doubtless enjoyed better protection than their Anglophone peers.[156] Anglo-American authors saw their works mutilated and distorted in ways that had few counterparts on the Continent. In 1878 Arthur Sullivan (of operetta fame) complained to the Royal Copyright Commission about simplified editions with digestible harmonies published against the will of composers. If they had ceded their rights, all they could do was sputter in indignation.[157] A publisher who left out the most valuable part of a work, a British parliamentary committee heard in 1909, would be liable only if the result was libelous.[158] Nothing could be done when advertisers used figures from paintings or photographs, a US Congressional hearing was told in 1905.[159] In Hollywood, the novelist Ben Lucian Berman recounted, writers sometimes could not tell which movie set was filming their story. So much had been changed that they could not recognize their work in the rushes. In filming the John Ford movie *Steamboat Round the Bend* (1935), a typing error rendered a minor character Dr. Boax, rather than Boaz. And so, despite Berman's protests, he remained. "That is about all the influence a writer has over his own material," was his resigned conclusion.[160] This was the madcap world of producers and writers in mortal combat that provided P. G. Wodehouse with fodder for his Hollywood stories.[161]

In the Anglophone nations the author's personal rights were protected, if at all, largely by statutes other than copyright: contract, laws on defamation, unfair competition, and privacy. Case law was spotty. What convinced one court might not move another. Using court cases to illustrate how moral rights were protected under copyright provides only an impressionistic account. At times protections could be pieced together that were broadly analogous to the Continental ones. But it was a rickety edifice, banged together from different sources, patched and repatched, jerry-rigged, and leaky to boot. In 1988, the year before the United States joined Berne, one observer tallied up no fewer than eight different ways to protect the author's personal interests: the 1976 Copyright Act; common law copyright; rights of privacy and publicity; laws on unfair competition, defamation, and contract; and the doctrine of waste.[162]

Nonetheless, though the Anglophone nations legally enshrined specific moral rights only late in the twentieth century, broadly equivalent protections were partly afforded by other means. Upholding integrity, Britain's Engravers' Act of 1735 prohibited reproductions that sought to sidestep charges of counterfeiting by varying an image slightly. Arguably the 1862 Fine Art Copyright Act was the first legislation anywhere on moral rights.[163] It forbade selling altered works without permission (integrity) and attributing them to someone else.[164] Here, too, dogs played a role. The attribution right was raised in a case where Charles, the lesser-known brother of the famous animal portraitist Edwin Landseer, painted two dogs. After touch-up by Edwin, the picture was sold to a dealer, who cut out the animals and framed and sold them as Edwin's work. The hole in the original was then filled with two new dogs by someone else and the remaining painting flogged as a work by Charles.[165]

Among the four most common moral rights (disclosure, attribution, integrity, and withdrawal), the Anglophones least neglected disclosure. True, a moral right of disclosure was not recognized separately from the economic right of first publication. And, of course, work-for-hire undermined employed authors' ambitions. But in other respects the exploitation right of determining the how and when of reproduction largely overlapped with disclosure.[166] In his 1782 open letter to the abbé Raynal, Thomas Paine consoled him for the purloined translation into English of a work that had not yet appeared even in the original French. A man's opinions are his own until he has published them, Paine wrote, "and it is adding cruelty to injustice to make him the author of what future reflection or better information might occasion him to suppress or amend."[167]

Queen Victoria and her consort, Prince Albert, prompted an early and celebrated assertion of disclosure. When sketches they had privately printed were described in a catalogue and readied for exhibition in 1848, the couple prevailed in their right to determine publication.[168] A century later in the United States, in 1949, Mark Twain's heirs successfully prevented publication of a manuscript. The court distinguished clearly between the ownership of the manuscript and the right of first publication.[169] The 1976 Copyright Act took over the disclosure right from state common law. The author now retained the right of publication even if he had sold or given away his manuscript.[170]

Repenting, in contrast, was not accepted even in every Continental system. From copyright's vantage it was an almost senseless claim, unilaterally violating contracts freely entered into.[171] And why should authors be entitled to tinker with history, erasing traces of their earlier selves to suit their current frame of mind? In the very few cases that arose, Anglophone judges showed little sympathy for authors' changes of heart.[172] Though sometimes compared to withdrawal, the US 1976 act's termination of transfer differed both in intent and effect.[173] Termination was a strictly economic renegotiation opportunity that allowed an author to take back assignment of his rights after thirty-five years, thus sharing in his own unexpected success. Withdrawal, in contrast, permitted an author to remove a work altogether after a change of heart. The point was to erase the past. Should the author change his mind again, the French and German laws required that the initial publisher be offered the original terms to ensure that the author's motives were strictly personal and not a cunning ploy for a better cut. In theory, the American termination right might be invoked to withdraw a work. But it was intended as an economic opportunity to reenter the market on better terms.

That left attribution and integrity. Anglo-Saxon law recognized no attribution right. To enforce recognition an author had to rely largely on contract. Defamation law helped him sue if works not his were attributed to him. Integrity, in turn, was an issue especially in heavily derivative art forms: engraving, theater, opera, and the ultimate magpie enterprise, film. Authors of primary works secured some measure of control as exploitation rights expanded. This did not entirely solve the integrity problem, however, since an authorized dramatization of a novel, say, might still be a travesty. But it allowed the original author to decide who used the work derivatively and how.

Integrity and attribution were often linked. If unauthorized alterations violated integrity, did changing attribution help? Did the author object to the changes as such or to being credited as the source of the mutilated work? In 1816 Byron persuaded a court to ban a volume of Byron poems, some of which he had not penned.[174] Fanny Fern was the nom de plume of an American journalist and novelist, author of a fictional autobiography, *Ruth Hall*, and the first woman with a regular newspaper column. When William Fleming published a cookbook under her name in 1856, she successfully sued in court, arguing that its poor style had tarnished her name. No one, she insisted, "has any more right to appropriate it than to take the watch from my girdle."[175] In 1894 a Pennsylvania court ruled for Henry Drummond, a Scottish evangelist and writer, on grounds that could be interpreted as validating either attribution or integrity. The Lowell lectures he had delivered on evolution (eventually to appear as *The Ascent of Man*) were published without permission, altered and incomplete. The court issued an injunction, recognizing his right not to have "any literary matter published as his work which is not actually his creation, and, incidentally, to prevent fraud upon purchasers."[176]

Mark Twain and a publisher who had issued a manuscript without his name fought over attribution.[177] Selling a book, one of the judicial opinions ventured, was not the same as selling a barrel of pork. An author was entitled both to be paid for his work and to have it published as he wrote it. The purchaser could not garble it nor issue it under another name, unless permitted by contract. That highlighted the weakness of moral rights in copyright systems since the author's claim depended on not having signed rights away. Alberto Vargas, famed for his drawings of leggy nudes, discovered the contractual nature of attribution when an American court ruled in 1947 that he—having assigned attribution—had no claim to be designated as the artist.[178] Others were luckier. The creators of Superman, originally a cartoon, signed away all rights in 1938 for the princely sum of $130. After their work had earned millions for others, they sued at least to be acknowledged as authors and won that small satisfaction (plus an annual pension) from Warner Communications in 1975.[179]

Statute also provided some protection against unauthorized alterations in the Anglophone world. The 1911 UK Copyright Act limited changes to mechanically reproduced musical works to those that were "reasonably necessary" to adapt them. In the US 1976 act licensees of nondramatic musical works were entitled to arrange them broadly as they pleased but forbidden to change their basic melodies or fundamental character.[180] Beyond such vestigial precautions, however, moral rights in the copyright systems were largely creatures of contract.

But things did sometimes improve, even in America and Britain—if not via statute or regulation, then by custom and habit. Testimony before Congress in 1886 outlined how completely a writer alienated his manuscript when selling it. The publisher could shut it up in his vault, throw it in the trash, sell it to a colleague, or have his own editors work it over. "[A] sale, delivery, and payment passes the title as completely with regard to a manuscript as to anything else. There is no sacredness, there is no concealed right or title or interest in a manuscript any more than in any other personal property."[181] Later evidence suggested change had occurred. Twenty years ago, an author testified before Congress in 1936, magazine editors used to alter manuscripts as they saw fit. He had once added a few lines to a Keats sonnet to show "how it would not hurt at all." But nowadays writers approved their editors' changes. That battle had been won.[182]

FINGERS CROSSED, THE ANGLOSPHERE ADOPTS MORAL RIGHTS

Despite French observers' plaintive laments, influence did not flow only one way. Yes, the media industries increasingly rested in Anglophone hands. And, yes, even behind Europe's protectionist local-content barriers, American output dominated the airwaves and the screens, big and small. But Hollywood, Motown, Nashville, New York, and later Silicon Valley had to accommodate the world's single largest developed consumer market: the ever-growing, ever-harmonizing EU. The client is always right, even if he is European. The US had to accept, and the UK live up to, the Berne Union's strictures. In so doing, the Anglo-American disseminating industries discovered interests of their own. There were advantages to tap-

ping into the Berne Union—but not unconditionally. While reciprocal protection within the union was tempting, media interests
shunned entanglement in requirements they disliked, especially
moral rights. They wanted Berne membership on their own terms:
"yes, with certain restrictions," as Edwin P. Kilroe, attorney for the
US Motion Picture Producers Association, put it in 1936.[183]

Early in the nineteenth century, as a populist democracy freely
appropriated Europe's cultural riches, the United States had been the
leading pirate. But by the 1950s America was the world's largest exporter of intellectual property and keenly interested in protecting its
cultural industries abroad. "In the four corners of the globe," Sydney
Smith, a founder of the *Edinburgh Review*, had sneered in 1820, "who
reads an American book?"[184] In 1838 the Senate Patent Committee
still agreed. American books were in no position to break into the
British market.[185] But already a decade later, in 1848, a memorial to
Congress cited over five hundred US books reprinted in England to
show that American authors stood to benefit from protection abroad,
just as their British colleagues would in America. Indeed, the charge
British authors used to level against US publishers, that their editions
mutilated works, was now returned in kind.[186] A million Britons
bought *Uncle Tom's Cabin* in 1852, the year of its publication, well
over thrice its American sales.[187] Who did *not* read an American book?
US observers now chortled.[188] Peter Parley and Louisa May Alcott
outsold any English authors of their day in Britain. Longfellow beat
even Tennyson in his homeland. Poe, Irving, Cooper, Hawthorne,
and Emerson were equally popular in America and Britain.[189]

By the mid-nineteenth century earlier objections to international
copyright were countered by claims that it would not harm the
American book trade. Prices would not rise because publishers now
understood the principle of individually small but collectively huge
profits on large sales. Given a manufacturing clause, jobs in printing
and publishing would not suffer. Only a quarter of books published
in the United States were now British reprints, the rest American
originals. By the end of the nineteenth century, American authors
and publishers, as well as librarians and educators, were solidly
aligned in demanding equal treatment for all authors, regardless of
nationality.[190]

A similar logic held half a century later as debate broadened beyond international copyright to American membership of Berne. By the 1930s travelers to Europe reported back that almost all the music in hotels and the films in movie theaters were American. European theaters often performed American plays. Economic self-interest spoke for participating fully in copyright's international regulation.[191] "We make a motion picture and carry the message of American life and American manufacture all over the known world; we carry the tunes of the American composers all over the known world," Louis Swarts, spokesman for the Motion Pictures Producers and Distributors of America, insisted before Congress in 1931. "If we go into foreign countries we want that material protected there."[192] When Berne membership was considered in the 1930s, the State Department highlighted the advantages of treaty protection for exports—factory goods, but increasingly also intellectual property and especially film.[193] A similar logic spurred the British when it came to popular music. In the 1980s a quarter of all hit records worldwide were British. "However much some noble Lords may dislike—and often despise—the form of music that is popular today," the Earl of Winchilsea and Nottingham cautioned his peers in 1987, "there is no doubt that it generates enormous sums of money for this country."[194]

Though a Berne member from the start, Britain had adhered to the 1928 Rome reforms only on the assumption that moral rights were safeguarded by existing legislation and required no change. In 1952 the Gregory Committee still agreed. But a quarter century later, in 1977, the Whitford Committee, reporting on how to ratify the convention's 1971 Paris revision, acknowledged deficiencies. The protection of moral rights afforded by the UK's 1956 Copyright Act did not last the requisite lifetime plus fifty. Britain should expressly recognize at least the attribution and integrity rights, though the committee also anticipated problems such as an author's heirs demanding to be bought off before blessing the changes needed to film a work or the difficulties of attribution for every participant in collaborative works. In any case, despite accepting moral rights the Whitford Committee imagined that they were to be waivable (unlike in France). Attribution, for example, was to be bindingly assigned by ghost writers, and novelists were to sign off in advance on any changes required to film their work.[195]

In 1988 the UK finally adopted moral rights.[196] Though now formally compliant with Berne, the British version was so hedged about with restrictions and exceptions that it amounted to only a partial implementation. "If US law has so far followed an ambling path to moral rights," one critic observed, "the new UK law has stepped briskly down the wrong road."[197] Attempts to hew closer to the Berne line were defeated in the House of Lords. Publishers and media barons clashed with peers and MPs claiming to speak for journalists and authors. Between work-for-hire and the waivability of their claims, journalists were largely deprived of both copyright and moral rights.[198] Advertising—another important British industry—also favored limiting moral rights in order to control authors on the payroll.[199] As in the United States, the British media self-interestedly sought to curb the excesses of a French-style approach. But the wider cultural pull of traditional copyright, and the reluctance to privilege authors, also remained strong.[200]

The British government openly planned to do only the minimum required to toe the Berne line. "Of course we defer to the Berne convention to the extent that we need to sign it in order to get appropriate protection for our works and our intellectual and industrial property rights in other countries," admitted John Butcher, parliamentary under-secretary for industry and consumer affairs, in response to protests that the bill did not follow the Continental spirit. But there were limits. "A convention is a convention and it is for national Governments to decide how far they go in slavish adherence to its provisions and in observing its spirit and practicalities."[201] The hard-nosed Anglo-Saxon approach to authors was summed up in 1987 by Lord Young, secretary of state for trade and industry: "Those with ideas deserve a fair reward for their labours but they cannot expect to be completely sheltered from the real world."[202] Lord Beaverbrook, grandson of the first Baron of Fleet Street and the government spokesman on the bill in the Lords, hammered the point home: "the person exploiting the work" was entitled to just as much justice as "the author, composer or artist whose work he is exploiting."[203]

The rights of disclosure and repenting were not introduced, while attribution and integrity were instituted only with detailed specifications that left courts little discretion. Distorting or mutilating changes that harmed the author's honor or reputation were forbidden. But putting the work in a possibly prejudicial context (a highbrow work surrounded by pop art, or worse) could be punished by Berne standards, but not in Britain.[204] Attribution and integrity also did not apply to exempted works: computer programs, works made for hire, periodical articles, or collective reference works. Violations of integrity were permitted if accompanied by a disclaimer indicating that the author had not consented—cold comfort at best. Blanket waivers allowed authors to consent to alterations—and also in advance for future works. Fearful magazine editors pleaded with the Lords: chaos would rule if they could not edit and change writers' work.[205] Though Britain's 1988 act made moral rights unassignable, the scope of waivers gutted any inalienability they might pretend to. The attribution right also curiously violated a fundamental premise of authors' rights by requiring the formality of written assertion.[206]

Oddly, the 1988 act also fobbed off as an author's moral right what in fact was an expanded privacy right for the commissioner of a work. The 1911 UK Copyright Act had given the copyright of commissioned works, including portraits, to the commissioner. This created an anomaly by which copyright of a landscape was vested in the artist, but of a portrait in its commissioner. The 1988 act now narrowed such work-for-hire by giving copyright to the author, not the commissioner. To guard the commissioner's privacy, it instead granted him control over the dissemination of works he had ordered. The commissioner received not copyright but the right to prevent paintings, photographs, and films he had ordered for private purposes from being shown or broadcast publicly. Though presented as a moral right, it was, if so, one of the commissioner, not of the author. In effect, the commissioner received a right of control in return for his lost copyright. An alleged moral right was thus used to grant some of the same powers as had been safeguarded earlier by work-for-hire—that nemesis of the Continental ideology.

At best Britain thus instituted the bare minimum of Berne's moral rights. The disseminating industries prevailed over most authorial concerns. Editors retained their ability to tailor content to their needs, and waivers of moral rights quickly became standard in film contracts.[207]

AMERICA FOLLOWS SUIT

Matters were no better in America. Reporting back in 1885, the British delegate to the Berne conference had optimistically calculated that the United States "will before long feel it difficult to abstain from becoming party to it also."[208] He was off by only a century. Though America did not join Berne until 1989, the gravitational force of the largest single copyright union increased relentlessly over the century. As the US moved from copyright outlaw to the paramount exporter of intellectual property, its content industries demanded harmony with the union. In the past the United States had not joined Berne, Representative Robert Kastenmeier—sponsor of the membership bill—explained in 1987, because "we did not want for our society the kind of copyright laws that the Convention requires." But now the "growing internationalization of copyright law, the trade imbalance, and so forth," required a course correction.[209] "We have gone from the biggest pirate in the world," Secretary of Commerce Malcolm Baldrige admitted, "to the biggest victim of pirates in the world, and it behooves us to strengthen this protection. It is in our self-interest."[210] Even though trans-Atlantic harmonization was never perfect, the trend was clear. On moral rights the United States accepted European guidelines, moving eastward at least in a pro forma sense to close the gap across the Atlantic.

At the state level the Americans introduced moral rights a few years ahead of the British. Starting in the 1980s, thirteen US states, including California and New York, legislated some variety of moral rights. At best these laws were faint echoes of the European version. All dealt only with visual arts and half only with works of recognized quality. All guarded against impairments of integrity, and some protected against more than violations of honor and reputation. Four explicitly protected works against destruction, which most European statutes did not. But they did not cover work-for-hire. Half did not

indicate any particular duration of protection, and half allowed re-
nunciation of moral rights, refusing to make them inalienable.[211] In
1977 California even adopted a droit de suite, or resale right for artworks, though that has recently been upended in court.[212]

In 1989 the United States finally joined Berne. Trading interests
were a crucial motive. US negotiators had made intellectual property
a focus of the Uruguay round of negotiations within the General
Agreement on Tariffs and Trade (GATT). But the Americans' absence
from Berne made their pose as a guarantor of intellectual property
implausible.[213] Why, Singapore and Korea demanded to know in bilateral negotiations, was the United States pushing hard for strong
copyright protection when it did not even belong to Berne? American membership would forestall appearances of a double standard.[214]
As of the mid-1970s the US began running a consistent trade deficit.
During the 1980s it became a debtor nation for the first time since
the end of the Second World War.[215] Nonetheless, the copyright industries stood out as a bright spot, generating a $1.5 billion annual
trade surplus.[216] America imported almost no software, and US computer program manufacturers dominated the European market in
the late 1980s.[217] Yet the United States was also estimated to be losing
many billions annually to piracy and lax enforcement of existing
statutes.[218] Membership in Berne, "the most prominent and effective
mechanism of defending copyright throughout the world," was part
of the answer.[219]

As in Britain the American collaborative cultural industries feared
that moral rights would obstruct efficient use of works. The National
Cable Television Association was "extremely suspicious" of moral
rights, especially as applied to work-for-hire. An author might have
signed a contract allowing cable companies to edit works to meet
local standards or even just shorten them to fit time slots. But, if
armed with moral rights, he could throw a wrench into the works.[220]
Like other major exporters, including the pharmaceutical firm Pfizer,
IBM, too, was pleased by the prospect of joining Berne. So long as
moral rights could be waived, formal adherence to the concept was
fine.[221] Though allergic to moral rights, Hollywood was also keen on
Berne's use in combatting piracy.[222]

The US print trade, in contrast, had mixed motives. Export publishers, like John Wiley, shared hopes with Hollywood for shelter from piracy. The domestic magazine press, from *Newsweek* to *Playboy*, was more worried by threats to editorial discretion. It banded together in the evocatively acronymed Coalition to Preserve the American Copyright Tradition (PACT). Giving journalists and photographers a final editorial say before press time, PACT argued, was a recipe for havoc. So was having to name every contributor or policing the immediate context in which photographs or articles appeared. The potential damage to authors' reputations, editors worried, was unquantifiable. Moral rights threatened to spark endless litigation.[223]

Against the serried ranks of the media industries even Hollywood's star power failed to dazzle. The great and the good of Tinseltown—directors Milos Forman and Sydney Pollack, actors Jimmy Stewart and Warren Beatty, Ginger Rogers and Jerry Lewis—all made the pilgrimage to Capitol Hill to plead for moral rights, often sounding like characters from a Woody Allen film. Director George Lucas evoked a scary future where movies were colorized, speeded up, and shortened, the actors replaced digitally with fresher faces, their lips altered to mouth new dialogue.[224] But he insisted on his own right to change a novel as he wished while filming it. Later, Lucas did to his most famous films, the *Star Wars* trilogy, what he here attacked. In 1997 he released an altered and supposedly final version that many fans considered mutilated and debased. Confiscating prints of the original versions, he claimed that "it's the director's prerogative . . . to go back and reinvent a movie."[225]

Steven Spielberg praised Berne for voicing the idea that "art and the artist are not commodities to be treated like sausage." Perhaps the public liked colorized movies, he conceded. But then this single most popular and commercially successful of all contemporary directors and producers struck the tortured pose of a Romantic artist: "the creation of art is not a democratic process, and in the very tyranny of its defined vision lies its value to the Nation. . . . The public does have the right to reject or accept the result but not to participate in its creation." Not to be outdone in questioning democracy's cultural credentials, Bo Goldman, screenwriter of *One Flew Over the Cuckoo's Nest*, gave a bathetic performance, worthy of a *schöngeisterisch* aesthete:

> Democracy is the last and best hope of mankind. It is great for mankind but terrible for art. A movie is not written by a committee. It is not shot by consensus. It starts with one man or woman alone in a room and then the director, despite the hordes around him, is alone on the stage. There is collaboration at every step, but the decision a costumer makes to sew a sequin here or a bow there, a cameraman to jell this window or not, an editor to go to the long shot from the closeup or the closeup from the long shot, every artist ultimately makes the decision, and it is a lonely one, forged by years of experience, the pain of trial and error, but made with the deepest of emotions. These movies are who we are, who we have been, who we will be. These movies are the litany of our existence and the food of our souls. They are absentminded laughter and they are unconscious tears. You can't change them any more than you can change the wart on Lincoln's face. They are sometimes not pretty, they are sometimes dispensable, but a thousand years from now they will still be us.[226]

The gentlemen of Hollywood certainly took themselves seriously. Alas, to little avail. Congress took advice indicating that the United States did not have to strengthen moral rights to qualify for Berne and that, in any case, moral rights would still be waivable by contract.[227] Senator Orrin Hatch, a major force behind the 1988 Berne membership bill, worried that magazine publishers and movie producers would be hobbled by lawsuits if work-for-hire was abrogated and every minor editorial decision required authorial consent. Much as John Butcher, the UK parliamentary under-secretary for industry and consumer affairs, had admitted in 1988, so too Hatch saw the point of membership as safeguarding American cultural exports, not protecting authors. If joining Berne required lip service to moral rights, so be it. But the bill explicitly did not increase existing rights for authors. It aimed "to enhance international protection for copyrights, not to interfere with existing domestic copyright relationships." The United States signed on for what was realistically described as a "minimalist approach."[228]

Unsurprisingly, when the US joined Berne, few changes followed.[229] The compulsory licensing of music played by jukeboxes was changed. Much more important, formalities were eliminated as a prerequisite of copyright. Berne's principles required this, and trading partners could otherwise reciprocate to hamper protection of American works.[230] With copyright notice made voluntary, every work was now protected as of creation.[231] On moral rights precisely nothing happened. Existing safeguards were deemed sufficient, and the act was carefully worded so as not to change moral rights protection—such as it was. Nor did the convention by itself become the law of the land, since it was not self-executing. Anyone seeking to litigate a moral right in the United States still had only domestic law to work with.[232]

Yet Washington did not wholly ignore the *cri de cœur* of Hollywood's auteur elite. That same year the National Film Preservation Act of 1988 indirectly protected a few significant movies against alteration. A Film Preservation Board, appointed by the librarian of Congress, could select up to twenty-five films annually for listing. If they were then modified, including being colorized, the films had to be so labeled. But cuts made to allow for commercials on TV were not considered mutilation, as they were in Europe, and no film could be listed during its first decade.[233] When the labeling requirement was removed in 1992, the law in effect reverted to an exercise in film preservation.[234]

In 1990, a year after the United States joined Berne, an American law on moral rights did pass. In some respects it was more inclusive than British legislation: attribution did not have to be formally asserted. But it remained very limited. For the first time in federal law, the author, and not just the copyright owner, was given rights. Integrity was not assignable and could not be waived except in writing, specifying what changes were allowed. But as the name, the Visual Artists Rights Act (VARA), indicated, the law's scope was very narrow.[235] It protected only fine art of recognized stature, as singular works or in limited editions of at most two hundred signed copies. As in the UK, work-for-hire artworks were excluded. Only attribution and integrity were protected—and integrity only from intentional or grossly negligent changes and only from harm to honor or reputation. A work's "public presentation, including lighting and placement" was excluded too, sidestepping the subjective question of damaging contexts. Curiously, however, almost uniquely in moral rights legislation worldwide, the law banned outright destruction.[236] Works that formed part of a building, like murals, could be removed only with the artist's permission. Thus in 1992 Kent Twitchell won a $1.1 million settlement when his Los Angeles mural depicting the artist Ed Ruscha was painted over. Rights could be waived but only for specific uses and not in the blanket sense of the UK law. Unlike in Europe, these moral rights lasted only for the author's lifetime.

PERPETUITY AND ITS DISCONTENTS

In the 1980s and '90s, trans-Atlantic antagonisms surfaced once again as the Europeans pushed the Anglo-Americans to slowly, grudgingly, and incompletely introduce reforms. The Europeans were impatient at the scale and pace of change. Corporate media industries, they charged, were flexing their muscle. The Americans worried more about exploiting works than protecting authors.[237] They were right. The American government's solicitude for collaborative cultural producers dated back to the subsidized postal rates granted newspapers in the 1790s and had not diminished two centuries later. The content industries wanted access to the Berne market without needless concessions. They saw moral rights as a sticking point: an inalienable claim to increase authors' leverage and annoy copyright owners. But American disseminators and authors did agree that following the Continental example of treating intellectual property like other property, with strong ownership rights, helped them all. Not moral rights but strong property rights were what the Americans learned from the Europeans.

From the public's vantage moral rights were ambiguous. If they made authors happier and more productive, the audience gained. So, too, if the authenticity guaranteed by moral rights outweighed their restrictive effect on derivative works. But moral rights also allowed authors to willfully and capriciously prevent their work from appearing except as it pleased them—or indeed from appearing at all. Moral rights fundamentally assumed that authors alone could judge their work. All other considerations—whether public preference or historical accuracy—were secondary. And, of course, they potentially pitted every author against all other authors and against every interpreter and performer who hoped to use the work.

The Anglosphere approached moral rights suspiciously. It was not merely, as French observers liked to pretend, that Anglo-Saxon courts could not understand the subtleties of moral rights.[238] The British and Americans often did not like what they saw. Enshrined in Berne, moral rights were nonetheless adroitly kept out or downplayed in the international treaties of the 1990s.[239] The Anglophones adopted moral rights more in name than substance. But in other respects the copyright nations did sacrifice some key features of their approach on the altar of Berne membership. Formalities, the gatekeeper function that had ensured a ready supply of works for the public domain, were now largely eliminated in American law. Even more important was the duration of term. The traditional copyright approach favored short terms, while the Continental natural rights view, with its focus on property claims, inherently pushed for more, even if it rarely achieved perpetuity. The Anglophone content industries disliked Berne's moral rights. But they could scarcely contain their glee at the prospect of the long and strong protection that Europeans enjoyed. With Berne membership the prize, the US Constitution's caution about "limited times" was doomed.

The length of terms had serious practical consequences. Although it was often discussed in similar terms, the duration question was not the same as whether intellectual property should last perpetually. The original advocates of perpetual literary property—les perpétuistes, as the anarchist Proudhon had called them—were the eighteenth century booksellers.[240] They had first introduced the idea of neverending copyright based on common law in hopes of grabbing for themselves the eternal property claims that natural rights allegedly gave authors.[241] They were stymied, however, by Donaldson in 1774 and the revolutionary edicts in France that cut short authors' property rights to balance their interests with the public's. Advocates of perpetual literary property rights clamored ceaselessly thereafter, well into the twentieth century. "Nothing is as persistent as a right," the jurist Adolphe Breulier reminded his readers, and the perpetuity of intellectual property put itself forth as a lodestar principle.[242]

But the perpétuistes rarely achieved their goals. Perpetuity was legislated in Guatemala, Venezuela, Mexico, Nicaragua, Holland, Portugal, and—the sources differ—possibly also Egypt.[243] Italy protected moral rights perpetually in 1925, as did Poland in 1926 and France as of 1957. As late as the early twentieth century, before the lockstep assumption that longer terms demonstrated progress and enlightenment, it was still argued that the higher the average educational level, the shorter terms should be.[244] In literate nations—so went the logic—authors could easily make a living in the thriving literary marketplace. In laggard countries longer protection was needed to match slower and smaller sales.[245]

The argument for perpetuity rested on the analogy with real property. As a reward for past performance, unconditional ownership made some sense. As a stimulus for future creativity, it was much weaker. If a short term offered some incentive, did not a long, possibly perpetual, one offer even more? A moment's reflection reveals a sentimental fiction here. As future rewards are discounted in proportion to the time until we collect them, the impetus they provide for current activity diminishes. A sixty-year term postmortem does not give the author thrice the pleasure of a twenty-year one. The British historian and campaigner against exaggerated authorial rights, Thomas Babington Macaulay, unflinchingly accepted this insight in 1841: "But an advantage that is to be enjoyed more than half a century after we are dead, by somebody, we know not whom, perhaps by somebody unborn, by somebody utterly unconnected with us, is really no motive to action."[246]

During France's July Monarchy, when perpétuistes battled more public-spirited commentators, Victor de Broglie, the third duke of that distinguished family, pointed out that, for all practical purposes, supporters of extending terms from twenty to fifty years postmortem, rather than the government's more limited proposal of thirty, were arguing for perpetuity.[247] When, prompted by the EU's adoption of seventy years postmortem in 1993, the United States also debated extended terms, economists detailed de Broglie's and Macaulay's insights. Dennis Karjala and his colleagues demonstrated that an extra twenty years on top of fifty, discounted to reflect the present value of monies, added only a smidgen to the worth of copyright.

Assuming interest rates of 7 percent, a dollar of royalty paid eighty years in the future had a present value of under half a cent. Add on the statistical unlikelihood of any given work being of commercial value seventy years hence, and it was highly implausible that the owner of a seventy-year copyright was any better off than one with fifty.[248]

But the main conceptual obstacle to perpetuity was the identity of the ultimate owners. Once no one could claim a personal connection to the author, why should the work belong to anyone in particular? Paying royalties to the heirs of Dante or Walther von der Vogelweide, one observer cautioned, was both laughable and utterly impractical.[249] A person could bar the public from the house he had inherited. But could an author's heir prevent a major cultural treasure from being reprinted? As Victor Hugo pointed out in 1878, in the long run the writer had only one heir: the human spirit and the public domain.[250] All the sillier, then, that it was his heirs who fought an unseemly battle against sequels to *Les Misérables*. Arguing against extending protection for Schiller's works, Jacob Grimm similarly concluded in 1859 that "the property of the world is worthier and greater claims follow than can be staked even by heirs and descendants."[251]

THE DURATION OF COPYRIGHT TERM

The United States was prevented from protecting intellectual property perpetually by the Constitution itself. To jump that hurdle, Jack Valenti, longtime president of the Motion Picture Association and tireless Hollywood spokesman, in 1988 slyly proposed copyright of eternity minus one day.[252] Nor did perpetuity have much traction left in the UK. Eighty years earlier the chairman of the Music Publishers' Association had naturally favored perpetual rights. Alas, he wistfully concluded in testimony to Parliament in 1909, "the public has always stepped in, and the rights of the public have always been recognized."[253]

In Europe, however, perpetuity remained a plausible argument for much longer. We have seen how eternal rights were one of Lamartine's preoccupations in the French debate of 1841 and how the idea faded only slowly thereafter.[254] In theory, perpetual rights were right and proper, an international congress on the subject concluded in 1859. Only the practical difficulties of implementation prevented their recommendation.[255] Well into the twentieth century, Europeans still clamored for perpetual rights. In Germany composers, a whole school of postwar reformers, and even the Ministry of the Interior advocated perpetuity in the 1950s.[256] At the 1967 Berne revision conference in Stockholm, attempts to make at least moral rights perpetual were defeated only after Anglophone resistance.[257] In a way that is inconceivable in the Anglophone literature, to this day standard-issue legal textbooks in France advocate perpetuity, not only for moral rights, which is already law, but also for economic rights.[258]

Perpetuity was not a practical ambition, however. Instead, battles raged over how long an author's claims should last. Over the past three centuries duration has consistently been shorter and more grudgingly extended in the Anglophone world than in France and Germany.[259] Thanks to the globalization of intellectual property law, most developed nations now share largely the same extensive terms—either the fifty years dictated by Berne in 1948 or the seventy required in the EU as of 1993. But it was not always so. Historically, the impetus and initiative for extension has invariably come from the authors' rights nations.

Until well into the nineteenth century neither the UK nor the US contemplated extending their initially short terms of fourteen years from publication plus a renewal of equal length. In 1831 the initial period was doubled in America to twenty-eight years. In 1909 so was the renewal period. That provided a maximum of fifty-six years of copyright from publication—if the author renewed, which very few did.[260] Only in 1976 did the United States begin following the now prevailing European norm of life plus fifty, which Berne recommended in 1908 and mandated in 1948.

In the UK the original fourteen years in the 1710 Statute of Anne was extended in 1831 to twenty-eight years or the author's life, whichever was longer. Talfourd's attempts to reward authors at the expense of the public with life plus sixty provoked outrage, prolonged parliamentary jousting, and finally a compromise that extended protection in 1842 to life plus seven years or forty-two in all, whichever was longer. Macaulay's celebrated riposte, that long terms were a "tax on readers for the purpose of giving a bounty to writers," summed up the Anglo-Saxon attitude: the general public took precedence over property owners, the common good over authors' rights. But, as one of the original Berne members, the UK could not escape Continental influences. By 1909 Macaulayian attitudes were gone, and fifty years postmortem was no longer considered prejudicial to the public interest.[261] In 1911 the UK adopted the Berne norm, though tempered by the possibility of licensing after twenty-five years that we have examined.

Initially the British and Americans dated protection from publication, rather than tying it to the author's lifespan. This underlined that his rights were a temporary monopoly to benefit him, as well as his heirs, but only if he did not survive his own term. Thomas Jefferson's actuarial calculations behind his recommendation of a nineteen-year term reflected his belief that, as the earth belonged to the living, copyright should be proportionate to average lifespans.[262] The author was not to rule over his works from the grave. In the event, the first US copyright statute of 1790 cut even that by following the British precedent of fourteen years. In contrast, the Continent regarded authors' rights as lifelong property that then passed to their heirs. The French royal edicts of 1777 assigned perpetual rights if the author acted also as publisher. This last whiff of the Old Regime was blown away by revolutionary edicts, which consciously followed the British precedent. The revolutionaries instituted short terms, though the author's life was now the measure of things (five and ten years postmortem, in the two revolutionary decrees).

But already by 1810, under Napoleon, property began to trump the public domain in France, and terms lengthened. Fearing that works owned by dispersed and squabbling heirs might vanish, Napoleon was skeptical of perpetual property.[263] Nonetheless, under his reign terms were extended to the life of both the author and his widow (marital property relations permitting) and then twenty years beyond their deaths for any children.[264] Under the Bourbon restoration in 1826, life plus fifty was proposed, as it was under the July Monarchy in 1836.[265] During the debates of 1841, Lamartine preferred per-petual rights but knew he had to settle for less. In 1854 life plus thirty was adopted, and all widows, regardless of their marriage's property terms, benefited from their spouse's rights. In 1863 a commission re-porting to Napoleon III favored perpetual rights, "without which there is no true property." But it grudgingly settled for life plus fifty, though it sneakily tacked on a perpetual royalty payment thereaf-ter.[266] In 1866 a term of fifty years postmortem was adopted, eighty years before Berne would require it. Later blanket extensions were added for works hampered by the two world wars: six and a half years for pre-1920 publications and eight and a half for those before 1941. The estates of authors who had died for *la patrie*, including Apollinaire and Saint-Exupéry, also received an additional thirty-year extension.[267] Among the unanticipated results, those parts of Proust's *À la recherche* published after the First World War entered the public domain earlier than the first volumes.[268]

The Germans thought less in terms of property than the French. By the late nineteenth century the concept of *geistiges Eigentum*, or intellectual property, was being superseded by *Urheberrecht*, or au-thors' rights as a personality right, independent of property.[269] But the Weimar Republic and the Third Reich were preoccupied by the social obligations of authorship. The Germans claimed to under-stand that literary works were not like conventional property and thus could not be held perpetually. The French approach struck them as bourgeois individualism, while they sought to care for soci-ety as a whole.[270] Correspondingly, the Germans took longer to move beyond the thirty-year term they adopted in 1837 for Prussia, in 1845 for the German Federation, and in 1871 across the new, united Ger-man nation. When terms were lengthened by an extra decade for Goethe, Schiller, and various other classic authors in 1856, scholars lamented the loss for critical editions and public enlightenment.[271]

In the mid-nineteenth century thirty years was thought to be how long an author would be remembered after death and thus an ap-propriate term.[272] Eighty years later, in 1927, this logic remained un-challenged. Authors really wanted to spread their works widely, the Prussian Academy of Sciences now reasoned. Long terms hampered that while benefitting their heirs, not them. Few authors would have living widows more than three decades after their deaths. Why bother lengthening the term?[273] Early in the twentieth century the Germans sounded almost Anglo-Saxon, arguing for the public domain and the general public.[274] The Germans stuck with thirty years until 1934, when the Nazis shifted to the French half-century standard. But after the war they went to town. Already in 1965 they were the first major nation to extend rights to seventy years postmortem, hoping thus to regain their high-culture credentials after the Third Reich.

Over the past three centuries protections for authors have almost never been lessened. They seem to ratchet ever upwards in a race to the top.[275] Having upped the ante for the rest of the world, the new German standard of 1965 could not be ignored. But things might have been even worse. In 1958 the Italian Society of Authors and Publishers recommended extending protection to the longest term then in effect, Spain's eighty years.[276] For some reason they ignored the Portuguese, who from 1927 to 1985 were true perpétuistes.[277] Indeed, at the 1928 Rome conference the Portuguese lambasted other attendees for falling behind, while congratulating Mussolini for supporting authors.[278] But the Spaniards and Portuguese were not a locomotive of change on a par with the formidable German publishing industry. The Federal Republic's seventy years became the gold standard to aim for. And aim the Europeans did.

In 1985 the French took the protection of musical works to seventy years.[279] In 1991 the European Commission heard no objections when sounding opinion on whether to protect databases (a category of work not covered at all in the United States) for as long as seventy years.[280] Then in 1993 the EU succumbed to the German precedent and made seventy years obligatory for member states.[281] The stated goal was to catch up with increasing lifespans, thus preserving Berne's traditional aim of granting property-like benefits during the life of the author and two full generations of successors.[282] As always, rights holders stood to gain most directly. The French recording industry feared the loss of its most valuable properties from the golden 1950s: Edith Piaf, Georges Brassens, Maria Callas.[283] Unlike earlier discussions of duration—whether Talfourd or Lamartine or the turn-of-the-century German disputes—the EU's 1993 term extension to seventy, decided in the back rooms of Brussels, sparked little controversy.[284]

CUI BONO? SONNY BONO: AMERICA
ADOPTS THE EUROPEAN NORM

The Americans were not obliged to extend terms since, in prepara-
tion for membership, they had legislated the Berne minimum of fifty
years postmortem already in 1976.[285] By then, the direction of influence was westward across the Atlantic. The content industries wanted
access to the Berne Union's markets and stronger claims to works but
not the bother of moral rights. The United States signed up for
"membership lite," adopting the European approach to property but
not to personality. But once in the club why should American disseminators not enjoy the same terms as their European colleagues?
When in 1993 the EU upped the stakes by making seventy the new
norm, American works had twenty years less protection than the
competition. American authors and disseminators saw eye to eye—
the public be damned.

Satisfaction arrived in 1998 with the Sonny Bono Copyright Extension Act, named after the former pop singer, then Republican congressman and fervent copyright advocate, after he was killed in a
skiing accident. The Bono Act has borne its share of criticism. It has
often been referred to as the Mickey Mouse bill, since the Disney
Corporation was a major beneficiary of term extension.[286] It was certainly warmly welcomed by authors and the content industries.[287] It
may have been "the biggest land grab in history" but only if we ignore what the Europeans had already done.[288] For it was fundamentally a reactive piece of domestic US legislation, catching up to the
EU's lead in extending protection from fifty to seventy years. Because
it wrenched US law further from its traditional concern with the
public domain, it sparked protest and debate without compare in
Europe, including a Supreme Court challenge. In Congress the act
was described as "a top priority for the entertainment industry," allowing American "copyright creators and owners . . . to enjoy the full
and appropriate term that European copyright owners have enjoyed
for some time now."[289] As Mary Bono, Sonny's widow and congressional replacement, testified, it made "our system conform to a strong
international standard."[290] Once Europe had taken its decision, Hol-

lywood's representatives argued, the United States had to follow or forfeit a tremendous trading advantage for its most dynamic export sector.[291]

It is often argued that the United States surpassed European norms by extending terms of work-for-hire to ninety-five years from publication (or 120 from creation, whichever was shorter).[292] In fact, US copyright duration was broadly adjusted to the European norm, taking into account the importance of work-for-hire in American cultural production. Terms for European work-for-hire, insofar as this was recognized in law, did tend to be shorter. But, more important, work-for-hire (that is, mainly collective works and sometimes, as in France after 1985, software) was a minor category in EU law, where most works were protected in relation to their authors' lifetimes. In practice, protection therefore still usually lasted longer in Europe.[293] Without the extended work-for-hire term much American work would have been protected for shorter times than its European equivalents.

Films, for example, treated as work-for-hire in the United States, were now protected for ninety-five years from their release. In Europe, treated as normal works, they were covered for seventy years from the death of the last survivor among the movie's many coauthors. Except for the work of very old authors, that was likely to be at least as extensive a term as the American.[294] To take one measure, as of 2003 no French film had yet entered the public domain.[295] By comparison, a compilation of US movies in the public domain from 2011 lists 284.[296] In addition, Continental wartime extensions, which had no American equivalents, were added on top of the blanket seventy-year term. One of Monet's *Water Lilies* paintings, executed in 1906 and hanging in the Art Institute of Chicago, entered the public domain in the United States in 1981. In France the war extensions kept it protected another thirty years, until 2010.[297]

Berne's policy had long been national treatment. Foreign authors were dealt with like their local peers. But for term durations the standards of the country of origin applied.[298] When the EU extended terms to seventy years, it exploited this loophole to impose a reciprocal "rule of the shorter term." Non-EU works would enjoy only the protection of their home country if that was shorter than in the

EU.[299] The United States was thus motivated to quickly adopt the longer European standard.[300] Arguably, term extension was thus forced on the US by the EU's imposition of a rule that violated Berne's spirit, if not its letter.

In American discussions arguments from property had long played second fiddle to the public good. Congress's power to grant copyrights was governed by the constitutional requirement that it promote the progress of science and the useful arts.[301] In the House committee report on the 1909 act, copyright was declared to exist "not primarily for the benefit of the author, but primarily for the benefit of the public."[302] In 1931 Karl Fenning, former patent commissioner, agreed: "The purpose of the copyright protection is not so much to give a living to an author as it is to get something for the public."[303] "The sole interest of the United States and the primary object in conferring the monopoly," Chief Justice Charles Evans Hughes pronounced in 1932, "lie in the general benefits by the public from the labors of authors."[304]

Four decades later, in 1975, the Supreme Court agreed. "The immediate effect of our copyright law is to secure a fair return for an author's creative labor. But the ultimate aim is, by this incentive, to stimulate artistic creativity for the general public good."[305] In all this, the court reflected in 1984, the law made "reward to the owner a secondary consideration."[306] Even the report on the Berne Convention Implementation Act of 1988 parroted this approach: "Under the US Constitution, the primary objective of copyright law is not to reward the author, but rather to secure for the public the benefits derived from the author's labors."[307] Such examples could be multiplied at will.[308]

But once the United States had joined Berne in 1989, the public good grew less important. Europe's property-dominated rhetoric crept in, and the very logic of encouraging authorial creativity subtly shifted. Copyright had traditionally promised the author only as much of the value he created as it took to persuade him to continue working.[309] The Continental ideology, in contrast, held out the possibility of a much larger share. Gradually this upping of the author's ante now spread into the Anglo-American realm too. No longer were authors to be rewarded only insofar as and because it stimulated their creativity. Now the algorithm assumed that reward encouraged creativity in a directly proportional way. The bigger the payoff, the better the works—or at least the more of them there would be.

The classic position had been stated by the Congressional Committee on the Library in 1873. The point of copyright, it reported, "is not the protection of authors as an object—not as the reward of genius independent of science, but as an incentive to the former in the interests of the latter."[310] In *Feist* (1991), the Supreme Court still upheld the traditional approach: "The primary objective of copyright is not to reward the labor of authors, but 'to promote the Progress of Science and useful Arts.'"[311] Rewarding the author was incidental to enhancing the public domain. It was the means to that end, not the end itself.

In *Eldred* (2003), the case that adjudicated the retrospective extension of term to seventy years, things were changing. Justice Ruth Bader Ginsburg argued that "copyright law serves public ends by providing individuals with an incentive to pursue private ones."[312] This logic was subtly different. By directly correlating reward and output, Ginsburg came closer to agreeing with Mary Bono, widow of the congressional crooner. "[B]y maximizing the incentives for original creation," she had argued, "we help expand the public store-house of art, films, music, books and now also software."[313] This approximated the traditional Continental logic. Enriching the cultural heritage, a guide to the Berne Convention explained, "depends directly on the level of protection afforded to literary and artistic works. The higher the level, the greater the encouragement for authors to create."[314] In other words, the more reward, the more good. This was a long way from the enlightened—and socially efficient—vision of the founding fathers.

Nonetheless, despite toying with a justification for strong rights built increasingly on property more than social utility, the American ideology had not wholly gone over to the other side in 2003. Both Ginsburg and Bono still spoke of incentives, and not—as in the logic of natural rights—of reward and just desert. But the incentives were no longer to be limited to the minimum that authors needed to keep creating. The idea of a maximum level of incentive, sufficient to stimulate creativity, beyond which no further profit need accrue to the author, was now being left behind. Authors and their assignees were increasingly seen to deserve as much of the monopoly rent as they could extract. The Continental natural rights tradition dwelled more on reward than incentive. The author *deserved* his due. Cost/benefit analysis was not crucial, and there was little sense of a cutoff after which further reward ceased serving a social purpose. This European argument—that there was a direct correlation between private reward and public good—was now being adopted also in America.

When in 1998 with the Bono act, the US followed the EU's unilateral term extension from fifty to seventy years, the sponsors of the legislation nonetheless complained that the public failed to benefit while authors and the copyright industries profited. "I feel strongly that extension of the copyright term should include public benefit," Senator Patrick Leahy insisted, "such as the creation of new works or benefit to public arts."[315] Senator Hank Brown lodged a minority protest in the committee report, venting traditional American concerns lest the public domain be overshadowed by private property. He lamented the ever-lengthening monopolies granted authors and quoted experts who put the conflict in traditional terms: as a battle between copyright owners and the public interest in lower prices and abundant works. "The European Union has resolved the tension in favor of the owners of old copyrights. We should rather favor the general public."[316]

But, in fact, the 1998 Bono Act took little account of the public. Senators Leahy, Ted Kennedy, and Paul Simon did insert two small changes: first, unpublished materials due to enter the public domain in 2003 (having had their common law protection removed by the 1976 act) would still be freed despite term extension; and second, libraries and educational institutions would still be able to copy research materials.[317] But other than authors, publishers, and heirs, the only beneficiaries were the owners of small restaurants, bars, hair salons, and the like. In a horse trade term extension was yoked to a measure that exempted such small businesses from licensing fees for playing the radio for their customers. A minor clawback from a few authors and their disseminators profited an arbitrary collection of retail businesses in return for a major extension of copyright term, severely disadvantaging the general public.

THE RIGHTS OF FAMILIES AND HEIRS

The question in the United States had traditionally been what copyright incentives sufficed to prompt creativity? As a 1961 congressional study asked, "what duration of limited time will best promote the progress of science and useful arts?"[318] But from the 1990s on, European-style property rhetoric sounded more often in America. The continental analogies between intellectual and conventional property now increasingly colored debates here too. And the claims of the heirs also received a hearing.

Authors' families had figured only tangentially in earlier American discussions of copyright duration. By definition European postmortem terms benefited the author's family and heirs. Anglo-Saxon terms, measured only from publication, did not. When at Noah Webster's behest the original term was doubled in 1831 from fourteen to twenty-eight years after publication, the right to that additional fourteen years was granted the author's spouse and children, even if the author had died. Here the authorial family first appeared on the American copyright stage, taking a small step toward the European position of works as heritable property.[319] American supporters of international copyright and long postmortem terms eyed the European situation enviously. In the 1890s George Haven Putnam, of the publishing family, argued for extended protection to give the author what other workers took for granted: "being able to labor for the advantage of his children and grandchildren."[320]

During the run-up to the 1909 act, however, only the author himself and his immediate family were the focus. Mark Twain, ardent supporter of long terms, testified that he did not worry about his grandchildren but that copyright should last long enough to support his daughters. He could take care of himself. But his daughters were "not as competent to earn a living as I am, because I have carefully raised them as young ladies, who don't know anything and can't do anything." Life plus fifty: "That would take care of my daughters, and after that I am not particular."[321] But when Congress heard evidence on Berne membership in the early 1930s, witnesses opposed extending terms to fifty years postmortem since that benefited grand- and great-grandchildren. The government report on the matter simply assumed that only the author and his immediate family should gain. There was "no logical reason to restrict the public's free access to the work by continuing the benefit to remote heirs, or to the distributors or his successors."[322]

When American copyright was extended in 1976 to European norms, a consideration was that, with longer life expectancies, the old fifty-six-year term fixed from publication no longer supported the author "and his dependents"—that is, one generation of heirs.[323] Twenty years later, in 1998, as it prepared to extend terms for yet another two decades, Congress had begun accepting the European insistence that copyright should benefit authors and two succeeding generations. The EU relied on this logic when it extended terms to seventy in 1993, arguing that increasing lifespans required longer durations.[324] At least three considerations escaped this argument. First, the average age at childbearing, not just lifespan, determined the timing of subsequent generations.[325] Whatever the changes in demographic behavior, European reformers presented no evidence on this point.[326] Second, not only were heirs living longer, but so were authors.[327] As average lives grew longer, postmortem copyright terms automatically lengthened. Why add to what nature and public health were already accomplishing?[328] Finally, since most authors assigned their rights, the main beneficiaries of any extension were the content industries, not grandchildren.[329]

Whatever its deficiencies, however, this European logic began infiltrating American discussions. Senator Orrin Hatch, active in copyright reform, now insisted that intellectual property should be treated like other property. Much like other owners, authors expected to pass on their possessions to their children and grandchildren.[330] Senator Diane Feinstein, whose Californian constituency included Hollywood, sentimentally welcomed term extension as allowing authors "to take pride and comfort in knowing that one's children—and perhaps their children—might also benefit from one's posthumous popularity."[331] The American discussion only gingerly seized the European three-generation rule. But the Old World idea that heirs were a legitimate focus of copyright was gaining foothold also in the New.[332]

Such arguments were old hat in Europe. There, families, lineages, and inheritances had always counted for more than in America, which celebrated self-made men and valued self-reliance among heirs. In his famous speech to the French National Convention in 1793, Joseph Lakanal had bewailed Corneille's distant relations, languishing in want. Forty years later Balzac agreed.[333] In 1841 Alfred de Vigny importuned the July Monarchy's deputies with a tearful tale of the penury of the dramatist Michel-Jean Sédaine's daughter.[334] Étienne Blanc lamented the fates of Racine's impoverished elderly descendants.[335] The introduction in France in 1920 of the droit de suite, the resale right to singular works of art, was motivated by pity for heirs in decline. Preposterous, one French deputy sputtered in 1937, that Jean-François Millet's grandchild was hawking flowers in a music hall when the painter's *Angélus*, which he had sold for twelve hundred francs, fetched three-quarters of a million gold francs in 1890.[336] Talfourd, too, had agitated for long protection to help the aging Wordsworth support his children. The poet held back his *Prelude* so that its posthumous publication would benefit his family.[337] In 1841 Lamartine argued for expanding protection from thirty years postmortem to half a century on familialist grounds: the moral person of the author was not just the creator but also his wife and children. The shorter term was insufficient to provide for "the father, the wife, the son."[338]

A century later, in the 1990s, such sentimentalism invaded American copyright discussions. Striking a jarringly unfamiliar note, the Senate worried that the children of prominent middle-brow composers—Richard Rodgers, Irving Berlin, Hoagy Carmichael, and the like—could no longer clip the coupons of their fathers' talents. Mark Twain had been content to abandon his grandchildren to their fates in 1906. But now Bob Dylan worried aloud about his songs falling into the public domain while his grandchildren were still teenagers.[339] Rarely had rentiers been spoken for so forcefully in Congress.[340]

Not all American senators and congressmen fell into line, however. Congress was not given copyright powers, Senator Herb Kohl complained, "for the sole purpose of ensuring that the heirs of copyrighted works can enjoy an unfettered income stream from a monopoly." Artists' heirs might be perfectly decent people. But that did not mean that "they should continue to receive royalties for an extra 20 years for work they did not create and at the expense of the American consumer."[341] Paying disingenuous homage to the fading traditions of the public domain, the senators who voted for the new longer copyright term shamefacedly insisted that authors' desire to benefit themselves, their children, and grandchildren "is consistent with both the role of copyrights in promoting creativity and the constitutionally based constraint that such rights be conferred for 'limited times.'"[342]

Upon joining Berne in 1989, the United States also had to retrospectively remove foreign works from the public domain. The convention required that new members protect all works that had not yet entered the public domain in their country of origin. Foreign works that had previously not been copyrighted in the US—usually thanks to neglected formalities—therefore now had to be protected. This consequence had earlier been one of the main stumbling blocks to US entry.[343] At first, the United States applied the convention only to works created after its admission in 1989. It refused to include noncopyrighted foreign works retrospectively. But after this unilateral approach was criticized abroad, the US grudgingly complied with Berne. Any hopes of striking out on its own were undermined by the negotiations over international trade of the 1990s, to which we come in the next chapter. The Americans were hoisted by their own petard. Seeking strong international protection for intellectual property, they could not neglect at home what they demanded abroad. They were therefore keen to file the burrs off their copyright legislation, making it fit international norms.[344]

The result was another blow to America's traditional concern for the public interest. Works that had fallen into the public domain were now reprotected.[345] James Joyce's *Ulysses*, for example, had never been copyrighted in the United States, thanks to an unfortunate combination of its supposed obscenity, the manufacturing clause, and missed filing deadlines. Snatched back from the public domain, it now enjoyed two full years of official protection before lapsing once again in 1998.[346] Users of works formerly in the public domain were helped in a small way in that rights holders of restored copyrights had to follow various formalities before asserting claims.[347]

While reprivatizing public domain works was controversial in America, an even larger pull-back into protection of public works in Europe ruffled few feathers, though protests were heard in Britain.[348] The EU Parliament, defying the European Commission, fought openly to make sure that lengthened terms were retrospective.[349] And this was no small matter. When in 1993 the EU extended terms to seventy years, two decades' worth of works once freely available were returned from the public domain to private control. As a modest counterbalance the EU permitted national legislation to exempt from payment those who in good faith had begun using these formerly public domain works.[350] A similar reprivatization occurred in 1990 when the former East Germany became part of the Federal Republic and adopted its longer term.[351]

FORMALITIES

On formalities, too, Berne obliged America to change its inherited approach. In 1976 the United States had ended many formalities required to protect works. By the time it joined Berne in 1989, it had done away with almost all remaining ones. The European approach had triumphed once again. In the continental view formalities were but artificial obstacles to what naturally belonged to the author from the moment of creation. This was the approach that had been expressed in debates over the French 1957 law. Formalities were initially proposed to free up the use of periodical articles. To retain exclusive rights journalists had to specifically exempt their works. But to thus expand the public domain provoked the legislature's ire. The Anglo-Saxons might impose formalities, deputies scoffed, but the French tradition safeguarded the work from the moment of creation. Journalists, too, should be protected without having to take further steps—the public be damned.[352]

By contrast, in the classic copyright view formalities ensured that only those works that someone specifically wanted to sell were kept out of the public domain. In Europe works were born as private property. In traditional copyright unless hoops were jumped, they were born free into the public domain. Formalities thus underlined the belief that intellectual property was not a natural right but an artificial creation of statute.

Nations had not differed dramatically on formalities in the eighteenth century. The 1710 Statute of Anne and the 1790 US Copyright Act had imposed formalities. But so did the 1793 French law. It made redress in court for unauthorized reproduction dependent on having deposited copies in the national library. So it remained until 1925.[353]

During the nineteenth century, however, a trans-Atlantic gulf opened in this respect too. Already in 1845 French case law swept away formalities for unpublished lectures, which by their nature could not be registered, deposited, or otherwise harnessed by bureaucratic procedure.[354] By contrast, in Britain the 1835 Publication of Lectures Act required anyone wanting to reserve rights in a lecture to notify two justices of the peace within five miles of the venue two days prior to its delivery.[355] This was rarely done, one might think, but standard forms were drawn up, just in case.[356] In 1908 the Berlin revision of Berne forbade making protection conditional on formalities, though many countries continued to require deposit in the national library. When the American 1909 Copyright Act then moved further from the European approach, emphasizing formalities, the trans-Atlantic gap was as wide as ever.

In 1911 the British adopted Berne's requirements, ending formalities. But, as always, the British straddled the fault line between copyright and authors' rights. When the UK finally introduced moral rights in 1988, it promptly violated a central Continental premise by making attribution contingent on its formal assertion.[357] The British logic remained firmly in the copyright tradition. The point of retaining that formality, the government emphasized, was to ensure that users of copyrighted material knew where they stood.[358] Lord Beaverbrook reasoned in a classically Anglo-Saxon way: the formality of assertion spared copyright owners the need to identify authors who could not be bothered to insist on attribution.[359] Copyright's default presumption remained for free use, not authorial rights.

In the United States formalities had been phased out starting in the 1970s as the nation prepared for Berne membership. The issue had always been ambiguous. As we have seen, collaborative media liked formalities for the clarity they brought to ownership rights.

But, as rights owners, the content industries also suffered if formalities became overly complicated, and claims were forfeited when technicalities were overlooked or neglected.[360] By the time Berne demanded an end to formalities, the system had become needlessly complicated. Many, in fact, welcomed this spring cleaning. Later, however, as the disadvantages became apparent of automatically protecting every scrap of creativity already from the gleam in its author's eye, formalities were rehabilitated. In recent years, as worries of copyright overreach have multiplied, the public utility of formalities has been celebrated. Reformers have regretted the trend toward the Continental approach. The American default position, as one complained, became European. Works were automatically protected, not inherently free.[361] When copyright was extended to seventy years in 1998 to meet the European norm, opponents sought repeatedly, though in vain, to reintroduce formalities.[362] If passed, the Public Domain Enhancement Acts of 2003 and 2005 would have required nominal fees after fifty years of protection and then again every decade. The majority of works were thus likely to become public domain then, rather than two decades later.[363]

Though based on natural rights, moral rights also surpassed them. On property rights authors and disseminators saw largely eye to eye. They might haggle about how to distribute the spoils, but both wanted long and strong protection. Insofar as authors' rights were founded on personality, however, market logic was left behind. No economic advantage flowed to the author from insisting on his continued aesthetic control. Quite the contrary. Asserting an author's (and his heirs') moral rights might have costs. How did Beckett's insistence on male actors benefit him financially? In what way did Joyce's grandson's iron grip on the canon profit the estate? Only if a narrow concept of authenticity commanded a sizable premium could authors hope to gain from personality-based decisions. But moral rights did potentially pit authors against disseminators. They chipped away at the rights otherwise assigned to the content industries by restricting the alienability of works. Disseminators wanted fully assignable rights, not inalienable authorial control.

From a historical perspective moral rights helped paper over the tension at the heart of intellectual property: how could the work be both personal and alienable? With conventional property alienability was not an issue. Once sold, it belonged fully to the new owner. But if the work expressed the author's personality, then alienability raised thorny issues. Thanks to the complications of Napoleonic family and property law, these were revealed first on the continent. While the Anglo-Saxon legal codes allowed largely free disposal of inheritance, Napoleon specified the claims of each family member. For conventional property that worked. But treating literary works in the same way gave spouses, widows, stepchildren, parents, creditors, or others a potentially inappropriate say over the author's aesthetic decisions.[364] Though the Anglophone nations could not wholly sidestep such problems, copyright's myopic focus on economic rights and the work's full alienability blended them out.

In the postwar era the American media industries came to understand that Berne membership would protect their now valuable exports abroad. They welcomed Berne insofar as it enhanced authors', and thus their own, property claims. But they were allergic to moral rights, which extended authorial powers. Viewed narrowly, American membership of Berne and the British adoption of moral rights may seem a grudging and half-hearted introduction of enlightened reforms that benefit authors and culture more generally. But seen in a broader historical context, the rapprochement with Berne in the 1980s obliged the Anglophone nations to adopt much of the Continental ideology, shifting copyright's traditional concern for the public toward authors and their assignees. After this, the major remaining difference across the Atlantic was work-for-hire, and here the Continental nations made concessions for economically important collaborative activities.

Copyright's evolution is often told as a story of American cultural hegemony. In fact, the opposite is more plausible. True, moral rights were only partly taken on board in the Anglophone nations. But in other, more important respects the Continental approach triumphed: the abolition of formalities, the extension of terms, and most fundamentally, the shift of copyright's philosophical underpinnings from statute back toward natural rights. Authors were now to be rewarded as deserving property owners, not incentivized for reasons of social utility. British and American law bowed to their content industries. As long as moral rights were kept in check, Hollywood and its ilk happily espoused the continental ideology—just as the eighteenth-century booksellers had recognized their advantage in natural rights. They tooted the horn of authors' rights all the way to the bank. But though they had managed to declare victory for the moment, the battle was far from over.

7

America Turns European

In the postwar era the idea that intellectual property was a variant of conventional property, therefore to be extensively protected, achieved its epitome. And yet at the same time, the shift to a personalist interpretation of authors' rights had partly supplanted this property-based view. Inalienable moral rights of the kind passed in France and Germany in the 1950s and '60s stayed with authors even after their work was sold, thus contradicting market logic. Nonetheless, in a broader sense personality-based rights rested on the same logic of natural rights as property. Thanks to authors' efforts, their works belonged firmly to them—whether due to the investment of their labor or as an emanation of their personalities. Such rights appealed to a higher justification than the mere statute that traditionally undergirded Anglo-American copyright.

The continental ideology thus founded authors' claims on both sweat and personality. After the Second World War, Anglo-American copyright, seeking to balance authorial claims with social utility, was unable to resist the triumphal march of the Berne Convention's principles of long and strong protection. At best, Britain and America mustered some surly resistance. They implemented moral rights only halfheartedly and clung to certain key features that suited the content industries (work-for-hire), even as other aspects of traditional copyright (short terms, formalities) were abolished. As intellectual property became an ever more important part of modern economies globally, the stakes in its governance grew. During the 1980s and '90s the content industries of the Anglophone world were able to win strong intellectual property rights. Their concerns called the tune, first in Washington and then increasingly in harmony with Brussels as the EU became an important policymaker on the international stage.

During the eighteenth-century Battle of the Booksellers, publishers had appealed to natural rights seemingly on behalf of authors, while in fact pursuing their own interests. Since their own rights could be no firmer than the creator's claims, publishers stood to gain from a solid authorial stake. A similar logic held in the twentieth century as the American media industries became the world's foremost content exporters. What was good for authors was good for disseminators. Robust authorial property claims, assignable to disseminators, served the content industries well. So long as they could avoid inalienable moral rights gumming up the workings of contract, they now signed on to the Berne ideology of treating intellectual property much like conventional property.[1]

Starting in the 1980s the stakes were also raised by the new digital technologies that promised to revolutionize how content was created, reproduced, and disseminated, much as Gutenberg's printing presses had four centuries earlier. Digitality allowed works to be reproduced exactly and cheaply. On the web all content could in theory now be made available effortlessly, perfectly, and globally. The pressing question was legal: how much control could rights holders still exert in this brave new world of possibly universal access? Would the new technologies' potential for global dissemination enhance access for the audience? Or would their ability to track, control, and charge for every use reinforce rights owners' prerogatives? Owners insisted that legal protection alone no longer sufficed to guarantee their claims when every digital copy could be reproduced at will. They needed new technological safeguards as well to control access and copying. Advocates for the public countered that adding technological protection on top of copyright threatened to give owners complete control over works, blocking even traditional exemptions like fair use.

During the 1990s the Clinton administration heeded the American content industries' concern that their products not be pirated abroad and their rights not be undermined by the new technologies. Reversing America's copyright isolationism of the nineteenth century, Washington now eagerly harnessed international conventions and agreements to the cause of strong intellectual property. In the Berne Union, which America joined in 1989, but even more in the 1994 TRIPs agreement of the GATT and the 1996 WIPO Copyright Treaty, America responded to the exporting content sector's desires to safeguard its products. To the inherited copyright laws were now added new regulations that reinforced technologies used to monitor and govern digital usage. Content merchants considered this a simple application of ownership in the new digital environment. Open access activists and others who fondly remembered erstwhile American copyright traditions, with their concern for the audience, feared a world where information was locked down by both law and technology.

And yet the US content industries were not the only players. In the nineteenth century reprint publishers, who wanted to reissue British books freely, had fought publishers specializing in American literature, who sought copyright for foreigners. In the 1990s various economic interests did battle too. Hollywood favored strong international protection for intellectual property. But in Silicon Valley the business model of the rising tech and internet industries was better served by a free flow of content through the infrastructure and devices that earned their keep. In America rights holders and audiences clashed once again. Open access activists, who had battled the content industries unaided at first, gradually discovered a pleasant coincidence of interests with the internet and high tech sectors. The fight was no longer just between Hollywood and idealistic downloaders, but it set rival business models against each other. While this twentieth-century Battle of the Booksellers was being fought in the United States, however, little hint of dissent from the primacy of rights owners' claims could yet be heard on the European continent.

In the late twentieth century two developments framed the renewed battles over authors' rights: the digital revolution and the increasing internationalization of intellectual property.

DIGITAL MIXES IT UP

Digital techniques of reproduction changed everything. Like pharmaceutical companies the cultural industries—music, film, television, publishing—had high initial costs, but their output was easy and cheap to reproduce and thus to pirate. Up to the mid-twentieth century reproducing and distributing works was expensive and complicated. It remained the province of large organizations. In the 1960s and '70s new analog technologies of reproduction allowed consumers to imitate the disseminators, though in a hobbled and imperfect way—taping music, photocopying texts, videotaping films. But with the digital revolution the inherent physical limitations of analog reproduction evaporated. Copies now became indistinguishable from originals, and marginal costs declined toward zero. To pirate works had once been almost as onerous as producing them in the first place. But digitality made every teenager with broadband a potential downloading site. Because each digital copy could be the source of thousands more, digitality required new protective technologies to prevent access and copying except as owners permitted. In the paper and analog eras, the sheer physical difficulties of reproduction had set inherent limits to piracy. Protection for rights owners could rely largely on the law alone. But with digitality the law needed to be bolstered by technology too.

Earlier, ideas had been what economists call nonrivalrous. They could be used by many at the same time without depriving anyone else. Digitality did the same for the works in which the ideas were expressed.[2] Everyone could now have a perfect, almost costless copy without taking it from anyone else. Within a decade, making the world's culture available to everyone on earth passed from wild imaginings of visionaries to the quotidian paragraphs of legal briefs. What did all this mean for authors and disseminators? Could they clamp into place new protective technologies and reinforce their legal claims? Or had digitality let the content cat out of the bag?

Like Dr. Doolittle's Pushmi-pullyu, digitality headed in two opposite directions. The new technologies promised/threatened to make works available to all. And they threatened/promised to make all information property, locking it up in owners' hands. The battle between audience and authors (the latter often spoken for by their disseminator proxies) flared up again in the digital era. An astounding opportunity to make culture available to all also threatened many commercial cultural producers.

Unlike their analog forerunners, digital technologies permitted tight monitoring of every copy, transmission, and use. Digitality also allowed authors and disseminators to segment and target markets. Works could be released in different versions at varying times and places—in cut-rate and luxury editions, student, home, and professional versions, in pristine formats at full price, or discount, ad-studded ones.[3] Owners could bargain with audiences for every use, charging differential prices. Thanks to ceaseless metering, the inherited exemptions, like fair use, were perhaps no longer needed. Instead of exceptions for certain uses, all content consumption could be charged through micropayments. Compulsory licensing—necessary in the analog world because of high transaction costs—might be replaced in new "high volume, low transactional value" business models with payments tailored to actual use.[4]

On the other hand, the ever-snowballing avalanche of works cascading through the internet's arteries has arguably outmoded the traditional model of exclusive rights altogether. Most disconcerting for inherited views, new cohorts of creators have found outlets for their work—whether YouTube videos, Wikipedia entries, or scholarly articles—motivated by generosity, a search for community and audience, for renown or some other nonmarket impetus. More mundanely, new business models have sought to reward digital creativity without resorting to exclusive authorial rights—through serializing delivery and payment, for example, or taxing digital and computer equipment to pay for downloaded content.[5] Most commonly, reformers have proposed updated forms of automatic licensing, skimming revenue for authors off the digital bounty.[6] So far, however, American and European official opinion has resisted new solutions.[7] Rather than exploring licensing, allowing untrammeled access tempered by statutory royalties, or other legal novelties, the US and the

EU have dragged the Berne template of exclusive authorial property rights awkwardly into the digital age.

Digitality undermined analog certainties. How could rights be asserted to works whose dissemination could barely be controlled? Was fair use outmoded now that every use could in theory be metered and charged via individual licensing?[8] Among the most important legal principles that digitality now threatened was first sale (in Europe known as "exhaustion of rights"). First sale had traditionally been another limitation of authorial exploitation rights.[9] Having once sold the work, the vendor lost his legal say over further sales and—with most works—rentals. The author controlled reproduction of the work but not the physical object sold. Composers were sometimes given rights over rentals of their scores. But first sale applied strictly to books, which could be rented, lent, resold, and otherwise freely disposed of once they had been sold. Hence libraries, used bookstores, and reading clubs were possible. Hence, too, Wordsworth's intemperate insistence that his friends not lend volumes of his poetry to anyone able to buy their own copies.[10]

In the 1990s digitality upended precedent. The first sale doctrine assumed that the physical work actually changed hands and that secondary uses were inferior to the original, whether involving a used book or an analog tape recording. The work's physicality limited possible infringement. Authors and disseminators could be expected to swallow the ensuing losses or be compensated by modest lending and copying fees. With digitality, however, the difference between original and copy, or other secondary uses, evaporated. A used DVD was as good as a freshly pressed one, and so was a copy of either. Forwarding a digital copy over the internet differed from selling or passing on a book or record, or even photocopying or taping it. The secondary market now threatened the primary. Digital copies were perfect facsimiles, clearly violating exclusive rights.

Adding insult to injury, "sharing" works on the internet meant copying and distributing them, not giving them away.[11] Should the first sale doctrine apply to digital distribution? Perhaps first sale could be reconciled with digitality if the original copy were destroyed once another had passed between users, leaving only one in existence. Would consumers agree? Commercial media interests saw digital copies among friends as sales foregone. Consumers regarded them as informal exchanges among people who would not have bought the work in the first place. What techniques would ensure deletion upon transmission?[12] As Amazon and Apple developed marketplaces for second-hand digital content starting in 2013, it was crucial that only one copy of the work changing hands continue to exist.[13]

Because digitality made copying works so easy, the first sale doctrine was curtailed for certain media. In the 1980s record rental stores also sold blank recording tapes, allowing patrons to copy works they rented. In response, US copyright owners were given the power to forbid rentals of sound recordings in 1984 and of software in 1990.[14] In 1991 the EU granted owners a rental right for computer programs and in 1992 for film.[15] The 1994 TRIPs agreement, to which we return below, internationalized such limitations of first sale, giving authors rental rights for films.[16]

E-books raised similar issues. The assumptions of first sale, developed for traditional books, followed the evolution of the medium into its digital format. As technological restrictions were imposed on digital books, readers objected when publishers decided how many times they might enjoy the work or what they could do with their copy once finished.[17] Publishers pushed back. They allowed only a certain number of loans before libraries had to renew their purchase, arguing that paper books too wore out and had to be bought again.[18] More generally, disseminators sought to retain control by leasing rather than selling, sidestepping first sale altogether. Software was increasingly licensed, library patrons used electronic journal subscriptions only at the publishers' sufferance, digital university textbooks remained on devices for the semester only, and music streaming made huge collections available but only as specified in contract. Ever more the issue facing consumers was not copying but how to access works.[19]

Digitality also forced a reconsideration of the right to make private copies. In the analog era private copying had not threatened disseminators' core markets. But the ease and perfection of digital copies posed a new challenge. While American law did not explicitly allow copies for private purposes, fair use generally covered them. In Europe the right to make individual private-use copies was spelled out in laws from the early analog era.[20] Hard hit by xeroxing, sheet-music publishers sometimes managed to win rental rights for scores. But as long as private copying meant photocopying a book or taping music, disseminators did not yet fear losing their primary markets.[21]

Even videotaping did not pose a dire threat. The US Supreme Court's 1984 Betamax decision allowed consumers to videotape television programs for some uses. Time shifting—copying programs for later viewing—was considered fair use. But making collections of taped shows was not.[22] Even so, already in 1955 the German Supreme Court had presciently anticipated the problem of private copying when it limited the use of magnetic tape. The judges foresaw digitality's threat. If uncompensated private taping was allowed, they predicted, the market for copyrighted content would vanish once new technologies eventually allowed users to make copies equal in quality to those for sale.[23] Indeed, as the cost of storage plummeted, digital copying became painless, perfect, cheap—and hugely popular. In 1982, when the Betamax case was first argued, Sony had sold five million analog video recorders in the United States. In 2005, at the time of the first peer-to-peer digital file sharing case, *Grokster*, forty to sixty million Americans were downloading.[24]

THE AESTHETIC CONSEQUENCES OF DIGITALITY

Digitality thus threatened content owners with sidestepping the usual avenues of reproduction and distribution. But digitality also called into question inherited aesthetic certainties. Many of the Continental ideology's Romantic assumptions were not readily compatible with the late twentieth century's postmodernism. That had knock-on effects for the legal incarnation of Romantic authorship in European authors' rights legislation. Postmodernism's tenets need no rehearsal here. But it is worth emphasizing the symbiosis between its aesthetic postulates and the technical possibilities now held out by digitality as a means not just of reproduction and dissemination but of creativity too. Above all postmodernism dethroned the Romantic author. No longer a solitary genius, he was now seen as the product of his society and age and as someone who created using other authors' materials. Nor were works regarded as singular and personal. While the author's intentions were an element of their meaning, they did not determine it exclusively. Revising his work, the author undermined any Archimedian point from which to understand his œuvre. Early versions of Wordsworth were more original, later ones more correct.[25] Were any definitive? The work's meaning was now seen to hinge as much on how it was received, understood, and reused by others as on the author's intentions—however those might be interpreted.

Such commonplaces of postmodernism not only became ingrained in contemporary culture, they also had implications for moral rights. The attribution right was hollowed out as author and work became ever less personally connected. If everyone stood on others' shoulders, the outcome was inherently collective. Contemporary literary theory relished exposing art's scavenger nature, unmasking the author's pretensions to solitary genius. Critics have gleefully shown how even the most venerable works embody the labor of others. Brian Vickers's *Shakespeare, Co-Author* (2004) speaks volumes in its title, as does Norman Carrell's *Bach the Borrower* (1967).[26] Even the high-cultural canon appropriated: Shakespeare from Montaigne and Saxo Grammaticus, Racine from Euripides, Coleridge from Schelling, Picasso from Manet, Joyce from Homer, Pound from Dante, T. S. Eliot from a veritable literary phonebook.

In the intertextuality of the postmodern view, attribution was fruitless. If it meant anything, the much-vaunted death of the author—announced by Roland Barthes in 1968 and then by countless obituarial epigones—also implied the demise of his attribution right—and integrity too for that matter. We might understand Marc Chagall when he tore up a drawing signed with his name by Lothar Malskat, a notorious forger. And we might sympathize with Maurice de Vlaminck as he destroyed signed imitations of his works in a gallery.[27] We might cheer on Richard Guino's son as he fought to have his father recognized as coauthor of sculptures that until 1971 had been attributed solely to Renoir.[28] But our inherited ideas of legally enforceable attribution rights were called into question when

Mark Kostabi claimed authorship over works created by others but commissioned by him.[29] And when James Patterson, who publishes several novels annually, tasked his five regular coauthors to draft chapters for his revision.[30] And when the very point of some art was to efface the personal craftsmanly investment of its author: Duchamp's Readymades, Warhol's Brillo boxes, the Dadaists' automatic writing.[31]

Digitality's challenges have split authors down the middle. Some have demanded that their rights be reinforced in the face of downloading, sampling, and other unauthorized uses. Their more iconoclastic colleagues, in contrast, gleefully smash the inherited pieties, dancing on the shards. Meanwhile, the born-digital generation barely grasps what the fuss is all about. Donning their berets, Hollywood's celebrity auteurs have appeared on Capitol Hill to assert their prerogatives, encouraging politicians to grant ever longer and stronger rights. The great, the good, and the aspiring among the writerly caste have contributed op-ed pieces and letters to the editor bemoaning digital pilfering and the decline of books-as-our-ancestors-knew-them: John Updike, Susan Cheever, Scott Turow, Mark Helprin, the executors of Joseph Brodsky, W. H. Auden, Thornton Wilder, and so forth.[32]

But other authors have actively undermined the very premises of Romantic authorship and its legal defenses. When Corot signed his students' paintings, Dali and de Chirico signed ones by other artists, and Dali put his name to blank pages for later printing, attribution was no longer taken seriously.[33] What, we may well ask, is the attribution right of the poet Kenneth Goldsmith, whose "uncreative writing" consists of allegedly verbatim traffic, weather, or sports reportage?[34] Or of Vanessa Place's novels, verbatim excerpts from the legal briefs of her day job as a criminal defense attorney?[35]

Nor has the integrity right fared much better. What is the integrity right of aleatory music, like John Cage's *Music of Changes*, and other pieces where sounds are randomly selected—or of improvisational compositions, a Stan Getz solo, say, or even Mozart's *Musikalisches Würfelspiel*, which generates minuets by combining measures according to the throw of dice?[36] Gustav Metzger's sculptures are designed to destroy themselves, leaving nothing to defend. Pierre Bonnard went to the Musée du Luxembourg to add some (final?) touches to one of his paintings.[37] Did the museum have a claim against him? Could Goya, or his heirs, sue when the Chapman brothers painted clown faces on his original prints? If the work stems from more or other factors than just the author's conscious decisions, then he cannot claim to guard it. If every text is a parasite on other texts, then integrity rights cannot belong to the immediate author alone.

If the work's meaning hinges on its reception and use, it cannot express a singular personality.[38] If the work stands independent of the author, if it is ultimately collaborative, integrity is fatally undermined. The integrity right was constructed to serve the primary author and to control derivative uses. If, as contemporary aesthetics teach, no one is really a primary author and all are derivative creators, then the dead hand of integrity rights arbitrarily favors a founding generation. If digital works are interactive, with users constantly changing them, integrity rights curtail, not encourage, creativity.[39] Who is the author when computer games and e-novels are changed by their users? When corporate owners assert their control over allowable uses for Barbie and Bambi, derivative works and secondary creativity are shut down.[40] But, as aesthetic bullies, Disney or Mattel do not seem to differ much from Beckett or Joyce *petit-fils*—high-culture authors and their heirs seeking to impose aesthetic restrictions on the canon.

Moral rights issues have also been raised by the internet's globalized audience. Integrity has typically protected authors from changes affecting honor or reputation (except in jurisdictions like France, where they could ban any alteration for any reason). Whether authors were harmed has been evaluated according to socially determined standards, not just their own judgment.[41] When works were transmitted globally and altered far away, hopes of determining damage to reputation or honor were undermined. The attribution right assumes a large measure of shared cultural background. An unidentified quotation immediately recognized by an audience is an allusion, testimony to the author's erudition. The same quotation, unrecognized at first and only later identified, may instead be branded plagiarism.[42] Even without changing them, the web can radically recontextualize works, affecting their integrity. By a simple link they can be inserted on possibly objectionable sites.[43] The moral right's prohibition of "derogatory action in relation to" the work thus vainly seeks to restrict the promiscuous interlinking of any- and everything allowed by the web. And it is hard to imagine what the withdrawal right means in practice once a work has been released into the web's elephantine memory.[44]

Technically digitality allows moral rights to be enforced: ensuring accurate attribution even as digital fragments are recombined into new works, locking down works in one authorized incarnation to preserve integrity.[45] Some believe that digitality's threat to individual authorship requires reasserting moral rights.[46] The digital dematerialization of the work threatens its sacred aspects, one prominent French reformer has fretted, and the ability to manipulate it practically invites the audience to participate.[47] The ability of users to modify works has been hailed as a great advance. But many authors fear it undermines their control.[48] Equally fervently, others consider moral rights an anachronistic vestige of past attitudes, a conservative preserving in aspic of culture that is unworthy of digital modernity.[49] Given digitality's encouragement of artistic fluidity, hybridity, and collaboration, should moral rights be abandoned or vigorously enforced?[50] As cultural production shifts from artisanal methods to more corporate forms, some have favored emulating Anglo-Saxon work-for-hire in Europe. Others, in contrast, claim that such changes require no reform of moral rights. Rather, it is time to help authors working for big corporations to face down dehumanizing employment conditions by reasserting moral rights and granting their claims even after they have changed jobs.[51]

GLOBALIZING INTELLECTUAL PROPERTY

In this new post-Romantic era intellectual property has also become increasingly global and everyone's business. Although each nation legislated on authors' rights at its own behest and pace, trade relations with other countries grew ever more important. Yet transnational relations had been an element of intellectual property from the start. To combat piracy at home, nations had to negotiate with the neighbors. Thanks partly to Belgian book pirates, French law dealt early in the nineteenth century with foreign authors and editions. Before unification in 1871, German publishers were unable to control the pan-Germanic market, and pirating was rife. But this fragmented market was also free and a boon to the public. Though without a national copyright law until 1871, German publishing bested heavily regulated Britain. German piracy stimulated a vast supply of inexpensive books on technical and scientific subjects, helping the nation overtake the UK as Europe's leading industrial power. Meanwhile British publishers issued expensive volumes of history, law, and theology.[52] British publishers also lost to American pirates—and pirated in kind those American authors popular in Britain. Such were the issues that the Berne Convention sought to address as of 1886.

Intellectual property continued to internationalize into the twentieth century, the issue picking up speed and urgency with ever easier dissemination technologies. Earlier battles had been fought among the European nations and across the North Atlantic. In the postwar era they increasingly set the West against the rest of the world. As intellectual property importers, the developing nations sought concessions over translation rights, compulsory licensing, and the scope of patenting. In general, they wanted to trim exclusive intellectual property rights.[53] High-profile battles were fought over HIV drugs and other expensive medicines. In trade negotiations the Third World insisted successfully on being allowed to sidestep patents and copyrights in public health emergencies as they licensed and manufactured generic medicines.

Developing nations also sought to control First World corporations as they used indigenous culture and nature for new products that would be sold back to them at world market prices. Whether plants, animals, and biological processes coveted by pharmaceutical concerns could be patented or should be made freely available to those among whom they had been found remains an ongoing dispute.[54] For their part, developing nations sought to copyright folklore and other indigenous cultural products. That raised the issue of how benefits would accrue to the inchoate *Volksmund* whence they had sprung. Disney had already grabbed *Snow White* and *Cinderella* from the Grimm brothers who, in turn, had transcribed them in the early nineteenth century from European peasants. Now they were on to the *Lion King* (based on the Bible and Shakespeare), *Aladdin,* and *Pocahontas.*[55]

Ever more economically important, intellectual property increasingly mattered to international trade. Broadly defined, industries based on copyright made up over 11 percent of US GDP in 2005.[56] Creative industries generated over 10 percent of UK exports in 2009 and 5 percent of total employment.[57] Digital creative industries were bested as UK exporters only by advanced engineering and financial and professional services.[58] In France similar sectors contributed over 17 percent of value added in 2003 and 13 percent of employment (outside of public administration).[59] Intellectual property became a growing element of most economic sectors. On average, intellectual capital provided 44 percent of the total market value of US firms in 2009, and intangibles made up a similarly large and growing part for British companies.[60]

While trade in goods and commodities and in intellectual property had earlier been treated apart, the two were now practically inseparable. As a rule importers of intellectual property have advocated free trade and exporters regulation. In the late twentieth century the global north saw its software, music, movies, and pharmaceuticals, as well as more traditional products like car parts and agricultural chemicals, pirated in China, India, Brazil, and the Philippines. By 2008 an estimated 37 percent of all CDs globally were bootlegged, and only one of twenty downloads was sold legally.[61] However much such figures may have been exaggerated by industry spokesmen, the problem was not just an artifact of statistics.[62] Counterfeiting accounted for as much as 7 percent of world trade by value.[63] Over $200 billion of internationally traded goods were estimated as counterfeit in 2005—larger than the GDPs of three-quarters of the world's nations.[64]

Global economic relations would strain the contours of this book. But it bears mention that the international trade treaties of the 1990s—the GATT, WIPO, and TRIPs agreements—subjected most countries to the strict standards of the First World and deprived the not-yet-industrialized economies of a means to modernize that Europe, the United States, and later much of Asia had already exploited. Europe had championed strict copyright legislation in the nineteenth century, while being weaker on patents. The US had played to its strengths by reversing matters. They now asked poor nations to regulate both.[65] Britain, France, and Germany in the eighteenth century, the European periphery in the nineteenth, Japan, Korea, and Taiwan after the Second World War, and most egregiously of all, the United States in the eighteenth and nineteenth centuries: all had pirated their way to economic maturity.[66]

During the 1880s Switzerland had laid the foundations of its formidable chemical industry unhampered by annoying considerations like patents. When Philips purloined Edison's incandescent lightbulb as it began building a vast corporation in the 1890s, Dutch law sympathetically threw up few obstacles.[67] Britain chose to exclude chemical products from patenting between 1919 and 1949 to counter the threat of superior German products.[68] Small surprise, then, that South Korea waited until 1961 to introduce a patent system. Or that in the early 1990s twenty-five developing nations offered no patent protection for pharmaceuticals and fifty-seven none for software.[69] But now World Trade Organization (WTO) sanctions curtailed access to First World markets in retaliation for unauthorized use of protected goods. The developing world therefore had to pay extra for intellectual property than if global trade had been more leavened by piracy.[70] In its pirating heyday the United States had simply thumbed its nose at Britain and Europe. When the US sent observers to the inaugural Berne meetings in 1886, Bismarck had lamented its refusal to join. But the Iron Chancellor added, "Am I supposed to dispatch warships?"[71]

In the 1990s, however, poor nations had to submit to international trade rules dictated by the industrialized world. In return, they were admitted to advanced markets on relatively equal terms. Playing by the TRIPs rules was an imprimatur for global investment. Whether toeing the line of global intellectual property rights benefits or harms developing nations remains an ongoing dispute, echoing the arguments heard during the nineteenth-century American debate over international copyright. How are importing nations served by the availability of foreign intellectual property? Does it undermine their ability to develop? Or allow them to springboard off the efforts of others?[72] Such were the issues. During the 1970s and '80s those Third World nations that insulated themselves from the world market, inefficiently creating their own substitute products when better ones were available for import, performed poorly. Meanwhile, other developing nations, like South Korea and Taiwan, profited from selling to Western markets, thus highlighting the advantages of joining the world market and playing by its rules. Already in the 1980s and '90s some emerging nations began showing an interest in strong intellectual property protection: India for its software and film industries and especially China, now on the verge of flipping from importer to exporter, from pirate to enforcer.[73] The emerging nations were thus not just losers from strict global intellectual property enforcement.[74]

Conflicts between First and Third worlds hampered the Berne Union during the postwar era. During its meetings in Stockholm in 1967 and Paris in 1971, developing nations insisted on easier access, with special provisions for translations, terms of protection, reprinting of press articles, radio broadcasting, and educational use. The industrialized world resisted what it saw as a giveaway of authors' property and dug in its heels. Significant concessions were achieved on paper but boycotted in practice.[75] With such harsh conflicts the prospects for future reform within the Berne machinery appeared dim.[76] Instead, America hoped to win greater protection abroad through the World Intellectual Property Organization (WIPO), created in 1967 as one of the UN's specialized agencies.[77] During the 1970s and '80s the United States also brought unilateral trade pressure to bear on nations considered insufficiently respectful of such protections: Brazil, Korea, Singapore, but also Australia, Germany, and Italy.[78] When the WIPO also proved susceptible to pressure from developing nations in the early 1980s, the Americans shifted their energies to international agreements on trade to secure intellectual property rights.[79]

Hopes of greater global protection for its intellectual property exports finally prompted the United States to join the Berne Union in 1989, a century after its launch. As we have seen, America had resisted international copyright agreements throughout the nineteenth century. But in the twentieth century the advantages promised by membership in the first and biggest copyright union became irresistible. Outside of Berne America's moral and negotiating position was weak. It was embarrassing for the US to insist on higher standards for others than for itself, Secretary of Commerce Malcolm Baldrige testified in 1988. Joining Berne would help establish an international consensus on standards "and it would not be just the US trying to use some kind of a stick on some poor developing country which is what we hear all the time."[80] Berne membership was needed for the United States to stand firm in defense of global intellectual property protection, Ralph Oman, the register of copyrights, testified to Congress.[81] The shift in America's position from culture importer to exporter had certainly changed its attitude. A century earlier America had regarded Berne as a nefarious European club of cultural monopolists seeking to stifle a nascent democracy in its quest for enlightenment on the cheap.

YOKING COPYRIGHT TO TRADE

From 1993 on, Bill Clinton's administration pursued global protection. The US president had been elected with enthusiastic backing from the copyright industries. Hollywood, Nashville, New York, Redmond, and Palo Alto all hoped to fight piracy. Linking global intellectual property protection to trade was the strategy. Access to the United States—on most metrics still the world's single largest market—was the quid offered in return for a quo of strict protection for American products abroad.[82] The official ideology of "free trade" and "open markets" was tweaked to become "fair trade" and a "level playing field."

American negotiators aimed for global intellectual property enforcement in order to protect the US's most dynamic and promising export industries. Strong rights were the condition of open trade. By enforcing property rights abroad the perils to American competitiveness could be addressed without abandoning free trade.[83] As in the 1980s, when the copyright industries' growing importance had prompted the United States to join Berne, now too intellectual property's economic implications were the primary consideration. Over 8 percent of the US economy was tied up with information technology, having almost doubled over a decade. At stake, the House Committee on Commerce reported in 1998, was the crucial field of digital and electronic commerce, expected to increase a hundredfold over a few years.[84]

Much of the traditional US approach to copyright, with its formalities and other obstacles to exclusive rights and its generous view of fair use exceptions, had already been sacrificed to Berne membership. The Clinton administration now moved further toward an expansive view of intellectual property rights, demanding that copyright be retooled for the digital era to grant owners full and exclusive control of works in the new media. Trade regulation became the means of enforcing property rights in works.

The first breakthrough came in 1994, with the Trade Related Aspects of Intellectual Property Rights (TRIPs) agreement, negotiated at the end of the Uruguay round of the General Agreement on Tariffs and Trade (GATT). After the Uruguay round the GATT became administered by the World Trade Organization, starting in 1995. Services and intellectual property were now included for the first time in an international trade agreement. The TRIPs agreement covered a broad spectrum of intellectual property, from copyrights and patents through appellations of origin, industrial designs, and integrated circuit layouts, to new plant varieties. It swiftly catapulted into practice reforms that had only slowly been winding through the Berne machinery: protecting software and databases as literary works and giving authors rights to authorize rentals of films, sound recordings, and computer programs.

Most important, while Berne had provided no effective enforcement, TRIPs members could invoke the WTO's dispute settlement mechanism. Industrialized countries could thus retaliate against pirate nations with no intellectual property of their own to protect, levying sanctions on other products.[85] This was the tactic that a German Reichstag deputy had formulated pithily in 1906. "If we pay for your wheat," he fulminated at American pirates, "then you damn well have to pay for our literature."[86] What had been an empty threat then was now built into the global enforcement of trade. To underline the new trade-based emphasis on property rights, the United States also ensured that moral rights were excluded from the standards enforceable under TRIPs—lest America be punished for noncompliance.[87]

The 1994 TRIPs agreement was a major victory for the rich world's intellectual property exporting economies. The United States was the initiator and driving force behind negotiations. The Europeans, as so often, found it hard to arrive at a single position even though their economic interests, like those of the Japanese, clearly favored heightened global protection.[88]

AMERICA TAKES THE INITIATIVE IN GENEVA

Then, in 1996, came the WIPO's copyright treaty. The Clinton administration sought to act in tandem at home and abroad. A white paper laying out the government's goals was issued by a subgroup of the Information Infrastructure Taskforce, chaired by Bruce Lehman, a patent lawyer appointed assistant secretary of commerce. It defended authors' rights, seen primarily as property claims. The public interest, it argued, was not necessarily best served by easy access. Illustrating how European America was becoming, the white paper explicitly rejected the nineteenth century belief that the public good lay in cheap and widespread access to works. "While at first blush," it now lectured, "it may appear to be in the public interest to reduce the protection granted works and to allow unfettered use by the public, such an analysis is incomplete." Copyright protection should instead be bolstered to stimulate high-quality content.[89] As in Europe, the focus was slipping from the audience to center on authors and owners.

True, the white paper also argued that authorial rights should not be unduly strengthened. It might be technically possible to meter and charge for each digital use, it conceded. But fair use remained relevant. The goal was to fine-tune for technological changes so as to maintain the existing balance between author and audience in the digital era.[90] Fair use was to be transferred seamlessly into the new technologies.[91] Indeed, new fair uses for libraries and archives were proposed, as well as editions for the blind. The administration's stance on devices used to circumvent technical safeguards of digital content was also moderate. It sought to ban only those whose primary purpose was to sidestep protection.[92] The white paper's overall goals may thus not have been fire-breathing. But individual proposals shifted toward market principles. Compulsory licensing was dismissed as a way forward. New technologies, the paper speculated, would allow individual licensing at market rates. Ominously, libraries were told to expect curtailment of the very base of their lending, the first sale principle. Instead, they should explore institutional licenses, with fees per reader.[93] The Clinton administration firmly focused on rights holders' prerogatives. It explicitly rejected any idea that copyright owners should be "taxed" or otherwise forfeit their claims to ensure widespread access for the public.[94]

Clinton's proposals proved controversial in America. Critics highlighted problems like the white paper's proposed liability for phone and internet companies if every copy made in computer memory of a digital work traversing the web was considered infringing. Bills to implement the government's objectives stalled for the moment in Congress.[95] Stymied, the administration shifted its attentions to the WIPO, seeking to win abroad what was denied at home.[96] In Geneva the United States then presented a property-based vision of how to extend owners' control over digital works, minimizing exceptions to exclusive rights and making licensed and other paid uses the standard mode of access.

To this end the Clinton administration encouraged the WIPO to adopt a number of points: (1) to include digital transmission as part of the author's exclusive right of distributing works; (2) to declare as infringing even the temporary copies of works that are inherently created in computer memory as they pass across the internet, thus giving rights owners full control of transmitted works; (3) to make internet providers liable for works transmitted, thus requiring them to police the web; (4) to limit exceptions like fair use, especially if licensing was possible; (5) to punish manufacture and sale of technologies used to circumvent technical safeguards that prevented consumers from accessing and copying copyrighted materials; (6) to ensure that digital rights management information was attached to works (electronic tattooing) so that owners could track, control, and charge for use. In short, digital works were to be fully under the control of their owners, who were to be paid for any and every use.

The most drastic of the Clinton administration's proposals were cut down to size during negotiations. But the final outcome in the WIPO Copyright Treaty of 1996 gave voice to the emergent, Berne-based, Euro-American consensus that intellectual property was much like conventional property, that owners deserved strong protection, and that exceptions to exclusive authorial rights should be strictly limited. The WIPO treaty sought to preserve owners' claims even in the fluid digital era. It defended their right to control works transmitted via the internet, which was gnomically described as "in such a way that members of the public may access these works from a place and at a time individually chosen by them." It required member nations to punish circumvention of protective technologies and demanded that they safeguard digital rights management information.[97]

Nonetheless, the WIPO treaty tempered the maximalist starting position in at least two ways. Disagreement marred discussion of how to deal with the temporary copies of works that are generated in computer memory during internet transmission. Though the Clinton administration had proposed to keep these firmly under rights holders' control, in fact the American negotiators in Geneva shied away from so drastic a shoring-up of the owners' position. Likewise, internet, telecom, and high tech companies were fearful of being held liable for infringement as works traversed their infrastructure.[98] In the absence of any consensus, a diplomatic waffle in the treaty reaffirmed Berne's reproduction right as fully applicable in the digital age. WIPO thus hewed to the already existing Berne position that guaranteed authors protection against unauthorized reproduction "in any manner or form."[99]

The original draft had also banned devices whose primary purpose was to circumvent technologies that blocked access to copyrighted works.[100] Since this would have allowed protective technologies to hinder all unauthorized uses, whether infringing or legal, it was controversial. A vaguer version emerged instead that committed members only to effective legal measures against circumvention.[101]

REIMPORTING THE DISPUTE

With the WIPO treaty the new international norm as of 1996, the Clinton administration shifted its attention back home. The outcome in domestic legislation was the Digital Millennium Copyright Act (DMCA) of 1998. This implemented the WIPO treaty, but also pushed beyond it to set an intended gold standard for other nations.[102] The cluster of copyright regulations from TRIPs to the DMCA has been attacked in America as in thrall to commerce and as departing from native copyright traditions.[103] Almost no one has had praise for the DMCA. Verbose, imprecise, and yet overly detailed, complicated, and opaque, it was a law whose reading one would not inflict on an enemy.[104] Even by the standards of copyright legislation, it was highly technical, dealing with matters from copies made incidentally during computer repairs to boat hull designs. The following discussion necessarily involves technical detail. But the overall point to keep in mind is that, even in the minutiae of the precise legislative wording, the battle fought was between rights holders seeking to enforce their claims in the digital age and the champions of the audience and its hopes for at least as much access as it had enjoyed in the analog era.

The WIPO treaty had been vague on the technologies that protected copyrighted digital works. Now the United States threatened to go further.[105] The DMCA initially forbade any unauthorized use of protected works, including fair use.[106] The bill prohibited both violating copyright and the act of circumventing the technical protection of digital content—something like using particular software to transfer a film from a DVD to a computer's hard disk. The legal powers that copyright already granted to owners were thus to be beefed up by an additional layer of technological controls. Critics dubbed this "paracopyright." Defenders likened them to antishoplifting devices in stores. Physical property was protected not just by laws against stealing but also by tangible security—locks, bars, alarms, guards—as well as by laws (against breaking and entering) that prohibited their circumvention. The DMCA now promised intangible property the same panoply of protection.[107]

But critics worried lest control technologies combine with new legal powers of enforcement to create a "pay-per-view" world.[108] One congressman defined that as where "the use of a library card always carries a fee and where the flow of information comes with a meter that rings up a charge every time the internet is accessed."[109] In the future, when all works were digital and transmitted via the web, the technical ability to prevent access and copying would effectively supplant copyright. Owners would then exert complete control, unmitigated by the usual limitations on copyright—fair use, first sale, the idea/expression dichotomy—or even by the inevitable leakiness of the old hard-copy and analog worlds.[110] Control could be directly enforced by the technologies of transmission (an e-book read only so many times, say, and not copied at all). The legal system's inherent wiggle room threatened to shrink. A transgressor being caught, arraigned, awaiting the court's judgment, deciding whether punishment was a price worth paying for the advantages of his crime: all such buffers between what the law prescribed and what it actually implemented collapsed when computer code, and no longer the legal code, did the enforcing.[111] And unlike copyright, technological barriers never expired. The public law of copyright would be supplanted by the private law of shrink- and click-wrap contracts, with sales conditions imposed unilaterally by vendors on their digital consumers.[112] In effect, critics charged, the Clinton administration sought to reintroduce the monopoly that the London Stationers' Company had enjoyed on printing books until the Statute of Anne ended it in 1710.[113]

And yet America's traditional emphasis on the public domain had not entirely vanished. Congressmen still pondered how to balance between "the interests of content creators and information users." Ensuring that fair use remained a cornerstone was crucial, one of the bill's shepherds, Thomas Bliley, insisted, since owners were being given new controls. Copyright, he continued, "is not just about protecting information. It's just as much about affording reasonable access to it."[114] Congressman John Dingell feared that the technological protection granted works was too hermetic, depriving all who could not afford commercial rates. That might sound like the American way, he conceded, but there was another side to the story. American copyright law had historically carved out important exceptions to owners' exclusive rights. This balance had to be maintained.[115]

The Clinton administration's initial proposals sought to ban both the manufacture and use of circumvention devices, thus leaving rights owners in full control of their works. But after protests in the House Committee on Commerce that the bill overly favored copyright holders, changes followed.[116] The Judiciary Committee's version had flatly prohibited all circumventing of technological protection. The Commerce Committee now rejected this. Indiscriminate protective technologies might block even lawful access.[117] To cover students, library patrons, journalists, and the like, it excepted users who had gained legitimate access.[118] The final version drew a complicated but important distinction between circumventing protective technologies that governed *access* to copyrighted works and those that prevented their *copying*. For access, circumvention remained illegal. No one could gain access to digital works except as rights holders permitted, any more than they could see a movie in a theater without buying a ticket. Circumventing to copy, in contrast, remained legal in some instances—for fair use, for example. Once having gained access, in other words, users could exercise rights to copy, like fair use quotation, even if they had to circumvent protective technologies to do so.

Congress also emphasized the continued validity of fair use for digital media. The initial bill had not mentioned fair use. But Congressmen Howard Coble and Barney Frank sought to enhance exceptions, including ones for libraries.[119] The new anticircumvention technologies, they insisted, must not restrict established exceptions to authors' exclusive rights.[120] And yet nothing in the final law directly concerned fair use. Though it remained in effect, it did not apply to circumventing protective technologies. Instead, the law instituted a triannual review by the librarian of Congress to hear from groups that claimed to have been excluded from fair use by overly restrictive practices. The librarian could then permit circumvention for certain uses three years at a time. This he eventually did for constituencies like film professors and documentary film makers, who sought greater ability to use digital content.[121]

In its final version the DMCA struck a series of compromises. It forbade users from circumventing protective technologies to access digital content. It left in place existing copyright exemptions, including fair use, and added new ones for law enforcement, reverse engineering (to ensure the interoperability of computer programs), and encryption research. Nonprofit educational institutions and libraries were permitted to circumvent protective technologies while accessing works to determine whether to buy them. They were allowed to make and keep digital copies of endangered materials and exempted from paying damages if their employees innocently infringed. The law prohibited removing digital rights management information. But most important, as a concession to computer and web interests, the so-called "safe harbor" provision exempted internet providers from liability if their systems were used to transmit infringing material, so long as they responded to rights owners' demands to remove it. After lengthy battles that allowed skeptics to prune back some of the administration's excess, the DMCA thus emerged as a moderated version of the maximalist agenda that the Clinton administration had originally taken to Geneva.

The administration portrayed the DMCA as taking copyright's traditional balance between users and owners and neutrally extending it into the digital era. But few were satisfied. Digital works were now protected not only by the usual copyright laws but also by new protective technologies, as well as the legal muscle that forbade their circumvention.[122] The pay-per-use world loomed ever closer. Fair use, critics charged, was being squeezed by technological protections outside of copyright law itself. Fair use, defenders countered, could be achieved by other means: copying a text by hand from a screen or videotaping images from a monitor. No one was promised fair use by the most up-to-date methods. Arguments revolved as much around convenience as the sheer physical ability legitimately to make use of content.[123] "Fair use," in the astringent words of the Second Circuit Court of Appeals in 2001, "has never been held to be a guarantee of access to copyrighted material in order to copy it by the fair user's preferred technique or in the format of the original."[124] Though this undeniably preserved a residual form of fair use, there was still reason to object. The rising tide of technology lifts everyone's boat. If all citizens were entitled to universal goods, they also deserved broadly the same level of quality. Though doubtless cheaper, it would hardly be adequate today to promise health care for all at the standard of, say, 1970. To offer fair use access with paper and pencil in the era of digital cut-and-paste reflected a united-but-unequal logic.

The DMCA outlawed the manufacture, sale, and use of circumvention technologies in order to *access* works. But in order to allow circumvention for protected uses, it banned only their manufacture and sale but not their use, for *copying* works. Copying a technologically protected work was thus not criminalized in itself, though—depending on why the work was copied—it might of course infringe and thus be actionable. This allowed rights holders to control access to digital works while not letting them block fair use or other permitted copying of legitimately acquired works.[125] That seemed like a concession to traditional copyright ideas of fair use. However, because trafficking in—though not use of—copying technologies was also forbidden, only users able to write their own circumvention programs could legally use them.[126] What was offered with one hand was thus withdrawn by the other.

Yet the safe-harbor exemption allowed even infringing content to be posted online until its owners protested. This opened a large loophole in rights holders' hopes of controlling works on the web. In retrospect, this was among the DMCA's most important decisions. Already then, in 1998, it signaled the coming power of the internet industrial complex that would burst into public view fifteen years later. So long as they removed infringing material once notified of its presence, internet providers were not liable for hosting it. Companies like Google and YouTube could thus host any content, copyrighted or not, while the policing function remained the duty of rights owners.

The sharp disputes unleashed by the DMCA showed that the copyright consensus of the analog era had come undone. Digitality had changed the playing field. Most vexing was the need—created by digitality's ease of reproduction—to beef up existing legal copyright protections with new technological measures. As during the nineteenth-century debates over international copyright, the gloves were off again. Many of the arguments were similar. But new actors from the internet and high tech sectors had in the meantime appeared on the scene—whom we will discuss below.

THE INTERESTS REGROUP

The property-based understanding of authors' rights that came to dominate at the end of the twentieth century was advocated at home and abroad by the recently converted American authorities. Emphasizing authors' and assignees' inherent claims to works, the new view approximated the European natural rights model. To undergird copyright's practical shift in favor of rights holders, a new ideology was needed, justifying long and strong protection. Economics had flourished as a discipline in postwar America.[127] A new approach to intellectual property in this period, the so-called "law and economics" school, allowed the queen of the social sciences to formulate a theory that claimed to harness heightened protection to the public interest.

In the Continental ideology the author deserved a stake in his works much like all owners of property. The public good was a concern only insofar as securing property averted anarchy. Rewarding the author might, of course, indirectly stimulate his creativity. But the natural rights argument did not take such stimulus as its primary goal. It was merely an incidental effect. The author deserved the fruits of his labor tout court. If rewarding him lavishly meant that he retired instead, then so be it. The public goods that derived from the natural rights argument were tangential to the primarily private goods it sought.

Even while justifying thick protection on the European model, the law and economics school sought to push beyond such fundamentally private goals. The motives were not the demands of justice, alleged by European natural rights. Instead, it presented an economic calculus of how best to stimulate the author's creativity and thereby promote the public interest.[128] Strong property rights were intended as an incentive not a reward. Insisting on its merely statutory basis and its social utility, Anglo-American copyright had traditionally provided only the minimum reward thought necessary to stimulate creativity. Now the argument shifted. Strong protection was believed to promote creativity, allocate resources, and reward efforts efficiently. Not by depriving the author of his property rights, but by fulfilling them, would the market deliver the highest private benefit as well as the greatest public outcome. In the law and economics approach, copyright served not—as in the traditional American view—merely to incentivize authors. In some formulations it also sent market signals via the price mechanism, indicating which works to exploit and how best to do so.[129]

This new take on copyright was, of course, part of the broader neoconservative shift of the 1970s and '80s across many fields. Restricting authors' claims on behalf of the public served little purpose in this view. Term durations should be increased, not limited. Baroquely, the one argument where even Europeans hesitated, and that was constitutionally ruled out in the United States, was now housebroken by some of these new masters of market logic. They advocated copyright in perpetuity—or at least renewing it as long as the work retained market value. Yet, if continuous terms were limited by high renewal fees and the initial term shortened, the overall average length of copyright might actually diminish.[130] Stronger controls, in other words, yet less actual lock-up of works. Fair use was no longer seen as a safety valve, allowing the public legitimate access, but as a means to sidestep prohibitive transaction costs.[131] With digital technologies, however, each use could be tracked and costs contained. Market pricing could therefore replace fair use. Once an answer to market failure, compulsory licensing could now also be replaced by precise measuring and charging for individual use.[132]

Yet even this new economistic ideology of strong authorial property rights did not cast off copyright's heritage of concern for the public interest. The Anglo-American emphasis on the public domain continued, now harnessed to the logic of the market rather than contradicting it. Royalties were not considered reward for past work, as in a standard property rights view, but as stimulus to promote future creativity.[133] Incentive remained the goal, even though the payoff might be more than the minimum required in the traditional approach. In *Eldred*, the 2003 case that tested the constitutionality of retrospectively extending copyright terms (see chapter 6), Justice Ruth Bader Ginsburg seemed influenced by this logic. Public and private goals were fully compatible, she insisted. "The two ends are not mutually exclusive; copyright law serves public ends by providing individuals with an *incentive* to pursue private ones."[134] Her focus on incentive kept the public interest firmly in the foreground.

The extent to which the new American discourse remained indebted to traditional utilitarianism can be gauged by the European reaction. Anglo-Saxon discourse still assumed that, to be justified, property also had to serve the public good. While the European natural rights approach regarded ownership as inherently deserving its rewards, in the Anglophone view property and the public interest had to be reconciled. This concern for the public—even as it justified stronger protection for rights holders—made the law and economics approach suspect in European eyes.[135] What surprised Europeans was the argument that private advantage could also provide for the public interest.[136] The increasingly economistic view of authors' rights has so lowered our defenses against the utilitarian approach, one Swiss commentator tellingly remarked of such new arguments, "that the idea of authors' rights being protected in the interests of the public good is now considered positively."[137]

For the Europeans, this was a win-win outcome. Insofar as they paid attention to such law and economics arguments, they could marry their traditional concern for rewarding authors to a claim that this served the public interest too. But for the Anglophones the law and economics school testified to the difficulties of reconciling traditional copyright with property rights traded on the market. Property and the public good still needed to be balanced against each other. The new economistic ideology might be tilted in favor of the author. But it remained deeply colored by the traditional copyright exercise of weighing interests. Seeking to square circles, the law and economics school claimed that public and private could be harmoniously strengthened together. This insistence on reconciling what in the Anglophone view were conventionally regarded as opposites both placed the new approach firmly in the copyright tradition (with its focus on the public domain as the ultimate good) *and* explained the resistance it provoked (through the claim that the market was the way to achieve this goal).

CIVIL WAR IN CALIFORNIA

In the nineteenth century America had been in much the same position as today's developing nations during the TRIPs negotiations—insistent that copyright protection was as much an instrument of public policy as a property right.[138] Besides the sea change in perspective that followed its shift from importer to exporter, the American volte-face is often attributed to the imperialism of Disney—the influence of its copyright industries and their demands for long and strong protection.[139] Doubtless the content sector and its political clout in Washington spurred the US government's conversion to European norms. With a rising trade deficit in the 1970s and '80s and freer global trade ushered in by the new GATT round and the North American Free Trade Agreement, the American authorities were eager to support those industries able to compete abroad.

But in a longer historical perspective that is too simple a story. However tempting a villain, it was not just Disney and its hopes of forever exploiting its adorable rodent that swung the authorities around. Mobilizing international regulation to protect intellectual property demonstrated Hollywood's influence as it collaborated with European and Japanese colleagues.[140] But there was more. Though the content industries favored long and strong protection, other powerful and corporate interests did not. As in the nineteenth century, disseminators disagreed amongst themselves. Back then, reprint publishers had crossed swords with colleagues specializing in American authors. At the cusp of the century, player-piano manufacturers had stolen a march on sheet-music publishers. Now Hollywood and Silicon Valley were at odds. Corporations were not pitted monolithically against the public. Rather, one set of corporate interests faced other, competing ones. Internet and high tech companies managed to align their goals with consumers, scaling the tactical heights of public spiritedness. The content industries, in contrast, were dismal public relations failures. But who won what battles and when and why?

New technologies made for new bedfellows. Predictably, libraries, schools, universities, and research institutes promoted a more expansive public domain. Consumer advocates joined in too, and grassroots open access movements sprang up. Some digital interests also participated: home electronics manufacturers, some software firms, and especially the telecom, internet, and web media companies that would emerge as major players early in the new millennium.[141] That some industrial sectors aligned with public domain advocates was hardly new. During the early 1960s German manufacturers of photocopiers and tape recorders had opposed restricting private copying. If users were forbidden to make recordings, they worried, consumer electronics would never take off.[142] During the early 1980s American video recorder manufacturers banded together with video rental outlets to defeat Hollywood's campaigns for rental rights in videos and levies on recorders and blank tapes.[143] In 1984 the Betamax case, mentioned above, handed Sony and other manufacturers of videotaping devices a major victory, allowing recording of television broadcasts for later viewing (time shifting) and thus legalizing the recorders despite their ability to infringe on television content.[144] Now the computer and software industries, together with the telecom and internet companies, assumed the job of being Hollywood's nemesis.

During negotiations for the WIPO treaty, computer and internet companies resisted proposals to require authorization for every temporary copy that computer memories might hold. They feared being held liable for infringing material they could not control, simply by providing the hardware for its journeys.[145] Silicon Valley firms also worried that too-restrictive anticircumvention regulations, insisted on by the content industries to prevent unauthorized use of their works, threatened their ability to reverse-engineer, test computer security, and do encryption research.[146] Computer companies wanted to keep their devices general-purpose consumer items, unencumbered by the content industries' protective technologies. Suppliers of such technologies naturally disagreed. But mostly, the high tech sector favored the unimpeded flow of content through the internet. Already in 1981 the Consumer Electronics Association had funded a pretend consumer rights organization, the Home Recording Rights Coalition. A quarter century later, in 2007, it sponsored a Digital Freedom Campaign, again to mobilize public opinion in its favor.[147] Google and other internet companies supported nonprofits to battle current copyright laws, like Creative Commons. Often thought of as underdogs to the film and music industries, Silicon Valley corporations actually spent even more money lobbying in Washington.[148]

As Silicon Valley overtook Hollywood and the music industry in economic importance, American corporate interests realigned.[149] In 2007 the industries dependent on fair use—everything from Amazon to fiber optics via computers, photocopying, and finance—tabulated (however generously) their contribution to American GDP at 16 percent and growing.[150] Unlike the old big media, these new consumer companies did not necessarily want technology to clamp down on piracy. As in the eighteenth-century savvy businessmen knew better than to lobby for their own unvarnished self-interest. They donned the rhetorical vestments of principle. The computer and internet sectors cleverly seized the moral high ground of open access and free-flowing information. Silicon Valley presented its position as broadly synonymous with the public interest.

By contrast, the copyright industries thumped the tub of property rights. Three hundred years earlier, during the Battle of the Booksellers, publishers had argued for the author's natural property rights, expecting to reap the benefits by assignment. Now Hollywood applied much the same argument and tactics.[151] Authors' rights needed protection! Digital technologies created the illusion that downloading hurt no one. But violating intellectual property rights was theft—and so forth and so on. The film and music industries hoped to convince the audience of the rightness of their cause through annoying film and DVD trailers that warned in dire tones against downloading and copying. The content owners hoped to catch them young by developing intellectual property awareness curricula for grade and high schools, but—hopelessly gauche—these commonly had all the street savvy of a Planned Parenthood blitz on safe sex.

Thanks to Silicon Valley's lobbying, the 1998 DMCA did not bar devices—like personal computers—that could illegally download or copy works so long as they could also be used for legitimate purposes, what lawyers called "significant noninfringing uses." This confirmed the 1984 Betamax decision where video recorder manufacturers had dodged liability for users taping television programs.[152] The movie studios had then feared that Sony's devices would bleed them dry. But not only did the Betamax standard die out a few years later, sales of recorded videotapes and then DVDs went on to trump ticket sales on the film industry's balance sheets. In 2001 the peer-to-peer downloading site Napster defended itself with a Betamax-style argument—that its technology, too, had noninfringing uses. This time the US courts were less persuaded. Napster did have legitimate uses, like downloading works in the public domain. But, unlike Sony's videotaping machines, the court reasoned, Napster could distinguish between authorized uses and piracy. It was therefore banned in its first incarnation.[153]

A more ambivalent decision followed in 2005 with another case against a downloading site, *Grokster*.[154] Though distributed peer to peer, Napster had channeled content through a central instance under the company's control. Grokster, in contrast, merely provided the downloading software so users could swap files directly with each other, thus seeming to keep its hands clean. Letting the Betamax decision stand, the Supreme Court did not rule on peer-to-peer technologies as such. But, with its download streams awash in copyrighted material, Grokster could scarcely portray its clients' activities as private copying for noncompeting uses. Though its potentially infringing technologies were left untouched, the court held Grokster liable for a new crime of inducing customers to commit infringement.[155] And yet, despite its best efforts to enforce exclusive rights, the music industry did not walk away with a clear victory in either case.

Broadly speaking, the battle over the DMCA pitted Hollywood against Silicon Valley, content providers against content distributors. However bohemian the pose affected by the dot-com sector, it was one set of corporate interests against another. Southern California battled middle California. Did big media win as the DMCA imposed stringent anticircumvention provisions on the use of content? Or did the software, electronics, and internet interests get their way with generous safe-harbor provisions, permitting them to transmit content without policing infringement? It all depends. With corporate interests locked in battle, both arguments have been advanced with equal conviction.[156] But to declare a winner already now would be premature. What we can say is that the outcome so far has been as much an uneasy compromise between two powerful economic actors, both with pull in Washington, as a resolution of tensions between corporate and public interests. Silicon Valley portrayed itself as siding with the angels of free access. The content industries were routinely branded as greedy, swollen leeches. But that testified more to savvy tactics than to a difference in principle.

When they extolled expansive access to content, the telecom and computer companies pursued their own corporate interests no less resolutely than Hollywood. Like newspapers, the fair use industries depended on content to attract an audience and generate revenue. But their money was made in different ways. While internet and technology companies distributed content—copyrighted or otherwise—they earned their keep from advertising posted against it (Google, Yahoo, Facebook) or from the gadgets that handled the media (Apple, Amazon). Content flowed through the pipes organized by Google and powered by Intel, and it was increasingly fed from sources abroad and beyond the control of national governments. The logic of networks dictated that as more participants joined, the value added by the activity grew even faster. The more consumers were lured in by promises of cheap or free content, the higher the price advertisers paid per eyeball.[157] Free content was the loss leader that tempted paying customers through the door.

Arguably, the content industry's nagging insistence on protective technologies and legal backup testified less to strength than impotence, as it watched its product siphoned off into the maw of the internet.[158] Certainly the music business faced a seemingly unstoppable hemorrhaging of content through the web. Yet, even there, having fallen 40 percent from its peak in 1999, it grew for the first time in 2012, slowly accumulating digital pennies to replace its lost analog dollars.[159] Commercial publishing, newspapers, and film in turn appeared better able to control and charge for their product. The paper-based media's audience had not yet made the transition wholly to the digital and were not born downloaders. Film retained some of the analog media's advantages even in the digital era and remained simply too bothersome for effortless downloading. Meanwhile, other enterprises seemed to be radiantly prospering in the new environment. Gaming was mushrooming: twice the size of recorded music, three-fifths the size of film. Not bad for an industry that had barely existed two decades earlier![160] Similarly lucrative was the scientific publishing industry. Elsevier, Wiley, Springer, and other such firms pursued a notorious rent-seeking boondoggle where a few monopolistic players made net profit margins of 30 or 40 percent by usuriously selling back to the universities works that taxpayers and philanthropists had already once paid to create, review, and edit.[161]

At this writing the most recent round of the American copyright wars has been the Stop Online Piracy Act (SOPA), debated in the House during the winter of 2011–12, and its companion Senate bill, the Protect Intellectual Property Act (PIPA). Aiming to clamp down on internet pirates abroad, these acts would have cut off Americans' access to infringing foreign websites by imposing controls on intermediaries. Credit card firms and other payment mechanisms would have been forbidden to channel funds to pirate sites. Search engines would have been required to take down links, and domain names would have been blocked. This revived the solution the DMCA had sought in vain by making internet providers, not copyright owners, police content on the web. Once again, as during the disputes over the DMCA, the content industries, especially film and music, battled an alliance of public access activists and the technology and internet sectors. This time the opposition was vociferous, and the Obama administration was less beholden to big media than Clinton's had been. When the administration failed to support the bills wholeheartedly, Rupert Murdoch, megaphone of the media interests, accused the president of having "thrown in his lot with Silicon Valley paymasters who threaten all software creators with piracy, plain thievery."[162]

The tech industry claimed that suppressing rogue sites threatened to introduce Chinese- or Iranian-style internet regulation and censorship. However exaggerated, such rhetoric struck a nerve in Washington, and the Obama administration withdrew its support of the bills. Whatever threat piracy posed, it was not prepared to agree to a law that "reduces freedom of expression … or undermines the dynamic, innovative global Internet."[163] Using social networks and chat rooms, high tech and open access interests mobilized unprecedented protest. So far, Wikipedia is the consummate product of a wide-open internet of free exchange and open access. Its achievement is all the more remarkable considering that its contributors are largely shut out of the mass of academic research, which—though digitized—remains paywalled within the ivory tower. In solidarity with the protesters, this crown jewel of the internet shut down for a day on 18 January 2012. As the scale and extent of opposition to the bills became apparent, the political tide turned, and several of the bills' sponsors backed off. Though consummate Washington insiders, the content industries still lost. They were left to ponder how they might prevail against opponents who, astraddle the social networks, could generate emails to politicians on a spammer's scale. Commentators spoke of the political coming-of-age for the technology sector.[164]

VOX POPULI

Alongside Silicon Valley's interests in the free-access agenda, a powerful grassroots consumer movement also sprang up on behalf of the public domain. In the nineteenth century no one, other than politicians, had spoken for the audience—except as the reprinting publishers made common cause with their book-buying public.[165] A century later consumers were no longer to be trifled with. Movements to organize their vast—though shallow and diffuse—common interests had arisen in many realms, the digital among them.[166] In the late twentieth century, libraries, colleges, and research institutions had also become major players in their own right. Universities were among the most competitive American products globally. The federally funded US research establishment was by far the largest worldwide, with serious political heft in Washington. Its biomedical research underpinned large, prosperous, and growing industries.[167] Software emerged from a huge, intertwined complex of university, governmental, and corporate interests.

On copyright, the research establishment's political muscle had been felt already in 1973 when the National Library of Medicine was allowed to continue its massive photocopying of articles from scientific periodicals for researchers.[168] The 1976 Copyright Act followed up by codifying fair use in statute, specifically including copying for research. At times the concern of the university and government research world for accessible information was seconded by corporations. In the *Texaco* case of 1994, a major company failed in its grab for a free ride on the scholarly world's fair use exemption, hoping to supply its scientists with the latest research findings without the expense of journal subscriptions.[169]

Beyond libraries and universities lay the grassroots open access movement—a wildfire of popular opposition, nourished by belief in the common good, defiant of the ideology of intellectual property, spread via the web, and whipped to combustion by the copyright industries' overreaching claims. Political scientists remind us that the diffuse and tepid interests in public goods, where many stand to gain only a little, are rarely as organized and effective as the defense of well-defined economic stakes.[170] When, in 1839, the Chamber of Peers of the July Monarchy weighed the choice between term durations of twenty and fifty years, the duc de Broglie pointed out that, though they were considering the equally important claims of authors and public domain, one of these interests was much louder than the other. "Though men of letters are few, compared to the public they have all the trumpets of renown. They make themselves better heard than the public, which is patient and accepts everything. Precisely because it does not speak as volubly, you should pay attention to its concerns."[171]

Now, nearly two centuries later, the public finally did speak loudly. As we have seen, during the debates surrounding the Sonny Bono Act, TRIPs agreement, WIPO treaty, and the DMCA, advocates of traditional American copyright values opposed the thickening and lengthening of protection and, more generally, the harmonizing of US policy with Berne and the EU.[172] Putting forth its white paper and draft bills in 1995, the Clinton administration genuinely seems to have believed that it was neutrally adjusting copyright law to the digital age while maintaining the inherited balance between owners and users. Its spokesmen—Assistant Secretary Lehman and Mary-beth Peters, the register of copyrights—both testified that this was only a minor technical adjustment to keep up with the times. Both seemed nonplussed by the critical reactions they provoked.[173]

Around this time, in 1995, the grassroots movement against the Clinton administration's departure from native traditions first appeared on the American authorities' radar. A law professor, Peter Jaszi, brought together opponents of the Clinton white paper in Washington to form the Digital Future Coalition.[174] In a *Washington Times* op-ed another law professor, James Boyle, warned of the radical changes proposed: outlawing reading documents online, making internet providers police surfing, and cutting off those too poor to pay licensing fees from the web's cornucopia.[175] Secretary Lehman brushed Boyle aside as failing to understand the administration's proposals.[176] But he underestimated the popular resonance of Boyle's views. During passage of the DMCA, the Digital Future Coalition and other such groups lobbied hard for the public interest.

The copyright industries were taken by surprise, having apparently expected to push through broad anticircumvention measures with little notice.[177] The United States now proposed to align itself with Berne and even to go beyond what the international treaties required. No wonder that protesters saw themselves as conservatives, seeking to preserve American traditions. No more protection than necessary, they argued, should be granted to stimulate creativity.[178] What would happen to traditional exemptions, like fair use, and to free speech if European-style moral rights were enforced? What if the integrity right gave authors powers to prevent parodies?[179] History was marshaled to argue that a nefarious alliance of Europeans and Hollywood was conspiring to lead America astray from the founding fathers' vision of the public sphere and enlightenment for the common man. Founded as a pirate nation, America should return to its native tradition of emphasizing access over ownership.[180]

Resistance mounted in the legislature and courts. Chagrinned at the DMCA's anticircumvention provisions, some policymakers sought to unravel what had been wrought. Along with others, Representative Rick Boucher began an almost annual ritual of introducing bills to pull the DMCA's anticircumvention teeth and to relax strictures on users' rights.[181] Other congressmen introduced reforms to implement what they claimed had been the DMCA's original purpose. Congress, they argued, had intended to preserve the inherited balance between rights holders and users. But the law hindered lawful fair use. The time had therefore come "to restore the traditional balance between copyright holders and society." Copyright laws should "prevent and punish digital pirates without treating every consumer as one."[182] Bills to enhance the public domain by freeing up orphaned works—out of print but still in copyright—made regular appearances.[183] In search of the perfect acronym, the Benefit Authors without Limiting Advancement or Net Consumer Expectations (BALANCE) Act was introduced in 2003. In return, the copyright industries countered with the Intellectual Property Protection Act of 2006.[184] The battle continued.

FRUITS OF EUROPEAN VICTORY

In converting to thick protection, the Clinton administration was not alone. Despite America's missionary zeal during the GATT, TRIPs, and WIPO negotiations, the door it pushed against stood open. As the single-largest monolingual developed market, the US bested the EU in the network advantages that internet-based enterprises thrived on.[185] But the American economy was not markedly more reliant on intellectual property than Europe.[186] And European corporations, along with the Japanese, were as concerned as the Americans to avoid piracy.[187] During the GATT negotiations the Europeans and Japanese had agreed with the Americans in strengthening intellectual property protection globally, though they differed on tactics.[188] Content businesses across the industrialized world varied less in what they wanted—thick protection—than in how they organized themselves and influenced their governments. Some, like the French, had close relations to the state cultural authorities, depending on them for subsidies and trade barriers. Others, like the British, thrived in a freer, American-style market.[189]

Despite taking the initiative in the trade negotiations of the 1990s, however, America could not ram just anything down its partners' throats. Though the EU itself was not formally a member of the GATT, by speaking through its commission with one voice on foreign trade issues, it could match bargaining clout with the United States.[190] Negotiations were very much a two-way street. During the WIPO discussions, for example, the Europeans insisted on granting audiovisual performers extensive rights, while the Americans, with their film industry's well-functioning contractual labor relations, vainly resisted change.[191] Digging in their heels, the Europeans also managed to protect culture from the GATT's free-trading strictures. They kept their rules on domestic broadcast content and their cinema taxes, used to finance local film industries. Canada, too, had resisted US pressure and exempted its culture producers from the North American free trade agreements of the 1990s.[192] Thus, the French exulted, was the "American Goliath" vanquished.[193]

Nor did the initiatives run in only one direction. The Europeans too exerted their political strength, holdin[g] [Amer]ica's feet to the fire. The United States was the first country t[o] [ ] the formal dispute settlement measures it had be[ ] [ ]king part of the TRIPs agreement.[194] The "h[ ] [ ]e US 1976 Copyright Act allowed small sh[ ] [ ]o play the radio to their customers witho[ ] [ ]ry time Edith Piaf belted out a number o[ ] [ ]c Bar in Tupelo, Mississippi, a European [ ] [ ]-changed. When this exemption was expanded in [ ] [ ]led the US before the WTO and had it fined.[195] The Europea[ ] [ ] successfully lobbied to have the TRIPs agreement give rights holders the power to authorize rentals of all works. The developing world (excluding India, wagged by its Bollywood tail) opposed such rental rights, and the United States resisted for film.[196] America also bowed to European imperatives when—as discussed in the previous chapter—it was finally shamed into enforcing Berne's requirement that works remain protected as long as held true in their country of origin, thus bringing public domain works back under copyright once Europe had extended terms to seventy years.[197]

True, the United States was the single largest exporter of intellectual property and the place where, as one European observer saw it, "the main right holders of the world reside."[198] But that was a matter of sheer bulk. In per capita terms or as a percentage of GDP, the intellectual property intensities of the West European and North American economies were roughly similar—although, thanks to the EU's self-hobbling in fields like genetically modified organisms and patentable animal and plant varieties, much European-financed research had moved offshore.[199] That gave the Europeans largely the same interest in firming up intellectual property rights as the Americans. In 2000 the Lisbon Agenda spelled out the EU's economic development strategy for the coming decade, including the intention of becoming the world's "most dynamic knowledge-based economy." Though failing to meet its own benchmarks, the EU's ambitions firmly positioned it alongside the US in the fight against global piracy. Its prowess in luxury brands equally gave Europe a stake in preventing counterfeiting. And while Mickey Mouse may have been the world's most widely recognized literary character, Tintin, the Belgian boy sleuth, was no slouch either, with 135 million volumes in forty-five languages. His merchandizing was equally vulnerable to rip-off.[200] Like the Americans, the Europeans hoped to ride the dynamic economic growth promised by the new intellectual property-based industries.[201] Facing the need to harmonize their fragmented markets, they were keenly aware of the competition they could expect from linguistically uniform and more integrated America.[202]

In sum, America was not the only mover behind ever stronger property rights. However much Washington had swaggered during international negotiations, Brussels was a contender in the same class. Starting in the 1980s, the EU had begun to call the European tune on intellectual property, issuing a steady stream of directives to member nations and deftly shaping the continent's stance. Brussels's increasing authority directly challenged the WIPO and especially Berne.[203] In particular, the EU's largely free-market attitude cut against some members' more dirigiste assumptions in cultural matters, France especially.[204] And the EU's need to represent not just the grand *Kulturnationen* but also the small and Anglophonically attuned Scandinavian countries, as well as the Netherlands, whose copyright attitudes tended toward the Anglo-Saxon, meant that France and Germany no longer enjoyed their accustomed heft without challenge.

More important, what the Americans had now signed up for was, broadly speaking, the traditional Continental position. Insofar as the two camps—copyright and authors' rights—were approximating each other, the Americans moved more in Europe's direction than vice versa. The now dominant First World consensus held that works were property and deserved thick protection. This position was more of a change for the Americans (and to a lesser extent for the British) than for the Continentals. Hardly surprising, then, that in the debates of the 1990s, Europe approximated the maximalist stance that the Clinton administration had brought to the WIPO negotiations. Intellectual property, the EU declared flatly in 2000, has "been recognized as an integral part of property."[205] Its protection was sanctified directly in the EU Constitution that then failed to be ratified in 2005.[206] Intellectual property, French President Nicolas Sarkozy parroted in 2007, is as important as conventional property.[207] The Europeans had already largely instituted what the United States now sought to emulate. And where they had not, they scurried to follow and even trump the American example.

The EU's directives, to be implemented in member nations' domestic legislation, invariably favored ever stronger protection. To foster a common, unified market during the 1980s and '90s, Brussels sought to coordinate laws and regulations that otherwise impeded the exchange of goods and services among its members.[208] Since it was politically simpler to harmonize different national regimes at the highest common denominator than to fight to scale back acquired privileges, the ratchet effect was always upward.[209] Much the same held true for the Berne Union, and perhaps inevitably for all transnational agreements. Berne had been founded to prevent nations from exploiting foreign authors and to protect their own. With a mandate to enhance authorial rights, it never paid much attention to the public domain.[210] The speed of a convoy may be its slowest ship. But harmonization is best achieved at the level of the most expansive rules.

Harmonization thus pressed authors' rights skyward everywhere—and nowhere more than in the EU. Protecting intellectual property uniformly across its member nations, the EU declared, was essential to developing Europe's internal market.[211] The EU introduced protection for software in 1991 because less than half the continent had legislated at all on the matter, thus hampering the cross-national market.[212] When the resale right (droit de suite) for artworks was mandated in 2001 for all European countries, again the goal was continent-wide uniformity. Otherwise those national art markets (primarily the UK, finally forced to comply in 2012) that had earlier resisted this new cost of doing business would be favored.[213] When the EU extended terms to seventy years postmortem in 1993, it was largely because national variations otherwise threatened to hobble single-market uniformity. German authors had won this expansive term already in 1965, and no one was willing to fight them. "[H]armonization of the terms of protection," the EU explained, "cannot have the effect of reducing the protection currently enjoyed by the rightholders in the Community."[214]

Across the Atlantic, as we have seen, the upward ratchet effect held equally, as US copyright was aligned with European standards and terms.[215] Databases illustrated the iron logic of upwards harmonization, though in this instance the United States has not yet succumbed to the EU's expansionary pressures. Since they were generally collections of information with few expressive aspects, databases were not yet copyrightable early in the 1990s. Hoping to compete commercially with the US, however, the EU mandated protection in 1996.[216] By encompassing the broadest possible definition of database, the EU aimed to stimulate European innovation.[217] It therefore covered original databases but also added a special protection for ones containing merely nonoriginal information. Even more drastic, so long as substantial investment continued in a database, the fifteen-year term could be continually renewed, thus effectively protecting it perpetually. The outcome has been described as "one of the least balanced and most potentially anti-competitive intellectual property rights ever created."[218] But it fit the mold of European thinking. Europeans needed to harmonize their approach, a French EU delegate exhorted. Only thus could they hold their own "against the might of the American system, which is so alien to the European culture."[219]

Since the EU 1996 database directive required non-EU Berne member states to offer similar protection in order to enjoy reciprocal benefits, upward harmonization was all but mandated. The US now needed database protection too, one American senator resignedly concluded, or EU coverage would be denied American publishers.[220] Thanks to the EU, perpetual database protection was thus forced onto the global agenda. As two observers gloomily noted, one government's legislative initiative could become an international minimum standard before anyone else even knew what had been proposed.[221] Sure enough, proposals for similar database protection followed both in the WIPO and the United States. But for once the upward momentum was blocked—at least for now. American scientists and researchers, backed by developing nations, objected that database protection would needlessly lock up information, crippling intellectual and scientific progress.[222] And businesses with a stake in freely available data, like Bloomberg News, lent economic muscle to counter rival interests that favored treating all information as property.[223]

Like the American content industries, the Europeans aimed to bolster the author's property rights even in the digital era. Unlike US big media, however, they also continued to insist on the author's personal rights. Even with digitality's mash-ups, bricolage, and collective creativity, Europe still venerated authors. Cultural workers, the European Commission announced in 1989, were entitled to a fair standard of living so that they could carry on "free from any ideological or aesthetic pressures and without compromising their personal integrity." The point of authors' rights was more to safeguard their interests than to balance between them and the audience. Their primary purpose, Brussels considered, was to guarantee authors "a living from their intellectual work and a right to a fair share in the income which others, particularly publishers, likewise derive from it."[224]

But the continental approach to authors' rights also promised Europe to enhance its global political, cultural, and economic standing. European culture was essential to ensure the continent's independence on the world stage, the French Senator Michel Thiollière insisted in 2008. That meant vigorously defending the rights of authors.[225] In the internet era European culture also had an economic value. Once digitized, an EU report promised, Europe's libraries would be a driver of networked traffic and a rich source of raw material for services and products in tourism and education.[226] Intellectual and artistic creativity was a precious asset, the European Commission green paper on copyright lectured in 1988. It was "a vital source of economic wealth and European influence throughout the world."[227]

To Europeans, that authors should be richly rewarded was a self-evident truth. A 1995 EU green paper extolling European culture's lucrative digital uses argued that protecting authors' rights would ensure incentives to invest in culture.[228] "It cannot be stressed often enough," insisted Jörg Reinbothe, representing the European Commission in 2002, "that intellectual property rights constitute a significant merchandise; they are the rightholders' 'currency.'"[229] Europe's traditionally high levels of authorial protection should be maintained, a European Commission report noted, indeed further developed, to reflect "that the subject matter is property and is, as such, guaranteed by the constitution in many countries."[230] As always, what was good for the culture business was assumed to be good for culture. Strong legal protection of rights would guarantee returns on investment, the EU instructed in 2001.[231] Though they normally favored consumers over producers, a broad spectrum of left-of-center parties in the European Parliament—Socialists, Liberals, and Greens—asserted in 2001 that, for intellectual property, they supported rights holders.[232]

Europe bravely reaffirmed inherited aesthetic certainties just as digitality, leaching away authorial integrity and coherence, blurred the line between creator and audience. With multimedia creations, for example, many—sometimes thousands—of authors recombined snippets of existing works into new expressions. Some Europeans hoped that the traditional Anglo-American copyright doctrines of fair use, full alienability, and work-for-hire might facilitate such novel works.[233] Eager to defend the Continental ideology in the freewheeling new age, a 1994 French report robustly disagreed. Digital tattooing, it argued, guaranteed that each author's individual contribution to collective works remained attributable, even as borrowing grew polymorphous.[234] Multimedia, another French report agreed, was no reason to change the personalist definition of the flesh-and-blood author. *Au contraire*, it should prompt renewed efforts to ensure that all authors were credited.[235]

Tweaked for the new technologies, traditional authors' rights remained useful, the European authorities maintained. "It is the environment in which works and other protected matter will be created and exploited which has changed—not the basic copyright concepts," one EU report cautioned in 1996. The author's reproduction right should be expanded to include scanning and digitizing. If this was not feasible, then licensing—royalties instead of authors' exclusive rights—might be considered.[236] But the Europeans continued to eye licensing suspiciously.[237] It was wrong, an EU green paper insisted in 1995, to allow just anyone to reproduce works—depriving authors of their exclusive dissemination rights—so long as they paid royalties. As digitality made works easier to copy, so the author's rights should grow stronger.[238] Enhancing exclusive rights for the author—not compulsory licensing—was Europe's answer also for cable and satellite broadcasts.[239] In contrast, the United States had instituted compulsory licensing for these new technologies as of 1976.[240]

The Europeans were as eager as the Americans to use technology to enforce authors' digital property rights. As we have seen, the 1998 DMCA's strictures on circumventing protective technologies prompted major disputes in the United States. Though the EU implemented measures broadly as restrictive, the controversy was far milder. The differences between the anticircumvention regulations of the DMCA and those in the EU's 2001 Information Society Directive are highly technical and detailed. Like the DMCA, the Information Society Directive outlawed the commercial manufacture, sale, and possession of circumvention devices with only limited other uses.[241] Like the DMCA, it too went beyond the WIPO's requirements by allowing the blocking of even lawful uses.[242] In certain specific ways that need not detain us here, it was less stringent than the DMCA.[243] But it was stricter than the DMCA in outlawing the circumvention not just of technologies preventing access to works but also those preventing copying.[244] Though such detailed issues distinguished the two instruments, ultimately they differed little.[245]

In other respects, too, the Europeans enthusiastically used digitality's powers to enhance property owners' rights. Digital rights management, an EU report argued, would benefit both rights holders and consumers by making more works available and counteracting the common belief that, if protected content was on the internet, it was for free.[246] The EU held internet providers more to account for their customers' infringement than did the US. On both sides of the Atlantic, internet companies were relieved of liability for temporary copies of copyrighted works made as technical necessity in the course of transmission.[247] Nonetheless, European internet providers were held more responsible for infringing content than their American peers and could be required to perform bottleneck policing functions. That spared the European content industries from having to attack their retail customers directly, as they had in the US when they prosecuted downloading teenagers, college students, and single mothers, not just large-scale pirates.[248]

Though the EU allowed exemptions similar to the DMCA's safe harbors clause, European internet providers were less sheltered from responsibility for infringing material. As in the DMCA, mere conduit and caching functions were allowed, as was (unknowing) storage of infringing content. But no mention was made of exemption for providing the tools (search engines, hyperlinks, directories, etc.) that linked users to unauthorized data. And the EU set little limit to the measures allowable in any member state to force internet providers to police and take down information. Providers could not be required to monitor transmitted or stored data. But they could be obliged to alert the authorities to illegal activities on their networks and to identify clients who stored data.[249] Once a site had taken down allegedly infringing material, the American law also allowed those who had posted in the first place to issue a counter-notice and repost the content until the issue had been settled. The EU had no equivalent to this put-back requirement.[250]

DIGITAL EXCEPTIONS

In such ways, the Europeans proved themselves at least as enthusiastic defenders of property owners' rights in the digital age as the Clinton administration. The other side of the copyright coin to strong property claims is the exceptions, like fair use, that have traditionally leavened owners' control of their works. As we have seen, such exceptions were generally more expansive in the Anglophone realm than on the Continent. The contrast between the broad and undefined fair use exemption in US law and the specified, precise, and exhaustive lists of exceptions in European legislation also continued into the digital age. Americans extensively discussed how digital rights management threatened lawful exemptions. The EU paid such concerns little mind.[251] Once exclusive rights and licensing arrangements had exhausted their possibilities, an EU green paper reluctantly conceded in 1996, "closely defined" fair use exceptions were perhaps needed in a few instances to accommodate the public.[252] The EU 2001 Information Society Directive allowed member nations to institute such loopholes for the disabled and for educational, research, journalistic, and other uses. It went beyond American fair use in explicitly mentioning parody, caricature, and pastiche—protected in the United States by case law, not statute. It allowed private copying, which was also not explicitly mentioned in US law, though generally permitted under fair use. But, seeking to outlaw peer-to-peer sharing, the Europeans restricted private copying to natural persons for strictly noncommercial uses—and even then only if rights holders were paid.[253] Digital technologies threatened to expand the consequences of fair use for rights holders, the EU cautioned. It might have to be restricted.[254]

In the EU the main obstacle to expansive fair use was Berne's "three-step" test. Once Berne had finally incorporated the disclosure right in 1967, reformers did not want member nations gutting it via overly expansive exceptions.[255] The Berne three-step test therefore permitted exemptions from authors' exclusive rights only if they were (1) exceptional, (2) did not conflict with the work's normal exploitation, and (3) posed no unreasonable prejudice to the rights holder's legitimate interests. The United States was in theory equally obliged by these strictures, but the Europeans seem to have taken them more seriously. Indeed, American fair use was considered possibly incompatible with Berne's requirements. A 2003 WIPO study suggested that American fair use might not meet the three-step test.[256] And the 2011 Hargreaves Report in the UK concluded that importing American fair use was impossible under European law.[257]

The Berne three-step test was quickly incorporated not only into the international agreements—the WIPO copyright treaty and TRIPs—but also into numerous EU directives, becoming a norm of European law.[258] The test was invoked on frequent occasions to block reforms that otherwise threatened to loosen authors' control of works.[259] The Information Society Directive listed twenty possible exceptions that EU members were free to adopt. But it mandated only one: temporary copies made during internet dissemination. Normally EU directives aimed for Europe-wide harmonization. But for fair use members could choose freely among the smorgasbord of possibilities. Since the list was offered to prevent additional exceptions, there was no pressure to expand fair use.[260] Every country was allowed to be less generous to the public than the EU, but none more so. Not that any European nation was pushing very hard in any case. Both the French and Germans implemented the directive quite restrictively. Their fair use exceptions for research and educational purposes were miserly, setting strict limits. In fact, they were arguably not exceptions at all, since they mandated royalties.[261] By comparison, the American exception for teaching and scholarship was folded into the fair use clause itself, giving it the imprimatur of a core copyright doctrine.[262]

The German law of 2003 implementing the EU Information Society Directive provoked the publishing industry's hostility even though it allowed reproduction of only short excerpts of works (against royalty payment) for teaching in schools and universities and for research. Excerpts from school textbooks and recent films could be used only with the author's permission.[263] These exceptions did not become permanent parts of the law on authors' rights, though they have been renewed intermittently since. The second German implementation law in 2006 allowed copying of excerpts for use in examinations in schools and universities—but for teaching only in schools and not in universities.[264]

The limited scope of such exceptions in Europe also played a role in the sparring over the Google Books project (discussed in the following chapter). Google proposed to give every American public library a terminal allowing patrons access to its digitized collection—thus turning the humblest branch institution into the Library of

Congress, even if only at one screen.[265] In the United States this was widely considered stingy public access. In Germany it was regarded as a rank giveaway of publishers' property.[266] German law allowed libraries to display on in-house terminals only those works they already owned in physical form. Not only that, they could display them only on as many terminals as they owned copies of the work. Adding insult to injury, the author still had to be paid royalties.[267] It is hard to see what was gained by this supposed exception to authors' exclusive rights, other than perhaps avoiding some wear and tear to library-owned copies.

French law had no fair use exemption for educational purposes at all until the EU Information Society Directive posed the possibility in 2001. Even then, France's first attempt at implementing the directive rejected any exemptions for research, teaching, or libraries as upsetting the balance of interests between authors and users.[268] Although France finally allowed use of brief excerpts for pedagogical purposes in return for royalty payments, the government made a point of emphasizing how this cut into authors' exclusive rights. In 2005 it sought instead to establish a framework within which educational institutions and the content industries could negotiate an agreement.[269]

The French publishing industry argued formidably in defense of its perquisites. French authors, it claimed, were bypassing them by writing and publishing directly in English. (The only example advanced in the literature of such treachery, however, was Jean-Michel Rabaté—unconvincing since he was a professor of English literature at the University of Pennsylvania.[270]) French library budgets were dwarfed by their Anglophone and German peers, publishers continued, and could not compensate for income they lost through fair use exemptions.[271] A copyright law in 2006 finally introduced a restrictive exemption.[272] Textbooks, musical scores, and digital works were not covered. But excerpts from other works could be used—for illustrative purposes only—in teaching and research for an audience exclusively of students and scholars. Recreation and fun were explicitly ruled out. In any case, authors had to be compensated with royalties.

The French exception for use by the handicapped was also miserly. In the United States special editions for the disabled were permitted in various formats and media as an exception to exclusive rights.[273] In France the handicapped were allowed to "consult" works designed for their use only for strictly private purposes and only on the premises of authorized publicly accessible establishments like libraries, museums, and archives. The handicapped wishing to use such works had to prove their entitlement through elaborate procedures, and the institutions that facilitated their access were closely monitored. Once the use was finished, the local institution was to destroy the work it had borrowed from the central national repository.[274] In Germany rights owners were entitled to compensation for works made accessible to the disabled, unless only a copy or two were issued.[275]

Other exceptions also highlighted the customary distinction between the comparatively expansive American fair use doctrine and the European emphasis on exclusive authorial rights. While US copyright was amended in 1992 to apply fair use to unpublished works, the EU 2001 Information Society Directive limited allowable quotations to a work "which has already been lawfully been made available to the public."[276] This was commonly interpreted to rule out unpublished works. But critics argued that "making available" could also mean deposit in an archive.[277] Whatever the outcome of the legal hermeneutics, the European battles continued.

After much agony, late in the twentieth century Europe also finally allowed incidental use of protected works in news reporting. In the early 1990s a French TV news broadcast reported the reopening of a theater on the Champs-Elysées in Paris. Frescos painted by Edouard Vuillard were shown for a total of forty-nine seconds. The visual arts collection society (SPADEM) was eventually able to collect royalties after France's Supreme Court rejected the TV station's claim of a news-reporting exemption. In the same vein a French television station briefly showed some of Maurice Utrillo's paintings while reporting on an exhibition. When his estate demanded royalties, a lower court refused in 1999, for once elevating the public's interest in being informed above the owner's rights. On appeal, however, this was overturned, as once again authorial rights reigned paramount.[278] The French Supreme Court took a generally dim view of exceptions to exclusive rights.[279] Only with the 2006 DADVSI law (to which we return in the next chapter) was an exception carved out, allowing snippets of works to be shown in news reports.[280] The Germans had introduced much the same right already in 2003.[281] In comparison, in the United States such uses tended to be considered either fair or so minor as to be exempt (de minimis). American cases analogous to the European examples generally involved more egregious use of works—prominently featuring a poster of a quilt nine times during a television program, for example.[282] In Britain incidental use has long been provided for in law.[283]

MORAL RIGHTS AND DIGITALITY

At the cusp of the millennium, some differences across the Atlantic were thus narrowing. Pushed by the collaborative cultural industries, European legislation had accepted some of copyright's tenets. In film corporate authors were granted attribution rights, and these were later extended also to software and databases.[284] Moral rights remained a bone of contention. But even here there was trans-Atlantic rapprochement. The Americans introduced only the minimum required to join Berne, and the British too had grudgingly implemented but a truncated version. Though France and Germany legislated expansive moral rights during the early postwar decades, the EU—truth be told—did not pay much attention to them either. Authors should be paid well and offered new opportunities, the EU insisted in 1988, adding as an afterthought that protecting creativity also meant invoking moral rights.[285]

Such lackluster advocacy by the EU of the Continental ideology's central conceit was not due to the Anglo-Saxons' creeping influence, so feared by the French. Rather, the EU was hamstrung by its role as a transnational organization, obliged to herd its member cats. Its main concern was harmonizing the internal market to promote competitiveness. In this, moral rights played a minor—possibly obstructive—role. Its members were not all equally enthusiastic. The French, who liked to portray themselves as defenders of European civilization, were largely backed by their fellow Mediterranean and some former East Bloc nations. But other EU members were far more skeptical—not just the British, but also small, culture-importing nations like the Dutch and the Scandinavians, who were wary of exaggerated powers for rights holders. From Brussels's vantage, with little trans-European consensus on moral rights, they were best left to domestic legislation.

More important, were moral rights compatible with modern cultural trends? Could they be applied to collective works like software?[286] Disparities among European nations on moral rights, a 1996 EU report suggested, hampered the exploitation and use of works. It would be helpful if moral rights could be interpreted and applied more pragmatically.[287] Even the French began noticing their dysfunctional effects. A government commission, tasked with reforms to bring France into the information age, suggested that only people closely connected to the author be allowed to invoke them. Unusually for France, it worried lest moral rights hinder the diffusion and use of works in the public domain.[288]

An EU green paper in 1995 was also skeptical about moral rights. It noted the chasm between authors and performers, who insisted on strong protection, and publishers, the press, broadcasters, and employers, who saw moral rights as a needless complication hindering exploitation. Digitality threatened to accentuate matters, and the integrity right contradicted one of the new technology's great promises: allowing everyone to alter works.[289] Not every change that users might digitally make to works violated integrity, another EU report noted, so long as the author's reputation was left unharmed.[290]

Earlier, the case against enforcing moral rights too punctiliously had been largely economic—the increased efficiency of exploitation that was promised were authors divested of control. Now the arguments took on a creative logic of their own. Thanks to digitality, users could—and possibly should be allowed to—alter works for their own creative purposes. The battle over moral rights no longer pitted just Mammon against art. It was now joined also between the solitary, singular authorial vision of creativity and the new hive-mind, inherently collaborative creativity of the digiterati. The Romantic author found himself struggling upstream against new digital technologies. Even the EU's 2001 Information Society Directive seemed indifferent to moral rights, declaring them a matter for national legislation and not central to its own purpose.[291]

Late in the twentieth century reformers on both sides of the Atlantic often complained that, thanks largely to Hollywood's clout, works were increasingly treated as property. Strong rights were granted their owners, which generally meant the disseminators to whom authors had assigned their claims. France's partial acceptance for software of work-for-hire in 1985 was widely seen as a beachhead for what the French understood as the copyright mentality on the shores of authors' rights.[292] Such complaints escalated toward the end of the millennium. Digitality threatened to upend inherited assumptions, a French report noted in 1994. The logic of authors' rights would cede pride of place to copyright. Among the threats it identified was the commercialization of already amortized products at low prices.[293] In other words, cheap editions of public domain works—the holy grail of copyright—had become the bête noire of authors' rights. Europeans who supported traditional Continental ideas even in the digital age were perturbed by Brussels's willingness to discount moral rights and its focus on efficient exploitation of works to strengthen Europe's global competitiveness. Harmonization of European law was a race into the Anglo-Saxon gutter.[294] Copyright threatened to vanquish authors' rights in the EU's increasingly neoliberal mindset, focused on the disseminator, not the author. The work, no longer seen as a spiritual creation, they feared, was becoming a mere commodity.[295]

In a longer historical sweep, however, matters look different than if we focus only on the 1990s—indeed possibly reversed. Yes, the Continental ideology adopted certain elements of copyright, especially work-for-hire. But this was due less to Hollywood's influence than the technical and cultural imperatives of new collaborative forms of work. The French, too, were proud of their software, film, and music industries. They, too, sought to adapt traditional authors' rights to the new digital world. Equally, Brussels's ambitions to harmonize the EU market rested of necessity on those elements all members could accept (thick protection for authors and assignees), while scrubbing away the controversial ones (moral rights).

True, copyright might be better suited than authors' rights for digital, corporate, collaborative cultural products. For inherently multiauthor endeavors like film and software, work-for-hire permit-

ted efficient allocation of rights. It could clearly distinguish owner-
from authorship without the Continent's messy overlap between
assigned economic rights and residual moral rights. But that was
only part of the story. The dispute of the 1990s was more fundamental. Should intellectual property be seen in the traditional Anglo-
American copyright mode, as a limited monopoly temporarily conceded to authors? Or should it be considered a form of property,
sanctified by natural rights—the classic Continental view?

Seen thus, the battle within the Anglophone nations was over the
very soul of copyright. The Continental ideology robustly asserted
thick authorial protection, while correspondingly discounting the
public domain. The copyright tradition was forever engaged in a pre-
carious balancing act between the two. When the digital revolution,
promising universal and potentially free access, provoked the content industries to assert their claims aggressively, the Anglophone
nations recognized the dilemma earlier than the Continent. Digitality posed anew the choice that had faced policymakers for centuries now. Given binary technologies' promises and perils, was a new
balance to be struck between author and audience? Or were the
spoils to go, European-style, to creators and owners, in line with the
natural rights view of just desserts for their investment of labor and
personality?

In Europe the turn-of-the-millennium debates were few and novel
conclusions rare. It was business as usual—digital revolution be
damned. But the copyright nations struggled with core principles.
As Europe saw it, it was a trans-Atlantic battle, another iteration of
the long drawn-out struggle between copyright and authors' rights.
For the Anglophones, in contrast, this was civil war. Fifth columnists from the content industries advocated property rights on the
European model. The content industries mounted a cuckoo attack—just as during the eighteenth-century Battle of the Booksellers, when publishers had invoked authors' natural rights to works in
the expectation of receiving their property by assignment. Pretending to be the author's friend, they demanded thick protection for
works—in order to enjoy their own rights better. Their opponents—on Main Street, in ivory towers, in countless well-wired ga-
rages and cellars, and in Silicon Valley—fought a rearguard action

to preserve the copyright tradition of limited rights and an expansive public domain.

Of course, in a broad sense both copyright and authors' rights balanced the interests of author and audience—but not at the same angle. Perhaps the victories won in both the US and the EU by authors and disseminators during the 1990s were largely theoretical. In practice, they may have been hollowed out by the difficulty of actually enforcing property rights to the quicksilvery streams of binary data cascading through the net. The 1990s spasm of intellectual property legislation may, in that sense, have testified more to rights owners' frustrating inability to hold on to their property than to the actual enforceability of their claims. But, on paper at least, the victory of the fin de siècle went to authors and owners, and thus to the Continental ideology. In legislation, jurisprudence, and enforcement, the public and its domain were forced onto their back legs, fighting ever more fiercely for rights that had earlier been taken for granted. But the 1990s also turned out to be but the opening skirmish in a larger battle, to which we now turn.

8

The Rise of the Digital Public

THE COPYRIGHT WARS CONTINUE IN THE NEW MILLENNIUM

In our new millennium we are once again caught in the crossfire between rights owners—authors and assignees—and the audience. Digitality has both promised untrammeled access and strengthened the grip of owners on their property. At the extremes digital millennialists do battle with copyright fundamentalists. Binary technologies have changed the game, claim the millennialists. Allowing universal and largely costless access to all knowledge, they transform creativity into a collective endeavor, expose how all works are ultimately derivative, and outmode private ownership and individual control. Poppycock, retort the fundamentalists. No system has stimulated creativity more than individual property rights traded on a free market. We enjoy an unprecedented cultural surfeit today precisely because the market for exclusive authorial rights has allowed us to dispense with patronage and emoluments, turning authors into intellectual entrepreneurs. Digitality may ease transactions, rendering the intellectual marketplace ever more fine grained and flexible. But even as the techniques of exchange modernize, the basic rules of strong authorial property remain valid.

In the 1990s the battle was fought largely in the United States. Here, the conversion of the Clinton administration to the Berne ideology of iron-clad intellectual property rights yanked traditional American policy around in a volte-face. With so drastic a change of course, protest followed. Opposition to the content industries and their victories in the legislation of the 1990s was mobilized both in academia and on the emergent digital street. Hackers and cyberanarchists rallied along with law professors and librarians to proclaim the virtues of open access and demand a return to the copyright tradition of an expansive public domain. What was new in America, however, was old hat in Europe. There, the new technologies were not yet considered reason to tamper with authorial rights. But even on the Continent digitality eventually forced a reconsideration of inherited pieties.

The new technologies of cultural creation and dissemination posed both aesthetic and legal issues. When culture was produced ever more collectively and in full recognition of how even original works borrowed from others, did any one author deserve the veneration and power he was granted by the classic authors' rights ideology? If the Enlightenment vision of opening culture to everyone at almost no cost could finally be realized, were there not better ways of stimulating creativity than the old system of making works artificially scarce by pretending that they were a form of property? Such questions, first raised in the United States, were now taken up in Europe too. They were thrashed out with particular vehemence in France, where authors had hitherto enjoyed robust protection. The born-digital generation, unimpressed by the inherited orthodoxy of strong authorial rights, began to influence the French left. Even in the heartland of authors' rights, pirate parties and downloading activists broached themes that sounded suspiciously like those of classic Anglo-American copyright. For the first time since the interwar fascists had tainted its needs with their totalitarian populism, the audience was being actively spoken for on the continent. Having won the battle of the 1990s, Berne's ideologists suddenly found themselves at the dawn of the new millennium fighting a whole new war against a demanding, downloading public.

NOT AS UNIQUE AS WE MIGHT THINK

However current these debates, they also resonate with themes we have traced over three centuries. Above all, whose claims are paramount, those of author or audience? Until recently, the Continental nations played little role in these disputes. Thanks to their venerable authors' right tradition, they plumped for creators and owners. Only in the past few years have Europeans begun questioning their inherited orthodoxies. But in the Anglophone world current debates broadly continue the ongoing antagonism of author and audience that fired the Talfourd controversy in Britain in the 1830s and stoked the endless American discussions throughout the nineteenth century over the worth of copyright at all. *Plus ça change.*

Much of the commentary on digitality and its cultural consequences sounds like what precedes the burst of economic bubbles: the happytalk that this time is different. But historians are by instinct and training allergic to claims of absolute rupture.[1] Where others discern a radical break, they find precedents and continuities with the past. Rarely have the claims for far-reaching novelty been voiced as insistently as for the digital revolution and its cultural implications. Cultural theorists, jurists, and literary critics all agree. It is perhaps an exaggeration to suggest that the debates of our own era farcically repeat earlier ones—as Marx concluded when comparing Louis Napoleon to his uncle, the first Napoleon. But healthy skepticism can usefully be applied to the millennial, sometimes apocalyptic, tenor of today's discussion.

Every age narcissistically considers itself unique. How quickly we moderns forget! In the past, many disruptive technologies have provided an expanding public with new, more accessible, and cheaper versions of art and culture. Those left behind—like the sheet-music publishers, outmaneuvered by the sound-recording industry in the late nineteenth century—have often cried foul. Sometimes, after an initial stumble, they have seized the opportunities again. Painters did it with engraving in the eighteenth century and so did the film industry a hundred years later, when videos and DVDs went from being bugbears to boons. Each broadening of accessibility has provoked grumbling from cultural conservatives, fearful lest the masses use their newfound enlightenment for their own purposes—as well as overjoyed optimism from reformers, delighted at similar prospects. The monks with their chained and locked illuminated manuscripts were aghast at the flood of print books that Gutenberg unleashed. So were bibliophiles at cheap reprints in the nineteenth century, not to mention the paperback avalanche of the twentieth.

A few reminders are in order. "Quantity is the new quality," it is claimed in this era of data surfeit.[2] But we are not the first to live in an information age nor to fear information overload. The *Siku Quanshu*, a compendium of works produced during the Qing Dynasty in the 1770s and '80s, comprised 36,000 volumes in seven copies (one of which survives in Beijing's Forbidden City). In words (800 million) it was surpassed only recently by the English-language Wikipedia (one billion as of June 2010).[3] Nor is piracy new. Hollywood fears videotapers in first-run cinemas. Nineteenth-century London theaters had stenographers in the audience. A West End hit could open on Broadway within the week.[4] The US edition of one of Walter Scott's last works, printed from purloined sheets, appeared earlier than the London one.[5]

Today, as well as yesterday, print pirates have been hailed as the Robin Hoods of intellectual property—fighters against censorship and for unhampered circulation, broad access, and universal illumination.[6] Eighteenth-century Europe was lousy with pirates. Scoffing at the Parisian publishers' claims to own works perpetually, the booksellers of the French provinces justified their piracy as enlightening the public.[7] Ludwig Christian Kehr could hardly have been more explicit in his *Defense of Piracy* (1799). The rich often buy books but do not read them, he argued. Meanwhile, others cannot afford even indispensable works. Only unauthorized reprinting keeps such evils in check, spreading enlightenment to all.[8] To keep the heirs of men of genius protected for fifty years after their deaths, Frederick Booth argued in Parliament in 1911, contravened British liberty. Time instead to celebrate the pirate, poacher, and smuggler—the practitioners of the fine art of free trade.[9]

Nineteenth-century America was unrepentantly the world's premier pirate. Sucking the marrow of British and European publishers' lists, it justified itself by ringing appeals to universal literacy, broad education, and the needs of a populist democracy. Cheap books, William Leggett, Jacksonian democrat and journalist, insisted in 1837, are the friend of humanity. "If there were no copyright laws, all literature would take a cheap form, and all men would become readers."[10] Such pronouncements are echoed in today's arguments for a freewheeling web of bottomless information and universal access.

One justification for pirating, often heard in the digital age, is that, by increasing a work's renown and market appeal, unauthorized editions actually benefit the original author. Information wants to be free, is the digiterati mantra. A work gains in value not from copyright's corset of artificial scarcity but by wide dissemination, argues John Perry Barlow—Grateful Dead lyricist, rancher, and internet visionary.[11] Such logic has been a leitmotif across the history of the printed word. In 1824 Leopold Neustetel conceded that a cheap and corrupted edition might whet the appetite for the better and pricier version. A book was recommended, as it were, when a pirate edition appeared.[12] This was the Lebenslüge of the nineteenth-century American publishing industry. Though British authors were not paid, US editions buffed their reputations and enhanced their rewards at home.[13] "Books, it is quaintly said, sell one another," the Senate reported in the early nineteenth century. "Every book that is read makes a market for more even of the same character. Mind, unlike matter, hungers upon that on which it feeds."[14]

Copyright imposes an artificial scarcity to create value for authors. But the public craves cheap, easy access. How to reconcile such opposites? A common proposal for the digital age is to license works, guaranteeing authors royalties and the audience access. Such ideas are not new either. Testifying before the Royal Copyright Commission of 1878, Louis Mallet argued that compulsory licensing and free competition among publishers benefited both authors and public, "the first by an extended circulation of his works, and the second by a reduction in their cost."[15] In 1928 Julius Kopsch, the reforming Weimar jurist who remained active under the Nazis, presciently anticipated why digitality and licensing would come to seem a perfect couple. Granting publishers exclusive rights is unnatural, he argued, since authors prefer to have their works widely disseminated in many editions. But given the expense of issuing works, publishers require a temporary monopoly to recoup costs. If one day a new technology allowed dissemination at a negligible cost, authors would naturally want to license.[16]

The content industries are often accused of having been especially active in reaffirming possession of works in recent years.[17] Much as owners fenced common lands in the eighteenth century, expelling the peasants who had worked them and rationalizing agriculture, this modern lockup of works has been described as "the second enclosure movement."[18] But the current appropriation of works is no greater than during the vast expansion of rights in the late nineteenth century, when film, photography, phonograph, radio, and other new media became protected. If anything, it is the contrast with digitality's promise of universal access that makes content owners' reasserted claims so provocative today.

Many of the aesthetic developments that postmodernism and digitality stake as their particular claims are also not as new as often thought. The audience's participation in creativity and the consequent blurring of the line between authors and their recipients is far from unprecedented. Think only of the cheap pamphlets and the penny press in Britain, France, and the United States from the latter half of the eighteenth century on. Every Grub Street publisher fired off blunderbuss salvoes of ephemera. Everyone who could write was a writer. The first recognizably modern and democratized mass media emerged two and a half centuries ago.[19] Those armies of hacks, titillating readers with scandal, sex, and sedition, were at least halfway to the audience-as-author concept that is supposedly so characteristic of digitality. They can reasonably be compared with today's bloggers. With wood-pulp paper and steam-driven presses, the price of information plummeted. The vast dissemination of works in nineteenth-century America—entire novels in single, affordable broadsheet periodicals, Dickens serialized on the back of railway timetables—spread enlightenment as efficiently and effectively as the age of paper allowed. The cheap press, as one mid-century observer hailed it, "puts every mind in direct communication with the greatest minds. . . . It is the great leveler, elevator and democratizer."[20]

Contemporaries then described themselves as living in "the era of broad-cast publication."[21] When nineteenth-century British publishers issued leather-bound, triple-decker editions for the wealthy, the gulf between expensive and cheap was not appreciably wider than it is today, when we compare the overpriced CD (ask your parents) and the MP3 download that may seem free but requires devices, broadband, and electricity.[22] Yes, digitality has almost banished the physical scarcity that still hobbled analog reproduction. But the basic dilemma of dealing with cheap and illicit plenitude has been with us for some time now.

Much the same holds for the actual creation of works. The narrator of Washington Irving's essay "The Mutability of Literature" (1819) heralded the age of "excessive multiplication" where paper and the press had ended the physical restraints of the parchment and quill era and made "every one a writer, and enabled every mind to pour itself into print, and diffuse itself over the whole intellectual world."[23] The eighteenth century would not have been surprised by staples of the modern aesthetic, like the idea that works are partly created in their reception, or even a sense of the hive mind and the public's beneficent influence in improving and changing works. Already then the themes of what we now consider postmodernist reception theory could be heard. "Knowledge has no value or use for the solitary owner," Lord Camden argued during *Donaldson* (1774), the fountainhead case of the classic copyright tradition. "To be enjoyed it must be communicated."[24]

In 1793 J. G. Fichte emphasized how the reader reformulated a work's ideas in his own mind, making it as much his as the original author's.[25] For Wilhelm Kramer in 1827, its reception was even more important than the work itself. The reader's thoughts, though prompted by the work, were his own, not the author's, and were often very different.[26] "Without the public, literary property would not exist," Narcisse-Achille de Salvandy, minister of education in the French July Monarchy, pronounced in 1839. "The poet, the historian or the playwright creates the writing [*l'écrit*], the public turns it into a work [*le livre*]."[27] Othmar Spann, the conservative interwar Austrian social philosopher, insisted that the individual creator was nothing without a community to receive his thoughts.[28] As the Nazis put it, "A radio program without an audience is not broadcasting [*Denn eine Sendung ohne Hörer ist kein Rundfunk*]."[29]

THE BATTLE HEATS UP

New technologies have changed how works are produced and disseminated. But the fundamental disputes over authors' rights have remained remarkably consistent during the past three centuries. Alongside exclusive authorial rights and royalties other means to reward creators survive. Patronage for officially favored authors continued in the socialist nations. It also endured, and even thrived, under capitalism. In Western Europe the cultural bureaucrats have been latter-day Medicis, from the BBC to the FilmFernsehFonds Bayern. Selected Swedish artists and writers are directly salaried by the state. Absent government initiative in America, universities have taken up the slack. Without them, what we quaintly call "serious" music would scarcely exist, and many more novelists and poets—now teaching creative writing—would be seeking day jobs. And for the sciences, vast government funding supports a mega-billion-dollar global research complex. Though theoretically unnecessary in an efficiently functioning cultural market, prizes to reward creativity are not only still with us, they are enjoying their best years ever. Think only of the Nobel, Field, Pritzker, Pulitzer, MacArthur, Goncourt, Booker, and so forth.[30]

Yet the authorial marketplace remains the system of choice. Despite the claims that property is based on natural rights, in practice its possession hinges entirely on the rights granted owners in statute. Since—thanks to its intangibility—intellectual property is even more contrived than conventional property, the defining, validating, and enforcing of its claims requires constant negotiation. Except for the most hermetically private pleasures, the "owners" of intellectual property have to disgorge it. There is no naturally exclusive right to its use, as for tangible property. Indeed, by virtue of its nature, the point of intellectual property is to ensure its widest possible dissemination, not to keep it for private enjoyment. But having in effect given it away, intellectual property's owners also want to control it sufficiently to reap their reward.

The two systems of protecting creativity—authors' rights and copyright—diverge over how to deal with what follows then, upon dissemination. If authors are to be rewarded only as required to stimulate them to further efforts, then their claims will be minimized to the most efficient levels—enough to keep them productive but no more. If, in contrast, we assume that authors own their works as farmers own their land, then their claims will start at perpetuity and be beaten back only by the practicalities of enforcing eternal claims to matters intellectual (who are Homer's heirs?) and a grudging admission that in the (distant) future, works should perhaps pass from private possession to the common patrimony.

The United States is often accused of having been motivated by its content industries, with Disney in the vanguard, to push through a new property-based approach to authors' rights during the 1990s.[31] Though true for the late twentieth century, in a longer historical perspective this seems anomalous. Traditionally, American priorities favored the public domain, not authors. As it joined Berne in 1989, the United States adopted the European idea of strong authorial property rights. Admittedly, it also viewed moral rights skeptically, but not more so than the British, nor even than the Scandinavians, the Dutch, and other European nations outside the Franco-German core.

Seen historically, the main shift of recent years has followed the direction espoused all along by the Berne tradition, favoring thick protection for authors and assignees. It has been the Anglophones— not France or Germany—who have readjusted their overall approach most, although certain economic interests naturally cheered them on. During the 1990s the Anglo-American content industries managed to hijack a national agenda that had not traditionally favored strong claims for rights owners. In Europe, where the Berne ideology had dominated since the late nineteenth century, little change was required. The Americans, as one French observer noted, have dramatically reoriented themselves, moving from an almost blanket rejection of intellectual property to now favoring it in order to conquer new markets.[32] The standard European position of support for authors' claims had become the new normal. But the battles of the current era have called this cramped consensus on the Berne ideology into question.

CREATIVITY IN THE DIGITAL AGE

First and foremost, digitality has questioned the Romantic idea of the artist creating solo from his own unique resources. Both the production and dissemination of works, the heralds of the digital era have claimed, were changed fundamentally by the new technologies. Culture is produced not ex nihilo by the solitary artist in his garret. It emerges out of collaboration, sharing, and borrowing across time and borders. The audience does not just consume culture but creates it too. As decentralized and cooperative networks of far-flung individuals connect via the web, the old centralized mass media and their large, highly capitalized corporations seem outmoded. Today's distributed networks trump yesterday's pantopticon media. The digiterati claim that open source tools, universally available content, and free expression are replacing intellectual property and exclusive rights as the pertinent concepts.[33]

In some respects this post-Romantic attitude to authorship and creativity has returned to earlier conceptions. Our view of the author as socially embedded in his age and society would not have surprised the Renaissance. Then as now authors were seen as artisans. Working in groups they readily used others' ideas and drew on their culture's common patrimony. They rarely earned their keep by selling their art. As the digiterati see it, our culture too is collaborative, derivative, and based on reassembling existing materials. Appropriation Art and Plunderphonics elevate plagiarism to a cultural strategy.[34] Digitality's effortless scavenging allows fragments of existing works to be mashed up, altered, commented on, and resituated. Bricolage, along with pastiche and parody, are hailed as the building blocks of the postmodern aesthetic.[35] Copying becomes the foundational creative act.[36]

Beginning already at the end of the analog age, in the 1970s and '80s, such socialized creativity has accelerated in the digital era. Musical sampling in rap and hip-hop was made possible, or at least easy, by digitality.[37] Reversing Sousa's turn-of-the-century railing against canned music and cultural decline as sound recordings undermined music making, law professors now celebrate mash-ups (compilations of favorite music) and other pastiches as digital folk creativity. They represent a return to the participatory culture of the era when music was played and not just listened to.[38] Sampling's popularity has made it a testing ground for what artists can borrow, spawning case law and a large literature.[39] Remixology uses similar techniques on written and video works.[40] Patchwriting appropriates others' texts in new combinations.[41] The Flarf poets trawl the net, combining the results of their searches into novel works. The new ethos can be found across digital creativity. Devotees churn out fan fiction—rewritings, elaborations of original works, and spin-offs. So active are they that original authors have sometimes been accused of plagiarizing their own fans' plotlines.[42] Remix culture elevates cut-and-paste from a software command to a cultural habit of mind. Why bother inventing fictional realities, David Shields has wondered, when the world provides so much that literature can just take?[43]

Whatever the truth of such claims for modern collaborative creativity, they are widespread and influential.[44] Crowds are wise, the advocates of the new digital creativity insist. Bacteria are cleverer than chimps.[45] Great engineering feats, whether airplanes or software, are the work of large teams. Excepting a couple antiquated genres, few major creations today are accomplished by one person—be it a car, bridge, building, medicine, computer program, or film. In the hard and social sciences, engineering, and even the humanities, work is done by teams rather than solo authors. Measured by citation intensities, the quality of group work has surpassed that of individual authors.[46] In every field except literature, and possibly economics, the Nobel Prize committees struggle annually with their inherited maximum of three awardees, when easily dozens are equal participants.

Digitality has affected the author, too, and not just the work. If not dead, he has moved from his garret into an open-plan office or an internet café. And he shares the limelight with his audience. The distinction between creators and the public has been effaced, the Swedish Pirate Party announced confidently in its election manifesto for 2010. In today's new participant culture everyone writes blogs, comments on others' postings, and uploads clips to YouTube.[47] Consumer and author seem to meld.[48] Presuming a Romantic authorial singularity, the classic moral rights—as we have seen in the previous chapter—seem out of place in our era of collaborative creativity and derivation. If the post-Romantic author is a magpie, assembling existing materials into new works, are his creations original or authentic? If art is self-expression, whose personality is voiced when creativity means reassembling others' self-expressions?[49] Sherrie Levine rephotographed Walker Evans's photographs. Having trampled on his disclosure, attribution, and integrity rights, did she expect her own?[50]

At its most messianic the digital vision has heralded a new hive-mind creativity and a faith in the wisdom of crowds. In 2006 Kevin Kelly, co-founder of *Wired* magazine, portrayed the Google Books project in Dionysian terms. To have the world's cultural patrimony universally available would be bliss. But it also announced a whole new approach to content itself. Once all works are digitized and searchable, the identity of each individual work—book, chapter, article, poem, blog—could dissolve into the oceanic textual whole. As every reference hyperlinks to all others, the boundaries would fall apart, readers plunging and dipping, recombining and reshaping what they find into a personal collage. "Once text is digital, books seep out of their bindings and weave themselves together." Digitally combined, books would merge into the "collective intelligence of a library." All books together become one massive tome, "a single liquid fabric of interconnected works and ideas."[51]

As the digiterati saw it, modern collectivist cultural production would replace the old model of individuals selling rights to their autonomously created works. Given that works were inherently collective, they were for the taking. New models of dissemination were based on free sharing more than on market exchange. The new paradigm was no longer the house but the village commons. Creative Commons and similar organizations developed alternatives to copyright's individualized markets. Open access spread, especially in the universities where authors are salaried and motivated mainly by reputation and truth seeking.[52] The digital millennialists held out little comfort for the Romantic creator. As in the age of the bards, digital culture was ever fluid, not belonging to any one person. The author was, like Homer, simply someone through whom the work passed. Authors' social importance would diminish as digitality leached away the myth of singular creativity, Barlow warned in 1994. "Creative people may have to renew their acquaintance with humility."[53] The independent author was advised to get a regular job. Musicians would earn more from performing than recording and more on selling paraphernalia than on their albums.[54] Writers would have to become teachers as well.[55]

THE REFORMERS REGROUP

Digital technology made reproducing content faultless, easy, and cheap. The remaining physical and economic limits to distribution, possession, and use paled compared to the legal ones. By allowing universal dissemination, digitality forced a rethinking of how to distribute and reward works. In the analog era price was a mechanism of allocating scarce resources. Above and beyond the manufacturing costs of reproduction, copyright imposed artificial scarcity, generating extra, socially created value for owners. Digital media's almost costless dissemination therefore shone a harsh and unforgiving light on copyright's monopoly, exposing the palisades it threw up to universal enjoyment. As the album, film, and book etherealized into the digital download, seat-of-the-pants economics discounted the real expenses of production to focus on the falling price of reproduction. Should content not be cheap, or even free?

Yet in legal terms, the rights holders' position in the digital age remained broadly what it had been since the eighteenth century. Though owners never achieved perpetuity, their claims had expanded and lengthened. At the close of the twentieth century, they were stronger than ever. Three centuries earlier, booksellers alone had faced down the royal administration. Now large and powerful content industries lobbied for their privileges. Those who violated their claims were harshly punished. Increasingly, all copyright breaches were criminalized. Earlier, only commercial pirates who made thousands of copies for profit risked prosecution. Now, even individuals who copied for private use or shared copies for free were pursued.[56] American law allowed infringers to be pursued for statutory damages, in addition to actual harm. Six- or even seven-figure fines were the possible outcome. Few other countries followed suit.[57]

But in criminal law the distinctions were less stark. In America pirates could be sentenced to between one and ten years in prison and up to million-dollar fines, depending on the gravity of the offense and whether they were repeat offenders.[58] The French threatened ordinary infringers with punishments of three years and €300,000, escalating to five years and half a million euros for organized criminal groups.[59] In France someone who violated moral rights—a publisher, say, who omitted the author's name—was liable too.[60] Civil damages of a million euros for transgressing moral rights were not unheard of.[61] In 2002 the UK increased criminal penalties for copyright infringement from a maximum of two years' imprisonment to ten, the same as for assault and other violent crimes.[62]

But if rights holders were robustly asserting their claims, the public had also become more truculent. The content industries' extreme position was met by the audience's equally uncompromising insistence that digitality had changed the rules. As in the eighteenth century, piracy became a political issue. Whether on Canal Street in New York or in Chungking Mansions in Hong Kong, conventional intellectual property pirates still plied their trade, peddling bootleg CDs and DVDs and seeking nothing loftier than a slice of someone else's pie. The real danger for rights holders lay elsewhere, with the novel breed of do-it-yourself pirate. Peer-to-peer networks allowed everyone to be their own pirate, heaping their plates at the celestial jukebox's ever-expanding smorgasbord of content.[63]

With past technologies even pirated reproduction required some investment and thus a profit incentive. But in the digital age other motives predominated. The average pirate might well be a teenager whose musical appetites exceeded his disposable income. But other downloaders were ideologically motivated buccaneers who fought for a higher cause. Aaron Swartz, the first open access martyr, who committed suicide in 2013 when threatened with prosecution, sought to release JSTOR, the storehouse of Anglophone social science periodicals, to those outside academia's digital walls. In the nineteenth century American reprint publishers had made a living pilfering British works while also arguing that they were enlightening a fledgling nation. The mercenary and the aspirational blended into a self-serving yet socially justified concoction that had left the Old World's authors and publishers apoplectic with indignation. In much the same way, digital pirates now invoked the high moral stance of universal enlightenment and accessibility, even as the result was as likely to be First World adolescents listening to Britney Spears as Kenyan field biologists reading *Nature*.

At their most articulate, the political pirates dreamed of a future where creativity did not depend on property rights and economic incentives. Adam Smith had rejected copyright in the late eighteenth century. Authors, he thought, were sufficiently rewarded by their first-mover advantage in the market. Everyone had a right to copy by hand a book they owned. Printing, he insisted, "is no more than a speedy way of writing."[64] Reprinting thus did not violate the author's rights. The modern pirates now followed the lead of laissez-faire's apostle. Digital reproduction and dissemination was just an even speedier way of writing. Nothing was taken from authors that they had not already lost by first publication. The English language, the French authorities sniffed, encouraged an unjustified conceptual elision between "free" and "freedom."[65]

Like the graffiti in Harvard's Widener Library elevators of the mid-1980s, pirates yearned to "Free the bound volumes." They believed that information belonged to the people. Piracy was thus a public good, indeed as innocuous and well meant as "a type of library service."[66] Peer-to-peer networkers were hailed by fellow travelers in the universities "not as buccaneers, but as privateers—the patriots of the information age."[67] But they would not have been pirates without a less couth side too. As put by one of the founders of Pirate Bay, the Swedish peer-to-peer downloading hub, "If I want it, I take it, 'cause I can. It might be [im]moral to some people but I think it's up to me to decide."[68] "Intellectual property is theft," Daniel Cohen, channeling Proudhon, proclaimed in 2001 in *Le Monde*. He had the jejune temerity to draw analogies between adolescent music downloaders and the doctors supplying Third World AIDS victims with cheap generic medicines.[69]

IN THE IVORY TOWER

The American legal professoriate also broadly supported a pruning of strong intellectual property rights. *Eldred*, the 2003 Supreme Court case that challenged seventy-year terms for existing works, revealed widespread sympathy for curbing copyright's relentless extension. The vehemence of the American battle surprised Europe, where similar opinion was found only at the fringes of the legal profession.[70] On the whole, university-based jurists favored reform of overly expansive protection. An upholder of strong copyright found herself disconcertedly the defender of a fallen faith among her colleagues.[71] Within the reform consensus moderates worried at the content industries' claims to overly strong protection, feared a consequent stifling of culture and debate, and hoped to expand fair use exceptions in the digital age.[72] We should counter the authors' private property rhetoric with similar claims in favor of the public domain, some suggested.[73] Others drew postmodernism's logical consequence to consider the public a coauthor of all works and thus entitled to its own copyright alongside the author's.[74] The most vehement jurists rejected moral rights and other strong authorial claims altogether as an unjustified power grab.[75]

Upstanding members of the professoriate advocated civil disobedience against "increasingly unjust" copyright laws that left citizens "no choice but to disobey."[76] Law professors, whose deans probably thought they were paid to worry about more pedestrian matters, issued pronouncements to the effect that, "In the post-literate millennium ... technology finally will sweep away all resistance to meaning, and all constraints beyond the individual."[77] Or, they suggested, the public domain was "a place like home, where, when you go there, they have to take you in and let you dance."[78] The law faculties (where some members were retooled humanities PhDs, refugees from the academic downturn of the 1980s and '90s and where the journals are edited by freshly-minted BAs) were heavily influenced by literary theories from English and comparative literature departments.[79] Such interests meant that, cheek by jowl with the usual fare on, say, "Implications of the Precautionary Principle for Environmental Regulation in the United States," the law journals now also carried learned disquisitions on "Romans, Roads, and Romantic Creators."[80]

The consensus in America's law schools was that copyright had overreached to damage the public sphere. Even moderates, who favored something less than wide-open access, did not simply defend authorial rights. Starting in the 1990s, as we have seen, the law and economics theorists advanced arguments for strengthened copyright based on considerations of public interest. For all their faith in property rights and the market, this still distinguished them from the continental ideology of absolute ownership for creators. Their aim was a balance between author and audience. By weakening incentives, they claimed, in the long run open access would diminish the public domain. Other moderates agreed with copyright's critics that fair use must be upheld, especially for transformative new production. But they were skeptical of the most far-reaching postmodernist claims for a new division of labor between audience and author. They questioned whether most of the digital audience was actively engaged with the work, and they remained unpersuaded by the digiterati's arguments that the average consumer deserved full, free access.[81]

AND ON THE DIGITAL STREET

Influential as such debates were in New Haven, Madison, Berkeley, and the other ivory tower exurbias, rumblings could also be heard on the digital street—in the chat rooms, the blogs, and the flamed-out e-manifestos—and sometimes even in the traditional media. For the first time since the nineteenth century, the American public intervened directly in debates over copyright. By 1995, when the law professor James Boyle sounded the alarm in the *Washington Times* about the Clinton administration's intentions to strengthen intellectual property rights, a grassroots movement was organizing to defend the public domain. It was a broad church. Digital anarchists proclaimed the internet a new extragovernmental dimension, a haven in the electronic ether, offshore from everywhere. At the watering hole of the über-connected in Davos, Barlow declared cyberspace's independence in 1996. Legal concepts of property, he announced, had no purchase there. "In our world, whatever the human mind may create can be reproduced and distributed infinitely at no cost. The global conveyance of thought no longer requires your factories to accomplish."[82]

Digital guerillas went beyond mere exit, threatening to fight fire with fire. As we have seen in chapter 7, much of the debate in the late

1990s over the Digital Millennium Copyright Act concerned digital rights management and protective technologies. Would the technical shut-in of content, reinforced by laws against picking digital locks, allow rights owners to sidestep fair use, first sale, and other limitations of authorial rights, leading to a pay-per-view world? Most moderate critics of the Clinton administration sought to ensure continued respect for traditional exceptions, thus restricting the role of protective technologies. More radical opponents, in contrast, saw such devices as the very tools they themselves could use to fight content owners' overweening ambitions. So-called cypherpunks turned protective technologies back on themselves. Let's equip all users with unbreakable encryption and snatch back privacy from the authorities' surveillance! Trackless in the net, encrypted citizens would regain the anonymity of the predigital world. Electronic drivers' licenses could be verified without revealing their holders' name. Digital cash left no traces.[83]

The most extreme cryptoanarchists simply accepted that iron-clad encryption protected both criminal and citizen. They predicted a new age of governments stymied by high tech privacy and corporations gutted of trade secrets by insouciantly untraceable whistleblowers. The same technological protective mechanisms that had marred the DMCA in the eyes of open access activists were now, in hacker hands, to create a liquid and open market for digital data.[84] Sheer transparency would, paradoxically, emerge from impenetrable secrecy. Hackers orchestrated attacks on enforcers of antipiracy measures. In 2010 Operation Payback targeted not just American organizations, like the Motion Picture and Recording Industry Associations, but also the British Phonographic Institute, the Australian Federation against Copyright Theft, the Stichting Bescherming Rechten Entertainment Industrie Nederland, and AiPlex Software, an Indian firm contracted by Bollywood to take down the Pirate Bay peer-to-peer site. The 2010 Wikileaks and 2013 National Security Administration data disclosures showed that governments were only as reliable as their least-paid employees with top-security clearance.

The cyberanarchists were furious at big media. The Operation Payback hackers sought to liberate content from its owners, distributing it to those who otherwise had to pay for access. They saw themselves as fighting "extremist capitalism," which locked up the knowledge that was humanity's birthright. "All should have the right to listen to that beat, experience that twist in a plot, or learn from the mass volumes of literature now made available."[85] The digital street was no pushover. Much as the faux bohemians of Silicon Valley might plead their alternative values and commitment to free-flowing information, the street eyed them warily. Like Hollywood's content hogs, these cyberlords' claims to control data conflicted "with the information freedoms sought by the vast majority of information users"—to use, share, and modify it.[86]

The digital downloaders followed the hacker shock troops. As millions of them soaked up data at the peer-to-peer downloading sites, they threatened to bleed the content industries dry—not just to top up their MP3 players for free but also in the name of higher principles. The cast of pirates, thieves, civil disobedients, and anarchists; the blurring of goals, tactics, and principle; and the unapologetic coexistence of ethical ambition and mercenary gain: all this made fighting the activists fiendishly difficult. Since downloading was committed largely at home, detecting, prosecuting, and convicting meant violating privacy.[87] What seemed to most people like normal private activity—browsing, downloading, mailing friends—proved to be infringing. Governments, in turn, were forced into an unpalatable choice between protection and privacy. Why, the Swedish Pirate Party demanded to know, should the authorities paw through downloads and e-mails when letters were sacrosanct?[88]

BORN DIGITAL

The ideological clash between open access enthusiasts and rights owners was reinforced by a generational divide. The born-digital generation simply refused to regard content as anything like conventional property. Absent police-state methods democracies could not enforce laws that were broadly out of tune with social mores. "A law deliberately disobeyed is demoralizing, and must either be enforced or repealed," the *Edinburgh Review* had insisted in 1878, discussing copyright reform. A good law, a French deputy echoed over a century later, is one that is accepted and not imposed.[89] Piracy remained illegal. But was it still immoral? The digitally native generation—the internauts—was accustomed to ubiquitous broadband accessibility and approached infringement and piracy in a new spirit.[90] Content should be both free and costless, demanded a cohort—generation gratis—that had suckled at the web's informational teat and was puzzled that it could be otherwise.[91]

Ever fewer citizens believed that digital piracy was a serious crime. Forty million Americans downloaded illegally per year. The number of illegal file sharers in France at any given time was estimated at 4.6 million. Fifty percent of Europeans surveyed did not feel guilty about illegal downloads.[92] The 2011 Hargreaves report in the UK despairingly noted that existing legislation was not fit for purpose if millions of Englishmen were in daily breach of copyright simply for shifting works from one device to another. French magistrates pondered the sense of punishing young violators who barely recognized the criminality of their actions.[93]

Generational tensions were laid bare when the aptly named Socialist senator Serge Lagauche in France grumbled that the habits of the young harmed creators. The net was their "far west," as the French call the American Wild West.[94] President Sarkozy spoke darkly of the demagogy and "youthism" (*jeunisme*) of the debates over downloading.[95] His administration paternalistically regarded France's epidemic of downloading as a "childhood disease of the net," which the law would soon cure. The young seemed to prefer the net as an anarchic jumble, the French minister of culture complained, rather than protecting the rights of all—authors as well as their fans.[96] In 2012 Emily White, a young intern at National Public Radio, provoked outrage among authors and her older listeners in America by admitting she had a downloaded library of 11,000 songs, despite having bought only fifteen CDs.[97]

The public increasingly assumed that anything found on the web should be theirs for free, the European Commission noted in 1995, fretting at the implications for rights holders of this growing sense of entitlement.[98] During the nineteenth century Americans had found it politically impossible to impose copyright on foreign books. Now it was becoming similarly difficult to enforce old-fashioned strictures on the new digital cornucopia.[99] Should forty million Americans be punished for downloading? Well, forty million speeding tickets were issued annually. Few argued that traffic rules were irrelevant, outmoded, or unenforceable.[100] Certainly President Sarkozy knew his mind about ubiquitous downloading, ironically asking whether France should also legalize assassination just because murder had become widespread.[101]

If downloading was becoming ever less a crime, plagiarism, too, was increasingly seen as a mere peccadillo. Redubbed as intertextual mixing, plagiarism was granted absolution by prominent thinkers as diverse as the postmodernist literary critic Stanley Fish and the economistic social scientist and judge Richard Posner.[102] Raised in an ethos of expansive appropriation, secondary school and university students' conception of plagiarism was becoming hazy.[103] Plagiarism, piracy, and downloading increasingly intertwined into an emergent ethos that regarded the web as a candy store of content, free for the helping.[104] Teen novelists, like Helene Hegemann in Germany, became literary sensations with books that were heavily borrowed.[105]

With plagiarism digitality cut two ways. It facilitated appropriation but also its discovery. If the young literati borrowed others' content, so too did the politicians. A startling number of prominent Europeans have recently been caught in flagrante. In 2011 the German defense minister Karl-Theodor zu Guttenberg resigned when much of his dissertation turned out to have been plagiarized. So did the German education minister, Annette Schavan, two years later. Among the many others caught having plagiarized their way to the coveted *Doktortitel* were the Hungarian and Romanian prime ministers, the Romanian education minister, and the culture minister of Lower Saxony.[106] Entire websites were now devoted to uncovering plagiarism in German dissertations.[107]

THE EUROPEAN DEBATE SPUTTERS TO LIFE

Until recently, the most heated debates over open access, freedom of the net, open source software, thick copyright protection, and the claims of the public interest have been Anglophone and largely

American. At the turn of the millennium, the single largest group defending the public domain were American academics.[108] We saw in the previous chapter that during the 1990s the Clinton administration began cheerleading for strong intellectual property protection. This radical policy shift away from America's native copyright tradition helps explain why the reaction against the Berne ideology was also especially American. The US content industries naturally welcomed, and even initiated, America's Berne-like reforms. But in doing so they upended what had been the founding principles of the American approach since the early nineteenth century. Copyright's public purpose was once the focus of American discussions.[109] When that changed with the globalization of the Berne ideology in the 1990s, debates flared up again in the United States.

By comparison, the European discussion was disjointed and slow, taking off only in the new millennium. The 1998 DMCA's proposals for technical protection of content aroused heated dispute in the US. The equivalent impositions in the EU after 2001, with the Information Society Directive, were received largely in silence.[110] The early Continental literature on authors' rights in the digital age typically compiled Anglophone writings, outfitting them with introductions to orient a European audience.[111] In Germany one critic dated the start of domestic debate from 2002.[112] Two years later another commentator reported that discussion of the public domain was no longer only an American phenomenon.[113] But the same year a Swedish observer noted the American domination of the debate and the Europeans' curious absence.[114] In 2004 an otherwise well-informed European critic puzzled at the "move afoot in the US which does not hesitate to throw into doubt the necessity of strong copyright protection."[115] The European establishment—authors, content industries, government authorities, jurists—lined up largely in unison behind the Berne position, defending strong protection for authors and rights holders. Since the Continental ideology obscured the distinction between authors and rights owners, corporate disseminators basked in the goodwill generated by Europe's supportive attitude toward authors' claims to thick protection.

While their American colleagues let the fur fly in favor of broadened access, the European legal professoriate generally welcomed how the international treaties strengthened property claims.[116] The EU's protection of rights holders was sometimes mildly criticized. One nonofficial report noted the EU's assumptions that strong protection stimulated investment and creativity and worried lest the balance between owners and users go askew.[117] But on the whole European jurists firmly supported authors' property rights. One study lauded Germany for restricting fair use to a few especially needy cases—and then making them pay anyway.[118] No need for new regulations on authorship for digital or multimedia works—or so went a typical expression of the European consensus; no need to reform authors' rights just because technology had changed.[119] The aim of the Continental systems was to ensure the author's rights, not to balance between him and the public.[120]

In the United States many voices resisted thick protection: digital anarchists, librarians, researchers, law professors, and Silicon Valley's magnates. But in Europe the main opposition was heard from shrill and narrow, single-issue pirate parties that arose to fight only this battle. The people spoke, even if the establishment did not. With little debate among bien-pensant opinion, dissent was forced to the extremes. A French Senate report of 2008 exemplified the authorities' bias on downloading and thus the inflexible attitude that faced the European pirates. In its Manichean view authors and rights holders who favored "civilized" relations on the internet opposed supporters of absolute freedom. For these open access activists, it claimed, society's rules did not apply to the web, and they sought to convince the young that "pillaging the fruits of others' talent and work" was "an almost sacred right."[121] When the nation's (indirectly) elected representatives took so unabashedly partisan an approach, it is no surprise that the opposition was driven to drastic measures.

THE RISE OF THE PIRATES

And so, Europe's pirates set sail. The European pirate parties were a subculture venturing into politics. Technologically they were digital, politically anarcho-communist, socially lumpen bourgeois, and aesthetically avant-gardistic, urban, and aristocratic. Their music was the

techno-pop that flourished in the Eurovision Song Contest au-
dioshed. Their peers were the social movements—feminist, eco, gay.
Their prophets were the French psycho-philosophical duo, Gilles
Deleuze and Félix Guattari.[122] Their denizens inhabited what they
saw as an independent technosphere, the internet-as-universe. The
technical realities of the net, Christopher Lauer, cultural policy
spokesman for the Berlin Pirate Party, insisted, "For us they are like
laws of nature."[123]

Pirates flourished in Scandinavia and Germany but not in the
United States or elsewhere in Europe. The reasons go beyond copyright. During the 1990s a No-Copyright Party campaigned in the US
against the Bono term extension, only to evaporate later.[124] Its fate
was that of most novel political actors in established two-party systems. New contenders find two-party systems hard to crack. Multiparty democracies, in contrast, especially if they have proportional
representation and low voting thresholds to entry, are easier. The
UK—which is now at least a two-and-a-half-party system—also had
no pirate party worth mentioning. But, then again, nor did France.[125]
In two-party systems the existing organizations have to accommodate novel opinions, and integrating new social forces generally takes
place at the party level. In multiparty systems, however, new issues
often lead to new parties. The radicality and fringiness of the Swedish and German pirate parties testified to the established institutions'
unwillingness to be accommodating.

While not notorious scofflaws, the Swedes nonetheless led the
way. Their Pirate Party (Piratpartiet) was founded in 2006. It was
widely noticed when, in May that year, the police raided the Pirate
Bay, a file-sharing site associated with it. The Pirates took a radically
consumerist approach. Their 2010 election manifesto argued that,
thanks to the internet, culture was infinitely available and no longer
governed from above. All noncommercial downloading, use, refine-
ment, and distribution of content should be legal.[126] Earlier, pirates
had skulked in the interstices of the internet. Their low profile implicitly acknowledged that many regarded their activities as illicit or
immoral. Now the Pirate Party made no bones about its objectives:
"We think that pirate copying is a positive force that should be encouraged in all ways. We don't give a shit what happens to the record-

ing industry."[127] In 2009 the party won 7 percent of the vote in the Swedish European parliamentary elections, campaigning largely on a platform of refusing to pay for downloads. Taking advantage of the dethroning of Lutheranism as the official Swedish state religion in 2000, the Church of Kopimism registered in 2012 as a religion. Kopimism (pronounced "copy-me-ism") theologized piracy, made file copying a sacrament, proclaimed originality an illusion, and insisted that the world is built on copies.[128]

A Berlin Pirate Party, founded shortly after the Swedish one in 2006, captured almost 9 percent of the vote and fifteen seats in the local legislature in September 2011. During the spring of 2012, similar victories followed in other German states. Berlin's unique politosphere was a pirate haven. Imagine a city of three million made up of equal parts East Village, Foggy Bottom, and downtown Detroit, combining bohemians, lumpen bourgeoisie, civil servants, and the ex-DDR unemployed, alongside a large and largely unassimilated Turkish community, all simmering in a sociologically unique metropolitan stew.

Unsurprisingly, this anarchist party thrived. Its platform went well beyond the Swedes' narrow download agenda. Besides being for privacy, against copyright, and outraged by the prosecution of downloaders, the Berlin Pirates advocated civil unions for threesomes and considered gender a private matter not to be recorded on census forms (since it might change). They were against prohibiting dangerous dog breeds, charging for public transportation, and banning first-person shooter video games. They wished to nationalize water and electricity and extend the vote to fourteen-year-olds and foreigners. They believed in direct internet democracy. Liquid Feedback, an electronic plebiscite that continuously sampled opinions, weighing them algorithmically, promised unmediated popular decision making. The Pirates dismissed the Greens, aging spokesmen of the ecology movement, as an establishment party.[129] Not surprising for a constituency of techno-nerds, most members were men.[130]

Naturally rights owners, the content industries, and the right-of-center parties in northern Europe were outraged at the pirates' attempts to justify digital theft as a blow for the public interest. But the formerly anti-establishment left, which saw itself as the natural defenders of authors and creativity more generally, was equally hostile to these new provocative upstarts. European bien-pensant opinion spoke for an older generation, still firmly in the saddle. Aging 68'ers reluctant to acknowledge that they were no longer the young rebels, they approached the web gingerly. They viewed the net through the lenses of Theodor Adorno and Max Horkheimer's 1930s critique of mass culture and suspected it was a mere technological sizzle with nefarious implications for high culture and civil society. Worse, it was an avenue down which the American media corporations could drive the tanks of globalization and cultural homogenization. The internet conveyed "un mode de pensée américain."[131] In 2006 Germany's most influential philosopher, Jürgen Habermas, issued a partial benediction, conceding that the internet might have positive democratic effects. But even so, caution was the watchword. Only in authoritarian regimes, he thought, was it a force for good, as it undermined censorship. In liberal democracies it balkanized the citizenry into isolated publics, each in its own chat room fighting its parochial issues.[132]

Despite their Marxist posturing, the European postwar cultural elites remained very traditional in their high-culture, print-based attitudes and their suspicion of mass media and pop culture as Trojan horses for American vulgarity. In the 1960s and '70s they had vigorously opposed Broadway musicals, pop records, comics and cartoons, Hollywood, theme parks, and mass tourism. Now, with practiced ease they transferred such views to the internet. The internet, they railed, was "full of profoundly anti-humanist values, shot through with the specter of the death of the human being."[133]

Starting in 2009, over two thousand of the great and the good among traditionally minded German authors and scholars signed the Heidelberg Appeal. This petition (not to be confused with the anti-global-warming declaration of the same name) was a cri de cœur of prominent humanities and social science professors and writers against what they regarded as their two worst enemies: digital downloaders and the hard science establishment. Google and YouTube were stealing works with impunity, they complained. Worse, the scientific research organizations dared to insist that works be published in broadly accessible formats. The authorities should step in to protect authors' rights against the American pirates and the dangerously modernizing science establishment.[134] Typically beholden to parties of the left and self-professedly eager to welcome new entrants in pursuit of egalitarianism and democracy, European intellectuals and artists of a certain age nonetheless discovered that they did not actually favor free downloads. Why did downloaders not go to the baker and demand bread for free, railed Hans Magnus Enzensberger, aging lion of the left. "Why does it have to be against us, the authors?"[135] "Stealing is not socialism," insisted his Swedish pendant, Jan Guillou, detective fiction author, former Maoist, and KGB informant, shaking his fist at the downloaders.[136]

Into this vacuum left by Europe's elders stepped the internauts and the pirates. They agreed with their parents that mass media could be centralizing, pacifying, and undemocratic. The net could be too. But the web 2.0, with its feedback and participation, was different and might encourage a Habermassian global civil society.[137] As a French deputy put it in 2006, the internauts were inventing a new form of democracy, one that would radically change relations between politics and citizens.[138] The pirates did not suffer from what the Germans call *Berührungsangst*, a fear of contact with the web. They embraced it—warts and all—as unavoidably part of the future. With their anarchic proclivities the pirates were more "American" than the Continent's classic left. As a "chaotic band of cyber-hippies," they provided a European pendant to what has been called the Californian ideology of the web.[139] French skeptics detected an unholy alliance of leftists and neoconservative hyperliberals, the first hoping to bring down the market altogether, the second to scour away its encrustations in a fit of creative destruction.[140] Both groups—Prenzlauer Berg and Silicon Valley—amalgamated new-left egalitarian, emancipatory, and reformist goals with a libertarian and antigovernment stance that traditional European thinkers were forced by their cognitive blinders to interpret as a new-right ideology.[141]

To illustrate the Atlantic divide most sharply: in Sweden it was left to the Pirate Party—a gaggle of ill-mannered young hackers whose vainglorious political pretensions masked their one-plank concern for discount downloading—to argue that culture and knowledge were public goods whose value increased the more they were shared.

Alone among Swedes, they saw that the internet could found the greatest public library ever.[142] In the United States it was Google—a major corporation valued at almost five times General Motors—whose Books Project set about putting such ideas into practice, despite the best efforts of the European cultural establishment to thwart this new Alexandrian library, free to all.

EUROPE JOINS THE FIGHT

During the 1990s the ideology of strong intellectual property rights had prevailed worldwide, with the WIPO Copyright Treaty and the TRIPs agreement, the DMCA, the EU Information Society Directive, and term extensions in Europe and then the United States. The Berne doctrine of thick protection for authors and their assignees carried the day, though with moral rights held to a minimum. This was business as usual in Europe. But for Britain and especially for America, the balance had tipped too far in the direction of rights holders. During the new century's first decade, the pendulum slowly began to swing back. In the US resistance flared up against the content industries' overreaching ambitions. We have already touched on the bills seeking to temper the DMCA's worst aspects and the fights over the SOPA and PIPA bills in 2012. In 1999 content owners had also run into resistance when the recording industry's trade association, the RIAA, successfully lobbied Congress to amend the definition of work-for-hire to include sound recordings. Without debate, recording artists thus found themselves stripped of their ability to terminate assignment of rights after thirty-five years. This had been a loophole allowing freelancers to renegotiate terms if they thought they could get a better deal for works that had, after thirty-five years, proven to be unexpectedly popular and profitable. When it became clear that the recording industry was surreptitiously trying to expropriate its artists, the protest was so vehement that the amendment was quickly repealed.[143]

Having passed the 1990s in silence, Europe now too finally joined the digital debates. In the new millennium the Continent moved from nary a murmur of dissent to an even more polarized confrontation than in the United States. Authors' rights defenders in the establishment confronted tattooed digiterati at their laptops. It no longer sufficed simply to pronounce that authors deserved protection, as always, and that new technologies were no cause for change. In the 1990s it had pained many Americans to lengthen terms yet again, to trim fair use, and to expand protection for rights holders. Now the Continental ideology too came under strain. The generational shift in expectations, expressed through the pirate parties, could no longer be ignored. Received opinion gradually acknowledged that the Anglophone copyright tradition did not just do the content industries' bidding but also defended an expansive public domain. Early in the new millennium some European intellectuals began arguing that Continental law had perhaps become overprotective of authors.[144]

Even the innately conservative legal profession in Europe began to thaw. A new generation of Continental jurists slowly adopted attitudes akin to the Anglo-Saxon. Unimaginably to Anglophone jurists, older French lawyers still insisted that authors' rights should be perpetual.[145] But younger ones began to suspect that protection had been extended too far. Perhaps a happy synthesis of the copyright and authors' rights traditions could be achieved.[146] Careful not to identify themselves as activists, several scholars associated with the Max Planck Institute for Intellectual Property and Competition Law in Munich—an important hatchery for reform ideas within the EU—published a declaration in 2008, arguing for a more balanced interpretation of Berne's three-step rule. As we have seen, this rule tightly limited fair use exceptions. By definition fair use was not allowed to harm the author's property rights. The 2008 Planck declaration now took issue with this.[147] Embracing the classic Anglo-American copyright logic of balancing interests among authors, disseminators, and audience, it supported exceptions as important tools to safeguard the public's concerns. And it broke with a core principle of the Continental ideology that—like any other owner—the author deserved whatever rewards the market offered. Instead, the Planck declaration now argued, below-market payments were justified when required by public ("third-party") interests "as long as there are sufficient incentives for the continued creation and dissemination of works." This was not the inherent logic of property but that of the public interest finally peeping through.

In a similar spirit the Wittem Project, initiated in the Netherlands in 2010, brought together European jurists to advocate reform of the opaque EU process of legislating on authors' rights. These lawyers explicitly sought to combine principles from both the authors' rights and copyright traditions, both natural rights and utilitarianism.[148] The Anglo-Saxon influence showed up in their critique of the closed European approach to fair use exceptions. In addition to an explicit catalog of exceptions, Wittem offered an opening clause that extended their scope. Though careful to explain that they were not proposing "mere" fair use on the American model "without any guidelines," they were clearly impatient with the EU 2001 Information Society Directive's list of specific enumerated exceptions, which no member nation could expand.[149] Also notable was Wittem's dethroning of moral rights, otherwise the holy grail of the Continental ideology. If moral rights threatened to harm the disseminators' legitimate interests, they should not be enforced. Nor should they be implemented if they impeded the public's interests—for example, in facilitating access to the work. The author could waive his moral rights, and they could be curtailed after his death. Other observers dared to suggest that perhaps moral rights should be more flexible for digital works on the web.[150]

In other respects, too, Berne's traditional priority for rights holders was questioned, though it was not yet changed in practice. The Berlin Declaration was spearheaded in 2003 by the Max Planck Society, German's primary scientific research institution (of which the intellectual property institute mentioned above was only one of some eighty branches). The Planck Society now advocated open access for state-financed research. It was such initiatives that had prompted more old-fashioned colleagues in the humanities and social sciences to sign the Heidelberg Appeal in protest. The Berlin Declaration's aim was to break the pricing monopoly of the science periodical publishers.[151]

Recent European court cases have also signaled an approach less beholden to the supremacy of authors' exclusive claims and even their moral rights.[152] As we have seen, in 2007 Victor Hugo's heirs ultimately failed to persuade the French courts to block sequels to Les Misérables, first published in 1862. Two polarized cases revealed the continuing tensions in German law—but also a possible shift in favor of the audience. In 1998 a Munich court found for the estate of Erich Kästner, author of *Emil and the Detectives*. It ruled that the Hollywood movie *It Takes Two* (1995) violated his 1949 novel, *Das doppelte Lottchen*, since both were about identical-looking nine-year-old girls who befriended each other and brought two adults together (in one case divorced parents, in the other a caretaker and a widowed father).[153] The author thus won purchase on something more than just his expression, indeed on something close to the idea of his story. The court also dismissed the differences between the two works as largely the effect of typically American entertainment movies and their exaggerated narrative techniques. The core of the protected work was declared to be the solid German novel (though actually Kästner's work had first seen life as a screenplay during the Third Reich).[154]

If the court here strengthened the traditional authors' rights, a new precedent quickly followed. In 2000 the descendants of two literary lions of the left, Heiner Müller and Bertolt Brecht, squared off.[155] Müller's play, *Germania 3: Gespenster am toten Mann*, collaged together large chunks of two Brecht pieces. When accused in 1930 of importing many verses of François Villon's poetry into his *Threepenny Opera*, Brecht himself had declared copyright to be medieval and superseded.[156] His less lofty heirs were known, however, for keeping interpreters on a short leash.[157] When they sued Müller's estate, the Supreme Court ruled that, since Brecht was a character in *Germania 3*, Müller had a right to quote him at length. Once published, the court lectured the plaintiffs, a work no longer belonged exclusively to its author. It joined society's common cultural heritage. Artists had to tolerate other creators making incursions into their authorial rights.[158]

FRANCE HAS ITS MACAULAY MOMENT

Even in the digital era France self-consciously remained the main defender of the Continental ideology. Around the turn of the millennium, this French self-image became intertwined with a broader sense of the nation's own cultural exceptionalism. Partly reacting to the growing dominance of the English language, the French also resisted including intellectual property in the global trade system. They rejected what they saw as the Anglo-Saxon commodification of culture, seeking instead to exempt it from the WTO's liberalization of international trade.[159] Late in the 1990s the French shorthand for the battle against Anglophone dominance gradually morphed from "cultural exceptionalism" to "cultural diversity."[160] Rather than setting up France as the only exception to the English-language hegemon, the French now implicitly accepted other cultures and languages as allies in their quest to beat back the Ango-Saxons. As a slogan "diversity" spared the French from painting themselves into their own culturally unique corner. They thus hoped for broader backing both from other Europeans and also the Third World, where French cultural exceptionalism seemed simply a parochial subvariant of Eurocentrism.[161]

The French were caught in pincers of their own making. The EU strove to harmonize the European economies, girding them for increasingly global competition. With its exporting content industries and ambitions to punch above its cultural weight, France had a vested stake in EU harmonization. A French commission reported in 2006 that if France aspired to best its competitors in the new global intellectual property market, then nostalgia, immobilism, and protectionism must go.[162] But France's "civilizing mission" was also defined as defending European culture against the Anglophone barbarians. Globalizer or cultural exception? The two goals conflicted. Domestic French battles over how to implement the EU's directives on authors' rights became part of a larger Kulturkampf that set the French—and to a lesser extent the Europeans—against the rest of the world. It was in France that the most telling battles were now fought. True, the nation's authors emerged victorious yet again. But, perhaps for the first time in French history since the revolution, the outcome was not foreordained.

Battles like those of the 1990s in America over the DMCA arrived in Europe early in the new millennium. The debate was sharper and more polarized now. The French content industries and their right-of-center political allies sought to keep France exceptional by strengthening authors' legal protection. The left-wing parties also supported French exceptionalism and were no fans of Anglophone capitalism either. But now they were attracted also by the egalitarian promise of universal access. For the first time the French left began to suspect that authors' rights had been pushed too far. Even allowing for the rhetorical excesses of French parliamentarians, the debates were raucous and unfocused. The center-right government and its Socialist opposition swiveled from discussing flat-rate licensing or the price of CDs at one instant to accusations of French thralldom to American media enterprises or totalitarian ideologies the next.[163]

The first round in France was fought over the 2006 DADVSI law, which implemented the EU 2001 Information Society Directive.[164] Media coverage was intense, spiced with public protest and comment. As a sop to French traditions, the government's first initiative was to extend authors' rights ("the personalist and liberal concept of authors' rights *à la française*") to—of all people—civil servants.[165] Primarily a tactical move, these provisions were largely ignored in the debates. In any case, they were carefully crafted to be anodyne. Though accorded a disclosure right, for example, government employees could invoke it only if not in conflict with their duties. Nor could they withdraw works except as authorized by their superiors. With little actually at stake, recognizing civil servants' moral rights was largely symbolic.[166] The interesting bits lay elsewhere.

Much like the Clinton administration with the 1998 DMCA, the Chirac government presented its ambition as a moderate adjustment of existing law to bring authors' rights into the digital age. Circumventing protective technologies was to be outlawed and two new exceptions to authors' exclusive rights were proposed: for copies made in computer memory as works moved across the internet and for works adapted for the handicapped.[167] But the government also struck another blow in the trans-Atlantic cultural battle, reaffirming French traditions even in the internet era. Opponents of the draft bill wanted much more radical changes. They argued that instead of traditional exclusive rights for authors, digital works should be compulsorily licensed, allowing unlimited access for flat-rate fees. The government, however, insisted that digitality's ability to track individual usage strengthened the nation's humanistic tradition and allowed

France to remain at odds with Anglo-Saxon copyright. The law was there to protect the author's exclusive rights, threatened as they were by unauthorized copies and downloads.[168]

Unexpectedly, the parliamentary opposition in both chambers violently denounced this supposedly harmless bill for criminalizing peer-to-peer file sharing and private copying. Free access was glorified and the content industries vilified. Microsoft and Apple were made the whipping boys. The parties of the left—Socialists, Communists, and Greens—attacked protective technologies as hobbling the right to private copies and more generally as stifling open access. France, they warned, was on the verge of implementing the most restrictive measures of any EU nation.[169] "It was rather odd to witness such a focus on [the] anti-copyright position in a country where the *droit d'auteur* is still so important," one commentator noted.[170] But that was precisely the point. In France kowtowing to authors had long trumped all other considerations. Now the audience was finally being spoken for. A century and a half later, Victor Hugo's homeland was having the fight that, in Britain, Macaulay had picked with Talfourd in the 1830s.

The French government was surprised that authorial rights no longer enjoyed the acquiescence it had complacently anticipated. Along with Communists and Greens—and with occasional support from defectors from the right-of-center government party, the UMP—the Socialist opposition introduced new themes to the French discussion. Deputies predictably attacked the monopolistic American media and high tech corporations. Yet behind the conventional bluster change was afoot. The French left now hesitantly embraced elements of the hated Anglo-Saxon copyright ideology.[171] Compulsory licensing, normally regarded in France as undermining the author's exclusive rights, was the solution for online works that the Socialist deputy Christian Paul advocated during the parliamentary debates. He also insisted that French law make exceptions for scholarship, teaching, and private copying modeled on the open-ended American practice of fair use.[172] And as an example of how to deal with peer-to-peer file sharing, Paul held up the US Supreme Court's 1984 Betamax decision, which allowed potentially infringing technologies so long as they also had significant legitimate uses.[173]

During the debates other Socialist deputies repeated the customary mantra that French cultural exceptionalism expressed itself
through authors' rights—a venerable achievement not to be diluted
into mere Anglo-Saxon copyright, and so forth.[174] Yet they also agreed
that modern knowledge production posed new challenges. Authors'
rights were part of a social give-and-take. The idea of a balance between creators and audience, formerly shunned in France as a weakening of authorial prerogatives, was now identified as the heart of the
issue—whether that was expressed explicitly as in the United States
or implicitly as in France.[175] Even the most sacred of French beliefs
was queried as the audience's concerns received attention. Was it really logical that the author should be protected for seventy years after
his death, a centrist deputy wondered. Perhaps it was time to dare
question this.[176] France had traditionally restricted exceptions to authorial rights. Should not the allowable use of works beyond the
author's control now be expanded?[177]

Socialist deputies proposed a flat-rate license, allowing unlimited
access to digital content for a fixed (and unrealistically low) levy on
broadband subscriptions (€5 monthly was an oft-mentioned figure).[178] The inherited system, they argued, mainly benefitted large
and usually American media and computer corporations.[179] Instead
of criminalizing downloading, why not allow surfers access for a
regularized fee? Exceptions to authors' exclusive rights were crucial,
they continued, especially making private copies. Otherwise consumers' interests—rarely a pressing concern in French debates before—
would be neglected, leaving digitality's "cultural democratization"
unfulfilled.[180] Yes, Macaulay could have said it better. But the gist of
this new-found concern for the audience was much the same.

The government's supporters, however, demanded exclusive authorial rights. They claimed that licensing was favored by only a few
performers' organizations. Perhaps licensing worked for music. But
it would choke off funding for film, which remained a jewel of
French culture. Digital technologies should not be held hostage to
an outmoded collectivism. Instead, each author should be rewarded
precisely for usage of his work.[181] Individualized tracking promised
to continue a "personalist conception of the law," calibrating reward
equitably to the work's appeal.[182] The government bill corresponded

to traditional French views, these supporters insisted. It celebrated the work, upheld France's cultural exceptionalism, and asserted her national identity.[183]

The French blamed academia and the American countercultures for the notion that internet content should be gratis.[184] But the French and Americans were entangled culturally in other ways too. In exceptionalist France culture was heavily regulated. The French government redistributed money from foreign to domestic authors, from blockbusters to bohemians. With its protectionist barriers and tariffs on foreign film imports, the system rested on a dirty little secret. French intellectuals might rail against Hollywood. But California was the locomotive that pulled their train. The more Hollywood blockbusters packed the cinemas, the more money the French state redistributed through the Centre national du cinéma, its Vichy-era institution for promoting local movie making.[185] Downloaders were thus sawing away at the limb on which the French cultural establishment perched. An end run around the Hollywood studios, "the majors," meant that much less money would trickle down to the minors. "Cyber gratuity" threatened to upend this carefully balanced ecosystem of tariffs and taxes.[186]

As though to cap a debate whose opening salvo had been fired two centuries earlier, both sides in the National Assembly and Senate reached back to the French Revolution. To reinforce its claim to be carrying on French exceptionalism, the right-of-center government quoted le Chapelier's hoary insistence from 1791 that no property was as sacred, legitimate, and personal as work springing from the author's mind.[187] The leftist opposition invoked his oft-ignored subsequent argument that, having published his work, the author had in effect given it away. The only rights he retained were those society granted him.[188] The classic tension between audience and author, which the Continent had largely resolved during the nineteenth century in favor of creators, returned here in full force to the center of debate.

But with a center-right majority in the French Assembly, even vehement debate did not prevent the outcome in 2006 from toeing the traditional line. Governmental maneuvering eliminated an amendment in favor of flat-rate licensing. Instead, the author was allowed to choose his means of remuneration and distribution. As the government spokesman trumpeted, the author was back at the center of events.[189] But the opposition had also left its mark. The government now at least spoke of achieving a balance between internet downloaders and authors.[190] Punishments were moderated. A graduated response to infringement (warnings followed by disruption of internet access) served as an alternative to more draconian penal sanctions. Personal, noncommercial downloads would no longer mean prison. But when the Constitutional Council later ruled that even personal downloads infringed and were punishable by up to three years in jail and fines of €300,000, the graduated response approach failed for the moment.

French audiences also benefited when this new DADVSI law, which passed in 2006, mandated that digital works should be interoperable across proprietary and incompatible formats. Interoperability appealed to the opposition's conversion to free-access principles. It also conveniently allowed left-of-center deputies to play to their core constituencies by fulminating against American media corporations. In effect, the hope was to force Apple to open its otherwise incompatible iPod format.[191] "Interoperability is the republic in digitality," argued Christian Paul, the tireless and often tiresome Socialist advocate for free access. It counteracted informational clannishness.[192] The right-leaning UMP government party agreed, and interoperability was adopted at its deputies' behest. Nonetheless, it did not meet a happy fate.[193] First the Senate watered down its provisions. Then the Constitutional Council struck out the exemption for interoperability altogether as too vague.[194] In the end the law banned circumventing technological protection for commercial purposes, thus implicitly exempting private users. But it also created a new criminal offense of supplying software for unauthorized access to works—file sharing—punishable by up to three years in jail and fines of €300,000.[195]

Despite such newfound support for the audience mustered on the parliamentary left, the DADVSI law in fact bolstered authors by punishing downloading severely. Yet French youth paid little heed. As massive downloading continued, the politicians responded quickly. The French faced a dilemma. They had something worth stealing.

Alone in Europe, the French liked to pride themselves, they had competitive music and film industries.[196] At 2.5 percent of GDP, the culture business was larger than in most comparable economies.[197] And content was easy to steal. Blessed with widespread and cheap broadband, French downloaders found piracy convenient and tempting. With important content industries and avid downloaders, French politicians were squeezed between two demanding constituencies. French internauts spent twice as much time illegally downloading as their American, British, or German peers.[198] Nearly 94 percent of recently released films were available on peer-to-peer networks before they appeared on DVD.[199] At the same time, the French public shunned dematerialized products.[200] Digital sales made up a quarter of the American market, but only 7 percent in France.[201] Veneration of the author was a national tradition. But the young demanded widespread access and were helping themselves to what they wanted. Now the political left eagerly catered to their consumerist populism.

Sarkozy's wife, Carla Bruni, a recording artist, spoke out for strict enforcement of intellectual property rights during his presidential campaign. Soon after his victory, in November 2007, a deal was brokered—the Elysée Agreement—between content producers and internet providers. Denis Olivennes, its shepherd, was a less than impartial outsider. Former lover of the presidential spouse, he also headed FNAC, the largest French retailer of books, media, and electronics.[202] Brandishing both carrots and sticks, the agreement gave voice to French officialdom's realization, born of the DADVSI debates, that the public could not be banned from unauthorized downloading without also being given a chance to pay for digital works. The Elysée signatories promised consumer-friendly digital works without noisome protective technologies. Music producers agreed to remove technical restrictions from French works; the movie industry promised to quicken the schedule by which films could be downloaded legally after their theatrical release.[203]

Merely an agreement, the Elysée accords still needed backing in statute. A year later, in 2008, the authorities drafted a bill to impede unauthorized downloading.[204] The Sarkozy government's core principle was that each author, performer, and producer be paid in the usual way for his work. There would be no "far west" fantasies of a lawless internet. France must resist the "illusion and the lie that works could be costless [la gratuité]." Nor should it allow (in the words of a Senate report) "a certain ideology" to advocate the pillaging of cultural works.[205] Enshrining cultural exceptionalism, this new law, France's cultural minister boasted, would continue France's long fight for authors' rights even in the internet era.[206]

To police downloading, the law established an administrative authority, the Haute autorité pour la diffusion des œuvres et la protection des droits sur internet (HADOPI). Avoiding penal sanctions, the law instead imposed graduated responses that slowed down and eventually cut off illicit downloaders' internet connections. Such moderated punishments were meant to demonstrate official solicitude for internauts, enticing them from their false ideology of laissez-faire and the "ultra-liberalism of the net." But the authorities were also determined to uphold creators' property rights and the "personalist" vision of authors' rights on the internet.[207] French cultural exceptionalism was the nation's pride, an element of its identity. At its core lay respect for property, especially intellectual property.[208]

Old ideological certainties were now partly reestablished. No partisan cleavages, the minister of culture insisted in 2008, undermined the grand French tradition of authors' rights.[209] Leftist deputies in the Assembly kept up the drumbeat for open access. But Socialists and Communists in the Senate vied with each other to support French cultural exceptionalism and authors' rights. They vividly expressed their distaste for the mercantile Anglo-Saxons and squelched proposals of free access for young internauts. Cutting off downloaders' connections, Socialist and Green senators insisted, violated rights no more than shutting off the phones of those who did not pay their bills.[210] Communist senators sought in vain to add an amendment reaffirming traditional French values and later even pondered a motion to anchor moral rights in the constitution itself.[211] But in the lower house Manichean dichotomies remained. Christian Paul, the excitable Socialist deputy, asked his fellow parliamentarians to choose between the infinite possibilities of the open internet and the closed world of the status quo. Paying for content was outmoded. The old regime—false scarcity through repression—was like scooping water with a butterfly net. Streaming would soon make even downloading obsolete, and so forth. The now familiar messianic tones of the digital visionaries sounded yet again.[212]

Though shrill, resistance was ineffectual. The left was hamstrung by at least three contradictory positions: its traditional veneration of authors (shared with the right) and its dislike of the media industries (undermined by the government's clever insistence that its bill would benefit local French producers more than the loathed American multinationals). Finally, a newfound interest in consumers and the audience was spiced by a sense that the internet was democratic and emancipatory and that here might be a way of winning the internauts' votes.[213] Socialists in the Senate generally supported the government. In the Assembly the tone was raucous and oppositional.

After an interminable and chaotic parliamentary passage the HADOPI law finally emerged in the spring of 2009—only to be partly quashed yet again by the Constitutional Council. The Council rejected having an administrative entity, the HADOPI, mete out severe punishments like cutting off internet access. To pass constitutional muster the government added final tweaks in yet a new law, shifting to the courts the authority to impose service cutoffs.[214] Dissent on the left in the Assembly during these prolonged debates had revealed that even France could not sidestep digitality's imperatives. Here, too, the audience was staking claims. Nonetheless, this cluster of laws (DADVSI, HADOPI, and the final 2009 law) reaffirmed traditional French views. Digital age or not, the author remained firmly in the saddle. Outright infringement still meant punishments of up to three years and €300,000. But garden-variety downloaders were warned, their connections then hobbled and eventually suspended. The left's hopes for an audience-friendly approach with more open access and downloading at flat-rate fees went nowhere.[215]

Historians commit few sins worse than assuming that the recent story they narrate has ended. France's attempts to grapple with digitality have not been resolved. Whatever is written here will be outmoded—no doubt by publication date. The point is that the debate—though not over—continues to be framed in terms that would have been entirely recognizable to Macaulay and Talfourd in the 1830s and even to Condorcet and Diderot in the 1760s. The digital age challenged even France's singularly insistent approach to authors' rights. For the first time in a century and a half, the inherited pieties of the author's predominance were being questioned. France was finally having its Macaulay moment. As in Britain in the 1830s, when Talfourd's hopes of extending protection for works to sixty years postmortem had been beaten back by Macaulay's eloquent defense of an expansive public domain, so in France the audience was now finally being spoken for and authorial prerogatives challenged. But, unlike in the UK and the US, Talfourd was besting Macaulay, and the French author remained ascendant—at least for now.

Seen more broadly, new fronts were opening up within Europe itself. While the French were beginning to debate digitality's imperatives, the German authorities clamped down, refusing concessions. "Authors' rights remain first and foremost the rights of authors," the German cultural minister insisted in 2010. "There is no reason to loosen the law on behalf of consumers. Free access for the public cannot be achieved by changing it from protecting the creative classes to serving consumers."[216] More widely still, new disputes pitted Eastern against Western Europe. Just after the SOPA and PIPA battles in the United States in 2012, when the content industries were bested by consumers and new technology firms, protests flared up across Europe against the Anti-Counterfeiting Trade Agreement (ACTA). ACTA had been worked out in secretive circumstances that did not endear it to internet activists, and it granted authorities disturbingly broad powers. Signed by thirty states, it sought to create an international regime for punishing counterfeiting and piracy. Especially the new EU nations of the former East Bloc now protested. There, Communism had scoured the cultural landscape. Credible newspapers and publishers had only recently reemerged. Coming of political age with the internet, the new Europeans had embraced the web far more enthusiastically than the older EU members. In the former East slogans of free and universal access were proclaimed on blogs and chanted in the streets. In July 2012, when the European Parliament rejected the ACTA, Easterners hailed it as their victory.

The ACTA's defeat was a rare grassroots triumph within the EU machinery. Parliament held out against the Commission, and the new nations—lacking big media businesses to influence local politicians—prevailed over Western Europe, with its powerful corporate content owners.[217] The Poles especially congratulated themselves on rallying protest in the dead of winter. The Western political elites, in contrast, fretted that digital populism had run amok. The ACTA should be supported, the German cultural minister argued, because it did for Europe what German law already had accomplished at home.[218] Most ACTA rules were already in European national law, Italy's premier newspaper, the *Corriere della Sera*, pointed out, so rejection at the EU level meant little. Internet activists, the *Financial Times Deutschland* grumbled, were lobbyists, no less than the pharmaceutical or the energy companies. By contrast, the conservative Slovenian paper, *Večer*, trumpeted that rejecting the ACTA meant "that Europe's understanding of copyright triumphs over that of the US."[219] That, of course, was nonsense. The new fault line no longer ran only through the Atlantic. It also followed the Iron Curtain. Fully half of the few European parliamentary deputies voting in favor of the ACTA were French.[220] Those opposed were young West Europeans of the internet generation and the Easterners, "who know what it is to have their freedoms curtailed and have expressed great concern about the way ACTA might be implemented," according to David Martin, rapporteur of the proposal.[221]

ALEXANDRIA REBORN? GOOGLE DOES BOOKS

Why these latest debates between author and audience were fought later and with different accents in Europe than in the United States can best be understood in light of the long historical trajectory outlined here. Thanks to the lobbying of its content industries, America decided in the 1990s to adopt the Berne line. Jack Valenti trumped Thomas Jefferson. Because this was a major shift from inherited domestic copyright traditions, American debates were heated. The United States had responded to digitality's challenges earlier than Europe. But global trends spared no one. Europe, too, had to face the new world. The Berne doctrine having triumphed in the 1990s, Europe now discovered the difficulties of reinforcing authors' prerogatives in the digital age while pretending that nothing had changed.

Since the United States had preceded Europe along the digital learning curve, American commercial interests took the lead. To be the world's (so far) largest, most economically integrated, monolingual cultural market was an advantage in the network era. The logic of networks dictates that, as they add members, their value grows exponentially. A phone system with four subscribers is more than twice as good as one with only two. As the web grew and densified, America's first-mover and scale advantages favored the half-billion Anglophones. Worse off were Europe's many linguistically distinct cultures, few of whom (other than the Iberians and to some little extent the French) had market depth in cultural hinterlands abroad. Back in the analog era this had merely meant being swamped by the Beatles and Clint Eastwood. But the web turbocharged the logic of networks. By ranking net surfers' choices, Google's algorithms reflected the universal suffrage of the mouse click. Inevitably, English-language sites percolated to the top. Europe understandably feared being doubly swamped: not just by Anglophonia's content but also by the very logic of the system imposing a digital Matthew Effect: giving more to those who already had plenty.[222]

As Europe reacted to the internet, nationalism and hostility to Americans grew. Instead of seeing the web as a global challenge for all nations, Europeans often regarded it as a particularly American threat. US media, especially Hollywood, were feared as predatory. Perhaps that was understandable. A wave of American film, TV, and music had washed over Europe ever since the 1930s, submerging local production with cheap, good-enough competition that delighted audiences but worried politicians and intellectuals.[223] Europe had imposed elaborate protectionist restrictions already early in the twentieth century: local-content requirements for radio and TV, regulation of the book and film markets, government subsidies, and the like. Bulwarks, palisades, dikes, and canals: such were the techniques Europe had employed against the Anglophone analog tsunami. But now the very tools of the internet—the search engines that increasingly mediated most knowledge—were tuned to reward one language, discounting the others. The threat had escalated. And when in 2004 Google proposed to recreate the Alexandrian library on a modern scale by digitizing the world's books, the possibility that Anglophone dominance would be woven into the very fabric of content delivery roused angst on the Continent.

This was not the first time Europeans had reacted allergically to American plans to safeguard and disseminate culture. In the mid-1930s Americans had proposed new photographic techniques to copy documents from European archives for research use in the United States. Inspired by Robert C. Binkley, Americans had then regarded microfilm as opening new technological vistas, comparable to Gutenberg's invention of printing. Mass microfilming would apply Fordist methods to reproduce documents from the great European libraries. The old distinctions between published and unpublished work would be overcome. "The library," Binkley foresaw, "may come to be, not only a depository of printed material, not only a collector of existing records, but even a maker of new records."[224] Microfilm promised to make obscure works affordably available. American scholars could gain access to European riches without having to travel. Many such themes of enhanced accessibility that we regard as particular to digitality were broached already then. Both in the 1930s and some seventy years later, the Americans presented plans to preserve and broaden access to European culture. But what the New World saw as the free flow of information, the Old feared as a sinister grab for treasures it preferred to keep under lock and key.

Affecting a high moral tone against the Google Books project, the Europeans now claimed to speak for cultural diversity against the relentless anglicization of the world, in thrall to "the hyperpower of a dominant civilization."[225] Digitizing Anglo-American libraries, they accused, would cement the ascendance of Anglophone literature, marginalizing European culture even further.[226] Google, they warned, was proffering a Faustian pact, luring Europeans with the illusion of free availability.[227] Perhaps Europeans' fears were understandable. Their answer was less so. Doing their utmost to shut down Google Books, they hobbled themselves too.

In using the pretext of feared anglicization to resist Google, the Europeans were in effect universalizing their own provincialism. Google's aim, after all, was to disseminate the already existing repertoire. It did not seek to tilt the present balance of cultures in any particular direction. Rather than throwing up obstacles, the Continent might have been better off rushing to participate, diluting the feared Anglophone overrepresentation.[228] Instead of snarling from the sidelines, why did the Bibliothèque nationale not join with the New York Public, Chicago, and Oxford libraries, alongside the other Google partners, to share its patrimony with the world?[229] The answer lay in Europe's fundamental assumptions about who gained. "In Google's attitude," one French observer sniffed of the books project, "one recognizes the Anglo-Saxon tendency to give the advantage to public interests over those of authors."[230]

The European charge of Anglophone myopia stuck only if the English-language libraries now to be digitized were as monocultural as the Continent's. Though accurate figures are scarce, over half the holdings of repositories like Harvard's Widener Library or the Library of Congress—two of the world's biggest—are in languages other than English. The Bibliothèque nationale claims that 60 percent of its books are in languages other than French. Again, figures are incomplete and approximate, but it appears that a quarter of all books published in recent years have been in English and 6 percent in French.[231] Such ratios will not, of course, have held throughout the book's long history. But with the vast increase of publishing in the last century, they will be broadly representative of the linguistic makeup of the collection that a globally representative and universal library would have acquired. With similar fractions (around half) of holdings in their native language, French books were thus four times overrepresented in the Bibliothèque nationale compared to English-language books in the Library of Congress. Books in German make up more than 12 percent of Widener's fourteen million volumes. Once the Harvard library has been digitized, as many German books will have come on line as if the entire University of Heidelberg library had been scanned.

By 2010 Google had digitized twelve million volumes in six years, twenty million by 2013. Over half of the first ten million books scanned were in languages other than English.[232] Where Google had pressed ahead, not asking for permission from rights holders on the assumption that fair use sufficed, the official European attempts to respond in kind were hampered by punctilious observance of authors' property rights. They were therefore slow, expensive, and limited. Gallica—founded in 1997 as the official French riposte to Google and dubbed by the French "the honest person's virtual library"—had scanned only 145,000 books by 2010.[233] The German equivalent, the Deutsche Digitale Bibliothek, got under way only in 2009. Europeana, the all-Europe digitization agglomerator, offered access to only some 200,000 books as of 2010.[234] Even the EU recognized that Google was outstripping European efforts.[235] At the rate of French digitization, another two generations would still have to trek to the libraries if they were to read at all.

In the United States authors and publishers—the ones with most to lose from an expanded public domain—also resisted Google's ambitions. Other, disinterested objectors worried at entrusting so important a public function as a universal digital library to private hands.[236] Europe, in contrast, was most concerned with the threatened violation of private property. Besides fears of cultural marginalization, Europeans sought to foil the Google Books project in order to protect content owners' claims. "Since intellectual property rights are a key tool to stimulate creativity," the European Communities Commission insisted, "Europe's cultural material should be digitised, made available and preserved," but only "in full respect of copyright and related rights."[237]

French senators portrayed Google as an amoral enterprise with massively destructive and hegemonic intentions. Under cover of the confusion introduced by digital technology, it planned to attack and dismantle authors' rights.[238] "Placing entire books online, even if encoded," Jean-Noël Jeanneney, former head of the Bibliothèque nationale, warned, "is a dangerous game."[239] It was dangerous also because the European publishing industry was well organized and ready to fight. We have already noted its power to block or restrict significant exceptions for research, education, or the handicapped during implementation of the EU Information Society Directive. European content industries were also shielded from outside competition by protectionist bulwarks and obligingly bolstered by corporatist pricing arrangements on the domestic market.

In the United States Google, the Authors Guild, and some publishers eventually arrived at a settlement in 2008. After vigorous lobbying by US and European publishers and authors, it was rejected in an American court in 2011. In Europe Google achieved no settlement at the time. In France Google was sued for violating both the economic and moral rights of authors. Whatever American fair use might dictate, the court ruled, the snippets of books displayed by Google were illegal. The American concept of fair use, the French minister of culture agreed, was but a legal loophole used by Google to despoil thousands of authors of their rights.[240] Yes, French law had a short quotation exemption. But Google's brief citations did not count since, as random excerpts, they allegedly conveyed no coherent information. Moreover, the French court added, by presenting only excerpts from books (so as not to violate the author's economic rights) and running them as a continuous banner, Google violated the moral right of integrity by distorting the work's appearance. France also rejected Google's claim that the publishers did not hold the rights to digital dissemination and that books were thus free to be digitized. Authors, the court insisted, had signed away their rights to any and all future uses in their publishing contracts. Curiously, these were precisely the sort of blanket waivers that European law normally rejected.[241]

The very act of collectivizing books in one mass database—the idea that so inspired *Wired*'s founder Kevin Kelly—raised French hackles. Google could rank books, formulating the algorithms that chose which ones were to be displayed and when. But this apparently demeaned "those special elements that distinguish the unique cultural traditions of France by turning books into merely industrial byproducts of a computer database."[242] Such French objections stemmed from a profoundly traditional approach to books as physical objects. "A book cannot be reduced to information," the French Communist senator Jack Ralite, insisted in 2009. "Libraries are not databases." Reading on the screen, he continued, "is not reading a work in its coherence and integrity. It fragments the text and its reading. It disintegrates works and mutilates moral rights. . . . Google is interested in pages and not in works in their entirety." It was absurd, he concluded—blithely oblivious to big-data research projects—to digitize all books. Two million books in the National Library had never been consulted. Why bother with them?[243]

As the Google Books settlement was adjudicated before New York's Southern District Court starting in 2005, European governments and publishers submitted numerous briefs. France and Germany weighed in to burnish their bona fides as bearers of high culture (their glorious literary pasts, the number of their Nobel prizes). Both claimed to be the third-largest producer of books worldwide (though the numbers cited gave the advantage to the Germans). Both governments staunchly backed their publishing industries.[244] Of slightly more than a thousand documents submitted to the court, at least three hundred were largely identical form letters from European publishers. The Germans alone provided half. One of the first outcomes of these protests was that, to placate European publishers, Google agreed to display only works published in the United States and other common law nations with sufficiently robust fair use provisions. Books from France and Germany were removed.[245] In this way precisely the outcome that Jeanneney, former head of the French National Library, had fearfully described as the "inevitable American self-centering of the selections" was coming to pass.[246] Google Books did indeed become a largely Anglophone project but not because of American provincialism. It was thanks to Continental publishers' insistence on protecting what they liked to portray as European culture but which in fact amounted to their own claims as rights owners.

In their court submissions the Germans and the French warned that accepting the settlement would embarrass the United States since it insisted on high standards of protection for others while refusing to hold itself to the same.[247] Given America's commitments to international treaties, endless litigation from its trading partners was sure to follow. Once again international standardization ratcheted authorial rights upward. Tied down by the Lilliputian strings of global treaties, one nation, however large and powerful, could no longer go its own way.

The role of intellectual property bruiser, played to the hilt by Hollywood in the 1990s, now passed to Europe's publishers. It was no coincidence that seven of the world's eight largest publishing corporations were European in 2010, while only the smallest one (McGraw-

Hill) was American.[248] Most rapacious of all were the scientific publishers. From the 1980s and on, two of the three publishers (Reed Elsevier, Springer, and Wiley) with a monopoly (42 percent) of the 25,000 leading English-language scientific periodicals were European. No other publisher controlled more than 3 percent of the market. They dictated prices, driving costs of journal subscriptions skywards, and gutting university library budgets. Their business model was a marvel: sell scholarship back to the same universities whose scientists had produced, written, peer reviewed, and edited it largely for free. Profit margins of between 35 percent and 40 percent were the happy outcome.[249] Since their products were unique, no substitution possibilities threatened their monopoly. As Deutsche Bank observed of Reed Elsevier in 2005, "If the process really were as complex, costly and value-added as the publishers protest that it is, 40% margins wouldn't be available."[250] Scientific publishers, the *Guardian* noted in 2011, make Rupert Murdoch look like a Socialist.[251] Besides banknotes, the *Frankfurter Allgemeine Zeitung* agreed in 2012, scientific papers are the most lucrative thing you can print.[252]

The scandal of the scientific journal publishers is well known. Less publicized, but worth telling, is another peculiarity of the (central) European publishing industry—the dissertation presses. In Anglophone universities a doctoral dissertation is not a book. Typically it is filed as a typescript or digitally online with the certifying university and usually, as in the US and now also the UK, with a centralized institution that supplies paper reproductions at reasonable cost. Anglophone scholars sometimes turn dissertations into proper books, but that is another matter. A German doctoral dissertation, however, is not official, nor part of a degree, until it has been "published." Published in this sense, however, does not mean submitting it to a publisher, having it peer reviewed, revised, edited, and proofread. Until recently, "publishing" a German dissertation meant having a so-called dissertation press (*Dissertationsdruckerei*) photocopy the typescript, slap it between boards with some glue slicked down the spine, and deliver a few copies to the university library.

Today things are somewhat different. A sufficiently interesting German dissertation might be accepted by a commercial publisher, bypassing the university publishing ritual and going straight to the normal book market. Sometimes German students pay to have their books published by commercial publishers, thus blurring the line between them and the dissertation presses. To avoid scams, universities usually require a minimum commercial print run.[253] For doctoral candidates who stick with the dissertation presses, things have also changed somewhat. Thanks to desktop publishing the final product looks more like a proper book, even if there is still no editorial process. Little, if anything, is added between finishing the PhD thesis and having it appear in print. The dissertation presses no longer command the German landscape unchallenged. Many dissertations in the natural sciences are now published digitally or in periodicals. But in the social sciences and humanities paper and binding are still preferred. It is unclear what percentage of German dissertations are published by these specialized presses. But even if it is only a fraction of the 25,000 dissertations written annually in Germany, it still represents a significant slice of the 78,000 German books issued every year.[254]

Indeed, in Germany scores, if not hundreds, of small and otherwise wholly obscure presses exist solely to "publish" dissertations. They are businesses set up only to profit from the monopoly created by the dissertation publishing requirement. Earlier the costs were borne entirely by the student, as with vanity presses. Today the student is occasionally spared the production costs, if the press can recoup its outlays from a captive audience of scholarly libraries. But mostly students cover the expenses.[255] Some websites even provide a convenient calculator for prospective authors to tally what bringing forth their book will cost them.[256] Among the hundreds of German publishers submitting briefs to the New York court that rejected the Google Books settlement were doubtless ones whose profits derive from such academic bottom-feeding. And certainly their interests were aligned with their more conventional peers. To the extent that Judge Denny Chin paid the European publishers' many submissions any heed, he listened also to foreign rent-seekers who enrich themselves among the pointless obstacles the German state governments throw up to the dissemination of taxpayer-financed academic research. They were among the forces thwarting Google's Alexandrine ambitions.

The attempted settlement tarnished Google's credentials among American open access activists. A deal with the publishers seemed to be placing its hand in the lion's mouth. From our vantage, however, the important point is that, in the United States the publishers' and authors' opposition was the lobbying of one interest group. In Europe, government authority once again allied with the content industries to protect the private property of rights owners, all the while beating the drum of high-cultural principle.

Pressured by European publishers, Google abandoned its ambitions to digitize worldwide. The settlement between Google, authors, and publishers was rejected by Judge Chin in March 2011. When further negotiations between the three parties bore no fruit, the Authors Guild again sued for copyright violation. Pending appeal, it lost in November 2013 when Judge Chin determined that, because Google put works to transformative new purposes, the Books Project was fair use. That allowed Google to continue digitizing and showing snippets of works, while users could search books which were not, unless in the public domain, displayed online in their entirety. By 2013 Google's digitization had become an ingrained part of online culture, no longer as controversial as a decade earlier. Searching Google's books, Judge Chin pointed out, was now an essential research tool, spawning new scholarly fields like text and data mining. It allowed more efficient discovery of little-known works and the preservation of obscure and endangered ones. Even publishers, he admonished, should be thankful for increased sales. And Google expanded access for the handicapped and where traditional libraries were sparse.[257]

In the meantime, Google signed an emasculated version of the US settlement with the French publishing industry in June 2012. Rights holders had to opt in, rather than being included by default. That left unattended most "orphaned" works—ones that were out of print but still in copyright. Their rights holders were unknown, and they were therefore suspended in legal limbo. (Thanks to Berne's principle of automatically protecting works as of creation, the majority of twentieth-century works are orphaned and therefore unusable by others.) The original publishers also had the final say over which works Google could digitize.[258] In effect, the agreement allowed French publishers to outsource digital editions to Google if they choose not to issue them themselves. While acceptable, this was far from Google's initial ambitions.

But to their credit the French have also begun replicating what Google was attempting. The first installment of that story has been the French law of 1 March 2012, permitting the digitization of works still in copyright but out of print.[259] Seeking to counter Google's "savage" attempts to digitize before having secured rights—motivated by profit, as they saw it, and not respect for the author—the French appointed a government entity to accomplish similar ends while saving Europe's patrimony from an American corporation.[260] Pleased with their defeat of Google, the French now took pride in passing the first law worldwide on out-of-print works—jumping the gun on the EU's directive that emerged only half a year later.[261] That directive permitted educational and cultural institutions to digitize orphan works after conducting a diligent search for rights holders and coming up empty.[262] The earlier debates now left traces as the French once again discussed how to balance the interests of authors and audiences. Nonetheless, digitization was approached in a traditionally Gallic spirit. As always, French politicians saw their duty as upholding "a conception of the book and of culture that is diametrically opposed to the Anglo-Saxon view."[263] The law allowed out-of-print books to be digitized—but not just by anyone. An organization, composed of authors and publishers, could digitize if the rights owners did not commit to do so themselves within six months of the work being listed.

The French hoped to make books available that could otherwise be read mainly at the National Library in Paris. But they differed from Google. Owners' property rights still reigned supreme. Fair use was not to be a wedge to pry open ownership. Ensuring authors' and publishers' stake in the new medium was as much the law's point as making works available. Digitized out-of-print books were to be sold like any other, the proceeds divided between writers and publishers. Rights owners, the government noted approvingly, were given pride of place in exploiting digital works. The problem

with digitization, a senator agreed, was that the "myth of universal-
ity was accompanied by the temptation of giving it away for free."[264]
That had been Google's fallacy.

But, thanks to the new spirit of open access, in one respect a
Google-like approach triumphed. An amendment proposed allowing costless digital dissemination of works whose owners had not
objected within a decade. The Sarkozy government fought this suggestion as a "confiscation of authors' rights," and a "brutal rupture"
with the inherited system. The Assembly rejected it as dispossessing
authors of their rights.[265] Nonetheless, a watered-down version survived into the final law, allowing public libraries to digitize for their
patrons out-of-print books from their holdings whose rights owners
could not be found.[266]

French traditions were also respected in the continued role of
moral rights. Authors retained the final say over new electronic editions, modeled on the withdrawal right. If they felt their honor or
reputation threatened, they could refuse permission to digitize.[267] Yet
such solicitude was motivated by less than noble sentiments. Imagine an author had written something—oh, say, during the occupation of the Second World War—that he now regretted, a leading
senator explained. Surely, he should be able to prevent it from reap-
pearing.[268] Rarely had the unappetizing aspects of moral rights been
so baldly stated. The Senate, however, did reject an even more indul-
gent proposal to allow heirs to express their distaste in forewords to
digitized editions of works that they disliked or were ashamed of.[269]

THE CHATTERING CLASSES DIVIDE

Thanks to divergent historical trajectories, disputes over digitality's
effects came earlier in the United States than Europe. But the intellectual classes also aligned themselves differently across the Atlantic.
In chapter 4 we touched on how the cult of Romantic authorship
did not flourish in the Anglo-American world. The British and
Americans resisted the Continental ideology in part because they
had a less exalted view of what authors did. As early as 1762, William
Warburton had noted the shameless use that authors made of others'

efforts when he argued against works being considered property.[270] In "The Art of Book-Making" (1819) Washington Irving took this view of literary creation as parasitical even further. Like birds, who served nature's intent by excreting fruit seed, so authors were but a means of conveyance, passing ideas from old works into the present.[271] If disseminating others' ideas was their primary function, little purpose was served by guaranteeing authors inalienable rights to their particular interpretation of society's common themes. The work was as much the reader's as the poet's. "For every atom belonging to me as good belongs to you," as Walt Whitman assured his audience in 1855.[272] Originality and creation ex nihilo were discounted in the Anglophone world, which emphasized instead the social nature of knowledge, the borrowing and use of others' works. "Every book in literature, science and art, borrows, and must necessarily borrow, and use much which was well known and used before," Justice Story pronounced in 1845.[273]

In the twentieth century postmodernism's focus on how works are socially constructed and how authors rely on their cultural inheritance comfortably fit longstanding domestic American intellectual traditions. Postmodernism sparked less controversy than in Europe with its Romantic leanings.[274] It is a commonplace that the French philosophers of postmodernism—Althusser, Barthes, Foucault, Lyotard, Derrida, and Deleuze—had far greater impact in the United States than at home.[275] Postmodernism meshed well with the nineteenth-century pragmatist school of American thought that in many respects anticipated it.[276] Pragmatists, too, considered ideas to be socially generated. They were neither just out there, waiting to be uncovered, nor the product of solitary genius.[277] Such pragmatist concepts had influenced judicial thinking, paving the way for work-for-hire in the late nineteenth century.[278] A century later they prepared the ground for postmodernism's triumphal march through the American academy and its law schools. One jurist dates the entry of postmodernism into American jurisprudence to 2006, with Jeff Koons's vindication as a bricolage auteur for his use of an advertising photograph in a painting.[279]

The Romantic author thus started at a disadvantage in the Anglophone world. From there it went downhill. European intellectuals marshaled in support of the independent author. Their Anglo-American peers more often fought for the public domain. The disseminator's role was crucial here. Competitors for the same pot of gold, authors and disseminators were natural antagonists. A story had Antoine Choudens, the composer Charles Gounod's publisher, out for a walk, dressed in a sumptuous fur coat and a battered old hat. Gounod approached him, eyed the coat and said bitterly, "Ah, *Faust*." "Yes, but," replied Choudens, indicating the hat, "the *Tribut de Zamora*." Choudens had paid Gounod ten thousand francs for *Faust*, but ten times as much for *Zamora*.[280] Yet the mutual hostility of author and disseminator paled in comparison to what united them against the public. However the spoils were divided between them, they agreed on resisting the public's demand for cheap enlightenment.

In turn, the public's view of authors and disseminators was influenced by differences between copyright and authors' rights. In the web era Anglophonia saw a sharp conflict between consumers and rights holders. Thanks to the work's physicality, cultural transactions had earlier seemed akin to exchanges of other goods. Now, with the decrease—ostensibly to zero—in marginal costs of each extra digital copy, the consumer was apparently getting an unprecedentedly raw deal. As digitality promised ever cheaper copies, the owners' insistence on their cut made them appear greedy. These owners—publishers and media corporations—faced the public as the chief culprits. Authors were but their appendages. Copyright's practice of full assignment of rights and work-for-hire, where the corporation pretended to be the author, compounded this basic market asymmetry.

On the Continent, in contrast, to the extent there was any tension, it was between the real authors, supported of course by their disseminators, and the audience. Disseminators were shielded by the goodwill that still extended to authors. But in the Anglosphere it was the rights holders—largely the disseminators—whom the audience viewed as the exploiters.[281] Consumer fury was here vented with none of the residual sympathy that still tempered hostility toward authors in Europe. Naturally, authors in America lined up to support the disseminators. But they were so clearly the stooges of Hollywood and New York's corporate interests that they garnered little sympathy. That bestselling and celebrity authors were the ones trotted out at the congressional hearings and in paid ads did little to boost their cause. Were the titans of Tinseltown really to be pitied as *artistes* in their garrets? Who cried if rock stars had to fly commercial? America's traditional disregard for its authors, its refusal to succumb to the Romantic myth of the tortured genius, bit the creator once again. Like the original Battle of the Booksellers, the digital defense of authors in the Anglosphere was a cuckoo exercise, disseminators squeezing their oversized eggs into the creator's nest. Pretending that they benefited authors, the bitter pill of ever-stronger property claims for disseminators was sugarcoated for consumers to swallow.[282]

Since moral rights had never played an important role in the Anglo-American world, public discussion dealt primarily with authors' economic rewards. So long as they got a fair—if perhaps no longer extravagant—shake, the audience was unlikely to man the ramparts on their behalf. But in Europe authors were the focus and disseminators only their unavoidable sidekicks. Moral rights reinforced the fiction of authorial predominance, even as exploitation rights were signed away. European intellectuals thus found it easier to support authors while ignoring how the stronger rights granted them were pocketed largely by their disseminators. Insofar as the European left abandoned its traditionally unconditional support for authors and began to consider also the audience's claims, its own bohemian flank attacked it for treason. Having failed to punish digital downloading severely, French Socialists stood accused by authors of spurning culture and joining the camp of unbridled capitalism. The CEOs of the multinational internet corporations might wear jeans and T-shirts, authors warned left-wing politicians. But they were still greedy, savagely predatory digital capitalists.[283]

In Europe, then, the myth of the independent author still commanded veneration. In America, however, it was the salaried intelligentsia which dominated the airwaves. No well-organized class of literati had sprung forth in nineteenth-century America. In the fledgling republic it was a common lament that authors had little clout. Witness only the disregard with which the nation had imposed copyright on its own writers while flooding the market with cheap foreign works.[284] Cornelius Mathews complained in 1843: "Here an author is an anomaly; a needless excrescence of nature; a make-trouble and mar-plot, a mere impertinence. A book is supposed to grow up by some sort of spontaneous process beyond the seas, and to be imported into this country with Rootabaga and Yellow Hop."[285] Authors with day jobs were common. In the first half of the nineteenth century, at most one-fifth of American writers counted literature as their primary source of income.[286] Not until James Fenimore Cooper did America produce its first "professional" author. As he liked to point out, thanks to the trade in British writers, in America "the printer came into existence before the Author."[287]

Henry Wadsworth Longfellow and James Russell Lowell were professors, Nathaniel Hawthorne was US consul in Liverpool, Washington Irving was a merchant, Ralph Waldo Emerson lectured and was a minister, Edgar Allan Poe was an editor, Henry David Thoreau a jack-of-all-trades.[288] T. S. Eliot was a banker, William Carlos Williams a physician, and William Faulkner wrote *As I Lay Dying* while working in a power plant. Dashiell Hammett was employed by Pinkerton's and the railroads, and Nathanael West was the night manager of a hotel. Wallace Stevens was an insurance executive and turned down a faculty position at Harvard to remain vice president of his Hartford firm. Charles Ives, also an insurance executive, helped develop modern estate planning.[289]

A 1976 study calculated that only three hundred writers in the United States could live off their literary earnings (of ten million aspiring colleagues).[290] A 1979 survey of over two thousand writers found that almost half held paid positions besides freelance writing.[291] Whatever the precise figures, the number of successfully self-employed writers was small. On the other hand, many American writers and composers did well in Hollywood. Though mostly salarymen, they enjoyed some of the strongest union protection on the planet.[292] "The creative motion picture community is not helpless in any way," a spokesman for the other side, the Motion Picture Association, argued in 1988. "As we speak, the writers of Hollywood are in the process of either striking or not striking on a matter which would involve creative rights. They have high-priced lawyers, experienced labor negotiators. They are not supine."[293]

Was the situation different in Europe? During the late nineteenth century a "respectable man of letters" in Britain was able to earn an income and hold a position comparable to that of a doctor or lawyer.[294] In Germany, where patronage was less common than in England or France, by the late eighteenth century an "epidemic of reading" (*Leseseuche*) had created a large and eager public. Alas, it was not yet able to sustain many authors on their writings alone. Gotthard Lessing was a librarian and Christoph Wieland a professor.[295] Goethe was a lawyer, but as a civil servant and advisor to the court of Weimar, he belonged more to the era of patronage. Friedrich Klopstock found a patron in Frederick V of Denmark. Lamartine is perhaps best understood in the French tradition of literary statesmen, followed down to the current day by François Mitterrand, Dominique de Villepin, and others. Kafka worked in insurance before becoming a workman's compensation actuary and made no attempt to live off his writing. J. K. Huysmans worked for thirty years in the French Ministry of the Interior, Primo Levi was a chemist, and Carlo Levi pinchhit as a physician during his exile to Lucania in the 1930s. Ibsen was a pharmacist in his youth, W. H. Auden was briefly a schoolmaster, J.R.R. Tolkien and C. S. Lewis were dons, and Philip Larkin a librarian. Dorothy Sayers worked as a teacher and copywriter. So, perhaps the contrast across the Atlantic is not stark.

Whatever the sociology, the ideology of those authors who did not live from selling their works neatly dovetailed with the prospects held out by digitality. This included some already well-off authors. But primarily it was the salaried intelligentsia that rallied behind the digital ideology. They could most conveniently insist on the planks of the digital dogma: creativity is collective, sharing stimulates productivity more than property does, freely flowing information is the ultimate good, and so forth. It was easy enough for them to suggest that the "reputational capital" of widely disseminated works was more valuable than actually selling books. Or that authors would be paid for performance and service, not for marketing works.[296] Their well-upholstered position allowed them to speculate whether perhaps authors were motivated by considerations other than the market's incentives.[297] Only the salaried could suggest that selling works be replaced by mutual gifts of self-expression—the adult equivalent of childish play.[298]

The few American men of letters who sided with traditional "European" authors' rights unwittingly presented themselves as genteel dinosaurs—and were mocked accordingly. John Updike rather feebly critiqued Kevin Kelly's vision of a digital Alexandrian library by nostalgically recalling his days of privilege and access at Harvard and Oxford, browsing the shelves at Grolier's and Blackwell's. He evoked his quaint New England town with its independent bookstore as the foil to what he considered the Marxist Moloch of the Google library.[299] Mark Helprin, old-school novelist and conservative pugilist, posing for his jacket photo by a baby grand, presented himself as the sort of literary fop who drives the digiterati to apoplexy, his prose oozing the ambiance of the gentleman's club, his faux cold shoulder to the modern world. Helprin's unremarkable arguments in favor of extending copyright terms provoked outrage. His initial piece ran on the *New York Times* op-ed page, which had invited him to fill the doldrums with what he judged to be an anodyne topic.[300] Within ten days it had been widely commented upon online. Helprin then decided that a book-length version, expanded into a jeremiad against the modern world, would calm things down.[301] So tightly into the wind of self-parody did Helprin tack that we cannot dismiss the possibility that he is a fifth columnist. But taken at face value, he argued the classic postulates of the moral rights ideology, especially the integrity right and the author's claim to have his voice heard precisely as intended. His views would not have raised an eyebrow in France. But in America such studied anachronism was a red flag to the digital bulls.

Nonetheless, the aging Romantic authors did have a point. Digitality has gutted the inherited business models and few new means to earn a living have emerged. Authors should earn their keep in other ways, Kevin Kelly suggested. "They can sell performances, access to the creator, personalization, add-on information, the scarcity of attention (via ads), sponsorship, periodic subscriptions—in short all the many values that cannot be copied."[302] The slapdash, unrealistic, in parts unintelligible, nature of this list testifies to its unresolved contradictions. Updike might be fusty, but he rightly took Kelly to task for this naïve view—a "grisly scenario" of the author singing for his supper.

Another digital insider, the dreadlocked computer scientist, composer, and inventor of virtual reality, Jaron Lanier, agreed with Updike. He defied anyone to point to more than a handful of musicians living from the web's supposedly "new" economy.[303] Perhaps the Grateful Dead, who sold special tickets to a section of seats reserved for bootleg tape recorders back in the analog era, had managed to find an alternative business model.[304] But they were largely alone. Independent musicians have often cried foul. The same generation that willingly paid extra for fair trade coffee and stood in line overnight to snap up Apple's latest sleek device proved reluctant to pay for content. "Congratulations," one musician mocked, "your generation is the first generation in history to rebel by *unsticking* it to the man and instead sticking it to the weirdo freak musicians!"[305] Thanks to downloading, musicians now faced the "Bowie Theory," the unforgiving syllogism by which tours and concerts alone earned them money.[306]

For all their foppish airs the old-schoolers who defended authors were canaries in the digital mine. Their objections marked a largely ignored fault line between salaried and self-employed literati. "Why is it always the guys with the cushy and secure jobs who tell you tweedle de dee, ideas should be free?" complained Ted Nelson, coiner of the phrase "hypertext."[307] Independent writers were civilization's bastion, Helprin insisted. The drones of "the academy, think tanks, or various other corporate bodies" owed allegiance to their department heads.[308] Tenured professors, *New Yorker* staff writers, think tankers— all had their feet on dry land. Independent authors were angered by their salaried peers' sellout to what they saw as the false idols of open access. In America these last few Romantic creators remained staunch defenders of authorial privileges—alongside aging rockers. Metallica's drummer, Lars Ulrich, and Kiss's bassist, Gene Simmons, aggressively supported copyright and musicians' claims to make a living selling their wares. In return radical digiterati hacked their websites and boycotted their music. "Make sure there are no incursions," was Simmons's message. "Be litigious. Sue everybody. Take their homes, their cars. Don't let anybody cross that line."[309] In 2007 Prince accused YouTube of being perfectly able to filter out porn and pedophilia while turning a blind eye to copyrighted music.[310] Mark Helprin and Gene Simmons, united at last to defend the young Werther school of Romantic creativity: we are uncomfortably close to the farcical possibilities with which this chapter began.

EUROPEAN HEGEMONY?

Left-of-center Americans often support and admire European policies: on the death penalty, state welfare, health care, and public education. But on copyright (much as with free speech—another issue where trans-Atlantic differences are profound) the libertarian and anarchic strain of American liberal ideology has prevailed.[311] Only rarely—certainly not on the left nor even very often on the right—was the European model of thick authorial rights held up for praise in America. Of course, the content industries pursued their own concerns when adhering to the Berne ideology. Moral rights, in turn, were advocated by Hollywood's auteurs, hoping to curb the industry's corporate self-interest, as well as by other authors out to increase their aesthetic heft. But unlike their European peers many American liberals and intellectuals regarded such author-centrism as an outmoded obeisance to elitism. In any case it was seen as out of sync with the digital age and its polymorphously collaborative creativity.

It is all the more striking, then, that during the 1990s American policy bowed to the content industries' imperative and swung copyright's traditional emphasis on the public domain around to a more European focus on rights owners' claims. Impelled by the dictates of new collaborative cultural endeavors and digital technologies, the Europeans did make a few concessions to copyright practices, adopting limited forms of work-for-hire for film and software, for example. Yet, seen in long historical perspective, it is clear that those who were most smartly changing gear were the Americans—and to a lesser extent the British.[312] In 1954 the Senate Judiciary Committee had listed the three main reasons why the Berne Convention was at variance with "our basic theory and philosophy on copyrights" and why the United States could not join: automatic recognition of copyright without any formalities, protection of moral rights, and the retroactive application of protection to works already in the public domain.[313] Within a few years, first in the late 1970s and then a decade later, these supposedly insurmountable obstacles had all been swept away. America was being carried along in Europe's wake.

How was this possible? Clearly the content industries bent the Clinton administration's ear. But simply to identify the economic interests that benefited most from this American policy volte-face is not enough. Corporate interests rarely had a uniform position on strong intellectual property rights. In the nineteenth century reprinting publishers had opposed international copyright while publishers who issued domestic authors were in support. The sound-recording industry had thrived in the absence of copyright during the 1890s, while the sheet-music publishers cried out for stronger protection. Today Hollywood's moment of supremacy in the 1990s has been challenged as Silicon Valley's internet and computer industries base their business models on web data's free availability. Inevitably both author and audience align with some economic interests. However tempting to vilify those who profit from strong protection as though they were a unified class, the battle has rarely been between corporate interests tout court and the general public. Though colored by the economic concerns of a varying cast of actors, the fundamental dispute has been ideological: whose concerns should prevail, the author's or the audience's.

In an era of much ballyhooed US cultural imperialism, it is not facetious to speak of European hegemony too. Much like the United States, the EU presented its model as a universally valid example to be commended to nations abroad.[314] EU harmonization pushed levels of intellectual property protection upward. Across the Atlantic, too, rights strengthened. "In recent years," one American observer complained in 2004, "'the labor-equals-property principle' has come to dominate."[315] The battles detailed in this chapter were the outcome of the still unresolved popular reaction against the pendulum's swing toward Berne's dogma of authorial preeminence. Authors' rights were but one policy where the Americans followed European examples. The ensuing Europeanization of American policy was, of course, a victory for some within the bestiary of US economic interests. More important, the outcome was major change to long-standing American political and cultural traditions.

Copyright was not the only field where globalization meant Europeanization. American patent legislation, too, has been Europeanized. Arguably, the US Constitution required that credit be given to the first to invent. The copyright clause empowered Congress to secure to authors and inventors "the exclusive right to *their* respective writings and discoveries" (emphasis added). Until recently America stuck to first-to-invent, rewarding the creator, not his corporate employer. But under pressure from the Europeans, things have changed. First-to-file offered certain advantages. By eliminating disputes over priority, it was simpler and more certain. And it encouraged making inventions public at the earliest moment.[316] But first-to-file triumphed even in the United States because it had become the global standard. If the US inventor was not also the first to file, then he lost his foreign markets. With some globally marketed products, like biotech and pharmaceuticals, the American inventor who did not file first for patent rights might recoup what he had foregone abroad by cross-licensing his US rights in exchange for foreign ones.[317] But clearly the advantage lay with the majority. When the America Invents Act of 2011 adopted first-to-file, the European approach had triumphed.

Bankruptcy law is another example of America's gradual Europeanization. Historically a debtor nation, America has traditionally allowed citizens second chances to bounce back from insolvency. This too has been leached away by the European approach of releasing debtors from their obligations only reluctantly. Bankruptcy has long been more debtor-friendly in the United States than Europe, in some measure to fill a vacuum in social policies.[318] But recent changes to consumer bankruptcy law have made student loans, for example, no longer dischargeable via ordinary bankruptcy. They now require separate proceedings and a demonstration of special hardship.[319] The bursting of the most recent housing bubble in 2008 thrust a new issue, again imported from Europe, into American discussions. Should house owners with loans be able to walk away from mortgages, leaving the bank with the property as collateral? Or should they, as in most of Europe, remain personally responsible for continued payments, regardless of what happened to the house? In the United States debt has traditionally been shrugged off via the backdoor socialism of lenient bankruptcy laws. But that is becoming harder as European-style standards spread to America.

Privacy has also been a bone of contention across the Atlantic. True, the Americans have whittled away at banking privacy and the attendant possibilities of tax evasion in Switzerland, Liechtenstein, Austria, and elsewhere in Europe. But the fiscal authorities of Germany, Scandinavia, and even some Mediterranean nations have welcomed the United States here in its role as bad cop. Claiming national security concerns, the Americans have only partly succeeded in requiring information on airline passengers.[320] But, more generally, US firms whose business relies on transparency and accumulating information about clients and customers—Google and Facebook—have faced increasingly stiff obstacles as the EU strictly enforces privacy regulations. The traditionally insouciant (Anglo-) American view of privacy as more a convenience than a fundamental right has been dampened by the EU's determination to clamp down on collecting private information. The new EU "right to be forgotten" on the internet contravenes American notions of free speech and will require internet companies to remove broadly defined personal information as demanded by their clients, however far it may have spread in the meantime.[321]

Examples of America's Europeanization could be multiplied. The death penalty has become less acceptable thanks to the "Strasbourg effect" exerted by the European Court of Human Rights on US Supreme Court justices.[322] More generally, the EU's status as the world's single largest consumer market permits it to set product and manufacturing standards that US corporations must follow.[323]

Copyright reform in the 1990s fit this larger pattern of cultural influence westward across the Atlantic. Globalization in such instances meant Europeanization. Converting to long and strong protection, the United States moved away from its traditional view of copyright as a limited monopoly and closer to the European natural rights tradition. "The United States should be leading the world toward a coherent intellectual property policy for the digital age," Dennis Karjala, copyright lawyer and activist, exclaimed in frustration before Congress in 1995 during debates on the seventy-year term, "and not simply following what takes place in Europe."[324]

And yet, while Berne may have won the battle in the 1990s, the war was not over. Digital technologies threw up new problems in producing and disseminating works that required a response in law. Ahead on the digital learning curve and favored by its market's size, integration, and uniformity, the United States travelled this path ahead of the Europeans. Both the attempts to impose new legal and technological protections for rights owners and the reaction against authors' and assignees' overweening demands therefore came earlier in the US than on the Continent. But in a longer perspective the imperatives for change were similar everywhere.

Digitality held out such promises of open and broad access that the Enlightenment dreams of a universal library for all humanity were reawakened early in the new millennium. Whether eventually achieved by Google or by others, the Alexandrian vision is now plausible. The downloaders have not, of course, all been motivated by higher causes. But mixed in with the digital piracy and pilfering has also been a robust commitment to the public domain. Having lost out in the 1990s to Hollywood and Berne's insistence on strong protection, the traditional vision of copyright as a limited monopoly that—while keeping authors happy—fundamentally serves the public interest has returned as an aspiration. Rejuvenated in the United States, where it had never entirely died, it is now echoed among the pirate parties and youthful downloaders of Western Europe and the digitally aspirational citizens of the former East. The battle between author and audience continues.

Conclusion

RECLAIMING THE SPIRIT OF COPYRIGHT

Anglo-American copyright and European authors' rights have dealt in distinctly different ways with the social role of creators, their control over works, and the audience's demands for access. Seen historically, authors submitted to the dictates of social utility more in the copyright systems, alienating their works largely to disseminators and losing them earlier to the public domain. On the Continent they retained stronger and more expansive rights for longer, indeed sometimes perpetually.

The cultural assumptions that underlay such distinctions also varied. Both the natural rights idea of property and Romanticism's veneration of the solitary artist had firmer roots on the Continent than in the Anglophone world. Literary property based on natural rights was propounded by Noah Webster in the United States and Talfourd in Britain. But already early on Anglo-Saxon copyright chose the path of a limited statutory monopoly, in Britain with *Donaldson* (1774) and in the US with *Wheaton* (1834).

The continental riposte was elaborated only later. While Kant and Fichte foreshadowed the philosophical argument in the late eighteenth century, authors' personal rights in works began being discussed in Parliament during the 1830s and '40s in France. Moral rights were partly embodied in the German laws of 1901 and 1907, entered the Berne Union in 1928, and finally achieved full statutory fruition during the postwar period. Romanticism may have marled the soil for such ideas. But curiously their legal implementation was most immediately the outcome of fascism—whether directly, as when Mussolini put moral rights into practice in Italy in 1925 and on the Berne Convention agenda in Rome in 1928, or reactively, as when France and Germany steered the course away from the totalitarian communalism of the 1930s to the cultural high ground in their laws of 1957 and 1965. With their pretentions to the status of a natural—thus eternal—right, it is easy to overlook just how recent a conceit authors' rights actually are. Like all traditions, they too were invented at a specific time and place.

With Berne's 1928 adoption of the core principle of moral rights, the Continental ideology of strong authorial claims continued its march to global dominance. In the mid-twentieth century Europeans increasingly regarded intellectual property as founded on natural rights in two ways: as a form of quasi-conventional property based on Lockean ownership via labor but also as an emanation of the author's personality. In the 1950s and '60s France and Germany adopted author-centric laws as they sought to reassert their high-cultural credentials. Traditional Anglophone copyright, with its utilitarian focus on the public domain, was marginalized. Now spoken for largely in the United States, even there it was increasingly on the defensive.

By the 1990s the Berne ideology had triumphed worldwide. The Anglo-Americans were increasingly influenced by the Berne Union's sway over international protection of literary and artistic rights. Even as the safeguarding of intellectual property shifted from Berne to the WIPO and then from there into trade legislation, overseen by the WTO, the fundamental Berne principles remained intact. Moral rights were ever more sidelined—and not just thanks to Anglophone skepticism. Aiming to make Europe competitive on the global market, the EU sought to avoid hobbling those industries reliant on intellectual property. Nor did France and Germany, the cultural heavy hitters of the nineteenth century and the main advocates of moral rights, enjoy their accustomed heft in the new postwar Anglophone world.

But moral rights had been only one element of the Berne ideology. Even more important was its assumption that works were a form of property, resting on natural rights. Its owners thus had near absolute claims, largely undiluted by social priorities or concerns. Treating works as property and their protection as a right, not the outcome of a utilitarian horse trade as in copyright's customary approach: that was the fundamental Berne premise of interest to the US content industries. That had encouraged them in the 1990s to turn American policy away from its traditional concern with the public domain. Instead, they pushed to outdo the Europeans by using the new international trade treaties to implement and enforce strong property rights.

The Anglo-Americans followed the European lead in several important respects. They lengthened terms, always chasing the Continental precedent: to fifty years postmortem in the UK in 1911 (importantly qualified by the loss of exclusive authorial rights after a quarter century) and the US in 1976 and then to seventy in the 1990s. They largely adopted the Berne refusal to predicate protection on formalities, thus making private ownership of all works the default position. On moral rights they formally toed the Berne line, though making sure that little emerged that was of any practical use to authors or inconvenience to disseminators. In other words, the Anglo-Americans did not adopt those aspects of the authors' rights ideology that specifically benefited authors at the expense of disseminators. But they did, more generally, abandon their traditional Jeffersonian and Macaulayian view of copyright as a limited monopoly granted rights owners primarily for socially utilitarian purposes. Instead, they accepted the European approach of natural rights to intellectual property and strong legal protection of works.

Today, twenty years later, the Berne consensus has begun to unravel. Not only has the native Anglo-American tradition of limited copyright been reasserted as an antidote to overweening rights holders' claims. But even in Europe digitality's promise of universal access coupled to a newfound understanding of creativity as collective and socially determined—not the work of solitary Romantic genius—has provoked a reconsideration of inherited verities. Strong authors' rights no longer command universal respect among the born-digital generation. We are once again gripped by a debate as intense as the Battle of the Booksellers in the eighteenth century or the controversy between Talfourd and Macaulay in the 1830s, not to mention the nineteenth-century American disputes over international copyright. Will digitality's promise of universal accessibility be fulfilled? Or will the new technologies be used to reinforce rights owners' property? Though the copyright tradition's focus on the public domain has been subordinated to owners' claims in recent years, there is good reason for cautious optimism that a return to its fundamental principles may guide us through the shoals of the digital revolution.

WHY THE DIFFERENCE?

Of course, the French were right that the Anglo-Saxons took a more matter-of-fact, possibly mercantile, approach to culture—generally speaking, as well as in their copyright legislation. The tropes of trans-Atlantic cultural antagonism are well known: the English are a nation of shopkeepers, the Americans capitalist barbarians, the French are bohemian artistes, the Germans otherworldly *Dichter und Denker*, at least when they are not being *Richter und Henker*. Such clichés did not originate with the copyright debates. But in the course of these disputes, they were undergirded by law. The disregard with which American authors were sacrificed on the altar of public enlightenment in the nineteenth century—inundated by noncopyrighted foreign literature until 1891—contrasted sharply with the ever stronger protection enjoyed by French and German writers.

The Americans' "love of trade," Charles Dickens reported sourly on tour in 1842, explained why literature would remain forever unprotected there.[1] But the French (and Dickens) were mistaken in interpreting the Anglo-American attitude as merely reflecting the content industries' sway and a blind worship of the market. Anglophone copyright was as ideological a choice as the Continental view of culture as sacrosanct and worthy of protection from market vicissitudes. It was democratic and populist, consciously rejecting the Continent's high-cultural premium on authorial interests. It reflected a political judgment that cheap and ready access for the audience was as worth defending as authors' creativity. The disputes over copyright and authors' rights thus cut to the core of broader political and cultural agendas.

Ultimately, the Anglophone nations were especially concerned with access for the audience because their political systems were more democratically porous, their leaders attuned to the needs and demands of an ever more literate public. With its limited suffrage and many literary men serving as deputies and ministers, France's July Monarchy was preoccupied with authors' claims. Meanwhile, the audience was already commanding the high ground in the Anglophone world. In nineteenth-century America the common people were well positioned to insist on access to the literature of their choice. Britain's suffrage was, of course, more limited, though as of 1832 the electorate was four times that of France. During the Talfourd debates British MPs pondered issues far removed from what preoccupied their French peers.

William Warburton was a free-trading radical, opposed to Talfourd's proposals to enhance authors' prerogatives. His outburst in 1839 that "any extension of the rights of authors was a robbery upon the public" was an extreme example of audience advocacy and would have been inconceivable in the French Chamber of the time. The chancellor of the exchequer's more moderate insistence during the same debate, that Talfourd's sixty-year term might "excite a certain degree of public feeling against the bill," came closer to the fears of popular unrest that the British authorities anticipated from excessively overt favoritism for authors.[2] The American authorities suffered similar anxieties throughout the nineteenth century. Cheap books were a necessity, the essayist Logan Pearsall Smith was quoted by a senator in 1891 as warning. The public would not tolerate steep price hikes.[3]

The debates over open access in our own time sound much the same political notes. "This *is* a war about basic American values," insists Lawrence Lessig, who favors reintroducing short terms and reimposing registration formalities, thus abandoning Berne principles to ensure that works fall quickly into the public domain.[4] American reformers who lament the triumph of the Berne ideology today often seek to bring back lost features of the traditional Anglo-Saxon approach: shorter terms, formalities, more extensive fair use.[5] The digital activists, hackers, and downloaders stand in what they consider the democratic and Enlightenment tradition of throwing open humanity's common patrimony to all. Unlike the nineteenth century, however, this is now a position heard on both sides of the Atlantic.

Though open access began in Europe early in the new millennium as the demand of the pirate party fringe, it is gradually—as in the United States—becoming more mainstream.

The open access activists in all nations position themselves as enemies of rights owners and especially the content industries, which seek to make private property of something that should, in their view, rightly belong to all. The strength of the open access movement in the universities reflects not just a general ideological penchant for widespread enlightenment (undergirded, of course, by salaries, benefits, and tenure) but also bitter experience with the grasping overreach of academic periodical publishers—rent-seekers at the public expense. Sadly, university professors and students are, in turn, often blind to how the general public, which ultimately finances such treasures, is locked out of the vast digital riches available only within the ivory tower. Jill Lepore's claim that "most of what academics produce can be found, by anyone who wants to find it, by searching Google," is simply false.[6] She should try Googling outside the well-feathered nest of her university proxy server. Such complacency was what drove Aaron Swartz in his ill-fated quest to release JSTOR's trove of Anglophone social science to those excluded from the MIT library's ambit. And all this, of course, concerns only the industrialized world. It ignores the data sluice gates that could today be opened for the Third World—were it not for rights owners' prerogatives.

AUTHORS, AUDIENCE, DISSEMINATORS: WHO ARE THE ACTORS?

Why have the Anglophone nations historically been less willing to protect authors than the Continent, and why did they switch course in the 1990s? Hollywood's influence has often been blamed for the increasing content lockdown of our time. But why should the disseminators in any one of these cultured nations have wielded especially much clout? The Continental publishing, music, and movie industries were no more to be trifled with than their American or British peers. More to the point, corporate interests have rarely spoken with one voice. Insofar as economic interests drove developments at all, they were hybridic and complex, pursuing few clear or enduring ambitions. Three main actors have engaged in a pas de trois over intellectual property: authors, disseminators, and the audience. But seen historically none has had a consistent and unified interest. Let us briefly consider the various combatants of the copyright wars.

Of course, authors sought renown and the translation of their reputations into royalties. Since their works were much like conventional property, they argued, they deserved long and strong, ideally perpetual, rights. When forced to choose between reputation and reward, they often proved to be precise bean counters. Dickens soured relations with his American fans on tour in 1842 when he brushed aside their adulation to insist on copyright for foreign authors. Sometimes authors worked both sides of the trade-off. Walt Whitman demanded strict authorial control even though he posed as the common man's friend, claiming that his works belonged as much to the reader as to their creator.[7]

Nor have authors sung in unison. Copyright was first formulated on the presumption that primary authors created ex nihilo and thus owned and should control their works. That distinction, between primary authors and their derivative colleagues, has now been questioned by postmodernist aesthetics, with its denial of autonomous authorship. Even the audience is seen to serve authorial functions. We are all interpreters now. But already from the very start of copyright, deep in the Romantic era, the use of works by other creators for inspiration and derivation undermined any unified authorial position. Primary authors, authors of derivative works, authors who use their colleagues' works for their own purposes, and performers of others' works (who are also authors in an interpretative sense) have rarely agreed on whether works should be free to use or stand as inviolate monuments to their creators' genius.

As a group authors have naturally sought their own immediate benefit by lengthening the duration of protection. But in a broader sense they are also fighting a losing battle against time itself. Unless terms expand continuously, the public domain will inevitably grow—eventually becoming overpoweringly vast compared to those few contemporary works that remain protected.[8] As their center of gravity shifts backward, modern cultures will age not only demographically but culturally.

Disseminators, in turn, have broadly shared interests with some authors. They supported their natural rights to literary property already in the eighteenth century, anticipating a stronger transfer of claims for themselves as the author's stake was beefed up. Of course, the precise division of spoils has always been contentious. What appeared a victory for authors—a term extension, say—often mainly benefited disseminators. Work-for-hire has almost invariably pitted disseminators against authors. And the two have clashed over moral rights. By promising authors a continued stake even after they alienated their economic rights, moral rights cut into what assignees received. Moral rights have set primary authors against a potential alliance of their derivative colleagues, disseminators, and the public that hoped to enjoy a broad array of works. Most generally, primary authors have shared interests with disseminators in strong rights, while authors who made use of others' works have aligned with the audience in seeking quick and uncomplicated access.

Disseminators' interests, however, have also depended on their niche in the market. Some were aligned with authors, like nineteenth-century American publishers of domestic works. Alongside performers and derivative authors, in contrast, the nineteenth-century American publishers who reprinted foreign works opposed strong rights for primary authors. Still other publishers were largely unconcerned with authors, making their money by flogging cheap public domain works, or pirated editions, to a broad public. These were the ones Mark Twain had in mind when he griped that publishers reaped the benefit of the public domain as much as the audience. "They live forever, the publishers do."[9] In the late nineteenth century the sound-recording industry ran roughshod over composers, blatantly reproducing their works in the new media. Given film's hybrid nature, Hollywood has often been an ambiguous actor: author, performer, *and* disseminator. It has pushed for authors' rights the better to own their works, treated its stable of writers and artists as employees, yet also hoped for an expansive public domain from which to poach its derivative creations.

Finally, the audience, too, has been at cross-purposes with itself. It has wanted cheap and good works but often could not have both—at least not at the same time. In nineteenth-century America popular movements arose both in favor of extending copyright to foreign authors and not doing so.[10] The audience's interests have rarely been spoken for directly. At best, those actors with whom it shared a concern at any given moment have claimed to represent it. The reprint publishers of nineteenth-century America trumpeted their concern for the public all the way to the bank. The sound-recording industry in the 1890s was even more shamelessly populist. How else, it asked as it fleeced composers, would the common folk far from metropolitan concert halls ever enjoy themselves?

This was an opportunistic speaking-for-the-public by economic interests that happened momentarily to overlap with audience demand. But the needs of a literate and increasingly demanding public hovered continuously in the background as the fundamental cause of the ever more pitched war between rights owners and the audience. The ease and range of reproducing works grew with every new technological development. The audience's consequent expansion vastly magnified the market from which authors and disseminators skimmed their cut. But it also amplified the consumer's demand for ready access. As the market for protected works grew, so too did the potential public domain. Day and night all homes now play musical recordings, a French observer warned in 1933. But authors have not been rewarded in proportion to this enormous expansion of consumption.[11] The consumers of recorded music are now everywhere, an Italian agreed. They insist on slashing royalty payments and play recordings in cafés or town squares without a thought for rewarding composers. And what the public wants, the government cannot refuse.[12] The imperative of universal access, which we now think defines our own digital age, in fact began its snowballing progress long ago.

With the digital revolution both sides have become even more clamorous. Rights owners have mobilized in defense of their property. But the audience has swelled too. Its consumption habits increasingly presume an ever greater degree of access. When, early in the 2000s, the French parties of the left abandoned their traditional veneration of the author to side tentatively with the audience, it was an ideological wrench. But the downloading generation's demands were becoming politically imperative. After the Swedish authorities sentenced the Pirate Bay's owners to fines and jail in 2009, voters promptly sent the Pirate Party to the EU parliament.[13] Authors who dared fight downloaders have been castigated and ridiculed. When Lars Ulrich, drummer for Metallica, insisted that fans pay for the band's music, file-sharers declared it Public Enemy Number One.[14]

Government authorities, in turn, have also been players. They have mediated debates among these actors, while also interjecting their own concerns. The French Old Regime monarchy sought to strengthen the Parisian publishers against their provincial competitors, but the eighteenth-century British authorities ended the London booksellers' monopoly, opening the market to competition. In the nineteenth century Macaulay better represented the new free-trading spirit of liberal government than did Talfourd. Having supported free reprinting in the nineteenth century, the American authorities switched position in the 1990s to agree with their postwar French and German colleagues in backing strong rights. But governments could also be as internally conflicted in their ambitions as business interests. Different parts of government have pursued divergent goals. In the 1970s, even as policy generally was moving in the Berne direction, the US educational authorities followed their primary constituency's lead to favor broad fair use exemptions for schools and universities. Even the military had its own stake in wanting to make computer copies of works at will.[15]

As governance has gone global international actors have also entered the stage.[16] Though many laws are enforced better as the authorities' geographical mandate widens, for copyright the connection has been crucial. Protection imposed in only one region could not stop piracy. Before unification in the late nineteenth century, the fragmentation of the Italian and German state systems effectively ruled out literary property.[17] Conversely, embedding copyright in national statute as of 1790, the United States solved the issue—insofar as copyright was applied at all—by consolidating the single largest protected market until the Berne Convention. Europe's interest in international standardization was early and pressing because only thus could its many small states hope to enforce authors' rights.

At the very least, the transnational organizations have provided a forum for interest groups to advance their cause. Hoping for economies of regulatory scale, nations have joined international organizations to standardize procedures across borders. Starting in 1886 the first of these, the Berne Union, has been a broad church. Though the major Continental nations' author-centric agenda eventually predominated, the Commonwealth nations, joined by small, populist, culture-importing polities like the Dutch and the Scandinavians, dug in their heels for more accessibility.[18] With the TRIPs agreement in 1994, internationalization accelerated as intellectual property became part of trade regulation. Any but the most autarchic hermit kingdoms now had to abide by rules made in Washington and Brussels if they hoped to find a market for their own wares abroad.

The fundamental antagonism between intellectual property importers and exporters—between pirates and policemen—most dramatically pitched the United States against the Old World in the nineteenth century. That clash was slowly squeezed down a century later, in the 1990s, as the developing world was brought into the global exchange system on terms dictated by the industrialized nations. Once China and other emerging economies develop intellectual property worth defending, transnational piracy will disappear. The influence of international organizations and agreements also helps explain the continuity of legislation over political shifts and ruptures that might otherwise have left more of an imprint. Though quitting the League of Nations, Nazi Germany remained a Berne member and—as the anticipated overlord of the European continent—continued to plan even in the depths of war for reform of authors' rights. However much it resisted other international organizations, the United States happily signed on to the dictates of the UN's WIPO Copyright Treaty.

By instinct and training historians are averse to generalizations, but in this case two may be ventured. First, even as conventional property, and especially real property, has become ever more subject to society's dictates, intellectual property has increased its scope, strength, and legal backing over the past three centuries for this reason: of the three main actors on the stage, two—authors and disseminators—have largely agreed on strong protection and acted forcefully to that end. With conventional property haves battle havenots, and the outcome has depended on their respective strengths. With intellectual property, however, the third actor, the authors, sounding the horn of natural rights entitlement, has tipped the balance in favor of the disseminators. Meanwhile, the audience has pursued its interest in broader access only in the characteristically tepid and diffuse way that public goods are sought. Second, culture exporters have sought strong protection of intellectual property, while importers have been more interested in the free movement and use of works.

The interaction of these two broad principles helps account for the more specific historical outcomes. Thus, until late in nineteenth-century America, the reprinting publishers dominated their colleagues who favored international copyright, domestic authors were few and ill-organized, and the audience, expressing its wishes through robust democratic institutions, was seconded and supported by official opinion. The outcome was possibly the most freewheeling and exuberant content cornucopia ever. Other nations, like eighteenth-century Austria, were pirates for similar reasons. In nineteenth-century France, conversely, authorial interests—well-represented in politics—were concerned to protect their disseminators' cultural exports by imposing bilateral and eventually broader international regulation of literary property rights. Few, other than Proudhon, spoke for the audience here.

As America began to export culture and as its authors and their disseminators persuaded the authorities to back strong protection, pirate became policeman. Today the hopes of a swing back in the direction of less protection and more access are based on the fissures that have opened up in the disseminators' hitherto monolithic front—Hollywood versus Silicon Valley—and the ability of the audience, now armed with the leverage of digital downloading and organized in the new spirit of consumer power, finally to flex its muscle.

IS COPYRIGHT A POLITICAL ISSUE?

The antagonism between the audience-friendly approach of traditional Anglophone copyright and the Continent's author-centric ideology is revealed most clearly through historical analysis. Thanks to the globalization of intellectual property regulation, many erstwhile contrasts have now faded. Formalities have been largely eliminated even in America. Durations are largely the same in most nations. Moral rights are in place everywhere—at least formally. Only a few clear differences remain: work-for-hire remains a core principle of Anglo-American copyright that the collaborative content industries will not relinquish. The flesh-and-blood author continues to cut a wider swath on the Continent. Fair use remains more generous in the US, and to some extent in the UK, than in France or Germany. Seen historically, this consensus—such as it is—was achieved by pushing the copyright systems toward the Berne standard. Since the Europeans had formed the first international union, thus reaping the network advantage, the United States had to creep to the Berne cross to protect its booming cultural exports. Long durations were invariably achieved earlier on the Continent and with less fuss than in America and Britain. Formalities were abolished at Berne's behest. Moral rights, with their curbing of the work's free alienability, were imposed in part on reluctant Anglophones. The only concession Europeans have made to copyright has been to adopt work-for-hire in a few limited instances.

However moderated, the antagonism between copyright and authors' rights nonetheless persists today in aspects of political ideology that go far beyond narrow technicalities. Copyright is a particular subset of law, subject to specific legal procedures and developments. But it is also an arena of bigger cultural battles.

Legal historians, however, often present the law as independent of, and irreducible to, the surrounding social, economic, and cultural circumstances. The law is seen as evolving on its own terms, in splendid isolation from the currents and battles that so obviously influence other human endeavors. However implausible such claims may seem to other historians, some credit is due. As copyright developed from the eighteenth century on, it was hard to read each particular twist and turn as indicative of specific political changes, novel ideologies, or new actors. The French Old Regime began reforms that then continued during the revolution. Despite his autocratic tendencies, Napoleon continued what the French revolutionaries regarded as world-historically democratic novelties. The postwar West German government built upon draft bills detailed under the Nazis, the French elaborated proposals first advanced under Vichy. To this day the Italians remain content with laws passed under Mussolini.

When the French first elaborated moral rights, they were less influenced by Kant and Fichte, or Romanticism, than by the dilemmas thrown up by Napoleonic procedures of property allocation at death and divorce. Community property and legally designated heirs meshed poorly with the personal aspects of authors' rights. Many developments were thus internal to each legal system. They were part of an institutional learning process whereby statute, once applied, revealed its practical inadequacies and the consequent need for tweaking. Historically speaking, paintings and sculpture were generally copyrighted only after books had been. That testified neither to the onslaught of new technologies nor to the rise of new and powerful interest groups, but rather to the eventual addressing of an oversight.[19]

But neither were reforms of copyright and authors' rights merely an ideologically neutral technical adjustment, something like the shift from imperial to metric standards of measurement. How they were formulated spoke of broader values and priorities. It would be hard to say that one approach was specifically left-wing and another rightist. True, supporting broad public access was generally a democratic position, while authors' interests were often backed by conservatives and moderates. But that is about as precise as one can be while remaining historically accurate. In the 1840s Whigs, like Macaulay, favored the audience. So did anarchists like Proudhon. Tories like Wordsworth or moderate republicans like Lamartine supported the author's claims for longer terms. Yet nineteenth-century Americans on both sides of the aisle rejected copyright altogether.

Early in the twentieth century conservative Germans favored protecting authors for high-cultural reasons, while Social Democrats agreed because they saw it as a form of worker's protection.[20] Because the Nazis sought to restrict authors' claims, postwar Germans of both right and left supported strong protection. So did the French. Ludwig Erhard's Christian Democratic government eagerly embraced moral rights in 1965, while Margaret Thatcher's Tories just as firmly refused to do more than nod grudgingly in their direction in 1988. Though some might regard strong authors' rights as conservatively narrowing the public domain, French Socialists continued to regard them as striking a blow against cultural capitalists and the mercantile Anglo-Saxon worldview.[21] But as the debates have progressed, even on the Continent leftists and rightists alike have come to think that perhaps authorial rights could sensibly be pruned.[22] Digital millennialists have been accused of both socialism and neoliberal free marketeering. Pirate parties, it has been said, do not recognize left or right, only starboard and port.[23]

While it is hard to spot the direct political coloring of copyright or authors' rights, at a more general level such laws were indeed socially inflected and ideologically permeable. Alfred Brockhaus, among the most interesting of Nazi Germany's reformers, thought that copyright allowed insight into an era and a society's political conceptions, above all whether the individual or the community was emphasized.[24] The copyright tradition demonstrated a concern with the audience, with education, and with democratic citizenship. That was clearest in the nineteenth-century American obsession with reprinting to provide widespread enlightenment on the cheap. But the British, too, were much more preoccupied with popular education than the continental nations, though the Germans were more alive to such issues than the French. Long copyright terms, British opponents of Talfourd's proposals made clear in 1840, would make books costlier and hinder workingmen from educating themselves.[25]

Copyright's populist coloring explains why it was only during the fascist 1930s that the themes so common in the Anglosphere were finally broached seriously on the Continent. Counterintuitive as it may sound, on copyright Macaulay had more in common with the

Nazis than with Lamartine. Left and right were less the ideological endpoints for copyright and authors' rights than populist and elitist—or possibly collectivist and individualist. Hence the French left's confusion in recent years as it has sought to reconcile the nation's traditional veneration of high culture with the need to pay attention also to the common people's cultural interests.

FROM ONE PROPERTY TO ANOTHER

Perhaps ideology is the wrong word for the social inflections of copyright and authors' rights. Left and right explain only a small part of the antagonism between these two approaches. Indeed, each position contains elements that are conventionally thought of as both left and right. Thus copyright is concerned with allowing entrepreneurial disseminators to exploit works efficiently in the cultural marketplace even while its ultimate goal is enhancing the socialized common property of the public domain. Authors' rights, in turn, hedge the free play of the market with inalienable authorial rights. But at the same time they foster a cultural conservatism, permitting authors to lock down works in one incarnation and preventing their free use and development by others.

At stake, therefore, is a deeper, more enduring cultural attitude or proclivity in each of these nations, a cleavage that is perhaps better captured by the contrast between populism and elitism than by left and right. Since intellectual property is the issue, it is scarcely surprising that similar differences can be found in how property more generally has been treated in these countries. Indeed, having spent time examining intellectual property, it repays the effort to look more broadly at conventional property too. Though this can be no more than a glance, the contrasts we have found in intellectual property across nations suggests the worth of also reconsidering views of property more generally. Anyone uninterested in how conclusions drawn from intellectual property might shed light on the larger topic of conventional property is welcome to skip to the next section.

The Anglo-Saxon world, especially the United States, is often thought to understand property as a natural right, something founded prepolitically as a claim more fundamental and inviolate than what mere statute conveys.[26] But, in fact, a potent combination of feudal law and utilitarianism has left property a concept shot through with social considerations on both sides of the Anglophone North Atlantic. In the meantime, with the revival of Roman law in the sixteenth century and its influence on the nineteenth century's legal codes that sought to eradicate the last vestiges of feudalism, the civil law nations of the Continent have implemented a more absolute and cohesive concept of property.

Thanks to the Norman Conquest in 1066, England found itself in a situation surprisingly similar to that of colonial America six centuries later, starting ab ovo with vast landholdings to be dispersed by the authorities. In Norman England almost all land was owned ultimately by the crown and held only secondarily by others via tenure from a higher power. Only late in the seventeenth century, coinciding with Locke, did law dictionaries begin to discuss land as owned directly and not as grants from the king.[27] Though it was common on the Continent, allodial real property, held free and clear, was rare in England. Feudal tenure gave ownership a far from absolute character. Any given piece of land could be the subject of multiple crosscutting claims to coexisting use and ownership rights, many of which were limited in time. In the absence of enforceable inheritance claims at death, land reverted to the lord by escheat. Rather than property as such, there were only property claims and little sense of any unitary, absolute, and perpetual ownership.

Feudal property relations evolved on both sides of the channel over the Middle Ages. Control was increasingly concentrated in the hands of the tenant, while the lord received only dues in cash or kind as acknowledgment of his ever more theoretical ownership. What had formerly been a personal relation of ownership and obedience became a primarily economic one. Possessors acquired the right to remain on the land for their lifetimes and then to bequeath it without their lords' permission.[28] Nonetheless, the English law of property remained more influenced by feudalism, and more variegated, than on the Continent. One British scholar has listed eleven elements of the ownership concept, which an American philosopher claims can be combined in 4,080 different ways.[29] Oscar Wilde once complained that the map of the Holy Roman Empire was such a patchwork that it made him itch. Such a "definition" of property might well elicit a similar reaction in a Continental jurist. In 1925 English law simplified land holding. Nonetheless, it still retained vestiges of the past in recognizing two forms of ownership: a term of years absolute (an interest for a limited time) and fee simple absolute in possession—or what Continental jurists would recognize as an approximation of absolute ownership. And even then the multitude of other forms of ownership was merely shifted from common law to equity.[30] Not until 2000 was the feudal system finally abolished in Scotland, with the transformation of the *dominium utile*, the use of land, into proper ownership.[31] On the Channel Islands, Jersey, Guernsey, and Sark, the old system remains largely in place.[32]

Land in England was held not directly but in estates, that is, an interest that lasted only for a certain time and often belonged to different people for various purposes: estate in fee simple, fee tail, for life, a leasehold estate. The idea of "simultaneous property," used by the French to designate feudal relations, remains alive and well in Britain.[33] The concept of uses, which eventually developed into trusts, arose within the parallel system of equity law and also distinguished British law from the Continent. It started as a means for monks to avoid the worst consequences of their vows of poverty. Property donated to monasteries could be officially owned via common law by one person, while its fruits remained available to others through equity.[34] Trusts divorced ownership, possession, and control in ways that—with some exceptions like German *Stiftungen*—have mostly remained out of bounds on the continent.[35]

Though America famously was born without feudalism, in fact colonial property concepts were deeply colored by the British feudal and common law inheritance. Even into the twenty-first century American property law remains heavily influenced by the feudal past.[36] Some of the North American colonies were owned by commercial companies; some by individuals, like William Penn; some were attached directly to the crown. Colonists like Thomas Jefferson and Henry Adams denied the reach of feudal law across the Atlantic.[37] But a widespread assumption held all lands to be concessions from the crown, the lord paramount.[38] The sovereign's eminent domain was recognized on both sides of the Atlantic, and the British common law model of estates predominated in the colonies. The exception was Louisiana, where the concept of absolute property derived from the same Roman law sources as would the Napoleonic Code eventually too.[39]

That, of course, changed with the revolution. Allodial views of property, as fully held by its owner, spread in America during the nineteenth century. By the time New York State—where large holdings subleased in return for quitrents on the British model had lasted longer than elsewhere—officially struck down feudal tenure in 1829, the law no longer had much practical consequence.[40] The heavy regulation imposed on property by the colonial authorities to achieve social goals gave way in the nineteenth century to a more classically laissez-faire approach. And yet the way in which land had been distributed at the federal state's behest contradicted the optimistic claims, as Jesse Root put it in 1798, that "every proprietor of land is a prince in his own domains, and lord paramount of the fee."[41]

With independence the new US government became the primary landowner. It put this enormous patrimony to the purpose of shaping a particular social vision, divesting itself of millions of acres to create a society of free-holding citizens. But the very act of distributing, on lenient terms, this vast mass of real estate as a matter of public policy meant that the buyers were the recipients of property alienated for a utilitarian social purpose. They bought on the government's terms and in fulfillment of its social ambitions. Just as massive grants of land were made to fulfill specific social goals—draining swamps, building railroads, founding universities—so individual citizens became owners in the quest for a higher goal. So too the homestead exemption—which protected against creditors up to fifty acres of land lived on and worked on by the debtor—demonstrated how dependent the "prince in his own domains" was on the state and its rules to preserve him from folly and misfortune.

In the West conventional property concepts arrived only late. Because vast acreage with little rain favored grazing, while fencing was expensive and difficult, ranchers asserted their claims to the product—by branding their cattle—not to the land. Only in the 1880s, with the coming of cheap barbed wire, did fencing, and thus land ownership in a conventional sense, spread.[42] When slavery was abolished without compensation, something that was then regarded as property was also subjected to social goals. Across the Atlantic, in contrast, taxpayers handsomely compensated slaveholders for their losses. Before communism this was the largest expropriation ever— the only comparisons being the taking of church lands during the Reformation and aristocratic properties in the French Revolution.[43]

In Britain and America absolute ownership was also undermined by another countervailing current. Beyond the contingent ownership claims, which were the best that feudalism and the common law offered, came also the Anglo-Saxon world's penchant for a utilitarian justification of property. Utilitarianism undermined any absolute view of property as the exclusive subject of one person's will.

First and foremost, despite Locke and a thousand epigones, it was a leitmotif of Anglo-American conceptions that property was a strictly man-made creation with little basis in nature. Benjamin Franklin thought that all property beyond the basic necessities of survival belonged to the public "who, by their Laws, have created it, and who may therefore by other Laws dispose of it."[44] Even Thomas Paine, who otherwise agreed with Locke on property's prepolitical origins, insisted in 1795 that "personal property is the *effect* of society."[45] The distribution of wealth, as John Stuart Mill continued this theme in 1848, was determined by human institutions. Property was disposed of only with society's consent. "Even what a person has produced by his individual toil, unaided by any one," Mill wrote, "he cannot keep, unless by the permission of society."[46]

Once that was admitted, all bets were off. If nature did not decree who owned, then let the contest of claims begin. Starting with David Hume in the mid-eighteenth century, utilitarianism scoffed at pretensions to ownership that paid no heed to what was done with property. Whatever the claims staked by one owner, if another competing property right was socially more useful, it took precedence. Rather than asking who owned a piece of land, the question was who *should* own it in order to maximize social utility? Adam Smith approved of a colony law that took away property in land left uncultivated, and Locke included a provision to this effect in the Fundamental Constitutions of Carolina, adopted in 1669.[47] Such utilitarian logic handily allowed the colonists to expropriate the natives who, from their vantage, were not using the land. But it applied to the colonists too. Headright grants required that—to be owned—land be brought under cultivation. Nevada mining law, memorably portrayed by Mark Twain in *Roughing It*, allowed prospectors to stake claims in other people's cellars and gardens. Nor was the European nobility safe. As US ambassador to France in the late 1780s, Thomas Jefferson recommended that aristocratic hunting preserves be redistributed to landless peasants.[48] Having applied economic rationality to expropriate one set of owners, why not to another?

The Anglosphere's utilitarianism elevated social priorities above private ownership. A market economy, as America's greatest nineteenth-century legal mind, Oliver Wendell Holmes, clearly understood, inherently undermines absolute property rights, condemning some otherwise perfectly legitimate claims to perish in the competitive battle.[49] Hoping to promote economic development during the early nineteenth century, American courts undermined property rights based on allegedly venerable ownership claims. The Americans, as one observer put it, preferred "property in motion or at risk rather than property secure and at rest."[50] Owners who wanted to construct new houses were allowed to violate "ancient lights" rules that gave existing buildings claim to their original natural illumination. If the economic outcome promised community advantages, riverside property owners who sought to erect mills upstream were permitted to divert water for industrial purposes, despite damage to older riparian rights downstream. Old-fashioned nuisance laws that punished offending owners for harming nearby property were relaxed so that neighbors' rights took a backseat to the imperatives of economic growth.[51] Society's interest in increasing prosperity took precedence over property owners' sovereign possession. Property belonged not to those with the firmest formal claims but to those who could make best use of it.

Conversely, feudal landownership was never as uniformly widespread on the Continent as in Britain. Starting in the sixteenth century, Roman law was widely revived. The still remaining feudal laws were swept away by the French Revolution and the great legal codifications in Austria, France, and then Germany. Roman law had perhaps a less absolute and unitary view of property than is sometimes portrayed. It knew the distinction between ownership (title) and possession (enjoyment). Even full owners had no absolute claims.[52] Yet the Roman ownership concept was more clear-cut than the fluid distinctions of better and worse claims along the spectrum between ownership and possession that was characteristic of both feudal law and the English common law.[53] On the continent Roman concepts combined during the nineteenth century with a Hegelian vision that saw property as innately connected to the person, as part of his ability to project his will onto the material world.[54] Much as the individual was made autonomous by sovereignty over his own person, so he demonstrated his freedom by commanding his property as its lord.[55] Property was an emanation of human personality.

The outcome in nineteenth-century Europe was a modernization of Roman ideas of absolute property. Unlike messy feudal and common law property relations, with their multiple and fragmented claims, Napoleon's Civil Code in 1804 enthroned property. It was declared to be "the right of enjoying and disposing of things in the most absolute manner."[56] Napoleon himself claimed that even he, with all his armies, could not violate so sacred a trust as property ownership.[57] The Austrian Code of 1811 went even further, granting permission for what utilitarianism forbade: allowing owners to use their property irrationally (*Sinnwidrig*), not making use of it at all, or even destroying it.[58] During the 1830s and '40s, at the time of France's Lamartine debates, this absolute conception of property as belonging wholly to the owner, whose personality it embodied and extended, reached its peak in Europe.[59]

What held for property generally was also true when the concept was extended to matters intellectual. The Europeans developed a more absolute and privatized concept. All property—of mind and matter alike—belonged absolutely, unitarily, and perpetually to its owner. Only imperative social concerns could remove it from its owner's full command. In the Anglo-Saxon concept of property, by contrast, the owner's claims were contingent on others' rights, and his sway was subordinated to society's needs and dictates. The Hegelian view of property as an integral part of personality found its legal solidification in the Continental doctrine of moral rights. The Continent's insistence on authors' absolute claims to their works mirrored the Napoleonic Code's belief in the owner's unitary and absolute ownership of his property generally. In Anglophone copyright, in contrast, the author's claims were subordinate to society's requirements. Authors were given temporary monopolies only as necessary to stimulate their creativity. Ownership depended on whose use was socially most desirable.

However contrary to received wisdom this may sound, when it came to property, both real and intellectual, the Anglo-Americans were thus more socialist, or at least communalist, while the Europeans paid private property greater homage. While the French revolutionaries elevated property to the status of a natural, imprescriptible, inviolable, and sacred right, their American forerunners preferred happiness as the goal to pursue.[60]

IDEOLOGICAL IMPORTERS

Whatever legal historians may think of the law's stately, hermetically buffered progress, nowhere did copyright or authors' rights legislation evolve without constant alertness to developments elsewhere. An accurate history of law can be written only comparatively and transnationally. The French revolutionaries paid homage to Britain's 1710 Statute of Anne, and the American colonists imitated it. The 1878 Royal Copyright Commission wished to emulate the Americans' low book prices. Britain quickly followed the US precedent of compulsory licensing of sound recordings in 1911, as had the Germans in 1910. Hitler's regime adopted the American model of first-to-invent for patents. In the 1990s the United States reversed course to follow Europe, toeing the Berne line of thick protection for authors.

In all countries both sides of the debate held up foreign examples of what to avoid too. National differences in legal provision for authors were understood to indicate broad cultural divergences. Postwar France and Germany defined their own high-culture bona fides by scorning the path of mercantile Anglo-Saxon copyright. And conversely many Americans have rejected the European example of strong protection—not only in the nineteenth century but even today.

The continental laws on authors' rights were first formulated in the era when Europe was a cultural exporter. Both interest and ideology had thus aligned to protect authors. Rights holders' strong claims gave them control both at home and abroad over both sales and then aesthetics. The economic and social policies of France and Germany thus dovetailed with the concerns of their cultural producers.

Britain, however, was poised halfway between Continent and colonies. Whatever the nineteenth-century British may have thought about America's disregard for copyright, they could not ignore it. Their authors' biggest literary market was in the United States. However little they gained directly in royalties before 1891, the sheer quantities of British books read across the Atlantic could not be denied. This was "the extreme importance of American copyright to English authors" that the Board of Trade signaled in 1884 when it cautioned against the changes to British law required to join the Berne Union.[61] The Commonwealth nations, eager to continue importing cheap US reprints rather than expensive British editions, only underscored the American influence in Westminster. Like the Continental nations, Britain was a cultural exporter. Nonetheless, its dependence on the US market, and its need to appease the vast Commonwealth public with its American-style interests, gave British policymakers willy-nilly an appreciation of the arguments from the other side. Both by tradition and geopolitics Britain was as much in the American camp as the European.

Over the past century and a half the single biggest development in the transnational history of copyright has been the shift of the United States from culture importer to exporter. In the nineteenth century America's interests, like those of the developing world today, lay in cheap, easy, untrammeled access to the world's patrimony. As US content began to flow outward early in the twentieth century, however, attitudes changed. The American content industries signed up for the Berne ideology that had long voiced the aims of the Continent's exporting *Kulturnationen*. That cemented the developed world's apparent consensus on the Berne principle of treating intellectual property much like conventional property. But ideology and interest were not identical.

America's political ideology, with its concern for popular education and its toleration of the piracy that efficiently achieved that end, had been formed while it was a culturally importing nation. American ideology therefore did not uniformly switch sides along with one segment of its industrial interests. Clamoring to protect its exports in the 1990s, Hollywood could not bring all other actors on board. Universal enlightenment did not give way entirely to exclusive authorial rights. Some Americans continued to fight a rearguard action against the content industries' insistence on strong protection. And the new powerful players from Silicon Valley did not see eye to eye with their fellow Californians from Hollywood. In the digital age, when the holy grail of universal accessibility suddenly seemed magically within reach, guerilla actions flared once again into a full-scale war that has now—less predictably—been taken up also in Europe.

AUTHORS AND THEIR PROPERTY

From the vantage of a transnational and longue durée historical approach to copyright, two points are worth making about our current battles. First, both copyright and authors' rights were based on treating the author as an intellectual entrepreneur, a self-employed independent agent selling his wares in the cultural marketplace. Master of his own destiny, he would be liberated from the servility of patronage and from the expectation that his occupation was more a calling than a profession. But whatever the reality of the eighteenth and nineteenth centuries, this assumption is increasingly out of sync with our current situation.

Of course, individual freelance authors still ply their trade. But if we define cultural production broadly to include not just fiction, music, and visual arts, but also science, research, and technology, most content today is produced by salaried employees working in academia, business, or government. Per capita Germany today has a dozen times more university professors than it did in 1835.[62] Even novelists and poets often hold day jobs, teaching creative writing.

The same goes for symphony orchestras, ballet companies, and museums—financed indirectly by the state in the United States via tax-deductible philanthropy and directly in Europe. Once we remove all the culture producers who one way or the other live off the public's dime, who is left other than a few novelists and the entertainment industry? However popular Hollywood's product, however well paid its top auteurs and moguls, the university world is orders of magnitude larger than film. American colleges and universities employ ten times as many people as the motion picture and recording industries, their income is at least five times as great.[63]

We live in a new age of patronage. Do we therefore need copyright at all any longer? To the extent that we do, should it not be limited to the niche market of commercially viable content produced by freelance authors or the content industries' work-for-hire? At the very least we need to distinguish between commercially marketed content and that produced by the university and research world. Whatever the rules for the commercial market, academic research must be treated separately. Through direct government subsidy and indirectly via the tax-deductability of much university and research funding, academic work is largely financed by taxpayers. What purpose then in having it paid for once again via commercial, and indeed monopolistic, academic periodicals and their aggregators? Even more senseless is that academic research should be locked up, unavailable to the public that funds it.

More broadly, history also instructs by reminding us just how contingent property is. Among the most enduring and fundamental disputes over three centuries has been whether intellectual property was founded on natural rights that justified strong, even perpetual claims or whether it was a temporary monopoly that society granted authors to stimulate their productivity. Seen historically, property was unquestionably a contingent, socially created right, in thrall to what the lawmakers of the day decided. Yes, it is broadly true that claims to intellectual property have become longer and stronger over the last three centuries, by now approximating what natural rights would dictate had they existed. Each expansion to new media and each extension to ever longer terms has created property rights where none existed before. But none of these creations rests in nature; none is any more solidly grounded than the laws that gave them life.

At times entire classes of rights holders have been expropriated in favor of new owners or on the public's behalf. If we seek a historical precursor for our era's technological upheavals and their possible legal consequences, sound recording in the 1890s serves well. With the new technologies music increasingly became its recording. It no longer existed abstractly, independent of its notation on paper. In this process various middlemen were cut out. As John Philip Sousa complained early in the twentieth century, we were transformed from amateur musicians—actively collaborating in making and spreading the art—into passive consumers of others' efforts. The audience as participant was largely eliminated. So were the sheet-music publishers who had once been the conveyors between composers and audience. By the time the legislators finally pronounced on the new technologies, the recording industry was too big and its audience too beholden for either to go willingly back into its bottle. The legal outcome effectively expropriated composers and their publishers in favor of the new manufacturers and their consumers. Ironically, that industry that today most loudly laments digital pilfering on its turf was built a century ago on the legal evisceration of sheet music. But if sheet music was not sacrosanct property in 1909, why should digital recordings be so today? What the law gives, it can take away.

Ultimately the issues at stake are political and ideological. Nature has precious little to say about how intellectual property is justified. Though phrased in legal terms, what the law decides is a political judgment. That we want to keep present and future authors happy and productive is clear. But why rights holders' claims to intellectual property should expand indefinitely, while those of other owners are ever more restricted by social concerns, is not. And that a vast existing cultural patrimony, already paid for and amortized, sits locked behind legal walls, hostage to outmoded notions of property, when at the flick of a switch it could belong to all humanity—that is little short of grotesque.

Acknowledgments

Historians are the magpies of the social sciences. With no discernible methodology of our own, we are united only by our interest in what has already happened. Jacks-of-all-trades, we pick up the necessary tools and specialized knowledge as our needs require. Transnational and comparative histories move us far from the coal face by diffusing attention among many nations. If we then decide to take a grand view of a broad sweep of development—three centuries, say, across four nations—the ice becomes perilously thin. Armed only with interest and good will, I am acutely aware of poaching on the turf of highly trained experts with their own finely honed methods and pressing agendas. But legal history is too important and interesting to leave to lawyers alone. I hope that its practitioners will forgive me the mistakes and misunderstandings I have inevitably committed as signs of eagerness, not bad faith.

I have relied on the help and counsel of many to guide me. Above all I am indebted to the wonderful collection of pre-1900 materials collected by a team of researchers under the direction of Professors Lionel Bently and Martin Kretschmer (*Primary Sources on Copyright (1450–1900)*, www.copyrighthistory.org). Secure in the knowledge that they have spared me countless hours of effort, I have made unabashed use of the primary sources there. I hope that is what they intended. As a small *Dankeschön* I have attempted to identify each first use of a document from that collection as "BK."

I am also indebted to research assistants and colleagues who have smoothed my way to other materials: above all, Michael Kellogg, but also Julie Kazdan, Matthew Luckett, Deborah Bauer, Daniella Perry, and Mary Momdjian. The Library of the Institute of Advanced Legal

Studies in London kindly allowed use of their collection. Experts have helped me with readings and advice: Mark Rose, Neil Netanel, Helle Porsdam, Zorina Khan, and Oren Bracha. Laurent Pfister kindly sent me unpublished articles. As a good friend and colleague, Peter Mandler read through an earlier, more bloated version of the manuscript. Brigitta van Rheinberg at the press was encouragingly enthusiastic about the potential appeal of the topic for a wider audience. Besides being a wonderful editor of the manuscript, she allowed me to sidestep the main moral dilemma of publishing a book on the ever strengthening grasp of copyright by agreeing that it would appear free to all under Creative Commons license after a year. Anne Hoy and Aimee Anderson gave the manuscript much needed editorial scrubbings.

I had very useful feedback at presentations of some of the material here and am grateful to William E. Nelson and Lauren Benton at NYU, Nomi Stolzenberg at USC, Emma Rothschild at both Harvard and Magdalene, Cambridge, Timothy Smith at Queens in Canada, Helle Porsdam at a conference at the Tate Modern in London, and Anjana Shrivastava and the Bundeszentrale für politische Bildung in Berlin. But, most of all, I am eternally grateful to my wife and colleague, Lisbet Rausing. Once again she has turned piffle into prose, slashed needless verbiage, and queried unsubstantiated assertions. J.E.D.

Notes

INTRODUCTION: THE AGON OF AUTHOR AND AUDIENCE

1. Peter Decherney, *Hollywood's Copyright Wars: From Edison to the Internet* (New York, 2012), 116–17.

2. *Shostakovich v. Twentieth Century Fox Film Corp*, 80 NYS 2d 575 (1948), p. 579. Discussed in William Strauss, "The Moral Right of the Author," *American Journal of Comparative Law* 4, 4 (1955): 533–35; Michael Rushton, "The Moral Rights of Artists: Droit Moral ou Droit Pécuniaire?" *Journal of Cultural Economics* 22, 1 (1998): 23.

3. André Bertrand, "Shostakovich and John Huston: The French Supreme Court on Copyright, Contracts and Moral Rights," in Christopher Heath and Anselm Kamperman Sanders, eds., *Landmark Intellectual Property Cases and Their Legacy* (Alphen aan den Rijn, 2011): 7–10.

4. "Kersauson n'a pas écrit Océan's songs—Retour sur un best seller," *La Lettrine* 26 (February 2010).

5. *Anne Bragance c. Olivier Orban et Michel de Grèce*, Cour d'appel (1st chamber), Paris, 1 February 1989, *Revue internationale du droit d'auteur* 142 (1989): 301–7.

6. The standard rider affecting all Beckett productions states, "There shall be no additions, omissions, changes in the sex of the characters as specified in the text, or alterations of any kind of nature in the manuscript or presentation of the Play." Quoted in Leonard Jacobs, "Beckett Estate Ends 'Godot,' Cites Casting Concerns," *Backstage* 29 (November 2002). Deirdre Bair, *Samuel Beckett* (New York, 1978), 632.

7. Justin Hughes, "The Philosophy of Intellectual Property," *Georgetown Law Journal* 77, 2 (1988): 294–95.

8. Cobi Bordewijk, "The Integrity of the Playtext: Disputed Performances of *Waiting for Godot*," in Marius Buning et al., eds., *Samuel Beckett 1970–1989* (Amsterdam, 1992), 145–46.

9. "Judge Authorizes All-Female 'Godot,'" *New York Times*, 6 July 1991.

10. Linda Ben-Zvi, ed., *Women in Beckett: Performance and Critical Perspectives* (Urbana, 1990), x.

11. *Guardian*, 4 February 2006; Jacobs, "Beckett Estate Ends 'Godot'"; *Jerôme Lindon et SACD c. La Compagnie Brut de Breton et Bruno Boussagol*, Tribunal de Grande Instance de Paris, 3rd chamber, 15 October 1992, *Revue internationale du droit d'auteur* 155 (1993): 227.

12. Matthew Rimmer, "Damned to Fame: The Moral Rights of the Beckett Estate," *Australian Library and Information Association* 5 (2003), http://archive.alia.org.au/incite/2003/05/beckett.html. In the 2000 New York Fringe Festival a company made light of this ongoing conflict between the Beckett estate and artistic directors. The work was entitled *The complete lost works of Samuel Beckett as found in an envelope (partially burned) in a dustbin in Paris labelled "Never to be performed. Never. Ever. EVER! Or I'll sue! I'LL SUE FROM THE GRAVE!"* The plot concerned a fight between three producers and the Beckett estate.

13. "Berne Convention Implementation Act of 1987: Hearings before the . . . Committee on the Judiciary, House of Representatives, . . . June 17, July 23, September 16 and 30, 1987, February 9 and 10, 1988," Serial No. 50, p. 413.

14. The merest smattering of examples: Simon Linguet in "Opinion de Linguet touchant l'arrêt sur les privilèges," (1777), 40 (BK); Cochu, "Requête au Roi," in Ed. Laboulaye and G.

Guiffrey, eds., *La Propriété littéraire au XVIIIe siècle* (Paris, 1859), 169; Commission de la propriété littéraire, *Collection des procès-verbaux* (Paris, 1826), 33–34; *Hansard* 3, 45 (27 February 1839): 935; Mark Helprin, *Digital Barbarians: A Writer's Manifesto* (New York, 2009), 27–31.

15. As is pointed out in "Report on H.R. 10881," (1890), 51st Cong., 1st sess., 1890, House Report 2401, p. 7 (BK); Lawrence Lessig, "The Solipsist and the Internet," pp. 9–10, at http://www .lessig.org/blog/2009/05/the_solipsist_and_the_internet.html.

16. Figuring in transfer and inheritance taxes, the expropriation takes place more often. Copyright is also subject to inheritance tax, at least in the US, but assessing the value is a more nebulous enterprise. Bridget J. Crawford and Mitchell M. Gans, "Sticky Copyrights: Discriminatory Tax Restraints on the Transfer of Intellectual Property," *Washington and Lee Law Review* 67 (2010): 52–53. Of course, inflation and appreciating property values also affect such calculations but no more than for the value of copyrights.

17. Pierre-Jules Hetzel, quoted in P.-J. Proudhon, *Les majorats littéraires* (Paris, 1868), 105.

18. Copyright Commission, *The Royal Commissions and the Report of the Commissioners*, c. 2036 (London, 1878), lvii.

19. A bitter lament from a music lover in Britain, where this was not true, in A.R.C., "Musical Settings of Poems: An Abuse of the Copyright," *Spectator*, 21 August 1931, p. 17, and in Charles V. Stanford's letter, *Times* (London), 3 March 1908, p. 4.

20. 1965 law, §24, which ended the *Vertonungsfreiheit* of the 1901 law, §20.

21. Ferdinand Roger, "The 'Carmen Jones Affair,'" *Revue internationale du droit d'auteur* 8 (1955): 10–12; Christopher L. Miller, *The French Atlantic Triangle: Literature and Culture of the Slave Trade* (Durham NC, 2008), 477.

22. http://www.mermaidsculpture.dk/productsandprices.php.

23. http://www.louisiana.dk/dk/Menu/Undervisning/Undervisningstilbud/Skoler /Samtidskunst+%232/ Michael+Elmgreen+%26+Ingar+Dragset.

24. Peter Garnsey, *Thinking about Property: From Antiquity to the Age of Revolution* (Cambridge, 2007), 204–5.

25. William Blackstone, *Commentaries on the Laws of England*, Bk. 2, ch. 1.

26. Art. 544.

27. Hélène Michel, *La cause des propriétaires: État et propriété en France, fin XIXe–XXe siècle* (Paris, 2006), 52–55; Karl Christian Führer, "Die Rechte von Hausbesitzern und Mietern im Ersten Weltkrieg und in der Zwischenkriegszeit," in Hannes Siegrist and David Sugarman, eds., *Eigentum im internationalen Vergleich* (Göttingen, 1999).

28. Quoted in Niall Ferguson, *The Ascent of Money* (New York, 2008), 89.

29. Henry Dunning Macleod, *A Dictionary of Political Economy* (London, 1863), 1: 552.

30. Carole Shammas et al., *Inheritance in America: From Colonial Times to the Present* (New Brunswick, 1987), 103.

31. Kenneth J. Vandevelde, "The New Property of the Nineteenth Century: The Development of the Modern Concept of Property," *Buffalo Law Review* 29 (1980): 333–37.

32. Morton J. Horwitz, *The Transformation of American Law, 1870–1960* (New York, 1992), 145.

33. Kevin A. Hassett and Robert J. Shapiro, "What Are Ideas Worth? The Value of Intellectual Capital and Intangible Assets in the American Economy," p. 3, Sonecon, http://www .sonecon.com/studies.php.

1. THE BATTLE BETWEEN ANGLO-AMERICAN COPYRIGHT AND EUROPEAN AUTHORS' RIGHTS

1. Following the approach adopted in his magisterial survey of the two traditions: Alain Strowel, *Droit d'auteur et copyright: Divergences et convergences* (Brussels, 1993).

2. Pierre Sirinelli, quoted in Alain Salles, "Les auteurs veulent garder leur droit," *Le Monde*, 2 May 2003; Strowel, *Droit d'auteur et copyright*, 538; Bernard Edelman, *Le sacre de l'auteur* (Paris, 2004), 225.

3. F. Pollaud-Dulian, "Moral Rights in France through Recent Case Law," *Revue internationale du droit d'auteur* 145 (1990): 128; P. Bernt Hugenholtz, "Copyright and Freedom of Expression in Europe," in Rochelle Cooper Dreyfuss et al., eds., *Expanding the Boundaries of Intellectual Property* (Oxford, 2001), 343–44; Jacqueline M. B. Seignette, *Challenges to the Creator Doctrine: Authorship, Copyright Ownership and the Exploitation of Creative Works in the Netherlands, Germany and the United States* (Deventer, 1994), 21–22.

4. Alfred C. Yen, "Restoring the Natural Law: Copyright as Labor and Possession," *Ohio State Law Journal* 51 (1990): 546.

5. Jon Baumgarten et al., "Preserving the Genius of the System: A Critical Examination of the Introduction of Moral Rights into United States Law," *Copyright Reporter: Journal of the Copyright Society of Australia* 8, 3 (1990): 3, 6; Jon A. Baumgarten, "On the Case against Moral Rights," in Peter Anderson and David Saunders, eds., *Moral Rights Protection in a Copyright System* (Brisbane, 1992), 88; Martin A. Roeder, "The Doctrine of Moral Right: A Study in the Law of Artists, Authors and Creators," *Harvard Law Review* 53, 4 (1940): 577–78; Ulrich Möller, *Die Unübertragbarkeit des Urheberrechts in Deutschland: Eine überschiessende Reaktion auf Savignys subjektives Recht* (Berlin, 2007), 4; Neil Turkewitz, "Authors' Rights are Dead," *Journal of the Copyright Society of the USA* 38, 1 (1990): 41.

6. Helle Porsdam, "On European Narratives of Human Rights and Their Possible Implications for Copyright," in Fiona Macmillan, ed., *New Directions in Copyright Law* (2007), 6: 335–58.

7. François Dessemontet, "Copyright and Human Rights," in Jan J. C. Kabel and Gerard J.H.M. Mom, eds., *Intellectual Property and Information Law* (The Hague, 1998), 117.

8. Henri Desbois, "Le droit moral," *Revue internationale du droit d'auteur* 19 (1958): 127.

9. André Lucas, *Droit d'auteur et numérique* (Paris, 1998), 14–15. Similarly, Séverine Dusollier, *Droit d'auteur et protection des œuvres dans l'univers numérique* (Brussels, 2005), 232–33.

10. Frédéric Pollaud-Dulian, *Le Droit d'auteur* (Paris, 2005), 47–48.

11. *Soc. Turner Entertainment c. Consorts Huston*, Cour d'appel de Paris, 6 July 1989, note Bernard Audit, *Recueil Dalloz Sirey*, Jurisprudence (1990): 156.

12. Serge Regourd, *L'exception culturelle*, 2nd ed. (Paris, 2004), 17–18.

13. Jules-Marc Baudel, *La législation des États-unis sur le droit d'auteur* (Brussels, 1990), 104.

14. Artur Wandtke, "Zur kulturellen und sozialen Dimension des Urheberrechts," *Archiv für Urheber- Film- Funk- und Theaterrecht* 123 (1993): 6; Markus A. Frey, "Die internationale Vereinheitlichung des Urheberrechts und das Schöpferprinzip," *Archiv für Urheber- Film- Funk- und Theaterrecht* 98 (1984): 62–63; Joëlle Farchy and Fabrice Rochelandet, "La Propriété littéraire et artistique," in Jean-Pierre Faugère et al., eds., *Politiques publiques européennes* (Paris, 2002), 82.

15. Thomas Oppermann, "Geistiges Eigentum: Ein 'Basic Human Right' des Allgemeinen Völkerrechts," in Albrecht Weber, ed., *Währung und Wirtschaft: Das Geld im Recht* (Baden-Baden, 1997), 458, 463.

16. Gérard Gavin, *Le Droit moral de l'auteur dans la jurisprudence et la législation françaises* (Paris, 1960), 300.

17. Henri Desbois, *Le Droit d'auteur en France*, 3rd ed. (Paris, 1978), 7, 539.

18. Bernard Edelman, "Entre copyright et droit d'auteur: L'intégrité de l'œuvre de l'esprit," *Recueil Dalloz Sirey* 40 (1990): 296; Michel Vivant, "Authors' Rights, Human Rights?" *Revue internationale du droit d'auteur* 174 (1997): 96.

19. Palacio Vallelersundi, European Parliament, 8 April 1997, *Official Journal of the European Communities* (1997/98): 4–498/99.

20. Bernard Edelman, "Applicable Legislation Regarding Exploitation of Colourised US

Films in France: The 'John Huston' Case," *International Review of Industrial Property and Copyright Law* 23 (1992): 639, 642; Dessemontet, "Copyright and Human Rights," 114.

21. *Journal Officiel*, Assemblée, Documents, Annexe 8612, 9 June 1954, pp. 985–87; Annexe 10681, 6 May 1955, p. 836.

22. Assemblée Nationale, Rapport 2349, 7 June 2005, p. 37.

23. *Journal Officiel*, Sénat, 29 October 2008, pp. 6356, 6361; 8 July 2009, p. 6813.

24. J. B. Laydu, "Droit moral et copyright: Les nouveaux frères ennemis?" *Les petites affiches* 87 (25 July 1994), quoted in Frédéric Rideau, *La Formation du droit de la propriété littéraire en France et en Grande-Bretagne: Une convergence oubliée* (Aix-en-Provence, 2004), 18; Dusollier, *Droit d'auteur et protection des œuvres dans l'univers numérique*, 296; Rudolf Monta, "The Concept of 'Copyright' versus the 'Droit d'Auteur,'" *Southern California Law Review* 32 (1959): 185; Strowel, *Droit d'auteur et copyright*, 6–7.

25. Christophe Geiger, "Constitutionalising Intellectual Property Law? The Influence of Fundamental Rights on Intellectual Property in the European Union," *International Review of Intellectual Property and Competition Law* 37, 4 (2006): 372. Elsewhere Geiger seeks to find common ground between the two approaches, though admitting that the emphasis remains different in each. Christophe Geiger, *Droit d'auteur et droit du public à l'information* (Paris, 2004), 36, 42–43.

26. Pollaud-Dulian, *Le Droit d'auteur*, 47–48.

27. John Perry Barlow, "Selling Wine without Bottles: The Economy of Mind on the Global Net," in Peter Ludlow, ed., *High Noon on the Electronic Frontier: Conceptual Issues in Cyberspace* (Cambridge MA, 1996), 12. Similarly, Peter Drahos, "Intellectual Property and Human Rights," *Intellectual Property Quarterly* 3 (1999): 368.

28. Maurice Lévy and Jean-Pierre Jouyet, "L'économie de l'immatériel: La croissance de demain: Rapport de la Commission sur l'économie de l'immatériel," December 2006, p. 12.

29. Economics and Statistics Administration, "Intellectual Property and the US Economy: Industries in Focus" (US Department of Commerce, March 2012), vi.

30. Commission of the European Communities, "Green Paper on Copyright and the Challenge of Technology: Copyright Issues Requiring Immediate Action," COM (88) 72 final, 7 June 1988, p. 3.

31. Duncan Matthews, *Globalizing Intellectual Property Rights: The TRIPs Agreement* (London, 2002), 31–33, passim.

32. Susan K. Sell, *Private Power, Public Law: The Globalization of Intellectual Property Rights* (Cambridge, 2003), 9.

33. WIPO, *2011 World Intellectual Property Indicators*, fig. A.3.1.2, p. 52.

34. L. Bently and B. Sherman, *Intellectual Property Law*, 3rd ed. (Oxford, 2009), 32; Leslie Kim Treiger-Bar-Am, "Authors' Rights as Limits to Copyright Control," in Macmillan, *New Directions in Copyright Law*, 6: 360–61. Strowel, having written a massive survey lovingly detailing the differences between the two approaches, concludes with a few pages curiously surmising that perhaps they are not so far apart after all. Strowel, *Droit d'auteur et copyright*. In a later article his examples of rapprochement are so marginal that his heart does not seem in it. Alain Strowel, "Droit d'auteur and Copyright: Between Nature and History," in Brad Sherman and Alain Strowel, eds., *Of Authors and Origins* (Oxford, 1994). Goldstein, one of the masters of international copyright, concludes that national laws on copyright are more similar than they are different, which he attributes largely to the influence of international agreements. Paul Goldstein, *International Copyright* (New York, 2001), vii, 4, 10. Similar arguments in Stephen Stewart, *International Copyright and Neighbouring Rights* (London, 1983), vi, 9; Gillian Davies, *Copyright and the Public Interest* (Weinheim, 1994). Yet Goldstein also insists that, for film, the view of authorial rights "differs dramatically" between the US and France, and he has waxed eloquent on the "two cultures of copyright" found on opposite sides of the Atlantic. Paul

Goldstein, *Copyright's Highway: From Gutenberg to the Celestial Jukebox* (Stanford, 2003), chap. 5.

35. Sénat, Report 308 (12 April 2006), p. 13; *Journal Officiel*, Sénat, 4 May 2006, p. 3508.

36. Cyrill P. Rigamonti, "The Conceptual Transformation of Moral Rights," *American Journal of Comparative Law* 55 (2007): 68–69, 72–73; Cyrill P. Rigamonti, "Deconstructing Moral Rights," *Harvard International Law Journal* 47, 2 (2006): 379–80 and passim; Cyrill P. Rigamonti, *Geistiges Eigentum als Begriff und Theorie des Urheberrechts* (Baden-Baden, 2001), 80–84.

37. Pamela Samuelson, "Economic and Constitutional Influences on Copyright Law in the United States," *European Intellectual Property Review* 9 (2001): 409–10.

38. The only exceptions are the current terms for work-for-hire and sound recordings, discussed in chapter 7.

39. Sam Ricketson, "The Copyright Term," *International Review of Industrial Property and Copyright Law* 23 (1992): 754–56.

40. Pollaud-Dulian, *Le Droit d'auteur*, 299–300; Desbois, *Le Droit d'auteur en France*, 416.

41. Section 301 of the 1988 Copyright Act. In the latter case the right is to a perpetual royalty. Catherine Seville, "Peter Pan's Rights: 'To Die Will Be an Awfully Big Adventure,'" *Journal of the Copyright Society of the USA* 51 (2003–4): 5. The Peter Pan right is sometimes confused by the French with Winnie the Pooh. Joëlle Farchy, *Internet et le droit d'auteur: La culture Napster* (Paris, 2003), 158.

42. Claude Masouyé, "Vers une prolongation de la durée générale de protection," *Revue internationale du droit d'auteur* 24 (1959): 101.

43. *Eldred v. Ashcroft*, 537 U.S. 186 (2003). There was also a half-hearted attempt to challenge the constitutionality of the Digital Millennium Copyright Act in 2001, arguing that it allowed copyright owners effectively to secure perpetual protection by mixing public domain works with copyrighted materials and locking both up with technological protection measures. *Universal City Studios, Inc. v. Corley*, 273 F. 3d 429 (2nd Cir. 2001), pp. 430, 436.

44. *Eldred v. Ashcroft*, transcript of oral arguments before the Supreme Court, No. 01–618, 9 October 2002, p. 23.

45. Geiger, *Droit d'auteur et droit du public à l'information*, 336–38, 294–95; André Lucas, "L'Intérêt general dans l'évolution du droit d'auteur," in *L'Intérêt général et l'accès à l'information en propriété intellectuelle* (Brussels, 2008), 86–87.

46. Pollaud-Dulian, *Le Droit d'auteur*, 22; Ysolde Gendreau, "The Criterion of Fixation in Copyright Law," *Revue internationale du droit d'auteur* 159 (1994): 112–26.

47. As in the French revolutionary law of 19 July 1793, art. 6.

48. "Copyright Law Revision," Senate Report 94–473 (1975), p. 126; "Copyright Law Revision: Report of the Register of Copyrights on the General Revision of the US Copyright Law," 87th Congress, 1st sess., House Committee Print, July 1961, p. 6.

49. Jane C. Ginsburg, "'Une Chose Publique'? The Author's Domain and the Public Domain in Early British, French and US Copyright Law," *Cambridge Law Journal* 65 (2006): 645.

50. Kevin Kelly, "Scan This Book!" *New York Times Magazine*, 14 May 2006; *Kahle v. Ashcroft* (2004), discussed in Dotan Oliar, "Making Sense of the Intellectual Property Clause: Promotion of Progress as a Limitation on Congress's Intellectual Property Power," *Georgetown Law Journal* 94 (2006): 1832–33.

51. "Lettres à un ami par l'abbé Pluquet," (1778–1779) in Ed. Laboulaye and G. Guiffrey, eds., *La Propriété littéraire au XVIIIe siècle* (Paris, 1859), 283.

52. Julia Ellins, *Copyright Law, Urheberrecht und ihre Harmonisierung in der Europäischen Gemeinschaft* (Berlin, 1997), 80–82; André R. Bertrand, "Multimedia: Stretching the Limits of Author's Rights in Europe," *Journal of Proprietary Rights* 7, 11 (1995): 4–5. Goldstein argues that the differences within each realm were as great as any between them, but on the basis of his own evidence this conclusion does not convince. There is clearly a general tendency for Continental

nations to regulate contract more than the Anglophone. Goldstein, *International Copyright*, 217–25.

53. For example, the EU Copyright (Rental and Lending Right), Council Directive No. 92/100, 1992, art. 4, made unwaivable the author's or performer's claim to equitable remuneration for rentals of his phonogram or film.

54. Arts. 31–37. *Journal Officiel*, Assemblée, Documents, Annexe 8612, 9 June 1954, p. 986. Similar attitudes in European Parliament, 9 February 1999, *Official Journal*, 1999, p. 4–533/65–66.

55. Jean Zay, *Souvenirs et solitude* (Le Rœulx, 1987), 219; *Journal Officiel*, Chambre, Documents, Annexe 3222, 6 December 1937, p. 238.

56. "Copyright and the Declaration of Human Rights," *Copyright Bulletin* 2, 1 (1949): 46.

57. But even here differences remained. While the motive of the French law was to help authors, temperamentally unable to pursue their own best interests and thus in need of the state's help, in the American reasoning the author was merely in an objectively and structurally weak position—no worse off than the publisher but simply less able to weather the unpredictability of the market. "Copyright Law Revision," House of Representatives, Report 94–1476 (1976), p. 124.

58. Thus the German laws of 1901 and 1907.

59. Jane C. Ginsburg, "The Concept of Authorship in Comparative Copyright Law," *DePaul Law Review* 52 (2003): 1088–90.

60. The attempt to argue that work-for-hire is actually a celebration of authorship, merely of the corporation, does not convince. Clearly work-for-hire violates the fundamental tenets of flesh-and-blood authorship in the Continental ideology and is one of the elements distinguishing the two approaches. Peter Jaszi, "On the Author Effect: Contemporary Copyright and Collective Creativity," in Martha Woodmansee and Peter Jaszi, eds., *The Construction of Authorship: Textual Appropriation in Law and Literature* (Durham NC, 1994), 34.

61. *Le Monde*, 3 May 1994, quoted in Joëlle Farchy, *La Fin de l'exception culturelle?* (Paris, 1999), 222.

62. Section 201(b). This is what is known also as deemed authorship, distinct from merely conferring authors' rights on someone who is not, in fact, the author. It is most notable for films.

63. Oren Bracha, "The Ideology of Authorship Revisited: Authors, Markets, and Liberal Values in Early American Copyright," *Yale Law Journal* 118 (2008): 248ff.

64. André Françon, "Authors' Rights beyond Frontiers: A Comparison of Civil Law and Common Law Conceptions," *Revue internationale du droit d'auteur* 149 (1991): 14; Farchy, *Internet et le droit d'auteur*, 87.

65. *Minutes of Evidence Taken before the Law of Copyright Committee* (Cd 5051, 1910), p. 33.

66. Robert Spoo, "Ezra Pound, Legislator," in Paul K. Saint-Amour, ed., *Modernism and Copyright* (Oxford, 2011), 49–50; Siva Vaidhyanathan, *Copyrights and Copywrongs: The Rise of Intellectual Property and How It Threatens Creativity* (New York, 2001), 76.

67. Roberto Verzola, "Cyberlords: The Rentier Class of the Information Sector," in Josephine Bosma et al., eds., *Readme! Filtered by Nettime: ASCII Culture and the Revenge of Knowledge* (Williamsburgh Station, 1999), 95.

68. *Feist Publications v. Rural Telephone Service Co.*, 499 U.S. 340 (1991), discussed in Ginsburg, "Concept of Authorship in Comparative Copyright Law," 1078ff.

69. Herman Cohen Jehoram, "The EC Copyright Directives, Economics and Authors' Rights," *International Review of Industrial Property and Copyright Law* 6 (1994): 828–29; Daniel J. Gervais, "Feist Goes Global: A Comparative Analysis of the Notion of Originality in Copyright Law," *Journal of the Copyright Society of the USA* 49 (2002): 974.

70. Luigi di Franco, "Der soziale Gehalt des Urheberrechts im neuen italienischen Gesetz," *Archiv für Urheber- Film- und Theaterrecht* 15 (1942): 111.

71. Accounts in Walter Bentivoglio, "Bemerkungen zum Filmrecht im neuen italienischen Urheberrechtsgesetz," *Archiv für Urheber- Film- und Theaterrecht* 15 (1942): 94–96; Willy Hoffmann, "Die filmrechtlichen Bestimmungen des neuen italienischen Urheberrechtsgesetzes in rechtsvergleichender Betrachtung," *Archiv für Urheber- Film- und Theaterrecht* 15 (1942): 122–38.

72. Pollaud-Dulian, *Le Droit d'auteur*, 373. It was used, for example, in *Simonin c. Syonnet et syndics Dieudonné*, 14 June 1844, *Dalloz*, 2 (1846): 41.

73. David Saunders, "Approaches to the Historical Relations of the Legal and the Aesthetic," *New Literary History* 23, 3 (1992): 508–9; Desbois, "Le droit moral," 123–25.

74. William M. Landes and Richard A. Posner, "An Economic Analysis of Copyright Law," *Journal of Legal Studies* 18, 2 (1989): 327.

75. Office Professionnel des Industries et Métiers d'Art et de Creation, *Travaux de la Commission de la propriété intellectuelle* (n.p., 1944–45), 71.

76. Baumgarten, "Preserving the Genius of the System," 4; Baumgarten, "On the Case against Moral Rights," 90. Generally in the same spirit: Robert A. Gorman "Federal Moral Rights Legislation: The Need for Caution," *Nova Law Review* 14 (1990): 423–24.

77. In a case similar to *Bragance*, the ghostwriter of several autobiographies, including that of Patrick Segal, a handicapped athlete, was allowed to be named as coauthor. *Etienne de Montpezat c. Editions Flammarion*, Cour d'appel de Paris (1st Chamber), 10 June 1986, *Revue internationale du droit d'auteur* 133 (1987): 193–99.

78. Though closely allied, the right of reproduction—or publication—and the right of disclosure are not quite identical. In both the author controls the terms under which the work appears. The right of publication is an economic right, that of disclosure a moral right. Some nations, like France and Germany, add the two together. What disclosure brings is some extra protection for unpublished works, insulating them from exemptions that might otherwise apply. And it may extend rights to authors of work-for-hire, otherwise excluded. In the US commissioned authors do not have control over when and how their work appears. But for primary authors the right of disclosure is largely folded into the right to control the first publication of a work.

79. Stig Strömholm, *Le droit moral de l'auteur en droit allemand, français et scandinave* (Stockholm, n.d. [1966]), 292–93; Laurent Pfister, "L'auteur, propriétaire de son œuvre? La formation du droit d'auteur du XVIe siecle à la loi de 1957," (diss., Strasbourg, 1999), 809–13.

80. A similar issue arose when the Massachusetts Museum of Contemporary Art sought to exhibit a vast unfinished work by the artist Christoph Büchel. The judge compared the months of labor put in by the museum staff to assemble the work with the few weeks spent by the artist himself and pronounced the outcome a collaboration. Amy M. Adler, "Against Moral Rights," *California Law Review* 97 (2009): 277.

81. Ludwig Gieseke, *Die geschichtliche Entwicklung des deutschen Urheberrechts* (Göttingen, 1957), 142–44; Elizabeth Adeney, *The Moral Rights of Authors and Performers* (Oxford, 2006), 38–39.

82. Other than, in the case of Kafka, perhaps his actuarial writings. Franz Kafka, *Amtliche Schriften* (Frankfurt, 2004).

83. Thomas H. Johnson, ed., *The Poems of Emily Dickinson* (Cambridge MA, 1955), 1: xxxixff; Daniel B. Smith, "What Is Art For?" *New York Times Magazine*, 16 November 2008, p. 40.

84. Jane C. Ginsburg, "The Right to Claim Authorship in US Copyright and Trademarks Law," *Houston Law Review* 41 (2004): 265–66. The Visual Artists Rights Act of 1990 did have an attribution right but only during the author's lifetime.

85. *Ellis v. Hurst*, 128 N.Y.S. 144 (1910).

86. Henry Hansmann and Marina Santilli, "Authors' and Artists' Moral Rights: A Comparative Legal and Economic Analysis," *Journal of Legal Studies* 26 (1997): 132.

87. Peter Decherney, *Hollywood's Copyright Wars: From Edison to the Internet* (New York, 2012), 128–29.

88. *Chaliapine c. URSS et Soc. Brenner*, Cour d'appel, Paris, 28 July 1932, *Dalloz*, 2 (1934): 143.

89. Stanislas de Gorguette d'Argœuves, *Le Droit moral de l'auteur sur son œuvre artistique ou litteraire* (Paris, 1926), 187–88.

90. Alphons Melliger, *Das Verhältnis des Urheberrechts zu den Persönlichkeitsrechten* (Berne, 1929), 5.

91. R. Besnier, "De la loi des douze tables à la législation de l'après-guerre: Quelques observations sur les vicissitudes de la notion romaine de la propriété," *Annales d'histoire économique et sociale* 46 (1937): 338; Pierre Recht, *Le Droit d'auteur, une nouvelle forme de propriété* (Paris, 1969), 9 and passim; Agnès Lucas-Schloetter, *Droit moral et droits de la personnalité: Étude de droit comparé français et allemand* (Aix-en-Provence, 2002), 1: 22.

92. Commission of the European Communities, "Follow-Up to the Green Paper on Copyright and Related Rights in the Information Society," COM (96) 568 final, 20 November 1996, p. 27.

93. Marjut Salokannel and Alain Strowel, "Study Contract Concerning Moral Rights in the Context of the Exploitation of Works through Digital Technology," ETD/99/B5–3000/E°28, April 2000, p. 208.

94. *Hansard*, 6 May 1861, p. 1635 (BK).

95. "Spielberg's Lament," *New Republic* 3818 (21 March 1988): 7.

96. John Henry Merryman, "The Refrigerator of Bernard Buffet," *Hastings Law Journal* 27, 5 (1976): 1040; Hansmann and Santilli, "Authors' and Artists' Moral Rights," 103. Tom Wolfe, *The Painted Word* (New York, 1975).

97. Gorguette d'Argœuves, *Le Droit moral de l'auteur*, 159–61.

98. Abdel-Moneim El-Tanamli, *Du droit moral de l'auteur sur son œuvre littéraire et artistique* (Paris, 1943), 85–91; "Le premier projet de loi concernant la protection du droit moral de l'auteur," *Droit d'auteur* 34 (1921): 59.

99. Art. 15. Adolf Dietz, "The Moral Right of the Author: Moral Rights and the Civil Law Countries," *Columbia-VLA Journal of Law and the Arts* 19 (1995): 224.

100. Salokannel and Strowel, "Study Contract Concerning Moral Rights," 36.

101. In British law the destruction of a work is actionable only if it is shown to constitute defamation. Gerald Dworkin, "The Moral Right and English Copyright Law," *IIC: International Review of Industrial Property and Copyright Law* 12 (1981): 484. On the other hand, strict heritage laws offer at least physical objects some protection from change and destruction. Arguably destruction affects the author's expression of his personality, since he is effectively rendered mute. Destruction could thus be prohibited by a strong interpretation of moral rights (no change for whatever reasons the author wishes), though not by a weak one (changes prohibited only if they affect his honor or reputation). Leslie Kim Treiger-Bar-Am, "Adaptions with Integrity," in Helle Porsdam, ed., *Copyright and Other Fairy Tales: Hans Christian Andersen and the Commodification of Creativity* (Cheltenham, 2006), 70–73.

102. Adolf Dietz, "The Artist's Right of Integrity under Copyright Law: A Comparative Approach," *IIC: International Review of Industrial Property and Copyright Law* 25, 2 (1994): 190.

103. Calvin Tomkins, *Duchamp* (New York, 1998), 185–86.

104. Wolfram Hamann, "Urheberrechtsprobleme um Beuys-Badewanne: Schadensbemessung für Beschädigung des Werkoriginals," *Film und Recht* 3 (1976): 166.

105. *Millar v. Taylor* (1769), Easter Term 9. Geo. 3. B.R., p. 2364 (BK).

106. "Entwurf eines Urhebergesetzes," *Gewerblicher Rechtsschutz und Urheberrecht* 44, 4/5 (1939), §§10, 28.

107. 22 April 1941 law, arts. 142–43.

108. 1957 law, art. 32; 1965 law, §42.

109. Raymond Sarraute, "Current Theory on the Moral Right of Authors and Artists under French Law," *American Journal of Comparative Law* 16, 4 (1968): 476–77; Rigamonti, "Deconstructing Moral Rights," 363.

110. Pollaud-Dulian, "Moral Rights in France through Recent Case Law," 178–80. The German law of 1965 (§§41–42) allowed heirs to withdraw a work but only if the author were entitled to during his lifetime and had for some reason been prevented from doing so.

111. *Congrès littéraire international de Paris 1878: Comptes rendus in extenso et documents* (Paris, 1879), pp. 148, 180, 212–13.

112. *Journal Officiel*, Sénat, 9 December 2011, p. 9642.

113. *Moniteur Universel*, 23 March 1841, p. 715; Alcide Darras, *Du droit des auteurs et des artistes dans les rapports internationaux* (Paris, 1887), 147.

114. *Congrès littéraire international de Paris 1878: Comptes rendus*, 214–15. See also Georges Michaélidès-Nouaros, *Le Droit moral de l'auteur* (Paris, 1935), 43–44; Josef Kohler, *Urheberrecht an Schriftwerken und Verlagsrecht* (Stuttgart, 1907), 6; J. Kohler, *Das Autorrecht, eine zivilistische Abhandlung* (Jena, 1880), 139.

115. *Minutes of the Evidence Taken before the Royal Commission on Copyright*, c.2036-I, (London, 1878), 149.

116. Thomas F. Cotter, "Pragmatism, Economics and the Droit Moral," *North Carolina Law Review* 76 (1997): 3.

117. That was her wish, fulfilled by the assignee of her rights, Hans Magnus Enzensberger, who has refused to reprint them in her collected works. Information from Aris Fioretos, author of *Nelly Sachs: Flight and Metamorphosis* (Stanford, 2012). More examples involving Jean-Paul Sartre and the Swedish writer Lars Norén: *Jean-Paul Sartre c. Editions Nagel*, Tribunal de Grande Instance de la Seine, 27 October 1969, *Revue internationale du droit d'auteur* 63 (1970): 238; Lars Norén, *Kung Mej och andra dikter* (Stockholm, 1973), 120. And there was, of course, also the Artist Formerly Known as Prince.

118. *Jerôme Lindon et SACD c. La Compagnie Brut de Breton et Bruno Boussagol*, Tribunal de Grande Instance de Paris, 3rd chamber, 15 October 1992, *Revue internationale du droit d'auteur* 155 (1993): 227.

119. *Minutes of the Evidence Taken before the Royal Commission*, c.2036-I, p. 148.

120. Wilhelm Freiherrn v. Weckbecker, "Richard Wagner, Johann Strauss und die Schutzfrist," *Archiv für Urheber- Film- und Theaterrecht* 3 (1930): 470.

121. Catherine Seville, *The Internationalisation of Copyright Law: Books, Buccaneers and the Black Flag in the Nineteenth Century* (Cambridge, 2006), 298–99.

122. James Thomson's *Seasons*, the work in dispute in both the *Millar* and *Donaldson* cases, was an instance of this.

123. James J. Marino, *Owning William Shakespeare: The King's Men and Their Intellectual Property* (Philadelphia, 2011), 1.

124. Catherine Seville, *Literary Copyright Reform in Early Victorian England: The Framing of the 1842 Copyright Act* (Cambridge, 1999), 193–95.

125. Joanna Demers, "Melody, Theft, and High Culture," in Saint-Amour, *Modernism and Copyright*, 114–15; Dorothy Lamb Crawford, *A Windfall of Musicians: Hitler's Emigrés and Exiles in Southern California* (New Haven, 2009), 224.

126. Manfred Rehbinder, "Die Beschränkungen des Urheberrechts zugunsten der Allgemeinheit," in Schweizerische Vereinigung für Urheberrecht, ed., *100 Jahre URG: Festschrift zum einhundertjährigen Bestehen eines eidgenössischen Urheberrechtsgesetzes* (Berne, 1983), 373–74.

127. *Hansard*, Commons, 5 February 1841, p. 355, Macauley.

128. Before she relented. Joanna Richardson, *Baudelaire* (London, 1994), 498.

129. Pierre Petitfils, *Rimbaud* (Charlottesville, 1987), 337; Graham Robb, *Rimbaud* (London, 2000), 444–43. Similar examples from Jules Michelet's second wife and Lilian Hellman: Oscar A. Haac, "A Spiritual Journey: Michelet in Germany, 1842," *Proceedings of the American Philosophical Society* 94, 5 (1950): 503; Lionel Gossman, "Michelet and Natural History," *Proceedings of the American Philosophical Society* 145, 3 (2001): 330–33; Roland Barthes, *Michelet* (Berkeley, 1992), 7; Lillian Hellman, ed., *The Dashiell Hammett Story Omnibus* (London, 1966), viii. More examples

in Alfred Wicher, "Schutz des Urhebers gegen seine Erben," *Börsenblatt für den Deutschen Buchhandel* (Frankfurter Ausgabe) 18, 79 (2 October 1962): 1694–95.

130. Dominique Eril, "D'Artaud à Zorn: 26 histoires d'héritage," *Lire* 138 (1987): 44–45.

131. Matthew Shaer, "Fitzgerald and Hemingway," *Los Angeles Times*, 26 July 2009.

132. Recht, *Le Droit d'auteur*, 142–43; Louis Vaunois, "Correspondance," *Le Droit d'auteur* 59 (1946): 31.

133. John Henry Merryman, "The Moral Right of Maurice Utrillo," *American Journal of Comparative Law* 43, 3 (1995): 449–52.

134. *Editions Gallimard v. Hamish Hamilton, Ltd.*, Tribunal de Grande Instance, Paris, 15 February 1984, *European Commercial Cases* 8 (1985): 574–79.

135. *New York Times*, 9 January 2012.

136. Of course the artist himself had done similar licensing while alive but not for as wide an array of merchandise. Alan Riding, "Moral Rights or the Outraged Heir: Real-Life Drama at House of Molière," *New York Times*, 29 May 2007, p. B3; Deborah Trustman, "The Ordeal of Picasso's Heirs," *New York Times Sunday Magazine*, 20 April 1980; Tim Jensen, "The Selling of Picasso: A Look at the Artist's Rights in Protecting the Reputation of His Name," *Art & the Law* 6, 3 (1981): 77–78.

137. "Communication de M. James Joyce sur le droit moral des écrivains," in James Joyce, *Occasional, Critical, and Political Writing* (Oxford, 2000), 288.

138. Paul K. Saint-Amour, *The Copywrights: Intellectual Property and the Literary Imagination* (Ithaca NY, 2003), 156–57; D. T. Max, "The Injustice Collector: Is James Joyce's Grandson Suppressing Scholarship?" *New Yorker*, 19 June 2006; Matthew Rimmer, *Digital Copyright and the Consumer Revolution: Hands Off My iPod* (Cheltenham, 2007), 38; Robert Spoo, "Copyright Protectionism and Its Discontents: The Case of James Joyce's *Ulysses* in America," *Yale Law Journal* 108 (1998): 656.

139. Heinz Püschel, "Rechte des Bühnenautors und Urheberrechtsschutzfrist aus historischer Sicht," in Robert Dittrich, ed., *Die Notwendigkeit des Urheberrechtsschutzes im Lichte seiner Geschichte* (Vienna, 1991): 236–37.

140. Paul K. Saint-Amour, "Modernism and the Lives of Copyright," in Saint-Amour, *Modernism and Copyright*, 13; Lewis Hyde, *Common as Air: Revolution, Art and Ownership* (New York, 2010), 71–75.

141. Walter Becker-Bender, *Das Urheberpersönlichkeitsrecht im musikalischen Urheberrecht* (Heidelberg, 1940), 132.

142. Jon Burlingame, "Underscoring Richard Wagner's Influence on Film Music," *Los Angeles Times*, 17 June 2010; Scott D. Paulin, "Piercing Wagner: The *Ring* in *Golden Earrings*," in Jeongwon Joe and Sander L. Gilman, eds, *Wagner and Cinema* (Bloomington, 2010), 228. The *Internet Movie Database* lists over 700 films and TV shows using Wagner's music, and that does not seem to include most non-English language ones: http://www.imdb.com/name/nm0003471/. A more useful listing is in the Joe and Gilman volume.

143. Hansmann and Santilli, "Authors' and Artists' Moral Rights," 100.

144. *Snow v. The Eaton Centre Ltd.*, 70 C.P.R. (2d) 105 (1983). A similar case: "Visual Artists Rights Amendment of 1986: Hearing Before the Subcommittee ... of the Committee of the Judiciary ... on S. 2796," Senate Hearing 99–1071, p. 22.

145. *Leger c. Reunion des Theatres Lyriques Nationaux*, Cour de Paris, 15 October 1954, discussed in Charles A. Marvin, "The Author's Status in the United Kingdom and France: Common Law and the Moral Right Doctrine," *International and Comparative Law Quarterly* 20, 4 (1971): 695; Salokannel and Strowel, "Study Contract Concerning Moral Rights," 37.

146. *Veuve Dwelshauvers c. Editions Payot*, Trib. Commerce Seine, 2 April 1951, discussed in Louis Vaunois, "Le Droit moral: Son évolution en France," *Le Droit d'auteur* 65 (1952): 66–67.

147. Edelman, "Entre copyright et droit d'auteur," 299.

148. Paris Court of Appeal, 31 October 1988, cited in Pollaud-Dulian, "Moral Rights in France

through Recent Case Law," 232. Similar examples: Elisabeth Logeais, "Post-Mortem Exercise of Copyright in French Law," *Entertainment Law Review* 2 (1991): 187–88.

149. Østre Landsret, *Ugeskrift for Retsvæsen* 124 (1990): 856–66.

150. Vaunois, "Correspondance," 31. The great German jurist Savigny asked what sense it made to grant the descendants of the sixteenth-century Meistersinger Hans Sachs perpetual property rights to his works when everything else he might have owned had long vanished. Elmar Wadle, "Savignys Beitrag zum Urheberrecht," in Gerhard Lüke, ed., *Grundfragen des Privatrechts* (Cologne, 1989), 132.

151. Peter Ruzicka, *Die Problematik eines "ewigen Urheberpersönlichkeitsrechts" unter besonderer Berücksichtigung des Schutzes musikalischer Werke* (Berlin, 1979), chap. 3.

152. Püschel, "Rechte des Bühnenautors," 228.

153. Peter Gast, "Grundsätzliches zur Stellung der Reichskulturkammer im Urheberrecht," *Archiv für Urheber- Film- und Theaterrecht* 8 (1935): 340–41; Julius Kopsch, "Der Schutz der Urheberehre," *Zeitschrift der Akademie für Deutsches Recht* 3 (1936): 377–78.

154. Adolf Dietz, *Das Droit Moral des Urhebers im neuen französischen und deutschen Urheberrecht* (Munich, 1968), 174.

155. Ferruccio Foà, *Manuale del diritto d'autore* (Milan, 1931), 151–52. Another case involved the manuscripts of Leopardi. Eduardo Piola Caselli, *Codice del diritto di autore* (Turin, 1943), 540.

156. *Société des Gens de Lettres c. Société "Les Films Marceau" et Roger Vadim*, 10 November 1961, *Recueil Dalloz* (1962): 113–16.

157. *Caisse nationale des Lettres c. Soc. d'Editions et de Diffusion artistiques, Agence parisienne de distribution et Marcireau*, 15 April 1964, *Recueil Dalloz* (1964): 746–48.

158. "Propriété intellectuelle: De la transmission du droit moral aux héritiers," *Le Dalloz* 117, 38 (1 November 2001): 3123.

159. Though the publisher also had to pay an indemnity of €10,000 and underwrite the costs of publishing the court decision. *Pierre Hugo et Société des gens de lettres de France c. Éditions Plon et François Cérésa*, Cour d'appel de Paris, 4e ch., 31 March 2004, *Revue internationale du droit d'auteur* 202 (2004): 292–300; Sylvia Nérisson, "Perpetual Moral Rights: A Troubling Justification for a Fair Result," *International Review of Intellectual Property and Competition Law* 36, 8 (2005): 959–60.

160. Cour de cassation, Première chambre civile, Arrêt 125, 30 January 2007, at http://www .courdecassation.fr/jurisprudence_2/premiere_chambre_civile_568/arret_n_9850.html#.

161. Quoted in the *Guardian*, 31 January 2007.

162. http://phugo.wtpromotions.com/.

163. Vincent Porter, "The Copyright Designs and Patents Act 1988: The Triumph of Expediency over Principle," *Journal of Law and Society* 16, 3 (1989): 342. Much the same distinction is made in André Kéréver, "Authors' Rights are Human Rights," *Copyright Bulletin* 32, 3 (1998): 18–19.

164. Michel Vivant, "Le Droit d'auteur, un droit de l'homme?" *Revue internationale du droit d'auteur* 174 (1997): 62.

165. Pollaud-Dulian, *Le Droit d'auteur*, 834–36; Pollaud-Dulian, "Moral Rights in France through Recent Case Law," 154.

166. *Recueil Dalloz Sirey* 1 (1990): 52–53; Ysolde Gendreau, "Colourizing Movies: Some International Ramifications," *Intellectual Property Journal* 5 (1990): 307.

167. Ysolde Gendreau, "The Continuing Saga of Colourization in France," *Intellectual Property Journal* 7 (1992–93): 342; Stephen Fraser, "The Copyright Battle: Emerging International Rules and Roadblocks on the Global Information Infrastructure," *John Marshall Journal of Computer and Information Law* 15 (1997): 803–4; Emmanuel Pierrat, *La Guerre des copyrights* (Paris, 2006), 64.

168. Edelman, "Applicable Legislation Regarding Exploitation of Colourized US Films in France," 638. This was seen as "juridical imperialism" in a more critical evaluation. Jane C.

Ginsburg and Pierre Sirinelli, "Authors and Exploitations in International Private Law: The French Supreme Court and the Huston Film Colorization Controversy," *Columbia-VLA Journal of Law and Arts* 15, 2 (1991): 141.

169. *Shostakovich v. Twentieth Century Fox Film Corp*, 80 N.Y.S. 2d 575 (1948), p. 579. In 1932 the Russian opera singer Feodor Chaliapin, then resident in France, won recognition of his moral rights against a Soviet publishing house for issuing an altered version of his memoirs in the USSR. *Chaliapine c. URSS et Soc. Brenner*, Cour d'appel, Paris, 28 July 1932, *Dalloz* 2 (1934): 139.

170. Pierre Sirinelli, "Note," *Revue internationale du droit d'auteur* 142 (1989): 319.

171. Mike Holderness, quoted in Porsdam, "On European Narratives of Human Rights," 347.

172. Bernard Edelman, "Une loi substantiellement internationale: La loi du 3 juillet 1985 sur les droits d'auteur et droits voisins," *Journal du droit international* 3 (1987): 562.

173. Desbois, *Le Droit d'auteur en France*, 470.

174. Gorguette d'Argœuves, *Le Droit moral de l'auteur*, 50.

175. F. Pollaud-Dulian, "Moral Rights in France through Recent Case Law," *Revue internationale du droit d'auteur* 145 (1990): 216–18.

176. "Le premier projet de loi concernant la protection du droit moral de l'auteur," 59; Willy Hoffmann, "Das neue österreichische Urheberrechtsgesetz," *Archiv für Urheber- Film- und Theaterrecht* 9 (1936): 249; Becker-Bender, *Das Urheberpersönlichkeitsrecht im musikalischen Urheberrecht*, 102, 127.

177. Stig Strömholm, "Droit Moral—The International and Comparative Scene from a Scandinavian Viewpoint," *IIC: International Review of Industrial Property and Copyright Law* 14 (1983): 39.

178. Olav Lid, "Classiques au crepuscule," *Revue internationale du droit d'auteur* 8 (1955): 87.

179. Lawrence Adam Beyer, "Intentionalism, Art, and the Suppression of Innovation: Film Colorization and the Philosophy of Moral Rights," *Northwestern University Law Review* 82, 4 (1988): 1033.

180. Neil Weinstock Netanel, "Copyright and a Democratic Civil Society," *Yale Law Journal* 106, 2 (1996): 296.

181. Sebastian Wündisch, *Richard Wagner und das Urheberrecht* (Berlin, 2004), 92–100; Joachim Köhler, *Wagner's Hitler: The Prophet and His Disciple* (Cambridge, 2000), 112–13.

182. Püschel, "Rechte des Bühnenautors und Urheberrechtsschutzfrist," 223–35; Lucy Beckett, *Richard Wagner* Parsifal (Cambridge, 1981), 94.

183. Engelsing, "Kann ein Schauspieler die Nachsynchronisierung eines alten Filmes, in welchem er die Hauptrolle gespielt hat, verhindern?" *Archiv für Urheber- Film- und Theaterrecht* 8 (1935): 157–60.

184. Pollaud-Dulian, "Moral Rights in France through Recent Case Law," 292.

185. Public Law 100–446.

186. "Berne Convention Implementation Act of 1987: Hearings before the . . . Committee on the Judiciary," Serial No. 50, p. 418.

187. Jack Matthews, "Film Directors See Red over Ted Turner's Movie Tinting," *Los Angeles Times*, 12 September 1986.

188. "Sinful to Color Old Movies, Woody Tells Senators," *Los Angeles Times*, 12 May 1987.

189. *Washington Post*, 28 February 1988.

190. Jane C. Ginsburg, "Moral Rights in a Common Law System," *Entertainment Law Review* 4 (1990): 128.

191. Michael Schudson, "Colorization and Authenticity," *Society* 24, 2 (1987): 18–19.

192. Beyer, "Intentionalism, Art, and the Suppression of Innovation," 1025–30.

193. Edelman, "Entre copyright et droit d'auteur," 300.

194. Commission of the European Communities, "Follow-up to the Green Paper: Working

Programme of the Commission in the Field of Copyright and Neighbouring Rights," COM (90) 584 Final, Brussels, 17 January 1991, p. 2.

195. http://www.piratpartiet.se/kultur.

196. Philippe Gaudrat, "Droits des auteurs—Droits moraux," in *Juris-Classeur*, Civil, Annexe, Propriété littéraire et artistique, Fasc. 1210, no. 60. The public's—not just creators'—interest in authors' rights is advanced in a sustained argument by Stéphanie Carre, "L'Intérêt du public en droit d'auteur," (diss. Montpellier 1, 2004).

197. Strowel, *Droit d'auteur et copyright*, 274; Carre, "L'Intérêt du public en droit d'auteur," 42–43.

198. This is something along the lines of what is argued by those who think that the copyright system's idea of the public interest, though seemingly collectivistic and social, is in fact a form of disguised utilitarian individualism. Copyright's definition of the public interest, in other words, is nothing more than the collectivity of the individual interests of all citizens. There is no public interest defined by reference to the state or another higher entity in some more nebulous Hegelian or Heideggerian sense. Mireille Buydens, "L'Intérêt général, une notion protéiforme," in *L'Intérêt général et l'accès à l'information en propriété intellectuelle*, 30–33. A similar opposition in the Conseil d'État's musings on the nature of the general interest: Le Conseil d'État, "Réflexions sur l'intérêt general: Rapport public 1999," http://www.conseil-etat .fr/fr/rapports-et-etudes/linteret-general-une-notion-centrale-de-la.html.

199. S. Conant, "International Copyright: An American View," *MacMillan's Magazine* 40 (1879): 158.

200. Leone Levi, "Copyrights and Patents," *Princeton Review* (1878): 751. This lesson was already firmly in place in Germany. Sometimes dropping the price by half does not just double the number of readers but increases it tenfold: Constantin Wrangell, *Die Prinzipien des literarischen Eigenthums* (Dorpat, 1866), 56.

201. Édouard Laboulaye, *Études sur la propriété littéraire en France et en Angleterre* (Paris, 1858), xliv.

202. Paul M. Zall, "Wordsworth and the Copyright Act of 1842," *Proceedings of the Modern Language Association* 70 (1955): 133; Susan Eilenberg, "Mortal Pages: Wordsworth and the Reform of Copyright," *English Literary History* 56, 2 (1989): 353; Edward Earle, "The Effect of Romanticism on the 19th Century Development of Copyright Law," *Intellectual Property Journal* 6 (1991): 286; Chris R. Vanden Bossche, "The Value of Literature: Representations of Print Culture in the Copyright Debate of 1837–1842," *Victorian Studies* 38, 1 (1994): 50–51.

203. *Hansard*, Commons, 5 February 1841, p. 348

2. FROM ROYAL PRIVILEGE TO LITERARY PROPERTY: A COMMON START TO COPYRIGHT IN THE EIGHTEENTH CENTURY

1. Eckhard Höffner, *Geschichte und Wesen des Urheberrechts* (Munich, 2010), 1: 310–23; Martha Woodmansee, "Publishers, Privateers, Pirates: Eighteenth-Century German Book Piracy Revisited," in Mario Biagioli et al., eds., *Making and Unmaking Intellectual Property* (Chicago, 2011).

2. Robert Darnton, *The Literary Underground of the Old Regime* (Cambridge MA, 1982), 187–95.

3. Robert Darnton, "The Science of Piracy: A Crucial Ingredient in Eighteenth-Century Publishing," *Studies on Voltaire and the Eighteenth Century* 12 (2003): 3–4.

4. The best overall survey of Locke's revolutionary position in the history of property concepts is Manfred Brocker, *Arbeit und Eigentum: Der Paradigmenwechsel in der neuzeitlichen Eigentumstheorie* (Darmstadt, 1992).

5. Jonathan Peterson, "Lockean Property and Literary Works," *Legal Theory* 14 (2008): 272–73.

6. E. S. de Beer, ed., *Correspondence of John Locke* (Oxford, 1979), 5: 791.

7. Brad Sherman and Lionel Bently, *The Making of Modern Intellectual Property Law: The British Experience, 1760–1911* (Cambridge, 1999), 20–23; Robert M. Reuss, *Naturrecht oder positivistisches Konzept: Die Entstehung des Urheberrechts im 18. Jahrhundert in England und den Vereinigten Staaten von Amerika* (Baden-Baden, 2010), 225–28.

8. Simon Marion, "Plaidoyé second sur l'impression des Œuvres de Seneque," p. 11 (BK).

9. "Mémoire sur la contestation qui est entre les libraires de Paris et ceux de Lyon au sujet des privilèges et des Continuations que le Roy accorde pour l'impression des livres," 1690, p. 2 (BK).

10. "Mémoire de Louis d'Héricourt à Monseigneur le Garde des Sceaux," 1725, pp. 2, 4–6 (BK).

11. See the commentaries on this case by Frédéric Rideau in BK. Background for all this is in Laurent Pfister, "L'auteur, propriétaire de son œuvre? La formation du droit d'auteur du XVIe siecle à la loi de 1957," (diss., Strasbourg, 1999), 206ff.

12. Denis Diderot, "Lettre historique et politique sur le commerce de la librairie" (1763) in his *Œuvres complètes* (Paris, 1876), 18: 30.

13. William H. Sewell, Jr., *Work and Revolution in France: The Language of Labor from the Old Regime to 1848* (Cambridge, 1980), 90–91.

14. Assemblée nationale, 13 January 1791, in *Archives Parlementaires de 1787 à 1860*, 1 series, 22: 212, or *Réimpression de l'ancien Moniteur* (Paris, 1847–1854), 7: 117. He was invoked as recently as 2005: *Journal Officiel*, Assemblée, 20 December 2005, p. 8551.

15. *Archives Parlementaires de 1787 à 1860*, Convention nationale, 19 July 1793, 69: 186.

16. Quoted in Mark Rose, *Authors and Owners: The Invention of Copyright* (Cambridge MA, 1993), 55.

17. *Millar v. Taylor* (1769), 4 Burr. 2303, pp. 2345–46 (BK). Similarly in William Enfield, *Observations on Literary Property* (London, 1774), 21; William Warburton, "A Letter from an Author to A Member of Parliament, Concerning Literary Property," in R. Hurd, ed., *The Works of the Right William Warburton* (London, 1811), 12: 405 (BK). Works, Disraeli said in 1838, "constituted a species of property better than any other." *Hansard*, Commons, 25 April 1838, p. 575.

18. *The Perpetual Laws of the Commonwealth of Massachusetts* (Boston, 1789), 369 (BK). Similar sentiments later from Senator Hoar. *Congressional Record*, 50th Congress, 1st sess., vol. 19, pt. 4, Senate, 24 April 1888, p. 3273.

19. Diderot, "Lettre," 30.

20. That is the position of Edelman, who refuses to accept that Diderot could have argued for the personal connection between author and work only in order that he be able to sell it off. As a result he claims to discern already here a kind of sleeper right that will eventually blossom into the personalist connection between author and work. The reality, of course, is that both English and French theorists were working with largely similar notions of natural rights to property and their total alienability. Bernard Edelman, *Le sacre de l'auteur* (Paris, 2004), 255. His opinion is based largely on Pfister, "L'auteur, propriétaire de son œuvre?" as is the argument in Frédéric Rideau's "Commentary on Linguet's opinion on the Decree of 30 August 1777 regarding privileges," in BK. A similar anachronistic reading is offered by Boncompain who argues that the personal nature of authors' property rights "founds their moral right," a phrase that was, of course, not in use during the 1790s. Jacques Boncompain, *La Révolution des auteurs (1773–1815)* (n.p., 2001), 278, 329, 419–20.

21. Cochu, "Requête au Roi," in Ed. Laboulaye and G. Guiffrey, eds., *La Propriété littéraire au XVIIIe siècle* (Paris, 1859), 160–63.

22. See also Roger Chartier, *The Order of Books: Readers, Authors and Libraries in Europe between the 14th and 18th Centuries* (Stanford, 1994), 33–35.

23. "Lettre du libraire Leclerc à M. de Néville, Directeur de la librairie" (1778), in Laboulaye and Guiffrey, *La Propriété littéraire au XVIIIe siècle*, 406–7.

24. "Opinion de Linguet touchant l'arrêt sur les privilèges" (1777), in Laboulaye and Guiffrey, *La Propriété littéraire au XVIIIe siècle*, 239–40.

25. "Lettres à un ami par l'abbé Pluquet" (1778–1779), in Laboulaye and Guiffrey, *La Propriété littéraire au XVIIIe siècle*, 315.

26. "Lettres à un ami par l'abbé Pluquet," 281–82, also 309.

27. Diderot, "Lettre," 30, 27.

28. *Archives Parlementaires de 1787 à 1860*, Assemblée nationale, 13 January 1791, 1 series, 22:212.

29. Jane C. Ginsburg, "A Tale of Two Copyrights: Literary Property in Revolutionary France and America," *Tulane Law Review* 64, 5 (1990): 1006–7. For an unsatisfactory attempt to argue against Ginsburg, see André Lucas, "L'Intérêt général dans l'évolution du droit d'auteur," in *L'Intérêt général et l'accès à l'information en propriété intellectuelle* (Brussels, 2008), 82–83.

30. Mich. 2 Geo. 3, pp. 333–34 (BK).

31. "The right of property in books and machines is therefore the same. Both have arisen from the extraordinary acts of the state." *Tonsor v. Collins* (1762), Trin. 1 Geo. 3, p. 308 (BK).

32. Marquis de Condorcet, *Fragments sur la liberté de la presse* (1776), in his *Œuvres* (Paris, 1847), 2: 308–11 (BK). For background, Carla Hesse, "Enlightenment Epistemology and the Laws of Authorship in Revolutionary France, 1777–1793," *Representations* 30 (1990): 115–16; Carla Hesse, *Publishing and Cultural Politics in Revolutionary Paris, 1789–1810* (Berkeley, 1991), chap. 2, pp. 97–114.

33. [Jean-François Gaultier de Biauzat], *Mémoire a consulter, pour les libraires et imprimeurs de Lyon, Rouen, Toulouse, Marseille et Nimes, concernant les privileges de librairie et continuations d'iceux* (1776), pp. 31–36 (BK).

34. *Millar v. Taylor* (1769), 4 Burr. 2303, p. 2341 (BK).

35. "Lettres à un ami par l'abbé Pluquet," 309, 332–33.

36. Commission de la propriété littéraire, *Collection des procès-verbaux* (Paris, 1826), 34 (BK). Similar ideas in Johann Caspar Bluntschli, *Deutsches Privatrecht* (Berlin, 1853), 1: 187–89 (BK).

37. Jefferson to Isaac McPherson, 13 August 1813, in Andrew A. Lipscomb and Albert Ellery Bergh, eds., *Writings of Thomas Jefferson* (Washington DC, 1905), 13: 333–35.

38. *Annales du Parlement français*, 18 January 1841, 3: 684.

39. L. Ray Patterson and Stanley W. Lindberg, *The Nature of Copyright* (Athens GA, 1991), 29–30.

40. 8 Anne, c. 19 (1710). The standard accounts include Lyman Ray Patterson, *Copyright in Historical Perspective* (Nashville, 1968), and Rose, *Authors and Owners*. These have recently been supplemented by Oren Bracha, *Owning Ideas: A History of Anglo-American Intellectual Property* (http://www.obracha.net/), Ronan Deazley, *On the Origin of the Right to Copy: Charting the Movement of Copyright Law in Eighteenth-Century Britain (1695–1775)* (Oxford, 2004), Isabella Alexander, *Copyright Law and the Public Interest in the Nineteenth Century* (Oxford, 2010), chaps. 1–3, Reuss, *Naturrecht oder positivistisches Konzept*.

41. *Correspondence of John Locke*, 5: 791.

42. John Feather, "The Book Trade in Politics: The Making of the Copyright Act of 1710," *Publishing History* 8 (1980): 35; W. R. Cornish, "Authors in Law," *Modern Law Review* 58, 1 (1995): 3.

43. *Millar v. Taylor* (1769), 4 Burr. 2303, p. 2399.

44. Howard B. Abrams, "The Historic Foundation of American Copyright Law: Exploding the Myth of Common Law Copyright," *Wayne Law Review* 29, 3 (1983): 1156.

45. *Hansard*, 1, 17 (1774), pp. 999–1000 (BK).

46. Reuss, *Naturrecht oder positivistisches Konzept*, 355–57.

47. Deazley, *Origin of the Right to Copy*, chap. 9; Ronan Deazley, *Rethinking Copyright: History, Theory, Language* (Cheltenham, 2006), 22–23.

48. In fact, the 1878 Copyright Commission found that the right was of minuscule value, with Oxford owning six such copyrights and Cambridge none. Copyright Commission, *The Royal Commissions and the Report of the Commissioners*, c. 2036 (London, 1878), xii.

49. Deazley insists on this broad social ambition of early British copyright law: Deazley, *Origin of the Right to Copy*, 46, 226; Deazley, *Rethinking Copyright*, 22–23.

50. This with the justified proviso that it remained unclear how exactly to define the public interest that was being served. This is Alexander's caution to what she sees as Deazley's overly emphatic interpretation of Donaldson as favoring the public interest. Alexander, *Copyright Law and the Public Interest*, 36.

51. Thomas Jefferson to James Madison, 6 September 1789, in Julian P. Boyd, ed., *The Papers of Thomas Jefferson* (Princeton, 1958), 15: 392–97 .

52. US Constitution, art. I, §8, cl. 8.

53. "An Act for the Promotion and Encouragement of Literature," 27 May 1783, *Acts of the General Assembly of the State of New Jersey* (Trenton, 1784), chap. 351, p. 325 (BK).

54. Abrams, "Historic Foundation of American Copyright Law," 1175.

55. This change may have rested on a misunderstanding by the drafters of the Copyright Act, who failed to grasp some of Anne's clauses that they were importing into American law. Patterson, *Copyright in Historical Perspective*, 200–201. But clearly the framers had plumped for a utilitarian understanding of copyright, resting it on statute and not natural law. Tyler T. Ochoa and Mark Rose, "The Anti-Monopoly Origins of the Patent and Copyright Clause," *Journal of the Copyright Society of the USA* 49 (2001–2): 691–95.

56. Oren Bracha, Commentary on the Copyright Act 1790, in BK.

57. The uses and meaning of "secure" are discussed in Edward G. Walterscheid, "Understanding the Copyright Act of 1790: The Issue of Common Law Copyright in America and the Modern Interpretation of the Copyright Power," *Journal of the Copyright Society of the USA* 53, 1–2 (2005–6): 324–32; Edward C. Walterscheid, *The Nature of the Intellectual Property Clause: A Study in Historical Perspective* (Buffalo, 2002), 212–26. The history of patents is brought to bear on the question in Jane C. Ginsburg, "'Une Chose Publique'? The Author's Domain and the Public Domain in Early British, French and US Copyright Law," *Cambridge Law Journal* 65 (2006): 663–66.

58. See, for example, Report 2401, 10 June 1890, *The Reports of Committees of the House of Representatives* (1889–90) (Washington DC, 1891), p. 7.

59. These were arguments raised in the Supreme Court in *Wheaton v. Peters* (1834). Richard Peters, *Reports of Cases Argued and Adjudged in the Supreme Court* (Philadelphia, n.d.; 1834), 8: 592, 661, 629, 641 (BK).

60. Patterson, *Copyright in Historical Perspective*, 199. British legislation of the period made no express distinction between natives and foreigners. Eaton S. Drone, *A Treatise on the Law of Property in Intellectual Productions in Great Britain and the United States* (Boston, 1879), 86; Catherine Seville, "Nineteenth-Century Anglo-US Copyright Relations: The Language of Piracy versus the Moral High Ground," in Lionel Bently et al., eds., *Copyright and Piracy* (Cambridge, 2010), 30–33. In 1852 France extended protection to nonresident foreigners who had first published outside France. By 1890, as Congress recognized, the US was the only nation refusing copyright to foreigners. House Report 2401, 10 June 1890, *The Reports of Committees of the House of Representatives* (1889–90), p. 2.

61. That the Constitution gives rights for only a limited time "was a confession that there was no absolute legal property in it [writings or inventions] at common law." *Congressional*

Record, 50th Congress, 1st sess., vol. 19, pt. 4, Senate, 24 April 1888, p. 3507. See also *Congressional Record*, 51st Congress, 2nd sess., vol. 22, Senate, 13 February 1891, p. 2608, Senator Daniel.

62. Report 1188, 21 May 1886, *Reports of Committees of the Senate* (1885–86), pp. 68–69.

63. Noah Webster, *A Collection of Papers on Political, Literary, and Moral Subjects* (New York, 1843), 176 (BK).

64. Jefferson to Isaac McPherson, 13 August 1813, in Lipscomb and Bergh, *Writings of Thomas Jefferson*, 13: 333–35.

65. Stuart Banner, *American Property* (Cambridge MA, 2011), chap. 5.

66. Wheaton's attorneys argued that governments were obliged to publish and make public laws—but not court decisions. Peters, *Reports of Cases Argued*, 8: 616.

67. Craig Joyce, "'A Curious Chapter in the History of Judicature': *Wheaton v. Peters* and the Rest of the Story (of Copyright in the New Republic)," *Houston Law Review* 42, 2 (2005): 383.

68. Peters, *Reports of Cases Argued*, 8: 615, 619–20.

69. Joyce, "Curious Chapter," 389.

70. Peters, *Reports of Cases Argued*, 8: 591.

71. Abrams, "Historic Foundation of American Copyright Law," 1126, 1185–86.

72. James Boswell, *The Life of Samuel Johnson, LL.D.* (London, 1791), 1: 421–22.

73. For the French and the British that is the theme of Frédéric Rideau, *La Formation du droit de la propriété littéraire en France et en Grande-Bretagne: Une convergence oubliée* (Aix-en-Provence, 2004).

74. "Arrest du Conseil d'Etat du Roi, Portant Règlement sur la durée des Privilèges en Librairie. Du 30 août 1777" (BK). The other decrees are in Laboulaye and Guiffrey, *La Propriété littéraire au XVIIIe siècle*, 127–50.

75. Protests from Simon Linguet in "Opinion de Linguet touchant l'arrêt sur les privilèges" (1777), pp. 29–30 (BK), and Cochu, "Requête au Roi," in Laboulaye and Guiffrey, *La Propriété littéraire au XVIIIe siècle*, 160–63, 217.

76. Decree 13–19 January 1791. *Archives Parlementaires de 1787 à 1860*, Assemblée nationale, 13 January 1791, 1 series, 22: 210–14.

77. Law of 19 July 1793, *Archives Parlementaires de 1787 à 1860*, Convention nationale, 19 July 1793, 69: 186–87.

78. Anne Latournerie, "Droits d'auteur, droits de public: Une approche historique," *L'économie politique* 22, 2 (2004): 22–23.

79. André Kerever, "The French Revolution and Authors' Rights," *Revue internationale du droit d'auteur* 141 (1989): 9–10.

80. "[U]ne chose qui pût entrer dans le commerce." *Dalloz* 1, Cour de Cassation, 27 May 1842, p. 303 (BK).

81. Assemblée nationale, 13 January 1791, *Réimpression de l'ancien Moniteur* (Paris, 1847–54), 7: 118. Art. 5 of the 1791 law said that heirs and assignees were the owners of their works during the term of protection and art. 2 of the 1793 law said that heirs and assignees enjoyed the same rights (of selling and distributing) as authors. The same was also said in "Droit de copie," *Encyclopédie, ou dictionnaire raisonné des sciences, des arts et des métiers* (Paris, 1755), 5: 146–47.

82. *Congrès littéraire international de Paris 1878: Comptes rendus in extenso et documents* (Paris, n.d.), 106.

83. *Journal Officiel*, Sénat, 29 October 2008, p. 6360; Assemblée nationale, 29 April 2009, p. 3739.

84. Höffner, *Geschichte und Wesen des Urheberrechts*, 1: chap. 4.

85. J. A. Schlettwein, *Grundfeste der Staaten oder die politische Oekonomie* (1779), §52, for example, quoted in Diethelm Klippel, "Historische Wurzeln und Funktionen von Immaterialgüter- und Persönlichkeitsrechten im 19. Jahrhundert," *Zeitschrift für neuere Rechtsgeschichte* 3/4 (1982): 137; Ludwig Gieseke, *Die geschichtliche Entwicklung des deutschen Urheberrechts* (Göttingen, 1957), 76–80.

86. Friedemann Kawohl, "Commentary on Kant's Essay, 'On the Injustice of Reprinting Books' (1785)," p. 2 and passim for other ideas that have been helpful here (BK).

87. *Two Treatises of Government*, bk. 2, chap. 2, §6, chap. 5, §27.

88. Helmut Coing, "Die Entwicklung der Persönlichkeitsrecht im 19. Jahrhundert," in Arthur Kaufmann, et al., eds., *Rechtsstaat und Menschenwürde: Festschrift für Werner Maihofer zum 70. Geburtstag* (Frankfurt, 1988), 80; Agnès Lucas-Schloetter, *Droit moral et droits de la personnalité: Étude de droit comparé français et allemand* (Aix-en-Provence, 2002), 1: 59–60.

89. Edelman would like to find a foreshadowing of the Kantian distinction between the work as a property and as an emanation of the author's personality a few years earlier in the work of Simon Linguet in 1768. Edelman, *Le sacre de l'auteur*, 257–64. His opinions are based on an uncharacteristically unconvincing reading of Linguet offered by Pfister, "L'auteur, propriétaire de son œuvre?" 326–39.

90. Immanuel Kant, "Von der Unrechtmäßigkeit des Büchernachdrucks," *Berlinische Monatsschrift* 5 (1785) (BK). The same ideas appeared more succinctly in his *Metaphysische Anfangsgründe der Rechtslehre* (Königsberg, 1797), 127–29.

91. Kant, "Unrechtmäßigkeit des Büchernachdrucks," 414–16, 406.

92. Gieseke, *Die geschichtliche Entwicklung*, 98; David Saunders, "Approaches to the Historical Relations of the Legal and the Aesthetic," *New Literary History* 23, 3, (1992): 506–7; Heinrich Hubmann, "Immanuel Kants Urheberrechtstheorie," *UFITA* 106 (1987): 151; Pascal Oberndörfer, *Die philosophische Grundlage des Urheberrechts* (Baden-Baden, 2005), 97–98.

93. Kant, "Unrechtmäßigkeit des Büchernachdrucks," 411.

94. Ibid., 416–17.

95. J. G. Fichte, "Beweis der Unrechtmäßigkeit des Büchernachdrucks," *Berlinische Monatsschrift* 21 (1793): 451–52 (BK).

96. Lessing had made a similar distinction in the 1770s: ownership and right to use were two separate things. He doubted that a publisher had ownership claims to a work. Gotthold Ephraim Lessing, "Leben und Leben Lassen: Ein Projekt für Schriftsteller und Buchhändler," in Herbert G. Göpfert et al., eds., *Werke* (Munich, 1973), 5: 783.

97. Fichte, "Beweis der Unrechtmäßigkeit," 457–59.

98. A similar argument in Johann Jakob Cella, "Vom Büchernachdruck," in his *Freymüthige Aufsätze* (Anspach, 1784), 86–87.

99. *Allgemeines Landrecht für die preussischen Staaten* (Berlin, 1794), §§ 996–98 (BK).

100. Martin Löhnig, "Der Schutz des geistigen Eigentums von Autoren im Preußischen Landrecht von 1794," *Zeitschrift für neuere Rechtsgeschichte* 29, 3/4 (2007): 201–3, 206–7.

101. §§1020, 1030.

102. Friedemann Kawohl, "The Berlin Publisher Friedrich Nicolai and the Reprinting Sections of the Prussian Statute Book of 1794," in Ronan Deazley, et al., eds., *Privilege and Property* (Cambridge, 2010).

103. §§1011–19. Gieseke, *Die geschichtliche Entwicklung*, 113–15; Löhnig, "Der Schutz des geistigen Eigentums," 211.

104. §§1029, 1012, 1016–17.

105. *Land-Recht des Grossherzogthums Baden* (Karlsruhe, 1809), §577de. (BK).

106. Verordnung vom 16ten Mai 1829, den Büchernachdruck betreffend, in *Sammlung von Gesetzen . . . für Kurhessen*, 5: 31–33 (BK).

107. Gesetz zum Schutze des Eigenthums an Werken der Wissenschaft und Kunst gegen Nachdruck und Nachbildung. Vom 11. Juni 1837, in *Gesetz-Sammlung für die Königlichen Preussischen Staaten*, 1837, pp. 165–71 (BK).

108. Ginsburg, "Tale of Two Copyrights," 995–96.

109. Édouard Laboulaye, *Études sur la propriété littéraire en France et en Angleterre* (Paris, 1858), xi–xiii.

110. Honoré de Balzac, "Notes sur la propriété littéraire" (1841), in his *Œuvres completes* (Paris, 1872), 22: 300.

3. THE WAYS PART: COPYRIGHT AND AUTHORS' RIGHTS IN THE NINETEENTH CENTURY

1. *Congrès littéraire international de Paris 1878: Comptes rendus in extenso et documents* (Paris, 1879), 138, 171.

2. Copyright Commission, *The Royal Commissions and the Report of the Commissioners*, c. 2036 (London, 1878), xlix.

3. *Minutes of the Evidence Taken before the Royal Commission on Copyright*, c.2036-I, (London, 1878), 16–17.

4. Ibid., 40–42 and passim.

5. Helmut Rittstieg, *Eigentum als Verfassungsproblem: Zu Geschichte und Gegenwart des bürgerlichen Verfassungsstaates* (Darmstadt, 1975), 26–27; Charles Donahue, Jr., "The Future of the Concept of Property Predicted from Its Past," in J. Roland Pennock and John W. Chapman, eds., *Property* (New York, 1980), 34.

6. Mich. 2. Geo. 3, pp. 340–41 (BK); Frederick G. Whelan, "Property as Artifice: Hume and Blackstone," in Pennock and Chapman, *Property*, 121.

7. Brad Sherman and Lionel Bently, *The Making of Modern Intellectual Property Law: The British Experience, 1760–1911* (Cambridge, 1999), 40–41.

8. *Land-Recht des Grossherzogthums Baden* (Karlsruhe, 1809), §577d. (BK).

9. *Pope v. Curl* (1741) 2 Atk. 342 (BK). See also Ronan Deazley, Commentary on *Pope v. Curl* (1741) in BK; Mark Rose, *Authors and Owners: The Invention of Copyright* (Cambridge MA, 1993), 60–64.

10. D. Roberton Blaine, *Artistic Copyright: Report Prepared at the Request of the Committee, Appointed by the Society of Arts* (London, 1858), 10 (BK).

11. "The Case of Designers, Engravers, Etchers, &c., Stated in a Letter to a Member of Parliament," Lincolns Inn Library: MP102, Fol 125, pp. 4–5 (BK). See also the commentary by Ronan Deazley in BK, as well as Ronan Deazley, *On the Origin of the Right to Copy: Charting the Movement of Copyright Law in Eighteenth-Century Britain (1695–1775)* (Oxford, 2004), 88–94.

12. Francis Hargrave, *An Argument in Defence of Literary Property* (London, n.d., 1774), 16, 36–38, 6–7 (BK).

13. "Lettres à un ami par l'abbé Pluquet" (1778–79), in Ed. Laboulaye and G. Guiffrey, eds., *La Propriété littéraire au XVIIIe siècle* (Paris, 1859), 315. Similarly: "Lettre du libraire Leclerc à M. de Néville, Directeur de la librairie" (1778), 406–7.

14. J. G. Fichte, "Beweis der Unrechtmäßigkeit des Büchernachdrucks," *Berlinische Monatsschrift* 21 (1793): 457–59. Similar arguments in Johann Jakob Cella, "Vom Büchernachdruck," in his *Freymüthige Aufsätze* (Anspach, 1784), 96–97, 103–5.

15. Robert Maugham, *A Treatise on the Laws of Literary Property* (London, 1828), 181–82.

16. *Archives Parlementaires*, Chambre de Pairs, 25 May 1839, 124: 644.

17. Ludwig Gieseke, *Die geschichtliche Entwicklung des deutschen Urheberrechts* (Göttingen, 1957), 21, 36–40.

18. Martin Luther, "Eyn Vermanung an die Drücker," 1541 (BK).

19. Lyman Ray Patterson, *Copyright in Historical Perspective* (Nashville, 1968), 71–77; Rose, *Authors and Owners*, 27–30. But, for a caution, see also Oren Bracha, *Owning Ideas: A History of Anglo-American Intellectual Property* (http://www.obracha.net/), 166–68, 174–75.

20. Daniel Defoe, *An Essay on the Regulation of the Press* (London, 1704), 18–22, 26–27 (BK).

21. *Burnet v. Chetwood* (1721), J. H. Merivale, *Chancery Reports* (London, 1817–19), 2: 442 (BK). Rose, *Authors and Owners*, 49–50.

22. Southey was also the author of the original version of Goldilocks and coined the term "autobiography."

23. *Southey v. Sherwood* (1817) 2 Mer. 435, p. 439. Isabella Alexander, *Copyright Law and the Public Interest in the Nineteenth Century* (Oxford, 2010), 71. In a later case the son of Charlie Chaplin, having assigned the copyright to his life story, sought to restrain publication. The court, however, refused to intervene. *Chaplin v. Leslie Frewin (Publishers) Ltd*. [1966] Ch. 71, discussed in Gerald Dworkin, "The Moral Right and English Copyright Law," *IIC: International Review of Industrial Property and Copyright Law* 12 (1981): 489.

24. Engravers' Act, 1735, 8 Geo. II. c. 13 (BK).

25. Fine Art Copyright Act, 1862, 25 & 26 Vict. c. 68, s 7.

26. An Act to Amend the Laws Relating to Dramatic Literary Copyright, 1833, 3 Will IV c. 15.

27. *Murray v. Elliston*, 3 May 1822, 5 B & Ald. 657, *English Reports*, vol. 106.

28. Quoted in Alexander, *Copyright Law and the Public Interest*, 86.

29. J. T. Atkyns, *Chancery Reports* (London, 1794), 2: 143 (BK). See also the instructive commentary by Ronan Deazley in BK.

30. *Millar v. Taylor* (1769), Easter Term 9 Geo. 3. B.R., p. 2399.

31. *The Cases of the Appellants and Respondents in the Cause of Literary Property, before the House of Lords* (London, 1774), 4, 44, 47 (BK).

32. Mark Rose, "Technology and Copyright in 1735: The Engraver's Act," *Information Society* 21, 1 (2005): 65; David Hunter, "Copyright Protection for Engravings and Maps in Eighteenth-Century Britain," *Library* 6, 9 (1987): 143–45.

33. Ronan Deazley, "Breaking the Mould? The Radical Nature of the Fine Art Copyright Bill 1862," in Deazley et al., eds., *Privilege and Property* (Cambridge, 2010), 293.

34. *Hansard*, Commons, 6 May 1861, pp. 1631–34.

35. 25 & 26 Vict. c. 68, s. 1 (1862).

36. 38 Geo. III. c. 71, s. 1 (1798). Similar wording in 54 Geo. III. c. 56, s. 1 (1814).

37. It also thought it monstrous that, if artists retained copyright, a photograph of the commissioner's wife or daughter should be able to be exhibited in shop windows "amongst actresses and like characters." *Minutes of the Evidence Taken before the Royal Commission on Copyright*, 184.

38. 5 & 6 Vict., c. 45, s. 18 (1842).

39. *Hansard*, Commons, 3, 43 (6 June 1838), p. 553.

40. *Congrès littéraire international de Paris 1878*, 40, 86–87.

41. Simon Linguet, "Opinion de Linguet touchant l'arrêt sur les privilèges," (1777), 31–32, 24, 29 (BK).

42. Pfister overinterprets Linguet here to make of him a proto-Kantian, and he is eagerly followed by Edelman and Rideau. Bernard Edelman, *Le sacre de l'auteur* (Paris, 2004), 255; Laurent Pfister, "L'auteur, propriétaire de son œuvre? La formation du droit d'auteur du XVIe siecle à la loi de 1957" (diss., Strasbourg, 1999), 332–39; Frédéric Rideau, "Commentary on Linguet's opinion on the Decree of 30 August 1777 regarding privileges" in BK.

43. Décret du 5 février 1810, contenant règlement sur l'imprimerie et la librairie, art. 40, in *Traité théorique et pratique de la propriété littéraire et artistique et du droit de représentation* (Paris, 1908), 885–86.

44. Commission de la propriété littéraire, *Collection des procès-verbaux* (Paris, 1826), 38, 329–32 (BK).

45. Daniel Defoe had made a similar complaint a century earlier, that pirates with their unauthorized editions acted as badly as though they had slept with the authors' wives and broken up their houses. Defoe, *Essay on the Regulation of the Press*, 28.

46. Honoré de Balzac, "Pro Aris et Focis. Lettre adressée aux écrivains du XIXe siècle," *Revue de Paris*, n.s., 11 (1834): 70–72.

47. Narcisse-Achille de Salvandy, in *Annales du Parlement français*, 5 January 1839, pp. 121–22.

48. *Annales du Parlement français*, 20 May 1839, pp. 133, 137.

49. *Archives Parlementaires*, Chambre de Pairs, 27 May 1839, 124: 716. Similar arguments in *Annales du Parlement français*, 18 January 1841, pp. 684–86.

50. Jean-Louis Halpérin, *Histoire du droit des biens* (Paris, 2008), 214–19; Donald R. Kelley and Bonnie G. Smith, "What Was Property? Legal Dimensions of the Social Question in France (1789–1848)," *Proceedings of the American Philosophical Society* 128, 3 (1984): 222.

51. *Moniteur Universel*, 14 March 1841, p. 634 (BK).

52. Ibid., 23 March 1841, pp. 714–15.

53. Julius Eduard Hitzig, *Das Königl. Preussische Gesetz vom 11. Juni 1837 zum Schutze des Eigenthums an Werken der Wissenschaft und Kunst gegen Nachdruck und Nachbildung* (Berlin, 1838), 61.

54. *Moniteur Universel*, 24 March 1841, p. 732.

55. Ibid., 26 March 1841, pp. 760–61.

56. Décret du 5 février 1810, art. 39.

57. *Moniteur Universel*, 26 March 1841, pp. 762–64.

58. Deputy Lherbette apparently thought that the power of bringing out new and possibly different editions was intended to pass from the author and vainly strove against this. On the other hand, the fact that, as per the Civil Code, half of that part of the author's "droit exclusif" that he had not already alienated became community property suggests that only the economic outcome was at stake. Ibid., 27 March 1841, p. 779.

59. Ibid., 27 March 1841, pp. 779–81.

60. Pierre-Joseph Proudhon, *What is Property?* (original ed., Paris, 1840). The quotation is from the postscript.

61. Jill Burk Jiminez and Joanna Banham, eds., *Dictionary of Artists' Models* (London, 2001), 74–76; Louis Vaunois, "Le Droit moral: Son evolution en France," *Le Droit d'auteur* 65 (1952): 67–68; Frédéric Poullaud-Dulian, *Le Droit d'auteur* (Paris, 2005), 278–79.

62. *Moniteur Universel*, 14 March 1841, p. 634.

63. *Charpentier c. Delprat*, Cour de Paris, 16 March 1865, *Dalloz, Jurisprudence générale* 2 (1865): 213–14.

64. Article 1382 of the Napoleonic Code required compensation in case of damage.

65. *Delprat c. Charpentier*, Cour de Cassation, 21 August 1867, *Dalloz, Jurisprudence générale* 1 (1867): 369–72.

66. Loi sur les Droits des héretiers et des ayants cause des Auteurs, 14 July 1866, no. 14,407, *Bulletin des lois*, 1866, no. 1405, p. 61. A detailed account of the possible interpretations of the 1866 law's approach in Marcel Guay, "De la propriété littéraire, ou explication de la loi française du 14–19 Juillet 1866 sur les droits des héritiers et des ayants cause des auteurs," in *Congrès littéraire international de Paris 1878*, 466–76.

67. Art. 1166. On Morillot, Pfister, "L'auteur, propriétaire de son œuvre?" 751–75.

68. André Morillot, "De la personnalité du droit de publication qui appartient à un auteur vivant," *Revue critique de législation et de jurisprudence*, n.s., 2 (1872–73): 29–33, 45–48 (BK).

69. André Morillot, *De la protection accordée aux œuvres d'art, aux photographies, aux dessins et modèles industriels et aux brevets d'invention dans l'Empire d'Allemagne* (Paris, 1878).

70. André Morillot, "De la nature du droit d'auteur, considéré à un point de vue général," *Revue critique de législation et de jurisprudence*, n.s., 7 (1878): 125–28 (BK).

71. J.N.Fr. Brauer, *Erläuterungen über den Code Napoleon und die Grossherzoglich Badische bürgerliche Gesetzgebung* (Karlsruhe, 1809), 1: 469–70.

72. Wilhelm August Kramer, *Die Rechte der Schriftsteller und Verleger* (Heidelberg, 1827), 58, 66.

73. Leopold Joseph Neustetel, *Der Büchernachdruck, nach Römischem Recht betrachtet* (Heidelberg, 1824), 11, 26–27, 46–47 (BK).

74. W. A. Hunter, *A Systematic and Historical Exposition of Roman Law*, 4th ed. (London, 1903), 145–56.

75. Carl Gareis, "Das juristische Wesen der Autorrechte, sowie des Firmen- und Markenschutzes," *Archiv für Theorie und Praxis des allgemeinen deutschen Handels- und Wechselsrecht* (1877), 35: 187–88, 197 (BK).

76. J. Kohler, *Das Autorrecht, eine zivilistische Abhandlung* (Jena, 1880), 41–46, 66–67, 83, 90–100, 74, 137, 146–47, 139, 152–54.

77. Ibid., 201–3.

78. Otto Gierke, *Deutsches Privatrecht* (Leipzig, 1895), 1: 756. Subsequent references are to pp. 760, 764, 759, 766–67.

79. Although on the same page (767) he also claimed that the author could give others full powers over the outer and inner substance of his work, even though, in that instance, he still retained the full rights of the author. Despite such unclarity the drift of his argument seems to have been that not everything could be alienated.

80. Gierke, *Deutsches Privatrecht*, 806. He illustrated this with the example of a manuscript assigned to a publisher for whatever uses he pleased, including destroying it and, if he decided to publish, shortening or otherwise changing the work.

81. Ibid., 767–68.

82. The standard account is Catherine Seville, *Literary Copyright Reform in Early Victorian England: The Framing of the 1842 Copyright Act* (Cambridge, 1999).

83. Chris R. Vanden Bossche, "The Value of Literature: Representations of Print Culture in the Copyright Debate of 1837–1842," *Victorian Studies* 38, 1 (1994): 42.

84. *Hansard*, Commons, 5 February 1841, p. 350.

85. Fritz Machlup and Edith Penrose, "The Patent Controversy in the Nineteenth Century," *Journal of Economic History* 10, 1 (1950): 3ff; Adrian Johns, *Piracy* (Chicago, 2009), chap. 10.

86. Paul M. Zall, "Wordsworth and the Copyright Act of 1842," *Proceedings of the Modern Language Association* 70 (1955): 134; John Feather, "Publishers and Politicians: The Remaking of the Law of Copyright in Britain 1775–1842," *Publishing History* 25 (1989): 47–48.

87. Catherine Seville, *The Internationalisation of Copyright Law: Books, Buccaneers and the Black Flag in the Nineteenth Century* (Cambridge, 2006), 16.

88. *Hansard*, Commons, 5 February 1841, p. 343.

89. William St. Clair, *The Reading Nation in the Romantic Period* (Cambridge, 2004), 209, 355–56.

90. Paul K. Saint-Amour, *The Copywrights: Intellectual Property and the Literary Imagination* (Ithaca NY, 2003), 55–57, can portray the outcome of the Talfourd debates as a victory for strong copyright and a defeat for the free traders only by failing to compare the British situation with what was brewing on the Continent.

91. *Hansard*, Commons, 29 January 1841, pp. 148–49.

92. *Hansard*, Commons, 5 February 1841, pp. 344ff.

93. Copyright Commission, *The Royal Commissions and the Report of the Commissioners*, ix, xlviii–l. He was supported by the jurist and statistician Leone Levi, who thought his compulsory licensing scheme useful in the colonies. Leone Levi, "Copyrights and Patents," *Princeton Review* (1878): 753.

94. *Minutes of the Evidence Taken before the Royal Commission on Copyright*, 2, 8, 270.

95. Ibid., 203–8.

96. Doron S. Ben-Atar, *Trade Secrets: Intellectual Piracy and the Origins of American Industrial Power* (New Haven, 2004), chaps. 2, 4, pp. 167–70.

97. Thomas Bender and David Sampliner, "Poets, Pirates and the Creation of American Literature," *New York University Journal of International Law and Politics* 29 (1996–97): 257.

98. Copyright Commission, *The Royal Commissions and the Report of the Commissioners*, li.

99. Quoted in Patrick Warfield, "John Philip Sousa and 'The Menace of Mechanical Music,'" *Journal of the Society for American Music* 3, 4 (2009): 435.

100. Eckhard Höffner, *Geschichte und Wesen des Urheberrechts* (Munich, 2010), 1: 310–23; Martha Woodmansee, "Publishers, Privateers, Pirates: Eighteenth-Century German Book Piracy Revisited," in Mario Biagioli et al., eds., *Making and Unmaking Intellectual Property* (Chicago, 2011), 185–86.

101. Senate Report 409, 7 February 1873, *Reports of Committees of the Senate of the United States* (1872–73), 1: 2.

102. Paul Starr, *The Creation of the Media: Political Origins of Modern Communications* (New York, 2004), 124–26.

103. Meredith L. McGill, *American Literature and the Culture of Reprinting, 1834–1853* (Philadelphia, 2003). The strength of McGill's work lies in portraying America's rogue status as a deliberate cultural choice and not, as does most of the previous literature, as an almost inexplicable and willful refusal to follow the Whiggish path of enlightened protection of authors. A very similar approach in B. Zorina Khan, *The Democratization of Invention: Patents and Copyrights in American Economic Development, 1790–1920* (Cambridge, 2005), chaps. 8, 9. The older view is well represented by Bruce W. Bugbee, *Genesis of American Patent and Copyright Law* (Washington DC, 1967), 146.

104. Report 622, 19 March 1888, *Reports of Committees of the Senate of the United States* (1887–88), 2: 40.

105. S. Conant, "International Copyright: An American View," *MacMillan's Magazine* 40 (1879): 153–54.

106. "Memorial of a Number of Persons Concerned in Printing and Publishing, Praying an alteration in the mode of levying duties on certain books, and remonstrating against the enactment of an international copyright law," 27th Cong., 2nd sess., 1842, Senate Rep. 323 (BK).

107. *Minutes of the Evidence Taken before the Royal Commission on Copyright*, 330.

108. Massachusetts representative Elbridge Gerry, quoted in Richard B. Kielbowicz, *News in the Mail: The Press, Post Office, and Public Information, 1700–1860s* (New York, 1989), 33, 147–48, 154–55.

109. By the 1840s every US newspaper received free an average of 4300 different exchange newspapers annually. Richard R. John, *Spreading the News: The American Postal System from Franklin to Morse* (Cambridge MA, 1995), 37.

110. McGill, *American Literature and the Culture of Reprinting*, 84.

111. On Carey, see Johns, *Piracy*, chaps. 7, 8, 11.

112. Ricketson and Ginsburg suggest that the US refusal to join the Berne Union, and presumably American resistance to international copyright, was largely the outcome of the influence of its publishing industry. Sam Ricketson and Jane C. Ginsburg, *International Copyright and Neighbouring Rights: The Berne Convention and Beyond*, 2nd ed. (Oxford, 2006), 1: 59.

113. *Minutes of the Evidence Taken before the Royal Commission on Copyright*, 89, George Haven Putnam.

114. James J. Barnes, *Authors, Publishers and Politicians: The Quest for an Anglo-American Copyright Agreement 1815–1854* (Columbus, 1974), 69. The figures here suggest that $5 million out of a total of $30 million invested in the publishing industry were aimed at reprints and that this sector was monopolized by three or four large firms. Memorial of a Number of Citizens of Boston, praying the passage of an international copyright law, 25th Cong., 2nd sess., 24 April 1838, Senate Doc. 398, p. 2 (BK).

115. Senate Report 409, 7 February 1873, p. 2.

116. *Punch*, 24 April 1847, p. 178, quoted in Melissa J. Homestead, *American Women Authors*

and Literary Property, 1822–1869 (Cambridge, 2005), 49. Such rhetoric was still being trotted out in the 1930s by aggrieved artists. *Revision of Copyright Laws: Hearings before the Committee on Patents, House of Representatives*, (February–April 1936), p. 700.

117. Homestead, *American Woman Authors*, 51; Michael J. Everton, *The Grand Chorus of Complaint: Authors and the Business Ethics of American Publishing* (New York, 2011), 104–5. During the July Monarchy, when France too was a slaveholding nation, Victor de Broglie had drawn parallels among monopolies, slavery, copyrights, and patents: law-imposed restrictions for the benefit of some of what should naturally be the domain of all. In other words, copyright and slavery were equally the creations of positive, not natural, law and could therefore be abolished. Pfister, "L'auteur, propriétaire de son œuvre?" 605.

118. For the self-contradictions of the natural rights approach when faced with slavery, William B. Scott, *In Pursuit of Happiness: American Conceptions of Property from the Seventeenth to the Twentieth Century* (Bloomington, 1977), chap. 6.

119. H. C. Carey, *Letters on International Copyright*, 2nd ed. (New York, 1868), 13.

120. Charles Dickens, *American Notes for General Circulation*, 2nd ed. (London, 1842), 1: 276.

121. Sidney P. Moss, *Charles Dickens' Quarrel with America* (Troy NY, 1984), 177, 190; John O. Waller, "Charles Dickens and the American Civil War," *Studies in Philology* 57, 3 (1960).

122. "Southern Feeling towards England," *Index*, 15 May 1862, p. 40 (BK).

123. Khan, *Democratization of Invention*, 260.

124. *Minutes of the Evidence Taken before the Royal Commission on Copyright*, 4; *Edinburgh Review* 304 (October, 1878): 304.

125. Seville, *Internationalisation of Copyright Law*, 147; Ronald J. Zboray, *A Fictive People: Antebellum Economic Development and the American Reading Public* (New York, 1993), 83.

126. St. Clair, *Reading Nation*, 386.

127. Craig Joyce, "'A Curious Chapter in the History of Judicature': *Wheaton v. Peters* and the Rest of the Story (of Copyright in the New Republic)," *Houston Law Review* 42, 2 (2005): 332; Memorial of the New York Typographical Society against the Passage of an International Copyright, 25th Cong., 2nd sess., 1838, Senate Doc. 296, p. 3 (BK); Report 1188, 21 May 1886, *Reports of Committees of the Senate* (1885–86), p. 32; *Congressional Record*, Senate, 9 February 1891, p. 2382; *Congrès littéraire international de Paris 1878*, 591; Johns, *Piracy*, 295.

128. *Minutes of the Evidence Taken before the Royal Commission on Copyright*, 287.

129. *Hansard*, Commons, 20 March 1838, pp. 1098–99; "Petition of Thomas Moore, and Other Authors of Great Britain," 24th Cong., 2nd sess., 2 February 1837, Senate Doc. 134 (BK).

130. *Gales and Seaton's Register of Debates in Congress*, Senate, 2 February 1837, p. 671 (BK).

131. Committee on Patents and the Patent Office, 25th Cong., 2nd sess., 25 June 1838, Senate Report 494, p. 3 (BK).

132. Other such firms included Monroe, Lovell, Seaside, and Franklin Square. *Congressional Record*, 50th Congress, 1st sess., vol. 19, pt. 4, Senate, 23 April 1888, p. 3236. Harpers, however, was held up by the US delegate to the International Literary Congress in Paris in 1878 as an example of a publisher who brought forth good editions of American authors. *Congrès littéraire international de Paris 1878*, 195.

133. *Gales and Seaton's Register of Debates in Congress*, Senate, 2 February 1837, p. 671.

134. Carey, *Letters on International Copyright*, 10–11; Reichstag des Norddeutschen Bundes, *Stenographische Berichte*, 26 March 1870, p. 508. Similarly in Adolf Fleischmann, "Die Berner Übereinkunft zum Schutze des Urheberrechts," *UFITA* 103 (1986): 48–49. Originally published in 1888.

135. Geo. Haven Putnam, *The Question of Copyright*, 2nd ed. (New York, 1896), 167–68.

136. Quoted in Siva Vaidhyanathan, *Copyrights and Copywrongs: The Rise of Intellectual Property and How it Threatens Creativity* (New York, 2001), 60.

137. Kielbowicz, *News in the Mail*, 128. The competition in size was the quadruple number

of the *Universal Yankee Nation* which was 4 feet 6 inches by 10 feet 8 inches. Isbelle Lehuu, *Carnival on the Page: Popular Print Media in Antebellum America* (Chapel Hill, 2000), 64.

138. Seville, *Internationalisation of Copyright Law*, 43–44.

139. David Saunders, *Authorship and Copyright* (London, 1992), 156.

140. In Britain the Copyright Commission of 1878 worried that the presence of lending libraries helped keep book prices high, at least those of first editions. *Minutes of the Evidence Taken before the Royal Commission on Copyright*, 40 and passim.

141. The Committee on Patents and the Patent Office, 25 June 1838, Senate Report 494, pp. 4–5. A similar accounting of prices across the Atlantic in Senate Report 409, 7 February 1873, *Reports of Committees of the Senate* (1872–73), 1: 5–7.

142. S. S. Conant, "International Copyright: An American View," *MacMillan's Magazine* 40 (1879): 152–53, 157–58; *Minutes of the Evidence Taken before the Royal Commission on Copyright*, 2–3.

143. *Edinburgh Review* 304 (October, 1878): 304.

144. Report 1188, 21 May 1886, *Reports of Committees of the Senate* (1885–86), p. 74.

145. See also Putnam, *Question of Copyright*, xvi–xvii, 83–84.

146. Report 1188, 21 May 1886, *Reports of Committees of the Senate* (1885–86), p. 35.

147. Edward Eggleston, "The Blessings of Copyright Piracy," *Century Magazine* 1 (1881–82): 944.

148. Report 1188, 21 May 1886, *Reports of Committees of the Senate* (1885–86), p. iii. Similar complaints: Report 2401, 10 June 1890, *Reports of Committees of the House of Representatives* (1889–90), pp. 9–10.

149. Report 622, 19 March 1888, *Reports of Committees of the Senate*, (1887–88), 2: 6.

150. Report 1188, 21 May 1886, *Reports of Committees of the Senate* (1885–86), p. 11.

151. Report 2401, 10 June 1890, *Reports of Committees of the House of Representatives* (1889–90), p. 4.

152. *Congressional Record*, Senate, 23 April 1888, p. 3234. Similar language in Report 622, 19 March 1888, *Reports of Committees of the Senate of the United States*, (1887–88), 2: 2.

153. "Memorials of John Jay and of William C. Bryant and Others, In Favor of an International Copyright Law," 22 March 1848, House of Representatives, Miscellaneous No. 76, p. 8 (BK).

154. Quoted in Barnes, *Authors, Publishers and Politicians*, 83.

155. *Congressional Record*, 50th Congress, 1st sess., vol. 19, pt. 4, Senate, 23 April 1888, p. 3235.

156. Report 622, 19 March 1888, *Reports of Committees of the Senate of the United States*, (1887–88), 2: 7.

157. *An Address to the People of the United States on Behalf of the American Copyright Club* (New York, 1843), 11 (BK).

158. McGill, *American Literature and the Culture of Reprinting*, chap. 3; Seville, *Internationalisation of Copyright Law*, chap. 5.

159. Moss, *Charles Dickens' Quarrel with America*, 3, 64–65, 86–89, 103, and passim.

160. Martin T. Buinicki, *Negotiating Copyright: Authorship and the Discourse of Literary Property Rights in Nineteenth-Century America* (New York, 2006), 64–65, 123.

161. Edwin T. Bowden, "Henry James and the Struggle for International Copyright: An Unnoticed Item in the James Bibliography," *American Literature* 24, 4 (1953): 538.

162. Thorvald Solberg, "Copyright Law Reform," *Yale Law Journal* 35, 1 (1925): 50ff.

163. Report 622, 19 March 1888, *Reports of Committees of the Senate of the United States* (1887–88), 2: 4–5.

164. Like the Americans, a German admitted, the Germans had long reprinted British and French works, but at least—unlike the Americans—they did not pretend to make a virtue of it. R.Klostermann, *Das geistige Eigenthum an Schriften, Kunstwerken und Erfindungen* (Berlin, 1867), 24–30.

165. Laurent Pfister, "Is Literary Property (a Form of) Property? Controversies on the Nature

of Authors' Rights in the Nineteenth Century," *Revue internationale du droit d'auteur* 205 (July 2005): 122ff; Christophe Geiger, *Droit d'auteur et droit du public à l'information* (Paris, 2004), 30–31.

166. Proudhon proudly emblazoned Lamartine's attack at the beginning of his own work. P.-J. Proudhon, *Les majorats littéraires* (Paris, 1868), 1. The original edition appeared in 1862.

167. Ibid., 12, 26, 95, and passim.

168. Albrecht Götz von Olenhusen, "'Ewiges geistiges Eigentum' und 'Sozialbindung' des Urheberrechts in der Rechtsentwicklung und Diskussion im 19. Jahrhundert in Frankreich und Deutschland," in Wilhelm Herschel et al., eds., *Festschrift für Georg Roeber zum 10. Dezember 1981* (Freiburg, 1982), 100–108.

169. Pfister, "L'auteur, propriétaire de son œuvre?" 691–92.

170. Reichstag des Norddeutschen Bundes, *Stenographische Berichte*, 26 March 1870, pp. 508–9.

171. *Congrès littéraire international de Paris 1878*, 143.

172. Ibid., p. 215.

173. Ibid., pp. 206–10, 223, 144. Jules Simon, the philosopher and later to be minister of education in the Third Republic, had also called attempts to limit the duration of literary property communism: Édouard Romberg, ed., *Compte rendu des travaux du Congrès de la propriété littéraire et artistique* (Brussels, 1859), 1: 120, 149. Similar tarring of opponents of intellectual property as communists in Constantin Wrangell, *Die Prinzipien des literarischen Eigenthums* (Dorpat, 1866), 28–33.

174. Reichstag, *Stenographische Berichte*, 18 April 1901, pp. 2175–92 and 1 May 1901, pp. 2458–65, contain much of this discussion.

175. Reichstag, *Stenographische Berichte*, 19 April 1901, p. 2222; 2 May 1901, pp. 2492, 2500, 2503, 2505; 12 April 1910, p. 2281; Wilhelm Freiherrn v. Weckbecker, "Richard Wagner, Johann Strauss und die Schutzfrist," *Ufita* 3 (1930): 466–68; Kai Bandilla, *Urheberrecht im Kaiserreich: Der Weg zum Gesetz betreffend das Urheberrecht an Werken der Literatur und Tonkunst vom 19. Juni 1901* (Frankfurt, 2005), 96–97, 122.

176. Reichstag, *Stenographische Berichte*, 12 April 1910, pp. 2279–80.

177. "Erklärung über die Schutzfrist des Urheberrechtes," *Sitzungsberichte der Preussischen Akademie der Wissenschaften*, 1927, Philosophisch-Historische Klasse, pp. 45–46; Ernst Heymann, "Die zeitliche Begrenzung des Urheberrechts," *Sitzungsberichte der Preussischen Akademie der Wissenschaften*, 1927, p. 103.

178. Declaration of the Börsenverein der deutschen Buchhändler, 14 February 1910, quoted in Manfred Rehbinder, "Die Parsifal-Frage oder der Gedanke des Verbraucherschutzes im Urheberrecht," in Robert Dittrich, ed., *Die Notwendigkeit des Urheberrechtsschutzes im Lichte seiner Geschichte* (Vienna, 1991), 94.

179. Isabella Löhr, *Die Globalisierung geistiger Eigentumsrechte: Neue Strukturen internationaler Zusammenarbeit 1866–1952* (Göttingen, 2010), 124–25.

180. Report 622, 19 March 1888, *Reports of Committees of the Senate of the United States* (1887–88), 2: 7, 25–26.

4. CONTINENTAL DRIFT: EUROPE MOVES FROM PROPERTY TO PERSONALITY AT THE TURN OF THE CENTURY

1. Felix Leinemann, *Die Sozialbindung des "Geistigen Eigentums"* (Baden-Baden, 1998), 163–64; Stanislas de Gorguette d'Argœuves, *Le Droit moral de l'auteur sur son œuvre artistique ou littéraire* (Paris, 1926), 6: Manfred Rehbinder, "Die Beschränkungen des Urheberrechts zugunsten der Allgemeinheit," in Schweizerische Vereinigung für Urheberrecht, ed., *100 Jahre URG: Fest-*

schrift zum einhundertjährigen Bestehen eines eidgenössischen Urheberrechtsgesetzes (Berne, 1983), 353.

2. Josef Kohler, *Urheberrecht an Schriftwerken und Verlagsrecht* (Stuttgart, 1907), 55.

3. André Morillot, "De la nature du droit d'auteur, considéré à un point de vue général," *Revue critique de législation et de jurisprudence*, n.s., 7 (1878): 124–25.

4. Alcide Darras, *Du droit des auteurs et des artistes dans les rapports internationaux* (Paris, 1887), 17.

5. Georges Michaélidès-Nouaros, *Le Droit moral de l'auteur* (Paris, 1935), 12. Similarly: Robert Michaelis, *Persönlichkeitsrechtliche Befugnisse im deutschen Urheberrecht und droit moral des französischen Rechts* (diss., Leipzig; Berlin, 1926), 34. A similar accounting, though in disagreement, in Const. Gheorghiu-Vieriu, *Le Droit moral de l'auteur* (Paris, 1939), 117.

6. Gorguette d'Argœuves, *Le Droit moral de l'auteur*, 62. A similar apotheosis: Pierre Masse, *Le Droit moral de l'auteur sur son œuvre littéraire ou artistique* (Paris, 1906), 35, quoted in Laurent Pfister, "Authors and Work in the French Print Privileges System," in Ronan Deazley et al., eds., *Privilege and Property* (Cambridge, 2010), 116.

7. Elmar Wadle, "Entwicklungsschritte des Geistigen Eigentums in Frankreich und Deutschland," in Hannes Siegrist and David Sugarman, eds., *Eigentum im internationalen Vergleich* (Göttingen, 1999), 257–58; Diethelm Kippel, "Die Idee des geistigen Eigentums in Naturrecht und Rechtsphilosophie des 19. Jahrhunderts," in Elmar Wadle, ed., *Historische Studien zum Urheberrecht in Europa* (Berlin, 1993), 125ff.

8. Leinemann, *Sozialbindung des "Geistigen Eigentums,"* 24–25; Cyrill P. Rigamonti, *Geistiges Eigentum als Begriff und Theorie des Urheberrechts* (Baden-Baden, 2001).

9. Georg Roeber, "Urheberrecht oder Geistiges Eigentum," *Archiv für Urheber- Film- Funk- und Theaterrecht* 21, 3/4 (1956): 156–57; Elizabeth Adeney, *The Moral Rights of Authors and Performers* (Oxford, 2006), 24.

10. *Annales du Parlement français*, 20 May 1839, pp. 133–34.

11. Loi no. 57–298 du 11 mars 1957 sur la propriété littéraire et artistique, *Journal Officiel*, 14 March 1957, pp. 2723–30. Pascal Kamina, "Author's Rights as Property: Old and New Theories," *Journal of the Copyright Society of the USA* 48 (2000–2001): 393–403; Alain Strowel, *Droit d'auteur et copyright: Divergences et convergences* (Brussels, 1993), 18.

12. *Gema w. Grundig*, Bundesgerichtshof, 18 May 1955, *Entscheidungen des Bundesgerichtshofes in Zivilsachen*, 17: 278.

13. Bundesverfassungsgericht, decisions of 7/8 July 1971 and 25 October 1978. Heinrich Hubmann, "Die Idee vom geistigen Eigentum, die Rechtsprechung des Bundesverfassungsgerichts und die Urheberrechtsnovelle von 1985," *Zeitschrift für Urheber- und Medienrecht/Film und Recht* 32, 1 (1988): 7. Gesetz zur Stärkung des Schutzes des geistigen Eigentums und zur Bekämpfung der Produktpiraterie, 7 March 1990.

14. Directive 2001/29/EC, 22 May 2001, recital 9, art. 3, *Official Journal*, L167, 22 June 2001, p. 10.

15. Treaty Establishing a Constitution for Europe, draft 18 July 2003, art. II-17(2).

16. Richard Schiff, "Originality," in Schiff and Robert Nelson, eds., *Critical Terms for Art History*, 2nd ed. (Chicago, 2003), 145–49.

17. Edward Earle, "The Effect of Romanticism on the 19th Century Development of Copyright Law," *Intellectual Property Journal* 6 (1991): 275–76.

18. Walter Bappert, *Wege zum Urheberrecht: Die geschichtliche Entwicklung des Urheberrechtsgedankens* (Frankfurt, 1962), 20–22.

19. Nick Groom, "Unoriginal Genius: Plagiarism and the Construction of 'Romantic' Authorship," in Lionel Bently et al., eds., *Copyright and Piracy* (Cambridge, 2010), 274–75; Carla Hesse, "The Rise of Intellectual Property, 700 BC–AD 2000: An Idea in the Balance," *Daedalus* 131, 2 (2002): 26–30.

20. Martha Woodmansee, *The Author, Art, and the Market: Rereading the History of Aesthetics* (New York, 1994), 35–40.

21. Gheorghiu-Vieriu, *Le Droit moral de l'auteur*, 121.

22. Honoré de Balzac, "Pro Aris et Focis. Lettre adressée aux écrivains du XIXe siècle," *Revue de Paris*, n.s. 11 (1834): 63. Similar ideas in "Pétition à l'Assemblée nationale," in *Œuvres complètes de Beaumarchais* (Paris, 1826), 6: 197 (BK).

23. Christopher Aide, "A More Comprehensive Soul: Romantic Conceptions of Authorship and the Copyright Doctrine of Moral Right," *University of Toronto Faculty of Law Review* 48, 2 (1990): 214.

24. *Donaldson v. Beckett* (1774), *Hansard*, 1, 17 (1774), pp. 999–1000.

25. *Hansard*, Commons, 7 April 1911, pp. 2634–37.

26. "An Act for the Encouragement of Literature and Genius," 1783, in *Acts and Laws of the State of Connecticut in America* (New London, 1784), 133–34 (BK).

27. *The Perpetual Laws of the Commonwealth of Massachusetts* (Boston, 1789), 369.

28. The Committee on Patents and the Patent Office, 25 June 1838, Senate Report 494, p. 5. Richard Hofstadter discussed the low value of genius in America in *Anti-Intellectualism in American Life* (New York, 1963), 255. The aptly named Paul Tough argues a similar line today. *How Children Succeed: Grit, Curiosity and the Hidden Power of Character* (New York, 2012).

29. Reichstag, *Stenographische Berichte*, 1875/76, vol. 3, Aktenstück 76, p. 294.

30. Ronan Deazley, "Commentary on Copinger's *Law of Copyright*," in BK; Catherine Seville, *Literary Copyright Reform in Early Victorian England: The Framing of the 1842 Copyright Act* (Cambridge, 1999), 243–45; Ronan Deazley, *Rethinking Copyright: History, Theory, Language* (Cheltenham, 2006), 26–27; Isabella Alexander, *Copyright Law and the Public Interest in the Nineteenth Century* (Oxford, 2010), chap. 6. The situation in France was similar: Laurent Pfister, "L'auteur, propriétaire de son œuvre? La formation du droit d'auteur du XVIe siecle à la loi de 1957" (diss., Strasbourg, 1999), 563–65.

31. *Stowe v. Thomas*, *Federal Cases*, 1853, 23: 201 (BK).

32. George Ticknor Curtis, *Treatise on the Law of Copyright* (Boston, 1847), 292–93.

33. Augustin-Charles Renouard, *Traité des droits d'auteurs, dans la littérature, les sciences et les beaux-arts* (Paris, 1838–39), 2: 38.

34. *Rosa c. Giradin*, Cour d'appel de Rouen, 7 November 1845, *Dalloz, Jurisprudence générale* 2 (1845): 212 (BK).

35. Eugène Pouillet, *Traité théorique et pratique de la propriété littéraire et artistique* (Paris, 1879), 429–30.

36. Robert Maugham, *A Treatise on the Laws of Literary Property* (London, 1828), 129–30.

37. Francis Lieber, *Manual of Political Ethics Designed Chiefly for the Use of Colleges and Students at Law*, pt. 1 (Boston, 1838), 133.

38. *Federal Cases*, 1839, 10: 1038.

39. *Federal Cases*, 1841, 9: 342 (BK). Some scholars go so far as to date the supposed decline of the American public-spirited utilitarian approach to copyright into natural rights private property from this case. John Tehranian, "Et Tu, Fair Use? The Triumph of Natural-Law Copyright," *UC Davis Law Review* 38 (2005): 466–67.

40. Oren Bracha, "Commentary on *Folsom v. Marsh* (1841)," in BK; R. Anthony Reese, "The Story of *Folsom v. Marsh*: Distinguishing between Infringing and Legitimate Uses," in Jane Ginsburg and Rochelle Cooper Dreyfuss, eds., *Intellectual Property Stories* (New York, 2006), 283–86.

41. Curtis, *Treatise on the Law of Copyright*, 237–38.

42. Eaton S. Drone, *A Treatise on the Law of Property in Intellectual Productions in Great Britain and the United States* (Boston, 1879), 436–38. Although in testimony leading up to the 1911 Copyright Act in the UK, abridgments were still lauded as serving worthy public goals:

"Report from the Select Committee of the House of Lords, on the Copyright (Amendment) Bill," *House of Commons Papers, Reports of Committees*, 1897, paper 385, 10: 213, 12.

43. Isabella Alexander, "Inspiration or Infringement: The Plagiarist in Court," in Bently, *Copyright and Piracy*, 6.

44. *Turner v. Robinson*, (1860) 10 Ir. Ch. 121, 510 and 10 Ir. Ch. 521. Randolph Jonakait, "Do Art Exhibitions Destroy Common-law Copyright in Works of Art?" *Copyright Law Symposium* 19 (1971): 82–88.

45. *Stowe v. Thomas*, *Federal Cases*, 1853, 23: 202.

46. Curtis, *Treatise on the Law of Copyright*, 273–74.

47. Drone, *Treatise on the Law of Property in Intellectual Productions*, 97–98, 384–85.

48. Oren Bracha, *Owning Ideas: A History of Anglo-American Intellectual Property* http://www .obracha.net/, chap. 3; Oren Bracha, "The Ideology of Authorship Revisited: Authors, Markets, and Liberal Values in Early American Copyright," *Yale Law Journal* 118 (2008): 225–38.

49. Pascal Kamina, *Film Copyright in the European Union* (Cambridge, 2002), 223–26.

50. Bracha, *Owning Ideas*, 326; L. Ray Patterson and Stanley W. Lindberg, *The Nature of Copyright* (Athens GA, 1991), 67–68.

51. An Act to Amend and Consolidate the Acts Respecting Copyright, 4 March 1909, Public Law 60–349, 35 Stat. 1075, sect. 1b, 26.

52. "Copyright Law Revision," Senate Report 94–473 (1975), p. 119.

53. *Congressional Record*, 22 September 1976, pp. 31983–85.

54. Ralph S. Brown, "Eligibility for Copyright Protection: A Search for Principled Standards," *Minnesota Law Review* 70, 2 (1985): 594.

55. William F. Patry, *The Fair Use Privilege in Copyright Law*, 2nd ed. (Washington DC, 1995), 288, 371, 433. The sections mentioned here are 107, 108, 504.

56. Indeed, the law took Justice Story's conclusions in *Folsom v. Marsh* almost verbatim: *Federal Cases*, 1841, 9: 348.

57. Paul Goldstein, *International Copyright* (New York, 2001), 293–94; Patry, *Fair Use Privilege*, 589–90; P. Bernt Hugenholtz, "Copyright and Freedom of Expression in Europe," in Rochelle Cooper Dreyfuss et al., eds., *Expanding the Boundaries of Intellectual Property* (Oxford, 2004), 352–53.

58. *Berlin v. EC Publications, Inc*, 329 F.2d 541, 544 (1964), quoted in Melissa de Zwart, "A Historical Analysis of the Birth of Fair Dealing and Fair Use: Lessons for the Digital Age," *Intellectual Property Quarterly* 11 (2007): 88.

59. A history in David Bradshaw, "'Fair Dealing' as a Defence to Copyright Infringement in UK Law," *Denning Law Journal* 10 (1995).

60. Patry, *Fair Use Privilege*, 595. The fair dealing sections are sect. 2 of the 1911 act, sect. 6 of the 1956 act, and sect. 29–43 of the 1988 act.

61. Robert Burrell and Allison Coleman, *Copyright Exceptions: The Digital Impact* (Cambridge, 2005), 37–38, 49–50, 204–5, 249; Mr. Justice Laddie, "Copyright: Over-strength, Over-regulated, Over-rated?" *European Intellectual Property Review* 18 (1996): 258–59.

62. *Rogers v. Koons*, 960 F.2d 301 (1992). And a case like *Kelly v. Ariba*, dealing with fair use of thumbnail images on the web, would probably have failed in the UK. William Cornish, *Intellectual Property: Omnipresent, Distracting, Irrelevant?* (Oxford, 2004), 65.

63. Sections 17, 67, 32, 70 of the 1988 act. The Gowers Report suggested that search engines like Google may have developed first in the US because of its flexible fair use standard. But, in fact, the case that vindicated Google's caching of internet content as fair use came in 2006 while the equivalent measure had been introduced in UK law already in 2002. *Gowers Review of Intellectual Property* (December 2006), 62.

64. Jules Romains objected to proposals for specified fair uses, as in school anthologies. *Journal Officiel*, Chambre, Documents, Annexe 3222, 6 December 1937, p. 242.

65. Bernard Edelman, "Une loi substantiellement internationale: La loi du 3 juillet 1985 sur les droits d'auteur et droits voisins." *Journal du Droit International* 3 (1987): 574.

66. §1025.

67. §4.

68. 1901 law, §§17–23, 27.

69. 1965 law, §§46, 52.

70. Paul Edward Geller, ed., *International Copyright Law and Practice* (Newark, 2005), 1: FRA-122.

71. Art. 41.

72. *Journal Officiel*, Assemblée, Documents, Annexe 553, 16 February 1956, p. 345.

73. In the US the logic seems to have been that to mention parody as an enumerated fair use would actually restrict the exemption. Patry, *Fair Use Privilege*, 282–83.

74. Information Society Directive 2001/29/EC, 22 May 2001, *Official Journal of the European Communities*, L167, 22 June 2001, p. 10, art. 5.

75. Burrell and Coleman, *Copyright Exceptions*, 193; Bernt Hugenholtz et al., "The Recasting of Copyright and Related Rights for the Knowledge Economy," (Institute for Information Law, University of Amsterdam, November 2006), 65–66.

76. Alain Salles, "Les auteurs veulent garder leur droit," *Le Monde*, 2 May 2003; Anne Latournerie, "Droits d'auteur, droits de public: Une approche historique," *L'économie politique* 22, 2 (2004): 22.

77. Early examples: Adrian Johns, *Piracy* (Chicago, 2009), 274–75; *Annales du Parlement français*, 5 January 1839, p. 128; Martin T. Buinicki, *Negotiating Copyright: Authorship and the Discourse of Literary Property Rights in Nineteenth-Century America* (New York, 2006), 159.

78. Goldstein, *International Copyright*, 309–10. The Stockholm revision of the Berne Convention in 1967 gave developing nations extensive licensing and fair use rights but met with widespread refusal among developed nations, leading to a scaling back of such concessions. Barbara A. Ringer, "The Role of the United States in International Copyright—Past, Present and Future," *Georgetown Law Journal* 56 (1967–68): 1072–74.

79. *Le Droit d'auteur* (1922): 19–20; Amedeo Giannini, *La Convenzione di Berna sulla Proprietà Letteraria* (Rome, 1933), 145; *Congrès littéraire international de Paris 1878: Comptes rendus in extenso et documents* (Paris, 1879), 148–50.

80. Report 1188, 21 May 1886, *Reports of Committees of the Senate* (1885–86), p. 113; *Testimony before the House Committee on the Judiciary on International Copyright*, 8 February 1890 (Washington DC, 1890), 34–35.

81. Henri Desbois, "L'Évolution des droits de l'auteur en matière de reproduction et d'exécution publique," *Revue trimestrielle de droit civil* 38 (1939): 41.

82. *Testimony before the House Committee on the Judiciary on International Copyright*, 8 February 1890, pp. 34–35.

83. Sect. 115.

84. *Revision of Copyright Laws: Hearings before the Committees on Patents of the Senate and House of Representatives on Pending Bills to Amend and Consolidate the Acts Respecting Copyright, March 26, 27 and 28, 1908*, pp. 191–92, 245.

85. Midge M. Hyman, "The Socialization of Copyright: The Increased Use of Compulsory Licenses," *Cardozo Arts and Entertainment Law Journal* 4 (1985): 111 and passim; *Revision of Copyright Laws: Hearings before the Committees on Patents* (1908), p. 361.

86. *Revision of Copyright Laws: Hearings before the Committee on Patents, House of Representatives*, (February–April 1936), 60.

87. Paul Goldstein, "Preempted State Doctrines, Involuntary Transfers and Compulsory Licenses: Testing the Limits of Copyright, *UCLA Law Review* 24, 5/6 (1977): 1128.

88. "Bill for the better Encouragement of Learning, and for the more effectual securing the

Copies of Printed Books to the Authors or Purchasers of such Copies, during the Times therein mentioned," 1737 (BK).

89. Paul K. Saint-Amour, *The Copywrights: Intellectual Property and the Literary Imagination* (Ithaca NY, 2003), 59.

90. 5 & 6 Vict., c. 45, s. 5.

91. *Hansard*, Commons, 6 April 1842, pp. 1353–54; Seville, *Literary Copyright Reform in Early Victorian England*, 230.

92. Copyright Commission, *The Royal Commissions and the Report of the Commissioners*, c. 2036 (London, 1878), ix; *Minutes of the Evidence Taken before the Royal Commission on Copyright*, c.2036-I (London, 1878), 257–58.

93. *Report of the Committee on the Law of Copyright*, Cd 4976 (London, 1909), 23–25.

94. Philip H. Nicklin, *Remarks on Literary Property* (Philadelphia, 1838), chap. 9; Aubert J. Clark, *The Movement for International Copyright in Nineteenth Century America* (Washington DC, 1960), 104; Catherine Seville, *The Internationalisation of Copyright Law: Books, Buccaneers and the Black Flag in the Nineteenth Century* (Cambridge, 2006), 202–3, 226; Geo. Haven Putnam, *The Question of Copyright*, 2nd ed. (New York, 1896), 67.

95. Art. 9, *Moniteur Universel*, 14 March 1841, p. 636.

96. "Rapport, fait au nom de la commission chargée d'examiner le projet de loi relatif aux droits des héritiers et des ayants cause des auteurs, par M. Perras," *Moniteur Universel*, 31 May and 1 June 1866, reprinted in Fernand Worms, *Étude sur la propriété littéraire* (Paris, 1878), 1: 266 (BK).

97. *Congrès littéraire international de Paris 1878*, 107.

98. Ralf-M. Vogt, *Die urheberrechtlichen Reformdiskussionen in Deutschland während der Zeit der Weimarer Republik und des Nationalsozialismus* (Frankfurt, 2004), 24–26. Other French discussion of the issue: *Le Droit d'auteur* (1919), 29–31.

99. *Journal Officiel*, Documents, Chambre, Annexe 3222, 6 December 1937, p. 244.

100. J. Kohler, *Das Autorrecht, eine zivilistische Abhandlung* (Jena, 1880), 231–32.

101. Monika Dommann, "Autoren und Apparate: Copyrights und Medienwandel (1850–1980)" (Habilitationsschrift, Zurich, 2011), 49–50. Evidence of the influence of the Swiss is in Report 7083, part 2, 2 March 1907, *House Reports* (59th Congress, 2nd sess.), 1: 2, 4.

102. Report 2222, 22 February 1909, *House Reports* (60th Congress, 2nd sess.), p. 5; *Journal Officiel*, Documents, Chambre, Annexe 3222, 6 December 1937, p. 234; Dommann, "Autoren und Apparate," 50–53; Kai Bandilla, *Urheberrecht im Kaiserrreich: Der Weg zum Gesetz betreffend das Urheberrecht an Werken der Literatur und Tonkunst vom 19. Juni 1901* (Frankfurt, 2005), 41–43.

103. *Kennedy v. McTammany*, 33 Fed. Rep. 584 (1888); *White-Smith Music Publishing Co. v. Apollo Co.*, 209 U.S. 1 (1908). *Boosey v. Whight* (1899) was the analogous case in Britain, *Massenet and Puccini v. Ullman & Co and Pathé Frères* (1905) in Belgium.

104. Art. 13.

105. Reichstag, *Stenographische Berichte*, 3 May 1910, p. 2843.

106. The story is told for the US in Stuart Banner, *American Property* (Cambridge MA, 2011), chap. 6.

107. *Revision of Copyright Laws: Hearings before the Committees on Patents of the Senate and House of Representatives* (1908), pp. 243–44.

108. *Arguments Before the Committees on Patents of the Senate and House of Representatives Conjointly on the Bills S. 6330 and H.R. 19853, to Amend and Consolidate the Acts Respecting Copyright, June 6, 7, 8, and 9, 1906*, pp. 23–25, 105–8.

109. *Arguments before the Committee on Patents of the House of Representatives on H.R. 11943, May 2, 1906*, p. 15.

110. *Revision of Copyright Laws: Hearings before the Committees on Patents of the Senate and House of Representatives* (1908), 281ff, 302, 319.

111. *Arguments Before the Committees . . . on the Bills S. 6330 and H.R. 19853 . . . June 6, 7, 8, and 9, 1906*, 24–25, 31, 186. This was also the testimony in the UK, where the plight of the sheet-music

industry was seen as due to competition from other pursuits entirely: golf, bridge, motoring, and other activities that had supplanted musical evenings. *Minutes of Evidence Taken before the Law of Copyright Committee* (Cd 5051, 1910), 97–98.

112. *Congressional Record*, 60th Congress, 2nd sess., vol. 43, no. 67, 2 March 1909, p. 3834.

113. *Arguments Before the Committees . . . on the Bills S. 6330 and H.R. 19853 . . . June 6, 7, 8, and 9, 1906*, 96–105, 156; *Congressional Record*, 59th Congress, 2nd sess., Report 6187, part 2, 7 February 1907, p. 3.

114. Such were the considerations in Germany: Reichstag, *Stenographische Berichte*, 12 April 1910, p. 2279. Report 2222, 22 February 1909, *House Reports* (60th Congress, 2nd sess.), p. 7.

115. *Publisher's Weekly* 1953 (3 July 1909): 19.

116. *Minutes of Evidence Taken before the Law of Copyright Committee*, Cd 5051 (1910), 32.

117. The Aeolian story is told throughout *Arguments before the Committees . . . on the Bills S. 6330 and H.R. 19853 . . . June 6, 7, 8, and 9, 1906*. The potential monopoly of the recording industry was also a theme in *Revision of Copyright Laws: Hearings before the Committees on Patents of the Senate and House of Representatives* (1908), 194ff, 245–46, 325–28.

118. 1909 Copyright Act, sect. 1e. This was expanded in 1976 for phonograph records, cable television, jukeboxes, and public broadcasting of music and other nonliterary works. The UK 1911 act dealt with licensing in article 19. It was continued in the 1956 law, section 8. But in 1988 compulsory licensing for recording musical works was abolished. The recording industry still supported it, but composers and music publishers thought it had outlived its usefulness. Department of Trade and Industry, *Intellectual Property and Innovation*, Cmnd 9712 (April 1986), 57. Other forms of licensing, however, like cable transmission, remained. The 1990 Broadcasting Act introduced licenses when licensing bodies needlessly restricted broadcasts of sound recordings. Geller, *International Copyright Law and Practice*, UK-135–36.

119. Gesetz zur Ausführung der revidierten Berner Übereinkunft zum Schutze von Werken der Literatur und Kunst vom 13. November 1908, 22 May 1910, §22.

120. Eugen Ulmer, "Das neue deutsche Urheberrechtsgesetz," *Archiv für Urheber- Film- Funk- und Theaterrecht* 45, 2 (1965): 33–34. And this is how things remained also after 1965, in deliberate contrast to the practice in the US and the UK.

121. Julius Kopsch, "Zur Frage der gesetzlichen Lizenz," *Archiv für Funkrecht* 1 (1928): 201–3.

122. §61.

123. Law of 16 May 1866. See J. B. Duvergier, ed., *Collection complète des lois, décrets, ordonnances, règlements et avis du Conseil d'état* (Paris, 1866), 66: 122–31.

124. Gustave Huard, *Traité de la propriété intellectuelle* (Paris, 1903), 1: 47–48.

125. Law of 10 November 1917, *Gazette du Palais* (1916–17): 1122.

126. *Minutes of Evidence Taken before the Law of Copyright Committee*, 130.

127. Willy Hoffmann, "Die Staatenvorschläge zur Revision der revidierten Berner Übereinkunft," *Archiv für Urheber- Film- und Theaterrecht* 1, 2 (1928): 169.

128. Law of 3 July 1985, art. 22, title 3.

129. Stig Strömholm, *Le droit moral de l'auteur en droit allemand, français et scandinave* (Stockholm, n.d. [1966]), 377.

130. Huard, *Traité de la propriété intellectuelle*, 1: 290–98.

131. The author's personality rights were recognized by the Supreme Court in its decision of 26 November 1954, *Entscheidungen des Bundesgerichtshofes*, 15: 249ff.

132. Stephen P. Ladas, *The International Protection of Literary and Artistic Property* (New York, 1938), 1: 578.

133. Ulrich Möller, *Die Unübertragbarkeit des Urheberrechts in Deutschland: Eine überschiessende Reaktion auf Savignys subjektives Recht* (Berlin, 2007), 4.

134. Rigamonti, *Geistiges Eigentum als Begriff*, 50–51.

135. Henry Hansmann and Marina Santilli, "Authors' and Artists' Moral Rights: A Comparative Legal and Economic Analysis," *Journal of Legal Studies* 26 (1997): 101.

136. William Blackstone, *Commentaries on the Laws of England* (1766), bk. 2, chap. 26.

137. *Dictionary of National Biography*; J. and J. A. Venn, *Alumni Cantabrigienses* (Cambridge, 1922–1958).

138. Edward Christian, *Notes to Blackstone's Commentaries* (Boston, 1801; original edition, London, 1793–95), 5: 45–46. It was in this spirit that Christian was quoted and invoked by Justice Thompson in his dissent to the ruling in *Wheaton v. Peters* (1834), which nailed fast US copyright as the product of statutory, not natural, law. Richard Peters, *Reports of Cases Argued and Adjudged in the Supreme Court* (Philadelphia, n.d., 1834), 8: 671–72.

139. Renouard, *Traité des droits d'auteurs*, 1: 473–74.

140. Morillot, "De la nature du droit d'auteur," 124, 126.

141. Alcide Darras, *Du droit des auteurs et des artistes dans les rapports internationaux* (Paris, 1887), 6.

142. *Veuve Vergne c. créanciers Vergne*, Cour royal de Paris, 11 January 1828, in Ledru-Rollin, ed., *Journal du Palais*, 3rd ed. (Paris, 1841), 21: 1030–31.

143. *Marie c. Lacordaire*, Cour d'appel de Lyon, 17 July 1845, *Dalloz, Jurisprudence générale* 1 (1845): 128.

144. Agnès Lucas-Schloetter, *Droit moral et droits de la personnalité: Étude de droit comparé français et allemand* (Aix-en-Provence, 2002), 1: 50–51; Gorguette d'Argœuves, *Le Droit moral de l'auteur*, 66–67; Pfister, "L'auteur, propriétaire de son œuvre?" 657–60.

145. *Dalloz, Jurisprudence générale* 2 (1898): 465–67.

146. Strowel, *Droit d'auteur et copyright*, 483–84; Cyrill P. Rigamonti, "The Conceptual Transformation of Moral Rights," *American Journal of Comparative Law* 55 (2007): 82. Whether an artist could be compelled to deliver a work he had contracted for in German law remains more of an open question: Adolf Dietz, *Das Droit Moral des Urhebers im neuen französischen und deutschen Urheberrecht* (Munich, 1968), 82–83.

147. *Dalloz, Jurisprudence générale* 1 (1900): 499.

148. It now hangs in the Hunterian Art Gallery in Glasgow.

149. Charles A. Marvin, "The Author's Status in the United Kingdom and France: Common Law and the Moral Right Doctrine," *International and Comparative Law Quarterly* 20, 4 (1971): 691.

150. John Henry Merryman, "The Refrigerator of Bernard Buffet," *Hastings Law Journal* 27, 5 (1976): 1023. In a similar case Joseph Beuys's sculpture, "Is It about a Bicycle," consisted of fifteen blackboards. Though exhibited together, as intended, they were owned by at least five different people. Fearing that they would be separated and having no means to prevent this, Beuys published a disclaimer denying authorship in the *New York Times*. "Visual Artists Rights Amendment of 1986: Hearing Before the Subcommittee … of the Committee of the Judiciary … on S. 2796," Senate Hearing 99–1071, 18 November 1986, Serial J-99–132, pp. 106–7.

151. Pfister, "L'auteur, propriétaire de son œuvre?" 661, 813–14.

152. In his *Cours de droit commercial*, quoted in Renouard, *Traité des droits d'auteurs*, 2: 327.

153. Strömholm, *Le droit moral de l'auteur*, 124–25.

154. *Teyssèdre c. Garnier*, Tribunal de Paris, 6 April 1842, discussed in Étienne Blanc, *Traité de la contrefaçon*, 4th ed. (Paris, 1855), 68. More examples of French integrity cases are in Stina Teilmann, "British and French Copyright: A Historical Study of Aesthetic Implications," (diss., Southern Denmark, 2004), 112ff.

155. As with Clement Greenberg's stripping the paint off David Smith's sculptures, mentioned in the introduction.

156. Pfister, "L'auteur, propriétaire de son œuvre?" 675.

157. Art. 1382. Strowel, *Droit d'auteur et copyright*, 487–88; Strömholm, *Le droit moral de l'auteur*, 138–39.

158. *Entscheidungen des Reichsgerichts in Zivilsachen* 79, 93 (1912): 397–402.

159. *Hansard*, Commons, 6 May 1861, p. 1634.

160. Although in France some case law favored the author in instances of work destroyed. Edward J. Damich, "The Right of Personality: A Common-Law Basis for the Protection of the Moral Rights of Authors," *Georgia Law Review* 23, 1 (1988): 18–21.

161. *Lacasse et Welcome c. Abbé Quénard*, Cour de Paris, 27 April 1934, discussed in Strowel, *Droit d'auteur et copyright*, 488–89; Martin A. Roeder, "The Doctrine of Moral Right: A Study in the Law of Artists, Authors and Creators," *Harvard Law Review* 53, 4 (1940): 569; Dietz, *Das Droit Moral des Urhebers*, 113.

162. Gerald Dworkin, "Moral Rights and the Common Law Countries," *Australian Intellectual Property Journal* 5, 1 (1994): 23; Gerald Dworkin, "The Moral Right and English Copyright Law," *IIC: International Review of Industrial Property and Copyright Law* 12 (1981): 484.

163. Cyrill P. Rigamonti, "Deconstructing Moral Rights," *Harvard International Law Journal* 47, 2 (2006): 371.

164. 17 U.S.C. §106A(a)(3)(B) (2000).

165. Strömholm, *Le droit moral de l'auteur*, 271.

166. *B. Gaudichot, dit Michel Masson, c. Gaudichot fils*, Cour de Cassation, 16 August 1880, *Dalloz, Jurisprudence générale* 1 (1881): 25–27.

167. *Cinquin c. Lecocq*, 25 June 1902, Cour de Cassation, *Dalloz, Jurisprudence générale* 1 (1903): 5–14 (BK).

168. *Dame Canal c. Jamin*, Tribunal civil de la Seine, 1 April 1936, *Dalloz, Jurisprudence générale* 2 (1936): 65–70.

169. Michaélidès-Nouaros, *Le droit moral de l'auteur*, 148–49.

170. *Jamin et Rempler ès qual. c. Dame Canal*, Arret of 14 May 1945, Cour de Cassation, civil, *Recueil Dalloz* 1 (1945): 285.

171. François Hepp, "Le droit d'auteur, 'propriété incorporelle'?" *Revue internationale du droit d'auteur* 19 (1958): 179–81. Similar issues were still being discussed also in Germany in 1944. Hans Otto de Boor, "Konstruktionsfragen im Urheberrecht," *Archiv für Urheber- Film- und Theaterrecht* 16 (1944): 349.

172. Lionel Bently and Brad Sherman, "Great Britain and the Signing of the Berne Convention in 1886," *Journal of the Copyright Society of the USA* 48 (2000–2001): 325–27.

173. "Correspondence Respecting the Formation of an International Copyright Union," *House of Commons Parliamentary Papers*, C.4606 (1886), 34–45.

174. *Congrès littéraire international de Paris 1878*, 77–78.

175. Peter Galison, *Einstein's Clocks, Poincaré's Maps: Empires of Time* (New York, 2003), 144–55.

176. Dealt with at length in Peter Baldwin, *Contagion and the State in Europe, 1830–1930* (Cambridge, 1999).

177. Sam Ricketson and Jane C. Ginsburg, *International Copyright and Neighbouring Rights: The Berne Convention and Beyond*, 2nd ed. (Oxford, 2006), 66–67.

178. Bently and Sherman, "Great Britain and the Signing of the Berne Convention," 324.

179. That the tide in favor of the author's control was inevitable was made clear in testimony already in 1897: "Report from the Select Committee of the House of Lords, on the Copyright (Amendment) Bill," *House of Commons Papers, Reports of Committees*, 1897, paper 385, 10: 213, 3. The issue continued to fester, however. The Stockholm revisions reflected the interests of developing nations by limiting translation rights to ten years and allowed compulsory licensing of translations after three. Ricketson and Ginsburg, *International Copyright*, 902–3. In the 1920s and '30s the issue had also arisen, with the revived emphasis on the public's interest now leading to restrictions on the author's control over translations—in the Soviet Union, for example—and in the Italian law of 1925 (art. 7), which gave authors rights over translations of scientific works for only a decade. *Journal Officiel*, Documents, Chambre, Annexe 3222, 6 December 1937, p. 230.

180. Ricketson and Ginsburg, *International Copyright*, 75; Sam Ricketson, "People or Ma-

chines: The Berne Convention and the Changing Concept of Authorship," *Columbia-VLA Journal of Law & the Arts* 16, 1 (1991): 7–8.

181. *Hansard*, Commons, 7 April 1911, p. 2595.

182. Reichstag des Norddeutschen Bundes, *Stenographische Berichte*, 1870, vol. 4, Aktenstück 138, p. 536. A similar approach in R. Klostermann, *Das geistige Eigenthum an Schriften, Kunstwerken und Erfindungen* (Berlin, 1867), 1: 219.

183. §6. Reichstag des Norddeutschen Bundes, *Stenographische Berichte*, 1870, vol. 4, Aktenstück 138, p. 537.

184. Gesetz, betreffend das Urheberrecht an Schriftwerken, Abbildungen, musikalischen Kompositionen und dramatischen Werken. Vom 11. Juni 1870, in *Bundes-Gesetzblatt des Norddeutschen Bundes* 19 (1870).

185. Gesetz, betreffend das Urheberrecht an Werken der Literatur und der Tonkunst, 19 June 1901; Gesetz, betreffend das Urheberrecht an Werken der bildenden Künste und der Photographie, 9 January 1907.

186. Dr. Esche. Reichstag, *Stenographische Berichte*, 8 January 1901, pp. 526–29. Other deputies pointedly described the new rights as personal ones, not just economic. Reichstag, *Stenographische Berichte*, 9 January 1901, p. 545, Dr. Oertel.

187. 1901 law, §10; 1907 law, §14. Reichstag, *Stenographische Berichte*, 1900–1902, vol. 1, Aktenstück 97, p. 395.

188. Reichstag, *Stenographische Berichte*, 1900–1902, Aktenstück 214, p. 1276.

189. 1901 law, §25. Reichstag, *Stenographische Berichte*, 17 April 1901, p. 2148.

190. 1907 law, §10, 1876 law, §8. In the earlier discussion the government bill had reasoned that, beyond the economic motives for preventing reproduction, an artist had "personal interests" at stake. Reichstag des Norddeutschen Bundes, *Stenographische Berichte*, 1870, vol. 3, Aktenstück 7, p. 141.

191. *Reichs-Gesetzblatt*, 1876, pp. 4–14. This was continued in the 1907 law, §18.

192. Reichstag, *Stenographische Berichte*, 1905–1906, Aktenstück 30, p. 1536.

193. Reichstag, *Stenographische Berichte*, 9 January 1901, p. 558; 30 April 1901, p. 2432, Ernst Müller-Meinigen, liberal deputy from Bavaria.

194. Reichstag, *Stenographische Berichte*, 1905–1906, Aktenstück 30, p. 1534.

195. Reichstag des Norddeutschen Bundes, *Stenographische Berichte*, 1870, vol. 3, Aktenstück 7, p. 132.

196. Reichstag, *Stenographische Berichte*, 1900–1902, vol. 1, Aktenstück 97, p. 392.

197. Ibid., 1900–1902, vol. 2, Aktenstück 214, p. 1274.

198. Ibid., 1900–1902, vol. 1, Aktenstück 97, p. 395.

199. Ibid., 1905–1906, Aktenstück 30, p. 1535.

200. 1870 law, §7; 1901 law, §19.

201. Reichstag des Norddeutschen Bundes, *Stenographische Berichte*, 1870, vol. 4, Aktenstück 138, p. 538.

202. 1870 law, §48; 1901 law, §20.

203. A German observer surveying the 1911 and 1909 laws in the UK and the US noted how radically different their approaches were—especially compared to the French. Ernst Heymann, "Die zeitliche Begrenzung des Urheberrechts," *Sitzungsberichte der Preussischen Akademie der Wissenschaften*, 1927, p. 57.

204. International Copyright Act, 1886, 49 & 50 Vict., c.33, s. 11; 1 & 2 Geo. 5, c.46, s. 5.1; Copyright Act, 1956, 4 & 5 Eliz. 2, c.74, cl. 4.

205. "Correspondence Respecting the Formation of an International Copyright Union," C.4606, p. 52.

206. By 1909 the consensus was that formalities should be abolished. *Report of the Committee on the Law of Copyright*, Cd 4976 (London, 1909), 12–13.

207. *Hansard*, Commons, 7 April 1911, pp. 2615–16, 2634–37, 2657–58.

208. *Hansard*, Commons, 28 July 1911, pp. 1959–60, 1964.

209. *Hansard*, Commons, 7 April 1911, pp. 2600–01; 28 July 1911, p. 1911.

210. *Hansard*, Commons, 28 July 1911, p. 1903.

211. *Hansard*, Commons, 7 April 1911, p. 2615, William Joynson-Hicks, Conservative MP. A very similar formulation by George Roberts at p. 2635, and 28 July 1911, p. 1963.

212. 1 & 2 Geo. 5, c.46, s. 3. The compulsory licensing provision lasted until abolished by the 1956 act.

213. In the eyes of many Europeans, this in effect meant that UK copyright lasted for only twenty-five years postmortem. Hoffmann, "Die Staatenvorschläge zur Revision der revidierten Berner Übereinkunft," 144–45.

214. *Hansard*, Commons, 7 April 1911, p. 2649, Birrell.

215. *The Cases of the Appellants and Respondents in the Cause of Literary Property, before the House of Lords* (London, 1774), 25 (BK).

216. Even though this safeguard had never actually been used since 1842, it was still considered crucial. *Hansard*, Commons, 7 April 1911, pp. 2642, 2654; *Minutes of Evidence Taken before the Law of Copyright Committee*, Cd 5051, 25.

217. *Hansard*, Commons, 7 April 1911, p. 2619; 28 July 1911, p. 1961.

218. International Copyright Act, 3 March 1891, 26 Stat. 1106, chap. 565; Report 622, 19 March 1888, *Reports of Committees of the Senate of the United States* (1887–88) (Washington DC, 1888), 2: 2.

219. Report 622, *Reports of Committees of the Senate* (1887–88), 2: 4–5.

220. Report 7083, 30 January 1907, *House Reports* (59th Congress, 2nd sess.), 1: 11–12.

221. 1909 Copyright Act, sect. 15, 62.

222. Joint Committee on the Library, Report 409, 7 February 1873, 42nd Congress, 3rd sess., reprinted in *Congressional Record*, Senate, 30 April 1888, pp. 3510–11.

223. *Minutes of the Evidence Taken before the Royal Commission on Copyright*, 65, 91–94.

224. *Testimony before the House Committee on the Judiciary on International Copyright*, 8 February 1890, p. 36.

225. *Congressional Record*, Senate, 23 April 1888, pp. 3233–34, 3242–44. Similarly, Senator John Reagan from Texas: *Congressional Record*, Senate, 9 February 1891, p. 2381.

226. *Congressional Record*, Senate, 9 February 1891, p. 2383. The Pearsall Smith quotation is from Senator Coke.

227. *Congressional Record*, Senate, 13 February 1891, p. 2611; *Testimony before the House Committee on the Judiciary on International Copyright*, 8 February 1890, pp. 8–9.

228. Report 1188, 21 May 1886, *Reports of Committees of the Senate* (1885–86), p. iv; *Congressional Record*, Senate, 24 April 1888, pp. 3269–70; *Testimony before the House Committee on the Judiciary on International Copyright*, 8 February 1890, p. 31.

5. THE STRANGE BIRTH OF MORAL RIGHTS IN FASCIST EUROPE

1. Burton Ong, "Why Moral Rights Matter: Recognizing the Intrinsic Value of Integrity Rights," *Columbia Journal of Law & the Arts* 26, 3/4 (2003): 299.

2. Hans Mommsen and Manfried Grieger, *Das Volkswagenwerk und seine Arbeiter im Dritten Reich* (Düsseldorf, 1996); Bernhard Rieger, *The People's Car: A Global History of the Volkswagen Beetle* (Cambridge MA, 2013); Robert Proctor, *The Nazi War on Cancer* (Princeton, 1999); George Davey Smith et al., "Smoking and Health Promotion in Nazi Germany," *Journal of Epidemiology and Community Health* 48 (1994).

3. Charles Lane, "The Paradoxes of the Death Penalty Stance," *Washington Post*, 4 June 2005;

Richard J. Evans, *Rituals of Retribution: Capital Punishment in Germany, 1600–1987* (Oxford, 1996), 785–86.

4. James Q. Whitman, "The Two Western Cultures of Privacy: Dignity Versus Liberty," *Yale Law Journal* 113, 6 (2004).

5. Frank Uekötter, *The Green and the Brown: A History of Conservation in Nazi Germany* (Cambridge, 2006); Franz-Josef Brüggemeier et al., eds., *How Green Were the Nazis? Nature, Environment, and Nation in the Third Reich* (Athens OH, 2005).

6. James Q. Whitman, "On Nazi 'Honour' and the New European 'Dignity,'" in Christian Joerges and Navraj Singh Ghaleigh, eds., *Darker Legacies of Law in Europe: The Shadow of National Socialism and Fascism over Europe and its Legal Traditions* (Oxford, 2003).

7. Art. 7. *Conférence Internationale pour la protection des œuvres littéraires et artistiques: Délégation Italienne: II. Protection du droit personnel (moral) de l'auteur* (Rome, 1928), 4.

8. Valerio de Sanctis, "Urheberrecht und Interesse der Allgemeinheit," *Archiv für Urheber-Film- und Theaterrecht* 7 (1934): 236.

9. Eduardo Piola Caselli, "Il Diritto Morale di Autore," *Il Diritto di Autore* 1, 1 (1930): 22–23; Amedeo Giannini, "Die Ausarbeitung des neuen Italienischen Urheberrechtsgesetzes Italiens," *Archiv für Urheber- Film- und Theaterrecht* 15 (1942): 113; Amedeo Giannini, *La Convenzione di Berna sulla Proprietà Letteraria* (Rome, 1933), 141, 165. Giannini was an enthusiastic fascist and editor of Mussolini's *La nuova politica dell'Italia* (Milan, 1923). Mabel Berezin, "Public Spectacles and Private Enterprises: Theater and Politics in Italy under Fascism, 1919–1940," (diss. Harvard, 1987), chaps. 2–3, presents the internal battles between playwrights and theater managers that formed the professional backdrop to the desire for reform among many in the theatrical classes.

10. E. Piola Caselli, "Les principes fondamentaux en droit d'auteur, d'édition et de radiophonie en Italie," *Archiv für Funkrecht* 3 (1930): 221; "Rapport de M. Ed. Piola Caselli sur la législation italienne," in *Congrès du Caire de l'Association Littéraire et Artistique*, 24 December 1929 (Cairo, 1930), 138.

11. Piola Caselli, "Il Diritto Morale," 26.

12. The law is in *Le Droit d'auteur*, 15 January 1926, pp. 2–7. The articles referred to here are 16, 15, 24, 56–57.

13. Arnold Raestad, *La Convention de Berne révisée à Rome 1928* (Paris, 1931), 152.

14. Marcel Plaisant and Olivier Pichot, *La Conférence de Rome: Commentaire pratique de la nouvelle Convention pour la protection internationale de la propriété littéraire et artistique* (Paris, 1934), 26; Heinz Püschel, *100 Jahre Berner Union: Gedanken, Dokumente, Erinnerungen* (Leipzig, 1986), 61.

15. Union Internationale pour la protection des œuvres littéraires et artistiques, *Actes de la conférence réunie à Rome du 7 Mai au 2 Juin 1928* (Berne, 1929), 162, 179–80. In addition to the original reports of the meeting, some of the documentation from the Rome Conference has been translated in *The Berne Convention for the Protection of Literary and Artistic Works from 1886 to 1986* (Geneva, 1986) and on the website associated with the standard work of Sam Ricketson and Jane Ginsburg, *International Copyright and Neighbouring Rights: The Berne Convention and Beyond*, 2nd ed. (Oxford, 2006), which includes material not in the book: http://www.oup.com /uk/booksites/content/9780198259466/.

16. National Archives, UK, FO 371/14173, 141–6, Foreign Office, S. G. Raymond, "International Copyright Conference. Rome, 1928 (Report of the New Zealand Delegate, Mr. S. G. Raymond, K.C.)."

17. National Archives, Dominions Office, DO 35/117/12, 20, Board of Trade, "Ratification of the Rome Copyright Convention of 1928" (1930), p. 20.

18. Hannes Siegrist, "Geistiges Eigentum im Spannungsfeld von Individualisierung, Nationalisierung, und Internationalisierung: Der Weg zur Berner Übereinkunft von 1886," in Rüdiger Hohls et al., eds., *Europa und die Europäer* (Stuttgart, 2005), 57–58.

19. Piola Caselli "Il Diritto Morale di Autore," *Il Diritto di Autore* 1, 2 (1930): 178–81.

20. National Archives, FO 371/14173, 175, "Rome Copyright Conference, 1928. Report of the British Delegates," p. 175.

21. Union Internationale, *Actes de la conférence réunie à Rome*, 178; Pierre Recht, "A propos de l'article 6*bis* de la Convention de Berne (droit moral)," *Le Droit d'auteur* 81, 1 (1968): 15.

22. Union Internationale, *Actes de la conférence réunie à Rome*, 201–04, 239.

23. Sam Ricketson, "Is Australia in Breach of Its International Obligations with Respect to the Protection of Moral Rights?" *Melbourne University Law Review* 17 (1989–90): 468–69; Ricketson and Ginsburg, *International Copyright*, 592–93.

24. Fritz Smoschewer, "Droit moral und Persönlichkeitsrecht des Urhebers," *Gewerblicher Rechtsschutz und Urheberrecht* (1930): 657–58.

25. "Kann ein Schauspieler die Nachsynchronisierung eines alten Filmes, in welchem er die Hauptrolle gespielt hat, verhindern?" *Archiv für Urheber- Film- und Theaterrecht* 8 (1935): 157–60.

26. *Le Droit d'auteur* (1928), 82; Bruno Marwitz, *Die revidierte Berner Übereinkunft und die Römische Konferenz* (Berlin, 1928), 37, 41.

27. Gerald Dworkin, "Moral Rights and the Common Law Countries." *Australian Intellectual Property Journal* 5, 1 (1994): 7.

28. Adrian Lyttleton, *The Seizure of Power: Fascism in Italy, 1919–1929* (London, 1973), 384.

29. Michael A. Ledeen, *The First Duce: D'Annunzio at Fiume* (Baltimore, 1977). The close connections between modernism and the cultural avant-garde have long been recognized as a facet of Italian Fascism. Ruth Ben-Ghiat, *Fascist Modernities: Italy, 1922–1945* (Berkeley, 2001), Walter L. Adamson, *Avant-Garde Florence: From Modernism to Fascism* (Cambridge MA, 1993). And also more generally in other nations too: Mark Antliff, *Avant-Garde Fascism: The Mobilization of Myth, Art and Culture in France, 1909–1939* (Durham NC, 2007), Andrew Hewitt, *Fascist Modernism: Aesthetics, Politics and the Avant-Garde* (Stanford, 1993), Laura Frost, *Sex Drives: Fantasies of Fascism in Literary Modernism* (Ithaca NY, 2002), Roger Griffin, *Modernism and Fascism: The Sense of a Beginning under Mussolini and Hitler* (Houndmills, 2007), Alice Yaeger Kaplan, *Reproductions of Banality: Fascism, Literature and French Intellectual Life* (Minneapolis, 1986).

30. Piola Caselli, "Il Diritto Morale di Autore," 183; Union Internationale, *Actes de la conférence réunie à Rome*, 292.

31. Stanislas de Gorguette d'Argœuves, *Le Droit moral de l'auteur sur son œuvre artistique ou litteraire* (Paris, 1926), 6–9.

32. Klauer, "Die Urheberrechtskonferenz in Rom," *Archiv für Urheber- Film- und Theaterrecht* 1 (1928): 373; Mittelstadt, "Das 'droit moral' nach den Beschlüssen der Römischen Urheberrechtskonferenz von 1928," *Gewerblicher Rechtsschutz und Urheberrecht* (1930): 47–48.

33. Union Internationale, *Actes de la conférence réunie à Rome*, 161–62, 199, 236. Similar arguments in Piola Caselli, "Il Diritto Morale," 8–11.

34. Though in general his view of Expressionism was negative. Thomas Mathieu, *Kunstauffassungen und Kulturpolitik im Nationalsozialismus* (Saarbrücken, 1997), 85–88.

35. Hildegard Brenner, "Art in the Political Power Struggle of 1933 and 1934," in Hajo Holborn, ed., *Republic to Reich* (New York, 1972), 421–25; Stephanie Barron, ed., *"Degenerate Art": The Fate of the Avant-Garde in Nazi Germany* (Los Angeles, 1991).

36. Berthold Hinz, *Art in the Third Reich* (New York, 1979).

37. Berndt W. Wessling, *Furtwängler: Eine kritische Biographie* (Stuttgart, 1985), 259–63; Bärbel Schrader, *"Jederzeit widerruflich": Die Reichskulturkammer und die Sondergenehmigungen in Theater und Film des NS-Staates* (Berlin, 2008), 68–69.

38. Simple trade-offs between individualism and collectivism in Nazi ideology have been replaced in the most recent historiography by a more complicated view of the way in which both concepts could be held in the Nazi mind at the same time. Their view of authors' rights fits well with this approach. Moritz Föllmer, "Was Nazism Collectivistic? Redefining the Indi-

vidual in Berlin, 1930–1945," *Journal of Modern* History 82, 1 (2010): 65–68. For an example of the usual view of the Nazis as wholly communalist, see: Mireille Buydens, "L'Intérêt général, une notion protéiforme," in *L'Intérêt général et l'accès à l'information en propriété intellectuelle* (Brussels, 2008), 10–11.

39. Willy Hoffmann, *Die Berner Übereinkunft zum Schutze von Werken der Literatur und Kunst vom 9. September 1886 revidiert in Berlin am 13. November 1908 und in Rom am 2. Juni 1928* (Berlin, 1935), 26; Alfred Brockhaus, *Gesamtheit und Einzelperson im faschistischen Urheberrecht: Ein Beitrag zur deutsch-italienischen Rechtsgemeinschaft* (Berlin, 1939), 44.

40. Alexander Elster, "Die sozialethische Grundlage des Urheberrechts (insbesondere bezüglich des Problems 'Persönlichkeit und Gemeinschaft') und die internationale Verständigung," *Archiv für Urheber- Film- und Theaterrecht* 11 (1938): 175–76.

41. Jlja Heifetz, "Il Diritto Sovietico d'Autore," *Il Diritto di Autore* 3 (1932): 54.

42. Alexander Elster, "Persönlichkeit und Sozialgebundenheit im Urheberrecht nach deutscher und französischer Rechtsauffassung," *Zeitschrift für Ausländisches und Internationales Privatrecht* 11 (1937): 530–31; Jean Escarra et al., *La doctrine française du droit d'auteur* (Paris, 1937), 23, 40.

43. Hoffmann, *Berner Übereinkunft*, 26–28; de Sanctis, "Urheberrecht und Interesse der Allgemeinheit," 237.

44. Herbert Meyer, "Die Schöpferpersönlichkeit im kommenden deutschen Urheber- und Verlagsrecht," *Zeitschrift der Akademie für Deutsches Recht* 3 (1936): 158.

45. Rudolf Brandt, *Das "droit moral" als Faktor im künftigen deutschen Urheberrecht* (diss., Jena, 1934), 24–33; Alexander Elster, "Die Rechtspersönlichkeit des Urhebers und ihr Recht in der Volksgemeinschaft," *Gewerblicher Rechtsschutz und Urheberrecht* 45 (1940): 405.

46. Mittelstadt, "Das 'droit moral,'" 44.

47. *Entscheidungen des Reichsgerichts in Zivilsachen* 123, 71 (16 February 1929): 312–20.

48. Brockhaus, *Gesamtheit und Einzelperson*, 43; Julius Kopsch, "Über die Einheit des Urheberrechtes," in Akademie für Deutsches Recht, *Das Recht des schöpferischen Menschen* (Berlin, 1936), 270.

49. Hoffmann, *Berner Übereinkunft*, 103; H. O. de Boor, "Der NSJ-Entwurf und die Urheberrechtsreform," *Archiv für Urheber- Film- und Theaterrecht* 7 (1934): 434; de Sanctis, "Urheberrecht und Interesse der Allgemeinheit," 238.

50. Gerhard Wank, *Das Persönlichkeitsrecht des Erfinders* (diss., Erlangen; Düren-Rhld., 1938), 2–3; Edgar Tatarin-Tarnheyden, *Werdendes Staatsrecht: Gedanken zu einem organischen und deutschen Verfassungsneubau* (Berlin, 1934), 144–45, 152–54.

51. Joseph Goebbels, *Die Tagebücher* (Munich, 1993), 7: 621. The Fascists had similar ideas: de Sanctis, "Urheberrecht und Interesse der Allgemeinheit," 259.

52. H. Barth, "Persönlichkeit und Volksgemeinschaft im Rechte der Erfinder und Erfindung," *Zeitschrift der Akademie für Deutsches Recht* 2 (1935): 823; *Die Neugestaltung des deutschen Urheberrechts: Die Vorschläge des Fachausschusses für Urheber und Verlagsrecht der Deutschen Arbeitsgemeinschaft für gewerblichen Rechtsschutz und Urheberrecht in der Akademie für Deutsches Recht* (Hans Frank, ed., *Arbeitsberichte der Akademie für Deutsches Recht*, 11) (Berlin, 1939), 34.

53. Brockhaus, *Gesamtheit und Einzelperson*, 3; "Kurzbericht von Gustav Kilpper über die Reform des Urheberrechts (1935)," in Werner Schubert, ed., *Akademie für Deutsches Recht, 1933–1945: Protokolle der Ausschüsse* (Frankfurt, 1999), 9: 587.

54. Ernst Hefti, "Das Urheberrecht im Nationalsozialismus," in Robert Dittrich, ed., *Woher kommt das Urheberrecht und wohin geht es?* (Vienna, 1988), 170–71.

55. Brockhaus, *Gesamtheit und Einzelperson*, 4; Luigi di Franco, "Der soziale Gehalt des Urheberrechts im neuen italienischen Gesetze," *Archiv für Urheber- Film- und Theaterrecht* 15 (1942): 104; Peter Gast, "Grundsätzliches zur Stellung der Reichskulturkammer im Urheberrecht," *Archiv für Urheber- Film- und Theaterrecht* 8 (1935): 336.

56. Elster, "Die sozialethische Grundlage des Urheberrechts," 180; Ferdinand Sieger, *Die*

künstlerische Entlehnung im neuen deutschen Urheberrecht (diss., Cologne, 1936), 13–16; Fritz Gloede, *Reichskulturkammer und Urheberschutz* (diss, Rostock; Gräfenhainichen, 1935), 35; Willy Hoffmann, "Die Aufgaben der deutschen Urheberrechtsreform" in Akademie für Deutsches Recht, *Das Recht des schöpferischen Menschen*, 250–51; *Die Neugestaltung des deutschen Urheberrechts*, 37–38.

57. Meyer, "Die Schöpferpersönlichkeit," 155; Walter Becker-Bender, *Das Urheberpersönlichkeitsrecht im musikalischen Urheberrecht* (Heidelberg, 1940), 8–10.

58. Ildephons Richter, "Urheberrecht und Reichskulturkammer," *Archiv für Urheber- Film- und Theaterrecht* 7 (1934): 330–31. Very similar language in Kopsch, "Über die Einheit des Urheberrechtes," 271; Julius Kopsch, "Vom sozialen Wesen des Urheberrechts," *Gewerblicher Rechtsschutz und Urheberrecht* 7 (1936): 452–53; Ausschuss für Urheber- und Verlagsrecht, minutes, 16 and 17 February 1934, in *Akademie für Deutsches Recht, 1933–1945: Protokolle der Ausschüsse*, 9: 560.

59. Adolf Hitler, *Mein Kampf* (London, 1969), 405–6. Hitler, however, also thought that the American democratic system of education accounted for the great number of inventions coming out of that nation. Ibid., 391.

60. Gloede, *Reichskulturkammer und Urheberschutz*, 35; Julius Kopsch, "Urheberrecht und Rechtsbewusstsein des Volkes," *Archiv für Urheber- Film- und Theaterrecht* 12 (1939): 42.

61. Ernst Heymann, "Die Neufassung der Berner Konvention und unsere Urheberrechtsreform," *Deutsche Juristen-Zeitung* 39, 3 (1934): 105–6; Meyer, "Die Schöpferpersönlichkeit," 158–59.

62. Kopsch, "Über die Einheit des Urheberrechtes," 271–72; Sieger, *Die künstlerische Entlehnung*, 53.

63. Bryan Gilliam, *The Life of Richard Strauss* (Cambridge, 1999), 146–48; Michael Kennedy, *Richard Strauss: Man, Musician, Enigma* (Cambridge, 1999), 285–86; Alan E. Steinweis, *Art, Ideology and Economics in Nazi Germany: The Reich Chambers of Music, Theater and the Visual Arts* (Chapel Hill, 1993), 51–53.

64. Richard Strauss, "Gedanken zum Urheberrecht," *Archiv für Urheber- Film- und Theaterrecht* 7 (1934): 217–18; "Ansprache von Richard Strauss, gehalten in der Sitzung vom 23.4.1934," in Schubert, *Akademie für Deutsches Recht, 1933–1945: Protokolle der Ausschüsse*, 9: 581–82.

65. Richard Strauss, "Appell," *GEMA-Nachrichten* 55 (25 February 1933): 3.

66. Willy Hoffmann, "Das Urheberpersönlichkeitsrecht in der Berner Übereinkunft," *Archiv für Urheber- Film- und Theaterrecht* 9 (1936): 115; Hoffmann, *Berner Übereinkunft*, 26.

67. Felix Leinemann, *Die Sozialbindung des "Geistigen Eigentums"* (Baden-Baden, 1998), 36–39; Elizabeth Adeney, *The Moral Rights of Authors and Performers* (Oxford, 2006), chap. 3.

68. Art. 153 III. Bernd Rüthers, *Die unbegrenzte Auslegung: Zum Wandel der Privatrechtsordnung im Nationalsozialismus*, 6th ed. (Tübingen, 2005), 351–52.

69. Kopsch, "Vom sozialen Wesen des Urheberrechts," 452–53.

70. Hoffmann, *Berner Übereinkunft*, 26–28.

71. Ausschuss für Urheber- und Verlagsrecht, minutes, 16 and 17 February 1934, in Schubert, *Akademie für Deutsches Recht, 1933–1945: Protokolle der Ausschüsse*, 9: 576; Gast, "Grundsätzliches zur Stellung der Reichskulturkammer," 337.

72. Broached in article 11*bis*.

73. Ausschuss für Urheber- und Verlagsrecht, minutes, 16 and 17 February 1934, in Schubert, *Akademie für Deutsches Recht 1933–1945: Protokolle der Ausschüsse*, 9: 558–59.

74. Willy Hoffmann, "Die Staatenvorschläge zur Revision der revidierten Berner Übereinkunft," *Archiv für Urheber- Film- und Theaterrecht* 1, 2 (1928): 169–70.

75. Julius Kopsch, "Zur Frage der gesetzlichen Lizenz," *Archiv für Funkrecht* 1 (1928): 201–3; Hefti, "Das Urheberrecht im Nationalsozialismus," 165.

76. Ludwig Wertheimer, "Gesetzliche Lizenzen im Urheberrecht und die Berner Übereinkunft zum Schutze von Werken der Literatur und Kunst," *Geistiges Eigentum* 2 (1936/37): 13–17.

77. Willy Hoffmann, "Nochmals: Die Zukunft der Berner Übereinkunft," *Gewerblicher*

Rechtsschutz und Urheberrecht 38 (1933): 761–62; Hoffmann, *Berner Übereinkunft*, 179. Nazi suspicions of Roman law and its allegedly materialist and individualistic tendencies were given expression already in point 19 of the party program, which demanded that German common law be substituted for Roman law. Ilse Staff, "Das rechtliche Steuerungspotential im NS-Staat im Blickwinkel des italienischen Faschismus," in Dieter Gosewinkel, ed., *Wirtschaftskontrolle und Recht in der nationalsozialistischen Diktatur* (Frankfurt, 2005), 390.

78. Willy Hoffmann, "Ziele der deutschen Urheberrechtsreform," *Gewerblicher Rechtsschutz und Urheberrecht* 43 (1938): 2, 5; Willy Hoffmann, *Ein deutsches Urheberrechtsgesetz: Entwurf eines Gesetzes über das Urheberrecht mit Begründung* (Berlin, 1933), 24; Brockhaus, *Gesamtheit und Einzelperson*, 78.

79. Richter, "Urheberrecht und Reichskulturkammer," 331; Kopsch, "Über die Einheit des Urheberrechtes," 272; Elster, "Die Rechtspersönlichkeit des Urhebers," 409–10; Elster, "Persönlichkeit und Sozialgebundenheit im Urheberrecht," 536.

80. Willy Hoffmann, "Die Zukunft der Berner Übereinkunft," *Gewerblicher Rechtsschutz und Urheberrecht* 38 (1933): 175; Bruno Marwitz, "Die Zukunft der Berner Übereinkunft: Eine Entgegnung," *Gewerblicher Rechtsschutz und Urheberrecht* 38 (1933): 547; Hoffmann, "Nochmals: Die Zukunft der Berner Übereinkunft," 761.

81. Elster, "Die sozialethische Grundlage des Urheberrechts," 181. Similar ideas in Sieger, *Die künstlerische Entlehnung*, 54.

82. Elster, "Die sozialethische Grundlage des Urheberrechts," 179; Meyer, "Die Schöpferpersönlichkeit," 157; Elster, "Persönlichkeit und Sozialgebundenheit," 531–33, 537–39; Bull, "Der Gemeinnutz im Urheberrecht," *Archiv für Urheber- Film- und Theaterrecht* 7 (1934): 378, 381.

83. Ute Frevert, *Men of Honour: A Social and Cultural History of the Duel* (Cambridge, 1995); Ute Frevert, "Honour and Middle-Class Culture: The History of the Duel in England and Germany," in Jürgen Kocka and Allan Mitchell, eds., *Bourgeois Society in Nineteenth-Century Europe* (London, 1993).

84. Julius Kopsch, "Der Schutz der Urheberehre," *Zeitschrift der Akademie für Deutsches Recht* 3 (1936): 376; Georg Müller, "Das Urheberpersönlichkeitsrecht im Gesetzentwurfe der Akademie für Deutsches Recht," *Archiv für Urheber- Film- und Theaterrecht* 12 (1939): 261.

85. Hoffmann, "Das Urheberpersönlichkeitsrecht," 116.

86. §10. *Gewerblicher Rechtsschutz und Urheberrecht* 44, 4/5 (1939): 243.

87. The scholarly works on Nazi authors' rights policy are few: Artur-Axel Wandtke, "Einige Aspekte zur Urheberrechtsreform im Dritten Reich," *UFITA: Archiv für Urheber- und Medienrecht* 2 (2002), and Ralf-M. Vogt, *Die urheberrechtlichen Reformdiskussionen in Deutschland während der Zeit der Weimarer Republik und des Nationalsozialismus* (Frankfurt, 2004).

88. Bekanntmachung, 31 October 1933, *Reichsgesetzblatt* 2 (9 November 1933): 889.

89. Discussions were still being held in August 1940, now in the expectation that Germany would soon be negotiating peace terms as a victor and imposing uniform patent and copyright law on a conquered Europe. Ausschuss für das Recht des geistigen Schaffens, minutes, 29 August 1940, in Schubert, *Akademie für Deutsches Recht, 1933–1945: Protokolle der Ausschüsse*, 9: 495–515. But after that things dried up.

90. Wertheimer, "Gesetzliche Lizenzen im Urheberrecht," 13.

91. The 1932 draft is discussed in Vogt, *Die urheberrechtlichen Reformdiskussionen*, 98–126.

92. de Boor, "Der NSJ-Entwurf und die Urheberrechtsreform," 414; Hans Otto de Boor, *Vom Wesen des Urheberrechts: Kritische Bemerkungen zum Entwurf eines Gesetzes über das Urheberrecht an Werken der Literatur, der Kunst und der Photographie* (Marburg, 1933), 72–73.

93. Hoffmann, *Ein deutsches Urheberrechtsgesetz*.

94. "NSJ-Entwurf eines neuen Deutschen Urheberschutzgesetzes," *Archiv für Urheber- Film- und Theaterrecht* 7, 4 (1934): 383–99.

95. The reworking from 1933 is discussed in Vogt, *Die urheberrechtlichen Reformdiskussionen*, 166–67. The 1934 version is in Ausschuss für Urheber- und Verlagsrecht, "Entwurf des Reichs-

justizministeriums zu einem Urheberrechtsgesetz vom 22.1.1934," in Schubert, *Akademie für Deutsches Recht, 1933–1945: Protokolle der Ausschüsse*, 9: 534–55. The final 1939 draft is in *Gewerblicher Rechtsschutz und Urheberrecht* 44, 4/5 (1939): 242–55; *Le Droit d'auteur* (1940), 28–41; *Die Neugestaltung des deutschen Urheberrechts*.

96. "Deutschland: Ministerialentwurf eines Urheberrechtsgesetzes vom 22. January 1934," *UFITA: Archiv für Urheber- und Medienrecht* 3 (2000): 779.

97. Vogt, *Die urheberrechtlichen Reformdiskussionen*, 167–78.

98. 1934 bill, §§10, 28; 1939 bill, §21.

99. §§10a, 53a. *Die Neugestaltung des deutschen Urheberrechts*, 44.

100. Hoffmann, *Ein deutsches Urheberrechtsgesetz*, 13, 76–77; "NSJ-Entwurf eines neuen Deutschen Urheberschutzgesetzes," §§30, 33; 1934 Justice Ministry bill, §§23, 24.

101. 1934 bill, §§28, 30, 31.

102. Dr. de Boor, "Zur Reform des Filmrechts," *Zeitschrift der Akademie für Deutsches Recht* 2 (1935): 831; de Boor, "Der NSJ-Entwurf und die Urheberrechtsreform," 430–35.

103. 1901 law, §3, 1907 law, §7, 1932 Justice Ministry bill, §7.

104. Hans Otto de Boor, "Soziale Gebundenheit des Urheberrechts," in Hans Frank, *Nationalsozialistisches Handbuch für Recht und Gesetzgebung* (Munich, 1935), 1016, 1025–26, 1030–31; Richter, "Urheberrecht und Reichskulturkammer," 331.

105. Julius Kopsch, "Steht dem Urheber das Recht zu, sein Werk nach dem Erscheinen zu ändern?" *Archiv für Urheber- Film- und Theaterrecht* 11 (1938): 28–30; Kopsch, "Urheberrecht und Rechtsbewusstsein," 41. A Swedish visitor to Berlin in 1934 reported that Kopsch was a strong backer of authors' moral rights. Petra Garberding, "'We Take Care of the Artist': The German Composers' Meeting in Berlin, 1934," *Music and Politics*, 3, 2 (2009): 6.

106. §31. Hoffmann, *Ein deutsches Urheberrechtsgesetz*, 79–80.

107. §§27–28.

108. H. O. de Boor, "Der Urheber als schöpferische Einzelpersönlichkeit," in Akademie für Deutsches Recht, *Das Recht des schöpferischen Menschen*, 240.

109. Hoffmann, "Die Aufgaben der deutschen Urheberrechtsreform," 250–51; Reinhard Höhn, "Der Führerbegriff im Staatsrecht," *Deutsches Recht* 5 (1935): 296–301; Sieger, *Die künstlerische Entlehnung im neuen deutschen Urheberrecht*, 13.

110. §4 and §6, respectively. Though various drafts also had the concept of "dependent creator" (*unselbständiger Urheber*), who participated, but only in a subsidiary position and therefore had no claims to be named as a creator or other moral rights. 1934 Justice Ministry bill, §21; 1939 bill, §§21, 29.

111. In contrast, the Italian law of 1925 (art. 17) gave the rights to collective works to the person directing them. Discussion and disagreement with this: Valerio de Sanctis, "Urheberrecht und Interesse der Allgemeinheit," *Archiv für Urheber- Film- und Theaterrecht* 7 (1934): 241–42.

112. Kees Gispen, *Poems in Steel: National Socialism and the Politics of Inventing from Weimar to Bonn* (New York, 2002), 193–95.

113. Gast, "Grundsätzliches zur Stellung der Reichskulturkammer," 339–41. Similar concerns in Brockhaus, *Gesamtheit und Einzelperson*, 45; Meyer, "Die Schöpferpersönlichkeit," 157; de Boor, "Soziale Gebundenheit des Urheberrechts," 1026–27.

114. Ausschuss für Urheber- und Verlagsrecht, minutes, 16 and 17 February 1934, in Schubert, *Akademie für Deutsches Recht, 1933–1945: Protokolle der Ausschüsse*, 9: 577; Elster, "Die Rechtspersönlichkeit des Urhebers," 410–11.

115. The Nazi Lawyers' Federation's bill (§§27–28); the 1933 and 1934 Justice Ministry bills (§53); the 1939 bill (§53); *Die Neugestaltung des deutschen Urheberrechts*, 43–44; Peter Ruzicka, *Die Problematik eines "ewigen Urheberpersönlichkeitsrechts" unter besonderer Berücksichtigung des Schutzes musikalischer Werke* (Berlin, 1979), 49–53.

116. Though their law (§9.6) required authorial permission to broadcast.

117. W. Harrison Moore, "The International Copyright Conference," *British Year Book of International Law* 11 (1930): 173–74. In this they had the same interests in new nonprint media that African and other developing nations would discover in the 1960s. Howard D. Sacks, "Crisis in International Copyright: The Protocol Regarding Developing Countries," *Journal of Business Law* (1969): 28.

118. Dr. Neugebauer, "Der Rundfunk auf der Romkonferenz," *Archiv für Rundfunk* 1 (1928): 295, 300; Union Internationale, *Actes de la conférence réunie à Rome*, 256–59; "Materialien zum Art. 11b der Berner Übereinkunft in Fassung der Beschlüsse der Romkonferenz," *Archiv für Funkrecht* 1 (1928): 387–88.

119. Hoffmann, "Ziele der deutschen Urheberrechtsreform," 3–4; de Boor, "Der NSJ-Entwurf und die Urheberrechtsreform," 430; Willy Hoffmann, "Der Entwurf eines Urheberrechtsgesetzes," *Archiv für Urheber- Film- und Theaterrecht* 5 (1932): 422, 450.

120. Hoffmann, "Die Aufgaben der deutschen Urheberrechtsreform," 255–56.

121. Becker-Bender, *Das Urheberpersönlichkeitsrecht im musikalischen Urheberrecht*, 5.

122. Alexander J. de Grand, *Fascist Italy and Nazi Germany: The "Fascist" Style of Rule*, 2nd ed. (New York, 2004), 50–51; Dick Geary, *Hitler and Nazism* (London, 1993), 48–49; David Schoenbaum, *Hitler's Social Revolution* (London, 1967), 139–43.

123. Gustavo Corni, *Hitler and the Peasants: Agrarian Policy of the Third Reich, 1930–1939* (New York, 1990), chap. 7; Daniela Münkel, "Bäuerliche Interessen versus NS-Ideologie," *Vierteljahrshefte für Zeitgeschichte* 44, 4 (1996): 549–53; Daniela Münkel, *Nationalsozialistische Agrarpolitik und Bauernalltag* (Frankfurt, 1996).

124. Meyer, "Die Schöpferpersönlichkeit," 157–60; de Boor, "Der NSJ-Entwurf und die Urheberrechtsreform," 435–38.

125. Gustav Kirstein, *Dreissig oder fünfzig Jahre?* (n.p., n.d. [Leipzig, 1926]).

126. de Boor, *Vom Wesen des Urheberrechts*, 74–75; Alexander Elster, "Deutsche Rechtsgedanken im Urheberrecht (unter Berücksichtigung des Entwurfs)," *Archiv für Urheber- Film- und Theaterrecht* 6 (1933): 203; de Boor, "Der NSJ-Entwurf und die Urheberrechtsreform," 428; de Boor, "Soziale Gebundenheit des Urheberrechts," 1028. This was also the position taken in 1927 by the Prussian Academy of Science: "Erklärung über die Schutzfrist des Urheberrechtes," *Sitzungsberichte der Preussischen Akademie der Wissenschaften* (1927) (Philosophisch-Historische Klasse), 44–46.

127. Ausschuss für Urheber- und Verlagsrecht, minutes, 16 and 17 February 1934, in Schubert, *Akademie für Deutsches Recht, 1933–1945: Protokolle der Ausschüsse*, 9: 561; Vogt, *Die urheberrechtlichen Reformdiskussionen*, 166–67.

128. Strauss, "Gedanken zum Urheberrecht," 220.

129. Gesetz zur Verlängerung der Schutzfristen im Urheberrecht, 13 December 1934, *Reichsgesetzblatt* 2 (1934): 1395; Steinweis, *Art, Ideology and Economics*, 51.

130. Ausschuss für Urheber- und Verlagsrecht, minutes, 16 and 17 February 1934, in Schubert, *Akademie für Deutsches Recht, 1933–1945: Protokolle der Ausschüsse*, 9: 560–62. The Austrian example had weighed heavily in German discussions also when the thirty-year term had been introduced in 1870. Reichstag des Norddeutschen Bundes, *Stenographische Berichte*, 24 March 1870, pp. 497–98.

131. Vogt, *Die urheberrechtlichen Reformdiskussionen*, 129–30.

132. Michael H. Kater, *Different Drummers: Jazz in the Culture of Nazi Germany* (New York, 1992).

133. Axel Jockwer, "Unterhaltungsmusik im Dritten Reich," (diss., Konstanz, 2004), 192–93.

134. Heymann, "Die Neufassung der Berner Konvention," 105; "NSJ-Entwurf eines neuen Deutschen Urheberschutzgesetzes," 386–87; Julius Kopsch, "Das Urheberrecht bei Schallplatte, Film und Funk," *Deutsches Recht* 6, 7/8 (1936): 155.

135. §13. This was an amplification of the 1870 law (§46) which forbade the verbatim poach-

ing of melodies—but not if they were further developed, as in variations or fantasias. Reichstag des Norddeutschen Bundes, *Stenographische Berichte*, 1870, vol. 4, Aktenstück 138, p. 543.

136. Bruno Marwitz, "Zur Neugestaltung des literarischen Urheberrechts," *Archiv für Urheber- Film- und Theaterrecht* 1 (1928): 10; Sebastian Wündisch, *Richard Wagner und das Urheberrecht* (Berlin, 2004), 35–47.

137. Dr. Bull, "Die Reinheit des Urheberrechts und das musikalische Potpourri," *Deutsche Juristen-Zeitung* 41, 23 (1936): 1412–13; de Boor, "Der NSJ-Entwurf und die Urheberrechtsreform," 426.

138. Gast, "Grundsätzliches zur Stellung der Reichskulturkammer," 339–41.

139. Becker-Bender, *Das Urheberpersönlichkeitsrecht im musikalischen Urheberrecht*, 60. The debate was still being referred to in the postwar period: Eugen Ulmer, *Urheber- und Verlagsrecht*, 3rd ed. (Berlin, 1980), 347.

140. *Amtliche Mitteilungen der Reichsmusikkammer* 17 (16 May 1934): 56.

141. Verordnung des badischen Ministers des Innern über das Singen des Deutschlandliedes und des Horst-Wessel-Liedes, 18 September 1933, *Bad. Gesetz und VBl.*, 193, quoted in Becker-Bender, *Das Urheberpersönlichkeitsrecht im musikalischen Urheberrecht*, 150.

142. Reichsgericht, 1. Zivilsenat, 2 December 1936, *Archiv für Urheber- Film- und Theaterrecht* 10 (1937): 96–100.

143. Gloede, *Reichskulturkammer und Urheberschutz*, 34; de Boor, "Soziale Gebundenheit des Urheberrechts," 1020.

144. Ausschuss für Urheber- und Verlagsrecht, minutes, 16 and 17 February 1934, in Schubert, *Akademie für Deutsches Recht, 1933–1945: Protokolle der Ausschüsse*, 9: 563–64.

145. Hoffmann, *Ein deutsches Urheberrechtsgesetz*, 53.

146. §§39, 35, respectively.

147. "Deutschland: Ministerialentwurf eines Urheberrechtsgesetzes vom 22. January 1934," pp. 785–86, 851–52.

148. 1934, §41.

149. "Gesetz über Vermittlung von Musikaufführungsrechten, 4 July 1933, *Reichsgesetzblatt* 1 (7 July 1933): 452; Hoffmann, *Ein deutsches Urheberrechtsgesetz*, 24.

150. Staatlich genehmigte Gesellschaft zur Verwertung musikalischer Aufführungsrechte. Wertheimer, "Gesetzliche Lizenzen im Urheberrecht," 23–25.

151. Heymann, "Die Neufassung der Berner Konvention," 105; Kopsch, "Das Urheberrecht bei Schallplatte, Film und Funk," 156.

152. H. G. Pridat-Guzatis, "Grundlinien eines nationalsozialistischen Rundfunkrechts," *Deutsches Recht* 5 (1935): 377–78.

153. Adam Tooze, *The Wages of Destruction: The Making and Breaking of the Nazi Economy* (New York, 2006), 147–49. Even TV was in the offing, with a *Fernseh-Volksempfänger* exhibited in 1939. Griffin, *Modernism and Fascism*, 314.

154. Hans Frank, *Nationalsozialistisches Handbuch für Recht und Gesetzgebung* (Munich, 1935), 532; Heinrich Spoerl, "Rechtsleben und Film," *Tag des Deutschen Rechts, 1939: 6. Reichstagung des Nationalsozialistischen Rechtswahrerbundes* (Berlin, 1939), 39.

155. Julius Kopsch, "Filmwerk und Filmschöpfer," *Gewerblicher Rechtsschutz und Urheberrecht* 42 (1937): 332; Steven Bach, *Leni: The Life and Work of Leni Riefenstahl* (New York, 2007).

156. Richard Taylor, *Film Propaganda: Soviet Russia and Nazi Germany* (London, 1998), 146.

157. Marwitz, "Zur Neugestaltung des literarischen Urheberrechts," 6.

158. *Revision of Copyright Laws: Hearings before the Committee on Patents, House of Representatives* (February–April 1936) (Washington DC, 1936), 525.

159. Pascal Kamina, *Film Copyright in the European Union* (Cambridge, 2002), 48.

160. John A. Fagg, *Urheberschaft und Urheberrecht am Film* (Berlin, 1928), 109–12; Hellmut Friedemann, "Grundfragen des Filmrechts," *Archiv für Urheber- Film- und Theaterrecht* 1 (1928):

557–59. A survey of the literature in Fritz Kanzow, *Das Urheberrecht in der Herstellung des Spielfilms* (diss., Jena, 1936), 45.

161. Kopsch, "Das Urheberrecht bei Schallplatte, Film und Funk," 158.

162. §14.

163. Stephen P. Ladas, *The International Protection of Literary and Artistic Property*, (New York, 1938), 1: 448–49.

164. Ordinance of 19 March 1935, arrêt of 16 March 1939, cited in Office Professionnel des Industries et Métiers d'Art et de Creation, *Travaux de la Commission de la propriété intellectuelle* (n.p., 1944–45), 15, 78.

165. Vogt, *Die urheberrechtlichen Reformdiskussionen*, 132–33, 150–51.

166. Contradictory testimony on the numbers of films produced: Horst Richard Pintsch, *Das Urheberrecht am Tonfilm: Ein Beitrag zur neuesten Entwicklung auf dem Gebiete des Urheberrechts am Tonfilm* (Leipzig, 1938), 2; Eberhard Aleff, *Das Dritte Reich*, 4th ed. (Hannover, 1963), 108; Griffin, *Modernism and Fascism*, 305.

167. Kopsch, "Das Urheberrecht bei Schallplatte," 158; Bull, "Der Gemeinnutz im Urheberrecht," 380; Armand von Zelewski, *Das Urheberrecht auf dem Gebiet der Filmkunst: Probleme des künftigen Filmrechtes* (Emsdetten, 1935), 50; "Deutschland: Ministerialentwurf eines Urheberrechtsgesetzes vom 22. Januar 1934," 790–91.

168. Arnold Raether, "Über die Aufgaben des Filmrechtsausschusses bei der Akademie für Deutsches Recht," *Zeitschrift der Akademie für Deutsches Recht* 6 (1935): 388; de Boor, "Zur Reform des Filmrechts," 830; Bruno Pfennig, "Film und Urheberrechtsreform," *Zeitschrift der Akademie für Deutsches Recht* 2 (1935): 828; de Boor, "Soziale Gebundenheit des Urheberrechts," 1020; Wilhelm Schlechtriem, "Die tatsächlichen Grundlagen des Rechts am Film," *Zeitschrift der Akademie für Deutsches Recht* 7 (1936): 713.

169. Werneburg, "Zur Lösung der Fragen von Miturheberrechten an Filmwerken in dem neuen Akademie-Entwurf eines Urhebergesetzes," *Archiv für Urheber- Film- und Theaterrecht* 12 (1939): 356; Elster, "Deutsche Rechtsgedanken im Urheberrecht," 200–201.

170. Meyer, "Die Schöpferpersönlichkeit im kommenden deutschen Urheber- und Verlagsrecht," 158; Pintsch, *Urheberrecht am Tonfilm*, 46–51; Alexander Elster, "Zum Urheberrechtsanspruch des Filmunternehmers," *Gewerblicher Rechtsschutz und Urheberrecht* 40, 10 (1935): 703–4; Julius Kopsch, "Die deutsche und die französische Lehre vom Urheberrecht: Eine Klarstellung zu dem Buch *La Doctrine Française du Droit d'Auteur* von Escarra, Rault und Hepp," *Zeitschrift der Akademie für Deutsches Recht* 4 (1937): 557.

171. Alfred Flemming, "Der künstlerische Film und sein Urheber," *Deutsche Juristen-Zeitung* 41, 12 (1936): 743; Dr. Bull, "Werk oder Ware? Ein Beitrag zur Klärung filmrechtlicher Grundfragen," *Zeitschrift der Akademie für Deutsches Recht* 2 (1935): 839; Walter Schubert, *Das Filmrecht des nationalsozialistischen Staates (unter Ausschluß des Filmarbeitsrechts)* (diss., Kiel, 1939), 32.

172. Julius Kopsch, "Zum Problem des Urheberrechts am Filmwerk," *Archiv für Urheber- Film- und Theaterrecht* 9 (1936): 113; Günther Krauß, "Wer ist der Urheber eines Filmwerkes?" *Deutsche Juristen-Zeitung* 41, 7 (1936): 424–27.

173. §§7, 21. Brandt, *Das "droit moral" als Faktor*, 60–64.

174. Hoffmann, *Ein deutsches Urheberrechtsgesetz*, 32–34.

175. §§5, 10, 21.

176. Oswald Lehnich, "Filmrechtsreform," in Akademie für Deutsches Recht, *Das Recht des schöpferischen Menschen*, 268.

177. "Urheberrecht am Film," *Völkischer Beobachter*, 21 July 1936, p. 2.

178. Justus Koch, "Filmhandschrift und Filmband," *Deutsche Juristen-Zeitung* 41, 19 (1936): 1147–48.

179. Dr. Bull, "Die Sicherung des Filmkredits," *Archiv für Urheber- Film- und Theaterrecht* 7 (1934): 479–80. Deep into the war, such subtle distinctions were still being parsed. Georg Roe-

ber, "Zum Rechtsbegriff 'Filmschaffender,'" *Archiv für Urheber- Film- und Theaterrecht* 16 (1944 [1943]): 401–2.

180. §19b. "Die Neugestaltung des deutschen Urheberrechts," 47–49.

181. *Le Droit d'auteur* (1940), 28.

182. Bundesgesetz über das Urheberrecht an Werken der Literatur und der Kunst und über verwandte Schutzrechte, §§38–39, *Bundesgesetzblatt für den Bundestaat Österreich*, 9 April 1936.

183. Accounts in Walter Bentivoglio, "Bemerkungen zum Filmrecht im neuen italienischen Urheberrechtsgesetz," *Archiv für Urheber- Film- und Theaterrecht* 15 (1942): 94–96; Willy Hoffmann, "Die filmrechtlichen Bestimmungen des neuen italienischen Urheberrechtsgesetzes in rechtsvergleichender Betrachtung," *Archiv für Urheber- Film- und Theaterrecht* 15 (1942): 122–38.

184. Eduardo Piola Caselli, "Le nouveau projet italien de réforme de la loi sur le droit d'auteur," *Le Droit d'auteur* (1939): 127–28, 133.

185. Piola Caselli, "Il Diritto Morale di Autore," 37–38.

186. The rhetoric thus emphasized the leader as an emanation of his people, distinguishing the "dictator," as a concept inherited from the previous individualistic era, from the "Führer." Höhn, "Der Führerbegriff im Staatsrecht," 296–301.

187. Elmar Wadle, *Geistiges Eigentum: Bausteine zur Rechtsgeschichte* (Munich, 2003), 2: 69.

188. Georg Klauer and Philipp Möhring, *Patentgesetz vom 5. Mai 1936* (Berlin, 1937), 122.

189. Ibid., 25.

190. Ibid., 123–24.

191. Wank, *Das Persönlichkeitsrecht des Erfinders*, 15–16.

192. Felix Kaiser, *Erfinder und Patent im neuen Staat* (Berlin, 1934), 5–6, 11–12.

193. Patentgesetz, 5 May 1936, §§3, 4(1), *Reichsgesetzblatt* (1936), 2: 117.

194. Barth, "Persönlichkeit und Volksgemeinschaft," 823–25.

195. Gispen, *Poems in Steel*, 144–45, and passim.

196. A story told in Catharina Maracke, *Die Entstehung des Urheberrechtsgesetzes von 1965* (Berlin, 2003).

197. Quoted in P. Grunebaum-Ballin, *Le Droit moral des auteurs et des artistes* (Paris, 1928), 5.

198. Piola Caselli, "Il Diritto Morale di Autore," 4, 183.

199. Adeney, *Moral Rights*, chap. 3.

200. Fritz Smoschewer, "Das Persönlichkeitsrecht im allgemeinen und im Urheberrecht," *Archiv für Urheber- Film- und Theaterrecht* 3 (1930): 128.

201. Willy Hoffmann, "Gedanken zur Systematik eines deutschen Urheberrechtsgesetzes," *Gewerblicher Rechtsschutz und Urheberrecht* 36 (1931): 706–8.

202. Alexander Elster, "Der Schutz des Geisteswerkes als Ausgleich zwischen Urheber und Allgemeinheit," *Archiv für Urheber- Film- und Theaterrecht* 4 (1931): 217–21.

203. Marwitz, "Zur Neugestaltung des literarischen Urheberrechts," 8–9.

204. Fritz Smoschewer, "Der Persönlichkeitsschutz in der neuesten Urheberrechts-Gesetzgebung des Auslandes und die Lehren für den deutschen Gesetzgeber," *Archiv für Urheber- Film- und Theaterrecht* 1 (1928): 505.

205. Elster, "Der Schutz des Geisteswerkes," 229–31; Georg Müller, "Bemerkungen über das Urheberpersönlichkeitsrecht," *Archiv für Urheber- Film- und Theaterrecht* 2 (1929): 402; Smoschewer, "Das Persönlichkeitsrecht," 127–28.

206. Hoffmann, "Die Staatenvorschläge," 169–70.

207. Ernst Heymann, "Der ewige Schutz der Geisteswerke gegen Entstellung," *Deutsche Juristen-Zeitung* 33 (1928): 278.

208. D. M. Kauschansky, "Evolution des Autorrechts, die moderne Auffassung über soziale Funktion der Erzeugnisse geistiger Tätigkeit und die Forderung des faktischen Schutzes des Autors," *Archiv für Urheber- Film- und Theaterrecht* 6 (1933): 25, 35.

209. Henri Desbois, "L'Évolution des droits de l'auteur en matière de reproduction et d'exécution publique," *Revue trimestrielle de droit civil* 38 (1939): 26–31; Georges Michaélidès-

Nouaros, *Le Droit moral de l'auteur* (Paris, 1935), 81–82. Const. Gheorghiu-Vieriu, *Le Droit moral de l'auteur* (Paris, 1939), gave the strongest version of this collectivist version of moral rights. The theories of Leon Duguit, who saw humans primarily as social beings who existed only in community and who defined property not as a right but as a social function, went in this direction too.

210. Projet de loi sur le droit d'auteur et le contrat d'edition, *Journal Officiel*, Documents, Chambre, 13 August 1936, Annexe 1164, pp. 1706–12.

211. Jean Zay, *Souvenirs et solitude* (Le Rœulx, 1987), 218.

212. Nord describes Zay's reform proposals as the product, not of the Popular Front and its enthusiasm but of the pessimism of the immediate prewar Daladier years. Even if that were true, which seems odd for a reform from 1936, it does not really clear up the curious similarities across so many different ideological regimes. Philip Nord, *France's New Deal: From the Thirties to the Postwar Era* (Princeton, 2010), 240.

213. In the sense that, hoping to keep them content and sedate, Bismarck gave workers social insurance benefits before universal suffrage.

214. *Journal Officiel*, Documents, Chambre, Annexe 3222, 6 December 1937, pp. 229–30.

215. Zay, *Souvenirs et solitude*, 219; *Le Droit d'auteur* (1936), 112; *Journal Officiel*, Annexe 3222, p. 237.

216. *Journal Officiel*, Annexe 3222, p. 229.

217. Ibid., Annexe 1164, p. 1708.

218. Hans Otto de Boor, "Konstruktionsfragen im Urheberrecht," *Archiv für Urheber- Film- und Theaterrecht* 16 (1944): 361.

219. Abdel-Moneim El-Tanamli, *Du droit moral de l'auteur sur son œuvre littéraire et artistique* (Paris, 1943), 85–87; Grunebaum-Ballin, *Le droit moral*, 20.

220. Union Internationale, *Actes de la conférence réunie à Rome*, 237.

221. Arts. 24, 5–6, respectively. Klauer, "Die Urheberrechtskonferenz in Rom," 374.

222. Law of 6 June 1930, §16. *Norsk Lovtidende* 22 (13 June 1930), p. 518. Indeed all the Scandinavian nations forbade demeaning treatment of works even after normal terms of protection had expired. Ruzicka, *Die Problematik eines "ewigen Urheberpersönlichkeitsrechts,"* 101–12.

223. A long list of examples in Torben Lund, *Om Forrringelse af Litteratur- Musik- og Kunstværker: Droit Moral og Undervisningsministeriet* (Copenhagen, 1944).

224. As in Simon Apel, "Das Reichsgericht, das Urheberrecht und das Parteiprogramm der NSDAP," *Zeitschrift für das Juristische Studium* 3, 1 (2010): 141–42; Hefti, "Das Urheberrecht im Nationalsozialismus."

225. Vogt, *Die urheberrechtlichen Reformdiskussionen*, 29.

226. One of the most contentious disputes in the historiography of Nazism has been the extent to which big or other business interests had the party and eventually regime in their pocket. The literature includes Arthur Schweitzer, *Big Business in the Third Reich* (Bloomington, 1964), Henry Ashby Turner, Jr., *German Big Business and the Rise of Hitler* (New York, 1985), Peter Hayes, *Industry and Ideology: IG Farben in the Nazi Era*, 2nd ed. (Cambridge, 2000), Simon Reich, *The Fruits of Fascism: Postwar Prosperity in Historical Perspective* (Ithaca NY, 1990).

227. Schubert, *Das Filmrecht des nationalsozialistischen Staates*, 32.

228. Elster, "Der Schutz des Geisteswerkes als Ausgleich zwischen Urheber und Allgemeinheit."

229. Still, the Nazi insistence on the socially determined nature of authors' rights followed in the tradition of some nineteenth-century German jurists, like Josef Kohler, who thought that property rights were social creations, and Otto von Gierke, who had rejected perpetual intellectual property as an exaggerated individualism that spurned culture and ignored the community. Otto Gierke, *Deutsches Privatrecht* (Leipzig, 1895), 1: 756; Christophe Geiger, *Droit d'auteur et droit du public à l'information* (Paris, 2004), 98.

230. Franz Wieacker, *Wandlungen der Eigentumsverfassung* (Hamburg, 1935), 25.

231. de Boor, "Der NSJ-Entwurf," 439; Brandt, *Das "droit moral" als Faktor im künftigen deutschen Urheberrecht*, 52; Becker-Bender, *Das Urheberpersönlichkeitsrecht im musikalischen Urheberrecht*, 48; Frank, *Nationalsozialistisches Handbuch*, 1027; "NSJ-Entwurf eines neuen Deutschen Urheberschutzgesetzes," 385; Kopsch, "Die deutsche und die französische Lehre," 247; Georg Müller, "Das Urheberpersönlichkeitsrecht im Gesetzentwurfe der Akademie für Deutsches Recht," *Archiv für Urheber- Film- und Theaterrecht* 12 (1939): 255.

232. A thought spelled out explicitly in the pre-Nazi era by one reformer who remained active in the new regime: Smoschewer, "Das Persönlichkeitsrecht," 127–28.

233. Law 5038 of 30 November 1941, *Journal Officiel*, 21 December 1941, p. 5482.

6. THE POSTWAR APOTHEOSIS OF AUTHORS' MORAL RIGHTS

1. Shelly Baranowski, *Strength through Joy: Consumerism and Mass Tourism in the Third Reich* (Cambridge, 2004); Hans Mommsen and Manfred Geiger, *Das Volkswagenwerk und seine Arbeiter im Dritten Reich* (Düsseldorf, 1996); Bernhard Rieger, *The People's Car: A Global History of the Volkswagen Beetle* (Cambridge MA, 2013).

2. General histories include Victoria de Grazia, *Irresistible Empire: America's Advance through Twentieth-Century Europe* (Cambridge MA, 2006); Richard Pells, *Modernist America: Art, Music, Movies and the Globalization of American Culture* (New Haven, 2011).

3. Martin Jay, *The Dialectical Imagination: A History of the Frankfurt School and the Institute of Social Research, 1923–1950* (London, 1973), 217, 248.

4. Stanislas de Gorguette d'Argœuves, *Le Droit moral de l'auteur sur son œuvre artistique ou litteraire* (Paris, 1926), 6–9.

5. Jean Escarra, "The Projected French Law on Artistic and Literary Property," *Revue internationale du droit d'auteur* 5 (October 1954): 32.

6. *Journal Officiel*, Assemblée Nationale, Débats, 21 April 1956, p. 1426; Documents, Annexe 1554, 18 April 1956, p. 1223. Earlier versions: *Journal Officiel*, Documents, Chambre, Annexe 3222, 6 December 1937, pp. 228, 237.

7. *Journal Officiel*, Assemblée Nationale, Débats, 21 April 1956, p. 1426. The same theme, 16 April 1992, pp. 552–53.

8. Examples below in the discussion of the 1965 German law.

9. de Boor, "Urheberrechtliche Grundsatzfragen in Schrifttum und Rechtsprechung," *Archiv für Urheber- Film- Funk- und Theaterrecht* 21, 3/4 (1956): 129, 136.

10. Union Internationale pour la Protection des Œuvres Littéraires et Artistiques, *Documents de la Conférence réunie à Bruxelles du 5 au 26 Juin 1948* (Berne, 1951), 97–98. In addition to the original reports of the meeting, some of the documentation from the Brussels Conference has also been translated in *The Berne Convention for the Protection of Literary and Artistic Works from 1886 to 1986* (Geneva, 1986) and on the website of Sam Ricketson and Jane Ginsburg, *International Copyright and Neighbouring Rights: The Berne Convention and Beyond*, 2nd ed. (Oxford, 2006): http://www.oup.com/uk/booksites/content/9780198259466/. An overview in Elizabeth Adeney, *The Moral Rights of Authors and Performers* (Oxford, 2006), chap. 6.

11. The debate over article 6bis is in Union Internationale, *Documents de la Conférence réunie à Bruxelles*, 184–200. See also Pierre Recht, "A propos de l'article 6bis de la Convention de Berne (droit moral)," *Le Droit d'auteur* 81, 1 (1968): 14–15.

12. Charles A. Marvin, "The Author's Status in the United Kingdom and France: Common Law and the Moral Right Doctrine," *International and Comparative Law Quarterly* 20, 4 (1971): 678.

13. Records of the Intellectual Property Conference of Stockholm, 1967, Report of the Work

of Main Committee 1, p. 299, on the website for Ricketson and Ginsburg, *International Copyright*.

14. Ricketson and Ginsburg, *International Copyright*, 128.

15. Art. 9(1). The problem had been that agreement also required harmony on the exceptions to the author's exclusive rights. This was now regulated in art. 9(2), where nations were allowed to make exceptions to such exclusive rights as long as they did not unreasonably contradict the author's rights to exploit his work. Paul Goldstein, *International Copyright* (New York, 2001), 22–23; Ricketson and Ginsburg, *International Copyright*, 593.

16. Sam Ricketson, "Is Australia in Breach of its International Obligations with Respect to the Protection of Moral Rights?" *Melbourne University Law Review* 17 (1989–90): 474–75.

17. Goldstein, *International Copyright*, 160.

18. Jean Vilbois, "Historique de la loi du 11 mars 1957," *Revue internationale du droit d'auteur* 19 (1958): 33–51; Anne Latournerie, "Petite histoire des batailles du droit d'auteur," *Multitudes* 5 (2001), at http://multitudes.samizdat.net/Petite-histoire-des-batailles-du. Cécile Desprairies, *L'Héritage de Vichy: Ces 100 mesures toujours en vigueur* (Paris, 2012), 120–21 also notes the continuities, but the facts are off.

19. Office Professionnel des Industries et Métiers d'Art et de Creation, *Travaux de la Commission de la propriété intellectuelle* (n.p., 1944–45).

20. Philippe Gaudrat, "The Eternal Quarrels of a Successful Couple: The Creator and the Investor," *Revue internationale du droit d'auteur* 190 (2001): 148.

21. Escarra, "Projected French Law on Artistic and Literary Property," 32. Similar sentiments in Office Professionnel des Industries et Métiers d'Art, *Travaux de la Commission de la propriété intellectuelle*, 7.

22. François Hepp, "L'esprit du nouveau projet de loi français sur la Propriété Littéraire et Artistique," *Archiv für Urheber- Film- Funk- und Theaterrecht* 23, 3/4 (1957): 135–37.

23. Loi no. 57–298 du 11 mars 1957 sur la propriété littéraire et artistique, *Journal Officiel*, 14 March 1957, pp. 2723–30. The hesitations at reintroducing the property concept expressed by some observers close to the bill were not mirrored in the bill itself. Jean Escarra, for example, apologized for use of the concept, insisting that it was but convenient shorthand for a right "in that twilight which reigns between real rights and personal rights." Escarra, "Projected French Law on Artistic and Literary Property," 6. And the various committees contemplated whether a property or a more ethereal authorial right was the correct approach. "Frankreich: Dokumente zur Urheberrechtsreform," *Archiv für Urheber- Film- Funk- und Theaterrecht* 21 (1956): 183–94.

24. François Hepp, "Le droit d'auteur, 'propriété incorporelle'?" *Revue internationale du droit d'auteur* 19 (1958): 163. Similarly, *Journal Officiel*, Documents, Chambre, Annexe 3222, 6 December 1937, p. 233.

25. *Annales du Parlement français*, 20 May 1839, pp. 133, 137; *Archives Parlementaires*, Chambre de Pairs, 25 May 1839, 124: 643.

26. For a general account of the postwar resurgence in continental law of the natural rights property paradigm, Cyrill P. Rigamonti, *Geistiges Eigentum als Begriff und Theorie des Urheberrechts* (Baden-Baden, 2001). For a similar reemergence of the concept in Germany: Georg Roeber, "Urheberrecht oder Geistiges Eigentum," *Archiv für Urheber- Film- Funk- und Theaterrecht* 21, 3/4 (1956): 150–51. For property more generally, Helmut Rittstieg, *Eigentum als Verfassungsproblem: Zu Geschichte und Gegenwart des bürgerlichen Verfassungsstaates* (Darmstadt, 1975), 289–90; Manfred Brocker, *Arbeit und Eigentum: Der Paradigmenwechsel in der neuzeitlichen Eigentumstheorie* (Darmstadt, 1992), 345–46.

27. Henri Desbois, "Le Droit moral," *Revue internationale du droit d'auteur* 19 (1958): 125. Very similar language from the German Supreme Court: *Gema w. Grundig*, Bundesgerichtshof, 18 May 1955, *Entscheidungen des Bundesgerichtshofes in Zivilsachen*, 17: 278.

28. This nature-based view of authors' rights was to continue as received orthodoxy in

French legislation. Discussing a draft law in 1964, the government spokesman described the French approach to authors' rights as recognizing that intellectual property was a "natural right of a universal nature." *Journal Officiel*, Débats, Assemblée nationale, 12 May 1964, p. 1147.

29. Office Professionnel des Industries et Métiers d'Art, *Travaux de la Commission de la propriété intellectuelle*, 21.

30. *Journal Officiel*, Assemblée, Documents, Annexe 8612, 9 June 1954, p. 985.

31. *Journal Officiel*, Assemblée, Documents, Annexe 553, 16 February 1956, p. 344; Vilbois, "Historique," 57; Jacques Isorni, "Le vote de la loi," *Revue internationale du droit d'auteur* 19 (1958): 23–25.

32. Henri Desbois, *Le Droit d'auteur en France*, 3rd ed. (Paris, 1978), 176.

33. Desbois, "Le Droit moral," 147.

34. Elisabeth Logeais, "Post-Mortem Exercise of Copyright in French Law," *Entertainment Law Review* 2 (1991): 186.

35. Pierre Recht, *Le Droit d'auteur, une nouvelle forme de propriété* (Paris, 1969), 140; Desbois, *Le Droit d'auteur en France*, 276–77.

36. *Dalloz, Jurisprudence générale* 2 (1936): 65–70. This decision was confirmed by the Paris Court of Appeal, 23 February 1938, but then overturned by the highest court in its arrêt of 14 May 1945. *Dalloz, Jurisprudence générale* 1 (1945): 285–88; Hepp, "Le droit d'auteur, 'propriété incorporelle'?" 179–81; Adolf Dietz, *Das Droit Moral des Urhebers im neuen französischen und deutschen Urheberrecht* (Munich, 1968), 44–45.

37. A similar provision had recently passed in the law of 25 February 1956, which assigned the Caisse Nationale des Lettres, established in 1946, the task of ensuring respect for literary works after the author's death and even after his works had entered the public domain. *Journal Officiel*, 26 February 1956, p. 2043.

38. Arts. 19–20. *Journal Officiel*, Assemblée, Documents, Annexe 8612, 9 June 1954, p. 985.

39. Louis Vaunois, "Correspondance," *Le Droit d'auteur* 59 (1946): 31.

40. Eugen Ulmer, *Urheber- und Verlagsrecht*, 3rd ed. (Berlin, 1980), 348.

41. *Journal Officiel*, Assemblée, Documents, Annexe 8612, 9 June 1954, p. 985; Annexe 10681, 6 May 1955, p. 836.

42. Art. 29. This was another "breach in the fortress of property" introduced by the law. Desbois, *Le Droit d'auteur en France*, 277.

43. Art. 41. Ricketson and Ginsburg, *International Copyright*, 759.

44. *Journal Officiel*, Assemblée, Documents, Annexe 10681, 6 May 1955, pp. 835–36; Annexe 553, 16 February 1956, p. 345.

45. *Journal Officiel*, Assemblée, Documents, Annexe 8612, 9 June 1954, p. 986.

46. Art. 153. Bernd Rüthers, *Die unbegrenzte Auslegung: Zum Wandel der Privatrechtsordnung im Nationalsozialismus*, 6th ed. (Tübingen, 2005), 351–52.

47. Art. 14(2). Continuities are highlighted in Roeber, "Urheberrecht oder Geistiges Eigentum," 165–66.

48. Heinrich Lehmann, "Die Neuordnung der Güterwelt nach ihrem wahren Lebenswert," in Lehmann et al., *Urheberrechtsreform: Ein Gebot der Gerechtigkeit* (Berlin, 1954), 8.

49. A detailed comparison of existing proposals, intended for use in the postwar reforms, took the late Weimar and Nazi drafts as "valuable earlier material" that was so "modern" that little new would have to be added, and the main task would be to select the best from them. Eduard Reimer, *Vergleichende Darstellung der geltenden deutschen Gesetzestexte und früherer Gesetzesentwürfe zum deutschen Urheberrecht als Grundlage für die Wiederaufnahme der Reformarbeit* (Weinheim/Bergstrasse, 1950), 5.

50. Catharina Maracke, *Die Entstehung des Urheberrechtsgesetzes von 1965* (Berlin, 2003), 54, 60–61, 724–25; Stig Strömholm, *Le Droit moral de l'auteur en droit allemand, français et scandinave* (Stockholm, n.d. [1966]), 462.

51. Bundesrat, Drucksache 1/62, 15 December 1961, pp. 27–28; Eugen Ulmer, "Das neue deutsche Urheberrechtsgesetz," *Archiv für Urheber- Film- Funk- und Theaterrecht* 45, 2 (1965): 19.

52. Alexander Elster was another Weimar jurist who had remained active throughout the Nazi period and whose writings (from before 1933) remained influential deep into the twentieth century. See favorable citations in Eric Pahud, "Zur Begrenzung des Urheberrechts im Interesse Dritter und der Allgemeinheit," *UFITA* (2000): 102, 118. Georg Roeber was also active on both sides of 1945.

53. Bundestag, *Stenographische Berichte*, 6 December 1963, 54: 4640–41. A similar reference in Eugen Ulmer, "Vom deutschen Urheberrecht und seiner Entwicklung," *Archiv für Urheber- Film- Funk- und Theaterrecht* 33, 1/2 (1961): 2.

54. High opinions of the 1965 law: Adolf Dietz, "Germany," in Paul Edward Geller, ed., *International Copyright Law and Practice*, (New York, n.d.), 2: GER-19; Gillian Davies, *Copyright and the Public Interest* (Weinheim, 1994), 121.

55. Hans Günter Hockerts, *Sozialpolitische Entscheidungen im Nachkriegsdeutschland: Aliierte und deutsche Sozialversicherungspolitik 1945 bis 1957* (Stuttgart, 1980).

56. Eugen Ulmer, "Vom deutschen Urheberrecht und seiner Entwicklung," *Archiv für Urheber- Film- Funk- und Theaterrecht* 23, 5/6 (1957): 261.

57. §§12–14, *Bundesgesetzblatt* 51 (16 September 1965).

58. §§41–42, 14, 39.

59. Maracke, *Entstehung des Urheberrechtsgesetzes*, 288.

60. Bundestag, *Stenographische Berichte*, 6 December 1963, 54: 4640–41. Very similar rhetoric in the committee report: Drucksache IV/3401, Bundestag, *Verhandlungen, Anlagen zu den stenographischen Berichten*, 98: 1.

61. Erich Schulze, *Recht und Unrecht: Eine Studie zur Urheberrechtsreform* (Munich, 1954), 5.

62. §31. This followed in the tradition enunciated already in the mid-nineteenth century whereby only the true author had a primal right to the work while all others could be given at most derivative rights. R. Klostermann, *Das geistige Eigenthum an Schriften, Kunstwerken und Erfindungen* (Berlin, 1867), 1: 293; R. Klostermann, *Das Urheberrecht an Schrift- und Kunstwerken* (Berlin, 1876), 105.

63. Dietz, *Das Droit Moral des Urhebers*, 129.

64. Bundesrat, Drucksache 1/62, 15 December 1961, p. 80. Perpetual moral rights, Hans de Boor (who, as an active participant in attempts to reform authors' rights during the Third Reich, knew something about this) warned after the war, would mean an unacceptable control by the state of the nation's spiritual life. De Boor, "Urheberrechtliche Grundsatzfragen in Schrifttum und Rechtsprechung," *Archiv für Urheber- Film- Funk- und Theaterrecht* 21, 3/4 (1956): 135.

65. Maracke, *Entstehung des Urheberrechtsgesetzes*, 73.

66. Dietz, *Das Droit Moral des Urhebers*, 150–51, 175–76, 181; Hauke Sattler, *Das Urheberrecht nach dem Tode des Urhebers in Deutschland und Frankreich* (Göttingen, 2010), 56–59.

67. Thomas Dreier et al., *Urheberrecht auf dem Weg zur Informationsgesellschaft* (Baden-Baden, 1997), 67.

68. §§7, 43, 26, 18, 44, 25, 36.

69. Bundesrat, Drucksache 1/62, 15 December 1961, p. 30.

70. §52. Schulze, *Recht und Unrecht*, 2–3.

71. Rigamonti, *Geistiges Eigentum als Begriff*, 103–7. Though free performances for various publicly valuable purposes were still allowed. Felix Leinemann, *Die Sozialbindung des "Geistigen Eigentums"* (Baden-Baden, 1998), 101–4.

72. *Gema v. Grundig*, Bundesgerichtshof, 18 May 1955, *Entscheidungen des Bundesgerichtshofes in Zivilsachen*, 17: 267. Heinrich Hubmann, "Die Entscheidungen des Bundesverfassungsgerichts zum Schutz des geistigen Eigentums," *Gewerblicher Rechtsschutz und Urheberrecht* (Internationaler Teil) 6/7 (1973): 272–73.

73. §24. Maracke, *Entstehung des Urheberrechtsgesetzes*, 160, 226–28.

74. Drucksache IV/3401, Bundestag, *Verhandlungen, Anlagen zu den stenographischen Berichten*, 98: 12; Heinz Püschel et al., *Urheberrecht der Deutschen Demokratischen Republik* (Berlin, 1969), 33.

75. Ulmer, *Urheber- und Verlagsrecht*, 340; Maracke, *Entstehung des Urheberrechtsgesetzes*, 534–37; Lehmann, "Die Neuordnung der Güterwelt," 12–13; Schulze, *Recht und Unrecht*, 53.

76. Maracke, *Entstehung des Urheberrechtsgesetzes*, 590.

77. §§14, 39, 42.

78. Thorvald Solberg, "The Present Copyright Situation," *Yale Law Journal* 40, 2 (1930): 193–94; Thorvald Solberg, "The International Copyright Union," *Yale Law Journal* 36, 1 (1926): 100–101.

79. The Vestal bill, 1930. HR 12549, House Calendar No. 395, Report No. 2016, 22 May 1930, §28.

80. *International Copyright Union: Hearing before the Committee on Foreign Relations United States Senate . . . on S.1928* (28 March 1934), pt. 1, pp. 10–12.

81. Thorvald Solberg, " La situation internationale du droit d'auteur aux États-Unis," *Le Droit d'auteur* (1935): 13–17.

82. *International Copyright Union: Hearing before the Committee on Foreign Relations United States Senate . . . on S.1928* (28/29 May 1934), pt. 2, pp. 64–65. Similar sentiments in *Revision of Copyright Laws: Hearings before the Committee on Patents, House of Representatives* (February–April 1936), 567–68.

83. *General Revision of the Copyright Law: Hearings before the Committee on Patents, United States Senate . . . on H.R. 12549* (28–29 January 1931), 54.

84. Monika Dommann, "Autoren und Apparate: Copyrights und Medienwandel (1850–1980)," (Habilitationsschrift, Zurich, 2011), 152–56.

85. *Le Droit d'auteur* (1937): 9–11.

86. *International Copyright Union: Hearing . . . on S.1928*, pt. 2, pp. 94–95.

87. *Revision of Copyright Laws: Hearings before the Committee on Patents*, 172.

88. *General Revision of the Copyright Law: Hearings . . . on H.R. 12549*, 184.

89. *Revision of Copyright Laws: Hearings before the Committee on Patents*, 64, 155–56, 159–62, 238, 496–97, and passim.

90. Martin A. Roeder, "The Doctrine of Moral Right: A Study in the Law of Artists, Authors and Creators," *Harvard Law Review* 53, 4 (1940): 558.

91. Isabelle Lehuu, *Carnival on the Page: Popular Print Media in Antebellum America* (Chapel Hill, 2000); Sidney P. Moss, *Charles Dickens' Quarrel with America* (Troy NY, 1984), 21; Susan S. Williams, "Authors and Literary Authorship," in Scott E. Casper et al., eds., *A History of the Book in America* (Chapel Hill, 2007), 3: 92–93.

92. *Le Droit d'auteur* (1930): 109–12.

93. Report 2016, House of Representatives, 24 June 1930, *House Reports*, 2 December 1929–3 July 1930, 4: 2; United States Senate, "Report of Proceedings, Hearings Held before Committee on Patents S. 2465," 8 May 1935, p. 53. Available at: http://www.lexisnexis.com/congcomp /getdoc?HEARING-ID=HRG-1935-PTH-0002.

94. Robert A. Gorman, "Federal Moral Rights Legislation: The Need for Caution," *Nova Law Review* 14 (1990): 423–24.

95. Senate, "Report of Proceedings, Hearings . . . S. 2465," 8 May 1935, p. 53.

96. *General Revision of the Copyright Law: Hearings . . . on H.R. 12549*, 221.

97. *Le Droit d'auteur* (1930): 109–12.

98. *International Copyright Union: Hearing . . . on S.1928*, pt. 2, pp. 86–87. Similarly: *Congressional Record*, Senate, 6 August 1935, p. 12561.

99. *International Copyright Union: Hearing . . . on S.1928*, pt. 2, pp. 74–78.

100. Ibid., pp. 84, 86–87.

101. "Statement of David Ladd on Behalf of the Coalition to Preserve the American Copyright Tradition," in "The Berne Convention: Hearings Before the Subcommittee on Patents, Copyrights and Trademarks of the Committee on the Judiciary . . . on S. 1301 and S. 1971," Senate, 18 February and 3 March 1988, Serial No J-100–49, p. 415.

102. *International Copyright Union: Hearing . . . on S.1928*, pt. 2, pp. 69–70, 74–78; Senate, "Report of Proceedings, Hearings . . . S. 2465," pp. 51–52.

103. *International Copyright Union: Hearing . . . on S.1928*, pt. 2, pp. 76–78.

104. Locke, *Second Treatise*, chap. 5, sect. 27–28; C. B. Macpherson, *The Political Theory of Possessive Individualism* (Oxford, 1962), 214–20.

105. Pascal Oberndörfer, *Die philosophische Grundlage des Urheberrechts* (Baden-Baden, 2005), 36–44.

106. 38 Geo. III. c. 71, s. 1 (1798). Similar wording in 54 Geo. III. c. 56, s. 1 (1814).

107. Copyright Law Amendment Act, 1842, 5 & 6 Vict., c. 45, s. 18. With the qualifications that the owner could not publish the work separately without the actual author's consent and the actual author regained his rights after twenty-eight years.

108. Sect. 5. Continued in the 1988 act, 11(2), 9(3).

109. Catherine L. Fisk, "Authors at Work: The Origins of the Work-for-Hire Doctrine," *Yale Journal of Law and the Humanities* 15 (2003): 32–33, 55; Catherine L. Fisk, *Working Knowledge: Employee Innovation and the Rise of Corporate Intellectual Property, 1800–1930* (Chapel Hill, 2009).

110. Edward C. Walterscheid, *The Nature of the Intellectual Property Clause: A Study in Historical Perspective* (Buffalo, 2002), 377–82.

111. L. Ray Patterson and Stanley W. Lindberg, *The Nature of Copyright* (Athens GA, 1991), 85–86.

112. Jacqueline M. B. Seignette, *Challenges to the Creator Doctrine: Authorship, Copyright Ownership and the Exploitation of Creative Works in the Netherlands, Germany and the United States* (Deventer, 1994), 37.

113. Sects. 201b, 101. "Copyright Law Revision," Senate Report 94–473 (1975), pp. 104–5.

114. Jane C. Ginsburg, "The Concept of Authorship in Comparative Copyright Law," *DePaul Law Review* 52 (2003): 1090–91; Laurent Pfister, "L'auteur, propriétaire de son œuvre? La formation du droit d'auteur du XVIe siecle à la loi de 1957" (diss., Strasbourg, 1999), 829.

115. Friedemann Kawohl, "The Berlin Publisher Friedrich Nicolai and the Reprinting Sections of the Prussian Statute Book of 1794," in Ronan Deazley et al., eds., *Privilege and Property* (Cambridge, 2010), 225.

116. §§1021–22. Martin Löhnig, "Der Schutz des geistigen Eigentums von Autoren im Preußischen Landrecht von 1794," *Zeitschrift für neuere Rechtsgeschichte* 29, 3/4 (2007): 208–9.

117. *Land-Recht des Grossherzogthums Baden* (Karlsruhe, 1809), §577da; Gesetz zum Schutze des literarischen und artistischen Eigenthumes gegen unbefugte Veröffentlichung, Nachdruck und Nachbildung, 19 October 1846, §1 (BK).

118. 1957 law, arts. 9, 13. Pierre-Yves Gautier, *Propriété littéraire et artistique*, 4th ed. (Paris, 2001), 646–48, thinks the distinction is night and day.

119. An anomaly puzzled over by outside observers. Jules-Marc Baudel, *La législation des États-unis sur le droit d'auteur* (Brussels, 1990), 101.

120. Sect. 102(a). "Copyright Law Revision," Senate Report 94–473 (1975), pp. 129–30.

121. Sect. 31, 17.

122. Schedule 1, sect. 12.

123. Patterson and Lindberg, *Nature of Copyright*, 109–10.

124. Sects. 301, 302a. "Copyright Law Revision," Senate Report 94–473 (1975), pp. 112–13.

125. *Salinger v. Random House, Inc.*, 811 F.2d 90 (1987). And in *Harper & Row Publishers, Inc. v. Nation Enterprises*, 471 U.S. 539 (1985), the Supreme Court held that unpublished works enjoy special protection against the fair use defense.

126. Mark A. Fowler, "The Quick in Pursuit of the Dead," in Paul K. Saint-Amour, ed., *Modernism and Copyright* (Oxford, 2011)

127. "The Berne Convention: Hearings . . . on S. 1301 and S. 1971," Serial No. J-100–49, p. 339.

128. *Hansard*, Lords, 30 November 1987, p. 892.

129. Ibid., p. 907.

130. Copyright Act, 1956, 4 & 5 Eliz. 2, c. 74, sect.13.

131. 1956 act, sect. 1; 1988 act, sects. 9, 77.

132. Copyright and Related Rights Regulations 1996, sects. 77(1) and 80(1).

133. US 1976 Copyright Act §201(b).

134. Pascal Kamina, *Film Copyright in the European Union* (Cambridge, 2002), 155–56.

135. Conversely, if the director had in fact not contributed to the artistic direction of the film but only followed the producer's instructions, then he could be denied his authorial claims by being considered a "simple exécutant." This from a case in Poitiers in 1999. Ginsburg, "Concept of Authorship in Comparative Copyright Law," 1072.

136. *Journal Officiel*, Assemblée Nationale, Documents, Annexe No. 8612; Débats, June 9, 1954, p. 985; Raymond Sarraute, "Current Theory on the Moral Right of Authors and Artists under French Law," *American Journal of Comparative Law* 16, 4 (1968): 474; Escarra, "Projected French Law on Artistic and Literary Property," 12.

137. Arts. 9, 13, 17, 16.

138. *Journal Officiel*, Débats, Assemblée, 21 April 1956, p. 1427.

139. *Journal Officiel*, Débats, Conseil, 30 October 1956, p. 2123; 31 October 1956, p. 2153.

140. Maracke, *Entstehung des Urheberrechtsgesetzes*, 62. *Spielleiter* is ambiguous, as is German terminology on this point generally, with *Régisseur* able to mean both director and producer. But the context here (the possibility that he would not have contributed artistically to the film) would seem to indicate that producer was meant. In British English, too, "producer" was sometimes used in the theatrical sense to mean director. Kamina, *Film Copyright in the European Union*, 28.

141. Bundestag, *Stenographische Berichte*, 6 December 1963, 54: 4641; Maracke, *Entstehung des Urheberrechtsgesetzes*, 112, 166, 207–8.

142. §§89, 90, 93.

143. Law of 3 July 1985, *Journal Officiel* (4 July 1985):7495.

144. Art. 63–1 changed art. 17 in the 1957 law in this respect. David Saunders, "Bridging the Channel? It's Copyright in France but Moral Right in the UK," *Copyright World* 1 (1988): 22. The other articles mentioned are 17, 4, 3, 21, 26.

145. Jane C. Ginsburg, "Reforms and Innovations Regarding Authors' and Performers' Rights in France: Commentary on the Law of July 3, 1985," *Columbia-VLA Journal of Law and the Arts* 10 (1985): 87–90.

146. Bernard Edelman, "Une loi substantiellement internationale: La loi du 3 juillet 1985 sur les droits d'auteur et droits voisins," *Journal du Droit International* 3 (1987); David Saunders, "Approaches to the Historical Relations of the Legal and the Aesthetic," *New Literary History* 23, 3 (1992): 516–17; David Saunders, "Some Implications of the 1985 French Law on Author's Rights," in Peter Anderson and Saunders, eds., *Moral Rights Protection in a Copyright System* (Brisbane, 1992), 57–58. More examples cited in Carolyn McColley, "Limitations on Moral Rights in French *Droit d'auteur*," *Copyright Law Symposium* 41 (1998): 427–28.

147. Bernard Edelman, *Droits d'auteur droits voisins: Droit d'auteur et marché* (Paris, 1993), 285; Edelman, "Commentaire de la loi no. 85–660 du 3 juillet 1985 relative aux droits d'auteur et aux droits voisins," *Actualité Législative Dalloz* 5 (1987): 20.

148. F. Pollaud-Dulian, "Moral Rights in France through Recent Case Law," *Revue internationale du droit d'auteur* 145 (1990): 130. As a government report later noted, these were but exceptions to a basic authorial right that remained unchanged. Assemblée Nationale, Rapport 2349, 7 June 2005, p. 37.

149. Council Directive 91/250/EEC, 14 May 1991, art. 2, *Official Journal of the European Communities*, L122 (17 May 1991): 44.

150. Directive 96/9/EC, 11 March 1996, *Official Journal*, L77 (27 March 1996): 20, recital 28, 29, art. 4.

151. Law 94–361, 10 May 1994, art. 3, *Journal Officiel* (11 May 1994): 6863.

152. On Canada: Ysolde Gendreau, "Moral Rights," in Gordon F. Henderson, ed., *Copyright and Confidential Information Law of Canada* (Scarborough, 1994), 161ff; Adeney, *The Moral Rights of Authors and Performers*, chap. 11.

153. Jane C. Ginsburg, "Moral Rights in a Common Law System," in Anderson and Saunders, *Moral Rights Protection in a Copyright System*, 17.

154. Board of Trade, "Report of the Copyright Committee," vol. 9, ¶¶ 219–226; Gerald Dworkin, "The Moral Right and English Copyright Law," *IIC: International Review of Industrial Property and Copyright Law* 12 (1981): 478.

155. Cyrill P. Rigamonti, "The Conceptual Transformation of Moral Rights," *American Journal of Comparative Law* 55 (2007): 72–73; Cyrill P. Rigamonti, "Deconstructing Moral Rights," *Harvard International Law Journal* 47, 2 (2006): 379–80 and passim; William Strauss, "The Moral Right of the Author," Study No. 4, in *Copyright Law Revision: Studies Prepared for the Subcommittee on Patents, Trademarks, and Copyrights of the Committee on the Judiciary* (US Senate, 86th Congress, 2nd sess., Pursuant to S. Res. 240, 1961), 141–42; William Strauss, "The Moral Right of the Author," *American Journal of Comparative Law* 4, 4 (1955): 537–38.

156. Broadly the conclusion of Russell J. DaSilva, "Droit Moral and the Amoral Copyright: A Comparison of Artists' Rights in France and the United States," *Bulletin of the Copyright Society* 28, 1 (1980); Neil Netanel, "Alienability Restrictions and the Enhancement of Author Autonomy in United States and Continental Copyright Law," *Cardozo Arts & Entertainment Law Journal* 12, 1 (1994). Also unflinching in its acceptance that authorial rights other than the economic simply concerned the Anglophones less is David Saunders, *Authorship and Copyright* (London, 1992), chaps. 5, 6.

157. *Minutes of the Evidence Taken before the Royal Commission on Copyright*, c.2036-I, (London, 1878), 108, 111–12.

158. *Minutes of Evidence Taken before the Law of Copyright Committee*, Cd 5051 (1910), 26.

159. Minutes, 31 May 1905, "Stenographic Report of the Proceedings of the First Session of the Conference on Copyright," in E. Fulton Brylawski and Abe Goldman, eds., *Legislative History of the 1909 Copyright Act* (South Hackensack, 1976), 1: 50.

160. *Revision of Copyright Laws: Hearings before the Committee on Patents*, 501–2.

161. The second half of *Blandings Castle* gives a good selection.

162. The headings in Edward J. Damich, "The Right of Personality: A Common-Law Basis for the Protection of the Moral Rights of Authors," *Georgia Law Review* 23, 1 (1988): 41ff. On moral rights in copyright systems generally, there is a large literature, including Robert C. Hauhart, "Natural Law Basis for the Copyright Doctrine of Moral Rights," *Catholic Lawyer* 30, 1 (1985); Živan Radojković, "The Historical Development of 'Moral Right,'" *Copyright: Monthly Review of the United International Bureaux for the Protection of Intellectual Property (BIRPI)* 2, 6 (1966).

163. Const. Gheorghiu-Vieriu, *Le Droit moral de l'auteur* (Paris, 1939), 136.

164. Fine Art Copyright Act, 1862, 25 & 26 Vict. c. 68, s.7. Background in Ronan Deazley, "Breaking the Mould? The Radical Nature of the Fine Art Copyright Bill 1862," in Deazley et al., *Privilege and Property*.

165. *Hansard*, Lords, 22 May 1862, p. 2019 (BK).

166. Goldstein, *International Copyright*, 289–90; Jon Baumgarten et al., "Preserving the Genius of the System: A Critical Examination of the Introduction of Moral Rights into United States Law," *Copyright Reporter: Journal of the Copyright Society of Australia* 8, 3 (1990): 4.

167. Thomas Paine, *A Letter Addressed to the Abbe Raynal on the Affairs of North America* (London, 1817), v.

168. *Prince Albert v. Strange*, 2 DeGex & Sm. 652, 64 ER 293, 1849.

169. *Chamberlain v. Feldman*, 89 N.E. 2d 863 (1949). *Salinger v. Random House*, 650 F. Supp. 413 (1986) was a similar instance.

170. §202. James M. Treece, "American Law Analogues of the Author's 'Moral Right,'" *American Journal of Comparative Law* 16, 4 (1968): 488–93.

171. Strauss, "Moral Right of the Author," 531. In the US, the closest analogy came with Howard Hughes's attempts to block a biography by buying copyrights of articles used as source material and withholding permission for their use. Jon M. Garon, "Normative Copyright: A Conceptual Framework for Copyright Philosophy and Ethics," *Cornell Law Review* 88 (2003): 1303–4. Although that was a third party trying to withdraw works from the public's vantage the difference from an author (and not just a copyright owner) attempting the same is slight.

172. *Southey v. Sherwood* (1817) 2 Mer 435, p. 439; *Chaplin v. Leslie Frewin (Publishers) Ltd.* [1966] Ch. 71.

173. Goldstein compares it to the right to repent: Goldstein, *International Copyright*, 156, 290.

174. *Byron v. Johnston*, 28 November 1816, *English Reports*, 35: 851.

175. Michael Newbury, *Figuring Authorship in Antebellum America* (Stanford, 1997), 195–96.

176. *Drummond v. Altemus*, Circuit Court, E.D. Pennsylvania, 23 January 1894, *Federal Reporter* 60 (April–May 1894): 338–39.

177. *Clemens v. Press Publishing*, 67 Misc. 183, 122 N.Y. Supp. 206 (1910).

178. *Vargas v. Esquire, Inc*, 164 F.2d 522, C.O. Bull. 26, 433 (1947).

179. *Siegel v. National Periodical Publications*, 508 F.2d 909 (2d Cir. 1974), discussed in Harold C. Streibich, "The Moral Right of Ownership to Intellectual Property: Part II—From the Age of Printing to the Future," *Memphis State University Law Review* 7 (1976–77): 79. Their story is told in Brad Ricca, *Superboys: The Amazing Adventures of Jerry Siegel and Joe Schuster—The Creators of Superman* (New York, 2013).

180. 1911 act, sect. 19; 1976 act, sect. 115.

181. Report 1188, 21 May 1886, *Reports of Committees of the Senate* (1885–86), 92–93.

182. *Revision of Copyright Laws: Hearings before the Committee on Patents*, 516–17.

183. Senate, "Report of Proceedings, Hearings ... S. 2465," p. 50.

184. *Edinburgh Review* 33 (1820): 79–80.

185. The Committee on Patents and the Patent Office, 25th Cong., 2nd sess., 25 June 1838, Senate Report 494, p. 4 (BK).

186. "Memorials of John Jay and of William C. Bryant and Others, In Favor of an International Copyright Law," 30th Cong, 1st sess., 22 March 1848, House of Representatives, Miscellaneous No. 76, pp. 4–5 (BK).

187. Amanda Foreman, *A World on Fire: Britain's Crucial Role in the American Civil War* (New York, 2010), 26.

188. H. C. Carey, *Letters on International Copyright*, 2nd ed. (New York, 1868), 62–63, 68; Michael Winship, "'The Greatest Book of Its Kind': A Publishing History of 'Uncle Tom's Cabin,'" *Proceedings of the American Antiquarian Society* 109, 2 (1999): 316.

189. Aubert J. Clark, *The Movement for International Copyright in Nineteenth Century America* (Washington DC, 1960), 50; Leone Levi, "Copyrights and Patents," *Princeton Review* (1878): 763.

190. Report on H.R. 10881 (1890), 51st Cong., 1st sess., 1890, House Rep. 2401, pp. 10–25.

191. *General Revision of the Copyright Law: Hearings ... on H.R. 12549*, 206. Similar testimony: *Congressional Record*, Senate, 31 July 1935, p. 12188; Report 2016, House of Representatives, 24 June 1930, *House Reports*, 2 December 1929–3 July 1930, 4: 3–4.

192. *General Revision of the Copyright Law: Hearings ... on H.R. 12549*, p. 221.

193. *International Copyright Union: Hearing ... on S.1928*, pt. 1, pp. 8–9.

194. *Hansard*, Lords, 12 November 1987, p. 1506. Indeed, the rest of the EU tried to piggyback

on this British market share by claiming that exceptions allowed in American copyright legislation to play radio and TV broadcasts in retail and food establishments cut into royalties that would otherwise have been due European authors. The evidence of the size of the infringement rested on the assumption that the size of the US market for European music was uniformly as great as the 23 percent share of US record sales held by UK performers in 1988—an unlikely extrapolation. World Trade Organization, "United States—Section 110(5) of the US Copyright Act: Report of the Panel," WT/DS160/R, 15 June 2000, p. 60.

195. "Copyright and Designs Law: Report of the Committee to consider the Law on Copyright and Designs," Cmnd. 6732, *Parliamentary Papers* (House of Commons and Command), 24 November 1976–26 October 1977, vol. 7, §§51–57; Dworkin, "Moral Right and English Copyright Law," 490–91; Strömholm, *Le Droit moral de l'auteur*, 430.

196. Copyright, Designs and Patents Act 1988, c. 48.

197. Jane Ginsburg, "Moral Rights in a Common Law System," *Entertainment Law Review* 4 (1990): 128. Rigamonti goes so far as to claim that the formal introduction of moral rights in the UK and the US actually lessened authors' protection. Rigamonti, "Deconstructing Moral Rights," 399–410. Similar sentiments: Peter Stone, *Copyright Law in the United Kingdom and the European Community* (London, 1990), 131; Irini A. Stamatoudi, "Moral Rights of Authors in England: The Missing Emphasis on the Role of Creators," *Intellectual Property Quarterly* 1 (1997): 505–6; Sheila J. McCartney, "Moral Rights under the United Kingdom's Copyright, Designs and Patents Act of 1988," *Columbia-VLA Journal of Law & the Arts* 15 (1991).

198. *Hansard*, Commons, 28 April 1988, pp. 568–70; 25 July 1988, pp. 177–78; Lords, 12 November 1987, pp. 1503, 1525. See also Hazel Carty and Keith Hodkinson, "Copyright, Designs and Patents Act 1988," *Modern Law Review* 52, 3 (1989): 372–73; Gerald Dworkin, "Moral Rights and the Common Law Countries," *Australian Intellectual Property Journal* 5, 1 (1994): 19.

199. *Hansard*, Commons, 25 July 1988, pp. 183–84.

200. An overly reductionist account of the law's formulation, attributing most of its features to the strength of the publishing industry and ignoring the extent to which it also stood in a long British tradition of skepticism about the French version of authors' rights is in Vincent Porter, "The Copyright Designs and Patents Act 1988: The Triumph of Expediency over Principle," *Journal of Law and Society* 16, 3 (1989).

201. *Hansard*, Commons, 25 July 1988, p. 181.

202. *Hansard*, Lords, 12 November 1987, p. 1476.

203. *Hansard*, Lords, 25 February 1988, p. 1337.

204. W.R. Cornish, "Moral Rights under the 1988 Act," *European Intellectual Property Review* 12 (1989): 450; Dworkin, "Moral Rights and the Common Law Countries," 22.

205. *Hansard*, Lords, 10 December 1987, pp. 375–76.

206. Sects. 79, 81, 87, 94, 78.

207. Porter, "Copyright Designs and Patents Act 1988," p. 344.

208. "Correspondence Respecting the Formation of an International Copyright Union," *House of Commons Parliamentary Papers*, C.4606 (1886), 55

209. "Berne Convention Implementation Act of 1987," Serial No. 50, p. 2.

210. Ibid., p. 182. Very similar wording in Statement of Donald J. Quigg, Acting Commissioner for Patents and Trademarks, *U.S. Adherence to the Berne Convention: Hearings before the Subcommittee on Patents, Copyrights and Trademarks of the Committee on the Judiciary*, Senate, 16 May 1986 and 15 April 1986, Serial No. J-99–25, p. 119.

211. Edward J. Damich, "State 'Moral Rights' Statutes: An Analysis and Critique," *Columbia-VLA Journal of Law & the Arts* 13 (1989): 293–94.

212. California Resale Royalties Act, 1977. Because it sought to control sales outside California, a judge declared it in violation of the commerce clause of the US Constitution in 2012. *New York Times*, 21 May 2012.

213. Clayton Yeutter to Robert W. Kastenmeier, *Congressional Record*, House, 10 May 1988, p. 10323.

214. "Berne Convention Implementation Act of 1988," House of Representatives, Report 100–609 (6 May 1988), pp. 18–19. Also *Congressional Record*, House, 10 May 1988, p. 10324; Senate, 2 March 1995, p. 6554.

215. Gail E. Evans, "Intellectual Property as a Trade Issue: The Making of the Agreement on Trade-Related Aspects of Intellectual Property Rights," *World Competition* 18, 2 (1994): 144; "US Trade in Goods and Services—Balance of Payments (BOP) Basis," http://www.census.gov /foreign-trade/statistics/historical/gands.pdf.

216. By 1998 intellectual property was the third-largest US export, accounting for almost 6 percent of total GDP, with the copyright industries providing 5 percent of total workforce employment and employing more than the four leading noncopyright manufacturing sectors combined. *Congressional Record*, Senate, 20 March 1997, p. 4573. Congress relied on reports produced regularly by Stephen E. Siwek and various collaborators. The most recent is *Copyright Industries in the US Economy: The 2006 Report*, available at http://www.iipa.com/pdf/2006 _siwek_full.pdf.

217. Commission of the European Communities, *Green Paper on Copyright and the Challenge of Technology: Copyright Issues Requiring Immediate Action*, COM (88) 72 final, 7 June 1988, pp. 171–72.

218. "The Berne Convention Implementation Act of 1988," Senate Report 100–352, 20 May 1988, p. 2.

219. "The Berne Convention: Hearings . . . on S. 1301 and S. 1971," Serial No. J-100–49, pp. 41–42.

220. *U.S. Adherence to the Berne Convention: Hearings before the Subcommittee on Patents, Copyrights and Trademarks of the Committee on the Judiciary*, Senate, 16 May 1985 and 15 April 1986, Serial No. J-99–25, p. 374.

221. "The Berne Convention: Hearings . . . on S. 1301 and S. 1971," Serial No. J-100–49, pp. 259, 283–90, 295–99, 331. And as we have seen, even when the 1988 act later passed, it did precious little to curtail waivers.

222. "The Berne Convention: Hearings . . . on S. 1301 and S. 1971," Serial No. J-100–49, pp. 340–43, 417.

223. Ibid., pp. 348–49, 378, 384–85, 392–93, 397–98; "Berne Convention Implementation Act of 1987," Serial No. 50, pp. 332–33, 401.

224. A mangled version of this curiously pointless fear reappeared some years later in an EC 1995 green paper: Commission of the European Communities, *Green Paper: Copyright and Related Rights in the Information Society*, COM (95) 382 final, 19 July 1995, p. 65. But, on the other hand, the possibility of new movies with old actors was taken seriously. Joseph J. Beard, "Casting Call at Forest Law: The Digital Resurrection of Deceased Entertainers—A 21st Century Challenge for Intellectual Property Law," *High Technology Law Journal* 8 (1993).

225. Quoted in "The Right to Cultural Heritage: Film Preservation and the Law," at http:// savestarwars.com/righttoculturalheritage.html.

226. "The Berne Convention: Hearings . . . on S. 1301 and S. 1971," Serial No. J-100–49, pp. 479, 525–27, 542, 502–3, 495.

227. "Final Report of the Ad Hoc Working Group on US Adherence to the Berne Convention," *Columbia-VLA Journal of Law and the Arts* 10 (1985–86): 547; "Berne Convention Implementation Act of 1987," Serial No. 50, pp. 312–17.

228. "The Berne Convention: Hearings . . . on S. 1301 and S. 1971," Serial No. J-100–49, pp. 41–42, 174; "Berne Convention Implementation Act of 1988," Report 100–609, pp. 7, 10.

229. Berne Convention Implementation Act of 1988, Pub. L. 100–568, 102 Stat. 2853 (1988).

230. "The Berne Convention Implementation Act of 1988," Senate Report 100–352, 20 May 1988, p. 4.

231. Some formalities remained. Affixation of copyright notice, though optional, could affect monetary recovery for infringement. Failure to make required deposit subjected copyright owners to a fine. Timely registration was required for a copyright owner to receive statutory damages and attorney's fees for infringement. Goldstein, *International Copyright*, 188–90.

232. Ricketson and Ginsburg, *International Copyright*, 613; Jane C. Ginsburg and John M. Kernochan, "One Hundred and Two Years Later: The US Joins the Berne Convention," *Columbia-VLA Journal of Law and the Arts* 13 (1988): 30–31; Ginsburg, "Moral Rights in a Common Law System," 18.

233. Public Law 100–446.

234. Public Law 102–307. Despite later attempts to beef things up, no reforms passed. Adeney, *Moral Rights of Authors*, 464–67.

235. Visual Artists Rights Act of 1990 (VARA), codified at 17 U.S.C. §§101, 102, 106(a), 107, 601. A good discussion in Robert A. Gorman, "Visual Artists Rights Act of 1990," *Journal of the Copyright Society of the USA* 38, 4 (1991).

236. Though the Swiss Urheberrechtsgesetz of 9 October 1992, art. 15(1), requires the owner of a work he intends to destroy to offer it to the author, demanding no more than its material value in return.

237. Adolf Dietz, "Les Etats-Unis et le droit moral: idiosyncrasie ou rapprochement," *Revue internationale du droit d'auteur* 142 (1989): 232–34.

238. Bernard Edelman, "Entre copyright et droit d'auteur: L'intégrité de l'œuvre de l'esprit," *Recueil Dalloz Sirey* 40 (1990): 300.

239. On NAFTA, Goldstein, *International Copyright*, 51. On TRIPs, Terence P. Stewart, ed., *The GATT Uruguay Round: A Negotiating History (1986–1992)* (Deventer, 1993), 2: 2288–89; Duncan Matthews, *Globalizing Intellectual Property Rights: The TRIPs Agreement* (London, 2002), 50–51. On the WIPO Performances and Phonograms Treaty, see Goldstein, *International Copyright*, 43, 277; Ricketson and Ginsburg, *International Copyright*, 173–74, 1252–59.

240. P.-J. Proudhon, *Les majorats littéraires* (Paris, 1868), 19.

241. John Feather, "The Book Trade in Politics: The Making of the Copyright Act of 1710," *Publishing History* 8 (1980): 35.

242. Adolphe Breulier, *Du droit de perpétuité de la propriété intellectuelle* (Paris, 1855), 16.

243. Senate, Report 6187, 5 February 1907, p. 38; J. Kohler, *Das Autorrecht, eine zivilistische Abhandlung* (Jena, 1880), 49. In 1842 Denmark, Sweden, and Norway were also reported as having perpetual protection. *Hansard*, Commons, 6 April 1842, p. 1373.

244. Reichstag, *Stenographische Berichte*, 3 May 1910, p. 2856, Spahn. The same argument, put conversely, in *Hansard*, Commons, 7 April 1911, p. 2636, George Roberts.

245. Union Internationale pour la protection des œuvres littéraires et artistiques, *Actes de la conférence réunie à Rome du 7 Mai au 2 Juin 1928* (Berne, 1929), 166.

246. *Hansard*, Commons, 5 February 1841, p. 349. "It is very probable, that in the course of some generations, land in the unexplored and unmapped heart of the Australian continent, will be very valuable. But there is none of us who would lay down five pounds for a whole province in the heart of the Australian continent. We know, that neither we, nor anybody for whom we care, will ever receive a farthing of rent from such a province. And a man is very little moved by the thought that in the year 2000 or 2100 somebody who claims through him will employ more shepherds than Prince Esterhazy, and will have the finest house and gallery of pictures at Victoria or Sydney."

247. *Archives Parlementaires*, Chambre de Pairs, 27 May 1839, 124: 715.

248. Depending on assumptions about the discount rate, the increased value varied from 0.1 to 5.4 percent. "The Copyright Term Extension Act of 1995: Hearing before the Committee on the Judiciary . . . on S. 483," 20 September 1995, Senate Hearing 104–817, Serial No. J-104–46, pp. 78–89. A version of this testimony is also in Dennis S. Karjala, "Comment of US Copyright Law Professors on the Copyright Office Term of Protection Study," *European Intellectual Prop-*

erty Review 16, 12 (1994). Very similar logic reigned in the amicus curiae brief to the Supreme Court filed in *Eldred v. Ashcroft*: George A. Akerlof et al., "The Copyright Term Extension Act of 1998: An Economic Analysis," No 01–618, 20 May 2002. Available at http://cyber.law.harvard.edu/openlaw/eldredvashcroft/supct.amici/economists.pdf.

249. Wilhelm Freiherrn v. Weckbecker, "Richard Wagner, Johann Strauss und die Schutzfrist," *Archiv für Urheber- Film- und Theaterrecht* 3 (1930): 473.

250. *Congrès littéraire international de Paris 1878: Comptes rendus in extenso et documents* (Paris, 1879), 214–15; Recht, *Le Droit d'auteur*, 241–43.

251. Jacob Grimm, "Rede auf Schiller" (1859) in his *Kleinere Schriften* (Berlin, 1864), 1: 396. Background in Elmar Wadle, *Geistiges Eigentum: Bausteine zur Rechtsgeschichte* (Munich, 2003), 2: 155ff.

252. *Congressional Record*, House, 7 October 1988, p. 24336.

253. *Minutes of Evidence Taken before the Law of Copyright Committee* , p. 36. But a last gasp of such arguments could be heard in the UK during debate on the 1956 act: *Hansard*, 4 June 1956, pp. 749–51.

254. Jules Mareschal, *Les Droits d'auteur et le droit du public relativement aux œuvres de l'esprit* (Paris, 1866), 8–9, 15–16.

255. Édouard Romberg, ed., *Compte rendu des travaux du Congrès de la propriété littéraire et artistique* (Brussels, 1859), 1: ii–iii.

256. Maracke, *Entstehung des Urheberrechtsgesetzes*, 121–23, 130, 155; Leinemann, *Sozialbindung des "Geistigen Eigentums,"* 47–49; Roeber, "Urheberrecht oder Geistiges Eigentum," 184–85; Peter Ruzicka, *Die Problematik eines "ewigen Urheberpersönlichkeitsrechts" unter besonderer Berücksichtigung des Schutzes musikalischer Werke* (Berlin, 1979), 74–78. Earlier examples: R. Dalidou, "Du droit d'auteur," *Mercure de France* 286 (15 September 1938): 761; Ernst Heymann, "Die zeitliche Begrenzung des Urheberrechts," *Sitzungsberichte der Preussischen Akademie der Wissenschaften* (1927), 59.

257. Records of the Intellectual Property Conference of Stockholm, 1967, Report of the Work of Main Committee 1, pp. 298–300, on the website for Ricketson and Ginsburg, *International Copyright*; Ruzicka, *Die Problematik eines "ewigen Urheberpersönlichkeitsrechts,"* 4.

258. Frédéric Pollaud-Dulian, *Le Droit d'auteur* (Paris, 2005), 299–300. In a more moderated way in Desbois, *Le Droit d'auteur en France*, 416. Intellectual property is property, and only because of "totally extrinsic economic and social reasons" does it not last forever. François Hepp, "L'esprit du nouveau projet de loi français sur la Propriété Littéraire et Artistique," *Archiv für Urheber- Film- Funk- und Theaterrecht* 23, 3/4 (1957): 140. By comparison, at the turn of the century, some French jurists rejected perpetuity even in theory: Gustave Huard, *Traité de la propriété intellectuelle* (Paris, 1903), 1: 78–79.

259. B. Zorina Khan, *The Democratization of Invention: Patents and Copyrights in American Economic Development, 1790–1920* (Cambridge, 2005), 237.

260. Only 15 percent of existing copyrights were renewed. Barbara A. Ringer, "Renewal of Copyright," *Studies on Copyright* 1 (1963): 617. That varied from 70 percent of films down to 7 percent of books and less than 1 percent of technical drawings. "Copyright Law Revision: Report of the Register of Copyrights on the General Revision of the US Copyright Law," 87th Congress, 1st sess., House Committee Print, July 1961, p. 51.

261. *Report of the Committee on the Law of Copyright*, Cd 4976 (London, 1909), 16. With one squawk on behalf of the public and its interest in short terms, p. 31.

262. Thomas Jefferson to James Madison, 6 September 1789, Julian P. Boyd, ed., *The Papers of Thomas Jefferson* (Princeton, 1958), 15: 392–97.

263. Jacques Boncompain, *La Révolution des auteurs (1773–1815)* (n.p., 2001), 862.

264. Décret Impérial contenant Réglement sur l'Imprimerie et la Librarie, No. 5155, 5 February 1810, art. 39 (BK).

265. Commission de la propriété littéraire, *Collection des procès-verbaux* (Paris, 1826), 329; *Annales du Parlement français*, 20 May 1839, p. 135.

266. Commission de la propriété littéraire et artistique, *Rapports à l'empereur, Décrets, Collection des procès-verbaux* (Paris, 1863), 251–52.

267. Pollaud-Dulian, *Le Droit d'auteur*, 306–7.

268. Dominique Eril, "D'Artaud à Zorn: 26 histoires d'héritage," *Lire* 138 (1987): 41. Otto Preminger could make *Carmen Jones* in 1954, and the French ban it, because, thanks to wartime extensions, *Carmen* remained protected in France until 1972. Ferdinand Roger, "The 'Carmen Jones Affair,'" *Revue internationale du droit d'auteur* 8 (1955): 6.

269. Generally, Rigamonti, *Geistiges Eigentum als Begriff*.

270. Heymann, "Die zeitliche Begrenzung des Urheberrechts," 74–77, 112.

271. Klostermann, *Das geistige Eigenthum an Schriften*, 1: 277.

272. Johann Caspar Bluntschli, *Deutsches Privatrecht* (Berlin, 1853), 1: 194, 201.

273. "Erklärung über die Schutzfrist des Urheberrechtes," *Sitzungsberichte der Preussischen Akademie der Wissenschaften* (1927), 44–55.

274. Heymann, "Die zeitliche Begrenzung des Urheberrechts," 90–96.

275. Among the few examples of authors' rights being curtailed in the course of legislative development, other than in the Soviet Union, are the Zay proposal in France in 1936 and the UK 1911 act. In both cases it depends on how to evaluate the shift from exclusive rights to a mixture of these and a period of compulsory licensing. Arguably the 1911 act shortened the author's exclusive rights from a maximum of forty-two (if the author died promptly after publishing) to twenty-five years. Also, the EU Database Directive of 1996 harmonized at a middle level, rather than at the most generous standard of originality. Brad Sherman and Lionel Bently, "Balance and Harmony in the Duration of Copyright: The European Directive and Its Consequences," in Patrick Parrinder and Warren Chernaik, eds., *Textual Monopolies: Literary Copyright and the Public Domain* (London, 1997), 35.

276. Claude Masouyé, "Vers une prolongation de la durée générale de protection," *Revue internationale du droit d'auteur* 24 (1959): 101.

277. Stephen P. Ladas, *The International Protection of Literary and Artistic Property* (New York, 1938), 1: 329–30.

278. Union Internationale, *Actes de la conférence réunie à Rome*, 164–65.

279. 1985 law, art. 8. The argument was that investment in serious music would produce returns only with a long term. Silke von Lewinski, "EC Proposal for a Council Directive Harmonizing the Term of Protection of Copyright and Certain Related Rights," *International Review of Industrial Property and Copyright Law* 23 (1992): 789.

280. Commission of the European Communities, *Follow-up to the Green Paper: Working Programme of the Commission in the Field of Copyright and Neighbouring Rights*, COM (90) 584 final, Brussels, 17 January 1991, p. 19.

281. Explicit among the motivations here was the desire to prompt nations other than Germany to offset the exploitation losses of the war generations. Council Directive 93/98/EEC, 29 October 1993, *Official Journal*, L290 (24 November 1993): 9, recital 6. A few grumbles were heard, for example, from a Danish MEP who thought that the extension meant "considering the interests of the dead above those of the living." *Official Journal*, 1992–93, No. 3–423 (26 October 1992): 27.

282. Council Directive 93/98/EEC, 29 October 1993, *Official Journal*, L290 (24 November 1993): 9, recital 5.

283. Joëlle Farchy, *Internet et le droit d'auteur: La culture Napster* (Paris, 2003), 35.

284. Sherman and Bently, "Balance and Harmony in the Duration of Copyright," 27–28.

285. "Copyright Law Revision," Senate Report 94–473 (1975), pp. 118–19.

286. Though, technically, the beloved rodent was trademarked, which meant he was protected for as long as Disney made good use of him.

287. As Attorney General Theodore Olson rather haplessly spelled it out during oral arguments before the Supreme Court in the case that tested the constitutionality of the extension, the copyright clause "provides incentives not just for . . . the creators, but to the disseminators, the publishers, the broadcasters, the film companies." *Eldred v. Ashcroft*, transcript of oral arguments before the Supreme Court, No. 01–618, 9 October 2002, p. 32.

288. Michele Boldrin and David K. Levine, *Against Intellectual Monopoly* (Cambridge, 2008), 100.

289. *Congressional Record*, House, 7 October 1998, p. 24334.

290. Ibid., p. 24336. Also, *Congressional Record*, Senate, 20 March 1997, p. 4569.

291. *Congressional Record*, Senate, 20 March 1997, p. 4573. "With so many of our trading partners moving to the longer term but preparing to recognize American works for only the shorter term, I believe it is time for us to act." Senator Leahy, p. 4575.

292. Neil Weinstock Netanel, "Copyright and a Democratic Civil Society," *Yale Law Journal* 106, 2 (1996): 367; Jessica Litman, *Digital Copyright* (Amherst, 2001), 32. For a complete misunderstanding of the simple numbers of such extensions, see Philippe Quéau, "Intérêt général et propriété intellectuelle," in Olivier Blondeau and Florent Latrive, eds., *Libres enfants du savoir numérique* (n.p., 2000), 167.

293. However, the US protected sound recordings for longer, ninety-five years from the date of publication, while in Europe this was fifty from the event that triggered protection for related rights. On the other hand, the "homestyle" exception for smallish food and retail establishments limited the amounts actually collected by rights holders for broadcasts in the US. Thus, while broadcast rights lasted for only fifty years in Europe and ninety-five in the US, and since only digital radio broadcasts were protected in the US, while all forms of radio were protected in Europe, it has been estimated that (with 70 percent of food and drink and 45 percent of retail establishments exempted) total revenues collected in the US may not have been more than in the EU. *Gowers Review of Intellectual Property* (December 2006): 49–50.

294. "The Copyright Term Extension Act of 1995: Hearing . . . on S. 483," Senate Hearing 104–817, p. 12; Goldstein, *International Copyright*, 244.

295. Farchy, *Internet et le droit d'auteur*, 158.

296. http://www.imdb.com/list/2RfGaIYkZPc/?start=251&view=compact&sort=listorian :asc.

297. Scott M. Martin, "The Mythology of the Public Domain: Exploring the Myths Behind Attacks on the Duration of Copyright Protection," *Loyola of Los Angeles Law Review* 36 (2002): 284–85.

298. Arts. 5 and 7(8).

299. Council Directive 93/98/EEC, 29 October 1993, art. 7, *Official Journal*, L290 (24 November 1993): 9. This counter-Berne principle of applying the standard of the originating nation, not that in which protection was sought, had been implemented in the 1993 Satellite and Cable Directive and was voiced again in the 1995 EC Green Paper on copyright. Stephen Fraser, "The Copyright Battle: Emerging International Rules and Roadblocks on the Global Information Infrastructure," *John Marshall Journal of Computer and Information Law* 15 (1997): 784–85.

300. "The Copyright Term Extension Act of 1995: Hearing . . . on S. 483," Senate Hearing 104–817, pp. 1–2.

301. Dotan Oliar, "Making Sense of the Intellectual Property Clause: Promotion of Progress as a Limitation on Congress's Intellectual Property Power," *Georgetown Law Journal* 94 (2006), and Oliar, "The (Constitutional) Convention on IP: A New Reading," *UCLA Law Review* 57 (2009).

302. Report 2222, 22 February 1909, *House Reports* (60th Congress, 2nd sess.) (Washington DC, 1909), p. 7. "The enacting of copyright legislation . . . is not based upon any natural right that the author has in his writings, . . . but upon the ground that the welfare of the public will be served."

303. *General Revision of the Copyright Law: Hearings . . . on H.R. 12549*, p. 24. Very similar claim in *Fox Film Corp v. Doyal*, 286 U.S. 123 (1931), p. 127.

304. *Fox Film Corp v. Doyal*, 286 U.S. 123 (1931), p. 127.

305. *Twentieth Century Music Corp v. Aiken*, 422 U.S. 151 (1975), p. 156.

306. *Sony Corporation v. Universal City Studios, Inc.*, 464 U.S. 417 (1984), p. 429.

307. "Berne Convention Implementation Act of 1988," Report 100–609, p. 17.

308. Information Infrastructure Taskforce, *Intellectual Property and the National Information Infrastructure: The Report on the Working Group on Intellectual Property Rights* (September 1995), 20–23; "Report of the Register of Copyrights on the General Revision of the US Copyright Law," July 1961, 87th Congress, 1st sess., p. 6, quoted in Lucie M.C.R. Guibault, "Contracts and Copyright Exemptions," in P. Bernt Hugenholtz, ed., *Copyright and Electronic Commerce: Legal Aspects of Electronic Copyright Management* (London, 2000), 154–55; *United States v. Paramount Pictures, Inc.*, 334 U.S. 131 (1948); *Congressional Record*, 60th Congress, 2nd sess., vol. 43, N 67, House of Representatives, 3 March 1909, p. 3850.

309. Stephen Breyer, "The Uneasy Case for Copyright: A Study of Copyright in Books, Photocopies, and Computer Programs," *Harvard Law Review* 84, 2 (1970): 285–86.

310. Joint Committee on the Library, Report 409, 7 February 1873, 42nd Congress, 3rd sess., reprinted in *Congressional Record*, 50th Congress, 1st sess., vol. 19, pt. 4, Senate, 30 April 1888, p. 3510.

311. *Feist Publications, Inc. v. Rural Telephone Service Co.*, 449 U.S. 340 (1991), p. 349.

312. *Eldred v. Ashcroft*, 537 U.S. 186 (2003), p. 212, nt. 18.

313. *Congressional Record*, House, 7 October 1988, p. 24336. Compare this assumption, that the more reward the more creativity, with the restatement of the traditional logic by Lawrence Lessig, a vociferous defender of the virtues of a limited copyright system: "The term should be as long as necessary to give incentives to create, but no longer." Lawrence Lessig, *Free Culture: The Nature and Future of Creativity* (New York, 2004), 292.

314. WIPO, *Guide to the Berne Convention for the Protection of Literary and Artistic Works* (Geneva, 1978), 3. In the same manner, the Digital Millennium Copyright Act of 1998 shifted the pricing structure of compulsory licenses for digital transmission from the traditional basis of a fair return for owners to an unabashed market rate. Neil Weinstock Netanel, *Copyright's Paradox* (New York, 2008), 79–80.

315. *Congressional Record*, Senate, 20 March 1997, p. 4576.

316. "Copyright Term Extension Act of 1996," Senate Report 104–315, 10 July 1996, pp. 29–36. He was quoting Dennis Karjala, "The Copyright Term Extension Act of 1995: Hearing . . . on S. 483," Senate Hearing 104–817, p. 88. A book-length argument against the extension was presented in Robert L. Bard and Lewis Kurlantzick, *Copyright Duration: Duration, Term Extension, the European Union and the Making of Copyright Policy* (San Francisco, 1999).

317. "Copyright Term Extension Act of 1996," Senate Report 104–315, 10 July 1996, pp. 25–28.

318. "The term should be long enough to provide an incentive for the author, ie. to encourage him to create by giving him the assurance that, if successful, his economic reward will be adequate." James J. Guinan, Jr., "Duration of Copyright," Study No. 30, in *Copyright Law Revision: Studies Prepared for the Subcommittee on Patents, Trademarks, and Copyrights of the Committee on the Judiciary* (Senate, 86th Congress, 2nd sess., pursuant to S. Res. 240, 1961), p. 74.

319. Meredith L. McGill, "Copyright," in Robert A. Gross and Mary Kelly, eds., *A History of the Book in America* (Chapel Hill, 2010), 2: 204.

320. Geo. Haven Putnam, *The Question of Copyright*, 2nd ed. (New York, 1896), vii.

321. *Arguments before the Committees on Patents of the Senate and House of Representatives, conjointly, on the Bills S. 6330 and H.R. 19853, to Amend and Consolidate the Acts Respecting Copyright*, 7, 8, 10, and 11 December 1906, pp. 116–17.

322. "It is basic to our economic system that profits in this area should be gained by more efficient manufacture, better distribution and the like, rather than by perpetual protection,

once the purpose of the protection for a limited time has been achieved." Guinan, Jr., "Duration of Copyright," 65, 74–75. "I do not see why authors feel that so long a term is necessary for their well being. The normal ambition of an individual today is to provide for himself and his spouse during their old age and to educate his children. I question the social utility of contributing to the support of even a posthumous child until he is forty-nine years old." Ibid., 101.

323. "Copyright Law Revision," Senate Report 94–473 (1975), p. 117; "Copyright Law Revision," House of Representatives Report 94–1476 (1976), pp. 134–35.

324. Council Directive 93/98/EEC, 29 October 1993, *Official Journal*, L290 (24 November 1993): 9, recital 3. Some such logic also seems to have been behind the German extension of terms to seventy in 1965. Sattler, *Das Urheberrecht nach dem Tode*, 24, 33.

325. Achilles C. Emilianides, "The Author Revived: Harmonisation without Justification," *European Intellectual Property Review* 12 (2004): 540; Patrick Parrinder, "The Dead Hand of European Copyright," *European Intellectual Property Review* 15 (1993): 393.

326. Though in the US the trend for children to be born later in marriage was adduced by Senator Orrin Hatch. And Alan Menken, a film score composer, pointed to the tendency for parents to support children for longer. "The Copyright Term Extension Act of 1995: Hearing ... on S. 483," Senate Hearing 104–817, pp. 3, 44.

327. Ibid., p. 74.

328. Mr. Justice Laddie, "Copyright: Over-strength, Over-regulated, Over-rated?" *European Intellectual Property Review* 18 (1996): 256; *Eldred v. Ashcroft*, 537 U.S. 186 (2003), p. 263.

329. von Lewinski, "EC Proposal for a Council Directive Harmonizing the Term of Protection," 789. If one seriously wanted to ensure benefits for two generations of descendants, the remedy would therefore be prohibitions of transfers by authors or the first generation of descendants and/or stronger termination rights allowing authors and descendants to win back rights from assignees. "The Copyright Term Extension Act of 1995: Hearing ... on S. 483," Senate Hearing 104–817, p. 86.

330. "The Copyright Term Extension Act of 1995: Hearing ... on S. 483," Senate Hearing 104–817, p. 2.

331. *Congressional Record*, Senate, 2 March 1995, p. S3393.

332. In the case that tested the constitutionality of the term extension, Attorney General Theodore Olson signaled that the government's position was protection for one generation of heirs. "We have a copyright term that's consistent with the concept of the creator plus the creator's first generation heirs." *Eldred v. Ashcroft*, transcript of oral arguments before the Supreme Court, No. 01–618, 9 October 2002, p. 47.

333. *Archives Parlementaires de 1787 à 1860*, Convention nationale, 19 July 1793, 69: 186; Honoré de Balzac, "Pro Aris et Focis. Lettre adressée aux écrivains du XIXe siècle," *Revue de Paris*, n.s. 11 (1834): 63.

334. Alfred de Vigny, "De mademoiselle Sédaine et de la propriété littéraire: Lettre à messieurs les Députés" (1841), in his *Œuvres complètes* (Paris, 1950), 1: 908–9.

335. Étienne Blanc, *Traité de la contrefaçon*, 4th ed. (Paris, 1855), 124.

336. *Journal Officiel*, Documents, Chambre, Annexe 3222, 6 December 1937, p. 248.

337. John Feather, "Authors, Publishers and Politicians: The History of Copyright and the Book Trade," *European Intellectual Property Review* 10, 12 (1988): 380; John Feather, "Publishers and Politicians: The Remaking of the Law of Copyright in Britain, 1775–1842. Part II: The Rights of Authors," *Publishing History* 25 (1989): 47.

338. *Moniteur Universel*, 14 March 1841, p. 634. A law that prevented an author from transmitting his works to his family would be against nature, Breulier argued. Breulier, *Du droit de perpétuité de la propriété intellectuelle*, 80.

339. "The Copyright Term Extension Act of 1995: Hearing ... on S. 483," Senate Hearing 104–817, p. 55. Others who testified in this vein included Alan Menken, Don Henley, Carlos Santana, Henry Mancini's widow, Ginny, and Arnold Schoenberg's grandson, the copyright

lawyer Randol, who was later to win prominence by wresting Klimt's portrait of Adele Bloch-Bauer from the Austrian government, thus allowing Ronald Lauder to buy it for his Neue Gallerie.

340. Contrast the opinion of the radical free-trader Booth during discussions of the 1911 bill in the UK on whether Adam Smith's *Wealth of Nations* should have enjoyed fifty years of copyright, when he asked whether it should be "in the power of degenerate descendants or trustees to prevent the masses from having a cheap edition." *Hansard*, Commons, 7 April 1911, p. 2658.

341. "Copyright Term Extension Act of 1996," Senate Report 104–315 (10 July 1996), pp. 37–38. Similar complaints about welfare for the rentier generations of copyright descendants in "The Copyright Term Extension Act of 1995: Hearing ... on S. 483," Senate Hearing 104–817, p. 86.

342. "Copyright Term Extension Act of 1996," Senate Report 104–315 (10 July 1996), pp. 10–11.

343. "Amending the Copyright Law in Implementation of the Universal Copyright Convention," Senate Report No. 1936, 19 July 1954, Calendar No. 1931, p. 2.

344. These provisions therefore raised no controversy at the time. *Congressional Record*, House, 29 November 1994, p. 29611.

345. 17 U.S.C. 104a.

346. Robert Spoo, "Copyright Protectionism and Its Discontents: The Case of James Joyce's *Ulysses* in America," *Yale Law Journal* 108 (1998): 660. Matters were even more complicated in the UK when *Ulysses*'s protection was extended. Victoria King, "James Joyce's 'Ulysses'—A Case of Preparatory Manuscripts and Revived Copyright," *Entertainment Law Review* 13 (2002): 86–90.

347. In at least two instances this retroactive expansion of copyright was challenged. In 2011 the Supreme Court agreed to review a lower court decision on the matter. Anthony T. Falzone, representing the challengers to the law, argued that Congress had thus taken speech rights of all Americans and "turned them into the private property of foreign authors, all on the bare possibility that might put more money in the pocket of some US authors." *International Herald Tribune*, 7 October 2011, p. 21. In January 2012 the Supreme Court rebuffed this challenge. *Golan v. Holder*, 565 U.S. XX (2012).

348. Parrinder, "The Dead Hand of European Copyright," 392; Patrick Parrinder, "Licensing Scholarship: Some Encounters with the Wells Estate," in Parrinder and Chernaik, *Textual Monopolies*, 57; Matthew Rimmer, "Bloomsday: Copyright Estates and Cultural Festivals," *SCRIPT-ed* 2, 3 (2005): 348–49. The Gowers Report recommended as a principle that term and scope of protection not be altered retrospectively. *Gowers Review of Intellectual Property* (December 2006), recommendation 4, p. 57.

349. Catherine Seville, "Copyright's Bargain—Defining Our Terms," *Intellectual Property Quarterly* 3 (2003): 327–28.

350. Council Directive 93/98/EEC, 29 October 1993, *Official Journal*, L290 (24 November 1993): 9, recital 27. Examples of authors dragged back into copyright in Saint-Amour, ed., *Modernism and Copyright*, 3–4.

351. Leinemann, *Die Sozialbindung des "Geistigen Eigentums,"* 119–20.

352. *Journal Officiel*, Assemblée, Documents, Annexe 553, 16 February 1956, p. 345. That the 1957 law's protection of works by virtue of creation alone was intended as a conscious antithesis to the American system is common opinion in the literature. Dietz, *Das Droit Moral des Urhebers*, 43. And the deputies themselves made this clear: *Journal Officiel*, Assemblée, Documents, Annexe 8612, 9 June 1954, p. 985; Annexe 10681, 6 May 1955, p. 836.

353. Art. 6. And a short-lived decree of 30 August 1792 had also added formalities. Stef van Gompel, "Les formalités sont mortes, vive les formalités! Copyright Formalities and the Reasons for their Decline in Nineteenth Century Europe," in Deazley et al., *Privilege and Property*, 161. Napoleon's Décret Impérial contenant Réglement sur l'Imprimerie et la Librairie, No. 5155, 5 February 1810, art. 48 required that publishers deposit five copies of works. Law of 9 May 1925, art. 22.

354. *Marie c. Lacordaire*, Cour d'appel de Lyon, 17 July 1845, *Dalloz, Jurisprudence générale* 1 (1845): 128.

355. 5 & 6 Will. IV. c. 65(a), (1835), s. 5.

356. Arthur Underhill, *An Encyclopedia of Forms and Precedents* (London, 1904), 5: 325.

357. Perhaps, as two experts argue, this followed from a perverse reading of the Berne Convention, turning a mandate for authors into an obligation to claim authorship in order to make the right enforceable. Ricketson and Ginsburg, *International Copyright*, 326.

358. Hazel Carty and Keith Hodkinson, "Copyright, Designs and Patents Act 1988," *Modern Law Review* 52, 3 (1989): 372.

359. *Hansard*, Lords, 12 November 1987, p. 1536.

360. "Berne Convention Implementation Act of 1987," Serial No. 50, pp. 232–33.

361. Lewis Hyde, *Common as Air: Revolution, Art and Ownership* (New York, 2010), 58–59. For other examples of this trend, see Ysolde Gendreau, "Intention and Copyright Law," in Frédéric Pollaud-Dulian, ed., *The Internet and Authors' Rights* (London, 1999), 8ff; Laurence R. Helfer and Graeme W. Austin, *Human Rights and Intellectual Property* (Cambridge, 2011), 206–11.

362. Arguments in favor of formalities in Lessig, *Free Culture*, 287–89; Lawrence Lessig, *The Future of Ideas: The Fate of the Commons in a Connected World* (New York, 2002), 240–61; Lessig, "Little Orphan Artworks," *New York Times*, 20 May 2008.

363. Matthew Rimmer, *Digital Copyright and the Consumer Revolution: Hands Off My iPod* (Cheltenham, 2007), 51–52. This was a reasonable assumption given that historically, the percentage of works whose copyright had been renewed back when that was required ranged only between 3 and 22 percent. William Patry, *Moral Panics and the Copyright Wars* (New York, n.d.), 68–69.

364. Authors' rights, as the Tribunal civil de la Seine ruled in 1936, are incompatible with the rules that govern community property. *Dame Canal c. Jamin*, Tribunal civil de la Seine, 1 April 1936, *Dalloz, Jurisprudence générale* 2 (1936): 70.

7. AMERICA TURNS EUROPEAN: THE BATTLE OF THE BOOKSELLERS REDUX IN THE 1990s

1. Though even here corporations were not too proud to invoke moral rights when to their advantage. Thus Microsoft claimed a moral right in its software when justifying why it hampered use of non-Microsoft browsers in Windows. *US v. Microsoft* (1998), discussed in Jonathan Band and Masanobu Katoh, *Interfaces on Trial 2.0* (Cambridge MA, 2011), 65–66.

2. Peter Suber, *Open Access* (Cambridge MA, 2012), 47.

3. Though this was not unprecedented. Rival formats of books, cheap and expensive editions, did much the same in the nineteenth century. Indeed, Balzac argued for perpetual literary property on the basis that authors could both receive absolute rights to works and the public interest still be upheld by ensuring that works were issued in different editions, formats, and prices and targeted at different audiences. Honoré de Balzac, "Notes sur la propriété littéraire" (1841) in his *Œuvres completes* (Paris, 1872), 22: 317.

4. Commission of the European Communities, "The Management of Copyright and Related Rights in the Internal Market," COM (2004) 261 final, 16 April 2004, p. 10. Trotter Hardy, "Property (and Copyright) in Cyberspace," *University of Chicago Legal Forum* (1996): 235–38; Jörg Reinbothe and Silke von Lewinski, *The WIPO Treaties 1996* (n.p., 2002), 140.

5. Diane Leenheer Zimmerman, "Authorship without Ownership: Reconsidering Incentives in a Digital Age," *DePaul Law Review* 52 (2003): 1124–26; Raymond Shih Ray Ku, "The Creative Destruction of Copyright: Napster and the New Economics of Digital Technology," *University of Chicago Law Review* 69 (2002): 312–13.

6. Michael Kretschmer, "Digital Copyright: The End of an Era," *European Intellectual Property Review* 25, 8 (2003): 333–41; Roberto Verzola, "Cyberlords: The Rentier Class of the Information Sector," in Josephine Bosma et al., eds., *Readme! Filtered by Nettime: ASCII Culture and the Revenge of Knowledge* (Williamsburgh Station, 1999), 95; Neil Weinstock Netanel, *Copyright's Paradox* (New York, 2008), 208–9; Jane C. Ginsburg, "Copyright and Control over New Technologies of Dissemination," *Columbia Law Review* 101 (2001): 1642–43; Assemblée Nationale, Rapport 2349, 7 June 2005, pp. 29–31, and see chapter 8.

7. Information Infrastructure Taskforce, *Intellectual Property and the National Information Infrastructure: The Report on the Working Group on Intellectual Property Rights* (September 1995), 52–53; Commission of the European Communities, "Green Paper: Copyright and Related Rights in the Information Society," COM (95) 382 final, 19 July 1995, pp. 25–26, 50, 72; David Lefranc, "The Metamorphosis of *Contrefaçon* in French Copyright Law," in Lionel Bently et al., eds., *Copyright and Piracy* (Cambridge, 2010), 71–74.

8. Melissa de Zwart, "A Historical Analysis of the Birth of Fair Dealing and Fair Use: Lessons for the Digital Age," *Intellectual Property Quarterly* 11 (2007): 62, 90. An analysis and criticism of this approach in Stephen M. McJohn, "Fair Use and Privatization in Copyright," *San Diego Law Review* 35 (1998).

9. Codified in the US in the 1976 Copyright Act, sect. 109.

10. Susan Eilenberg, "Mortal Pages: Wordsworth and the Reform of Copyright," *English Literary History* 56, 2 (1989): 353.

11. Jane C. Ginsburg, "How Copyright Got a Bad Name for Itself," *Columbia Journal of Law and the Arts* 26 (2002): 63.

12. National Telecommunications and Information Administration, "Report to Congress: Study Examining 17 USC Sections 109 and 117 Pursuant to Section 104 of the Digital Millennium Copyright Act," March 2001, in *The Digital Millennium Copyright Act: Text, History, and Caselaw* (Silver Spring, 2003), 459–60.

13. *New York Times*, 8 March 2013, p. B1.

14. *Congressional Record*, House, 4 August 1998, p. 18777. 17 U.S.C. § 109(b). Computer Software Rental Amendments Act of 1990.

15. Council Directive 91/250/EEC, 14 May 1991, art. 4, *Official Journal of the European Communities*, L122 (17 May 1991): 42; Council Directive 92/100/EEC, 19 November 1992, *Official Journal*, L346 (27 November 1992): 61. EU documents can usually be found by searching their titles or numbers on the internet. A good collection can also be had at the University of Pittsburgh's Archive of European Integration, http://aei.pitt.edu/view/eudocno/.

16. Although it did allow an exemption used in the US and elsewhere when rentals did not impair exclusive rights of reproduction. David Nimmer, "The End of Copyright," *Vanderbilt Law Review* 48 (1995): 1388; Manfred Rehbinder and Alesch Staehelin, "Das Urheberrecht im TRIPs-Abkommen: Entwicklungsschub durch die New Economic World Order," *UFITA: Archiv für Urheber- Film- Funk- und Theaterrecht* 127 (1995): 20.

17. In 1827 Kramer had foreseen the issue. He argued that if it were possible to sell a book that was physically impossible to copy, buyers—if warned about this beforehand—would generally not refuse to buy it. And then authors could sell them, for an extra fee, the right to copy from the work. Wilhelm August Kramer, *Die Rechte der Schriftsteller und Verleger* (Heidelberg, 1827), 130.

18. Randall Stross, "Publishers vs. Libraries," *New York Times*, 26 December 2011; "Literary Labours Lent," *Economist*, 28 July 2012.

19. Jason Mazzone, *Copyfraud and Other Abuses of Intellectual Property Law* (Stanford, 2011), chap. 6; Jane C. Ginsburg, "From Having Copies to Experiencing Works: The Development of an Access Right in US Copyright Law," in Hugh Hansen, ed., *US Intellectual Property Law and Policy* (Cheltenham, 2006), 40–42.

20. The EU Information Society Directive of 2001 permitted private copying so long as

owners were compensated. Directive 2001/29/EC, 22 May 2001, art. 5(2), *Official Journal*, L167 (22 June 2001): 10. The French law of 1985 had introduced the right to make private copies, as had the 1965 German law, art. 53.1.

21. Jane C. Ginsburg, "Reforms and Innovations Regarding Authors' and Performers' Rights in France: Commentary on the Law of July 3, 1985," *Columbia-VLA Journal of Law and the Arts* 10 (1985): 92–95.

22. *Sony Corp of America v. Universal City Studios, Inc.*, 464 U.S. 417 (1984), pp. 440–42.

23. *Gema w. Grundig*, Bundesgerichtshof, 18 May 1955, *Entscheidungen des Bundesgerichtshofes in Zivilsachen*, 17: 280–81.

24. Jessica Litman, "The Story of *Sony v. Universal Studios*: Mary Poppins Meets the Boston Strangler," in Jane C. Ginsburg and Rochelle Cooper Dreyfuss, eds., *Intellectual Property Stories* (New York, 2006), 386–87.

25. Zachary Leader, *Revision and Romantic Authorship* (Oxford, 1996), 72.

26. Oxford, 2004, and London, 1967. Further scholarship in this vein on Shakespeare includes Gary Taylor and John Jowett, *Shakespeare Reshaped, 1606–1623* (Oxford, 1993), M.W.A. Smith, "The Authorship of Acts I and II of *Pericles*: A New Approach Using First Words of Speech," *Computers and the Humanities* 22 (1988); James J. Marino, *Owning William Shakespeare: The King's Men and Their Intellectual Property* (Philadelphia, 2011), 41–45; Laura J. Rosenthal, "(Re)Writing Lear: Literary Property and Dramatic Authorship," in John Brewer and Susan Staves, eds., *Early Modern Conceptions of Property* (London, 1995). Similar ideas for music: J. Peter Burkholder, "The Uses of Existing Music: Musical Borrowing as a Field," *Notes* 50, 3 (1994).

27. Christopher Aide, "A More Comprehensive Soul: Romantic Conceptions of Authorship and the Copyright Doctrine of Moral Right," *University of Toronto Faculty of Law Review* 48, 3 (1990): 225.

28. Roland Dumas, *La Propriété littéraire et artistique* (Paris, 1987), 120–25.

29. Kathy Bowrey, "Copyright, the Paternity of Artistic Works, and the Challenge Posed by Postmodern Artists," *Intellectual Property Journal* 8 (1993–94): 316.

30. *New York Times Magazine*, 24 January 2010, p. 38.

31. Paul Edward Geller, "Must Copyright Be For Ever Caught between Marketplace and Authorship Norms?" in Brad Sherman and Alain Strowel, eds., *Of Authors and Origins* (Oxford, 1994), 180.

32. John Updike, "The End of Authorship," *New York Times*, 25 June 2006; Susan Cheever, "Just Google 'Thou Shall Not Steal,'" *Newsday*, 11 December 2005; Mark Helprin, "A Great Idea Lives Forever: Shouldn't Its Copyright?" *New York Times*, 20 May 2007, p. 12; Scott Turow et al., "Would the Bard Have Survived the Web?" *New York Times*, 14 February 2011; *New York Review of Books*, 26 March 2009, p. 49.

33. Henry Hansmann and Marina Santilli, "Authors' and Artists' Moral Rights: A Comparative Legal and Economic Analysis," *Journal of Legal Studies* 26, 1 (1997): 107. Other examples: Jon Baumgarten et al., "Preserving the Genius of the System: A Critical Examination of the Introduction of Moral Rights into United States Law," *Copyright Reporter: Journal of the Copyright Society of Australia* 8, 3 (1990): 12.

34. Marjorie Perloff, "Conceptual Bridges/Digital Tunnels: Kenneth Goldsmith's *Traffic*," in her *Unoriginal Genius: Poetry by Other Means in the New Century* (Chicago, 2010); Kenneth Goldsmith, *Uncreative Writing* (New York, 2011).

35. Vanessa Place, *Tragodía 1: Statement of Facts* (Los Angeles, 2010).

36. Dorothy Pennington Keziah, "Copyright Registration for Aleatory and Indeterminate Musical Compositions," *Bulletin of the Copright Society of the USA* 17, 5 (1970): 311–20.

37. Louis Vaunois, "Le Droit moral: Son évolution en France," *Le Droit d'auteur* 65 (1952): 67.

38. Indeed, some have argued that moral rights should go to the audience, the ultimate determinant of the work, not the author. Tom G. Palmer, "Are Patents and Copyrights Morally

Justified? The Philosophy of Property Rights and Ideal Objects," *Harvard Journal of Law and Public Policy* 13, 3 (1990): 848.

39. "Exposure '94: A Proposal for the New Rule of Intellectual Property for Multimedia," Institute of Intellectual Property (Feb. 1994), 14–15, 18. Bjork's 2011 album, *Biophilia*, allowed users to interact with the music, including limited remixing. No doubt this footnote will soon be out of date.

40. Jon A. Baumgarten, "On the Case against Moral Rights," in Peter Anderson and David Saunders, eds., *Moral Rights Protection in a Copyright System* (Brisbane, 1992), 87.

41. Thomas P. Heide, "The Moral Right of Integrity and the Global Information Infrastructure: Time for a New Approach?" *UC Davis Journal of International Law and Policy* 2 (1996): 227.

42. Joseph R. Slaughter, "It's Good to Be Primitive," in Paul K. Saint-Amour, ed., *Modernism and Copyright* (Oxford, 2011), 290–91.

43. André Françon, "Protection of Artists' Moral Rights and the Internet," in Frédéric Pollaud-Dulian, ed., *The Internet and Authors' Rights* (London, 1999), 79; Alain Strowel and Nicolas Ide, "Liability with Regard to Hyperlinks," *Columbia-VLA Journal of Law and the Arts* 24 (2001): 416–17, 428–29.

44. Françoise Benhamou and Joëlle Farchy, *Droit d'auteur et copyright*, 2nd ed. (Paris, 2009), 59.

45. Marjut Salokannel and Alain Strowel, "Study Contract concerning Moral Rights in the Context of the Exploitation of Works through Digital Technology," ETD/99/B5–3000/E°28, April 2000, pp. 208–9; Séverine Dusollier, "Some Reflections on Copyright Management Information and Moral Rights," *Columbia Journal of Law and the Arts* 25 (2003): 390.

46. Pollaud-Dulian, *The Internet and Authors' Rights*, vii; André Lucas, *Droit d'auteur et numérique* (Paris, 1998), 232.

47. Pierre Sirinelli, "The Adaptation of Copyright in the Face of New Technology," *WIPO Worldwide Symposium on the Future of Copyright and Neighboring Rights* (Geneva, 1994), 44–46.

48. "Green Paper," COM (95) 382 final, p. 65.

49. Amy M. Adler, "Against Moral Rights," *California Law Review* 97 (2009).

50. Guy Pessach, "The Author's Moral Right of Integrity in Cyberspace: A Preliminary Normative Framework," *International Review of Industrial Property and Copyright Law* 34 (2003): 252.

51. Adolf Dietz, "Transformation of Authors' Rights: Change of Paradigm," *Revue internationale du droit d'auteur* 138 (October 1988): 38–42; Adolf Dietz, "The Concept of Author under the Berne Convention," *Revue internationale du droit d'auteur* 155 (January 1993): 42; Felix Leinemann, *Die Sozialbindung des "Geistigen Eigentums"* (Baden-Baden, 1998), 162–63.

52. Eckhard Höffner, *Geschichte und Wesen des Urheberrechts* (Munich, 2010), 1: 168, 2: 211–14, 253–58, 383.

53. Gail E. Evans, "Intellectual Property as a Trade Issue: The Making of the Agreement on Trade-Related Aspects of Intellectual Property Rights," *World Competition* 18, 2 (1994): 166–68; Terence P. Stewart, ed., *The GATT Uruguay Round: A Negotiating History (1986–1992)* (Deventer, 1993), 2: 2270–72.

54. Keith Aoki, " Neocolonialism, Anticommons Property, and Biopiracy in the (Not-so-Brave) New World Order of International Intellectual Property Protection," *Indiana Journal of Global Legal Studies* 6 (1998): 46ff.

55. The *Lion King* song "The Lion Sleeps Tonight" was based on "Mbube," written by Solomon Linda in the 1920s. When Pete Seeger and the Weavers recorded it in 1951, bringing it to the attention of a Western audience, they mistakenly believed it to be a traditional folksong.

56. Stephen E. Siwek, *Copyright Industries in the US Economy: The 2006 Report*, http://www.iipa.com/pdf/2006_siwek_full.pdf. See also J. Thomas McCarthy, "Intellectual Property—America's Overlooked Export," *University of Dayton Law Review* 20 (1995): 809.

57. Department for Culture, Media and Sport, "Creative Industries Economic Estimates:

Full Statistical Release," 8 December 2011, p. 5, http://www.culture.gov.uk/publications/8682 .aspx. Creative industries were a narrow subset of intellectual property more generally, consisting of advertising, music, film, publishing, and the like.

58. Ian Hargreaves, *Digital Opportunity: A Review of Intellectual Property and Growth* (London, 2011), 3. Available at http://www.ipo.gov.uk/ipreview-finalreport.pdf.

59. Maurice Lévy and Jean-Pierre Jouyet, "L'économie de l'immatériel: La croissance de demain: Rapport de la Commission sur l'économie de l'immatériel," December 2006, p. 12; Sénat, Report 53, 22 October 2008, p. 12. Available at http://www.senat.fr/rap/l08–053/l08–053 .html.

60. Kevin A. Hassett and Robert J. Shapiro, "What Are Ideas Worth? The Value of Intellectual Capital and Intangible Assets in the American Economy," p. 3, Sonecon, http://www .sonecon.com/studies.php; *Gowers Review of Intellectual Property*, December 2006, p. 3.

61. Sénat, Report 53, 22 October 2008, p. 19.

62. Frank Emmert, "Intellectual Property in the Uruguay Round: Negotiating Strategies of the Western Industrialized Countries," *Michigan Journal of International Law* 11 (1989–90): 1326–28; William Patry, *Moral Panics and the Copyright Wars* (New York, n.d.), 30–36.

63. Commission of the European Communities, "Green Paper: Combating Counterfeiting and Piracy in the Single Market," COM (98) 569 final, 15 October 1998, p. 4.

64. OECD, *The Economic Impact of Counterfeiting and Piracy* (2008), 15.

65. B. Zorina Khan, *The Democratization of Invention: Patents and Copyrights in American Economic Development, 1790–1920* (Cambridge, 2005), 304–5; *Integrating Intellectual Property Rights and Development Policy: Report of the Commission on Intellectual Property Rights* (London, 2002), 8.

66. Rehbinder and Staehelin, "Urheberrecht im TRIPs-Abkommen," 34; Doron S. Ben-Atar, *Trade Secrets: Intellectual Piracy and the Origins of American Industrial Power* (New Haven, 2004), chap. 1.

67. Eric Schiff, *Industrialization without National Patents: The Netherlands, 1869–1912; Switzerland, 1850–1907* (Princeton, 1971), 59–63 and passim.

68. Khan, *Democratization of Invention*, 38.

69. Michael P. Ryan, *Knowledge Diplomacy: Global Competition and the Politics of Intellectual Property* (Washington DC, 1998), 145–46.

70. Rochelle Cooper Dreyfuss, "TRIPs—Round II: Should Users Strike Back?" *University of Chicago Law Review* 71 (2004): 21–22. Numbers in Christopher May and Susan K. Sell, *Intellectual Property Rights: A Critical History* (Boulder, 2006), 187.

71. Adolf Fleischmann, "Die Berner Übereinkunft zum Schutze des Urheberrechts," *UFITA* 103 (1986): 50. Originally published in 1888.

72. Moderately skeptical of the argument that strong global intellectual property is the sole solution is Keith E. Maskus, "Encouraging International Technology Transfer," UNCTAD-ICTSD Project on IPRs and Sustainable Development, Issue Paper 7, May 2004; Carlos M. Correa, "Can the TRIPs Agreement Foster Technology Transfer to Developing Countries?" in Keith E. Maskus and Jerome H. Reichman, eds., *International Public Goods and Transfer of Technology under a Globalized Intellectual Property Regime* (Cambridge, 2005), 227ff. Support for strong protection in Hassett and Shapiro, "What Are Ideas Worth?" 21–23. A belief that strong protection helps Third World nations above a certain level of development, with Singapore as an example, in Dru Brenner-Beck, "Do as I Say, Not as I Did," *UCLA Pacific Basin Law Journal* 11 (1992).

73. In 2010 China had the third-largest number of patents granted worldwide, trailing only Japan and the United States. WIPO, *2011 World Intellectual Property Indicators*, Figure A.3.1.2, p. 52. And it joined Berne in 1992.

74. Thomas Cottier, "The Prospects for Intellectual Property in GATT," *Common Market Law*

Review 28 (1991): 389–91; Peter Drahos with John Braithwaite, *Information Feudalism: Who Owns the Information Economy?* (London, 2002), 197.

75. Howard D. Sacks, "Crisis in International Copyright: The Protocol Regarding Developing Countries," *Journal of Business Law* (1969): 29–31, 128–29; Sam Ricketson and Jane Ginsburg, *International Copyright and Neighbouring Rights: The Berne Convention and Beyond*, 2nd ed. (Oxford, 2006), chaps. 3, 4.

76. Sam Ricketson, "The Future of the Traditional Intellectual Property Conventions in the Brave New World of Trade-Related Intellectual Property Rights," *International Review of Industrial Property and Copyright Law* 26 (1995): 878.

77. "US Adherence to the Berne Convention: Hearings Before the Subcommittee on Patents, Copyrights and Trademarks of the Committee on the Judiciary," Senate, 16 May 1986, and 15 April 1986, Serial No. J-99-25, pp. 123–25; Drahos and Braithwaite, *Information Feudalism*, 112–13.

78. Peter Drahos, "Global Property Rights in Information: The Story of TRIPs at the GATT," *Prometheus* 13, 1 (1995): 9–12; Evans, "Intellectual Property as a Trade Issue," 148–58; Eva Hemmungs Wirtén, *No Trespassing: Authorship, Intellectual Property Rights and the Boundaries of Globalization* (Toronto, 2004), 92.

79. Laurence R. Helfer and Graeme W. Austin, *Human Rights and Intellectual Property* (Cambridge, 2011), 36–37.

80. "Berne Convention Implementation Act of 1987: Hearings before the . . . Committee on the Judiciary, House of Representatives, . . . June 17, July 23, September 16 and 30, 1987, February 9 and 10, 1988," Serial No. 50, p. 183.

81. Ibid., p. 73.

82. John Braithwaite and Peter Drahos, *Global Business Regulation* (Cambridge, 2000), 61–62.

83. Susan K. Sell, *Private Power, Public Law: The Globalization of Intellectual Property Rights* (Cambridge, 2003), 15–17, 35–36, 52, chap. 4.

84. "Digital Millennium Copyright Act of 1998," House Report 105-551, pt. 2 (22 July 1998), pp. 21–22; Department of Commerce, "The Emerging Digital Economy," p. 2, http://govinfo.library.unt.edu/ecommerce/EDEreprt.pdf.

85. Ricketson and Ginsburg, *International Copyright*, 154–61; Nimmer, "End of Copyright," 1396–97.

86. Reichstag, *Stenographische Berichte*, 23 November 1906, p. 3860, Dietz.

87. Paul Goldstein, *Copyright's Highway: From Gutenberg to the Celestial Jukebox* (Stanford, 2003), 160–61.

88. Thomas Oppermann and Jutta Baumann, "Handelsbezogener Schutz geistigen Eigentums ('TRIPs') im GATT," *Ordo* 44 (1993): 123–24.

89. Information Infrastructure Taskforce, *Intellectual Property and the National Information Infrastructure*, 14–15.

90. Ibid., 17, 212.

91. This was also the position taken by the US delegation during the WIPO negotiations: WIPO, *Records of the Diplomatic Conference on Certain Copyright and Neighboring Rights Questions, Geneva 1996* (Geneva, 1999), 2: 704.

92. "NII Copyright Protection Act of 1995: Joint Hearing before the Subcommittee on Courts and Intellectual Property . . . on H.R. 2441 and S. 1284," 15 November 1995, pp. 33, 37–38, 40.

93. Information Infrastructure Taskforce, *Intellectual Property and the National Information Infrastructure*, 52–53, though somewhat contradicted at 225–26.

94. Ibid., 84.

95. "NII Copyright Protection Act of 1995: Joint Hearing," pp. 27–28. The bills were: "NII Copyright Protection Act of 1995," 28/29 September 1995, H.R. 2441, S. 1284.

96. The story is told in Pamela Samuelson, "The US Digital Agenda at WIPO," *Virginia Journal of International Law* 37 (1996–97). A shorter and more polemical version in Samuelson, "The Copyright Grab," *Wired* 4.01 (1996).

97. WIPO Copyright Treaty 1996.

98. WIPO, *Records of the Diplomatic Conference*, 2: 668–70; Ricketson and Ginsburg, *International Copyright*, 683–87.

99. Art. 9. Stephen Fraser, "The Copyright Battle: Emerging International Rules and Roadblocks on the Global Information Infrastructure," *John Marshall Journal of Computer and Information Law* 15 (1997): 777–78; "NII Copyright Protection Act of 1995: Joint Hearing," 53.

100. WIPO, "Committee of Experts on a Possible Instrument for the Protection of the Rights of Performers and Producers of Phonograms," 20 May 1996, BCP/CE/VII/1-NR/CE/VI/1, p. 3.

101. "The Digital Millennium Copyright Act of 1998," Senate, Report 105–190, 11 May 1998, p. 5; Thomas C. Vinje, "A Brave New World of Technical Protection Systems: Will There Still Be Room for Copyright?" *European Intellectual Property Review* 18 (1996): 433, 437.

102. "The Digital Millennium Copyright Act of 1998," Senate, Report 105–190, pp. 2, 11.

103. Nimmer, "End of Copyright," 1416; Goldstein, *Copyright's Highway*, 171–75, 184; Patry, *Moral Panics and the Copyright Wars*, 164–65; James Boyle, *The Public Domain: Enclosing the Commons of the Mind* (New Haven, 2008), chap. 5.

104. Pierre Sirinelli quoted in Séverine Dusollier, *Droit d'auteur et protection des œuvres dans l'univers numérique* (Brussels, 2005), 82.

105. Pamela Samuelson, "Intellectual Property and the Digital Economy: Why the Anti-Circumvention Regulations Need to be Revised," *Berkeley Technology Law Journal* 14 (1999): 521–22.

106. Goldstein, *Copyright's Highway*, 181; Fred von Lohmann, "Unintended Consequences: Twelve Years under the DMCA" (February 2010), available at https://www.eff.org/files/eff-unintended-consequences-12-years.pdf.

107. "Digital Millennium Copyright Act of 1998," House Report 105–551, pt. 2, p. 24; "NII Copyright Protection Act of 1995: Joint Hearing," pp. 32–33, 98, 117.

108. *Congressional Record*, House, 4 August 1998, p. 18772.

109. *Congressional Record*, House, 12 October 1998, p. 25812.

110. David Nimmer, "A Riff on Fair Use in the Digital Millennium Copyright Act," *University of Pennsylvania Law Review* 148, 3 (2000): 711–13; Paul Goldstein, "Copyright and Its Substitutes," *Wisconsin Law Review* (1997): 869–70. A book-length analysis in this vein in Tarleton Gillespie, *Wired Shut: Copyright and the Shape of Digital Culture* (Cambridge MA, 2007).

111. Lawrence Lessig, *Free Culture: The Nature and Future of Creativity* (New York, 2004), 151–52.

112. Stefan Bechtold, "Digital Rights Management in the United States and Europe," *American Journal of Comparative Law* 52 (2004): 355–56; Lucie M.C.R. Guibault, "Contracts and Copyright Exemptions," in P. Bernt Hugenholtz, ed., *Copyright and Electronic Commerce: Legal Aspects of Electronic Copyright Management* (London, 2000), 125–26.

113. Glynn S. Lunney, Jr., "The Death of Copyright: Digital Technology, Private Copying and the Digital Millennium Copyright Act," *Virginia Law Review* 87, 5 (2001): 814–15.

114. *Congressional Record*, House, 4 August 1998, p. 18773.

115. Ibid., p. 18778.

116. On the background to the Commerce Committee's interjection into the debate, see Jessica Litman, *Digital Copyright* (Amherst, 2001), 136–42.

117. "Digital Millennium Copyright Act of 1998," House Report 105–551, pt. 2, pp. 35–36.

118. *Congressional Record*, House, 4 August 1998, p. 18779.

119. Ibid., p. 18776.

120. "WIPO Copyright Treaties and Implementation and On-Line Copyright Infringement Liability Limitation," House Report 105–551, pt. 1, (22 May 1998), p. 20.

121. "Digital Millennium Copyright Act of 1998," House Report 105–551, pt. 2, p. 36; *Congressional Record*, Senate, 8 October 1998, p. 24464; Bill D. Hermann and Oscar H. Gandy, Jr., "Catch 1201: A Legislative History and Content Analysis of the DMCA Exemption Proceedings," *Cardozo Arts and Entertainment Law Journal* 24 (2006): 123–24 and passim; Patricia Aufderheide and Peter Jaszi, *Reclaiming Fair Use: How to Put Balance Back in Copyright* (Chicago, 2011), 9–13, 75–78, chap. 6.

122. Nimmer, "Riff on Fair Use," 727–32.

123. Gillespie, *Wired Shut*, 180; Mazzone, *Copyfraud*, 88–89; Jane C. Ginsburg, "Authors and Users in Copyright," *Journal of the Copyright Society of the USA* 45, 1 (1997): 4.

124. *Universal City Studios, Inc. v. Corley*, 273 F.3d 429 (2d Cir. 2001), pp. 433, 459.

125. "WIPO Copyright Treaties Implementation Act: Hearing before the Subcommittee on Courts and Intellectual Property of the Committee of the Judiciary, House of Representatives . . . on HR 2281 . . . and HR 2280," 16 and 17 September 1997, Serial No. 33, p. 49; US Copyright Office, "DMCA Section 104 Report," August 2001, pp. 11–12 in *The Digital Millennium Copyright Act*, 531–32.

126. Terese Foged, "US v. EU Anti-Circumvention Legislation: Preserving the Public's Privileges in the Digital Age," *European Intellectual Property Review* 11 (2002): 531; Gillespie, *Wired Shut*, 159, 179–80.

127. Two-thirds of Nobel prizes in economics have gone to Americans.

128. The early history and a clear mapping out of the distinction between economic and natural rights approaches is in Gillian K. Hadfield, "The Economics of Copyright: An Historical Perspective," *Copyright Law Symposium* 38 (1992).

129. Neil W. Netanel, "Why Has Copyright Expanded?" *New Directions in Copyright Law* 6 (2007): 17–21.

130. William M. Landes and Richard A. Posner, "Indefinitely Renewable Copyright," *University of Chicago Law Review* 70, 2 (2003): 474, 484. This argument had been anticipated in James J. Guinan, Jr., "Duration of Copyright," Study No. 30, in *Copyright Law Revision: Studies Prepared for the Subcommittee on Patents, Trademarks, and Copyrights of the Committee on the Judiciary* (US Senate, 86th Congress, 2nd sess., pursuant to S. Res. 240, 1961), 79–80. Guinan rejected the idea because it would benefit not the author but mainly remote heirs and assignees. And it would eliminate the public domain for works that retained commercial value, which were precisely those works which should be there.

131. Wendy Gordon, "Fair Use as Market Failure: A Structural and Economic Analysis of the Betamax Case and its Predecessors," *Columbia Law Review* 82 (1982): 1613–14; William M. Landes and Richard A. Posner, "An Economic Analysis of Copyright Law," *Journal of Legal Studies* 18, 2 (1989): 357–61.

132. Hardy, "Property (and Copyright) in Cyberspace," 235–38; Robert P. Merges, "The End of Friction? Property Rights and Contract in the 'Newtonian' World of On-Line Commerce," *Berkeley Technology Law Journal* 12, 1 (1997): 130–31.

133. Jeremy Waldron, "From Authors to Copiers: Individual Rights and Social Values in Intellectual Property," *Chicago-Kent Law Review* 68 (1993): 854–56.

134. *Eldred v. Ashcroft*, 537 U.S. 186 (2003), p. 212, nt. 18. Emphasis added.

135. Dusollier, *Droit d'auteur et protection des œuvres dans l'univers numérique*, 243, 271.

136. That would explain the otherwise peculiar claim that "economic arguments are gaining weight in European copyright doctrine." Insofar as property-based arguments are economic, economic arguments had always been primary to European doctrine. Indeed, the work that advances this claim also concludes that the outcome for authors of the property rights approach and the traditional European natural rights approach were similar and that the supposed conversion of the Europeans to the property rights approach was in fact not much of a

change at all. Kamiel J. Koelman, "Copyright Law and Economics in the EU Copyright Directive: Is the Droit d'Auteur Passé?" *International Review of Intellectual Property and Competition Law* 35 (2004): 604, 637–38.

137. Eric Pahud, "Zur Begrenzung des Urheberrechts im Interesse Dritter und der Allgemeinheit," *UFITA* (2000): 110–13.

138. Stewart, *The GATT Uruguay Round*, 2: 2273; Carla Hesse, "The Rise of Intellectual Property, 700 BC—AD 2000: An Idea in the Balance," *Daedalus* 131, 2 (2002): 43.

139. Reto M. Hilty, "Five Lessons about Copyright in the Information Society," *Journal of the Copyright Society of the USA* 53, 1–2 (2005–6): 110–12, 132.

140. Drahos and Braithwaite, *Information Feudalism*, 28.

141. They were lumped together in their interest in the DMCA as the "consumer electronic and fair use communities." *Congressional Record*, House, 4 August 1998, pp. 18773–76.

142. Catharina Maracke, *Die Entstehung des Urheberrechtsgesetzes von 1965* (Berlin, 2003), 90–92.

143. Thomas P. Olson, "The Iron Law of Consensus: Congressional Responses to Proposed Copyright Reforms since the 1909 Act," *Journal of the Copyright Society of the USA* 36, 1 (1988): 127; Litman, "Story of *Sony v. Universal Studios*," 366.

144. *Sony Corp of America v. Universal City Studios, Inc.*, 464 U.S. 417 (1984), pp. 440–42.

145. Samuelson, "US Digital Agenda at WIPO," 385–86.

146. Samuelson, "Intellectual Property and the Digital Economy," 522–23; Jonathan Band and Masanobu Katoh, *Interfaces on Trial: Intellectual Property and Interoperability in the Global Software Market* (Boulder, 1995); Band and Katoh, *Interfaces on Trial 2.0*.

147. Home Recording Rights Coalition website at http://www.hrrc.org/index.php?id=9&subid=9.

148. Verizon spent four times Disney on lobbying in 2010, Google more than the RIAA. Robert Levine, *Free Ride: How Digital Parasites are Destroying the Culture Business, and How the Culture Business Can Fight Back* (New York, 2011), 81.

149. Yochai Benkler, *The Wealth of Networks: How Social Production Transforms Markets and Freedom* (New Haven, 2006), 411–12.

150. Thomas Rogers and Andrew Szamosszegi, *Fair Use in the US Economy: Economic Contribution of Industries Relying on Fair Use* (Computer and Communications Industry Association, 2010), 8.

151. Patry, *Moral Panics and the Copyright Wars*, xviii–xix.

152. *Congressional Record*, House, 12 October 1998, pp. 25812–13; "WIPO Copyright Treaties and Implementation and On-Line Copyright Infringement Liability Limitation," House Report 105–551, 22 May 1998, pt. 1, pp. 10, 18.

153. *A&M Records, Inc. v. Napster, Inc.*, 239 F.3d 1004 (9th Cir. 2001). Jane C. Ginsburg, "Copyright Use and Excuse on the Internet," *Columbia-VLA Journal of Law and the Arts* 24 (2000): 37.

154. *MGM Studios v. Grokster*, 545 U.S. 913 (2005).

155. Litman, "Story of *Sony v. Universal Studios*," 386–93; Jane C. Ginsburg and Yves Gaubiac, "Infringement, Provision of Means and Fault: Outlook in the Common Law and Civil Law Systems Following the *Grokster* and *Kazaa* Rulings," *Revue internationale du droit d'auteur* 207 (2006): 11–14.

156. The former: Matthew Rimmer, *Digital Copyright and the Consumer Revolution: Hands Off My iPod* (Cheltenham, 2007), 158–59; Samuelson, "Intellectual Property and the Digital Economy," 522–23. The latter: Levine, *Free Ride*, 27–31. In this camp, too, but not specifically related to the DMCA: Alvise Maria Casellati, "The Evolution of Article 6.4 of the European Information Society Copyright Directive," *Columbia-VLA Journal of Law and the Arts* 24 (2001): 370.

157. Olivier Bomsel, *Gratuit! Du déploiement de l'économie numérique* (n.p., 2007), 29–30.

158. The argument of Levine, *Free Ride*.

159. *Economist*, 17 August 2013.

160. *Economist*, 10 December 2011.

161. Glenn S. McGuigan and Robert D. Russell, "The Business of Academic Publishing: A Strategic Analysis of the Academic Journal Publishing Industry and Its Impact on the Future of Scholarly Publishing," *Electronic Journal of Academic and Special Librarianship* 9 (2008): 1–11.

162. *New York Times*, 16 January 2012, p. B1. In fact, Obama no more wanted to alienate Hollywood than Silicon Valley. He shortly thereafter made fund-raising trips of appeasement to both these sites of significant Democratic support. *New York Times*, 15 February 2012, p. A14. But overall, tech businesses donated $14 million during the 2012 campaign to the president and Democrats, significantly more than in 2008. Nicholas Confessore and Jo Craven McGinty, "Obama, Romney and Their Parties on Track to Raise $2 Billion," *New York Times*, 25 October 2012.

163. *New York Times*, 15 January 2012, p. 22.

164. *New York Times*, 19 January 2012, pp. 1, B1.

165. Jessica Litman, "Copyright Legislation and Technological Change," *Oregon Law Review* 68, 2 (1989): 312.

166. Stephen Brobeck, ed., *Encyclopedia of the Consumer Movement* (New York, 1997).

167. The early history is in Stephen P. Strickland, *Politics, Science and Dread Disease: A Short History of United States Research Policy* (Cambridge MA, 1972).

168. *Williams & Wilkins Co. v. The United States*, 487 F.2d 1345 (1973), 420 U.S. 376 (1975). The magnitude of copying was impressive. In 1970 the NIH library's budget for journals and that for photocopying were approximately equal ($85,000 and $86,000 respectively), and it made some 93,000 copies of articles.

169. *American Geophysical Union v. Texaco Inc.*, 802 F. Supp. 1 (S.D.N.Y. 1992), *aff'd*, 37 F.3d 881 (2d Cir. 1994), p. 892.

170. Mancur Olson, *The Logic of Collective Action* (Cambridge MA, 1965) is the classic statement.

171. *Archives Parlementaires*, Chambre de Pairs, 27 May 1839, 124: 715–16. A similar statement a century later in Hans Otto de Boor, *Vom Wesen des Urheberrechts: Kritische Bemerkungen zum Entwurf eines Gesetzes über das Urheberrecht an Werken der Literatur, der Kunst und der Photographie* (Marburg, 1933), 72–73.

172. "The Copyright Term Extension Act of 1995: Hearing before the Committee on the Judiciary ... on S. 483," 20 September 1995, Senate Hearing 104–817, Serial No. J-104–46, pp. 77–79.

173. "NII Copyright Protection Act of 1995: Joint Hearing," 74–76.

174. Litman, *Digital Copyright*, chap. 9; Boyle, *The Public Domain*, 58–59.

175. James Boyle, "Overregulating the Internet," *Washington Times*, 14 November 1995.

176. "NII Copyright Protection Act of 1995: Joint Hearing," 68, 76.

177. Julie E. Cohen, "WIPO Copyright Treaty Implementation in the United States: Will Fair Use Survive?" *European Intellectual Property Review* 21 (1999): 238.

178. Peter A. Jaszi, "Goodbye to All That: A Reluctant (and Perhaps Premature) Adieu to a Constitutionally-Grounded Discourse of Public Interest in Copyright Law," *Vanderbilt Journal of Transnational Law* 29 (1996): 598–99.

179. Nimmer, "End of Copyright," 1413–14.

180. Lewis Hyde, *Common as Air: Revolution, Art and Ownership* (New York, 2010), 57–58, and passim; Siva Vaidhyanathan, *Copyrights and Copywrongs: The Rise of Intellectual Property and How it Threatens Creativity* (New York, 2001), 22–23, 161; John Tehranian, "Et Tu, Fair Use? The Triumph of Natural-Law Copyright," *UC Davis Law Review* 38 (2005).

181. HR 5544 (2002), HR 1066 (2003), HR 107 (2003), HR 4536 (2005), HR 1201 (2007). More examples in Peter K. Yu, "The Escalating Copyright Wars," *Hofstra Law Review* 32 (2004): 938–39; Band and Katoh, *Interfaces on Trial 2.0*, 94–98.

182. HR 5522 (2002).

183. HR 2408 (2005), S 2913 (2008).

184. Rimmer, *Digital Copyright and the Consumer Revolution*, 182–83.

185. Bomsel, *Gratuit!*, 264–65.

186. In 1989 copyrighted material made up 1.1 percent of US exports, the same as in the UK and a nose ahead of the EU-12 rate of 0.8 percent. WIPO, "Guide on Surveying the Economic Contribution of the Copyright-Based Industries" (Geneva, 2003), table 5.1, p. 42.

187. Thomas Dreier, "TRIPs and the Enforcement of Intellectual Property Rights," in Friedrich-Karl Beier and Gerhard Schricker, eds., *From GATT to TRIPs* (Weinheim, 1996), 255–57; Drahos and Braithwaite, *Information Feudalism*, 10–11, 90, 119, 121, 137; Lévy and Jouyet, "L'économie de l'immatériel," 14.

188. Carlos Alberto Primo Braga, "The Economics of Intellectual Property Rights and the GATT: A View from the South," *Vanderbilt Journal of Transnational Law* 22 (1989): 250–51.

189. Duncan Matthews, *Globalizing Intellectual Property Rights: The TRIPs Agreement* (London, 2002), 2–3, 13, 22–24, 27–28.

190. Jörg Reinbothe, "Der Schutz des Urheberrechts und der Leistungsschutzrechte im Abkommensentwurf GATT/TRIPs," *Gewerblicher Rechtsschutz und Urheberrecht*, Internationaler Teil, 10 (1992): 708.

191. WIPO, *Records of the Diplomatic Conference*, 2: 699–700; Mihály Ficsor, *The Law of Copyright and the Internet: The 1996 WIPO Treaties, Their Interpretation and Implementation* (Oxford, 2002), 71–74.

192. Stephen Fraser, "Berne, CFTA, NAFTA & GATT: The Implications of Copyright *Droit Moral* and Cultural Exemptions in International Trade Law," *Hastings Communications and Entertainment Law Journal* 18 (1995–96): 288–89, 304–6, 316–17.

193. Serge Regourd, *L'Exception culturelle*, 2nd ed. (Paris, 2004), 85.

194. Graeme B. Dinwoodie, "The Development and Incorporation of International Norms in the Formation of Copyright Law," *Ohio State Law Journal* 62 (2001): 734–35.

195. World Trade Organization, "United States—Section 110(5) of the US Copyright Act: Report of the Panel," WT/DS160/R, 15 June 2000.

196. Ana María Pacón, "What Will TRIPs Do For Developing Countries?" in Beier and Schricker, *From GATT to TRIPs*, 348.

197. Gloria C. Phares, "Retroactive Protection of Foreign Copyrights: What Has Congress Be-GATT?" *Journal of Proprietary Rights* 7, 4 (1995): 2–3.

198. Bernt Hugenholtz, "Why the Copyright Directive Is Unimportant, and Possibly Invalid," *European Intellectual Property Review* 11 (2000): 501–2.

199. Cottier, "Prospects for Intellectual Property in GATT," 406–7.

200. Jean-Claude Jouret, *Tintin et le merchandising: Une gestion stratégique des droits dérivés* (Paris, 1991).

201. Directive 2001/29/EC, 22 May 2001, recital 2, *Official Journal*, L167 (22 June 2001): 10; "A European Initiative in Electronic Commerce: Communication to the European Parliament, the Council, the Economic and Social Committee and the Committee of the Regions," COM (97) 157, 15 April 1997; Directive on Electronic Commerce, 2000/31/EC, 8 June 2000, *Official Journal*, L178 (17 February 2000): 1.

202. "Growth, Competitiveness, Employment: The Challenges and Ways Forward into the 21st Century," COM (93) 700, 5 December 1993; "Europe and the Global Information Society: Bangemann Report Recommendations to the European Council," Innovatia Documentation; European Commission, Directorate-General for Employment, Industrial Relations and Social Affairs, "Building the European Information Society for Us All: Final Policy Report of the High-Level Expert Group," April 1997, p. 13.

203. Ralph Oman, "Berne Revision: The Continuing Drama," *Fordham Intellectual Property, Media and Entertainment Law Journal* 4 (1993): 145.

204. Regourd, *L'Exception culturelle*, 70–74.

205. Common Position (EC) No. 48/2000, 28 September 2000, (2000/C 344/01), pt. 9, *Official Journal*, C344/1 (1 December 2000). Repeated in the Information Society Directive: Directive 2001/29/EC, 22 May 2001, recital 9, art. 3, *Official Journal*, L167 (22 June 2001): 10.

206. Treaty Establishing a Constitution for Europe, draft 18 July 2003, art. II-17(2).

207. "Discours de M. le Président de la République. Accord en faveur du développement et de la protection des œuvres culturelles dans les nouveaux réseaux de communication," 23 November 2007, http://www.culture.gouv.fr/culture/actualites/index-olivennes231107.htm.

208. Herman Jehoram, "The EC Copyright Directives, Economics and Authors' Rights," *International Review of Industrial Property and Copyright Law* 6 (1994): 821–22.

209. Bernt Hugenholtz et al., "The Recasting of Copyright and Related Rights for the Knowledge Economy" (Institute for Information Law, University of Amsterdam, November 2006), 7–8; Fabrice Rochelandet, "Le Droit d'auteur européen à l'ère numérique: Quelles leçons tirer de l'expérience américaine du Digital Millennium Copyright Act?" in Maurice Baslé and Thierry Pénard, eds., *eEurope: La Société européenne de l'information en 2010* (Paris, 2002), 332.

210. P. Bernt Hugenholtz and Ruth L. Okediji, "Conceiving an International Instrument on Limitations and Exceptions for Copyright" (Institute for Information Law, University of Amsterdam, 6 March 2008), 6–7; Isabella Löhr, *Die Globalisierung geistiger Eigentumsrechte: Neue Strukturen internationaler Zusammenarbeit 1866–1952* (Göttingen, 2010), 123–24.

211. Directive 2004/48/EC, 29 April 2004, *Official Journal*, L157 (30 April 2004): 46, recitals 1, 8.

212. Commission of the European Communities, "Report … on the Implementation and Effects of Directive 91/250/EEC on the Legal Protection of Computer Programs," COM (2000) 199 final, 10 April 2000, p. 5.

213. Directive 2001/84/EC, 27 September 2001, *Official Journal*, L272 (13 October 2001): 32, recitals 9–14.

214. Council Directive 93/98/EEC, 29 October 1993, *Official Journal*, L290 (24 November 1993): 9, recitals 2, 9.

215. "The Copyright Term Extension Act of 1995: Hearing before the Committee on the Judiciary," Senate Hearing 104–817, p. 79. On the upward direction of harmonization, L. Bently and B. Sherman, *Intellectual Property Law*, 3rd ed. (Oxford, 2009), 47.

216. Directive 96/9/EC, 11 March 1996, *Official Journal*, L77 (27 March 1996): 20, recitals 11–12.

217. The evidence was that, in fact, little was gained. Commission of the European Communities, "First Evaluation of Directive 96/9/EC on the Legal Protection of Databases: DG Internal Market and Services Working Paper," 12 December 2005, pp. 5, 15–16, 24; Stephen M. Maurer, "Across Two Worlds: Database Protection in the US and Europe," p. 2, http://www.ic.gc.ca/eic/site/ippd-dppi.nsf/vwapj/13-EN2%20Maurer.pdf/$file/13-EN2%20Maurer.pdf; Boyle, *The Public Domain*, chap. 9.

218. J. H. Reichman and Pamela Samuelson, "Intellectual Property Rights in Data?" *Vanderbilt Law Review* 50 (1997): 81.

219. Yves Frémion, European Parliament, 23 June 1993, *Official Journal*, 1993/94, pp. 3–432/154.

220. *Congressional Record*, Senate, 8 October 1998, p. 24467, Patrick Leahy.

221. Reichman and Samuelson, "Intellectual Property Rights in Data?" 76.

222. Mark Schneider, "The European Union Database Directive," *Berkeley Technology Law Journal* 13 (1998): 562–64; Maurer, "Across Two Worlds," 33; Michele Boldrin and David K. Levine, *Against Intellectual Monopoly* (Cambridge, 2008), 201; Paul A. David, "Koyaanisqatsi in Cyberspace: The Economics of an 'Out-of-Balance' Regime of Private Property Rights in Data and Information," in Maskus and Reichman, *International Public Goods and Transfer of Technology*, 104–5. Similar objections could also be heard in Europe, but to no avail: Commission of the European Communities, "First Evaluation of Directive 96/9/EC on the Legal Protection of Databases: DG Internal Market and Services Working Paper," 12 December 2005, pp. 3–7. In the

EU objections during debates were very few: European Parliament, 21 June 1993, Grund, *Official Journal*, 1993/94, p. 3–432/19, and also p. 3–432/154, Porto.

223. Robert P. Merges, "One Hundred Years of Solicitude: Intellectual Property Law, 1900–2000," *California Law Review* 88 (2000): 2237–38.

224. Commission of the European Communities, "Books and Reading: A Cultural Challenge for Europe," COM (89) 258 final, 3 August 1989, pp. 1–2, 4. A similar attack on the idea of balancing between the various interests as upsetting the traditional French preeminence for authors in Lucas, *Droit d'auteur et numérique*, 247.

225. *Journal Officiel*, Sénat, 29 October 2008, p. 6346.

226. "i2010: Digital Libraries," COM (2005) 465 final, 30 September 2005, p. 5.

227. Commission of the European Communities, "Green Paper on Copyright and the Challenge of Technology: Copyright Issues Requiring Immediate Action," COM (88) 72 final, 7 June 1988, p. 6. Similar considerations: *Official Journal*, 1992–93, No. 3–423, 26 October 1992, pp. 27–28. We have one of the strongest content industries on the planet, their representatives told the world in 2008. *Journal Officiel*, Sénat, Report 53, 22 October 2008, p. 165.

228. "Green Paper," COM (95) 382 final, p. 11. In the EU's vocabulary "copyright" was the word used to designate authors' rights in the English version of documents, thus undermining my attempt to preserve the terminological differences.

229. Jörg Reinbothe, "A Review of the Last Ten Years and a Look at What Lies Ahead: Copyright and Related Rights in the European Union," lecture at Fordham University, 4 April 2002, available at http://ec.europa.eu/internal_market/copyright/documents/2002-fordhamspeech-reinbothe_en.htm.

230. Commission of the European Communities, "Follow-Up to the Green Paper on Copyright and Related Rights in the Information Society," COM (96) 568 final, 20 November 1996, p. 8.

231. Directive 2001/29/EC, 22 May 2001, recital 10, *Official Journal*, L167 (22 June 2001): 10; Directive 2004/48/EC, *Official Journal*, L157 (30 April 2004): 45, recitals 1–3.

232. European Parliament, Debates, 13 February 2001, Boselli, Medina Ortega, Echerer.

233. André R. Bertrand, "Multimedia: Stretching the Limits of Authors' Rights in Europe," *Journal of Proprietary Rights* 7, 11 (1995): 2–3, 7–8; Irini A. Stamatoudi, *Copyright and Multimedia Products* (Cambridge, 2002), 60.

234. *Industries culturelles et nouvelles techniques: Rapport de la commission présidée par Pierre Sirinelli* (Paris, 1994), 71–72.

235. Conseil supérieur de la propriété littéraire et artistique, Commission sur les aspects juridiques des œuvres multimédia, "Le Régime juridique des œuvres multimédia: Droit des auteurs et sécurité juridique des investisseurs," 26 May 2005, pp. 24–25. Similar arguments in favor of no change in Thomas Dreier et al., *Urheberrecht auf dem Weg zur Informationsgesellschaft* (Baden-Baden, 1997), 204–8.

236. "Follow-Up to the Green Paper on Copyright and Related Rights in the Information Society," COM (96) 568 final, pp. 8, 11–12.

237. Lefranc, "Metamorphosis of *Contrefaçon* in French Copyright Law," 72. The Italians with their broad licensing provisions were an exception here.

238. "Green Paper," COM (95) 382 final, pp. 25–26, 50, 72. A similar conclusion in Assemblée nationale, Commission des lois constitutionnelles, de la législation et de l'administration générale de la république, Compte rendu 37, 31 May 2005.

239. Council Directive 93/83/EEC, 27 September 1993, arts. 2, 3, *Official Journal*, L248 (6 October 1993): 15.

240. The endlessly complicated negotiations leading up to 1976 are detailed in Litman, "Copyright Legislation and Technological Change," 326–32.

241. Directive 2001/29/EC, 22 May 2001, recital 48, art. 6, *Official Journal*, L167 (22 June 2001): 10.

242. Hugenholtz, "Why the Copyright Directive Is Unimportant, and Possibly Invalid," 501–2. Also "Report to the Council, the European Parliament and the Economic and Social Committee on the Application of Directive 2001/29/EC on the Harmonisation of Certain Aspects of Copyright and Related Rights in the Information Society," SEC (2007) 1556, 30 November 2007, p. 8.

243. Foged, "US v. EU Anti-Circumvention Legislation," 535; Nora Braun, "The Interface between the Protection of Technological Measures and the Exercise of Exceptions to Copyright and Related Rights: Comparing the Situation in the United States and in the European Community," *European Intellectual Property Review* 11 (2003): 499; Wencke Bäsler, "Technological Protection Measures in the United States, the European Union and Germany: How Much Fair Use Do We Need in the 'Digital World'?" *Virginia Journal of Law and Technology* 8, 13 (2003): 15–16.

244. Lucie Guibault et al., "Study on the Implementation and Effect in Member States' Laws of Directive 2001/29/EC" (Institute for Information Law, University of Amsterdam, February 2007), 79, 94, 96; Casellati, "Evolution of Article 6.4 of the European Information Society Copyright Directive," 374–75, 399–400; Markus Fallenböck, "On the Technical Protection of Copyright: The Digital Millennium Copyright Act, the European Community Copyright Directive and Their Anticircumvention Provisions," *International Journal of Communications Law and Policy* 7 (2002/03): 37–47, 56.

245. Will Hutton is misinformed when he portrays them otherwise: Hutton, *The World We're In* (London, 2002), 355–56.

246. "The Management of Copyright and Related Rights in the Internal Market," COM (2004) 261 final, pp. 10–11.

247. Rosa Julià-Barceló, "On-line Intermediary Liability Issues: Comparing EU and US Legal Frameworks," *European Intellectual Property Review* 3 (2000): 107–8, 112.

248. Ryan Bates, "Communication Breakdown: The Recording Industry's Pursuit of the Individual Music User, a Comparison of US and EU Copyright Protections for Internet Music File Sharing," *Northwestern Journal of International Law and Business* 25 (2004): 249–50; Eleanor M. Lackman, "Slowing Down the Speed of Sound: A Transatlantic Race to Head Off Digital Copyright Infringement," *Fordham Intellectual Property, Media and Entertainment Law Journal* 13 (2003): 1177.

249. Directive 2000/31/EC on electronic commerce, 8 June 2000, *Official Journal*, L178 (17 July 2000): 1, recitals 42–44, 46, 48, arts. 12–15. Christopher Kuner et al., *Study on Online Copyright Enforcement and Data Protection in Selected Member States* (November 2009, European Commission, DG Internal Market and Services), 6; Daniel J. Gervais, "Transmissions of Music on the Internet: An Analysis of the Copyright Laws of Canada, France, Germany, Japan, the United Kingdom, and the United States," *Vanderbilt Journal of Transnational Law* 34 (2001): 1377, 1409.

250. Ginsburg, "How Copyright Got a Bad Name for Itself," 68.

251. Stefan Bechtold, "Digital Rights Management in the United States and Europe," *American Journal of Comparative Law* 52 (2004): 366.

252. "Follow-Up to the Green Paper on Copyright and Related Rights in the Information Society," COM (96) 568 final, pp. 11–12.

253. European Parliament, Debates, 13 February 2001, Boselli.

254. Directive 2001/29/EC, 22 May 2001, recital 44, arts. 5, 6, *Official Journal*, L167 (22 June 2001): 10. Exceptions to the imposition of digital rights management technologies were also more limited than in the US. Bechtold, "Digital Rights Management in the United States and Europe," 376–79.

255. Martin Senftleben, *Copyright, Limitations and the Three-Step Test* (The Hague, 2004), 47–53.

256. Sam Ricketson, "WIPO Study on Limitations and Exceptions of Copyright and Related Rights in the Digital Environment," SSCR/9/7, 5 April 2003, pp. 67–69. For more on this, Senftleben, *Copyright, Limitations and the Three-Step Test*, 162–68.

257. Hargreaves, *Digital Opportunity*, 4.

258. Directive 2001/29/EC, 22 May 2001, recital 44, art. 5, *Official Journal*, L167 (22 June 2001): 10.

259. *Gowers Review of Intellectual Property*, December 2006, p. 6; "Green Paper: Copyright in the Knowledge Economy," COM (2008), 466/3, pp. 19–20; Assemblée Nationale, Rapport 2349, 7 June 2005, p. 31; *Journal Officiel*, Assemblée, 20 December 2005, p. 8550.

260. "Green Paper: Copyright in the Knowledge Economy," COM (2008), 466/3, pp. 4–5.

261. The German publishing association protested even this as violating the Basic Law. Guibault, "Study on the Implementation and Effect in Member States' Laws of Directive 2001/29/EC," 49–50.

262. 17 U.S.C. §107.

263. Gesetz zur Regelung des Urheberrechts in der Informationsgesellschaft, 10 September 2003, §52a.

264. Fünftes Gesetz zur Änderung des Urheberrechtsgesetzes, 10 November 2006, §53(3)1.

265. *Authors Guild v. Google* (S.D.N.Y.), Settlement Agreement, 4.8, at https://www.authors guild.org/advocacy/authors-guild-v-google-settlement-resources-page/.

266. "Memorandum of Law in Opposition to the Settlement Proposal on Behalf of the Federal Republic of Germany," 31 August 2009, pp. 4–5, *Authors Guild et al. v. Google Inc.*, document 179, http://dockets.justia.com/docket/new-york/nysdce/1:2005cv08136/273913/.

267. Urheberrechtsgesetz, §52b.

268. Assemblée nationale, Commission des lois constitutionnelles, de la législation et de l'administration générale de la République, Compte rendu 37, 31 May 2005; Assemblée nationale, Rapport 2349, 7 June 2005, p. 47.

269. Guido Westkamp, "The Implementation of Directive 2001/29/EC in the Member States," Queen Mary Intellectual Property Research Institute, February 2007, pp. 211–12.

270. Sophie Barluet, *Édition de sciences humaines et sociales: Le cœur en danger* (Paris, 2004), 56. No doubt the sciences provide other examples.

271. "Pourquoi l'université veut-elle la mort de l'édition universitaire?" *Le Monde*, 18 April 2003; Françoise Benhamou, *Les Dérèglements de l'exception culturelle: Plaidoyer pour une perspective européenne* (Paris, 2006), 177. Bernard Edelman was suspicious of EU directives and thought the union was giving investors more consideration than authors. Alain Salles, "Les auteurs veulent garder leur droit," *Le Monde*, 2 May 2003. Similar ad campaigns against exceptions by German publishers are mentioned in Michael Kretschmer, "Digital Copyright: The End of an Era," *European Intellectual Property Review* 25, 8 (2003): n22.

272. Code de la propriété intellectuelle, art. L 122–5(3e).

273. 17 U.S.C. §121.

274. Code de la propriété intellectuelle, art. L. 122–5(7). Guibault, "Study on the Implementation and Effect in Member States' Laws of Directive 2001/29/EC," 51.

275. Fünftes Gesetz zur Änderung des Urheberrechtsgesetzes, 10 November 2006, §45a.

276. Art. 5(3)(d).

277. Jonathan Bate, "Myths and Ambiguities in Copyright Law," *Times Literary Supplement*, 6 August 2010, p. 15.

278. P. Bernt Hugenholtz, "Copyright and Freedom of Expression in Europe," in Rochelle Cooper Dreyfuss et al., eds., *Expanding the Boundaries of Intellectual Property* (Oxford, 2001), 343–64; Christophe Geiger, "Constitutionalising Intellectual Property Law? The Influence of Fundamental Rights on Intellectual Property in the European Union," *International Review of Intellectual Property and Competition Law* 37, 4 (2006): 391–92.

279. Christophe Geiger, *Droit d'auteur et droit du public à l'information* (Paris, 2004), 345.

280. Code de la propriété intellectuelle, art. L 122–5 (9).

281. Gesetz zur Regelung des Urheberrechts in der Informationsgesellschaft, 10 September 2003, §50.

282. *Ringgold v. Black Entertainment Television, Inc.*, 126 F.3d 70 (2d Cir. 1997). Samuelson, "Unbundling Fair Uses," 2576.

283. 1956 act, sects. 6, 9; 1988 act, sect. 31.

284. Council Directive 91/250/EEC, 14 May 1991, art 2(1), *Official Journal*, L 122 (17 May 1991): 42–46; Directive 96/9/EC, 11 March 1996, art. 4(1), *Official Journal*, L 77 (27 March 1996): 20–28.

285. "Green Paper on Copyright and the Challenge of Technology," COM (88) 72 final, p. 6.

286. Ibid., pp. 7, 197.

287. "Follow-Up to the Green Paper on Copyright and Related Rights in the Information Society," COM (96) 568 final, pp. 3, 27–28. A similar worry in "Commission Staff Working Paper on the Review of the EC Legal Framework in the Field of Copyright and Related Rights," SEC (2004) 995, 19 July 2004, p. 16.

288. Its two examples of dysfunctional invocation of moral rights were those of Choderlos de Laclos and Victor Hugo, discussed in chapter 1. Lévy and Jouyet, "L'économie de l'immatériel," 125.

289. "Green Paper," COM (95) 382 final, pp. 65–67.

290. "Follow-Up to the Green Paper on Copyright and Related Rights in the Information Society," COM (96) 568 final, p. 27.

291. Directive 2001/29/EC, 22 May 2001, recital 19, *Official Journal*, L167 (22 June 2001): 10.

292. Bernard Edelman, "Une loi substantiellement internationale: La loi du 3 juillet 1985 sur les droits d'auteur et droits voisins," *Journal du Droit International* 3 (1987); David Saunders, "Approaches to the Historical Relations of the Legal and the Aesthetic," *New Literary History* 23, 3 (1992): 516–17; David Saunders, "Some Implications of the 1985 French Law on Author's Rights," in Anderson and Saunders, *Moral Rights Protection in a Copyright System*, 57–58.

293. *Industries culturelles et nouvelles techniques*, 41–42.

294. Frédéric Pollaud-Dulian, *Le Droit d'auteur* (Paris, 2005), 26, 52, 55.

295. Margret Möller, "Urheberrecht oder Copyright?" *Zeitschrift für Urheber- und Medienrecht/Film und Recht* 2 (1990): 65–66.

8. THE RISE OF THE DIGITAL PUBLIC: THE COPYRIGHT WARS CONTINUE IN THE NEW MILLENNIUM

1. Others have also traced parallels between today's discussions and those of the nineteenth century. Laurent Pfister, "Is Literary Property (A Form of) Property? Controversies on the Nature of Authors' Rights in the Nineteenth Century," *Revue internationale du droit d'auteur* 205 (July 2005); Monika Dommann, "Autoren und Apparate: Copyrights und Medienwandel (1850–1980)" (Habilitationsschrift, Zurich, 2011), 27.

2. Kenneth Goldsmith, *Uncreative Writing* (New York, 2011), 24.

3. Ann M. Blair, *Too Much to Know: Managing Scholarly Information before the Modern Age* (New Haven, 2010), 29–30.

4. Copyright Commission, *The Royal Commissions and the Report of the Commissioners*, c. 2036 (London, 1878), xxxvii.

5. *Hansard*, 3, 41, 20 March 1838, p. 1099.

6. Adrian Johns, *Piracy* (Chicago, 2009). Today the mantra is that "piracy is progressive taxation," viz, while it may shave the sales of prominent artists a tad, it helps the obscure ones enormously. Tim O'Reilly, "Piracy is Progressive Taxation, and Other Thoughts on the Evolution of Online Distribution," 11 December 2002, http://openp2p.com/pub/a/p2p/2002/12/11/piracy.html. Or even more radically, Aaron Swartz, "Guerilla Open Access Manifesto," July 2008, http://pastebin.com/cefxMVAy. More general appreciations of piracy include Peter An-

dreas, *Smuggler Nation: How Illicit Trade Made America* (New York, 2013), and Rodolphe Durand and Jean-Philippe Vergne, *The Pirate Organization: Lessons from the Fringes of Capitalism* (Boston, 2013).

7. Laurent Pfister, "L'auteur, propriétaire de son œuvre? La formation du droit d'auteur du XVIe siecle à la loi de 1957," (diss., Strasbourg, 1999), 247.

8. Ludwig Christian Kehr, *Vertheidigung des Bücher-Nachdruks* (Kreuznach, n.d. [1799]), 3–5 (BK).

9. *Hansard*, Commons, 9 April 1911, p. 2657.

10. William Leggett, "Rights of Authors," *Plaindealer*, 27 January 1837, in William Leggett, *Democratick Editorials: Essays in Jacksonian Political Economy*, ed. Lawrence H. White (Indianapolis, 1984), 394.

11. John Perry Barlow, "Selling Wine Without Bottles: The Economy of Mind on the Global Net," in Peter Ludlow, ed., *High Noon on the Electronic Frontier: Conceptual Issues in Cyberspace* (Cambridge MA, 1996).

12. Leopold Joseph Neustetel, *Der Büchernachdruck, nach Römischem Recht betrachtet* (Heidelberg, 1824), 78.

13. Philip H. Nicklin, *Remarks on Literary Property* (Philadelphia, 1838), 14–15; H. C. Carey, *Letters on International Copyright*, 2nd ed. (New York, 1868), 56–57.

14. The Committee on Patents and the Patent Office, 25th Cong., 2nd session, 25 June 1838, Senate Report 494, p. 7.

15. Copyright Commission, *The Royal Commissions and the Report of the Commissioners*, c. 2036, li.

16. Julius Kopsch, "Zur Frage der gesetzlichen Lizenz," *Archiv für Funkrecht* 1 (1928): 205–6.

17. Ronan Deazley, *Rethinking Copyright: History, Theory, Language* (Cheltenham, 2006), 149–52.

18. James Boyle, "The Second Enclosure Movement and the Construction of the Public Domain," *Law and Contemporary Problems* 66 (2003), 37–38; Christopher May, *The Global Political Economy of Intellectual Property Rights: The New Enclosures*, 2nd ed. (London, 2010).

19. Robert Darnton, *The Literary Underground of the Old Regime* (Cambridge MA, 1982).

20. J. Parton, *The Life of Horace Greeley*, quoted in Oren Bracha, "The Ideology of Authorship Revisited: Authors, Markets, and Liberal Values in Early American Copyright," *Yale Law Journal* 118 (2008): 245.

21. *An Address to the People of the United States on Behalf of the American Copyright Club* (New York, 1843), 9.

22. Kent Anderson, "The Hidden Expense of Energy: Print Is Costly, Online Isn't Free," *Scholarly Kitchen*, 19 January 2012; Kent Anderson, "Not Free, Not Easy, Not Trivial: The Warehousing and Delivery of Digital Goods," *Scholarly Kitchen*, 13 June 2012.

23. Irving, "The Mutability of Literature," in his *The Sketch Book* (New York, n.d.), 107.

24. *Hansard*, Lords, 1, 17 (1774), p. 1000.

25. J. G. Fichte, "Beweis der Unrechtmäßigkeit des Büchernachdrucks," *Berlinische Monatsschrift* 21 (1793).

26. Wilhelm August Kramer, *Die Rechte der Schriftsteller und Verleger* (Heidelberg, 1827), 128–29.

27. *Annales du Parlement français*, 5 January 1839, p. 122.

28. No thought or emotion can arise and endure in the individual without being mutually felt or thought by someone else. Othmar Spann, "Universalismus" in Ludwig Elster et al., eds., *Handwörterbuch der Staatswissenschaften* (Jena, 1928), 8: 455.

29. H. G. Pridat-Guzatis, "Grundlinien eines nationalsozialistischen Rundfunkrechts," *Deutsches Recht* 5 (1935): 377.

30. Arguably the very success of the modern patronage system has rejuvenated the need for prizes since salaries, being fairly flat and unresponsive to effort, do not serve to stimulate activ-

ity. Jerry Gaston, *The Reward System in British and American Science* (New York, 1978), argues that scientists are rarely motivated by their salaries but more by nonmonetary aims—renown in citation indexes, titles, prizes, and so forth.

31. Bernard Edelman, "Entre copyright et droit d'auteur: L'intégrité de l'œuvre de l'esprit," *Recueil Dalloz Sirey* 40 (1990): 295; Mireille Buydens, "L'Intérêt général, une notion protéiforme," in *L'Intérêt général et l'accès à l'information en propriété intellectuelle* (Brussels, 2008), 30–33.

32. Emmanuel Pierrat, *La Guerre des copyrights* (Paris, 2006), 60–61.

33. Yochai Benkler, *The Wealth of Networks: How Social Production Transforms Markets and Freedom* (New Haven, 2006), 469–70; Siva Vaidhyanathan, *The Anarchist in the Library: How the Clash Between Freedom and Control is Hacking the Real World and Crashing the System* (New York, 2004), chap. 2; John Tehranian, "Infringement Nation: Copyright Reform and the Law/Norm Gap," *Utah Law Review* 3 (2007): 540.

34. Nick Groom, "Unoriginal Genius: Plagiarism and the Construction of 'Romantic' Authorship," in Lionel Bently et al., eds., *Copyright and Piracy* (Cambridge, 2010), 293–96.

35. Rosemary J. Coombe, *The Cultural Life of Intellectual Properties: Authorship, Appropriation, and the Law* (Durham NC, 1998), 49; Thomas P. Heide, "The Moral Right of Integrity and the Global Information Infrastructure: Time for a New Approach?" *UC Davis Journal of International Law and Policy* 2 (1996), 220.

36. Hillel Schwartz, *The Culture of the Copy: Striking Likenesses, Unreasonable Facsimiles* (New York, 1996), chaps. 6, 7; Markus Boon, *In Praise of Copying* (Cambridge MA, 2010).

37. David Anjek, "'Don't Have to DJ No More': Sampling and the 'Autonomous' Creator," in Martha Woodmansee and Peter Jaszi, eds., *The Construction of Authorship: Textual Appropriation in Law and Literature* (Durham NC, 1994), 343ff.

38. Lawrence Lessig, *Free Culture: The Nature and Future of Creativity* (New York, 2004), 184–85; Lawrence Lessig, *The Future of Ideas: The Fate of the Commons in a Connected World* (New York, 2002), 9.

39. Lionel Bently and Brad Sherman, "Cultures of Copying: Digital Sampling and Copyright Law," *Entertainment Law Review* 5 (1992); Peter Dicola, "An Economic View of Legal Restrictions on Musical Borrowing and Appropriation," in Mario Biagioli et al., eds., *Making and Unmaking Intellectual Property* (Chicago, 2011), 236–37.

40. Mark Amerika, *Remix the Book* (Minneapolis, 2011).

41. Jonathan Lethem, "The Ecstasy of Influence: A Plagiarism," *Harper's Magazine*, February 2007.

42. Aaron Schwabach, *Fan Fiction and Copyright: Outsider Works and Intellectual Property Protection* (Farnham, 2011), 5, 111–13.

43. David Shields, *Reality Hunger* (New York, 2010).

44. Martha Woodmansee, "On the Author Effect: Recovering Collectivity," in Woodmansee and Peter Jaszi, *The Construction of Authorship*, 24–25.

45. Howard Bloom, "Who's Smarter: Chimps, Baboons or Bacteria? The Power of Group IQ," in Mark Tovey, ed., *Collective Intelligence* (Oakton, 2008), 251ff.

46. Stefan Wuchty et al., "The Increasing Dominance of Teams in Production of Knowledge," *Science* 316 (2007): 1036–39.

47. http://www.piratpartiet.se/kultur.

48. Matthew Rimmer, *Digital Copyright and the Consumer Revolution: Hands Off My iPod* (Cheltenham, 2007), 6–8.

49. Jeremy Waldron, "From Authors to Copiers: Individual Rights and Social Values in Intellectual Property," *Chicago-Kent Law Review* 68 (1993): 877; Guy Pessach, "The Author's Moral Right of Integrity in Cyberspace: A Preliminary Normative Framework," *International Review of Industrial Property and Copyright Law* 34 (2003): 252; *Industries culturelles et nouvelles techniques: Rapport de la commission présidée par Pierre Sirinelli* (Paris, 1994), 64.

50. Richard Schiff, "Originality," in Schiff and Robert Nelson, eds., *Critical Terms for Art History*, 2nd ed. (Chicago, 2003), 145–59.

51. Kevin Kelly, "Scan This Book!" *New York Times Magazine*, 14 May 2006. An adumbration in John Perry Barlow, "A Declaration of the Independence of Cyberspace," 8 February 1996, at https://projects.eff.org/~barlow/Declaration-Final.html. A start-up company, Citia, now dissolves books back into their basic ideas so that they can be recombined with others, much as Kelly advocates: www.citia.com.

52. Peter Suber, *Open Access* (Cambridge MA, 2012).

53. Barlow, "Selling Wine without Bottles," 21.

54. Raymond Shih Ray Ku, "The Creative Destruction of Copyright: Napster and the New Economics of Digital Technology," *University of Chicago Law Review* 69 (2002): 308–9. Though this advice ignored obvious contradictions. If bands were not to sell their albums but instead their T-shirts and other branded merchandise, did the vicious cycle of property and its pirating not just start over again?

55. Daniel Cohen, "La Propriété intellectuelle, c'est le vol," *Le Monde*, 8 April 2001.

56. Information Infrastructure Taskforce, *Intellectual Property and the National Information Infrastructure: The Report on the Working Group on Intellectual Property Rights* (September 1995), 228–29; Benkler, *Wealth of Networks*, 441–42; Yochai Benkler, "Through the Looking Glass: Alice and the Constitutional Foundations of the Public Domain," *Law and Contemporary Problems* 66 (2003): 216–17.

57. Pamela Samuelson et al., "Statutory Damages: A Rarity in Copyright Laws Internationally, But for How Long?" *Journal of the Copyright Society of the USA* 60 (2013).

58. 18 U.S.C. §2319; 17 U.S.C. §1204.

59. Code de la propriété intellectuelle, art. L 335–2.

60. David Lefranc, "The Metamorphosis of *Contrefaçon* in French Copyright Law," in Bently, *Copyright and Piracy*, 56–58.

61. Elizabeth Adeney, *The Moral Rights of Authors and Performers* (Oxford, 2006), 209–10.

62. Bently, *Copyright and Piracy*, xvii.

63. Paul Goldstein, *Copyright's Highway: From Gutenberg to the Celestial Jukebox* (Stanford, 2003), 169.

64. Adam Smith, *Lectures on Jurisprudence*, ed. R. L. Meek et al. (Oxford, 1978), 83.

65. Sénat, Report 53, 22 October 2008, p. 74.

66. "So You Want to Be a Pirate?" in Ludlow, *High Noon on the Electronic Frontier*, 110.

67. Kathy Bowrey, *Law and Internet Cultures* (Cambridge, 2005), 155.

68. Quoted in Robert Levine, *Free Ride: How Digital Parasites are Destroying the Culture Business, and How the Culture Business Can Fight Back* (New York, 2011), 202–03.

69. "It is often the nature of revolutions to unify under the same flag radically different vantages" was his lame argument. Cohen, "La Propriété intellectuelle." And because you can never have too much of a good slogan, repeated by Christian Paul, *Journal Officiel*, Assemblée, 30 June 2006, p. 4680. And Didier Mathus, *Journal Officiel*, Assemblée, 11 March 2009, p. 2497. And riposted by Denis Olivennes, *La Gratuité, c'est le vol: Quand le piratage tue la culture* (Paris, 2007).

70. Christophe Geiger, *Droit d'auteur et droit du public à l'information* (Paris, 2004), 336–38.

71. Jane C. Ginsburg, "Authors and Users in Copyright," *Journal of the Copyright Society of the USA* 45, 1 (1997): 1.

72. Waldron, "From Authors to Copiers"; William Patry, *Moral Panics and the Copyright Wars* (New York, n.d.); Neil Weinstock Netanel, *Copyright's Paradox* (New York, 2008), chap. 4 and passim; Stephen M. McJohn, "Fair Use and Privatization in Copyright," *San Diego Law Review* 35 (1998); Patricia Aufderheide and Peter Jaszi, *Reclaiming Fair Use: How to Put Balance Back in Copyright* (Chicago, 2011); Jason Mazzone, *Copyfraud and Other Abuses of Intellectual Property Law* (Stanford, 2011); Jessica Litman, *Digital Copyright* (Amherst, 2001); James Boyle, *Shamans,*

Software and Spleens: Law and the Construction of the Information Society (Cambridge MA, 1996), chap. 11.

73. David Fagundes, "Property Rhetoric and the Public Domain," *Minnesota Law Review* 94 (2010): 691–92.

74. Lior Zemer, *The Idea of Authorship in Copyright* (Aldershot, 2007), chap. 4.

75. Amy M. Adler, "Against Moral Rights," *California Law Review* 97 (2009); Tom G. Palmer, "Are Patents and Copyrights Morally Justified? The Philosophy of Property Rights and Ideal Objects," *Harvard Journal of Law and Public Policy* 13, 3 (1990): 843–49.

76. Glynn S. Lunney, Jr., "The Death of Copyright: Digital Technology, Private Copying and the Digital Millennium Copyright Act," *Virginia Law Review* 87, 5 (2001): 821; Peter K. Yu, "The Escalating Copyright Wars," *Hofstra Law Review* 32 (2004): 940.

77. David Lange, "At Play in the Fields of the Word: Copyright and the Construction of Authorship in the Post-Literate Millennium," *Law and Contemporary Problems* 55, 2 (1992): 151.

78. David Lange, "Reimagining the Public Domain," *Law and Contemporary Problems* 66 (2003): 470.

79. Ginsburg, "Authors and Users in Copyright," 7.

80. Both in *Law and Contemporary Problems* 66 (2003).

81. Ginsburg, "Authors and Users in Copyright," 1–11.

82. Barlow, "Declaration of the Independence of Cyberspace."

83. Steven Levy, "Crypto Rebels," in Ludlow, *High Noon on the Electronic Frontier*, 186, 200–201.

84. Timothy C. May, "A Crypto Anarchist Manifesto," in Ludlow, *High Noon on the Electronic Frontier*, 238. More examples in Peter Ludlow, ed., *Crypto Anarchy, Cyberstates, and Pirate Utopias* (Cambridge MA, 2001), section 2.

85. http://pastebin.com/kD52Af4N.

86. Roberto Verzola, "Cyberlords: The Rentier Class of the Information Sector," in Josephine Bosma et al., eds., *Readme! Filtered by Nettime: ASCII Culture and the Revenge of Knowledge* (Williamsburgh Station, 1999), 95.

87. Christophe Geiger, "Right to Copy v. Three-Step Test: The Future of the Private Copy Exception in the Digital Environment," *Computer Law Review International* 1 (2005): 9; Anne Baron, "Copyright Infringement, 'Free-Riding' and the Lifeworld," in Bently, *Copyright and Piracy*, 126.

88. Levine, *Free Ride*, 204.

89. *Edinburgh Review* 304 (October 1878): 305; *Journal Officiel*, Assemblée, 11 March 2009, p. 2550.

90. J.A.L. Sterling, "Creator's Right and the Bridge between Author's Right and Copyright," *International Review of Industrial Property and Copyright Law* 20 (1998): 305–6.

91. Johann Söderberg, *Allt mitt är ditt: Fildelning, upphovsrätt och försörjning* (Stockholm, 2008), 166.

92. Levine, *Free Ride*, 46–47; Jane C. Ginsburg, "A Common Lawyer's Perspective on *Contrefaçon*," in Bently, *Copyright and Piracy*, 81; Bernt Hugenholtz et al., "The Recasting of Copyright and Related Rights for the Knowledge Economy" (Institute for Information Law, University of Amsterdam, November 2006), 203–4; Lefranc, "Metamorphosis of *Contrefaçon* in French Copyright Law," 55.

93. Ian Hargreaves, *Digital Opportunity: A Review of Intellectual Property and Growth* (May 2011), 5; Assemblée Nationale, Rapport 2349, 7 June 2005, p. 26.

94. *Journal Officiel*, Sénat, 8 July 2009, p. 6804; *Journal Officiel*, Assemblée, 30 June 2006, p. 4681. Sarkozy then used the same phrase in the speech quoted in the following footnote.

95. And then went on helpfully to suggest that the young were more intelligent than one might imagine. "Discours de M. le Président de la République. Accord en faveur du développement et de la protection des œuvres culturelles dans les nouveaux réseaux de communication,"

23 November 2007. Available at http://www.culture.gouv.fr/culture/actualites/index-olivennes 231107.htm.

96. Assemblée nationale, Commission des lois constitutionnelles, Report 1486, 18 February 2009, p. 75; *Journal Officiel*, Assemblée, 29 April 2009, p. 3740.

97. Emily White, "I Never Owned Any Music to Begin With," 16 June 2012, http://www.npr .org/blogs/allsongs/2012/06/16/154863819/i-never-owned-any-music-to-begin-with.

98. Commission of the European Communities, "Green Paper: Copyright and Related Rights in the Information Society," COM (95) 382 final, 19 July 1995, p. 54.

99. Hugenholtz, "Recasting of Copyright and Related Rights," 197ff; Michael Kretschmer, "Digital Copyright: the End of an Era," *European Intellectual Property Review* 25, 8 (2003): 333–41.

100. Levine, *Free Ride*, 46–47. The same analogy was used by the French Senate: Sénat, Report 53, 22 October 2008, p. 77, and in Ginsburg, "Authors and Users in Copyright," 18.

101. "Discours de M. le Président de la République."

102. Stanley Fish, "Plagiarism Is Not a Big Moral Deal," *International Herald Tribune*, 13 August 2010; Richard A. Posner, "On Plagiarism," *Atlantic*, April 2002.

103. Susan D. Blum, *My Word! Plagiarism and College Culture* (Ithaca NY, 2010).

104. Jon M. Garon, "Normative Copyright: A Conceptual Framework for Copyright Philosophy and Ethics," *Cornell Law Review* 88 (2003): 1291–93.

105. Helene Hegemann's *Axolotl Roadkill*, published by Ullstein. Andrew Orlowski, "The Not-Invented-Anywhere-Syndrome," http://www.theregister.co.uk/2010/02/19/not_invented _anywhere/.

106. Other German politicians in trouble at around the same time for similar infractions included Silvana Koch-Mehrin, an MEP, and Jorgo Chatzimarkakis, another MEP, who wanted a PhD to counterbalance his foreign name. Bernd Althusmann was the minister of culture in Lower Saxony. *Dagens Nyheter*, 13 July 2011, p. 14. Most recently Frank-Walter Steinmeier, SPD foreign minister and former vice chancellor, and Norbert Lammer, senior member of the CDU, have come under scrutiny. The Hungarian Prime Minister was Pál Schmitt and the Romanian, Victor Ponta. Lest this be thought to be a particular problem of digitality, remember that in the late 1970s similar concerns were raised about Chancellor Helmut Kohl's dissertation on the postwar political history of the Palatinate, "Die politische Entwicklung in der Pfalz und das Wiedererstehen der Parteien nach 1945," Heidelberg, 1958. The German obsession with doctoral degrees is in large measure a function of the lack of a status hierarchy among German universities, generally treated with the polite fiction as being all about the same caliber. Thus, where the ambitious Anglophone buffs his resume with attendance at a top-tier institution, the German has to add an extra qualification. Hence the far greater numbers of PhDs among the ranks of top German businessmen than their Anglophone peers. Egon Franck, "Kurse lassen sich kaufen, Signale nicht," *Neue Züricher Zeitung Online*, 8 May 2012.

107. http://de.vroniplag.wikia.com/wiki/Home.

108. Peter Drahos and John Braithwaite, *Information Feudalism: Who Owns the Knowledge Economy?* (London, 2002), 16; Bowrey, *Law and Internet Cultures*, 87.

109. Jacqueline M. B. Seignette, *Challenges to the Creator Doctrine: Authorship, Copyright Ownership and the Exploitation of Creative Works in the Netherlands, Germany and the United States* (Deventer, 1994), 36.

110. May, *Global Political Economy of Intellectual Property Rights*, 130.

111. Olivier Blondeau and Florent Latrive, eds., *Libres enfants du savoir numérique* (n.p., 2000).

112. Pascal Oberndörfer, *Die philosophische Grundlage des Urheberrechts* (Baden-Baden, 2005), 9–10. One French observer began emphasizing the importance of the public domain at around this time: Philippe Quéau, "Intérêt général et propriété intellectuelle," in Blondeau and Latrive, *Libres enfants du savoir numérique*. Another blamed the importance of moral rights for why so

few French economists debated the issue at all: Joëlle Farchy, *La Fin de l'exception culturelle?* (Paris, 1999), 215.

113. P. Bernt Hugenholtz, "Copyright and Freedom of Expression in Europe," in Rochelle Cooper Dreyfuss et al., eds., *Expanding the Boundaries of Intellectual Property* (Oxford, 2004), 343.

114. Eva Hemmungs Wirtén, *No Trespassing: Authorship, Intellectual Property Rights and the Boundaries of Globalization* (Toronto, 2004), 143–44.

115. Martin Senftleben, *Copyright, Limitations and the Three-Step Test* (The Hague, 2004), 19.

116. Manfred Rehbinder and Alesch Staehelin, "Das Urheberrecht im TRIPs-Abkommen: Entwicklungsschub durch die New Economic World Order," *UFITA: Archiv für Urheber- Film- Funk- und Theaterrecht* 127 (1995): 33.

117. Hugenholtz, "Recasting of Copyright and Related Rights," 7–10.

118. Wencke Bäsler, "Technological Protection Measures in the United States, the European Union and Germany: How Much Fair Use Do We Need in the 'Digital World'?" *Virginia Journal of Law and Technology* 8, 13 (2003): 28.

119. Thomas Dreier et al., *Urheberrecht auf dem Weg zur Informationsgesellschaft* (Baden-Baden, 1997), 68–70. A largely similar approach in André Lucas, *Droit d'auteur et numérique* (Paris, 1998), 11 and passim.

120. Thus the summary of French opinion, and a survey of the very sparse literature that dared to disagree: Séverine Dusollier, *Droit d'auteur et protection des œuvres dans l'univers numéri- que* (Brussels, 2005), 232–33; Séverine Dusollier, "Le Domaine public, garant de l'intérêt public en propriété intellectuelle?" in *L'Intérêt général et l'accès à l'information en propriété intellectuelle*, 119.

121. Sénat, Report 53, 22 October 2008, p. 26.

122. A critical take in Richard Barbrook, "The Holy Fools: Revolutionary Elitism in Cyber- space," in Patricia Pisters, ed., *Micropolitics of Media Culture: Reading the Rhizomes of Deleuze and Guattari* (Amsterdam, 2001).

123. Thomas Hüetlin and Philipp Oehmke, "Just Shut Them Down, Man," *Spiegel Online*, 20 April 2012.

124. Traces of it in Scott M. Martin, "The Mythology of the Public Domain: Exploring the Myths behind Attacks on the Duration of Copyright Protection," *Loyola of Los Angeles Law Review* 36 (2002): 316.

125. "Le Parti pirate français rêve de suivre l'exemple allemande," *Le Figaro*, 20 September 2011.

126. http://www.piratpartiet.se/kultur.

127. Anders Rydell and Sam Sundberg, *Piraterna: Historien om The Pirate Bay, Piratpartiet och Piratbyrån* (Stockholm, 2010), 82, 91, 95.

128. Rollo Romig, "The First Church of Pirate Bay," *New Yorker*, 12 January 2012.

129. *Economist*, 22 October 2011, p. 62; 28 April 2012, p. 60.

130. Only 10 percent of the Swedish party was said to be women. Michael Brake, "Die Digital-Liberalen," *taz*, 11 September 2006.

131. Lucas, *Droit d'auteur et numérique*, 7.

132. Jürgen Habermas, "Political Communication in Media Society: Does Democracy Still Enjoy an Epistemic Dimension?" *Communication Theory* 16 (2006): 423, nt. 3.

133. Philippe Breton, *The Culture of the Internet and the Internet as Cult: Social Fears and Reli- gious Fantasies* (Duluth, 2010), 143.

134. "Für Publikationsfreiheit und die Wahrung der Urheberrechte," http://textkritik.de /urheberrecht/. 2636 very high-level signatories as of the moment it closed.

135. Sven Becker et al., "Artists Turn against Pirate Party," *Spiegel Online*, 20 April 2012.

136. Söderberg, *Allt mitt är ditt*, 217.

137. Stefan Münkler, *Emergenz digitaler Öffentlichkeiten: Die sozialen Medien im Web 2.0* (Frankfurt, 2009), 53–54; Bowrey, *Law and Internet Cultures*, 60–63.

138. *Journal Officiel*, Assemblée, 7 March 2006, p. 1612, Christine Boutin.

139. Nicholas Kulish, "Direct Democracy, 2.0," *New York Times*, 6 May 2012; Richard Barbrook and Andy Cameron, "The Californian Ideology," August 1995, http://www.hrc.wmin.ac.uk/theory-californianideology-main.html. A historical account of the countercultural roots of the web in Patrice Flichy, *The Internet* Imaginaire (Cambridge MA, 2007).

140. Olivennes, *La gratuité, c'est le vol*, 16–19.

141. Richard Barbrook, "The High-Tech Gift Economy," in Bosma, *Readme!*, 132.

142. Rimmer, *Digital Copyright and the Consumer Revolution*, 121.

143. Tehranian, "Infringement Nation," 541–42. In May 2012 Victor Willis, lead singer of the Village People, became one of the first to win back rights to his works. *New York Times*, 9 May 2012, p. B1.

144. Christophe Geiger, "Constitutionalising Intellectual Property Law? The Influence of Fundamental Rights on Intellectual Property in the European Union," *International Review of Intellectual Property and Competition Law* 37, 4 (2006): 371.

145. Frédéric Pollaud-Dulian, *Le Droit d'auteur* (Paris, 2005), 299–300. More moderately, portraying perpetuity as part of an "absolutist conception," Henri Desbois, *Le Droit d'auteur en France*, 3rd ed. (Paris, 1978), 416.

146. Geiger, *Droit d'auteur et droit du public à l'information*, 10, 36, 42–43. Similar skepticism about moral rights taken too far in Françoise Benhamou and Joëlle Farchy, *Droit d'auteur et copyright*, 2nd ed. (Paris, 2009), 26. A much more Anglo-Saxon approach to the French system infuses Stéphanie Carre, "L'Interêt du public en droit d'auteur," (diss., Montpellier 1, 2004), who argues that the French system, despite its reputation, actually takes the public into account. See 17–18 and passim.

147. Max-Planck-Institut für Immaterialgüter- und Wettbewerbsrecht, "Declaration: A Balanced Interpretation of the 'Three-Step Test' in Copyright Law," at http://www.ip.mpg.de/files/pdf2/declaration_three_step_test_final_english1.pdf.

148. "The Wittem Project: European Copyright Code," April 2010, p. 7, www.copyrightcode.eu; P. Bernt Hugenholtz, "The Wittem Group's European Copyright Code," in T.-E. Synodinou, ed., *Codification of European Copyright Law* (Alphen aan den Rijn, 2012), 342.

149. Reto M. Hilty, "Declaration On the 'Three-Step Test': Where Do We Go From Here?" *Journal of Intellectual Property, Information Technology and E-Commerce Law* 1 (2010): 84. In contrast, during discussion of the Three-Step Declaration, Rainer Kuhlen suggested that the EU follow a fair use principle rather than the EU's exhaustive list of twenty permitted exceptions. Monika Ermert, "IP Experts Sign Declaration Seeking Balanced Copyright Three-Step Test," *Intellectual Property Watch*, 24 June 2008, http://www.ip-watch.org/.

150. Though this observer advocated nothing more fire-breathing than allowing authors to waive their moral rights (otherwise impossible in countries like France and Germany) and accept technical adjustments to transfer film from the cinema to TV. André Françon, "Protection of Artists' Moral Rights and the Internet," in Frédéric Pollaud-Dulian, ed., *The Internet and Authors' Rights* (London, 1999), 80–83. A similar attitude earlier in Roland Dumas, *La Propriété littéraire et artistique* (Paris, 1987), 199.

151. Reto M. Hilty, "Five Lessons about Copyright in the Information Society," *Journal of the Copyright Society of the USA* 53, 1–2 (2005–06): 124–29; Volker Stollorz, "Ein guter Ruf is Gold Wert," *Frankfurter Allgemeine Zeitung*, 17 June 2012, p. 55.

152. Christophe Geiger, "Intérêt general, droit d'accès à l'information et droit de propriété," in *L'Intérêt général et l'accès à l'information en propriété intellectuelle*, 192–99.

153. A similar US case, *Nichols v. Universal Pictures Corp.*, 282 U.S. 902 (1931), evaluating two films with similar plots, had come to the opposite conclusion, upholding the idea/expression distinction with a famous ruling by Judge Learned Hand that formulated the "levels of abstractions test." But, on the other hand, in *Animal Fair, Inc. v. AMFESCO Indus.*, 794 F.2d 678 (8th Cir. 1986), and other more recent cases, the "total concept and feel" of a set of bedroom slippers was

allowed to be protected, shifting much closer to the idea than its expression. Netanel, *Copyright's Paradox*, 58–62.

154. Oberlandsgericht München, 29 U 3350/98, 17 December 1998, *Zeitschrift für Urheber- und Medienrecht* 2 (1999): 149–52.

155. The aesthetic clashes between Brecht and Müller are discussed in David Bathrick, *The Powers of Speech: The Politics of Culture in the GDR* (Lincoln, 1995), chaps. 5, 6.

156. Bertolt Brecht, "Der Dreigroschenprozess," *Versuche 1–12* (Berlin, 1959), 248.

157. Hauke Sattler, *Das Urheberrecht nach dem Tode des Urhebers in Deutschland und Frankreich* (Göttingen, 2010), 43.

158. Bundesverfassungsgericht, 1 BvR 825/98, 29 June 2000.

159. Serge Regourd, "Contradictions à la française," *Le Monde diplomatique*, February 2011, p. 27.

160. Frédéric Mitterrand, minister of culture in the Sarkozy government, put it thus: "While the internet offers unprecedented opportunities for the diffusion of knowledge and creativity, maintaining and promoting cultural diversity on the networks requires that states make efforts to assure the presence of a varied body of works in languages other than English." *Journal Officiel*, Assemblée, 19 January 2012, p. 276.

161. Serge Regourd, *L'exception culturelle*, 2nd ed. (Paris, 2004), 97–99; Françoise Benhamou, "L'exception culturelle, Exploration d'une impasse," *Esprit* 304 (2004): 104. Though in its most extreme formulations, the exceptionalist impulse falls victim to its own contradictions. Thus, we are assured, learning French will help keep the relentless Anglicization of the world at bay. Reviving the now faded universal language—the quondam hegemon—thus becomes the guarantee of diversity. Claude Hagège, *Contre la pensée unique* (Paris, 2012).

162. Maurice Lévy and Jean-Pierre Jouyet, "L'économie de l'immatériel: La croissance de demain: Rapport de la Commission sur l'économie de l'immatériel," December 2006, p. 9.

163. One example among many: *Journal Officiel*, Assemblée, 20 December 2005, pp. 8551ff.

164. Loi sur le Droit d'Auteur et les Droits Voisins dans la Société de l'Information, 1 August 2006. The legislative history is at http://www.assemblee-nationale.fr/12/dossiers/031206.asp.

165. *Journal Officiel*, Assemblée, 20 December 2005, p. 8551.

166. Sénat, Report 308, 12 April 2006, p. 207. Arts. 31–33.

167. Assemblée nationale, Projet de loi 1206, 12 November 2003.

168. Assemblée nationale, Commission des lois constitutionnelles, de la législation et de l'administration générale de la République, Compte rendu 37, 31 May 2005.

169. *Journal Officiel*, Assemblée, 20 December 2005, pp. 8553–54, 8558, 8563.

170. Guido Westkamp, "The Implementation of Directive 2001/29/EC in the Member States," Queen Mary Intellectual Property Research Institute, February 2007, p. 207.

171. *Journal Officiel*, Sénat, 29 October 2008, p. 6360.

172. Assemblée nationale, Commission des lois constitutionnelles, de la législation et de l'administration générale de la République, Compte rendu 37, 31 May 2005.

173. *Journal Officiel*, Assemblée, 15 March 2006, p. 1913.

174. Lest we overestimate the sea change, note also that in a later debate Communist senators insisted that France should resist the encroachment of Anglo-Saxon copyright, with its focus on investors not authors and their moral rights. *Journal Officiel*, Sénat, 29 October 2008, p. 6356; Sénat, 21 September 2009, p. 7737.

175. *Journal Officiel*, Assemblée, 21 December 2005, p. 8607, Patrick Bloche; Assemblée, 30 June 2006, p. 4689, Christian Paul. The idea that the goal was a "balance of interests," the fundamental idea of copyright, now began to be heard for the first time in France during these debates. André Lucas, "L'Intérêt général dans l'évolution du droit d'auteur," in *L'Intérêt général et l'accès à l'information en propriété intellectuelle*, 85.

176. *Journal Officiel*, Assemblée, 21 December 2005, p. 8588, Jean Dionis du Séjour of the UDF.

177. *Journal Officiel*, Assemblée, 21 December 2005, p. 8614.

178. At ten euros monthly and a 26 percent participation rate among all internet users, the sums raised would have been but one-tenth of the income from CD sales alone. *Journal Officiel*, Assemblée, 7 March 2006, p. 1607. Nor were the Socialists unanimous on this point. Though the parliamentary group supported the idea, heavy-hitters within the party, like former Minister of Culture Jack Lang and François Hollande, eventually to be president, did not. They favored instead the government's approach of royalties for individually metered usage. The calculations of Pierre Sirinelli's commission put the income of a €5 levy on 14 million subscribers at about the projected income of the CD market in 2010. But, overall, the income was expected to be but 6 percent of that from exclusive rights. Sirinelli report, pt. 4.3.3, no date, no title, but available at http://eucd.info/documents/rapport-sirinelli.pdf.

179. *Journal Officiel*, Assemblée, 20 December 2005, p. 8547; 8 March 2006, p. 1666.

180. *Journal Officiel*, Assemblée, 16 March 2006, p. 1974.

181. Assemblée nationale, Commission des lois constitutionnelles, de la législation et de l'administration générale de la République, Compte rendu 37, 31 May 2005, Christian Paul, Jean Dionis du Séjour, et al.; Assemblée nationale, Rapport 2349, 7 June 2005, pp. 29–31; *Journal Officiel*, Assemblée, 7 March 2006, p. 1607; 9 March 2006, p. 1768.

182. *Journal Officiel*, Assemblée, 7 March 2006, p. 1602; 9 March 2006, p. 1761.

183. *Journal Officiel*, Assemblée, 21 December 2005, pp. 8591, 8595. In a later debate a Socialist senator supercharged the rhetoric, claiming that the strict defense of authors' rights was a categorical imperative that founded the French approach, unique not only in Europe but the whole world. *Journal Officiel*, Sénat, 29 October 2008, p. 6361.

184. Joëlle Farchy, *Internet et le droit d'auteur: La culture Napster* (Paris, 2003), 47.

185. The Centre national du cinéma was the successor of Vichy's corporatist Comité d'organisation de l'industrie cinématographique. Françoise Benhamou, *Les Dérèglements de l'exception culturelle: Plaidoyer pour une perspective européenne* (Paris, 2006), 196.

186. Olivennes, *La gratuité, c'est le vol*, 13.

187. The original was in Assemblée nationale, 13 January 1791, in *Archives Parlementaires de 1787 a 1860*, 1st series, 22: 212 or *Réimpression de l'ancien Moniteur* (Paris, 1847–1854), 7: 117. The more recent in *Journal Officiel*, Assemblée, 20 December 2005, p. 8551.

188. *Journal Officiel*, Assemblée, 15 March 2006, p. 1883.

189. *Journal Officiel*, Assemblée, 21 March 2006, p. 2101.

190. Ibid., p. 2102.

191. This aspect grabbed the headlines and was widely understood to aim at Apple and its proprietary format for iTunes and iPods. Nicolas Jondet, "La France v. Apple: Who's the DADVSI in the DRMs?" *SCRIPT-ed* 3, 4 (2006): 479–80.

192. *Journal Officiel*, Assemblée, 20 December 2005, p. 8563.

193. Assemblée nationale, Rapport 2973, 17 March 2006, pp. 3–4.

194. Constitutional Council, Decision 2006–540 DC, 27 July 2006.

195. Code de la propriété intellectuelle, L 335-3-1, L 335-2-1.

196. Assemblée nationale, Commission des lois constitutionnelles, Report 1486, 18 February 2009, p. 19. They even had ambitions for video games, where they were surpassed on the European market only by the UK and Germany. UMP, "Croissance: Révolution numérique: Le Meilleur reste à venir," June 2011, p. 7, http://www.projet-ump.fr/wp-content/uploads/2011/06/ump_num%C3%A9rique_propositions_2012.pdf. For similar reasons they had defended their software industry in 1985: Jane C. Ginsburg, "Reforms and Innovations Regarding Authors' and Performers' Rights in France: Commentary on the Law of July 3, 1985," *Columbia-VLA Journal of Law and the Arts* 10 (1985): 87.

197. *Journal Officiel*, Assemblée, 11 March 2009, p. 2491.

198. Assemblée nationale, Commission des lois constitutionelles, Compte rendu 27, 17 February 2009, p. 4.

199. "Le Developpement et la protection des œuvres culturelles sur les nouveaux reseaux:

Rapport au Ministre de la culture et la communication. Mission confiée à Denis Olivennes," November 2007, p. 5. Available at http://www.culture.gouv.fr/culture/actualites/index-olivennes 231107.htm.

200. Something similar was true in Germany, where a cultural predilection for being able to collect tangible objects (*Sammlerwut*) helped explain why the sales of CDs and DVDs remained much higher than in comparable nations. In 2010 CD sales as a percentage of total recorded music sales was 81 in Germany compared to 49 in the US. *Economist*, 7 July 2011.

201. *Journal Officiel*, Sénat, 29 October 2008, p. 6341.

202. Since FNAC made more money selling computers than music, it is unclear which side—content or internet providers—Olivennes's economic motives would have favored. Assemblée nationale, Commission des lois constitutionelles, Compte rendu 27, 17 February 2009, p. 20.

203. "Accords de l'Elysée," http://www.culture.gouv.fr/culture/actualites/dossiers/internet -creation08/Accords_Fiche%20explicative.pdf.

204. The documents referred to here can be accessed via http://www.assemblee-nationale .fr/13/dossiers/internet.asp.

205. "Discours de M. le Président de la République"; Sénat, Report 53, 22 October 2008, p. 12.

206. *Journal Officiel*, Assemblée, 11 March 2009, p. 2495.

207. Sénat, Report 53, 22 October 2008, pp. 61, 75–76; Assemblée nationale, Commission des lois constitutionnelles, Report 1486, 18 February 2009, p. 10.

208. *Journal Officiel*, Assemblée, 29 April 2009, p. 3742.

209. Sénat, 29 October 2008, p. 6362.

210. Ibid., pp. 6361–62.

211. *Journal Officiel*, Sénat, 13 May 2009, p. 4434; Sénat, 8 July 2009, p. 6809.

212. *Journal Officiel*, Assemblée, 11 March 2009, pp. 2512–15.

213. An example of government's defense of small French cultural producers, despite having the head of FNAC draw up the Elysée Agreement, by its Minister of Culture, Frédéric Mitterrand, nephew of the former Socialist president: *Journal Officiel*, 21 July 2009, pp. 6673–74.

214. Law of 28 October 2009. The legislative history: http://www.assemblee-nationale.fr/13 /dossiers/protection_penale_proplitt.asp.

215. For the presidential elections of 2012, the UMP began to have second thoughts about graduated responses. "Pour 2012, l'UMP veut faire oublier la riposte graduée," *Le Figaro*, 29 June 2011. And in July 2013 the HADOPI was revoked.

216. "'Ohne Urheber, keine kulturelle Vielfalt.' Zwölf-Punkte-Papier des Staatsministers für Kultur und Medien zum Schutz des geistigen Eigentums im digitalen Zeitalter," 26 November 2010, p. 2, http://www.miz.org/artikel/2010_November_Kulturstaatsminister_Positionspapier %20geistiges%20Eigentum.pdf.

217. In the EU parliamentary debates it was a recurring theme that "civil society," as the Europeans call public opinion, had spoken largely in unison against the measure and that to vote it down would be a victory for the grassroots. Gerard Batten, Paul Murphy, Sandrine Bélier, Martin Ehrenhauser, European Parliament, 3 July 2012, http://www.europarl.europa.eu/sides /getDoc.do?type=CRE&reference=20120703&secondRef=ITEM-010&language=EN& ring=A7-2012-0204.

218. "Rede von Staatsminister Bernd Neumann zum Symposium 'Der Schutz des geistigen Eigentums—Urheberrecht in der digitalen Medienwelt,'" 8 March 2012, http://www.bundes regierung.de/Content/DE/Rede/2012/03/2012-03-08-neumann-urheberrecht.html.

219. *Corriere della Serra*, *Financial Times Deutschland*, *Gazeta Wyborcza*, *Večer*, 5 July 2012, cited in Eurotopics, 5 July 2012, http://www.eurotopics.net/en/home/presseschau/aeltere/NEWS LETTER-2012-07-05-Civil-society-wins-out-over-Acta.

220. "Le Parlement européen vote contre le traité anticontrefaçon ACTA," *Le Monde*, 5 July 2012.

221. European Parliament, 3 July 2012.

222. Kevin Kelly, *New Rules for the New Economy* (New York, 1998), chap. 2; Bomsel, *Gratuit!*, 270–71. The biases of Google's page rankings are discussed in Alain Strowel, *Quand Google défie le droit: Plaidoyer pour un Internet transparent et de qualité* (Brussels, 2011), chap. 6.

223. Though the net has equally seen a renaissance of local cultural production and its long-tail effects promise a much more differentiated market. Not to mention that the trope of Americanization has often been wildly overstated. Richard Pells, *Not Like Us: How Europeans Have Loved, Hated, and Transformed American Culture Since World War II* (New York, 1997), chap. 11.

224. Dommann, "Autoren und Apparate," 61–71, 141–49.

225. Jean-Noël Jeanneney, *Google and the Myth of Universal Knowledge* (Chicago, 2007), 33.

226. "Schwatzen, Schrillen, Schreien," *Der Spiegel* 34 (2005).

227. *Journal Officiel*, Sénat, 16 November 2009, p. 10530.

228. And, indeed, various European libraries did see the advantages of joining forces with Google: the Bavarian State Library in Munich, the municipal library of Lyon, the cantonal and university library of Lausanne. Sénat, Report 151, 30 November 2011, p. 12; Assemblée nationale, Report 4189, 18 January 2012, p. 11.

229. James Grimmelmann, "How to Fix the Google Book Search Settlement," *Journal of Internet Law* 12, 10 (2009): 18.

230. Pierrat, *La Guerre des copyrights*, 166. Obviously, he continued, consumers like this idea since they are given free and exhaustive access to culture under the very ambiguous (polyvalent) "right of the public to information."

231. Calculated on figures for the early 1990s. English percentage: 23.65 percent, French percentage: 5.75 percent. Figures on world production of books from the UNESCO Institute for Statistics, "Book production: Number of titles by UDC classes; Total" available at http://stats.uis.unesco.org/unesco/TableViewer/tableView.aspx?ReportId=202. Some important countries are missing from the tables, including Australia, Belgium, and China. Except Canada and Switzerland, the books of a country were marked as being written in the primary language of that country. To calculate the approximate number of French books in Switzerland, the total number of Swiss books was multiplied by 20.4 percent, the number of the Swiss who speak primarily French. Similar calculations done for Canada. India was not included since no clear figure could be found for what percentage of Indian books are in English.

232. Matthew Saltmarsh, "Google Loses in French Copyright Case," *New York Times*, 18 December 2009.

233. Sénat, Report 151, 30 November 2011, p. 5. *New York Times*, 15 January 2010; "Google Book Scanning: Cultural Theft or Freedom of Information?" CNN, available at http://www.cnn.com/2010/WORLD/europe/02/08/google.livres.france/index.html. In 2011 the French reported that Gallica had done a million and a half books but also that Google had done thirty-five million. Sénat, Report 151, 30 November 2011, pp. 5, 11.

234. Sophie Hardach, "France Proposes Digital Book Swap with Google," *Reuters*, 12 January 2010, at http://www.reuters.com/article/idUSLDE60B20K20100112.

235. "i2010: Digital Libraries," COM (2005) 465 final, 30 September 2005, p. 5.

236. Robert Darnton, *The Case for Books* (New York, 2009), 10–15.

237. "Commission Recommendation of 24 August 2006 on the Digitisation and Online Accessibility of Cultural Material and Digital Preservation," 2006/585/EC, recital 10.

238. *Journal Officiel*, Sénat, 16 November 2009, pp. 10534–35.

239. Jeanneney, *Google and the Myth of Universal Knowledge*, 79.

240. *Journal Officiel*, Sénat, 16 November 2009, p. 10547.

241. *Editions du Seuil c. Google Inc.*, T.G.I. Paris, 79 PTCJ 226, 1/1/10 (Tribunal de Grande In-

stance de Paris 3ème Chambre, 18 December 2009). French law allowed authors to sign away rights to unknown modes of exploitation but only if the contract was in writing and promised them a cut. Code de la propriété intellectuelle, art. L. 131–6. German law held such agreements null and void. Pascal Kamina, *Film Copyright in the European Union* (Cambridge, 2002), 190.

242. "Memorandum of Law in Opposition to the Settlement Proposal on Behalf of the French Republic," 8 September 2009, p. 1, document 287, *Authors Guild et al. v. Google Inc.*, at http://dockets.justia.com/docket/new-york/nysdce/1:2005cv08136/273913/.

243. *Journal Officiel*, Sénat, 16 November 2009, pp. 10532–33.

244. "Memorandum of Law in Opposition to the Settlement Proposal on Behalf of the French Republic," p. 5; "Memorandum of Law in Opposition to the Settlement Proposal on Behalf of the Federal Republic of Germany," 31 August 2009, p. 3, document 179.

245. "Google lässt Auslandstitel aus Buchvergleich fallen," *Frankfurter Allgemeine Zeitung*, 16 November 2009, p. 15; Robert Darnton, "Google and the New Digital Future," *New York Review of Books*, 17 December 2009, p. 82.

246. Jeanneney, *Google and the Myth of Universal Knowledge*, p. 11.

247. "Memorandum of Law in Opposition to the Settlement Proposal on Behalf of the Federal Republic of Germany," p. 15; "Memorandum of Law in Opposition to the Settlement Proposal on Behalf of the French Republic," pp. 12, 17.

248. Counting Reed Elsevier as European. "Livres Hebdo's 2010 Ranking of the World's Leading Publishers," p. 4, http://www.publishersweekly.com/binary-data/ARTICLE_ATTACHMENT/file/000/000/127–1.pdf.

249. Glenn S. McGuigan and Robert D. Russell, "The Business of Academic Publishing: A Strategic Analysis of the Academic Journal Publishing Industry and Its Impact on the Future of Scholarly Publishing," *Electronic Journal of Academic and Special Librarianship* 9 (2008): 1–11.

250. Deutsche Bank AG, "Reed Elsevier: Moving the Supertanker," *Company Focus: Global Equity Research Report*, 11 January 2005, p. 36.

251. George Monbiot, "Academic Publishers Make Murdoch Look like a Socialist," *Guardian*, 29 August 2011. In the longer run, however, it seems clear that this model is unsustainable. Open access journals have been successfully competing with those behind pay walls, and public opinion is running against the monopolists. Taking note of especially Reed Elsevier's problems, the financial community has recently cooled to the sector's prospects. Jared Woodward, "RUK: The Maturing Threat of Open Access," *The Street*, 30 May 2012, http://www.thestreet.com/print/story/11560589.html.

252. Jörg Albrecht, "Forscher, hört die Signale," *Frankfurter Allgemeine Zeitung*, 17 June 2012, p. 54.

253. Thus the philosophical faculty of the Humboldt University in Berlin requires that it be given six copies of a commercial publication with a minimum edition of 150 copies. "Promotionsordnung der Philosophischen Fakultät II," *Amtliches Mitteilungsblatt* 19, 4 (20 January 2010): 7.

254. Latest figures from 1998: http://stats.uis.unesco.org/unesco/TableViewer/tableView.aspx?ReportId=202. The Germans produce a higher per capita number of dissertations than the US (67,000 doctoral degrees in 2009) to some extent because certain degrees, like law, which in the US require no dissertation, do in Germany.

255. The Shaker Press, for example, proudly announces that "the most important aspect of our offer is that we do not ask for any advances for printing costs, i.e. the publication itself does not cost anything for authors or editors if it is accepted into our publishing program." This is a press with a list of 20,000 doctoral works. See http://www.shaker.eu/en/content/publication/index.asp?lang=en&ID=50. Others require the authors to buy a certain number of copies, that is to finance it themselves. See the Herbert Utz Verlag: http://www.utzverlag.de/info_autoren.php. Others make it clear what the student has to pay per hundred pages, as with the Wissenschaftliche Verlag Berlin: http://www.wvberlin.de/data/druckkostenzuschuss.htm.

256. €773.99 for 100 copies of a 350-page book from the Dissertations-Druck-Regensburg, for example: http://www.liskor.de/asp/css-0001.asp?strInput=100&strInput2=0350&strInput3=0 &strOutput=0+EUR.

257. *Authors Guild v. Google*, USDC S.D.N.Y., Case 1:05-cv-08136-DC, Doc. 1088, 14 November 2013, pp. 9–12, available at https://s3.amazonaws.com/s3.documentcloud.org/documents/834877 /google-books-ruling-on-fair-use.pdf.

258. *New York Times*, 17 November 2010, 7 August 2011, 25 August 2011, 11 June 2012.

259. Its legislative history is at http://www.legifrance.gouv.fr/affichLoiPubliee.do;jsessionid= 32929A0E1EB85624B326F7023A832355.tpdjo15v_3?idDocument=JORFDOLE000024946198& type=general.

260. Assemblée nationale, Report 4297, 1 February 2012, p. 3; *Journal Officiel*, Assemblée, 19 January 2012, p. 273; Sénat, 13 February 2012, pp. 1049–50.

261. *Journal Officiel*, Assemblée, 19 January 2012, pp. 273–74, 277; Sénat, 13 February 2012, p. 1047.

262. Directive 2012/28/EU, 25 October 2012, *Official Journal*, L299 (27 October 2012): 5.

263. *Journal Officiel*, Assemblée, 19 January 2012, p. 281.

264. *Journal Officiel*, Sénat, 9 December 2011, pp. 9629–30.

265. *Journal Officiel*, Assemblée, 19 January 2012, p. 276; Sénat, 9 December 2011, pp. 9630, 9645–49; Assemblée, 22 February 2012, p. 1457.

266. Law 1 March 2012, art. 134–8.

267. Art 134–4; *Journal Officiel*, Sénat, 9 December 2011, pp. 9626–27.

268. Ibid., p. 9642.

269. Ibid., p. 9643.

270. [William Warburton], *An Enquiry into the Nature and Origin of Literary Property* (London, 1762), 11–13.

271. Irving, "The Art of Book-Making," in his *The Sketch Book* (New York, n.d.), 65.

272. Walt Whitman, "Leaves of Grass," in *Poetry and Prose* (New York, 1982), 27. More generally on Whitman and copyright, Buinicki, *Negotiating Copyright*, chap. 3.

273. *Emerson v. Davies*, 8 F. Cas. 615 (1845), quoted in Bracha, "The Ideology of Authorship Revisited," 202.

274. Antoine Compagnon, "Le Postmoderne," in Compagnon and Jacques Seebacher, eds., *L'Esprit de l'Europe* (Paris, 1993) 3: 297–98.

275. While Derrida was the most cited author in the *Proceedings of the Modern Language Association* during the early 1980s, he did not make it onto a 1981 list of the thirty-six French intellectuals considered most influential by French intellectuals themselves. Jeffrey Mehlman, "Writing and Deference: The Politics of Literary Adulation," *Representations* 15 (1986): 8.

276. Katrin Amian, *Rethinking Postmodernism(s): Charles S. Pierce and the Pragmatist Negotiations of Thomas Pynchon, Toni Morrison and Jonathan Safran Foer* (Amsterdam, 2008); Larry A. Hickman, *Pragmatism as Post-Modernism: Lessons from John Dewey* (New York, 2007).

277. Louis Menand, *The Metaphysical Club* (New York, 2001), pt. 3.

278. Catherine L. Fisk, "Authors at Work: The Origins of the Work-for-Hire Doctrine," *Yale Journal of Law and the Humanities* 15 (2003): 9.

279. Peter Jaszi, "Is There Such a Thing as Postmodern Copyright?" *Tulane Journal of Technology and Intellectual Property* 12 (2009): 112–13.

280. *Journal Officiel*, Chambre, Documents, Annexe 3222, 6 December 1937, p. 238.

281. Ysolde Gendreau, "Digital Technology and Copyright: Can Moral Rights Survive the Disappearance of the Hard Copy?" *Entertainment Law Review* 6 (1995): 216.

282. Lucas, "L'Intérêt général dans l'évolution du droit d'auteur," 80; James Boyle, *Shamans, Software and Spleens: Law and the Construction of the Information Society* (Cambridge MA, 1996), 123.

283. "Quand vous redeviendrez de gauche, vous saurez ou nous trouver," *Le Monde*, 5 May 2009.

284. Thomas Bender and David Sampliner, "Poets, Pirates and the Creation of American Literature," *New York University Journal of International Law and Politics* 29 (1996–97): 264–65.

285. Quoted in Melissa J. Homestead, *American Women Authors and Literary Property, 1822–1869* (Cambridge, 2005), 83.

286. Lawrence Buell, *New England Literary Culture: From Revolution Through Renaissance* (Cambridge, 1986), 378.

287. *Notions of the Americans, Picked up by a Traveling Bachelor* (1828), quoted in Buinicki, *Negotiating Copyright*, 12. After international copyright was introduced in 1891, one observer estimated the number of professional writers to have increased tenfold. G. Herbert Thring, "United States Copyright Law and International Relations," *North American Review* 181, 584 (1905): 74.

288. Max M. Kampelman, "The United States and International Copyright," *American Journal of International Law* 41 (1947): 412–14; Edward Eggleston, "The Blessings of Copyright Piracy," *Century Magazine* 1 (1881–82): 944.

289. Though he is credited with writing a book on the subject, it was apparently more of a company pamphlet and cannot be found in any library. Vivian Perlis, *Charles Ives Remembered* (Champaign, 2002), 36.

290. John Tebbel, "The Book Business in the US," in David Daiches and Anthony Thorlby, eds., *The Modern World* (London, 1976), 3: 533.

291. Paul W. Kingston et al., "The Columbia Economic Survey of American Authors: A Summary of Findings," Center for Social Sciences, Columbia University, 1981, p. 14.

292. Jon A. Baumgarten, "On the Case against Moral Rights," in Peter Anderson and David Saunders, eds., *Moral Rights Protection in a Copyright System* (Brisbane, 1992), 193; Jon Baumgarten, et al., "Preserving the Genius of the System: A Critical Examination of the Introduction of Moral Rights into United States Law," *Copyright Reporter: Journal of the Copyright Society of Australia* 8, 3 (1990): 5; Rudolf Monta, "The Concept of 'Copyright' versus the 'Droit d'Auteur,'" *Southern California Law Review* 32 (1959): 185.

293. "The Berne Convention: Hearings Before the Subcommittee on Patents, Copyrights and Trademarks of the Committee on the Judiciary . . . on S. 1301 and S. 1971," Senate, 18 February and 3 March 1988, Serial No. J-100–49, p. 339, David Brown.

294. Guinevere L. Griest, *Mudie's Circulating Library and the Victorian Novel* (Bloomington, 1970), 4.

295. Martha Woodmansee, *The Author, Art and the Market: Rereading the History of Aesthetics* (New York, 1994), 22–25, 40–41.

296. David R. Johnson and David Post, "Law and Borders: The Rise of Law in Cyberspace," *Stanford Law Review* 48, 5 (1996): 1384; Barlow, "Selling Wine without Bottles," 29.

297. Lewis Hyde, *The Gift: Imagination and the Erotic Life of Property* (New York, 1979); Jeff Berg, "Moral Rights: A Legal, Historical and Anthropological Reappraisal," *Intellectual Property Journal* 6 (1991): 368–69.

298. Lange, "At Play in the Fields of the Word," 148; Bernard Edelman, "Une loi substantiellement internationale: La loi du 3 juillet 1985 sur les droits d'auteur et droits voisins," *Journal du Droit International* 3 (1987): 575.

299. John Updike, "The End of Authorship," *New York Times*, 25 June 2006.

300. The original piece was Mark Helprin, "A Great Idea Lives Forever: Shouldn't Its Copyright?" *New York Times*, 20 May 2007, p. 12.

301. Because Helprin prides himself on his lack of tech savvy, it is hard to know precisely what the impact was. He claims his article had three-quarters of a million "hits" but then goes

on to say that none of them was favorable, suggesting that he means comments. Mark Helprin, *Digital Barbarians: A Writer's Manifesto* (New York, 2009), 31.

302. Kelly, "Scan This Book!"

303. Jaron Lanier, *You Are Not a Gadget: A Manifesto* (New York, 2010). The examples of Death Cab for Cutie and Phish are among the success stories examined in Greg Kot, *Ripped: How the Wired Generation Revolutionized Music* (New York, 2009).

304. Alex Sayf Cummings, *Democracy of Sound: Music Piracy and the Remaking of American Copyright in the Twentieth Century* (New York, 2013), 158–59.

305. David Lowery, "Letter to Emily White at NPR All Songs Considered," *Trichordist*, 18 June 2012, http://thetrichordist.wordpress.com/2012/06/18/letter-to-emily-white-at-npr-all-songs -considered/.

306. Alan B. Krueger, "The Economics of Real Superstars: The Market for Rock Concerts in the Material World," *Journal of Labor Economics* 23, 1 (2005): 25–26.

307. Quoted in Johns, *Piracy*, 479.

308. Helprin, *Digital Barbarians*, 83.

309. http://arstechnica.com/tech-policy/news/2010/10/kiss-frontman-we-should-have-sued -them-all.ars; Kot, *Ripped*, 33–35.

310. *Billboard*, September 14, 2007, at http://www.billboard.com/articles/news/1049302 /prince-to-sue-youtube-ebay-over-unauthorized-content.

311. Erik Bleich, "Freedom of Expression versus Racist Hate Speech: Explaining Differences between High Court Regulations in the USA and Europe," *Journal of Ethnic and Migration Studies*, 2013.

312. Susan K. Sell, *Private Power, Public Law: The Globalization of Intellectual Property Rights* (Cambridge, 2003), 60; "Situation actuelle du droit d'auteur: Entretien avec Alain Berenboom," in Jan Baetens, ed., *Le Combat du droit d'auteur* (Paris, 2001), 172–73.

313. "Amending the Copyright Law in Implementation of the Universal Copyright Convention," Senate Report No. 1936, 19 July 1954, Calendar No. 1931, p. 2.

314. Jan Zielonka, *Europe as Empire: The Nature of the Enlarged European Union* (Oxford, 2006), chap. 6.

315. Rochelle Cooper Dreyfuss, "TRIPs—Round II: Should Users Strike Back?" *University of Chicago Law Review* 71 (2004): 26; Robert P. Merges, "One Hundred Years of Solicitude: Intellectual Property Law, 1900–2000," *California Law Review* 88 (2000): 2239–40; Graeme W. Austin, "Does the Copyright Clause Mandate Isolationism?" *Columbia Journal of Law and the Arts* 26 (2002): 45–46.

316. Thomas R. Nicolai, "Erstanmelder- oder Ersterfinderprinzip: Eine vergleichende Untersuchung des deutschen und amerikanischen Patentrechts," *Gewerblicher Rechtsschutz und Urheberrecht*, Int. Teil, 5 (1973): 170–71.

317. Harold C. Wegner, "TRIPS Boomerang—Obligations for Domestic Reform," *Vanderbilt Journal of Transnational Law* 29 (1996): 544–46.

318. Dieter Stiefel, "The Policy of Insolvency EU-US," in Barry Eichengreen et al., eds., *The European Economy in an American Mirror* (London, 2008), 385.

319. One expert in the field sees Europe as toeing the US line, but the evidence accumulating since this book's publication suggests a less clearly teleological development. David A. Skeel, Jr., *Debt's Dominion: A History of Bankruptcy Law in America* (Princeton, 2001), 240–43.

320. In 2000 the Safe Harbor Agreement was signed between the US and the EU, by which US organizations that agreed to participate promised to handle the data of European citizens according to EU rules, thus avoiding difficulties with EU privacy standards. See http://export .gov/safeharbor/.

321. Jeffrey Rosen, "The Right to Be Forgotten," *Stanford Law Review Online* 64, 88 (2012): 88–89.

322. Michael C. Dorf, "The Hidden International Influence in the Supreme Court Decision Barring Executions of the Mentally Retarded," *FindLaw*, 26 June 2002, http://writ.news.findlaw .com/dorf/20020626.html.

323. One of the themes of T. R. Reid, *The United States of Europe: The New Superpower and the End of American Supremacy* (New York, 2004).

324. "The Copyright Term Extension Act of 1995: Hearing before the Committee on the Judiciary . . . on S. 483," 20 September 1995, Senate Hearing 104–817, Serial No. J-104–46, p. 83. "The real conflict, in both Europe and the United States, is between the interests of the public in a richer public domain and the desires of copyright owners (who may or may not be relatives of authors) to control economic exploitation of the copyright-protected works that remain in their hands. That Europe has resolved the conflict one way does not mean that we should blindly follow suit," p. 88.

CONCLUSION: RECLAIMING THE SPIRIT OF COPYRIGHT

1. Charles Dickens, *American Notes for General Circulation* (original ed: London, 1842), chap. 18.

2. *Hansard*, Commons, 1 May 1839, p. 711.

3. *Congressional Record*, Senate, 9 February 1891, p. 2383. The Pearsall Smith quotation is from Senator Coke.

4. Lawrence Lessig, *The Future of Ideas: The Fate of the Commons in a Connected World* (New York, 2002), xvi.

5. James Boyle, *Shamans, Software and Spleens: Law and the Construction of the Information Society* (Cambridge MA, 1996); Lessig, *Future of Ideas*, 240–61; Neil Weinstock Netanel, *Copyright's Paradox* (New York, 2008), 205; Lewis Hyde, *Common as Air: Revolution, Art and Ownership* (New York, 2010); Laurence R. Helfer and Graeme W. Austin, *Human Rights and Intellectual Property* (Cambridge, 2011), 206–11.

6. Jill Lepore, "The New Economy of Letters," *Chronicle of Higher Education*, 3 September 2013.

7. Martin T. Buinicki, *Negotiating Copyright: Authorship and the Discourse of Literary Property Rights in Nineteenth-Century America* (New York, 2006), 107.

8. This was the concern of the Italian Society of Authors and Publishers in 1958. Claude Masouyé, "Vers une prolongation de la durée générale de protection," *Revue internationale du droit d'auteur* 24 (1959): 97.

9. *Arguments before the Committees on Patents of the Senate and House of Representatives, conjointly, on the Bills S. 6330 and H.R. 19853, to Amend and Consolidate the Acts Respecting Copyright*, 7, 8, 10, and 11 December 1906, p. 117.

10. That is the implication, though he resists drawing it, of Steven Wilf, "Copyright and Social Movements in Late Nineteenth-Century America," *Theoretical Inquiries in Law* 12 (2011).

11. *Le Droit d'Auteur* (1933): 53.

12. Roberto Forges Davanzati, "Solidarietà e necessarie cautele nell'esercizio del diritto d'autore," *Il Diritto di Autore* 3 (1932): 12–13; *Il Diritto di Autore* 2 (1931): 351–55.

13. Anders Rydell and Sam Sundberg, *Piraterna: Historien om The Pirate Bay, Piratpartiet och Piratbyrån* (Stockholm, 2010), 233.

14. Greg Kot, *Ripped: How the Wired Generation Revolutionized Music* (New York, 2009), 33–35.

15. William F. Patry, *The Fair Use Privilege in Copyright Law*, 2nd ed. (Washington DC, 1995), 452.

16. Isabella Löhr, *Die Globalisierung geistiger Eigentumsrechte: Neue Strukturen internationaler Zusammenarbeit 1866–1952* (Göttingen, 2010), 63, 233–36, 251–53.

17. *The Cases of the Appellants and Respondents in the Cause of Literary Property, before the House of Lords* (London, 1774), 24; Eckhard Höffner, *Geschichte und Wesen des Urheberrechts* (Munich, 2010), 1: 168; 2: 211–14, 253–58, 383.

18. For New Zealand and Australia: W. Harrison Moore, "The International Copyright Conference," *British Year Book of International Law* 11 (1930): 173–74; Sam Ricketson, "The Copyright Term," *International Review of Industrial Property and Copyright Law* 23 (1992): 759. For recent examples of Scandinavian adherence to the Anglo-Saxon side of things: European Parliament, 9 February 1999, *Official Journal*, 1999, pp. 4–533/66, 68.

19. Oren Bracha, *Owning Ideas: A History of Anglo-American Intellectual Property* (http://www.obracha.net/), 375–76.

20. Reichstag, *Stenographische Berichte*, 23 November 1906, p. 3858.

21. *Journal Officiel*, Sénat, 29 October 2008, p. 6360.

22. Florent Latrive, "Le Débat autour de l'appropriation de la pensée," in *L'Intérêt général et l'accès à l'information en propriété intellectuelle* (Brussels, 2008), 69.

23. Michael Brake, "Die Digital-Liberalen," *taz*, 11 September 2006; Rydell and Sundberg, *Piraterna*, 122.

24. Alfred Brockhaus, *Gesamtheit und Einzelperson im faschistischen Urheberrecht: Ein Beitrag zur deutsch-italienischen Rechtsgemeinschaft* (Berlin, 1939), 1, 5.

25. *Hansard*, Commons, 19 February 1840, p. 405.

26. Will Hutton, *The World We're In* (London, 2002), 61–63.

27. G. E. Aylmer, "The Meaning and Definition of 'Property' in Seventeenth-Century England," *Past and Present* 86 (1980): 93–96.

28. S.F.C. Milsom, *Historical Foundations of the Common Law*, 2nd ed. (London, 1981), 103.

29. A. M. Honoré, "Ownership," in A.G. Guest, ed., *Oxford Essays in Jurisprudence* (Oxford, 1961), 113ff; Lawrence C. Becker, "The Moral Basis of Property Rights," in J. Roland Pennock and John W. Chapman, eds., *Property* (New York, 1980), 192.

30. John H. Johnson, "The Reform of Real Property Law in England," *Columbia Law Review* 25, 5 (1925): 617.

31. Abolition of Feudal Tenures Act, 2000.

32. Sjef van Erp, "Comparative Property Law," *Oxford Handbook of Comparative Law* (Oxford, 2006), 1048, 1058; Jean-Louis Halpérin, *Histoire du droit des biens* (Paris, 2008), 340.

33. Anne-Marie Patault, *Introduction historique au droit des biens* (Paris, 1989), 15, 33–34.

34. Edward Jenks, *A Short History of English Law*, 6th ed. (London, 1949), 97–101.

35. Some parallels to trusts in continental law are noted in Hans W. Goldschmidt, *English Law from the Foreign Standpoint* (London, 1937), 105.

36. John Henry Merryman, "Ownership and Estate (Variations on a Theme by Lawson)," *Tulane Law Review* 48 (1973–74): 923; Francis R. Crane, "The Law of Real Property in England and the United States: Some Comparisons," *Indiana Law Journal* 36, 3 (1961): 282–83.

37. Eugene C. Hargrove, "Anglo-American Land Use Attitudes," *Environmental Ethics* 2, 2 (1980): 131–35; Stanley N. Katz, "Thomas Jefferson and the Right to Property in Revolutionary America," *Journal of Law and Economics* 19 (1976): 476.

38. Gregory S. Alexander, *Commodity and Propriety: Competing Visions of Property in American Legal Thought, 1776–1970* (Chicago, 1997), 50–52.

39. Halpérin, *Histoire du droit des biens*, 268–69; Robert W. Gordon, "Paradoxical Property," in John Brewer and Susan Staves, eds., *Early Modern Conceptions of Property* (London, 1995), 96–99.

40. Alexander, *Commodity and Propriety*, 114.

41. Quoted in Lawrence M. Friedman, *A History of American Law*, 2nd ed. (New York, 1985), 234.

42. Terry L. Anderson and P. J. Hill, "The Evolution of Property Rights: A Study of the American West," *Journal of Law and Economics* 18 (1975): 169–74.

43. Slaves represented between 40 and 60 percent of the South's total wealth, while the appropriations of the revolution affected some 20 percent of total land. Claudia Dale Goldin, "The Economics of Emancipation," *Journal of Economic History* 33, 1 (1973): 73–74; Peter McPhee, *The French Revolution, 1789–1799* (Oxford, 2002), 191.

44. Letter 1461 to Robert Morris, 25 December 1783, quoted in Richard McKeon, "The Development of the Concept of Property in Political Philosophy: A Study of the Background of the Constitution," *Ethics* 48, 3 (1938): 353–54.

45. Thomas Paine, "Agrarian Justice, Opposed to Agrarian Law, and to Agrarian Monopoly," in Paine, *Political Writings of Thomas Paine* (New York, 1830), 2: 412.

46. John Stuart Mill, *Principles of Political Economy* (New York, 1920), 1: 258, i.e., Book 2, chap. 1.

47. Andrew Reeve, *Property* (Atlantic Highlands, 1986), 62.

48. William B. Scott, *In Pursuit of Happiness: American Conceptions of Property from the Seventeenth to the Twentieth Century* (Bloomington, 1977), 16, 42.

49. Morton J. Horwitz, *The Transformation of American Law, 1870–1960* (New York, 1992), 129–30.

50. J. Willard Hurst, quoted in James W. Ely, Jr., *The Guardian of Every Other Right: A Constitutional History of Property Rights* (New York, 1992), 6.

51. Morton J. Horwitz, *The Transformation of American Law, 1780–1860* (Cambridge MA, 1977), 42–47, 70–78.

52. Barry Nicholas, *An Introduction to Roman Law* (Oxford, 1962), 101, 140.

53. W. W. Buckland and Arnold D. McNair, *Roman Law and Common Law*, 2nd ed. (Cambridge, 1952), 63–81.

54. Richard Teichgraeber, "Hegel on Poverty and Property," *Journal of the History of Ideas* 38, 1 (1977); Margaret Jane Radin, *Reinterpreting Property* (Chicago, 1993), 36, 44–46.

55. "Eigentum," in *Geschichtliche Grundbegriffe*, 2: 78.

56. Arts. 544, 537, 545. Richard Schlatter, *Private Property: The History of an Idea* (London, 1951), 232. In the German code, §903 was similar.

57. Quoted in François Terré, "L'évolution du droit de propriété depuis le code civil," *Droits* 1 (1985): 33.

58. *Allgemeines Bürgerliches Gesetzbuch*, 1811, §362.

59. Halpérin, *Histoire du droit des biens*, 214–19.

60. Peter Garnsey, *Thinking about Property: From Antiquity to the Age of Revolution* (Cambridge, 2007), 204–5, 222–25.

61. "Correspondence Respecting the Formation of an International Copyright Union," *House of Commons Parliamentary Papers*, C.4606 (1886), 34.

62. Forty per million in 1835, 507 in 2010: Claude Diebolt, *Die langfristige Entwicklung des Schulsystems in Deutschland im 19. und 20. Jahrhundert*, C.3. Anzahl der Lehrer in Deutschland (1835–1940), Deutschland, Professoren an den Universitäten, 1997 [2005], Gesis, histat: Historische Statistik. Available at http://www.gesis.org/histat/table/details/F19F3B6F210A682349F308 D8618F1D0C/020000000000000000000000000000000; Statistisches Bundesamt, H201—Hochschulstatistik, Professoren nach Geschlecht, Insgesamt. Excel file provided by Statistisches Bundesamt.

63. In 2009 four-year colleges in the US had a staff of 3.7 million. With enrollments of almost 13 million in 2009 and an average tuition of $21,657, that suggests an annual income from this source alone of $280 billion. To that came approximately $60 billion in federal and private R&D funding in 2011. 388,000 people worked in the motion picture and recording industries in 2013. Its gross intake was 61.2 billion in 2010. Figures from: Institute of Education Sciences,

Digest of Education Statistics, 2011 Tables and Figures, http://nces.ed.gov/programs/digest/d11/tables/dt11_196.asp; Congressional Research Service memo from Sue Kirchhoff, 9 December 2011 at http://www.techdirt.com/articles/20111212/02244817037/congressional-research-service-shows-hollywood-is-thriving.shtml; US Department of Labor, Bureau of Labor Statistics, *Industries at a Glance*; Motion Picture and Sound Recording Industries: NAICS 512; Workforce Statistics: Employment, Unemployment, and Layoffs; Employment, all employees (seasonally adjusted), http://www.bls.gov/iag/tgs/iag512.htm#workforce.

Index

À la recherché du temps perdus (Proust), 246
abolitionism, 116
abridgements, 5, 84, 89, 90–91, 125, 127, 132, 133–34
Academy of German Law, 189, 192
access, authors' to works, 211
ACTA, 358–59
Adams, Henry, 400
adaptation rights, 43
adaptations, 156; film, 132
Addison, Joseph, and Richard Steele, 63
Adorno, Theodor, 343
advertisement/advertising, 226, 233, 295
Aeneid (Virgil), 31
aesthetic control, 10, 11, 29–30, 48, 76, 100, 105, 127, 259; and compulsory licensing, 139; in copyright tradition, 93; in France, 99; in Germany, 106; and Kant, 78; and moral rights, 149–50; in the Statute of Anne, 89, 90
aesthetic theories, classic Greek and Roman, 130
AiPlex Software, 335
Aix-en-Provence, 43
Aladdin (Disney), 275
Albert, Prince (consort of Queen Victoria), 227
Alcott, Louisa May, 231
Alexander, Isabella, 428n50
Alexandria, library of, 345, 360, 376, 382
alienability of rights, 25, 30, 45, 72, 87, 95–96, 100, 130, 260; in digital era, 306; in Gierke, 109; in Kant, 77; limits of, 83, 96, 106, 127
Allegheny County, 40
Allen, Woody, 48, 49, 237
Allgemeines Landrecht. See Civil Code: of Prussia
altering works, 314
Althusmann, Bernd, 498n106
Amazon, 268, 293, 295
America Invents Act, 2011, 380

American Geophysical Union v. Texaco Inc., 298
American Repertory Theater, 2
American Revolution (1776), 69
American System, of protectionism, 115
analog era, 330
analog technologies, 265, 266, 284, 323
anarchists/anarchy, 98, 101, 334–35, 378
Andersen, Hans Christian, 6
Angélus (Millet), 255
anthologies, 124, 137–38, 212
anticapitalism: in Nazi ideology, 178, 182–83, 187, 191; in postwar German ideology, 210
Anti-Counterfeiting Trade Agreement. *See* ACTA
Anti-Machiavel (Frederick the Great), 36
Antiqua, 48
anti-Semitism, 35
Apocalypse Now (Coppola), 40
Apollinaire, Guillaume, 246
appellations of origin, 279
Apple Corporation, 268, 295, 354, 377, 502n191
Appropriation Art, 327
Archaeologia Philosophica (Burnet), 89
architecture, 33, 84, 127, 180
Armstrong, Louis, 46
art, social function, 19
Art Institute of Chicago, 249
art market, 39
Artaud, Antonin, 31
artistic quality, 46, 51, 52
As I Lay Dying (Faulkner), 374
ASCAP, 215
Ascent of Man (Drummond), 229
Asia, 19, 276
Asphalt Jungle (Huston), 1, 45, 48
assignees, 35
assignment of works, Germany, 25
Aston, Richard, Justice, 59, 63
Atlantic Monthly, 215

attribution right, 29, 31–32, 78, 91, 105; in Berne, 165, 168; of engravings, 90; in Germany, 106, 172, 180, 190, 209; and postmodernism, 270; in UK, 227, 228, 234, 258; in US, 228, 229
Auden, W. H., 271, 375
audience, 14, 391; as author, 79, 323, 328
Augustine, Saint, 35
Aupick, Caroline, 38
Australia, 2, 167, 182, 277
Australian Federation against Copyright Theft, 335
Austria, 55, 113, 179, 184, 381, 394, 403
auteur theories, 189, 222
authenticity, 33, 46, 49, 50, 51, 218, 242, 259
author: death of, 37, 270, 328; identity of, 26–27
authorial control, 46, 78
authorial personality, coherent, 35
authorial rights, personality-based, 60, 104–5, 127, 205
authors: American, 121; British, 117, 118; fascist views of, 163; primary, 272, 389, 390; social position of, 76
authorship, legal, 9
Authors Guild, 363, 368
author's intentions, 270
Authors' League, 215
authors' rights: defined, 15–17; as property, 94
Avant-garde culture, 168–69, 170
"Ave Maria," 47
Ave Verum (Mozart), 46
Avignon, 2

Babelsberg, 50
Bach, Johann Sebastian, 41
Baden, 185
Bahr, Hermann, 37
balancing interests in copyright, 16, 290, 316, 346; in France, 352, 369
Baldrige, Malcolm, 235, 278
Baltimore, 116
Balzac, Honoré de, 46, 81, 97, 131, 255
Balzo, Carlo del, 123
Bambi (cartoon character), 272
bankruptcy, 29, 380
Barbarella (film character), 42
Barbie, 272
Barcelona, 47
Bardot, Brigitte, 42
Barlow, John Perry, 18, 322, 329, 334

Barrès, Maurice, 31
Barrie, J. M., 23
Barthes, Roland, 270, 371
Basic Law, Germany, 130, 165, 208, 213
Battle of the Booksellers, 54, 56–58, 154, 262, 263, 293; twentieth-century version, 264, 316, 373, 385
Baudelaire, Charles, 38, 207
Baudouin, Manuel, 152
Bayreuth, 42, 47, 124
BBC, 325
Beatles, 360
Beatty, Warren, 48, 237
Beaumarchais, Pierre, 75
Beaverbrook, 3rd Baron, 233, 258
Beck, James, 71, 161
Beckett, Samuel, 2, 5, 272, 413n6, 413n12
Beethoven, Ludwig van, 125
Beijing, 321
Belgium, 29, 32, 40, 113, 195, 202, 274
Bell Telephone Company, 114
Benefit Authors without Limiting Advancement or Net Consumer Expectations Act, 300
Bergdorf Goodman, 44
Berlin, 2, 36, 47, 150; pirates and, 342–43
Berlin, Irving, 255
Berlin Declaration, Max Planck Society, 347
Berlin Wall, 150
Berman, Ben Lucian, 226
Berne Convention Implementation Act, US (1988), 250
Berne Convention/Union, 11, 19, 20, 112, 120, 129, 154–56, 302, 303, 393; and Britain, 11, 20; and compulsory licensing, 144, 175; differences within, 155; and France, 11; and national treatment, 155, 249; and Nazi regime, 178; and sound recordings, 141–42; UK membership of, 11, 154, 159; US membership of, 11, 20, 115, 119, 122, 136, 154, 161, 202, 213–15, 231, 232, 235–35, 258, 277–78
Berne Union, 1908 Berlin Conference, 125, 155, 156, 159, 160, 183, 258; and film, 187
Berne Union, 1928 Rome Conference, 125, 141, 172, 174–76, 185, 247; and film, 187; and moral rights, 145, 163–64, 181
Berne Union, 1948 Brussels Conference, 202, 244
Berne Union, 1967 Stockholm Conference, 203, 244, 277

Berne Union, 1971 Paris Conference, 203, 232, 277
Berté, Heinrich, 185
Berville, Saint-Albin, 99
bestseller clause, Germany, 211, 223
Betamax decision, US Supreme Court, 1984, 269, 292, 294, 351
Beuys, Joseph, 34, 445n150
B. Gaudichot, dit Michel Masson, c. Gaudichot fils, 151, 153
Biauzat, Jean-François Gaultier de, 63
Bible, 161, 275; King James translation, 23
Bibliothèque nationale, Paris, 362, 363, 364, 365, 369
Bicyclette bleue, La (Desforges), 134
big data, 364, 363
bilateral copyright agreements, 112
Binkley, Robert C., 214, 361
Birth of a Nation (Griffith), 40
Bismarck, Otto von, 276
Bizet, Georges, 5
Blackletter (font), 48
Blackstone, William, 6, 117, 146
Blackwell's, 376
Blanc, Étienne, 255
Bliley, Thomas, 284
blogs, 115, 323, 328, 334
Bloomberg News, 305
Board of Trade, England, 36, 159, 166, 406
boat hull designs, 283
Böcklin, Arnold, 150, 167
bohemians, 173, 183, 373
Bollywood, 301, 335
Boncompain, Jacques, 426n20
Bonnard, Pierre, 102, 271
Bono, Mary, 248, 251
Bono, Sonny, 248
book market: US, 117; UK, 231
book prices, 85, 111–12, 119, 231
books, UK, 51
booksellers, 20, 30, 53, 54, 55; Parisian, 58, 60, 61, 63, 96; provincial, 56, 63; and rights to works, 56, 67, 241, 260
Boor, Hans Otto de, 193, 202, 209, 463n64
Booth, Frederick, 321, 477n340
Boris Godunov (Mussorgsky), 40
born-digital generation, 319, 336–38, 344, 355, 392
Boston, 2, 118
Boswell, James, 38
Boucher, Rick, 299

Bourbon Restoration, France, 64, 96, 97, 245
Boursin, Maria, 102
Bowie Theory, 377
Boydell, John, 93
Boyle, James, 299, 334
Bragance, Anne, 2, 44–45
Brahms, Johannes, 124, 184
brand image, 18, 33
Brant, Sebastian, 88
Brassens, Georges, 247
Braun, Karl, 123
Brazil, 275, 277
breaking and entering, laws against, 284
Brecht, Bertolt, 39, 348
Brera Academy, Milan, 42
Breulier, Adolphe, 241
bricolage, 305, 327
British Museum, 140
British Phonographic Institute, 335
broadband, 337, 355
Broadway, 201, 321, 343
Brockhaus, Alfred, 397
Brodsky, Joseph, 271
Broglie, Victor de, 242, 298, 436n117
Brother Jonathan (periodical), 118
Brown, Dan, 4
Brown, David, 221
Brown, Hank, 252
Bruni, Carla, 355
Brussels. *See* EU
Buchanan, James, 118
Büchel, Christoph, 419n80
Buffet, Bernhard, 149
Buffon, Georges-Louis, 69
Bullets over Broadway (Allen), 49
Bundestag, Germany, 209
Burnet, George, 89
Burnet, Thomas, 89
Busch, Wilhelm, 172
Butcher, John, 233, 238
Buxton, Sidney, 159
Byron, George Gordon, 90, 117, 229

cable: broadcasts, 139, 307; companies, 236
Cage, John, 39, 271
Calder, Alexander, 40
Caldwell, Louis, 214
calico, designs on, 85
California, 4, 45, 235, 254, 291–97
Californian ideology of the web, 344
Callas, Maria, 247

Calmels, Edouard, 122
Cambridge University, 23, 68
Camden, 1st Earl (Pratt), 68, 131, 324
Camoin, Charles, 30
Camus, Albert, 39
Canada, 84, 117, 161, 225, 301
Canal. See Dame Canal c. Jamin
Canal, Marguerite, 153, 206
canned music, 143
capital, 7; intellectual, 8
Carey, Henry, 115, 116, 118, 123
caricature. *See* parody
Carlos, Wendy, 41
Carmen (Bizet), 5
Carmen Jones (Preminger), 5
Carmichael, Hoagy, 255
Carre, Stéphanie, 425n196, 500n146
Carrell, Norman, 270
case law: French, 144–45, 151, 162, 258; Anglo-
    phone, 226
Catholics, 222
CDs, 275, 323, 331, 337, 350
Céline, Louis-Fernand, 35, 169
censorship, 66, 217
Centre national du cinéma, 353
Chace, Jonathan, 120
Chagall, Marc, 270
Chaliapin, Feodor, 424n169
Chamber of Deputies, France, 83, 97, 98–103,
    387
Chamber of Peers, France, 298
Champs-Elysées, 312
Chaplin, Charles, 40; son of, 432n23
Chapman, Jake and Dinos, 272
chat rooms, 297, 334
chattels, 58, 88, 101, 146, 152, 206
Chatzimarkakis, Jorgo, 498n106
Cheever, Susan, 271
Chin, Denny, 367, 368
China, 19, 112, 275, 277, 393
Chirac, Jacques, 350
Chirico, Giorgio de, 31, 271
Choderlos de Laclos, Pierre, 42–43
Chopin, Frédéric, 46
Choudens, Antoine, 372
Christ, 41
Christian Democratic Party, Germany, 209,
    397
Christian Socialism, 208–09
Christian, Edward, 146
Christian, Fletcher, 146

Christianity, 209
Church of Kopimism, 342
Churchill, Winston, 150
Cinderella (Disney), 274
cinema taxes, 301
Cinquin v. Lecocq, 151, 153
citation, 137
Citia, 496n51
Citizen Kane (Welles), 26, 48
Citroën, 39
Civil Code: of Austria (1811), 404; of Baden
    (1809), 80, 86, 106, 149, 218; of France (*see*
    Napoleonic Code); of Prussia (1794), 79–80,
    106, 133, 137, 149, 218
civil law, 9
civil servants, and moral rights, 350
Civil War, US, 218
Clarissa (Richardson), 38
Clay, Henry, 115
Clinton Administration, 263, 296, 303, 308;
    and intellectual property, 278–79, 298–99,
    300, 318, 334; and WIPO, 280–82
Coalition to Preserve the American Copy-
    right Tradition, 237
Coble, Howard, 285
Cochu (French lawyer), 60
Cohen, Daniel, 332
Coke, Richard, 162
Cold War, 1, 50
Coleridge, Samuel Taylor, 270
collaborative cultural enterprises, 199, 203,
    215–19, 225, 240, 258; and moral rights, 216,
    236, 315, 378
collective works, 26, 93, 157, 181, 217–18, 221,
    249, 305, 306
colonies: British, and copyright, 155, 166; US,
    65
Colorado, 117
colorization, 1, 44–45, 46, 47–50, 237, 239
Coltrane, John, 41
Comedie Française, 2, 75
Comité d'organisation de l'industrie ciné-
    matographique, 502n185
Commentaries on the Laws of England (Black-
    stone), 117
commercialization of culture, 10
commercials, TV, 239
Commission on Intellectual Property,
    France, 204
commissioned works. *See* work-for-hire
commissioner of works, 217, 218

Committee on Commerce, US House of Representatives, 285

Committee on Film Rights, Germany (1933), 189

Committee on Patents, US Senate, 71, 118, 119, 131

Committee on the Library, US Congress, 161, 251

commodity, culture as, 15, 201, 237

common good, 15

common law, 10, 56, 128, 167, 203; and copyright, 54, 62, 63, 65, 67, 68, 71, 72, 91–92, 219–20, 241, 252; and moral rights, 227; and property, 85, 404; US state, 228

Commonwealth nations, 156, 166, 167, 168, 176–77, 213, 406

Communists/Communism, 18, 192, 201, 209, 358, 402; in France, 351, 356, 364

community property, 100, 102, 151, 152, 153, 206–7, 396

competition, 17

composers, 5, 28, 75, 139, 141, 143, 156, 174, 185, 212, 226, 244, 391; in film, 187, 215

compulsory licensing, 27–28, 111, 123, 126, 138–41, 224–25; and digital technology, 266–67, 281, 307; in France, 195, 204, 350–55; and new mass media, 170

computer games, 272, 296, 502n196

computer programs. See software

Comte, Auguste, 149, 150

Condorcet, Nicolas de, 63, 357

Confederacy, US, 116–17

Confédération Internationale des Sociétés d'Auteurs et Compositeurs, 175

Congress, US, 12, 49, 69, 113, 117, 142, 218, 220, 230, 231, 232, 238, 248, 278, 300

Conjectures on Original Composition (Young), 130

Conservatives. See right-wing parties

conservatives, cultural, 320

Constituent Assembly, France, 75, 204

Constitution, Bavaria (1946), 130

Constitution, EU (2003), 130, 303

Constitution, US, 23, 69, 214, 218, 250; and copyright, 69, 70, 71, 114, 123, 241; and limited terms, 243; and patents, 380

Constitutional Council, France, 354, 357

consumer electronics, 12, 18

Consumer Electronics Association, 292

consumer interests, 292, 297–98, 372

content, free, 337, 353, 356, 370

content industries, 11, 12, 17, 18, 20, 46, 300; and authors, 259, 263; and Berne, 231, 235, 242, 248, 260, 378; and Clinton administration, 278, 291–93, 379; in eastern Europe, 358; economic importance of, 275–76; as exporters, 264; and formalities, 259; in France, 247, 300, 315, 349, 355; and moral rights, 231, 233, 260; under Nazism, 174; position on intellectual property, 379, 389; in US, 154, 200, 236, 240, 263, 316

context, of works, 237, 239, 272

contracts, 25–26; click- and shrink-wrap, 284; and literary property, 58, 226, 227, 228, 229, 230

Cooper, James Fenimore, 231, 374

Copenhagen, 6

Coppola, Francis Ford, 40

copying artworks, 84; as creative act, 327; in digital age, 267

copyright: American views of, 70–71, 142–43; in art, 93; and citizenship, 70, 83, 109–10, 113, 119, 122, 125; in distinction to authors' rights, 21; in US, 161; public benefit of, 50, 252; renewal of, 218; social utility of, 68, 251; utilitarian approach to, 69, 290, 347

copyright, perpetual, 23, 45, 52, 53–54, 56, 58, 61, 67, 68, 71, 72, 95, 241–44; after 1945, 202, 289, 346; and compulsory licensing, 139, 141; in France, 74, 98, 122, 205, 245–46; in Germany, 123, 246; and International Literary Congress, 84, 124; in UK, 110

Copyright Act, Austria (1846), 218

Copyright Act, Austria (1895), 141

Copyright Act, Austria (1936), 190

Copyright Act, Bavaria (1865), 129, 156

Copyright Act, France (1791), 59, 74, 81, 117

Copyright Act, France (1793), 59, 74, 75, 81, 144, 258

Copyright Act, France (1941), 197

Copyright Act, France (1957), 17, 25, 35, 130, 138, 204–8, 218, 242, 257; and compulsory licensing, 144; and film, 222; moral rights in, 153

Copyright Act, France (1985), 26, 200, 211, 224

Copyright Act, France (2006), 311, 312, 350–55

Copyright Act, France (2009), 357

Copyright Act, Germany (1870), 123, 129, 137, 156–58, 146; fair use in, 158

Copyright Act, Germany (1901), 124, 137, 141, 157, 158; fair use in, 158; and melodies, 185

Copyright Act, Germany (1907), 124, 137, 157

Copyright Act, Germany (1965), 35, 138, 144, 208–13, 223–24, 247
Copyright Act, Germany (2003), 310
Copyright Act, Germany (2006), 310
Copyright Act, Italy (1925), 162, 165, 166, 190, 195, 242
Copyright Act, Italy (1941), 190
Copyright Act, Massachusetts (1783), 59, 131
Copyright Act, New Jersey (1783), 69
Copyright Act, Norway (1930), 182, 196
Copyright Act, Prussia (1837), 80, 99, 103, 106, 129, 137, 156, 246; and copyright duration, 183, 240–52; and fair use, 158
Copyright Act, Romania (1923), 195
Copyright Act, Saxony-Weimar (1839), 156
Copyright Act, Switzerland (1992), 33
Copyright Act, UK (1842), 28, 93, 140, 160, 217, 245
Copyright Act, UK (1906), 141–42
Copyright Act, UK (1911), 26, 123, 131, 137, 140, 143, 155, 195, 220, 229; and duration 159–60, 245; and formalities, 159, 258; and work-for-hire, 217–18, 234
Copyright Act, UK (1956), 137, 221, 232
Copyright Act, UK (1988), 137, 150, 200, 220; formalities in, 234, 258
Copyright Act, US (1790), 22, 65, 69, 70, 113, 161, 245, 258
Copyright Act, US (1831), 161, 244, 253
Copyright Act, US (1909), 26, 135, 139, 140, 143, 160, 244, 258; and work–for–hire, 218
Copyright Act, US (1976), 26, 135, 136, 139, 200, 218, 219–20, 227, 228, 230, 244, 252, 298
Copyright Acts, France (1777), 74, 245
copyright and foreign authors. See copyright: and citizenship
Copyright Association, US, 119
copyright duration, 4, 11, 21–24, 36, 54, 65, 66, 67, 72, 385; and Berne Union, 159, 203, 212, 242; in France, 98, 99, 352; in Germany, 80, 123, 124, 125, 174, 184, 212–13, 303; and Jefferson, 69; and lifespans, 247, 254; and Locke, 55–56; in UK, 110–13, 159; US, 136, 200, 248–52; wartime extensions of, 212, 246, 249
copyright industries. See content industries
Copyright Office, US, 219
copyright protection, measured from death of author, 219, 244, 253
copyright terms. See copyright duration
copyright tradition, Anglo-American, 12, 14–15

Corn Laws, 110
Corneille, Pierre, 255
Corot, Jean-Baptiste-Camille, 271
corporate authorship, 26, 31, 108, 205, 156; in Berne, 203; in Germany, 158, 181, 196
corporatism, 59
counterfeiting, 19; in digital age, 275
Cour de Cassation. See Supreme Court, France
Court of Appeals: New York, 136; Paris, 133, 150, 151, 152, 187
Court of King's Bench, 67
court records, 72
courts: France, 45; US, 50
Creative Commons, 293, 329
creative personalities in Nazism, 172–73, 178, 183, 193
creativity: in digital age, 314, 318, 327–28; incentives for, 51, 251, 253, 261, 289, 290, 306; mimetic view of, 130; reward for, 251–52, 261, 288, 289; stimulation of, 46, 52, 53, 242, 251, 288
creator, flesh-and-blood, 26, 164, 180, 189, 199, 217; and Berne, 203; in France, 205–6, 222, 306; in Germany, 211, 222, 223; and patents, 192, 219
creators, salaried, 329, 373–75, 377
creditors and copyright, 99–100, 103, 105, 127, 147, 152, 165, 180, 260
criminalizing infringement, 330–31, 352, 356
cultural conservatism, 15, 47
cultural exceptionalism, 17; in France, 348–49, 352–53, 356
cultural pessimism, 169
Curl, Edmund, 86
Curtis, George Ticknor, 133–34
cut-and-paste, 287, 328
cyberanarchists, 318
cyberspace, 334
cypherpunks, 335
Czechoslovakia, 165

Dadaism, 271
DADVSI law, France (2006), 312, 350–55
Dali, Salvador, 271
damage(s), 31, 32, 104, 107, 148, 150, 207, 222
Dame Canal c. Jamin, 153
Daniel, John, 162
Danish Film Institute, 41
D'Annunzio, Gabriele, 169
Dante, 242, 270

Darras, Alcide, 128
Darwin, Charles, 118
data mining, 368
databases, 224, 247, 279, 304–05
David, King (author of Psalms), 41
DDR, 201, 257, 342
death and copyright, 105
Death of Chatterton (Wallis), 134
Death of General Wolfe (West), 92
death penalty, 165, 378, 381
Deazley, Ronan, 428n50
debt, 151, 157; government, 7; US, 236
Deerfoot series, 31
defamation, 37, 167, 226, 227, 228
Defoe, Daniel, 88, 96, 432n43
degenerate art, Nazi Germany, 171
de Grey, William, Lord Chief Justice, 92
Deleuze, Gilles, 340
Delaware, 69
Delprat (French journalist), 103–4
democracy and copyright, 49, 386–87, 397;
    and creativity, 237–38
Denmark, 32, 41, 196
Depression, Great, 214
derivative works, 5, 127, 132, 134, 135, 144, 157,
    194, 228, 272, 318
Derrida, Jacques, 371, 506n275
descendants: moral rights of, 127, 152–53, 166,
    232; suppressing works, 140, 141, 160
descendants' interest in works, 30, 35, 42, 43,
    52, 55, 79, 123; in Gierke, 109
descendants' rights, 74, 99–103, 253–57, 152,
    228, 260; in France, 195, 206, 211; in Ger-
    many, 211; two generations of, 247
Desforges, Régine, 134
destruction of work, 33, 150–51, 235–36, 240,
    420n101, 471n236
Deutsche Bank, 366
Deutsche Digitale Bibliothek, 363
developing nations, 19; and compulsory li-
    censing, 28, 139, 274; and databases, 305;
    and intellectual property, 274–77, 291, 393;
    and global trade, 276–77
Deveria, Achille, 41
Dickens, Charles, 7, 51, 116, 117, 121, 323, 386, 389
Dickinson, Emily, 31
Diderot, Denis, 59, 60, 61, 63, 357
digital content: marketing of, 266; sales of,
    355; second-hand, 268
Digital Freedom Campaign, 293
Digital Future Coalition, 299

digital millennialists, 21, 318, 329, 397
Digital Millennium Copyright Act. *See*
    DMCA
digital revolution, 12, 265–69
digital rights management, 12, 282, 286, 306,
    307–8, 335
digital technology, 12, 263, 391; aesthetic ef-
    fects of, 269–73; business models of,
    266–67
digiterati, 322, 327, 329
digitization, 307
dignity, 165
Dill, Clarence, 214
Dingell, John, 285
Directive on Digitization of Orphan Works,
    EU (2012), 369
disclaimers, for moral rights, 234
disclosure right, 29–31, 105, 147–49, 167, 206,
    419n78; in Berne, 168, 203, 309–10; in Ger-
    many, 180, 209; in UK, 227
disco music, 46
Disney Corporation, 11, 37, 248, 272, 291, 326;
    cartoons, 41
dissertation presses. *See* publishers,
    dissertation
dissertations, Germany, 367
distributed networks, 327
divorce, 29, 105; and copyright, 102, 151, 153
divulgation. *See* disclosure
DMCA, 283–88, 293, 298, 307, 335, 339; put-
    back requirement, 308
doctrine of waste, 227
Dogme school of filmmaking, 41
Dognée, Eugene Marie, 123
dogs, 93, 227
domaine public payant, 204, 213
domestic content rules, 301, 360
Donaldson v. Beckett, 67, 68, 69, 71, 71, 74, 91,
    92, 94, 128, 160, 241, 324, 383
doppelte Lottchen, Das (Kästner), 348
dot.com sector, 294
downloading, 271, 275, 319, 336, 337–38, 341; in
    France, 351, 354–55; peer-to-peer, 12, 294,
    309, 331, 332, 336
dramatizations, 97, 127, 132, 156
Dreimäderlhaus, Das (Berté), 185
Dresden, 47
Dreyfus Affair, 152
Drinan, Robert, 136
droit de suite, 29, 203, 211, 236, 255, 304
droit moral. See moral rights

Drone, Eaton, 134
Drummond, Henry, 229
Dublin, 2
Duchamp, Marcel, 34, 271
Duguit, Leon, 459n209
Dühring, Eugen, 123
Dumas, Roland, 222
Dupin, André, 75
DVDs, 267, 283, 293, 294, 320, 331, 355
Dwelshauvers, Georges, 40
Dylan, Bob, 255

easements, 146
East Bloc, 12, 193, 201, 313, 358, 382
East Coast, US, 116, 119, 161
Eastwood, Clint, 360
Eaton Centre, Toronto, 40
e-books, 268, 272, 284
economic rights. *See* exploitation rights
Edelman, Bernard, 45, 426n20, 430n89,
    492n271
Eden, Lord and Lady, 148
Edinburgh Review, 119, 231, 336
Edison, Thomas, 276
editions, of books, 55, 80, 117
editors, 33, 157, 234, 235
education, mass, 113–15, 124, 125, 397
educational institutions, 252, 292, 296, 297,
    371, 388, 408
Eggleston, Edward, 120
Egypt, 242
8½ (Fellini), 40
Eldon, Lord, 90
Eldred v. Ashcroft, 23, 251, 290, 332
Eliot, T. S., 31, 169, 270, 374
Ellington, Duke, 46
Ellis, Edward S., 31
Elmgreen and Dragset, 6
Elsevier, 296, 366
Elster, Alexander, 175, 193, 463n52
Elysée Agreement, France (2007), 355
Emerson, Ralph Waldo, 231, 374
Emil and the Detectives (Kästner), 348
employee rights to works, 158, 211
employer as author. *See* corporate authorship
employers, 11, 158
enclosure movement, 323
encryption, 335; research, 292
encyclopedias, 93, 217, 218, 221, 234
Endgame (Beckett), 2
England, as model for French, 75

Engravers' Act, UK (1735), 86, 90, 227
engravings, 84, 86–87, 92, 127, 132, 228, 320
Enlightenment, 6, 11, 44, 319, 382, 387
entertainment industry, 16. *See also* content
    industries
Enzensberger, Hans Magnus, 344, 421n117
equitable remuneration. *See* compulsory
    licensing
Erhard, Ludwig, 397
Eriksen, Edward, 6
EU, 19, 138, 230, 252, 301, 303, 381; extension of
    term in, 1993, 242, 244, 247, 248, 254, 257,
    304; free market ideology of, 302; harmo-
    nization of rights within, 303–4, 310, 313,
    349, 379; as initiator in intellectual prop-
    erty developments, 302–3; as universal
    model, 379
EU Software Directive, 28, 224, 304
Euripides, 270
Eurocentrism, 349
European Commission, 50, 257, 305, 306, 337,
    358, 363
European Court of Human Rights, 381
European culture, economic worth of,
    305–6
European Parliament, 257, 306, 358, 392
European Union. *See* EU
Europeana, 363
Eurovision Song Contest, 341
Evans, Walker, 328
exceptions to author's exclusive rights. *See*
    fair use
excerpts, 137, 310
exclusive rights, author's, 27, 138, 160, 182, 267,
    351; in digital age, 281
Exhaustion of Rights. *See* First Sale
exhibition rights, 211
exploitation rights, 29, 72, 76, 88, 94, 100, 108–
    9, 127, 228; in France, 145, 151, 206; in Ger-
    many, 145–46, 211, 223
Expressionism, 171

Fables (La Fontaine), 58, 61
Facebook, 295, 381
fair abridgement, 135
fair dealing. *See* fair use
fair use, 21, 27, 126, 128, 134, 135–38; in Conti-
    nental nations, 137–38, 144, 347, 363; copy-
    ing, 137, 298; in digital age, 280–81, 289, 306,
    308–13; and digital technology, 266; and
    DMCA, 283–84, 285–87, 296; educational

exceptions to, 138; exemptions in US to, 136, 387; in France, 194, 208, 351, 369; in Germany, 124, 158, 186, 211–12; and Google Books project, 368; and handicapped, 281, 309, 311–12, 350, 368; and performances, 135, 212; in UK, 137, 160; of unpublished works, 220, 312

family, authors'. *See* descendants' rights

fan fiction, 328

Fantasia (Disney), 37

Farrer, Thomas, 36, 84, 112

fascism, 10, 29; and copyright, 50, 168

fascist. *See* Nazi

Fascist Italy, copyright laws, 35, 42, 145, 163, 184, 194

Faulkner, William, 374

Faust (Gounod), 372

Feinstein, Diane, 254

Feist Publications v. Rural Telephone Service Co, 28, 251

Fellini, Federico, 40

Fenning, Karl, 250

Fermoy, 1st Baron, 33

Fern, Fanny, 229

feudalism, and property, 399–400, 403–4

Feuerbach, Ludwig, 184

fiber optics, 293

Fichte, Johann Gottlieb, 77–79, 87, 106–7, 129, 144, 145, 199, 324, 383

file sharing. *See* downloading

Fille de Madame Angot, La (Lecocq), 151

film: as collective works, 93, 221–22, 228; and copyright ownership, 48, 187–91; economic importance of, 188; in France, 187; integrity right of, 48; under Nazism, 163, 180, 186–91; as new medium, 169; producer as author, 188–89, 222–24; rental right of, 268, 279, 292; rights of producers, 164, 187–91, 196, 221–23, 224; screenwriters, 48, 187–88; silent, 48, 168; talkies, 187, 222; 3-D, 48; US, 215

film adaptation of works, 233

film director, 48, 187–91; as author, 1, 222; moral rights of, 221

FilmFernsehFonds Bayern, 325

film industry, in digital age, 296–97 *See also* content industries

Film Preservation Board, US, 239

Fine Art Copyright Act, UK (1862), 33, 90, 93, 227

Firebird (Stravinsky), 37

First Sale, 267–68, 281, 284

First World War, 169, 201, 246

first-mover advantage, 332, 360

Fish, Stanley, 338

Flarf poets, 328

Fleet Street, 233

Fleming, William, 229

Fleurs du Mal, Les (Baudelaire), 38

Flightstop (Snow), 40

FNAC, 355

Förster-Nietzsche, Elisabeth, 38

folklore, 274

Folsom v. March, 133, 135

Fonda, Jane, 42

Fontane, Theodor, 124

Ford, John, 226

formalities, 4, 21, 24–25, 136, 387; in Berne, 156, 159, 160, 257–59; in France, 194, 207–8; in UK, 159; in US, 160–61, 213, 216, 219, 239, 241, 256

Forman, Milos, 26, 237

Foucault, Michel, 31, 371

founding fathers, US, 114

Fountain (Duchamp), 34

fountains, public, 33

4'33" (Cage), 39

Fourth Republic, France, 204

Fraktur, 48

France, Anatole, 31, 148

franchises, 8

Frank, Barney, 285

Frank, Hans, 192

Frankfurt, 47

Frankfurt school, 184, 201, 343

Franklin, Benjamin, 402

Frederick V of Denmark, 375

Frederick the Great, 36

free speech, 378, 381

free trade, 110, 115, 123, 291, 387, 392; in culture, 301, 321

French Revolution, 7, 17, 44, 73–76, 102, 109, 123, 132, 164, 173, 353, 402

frescos, 150, 167, 312, 240, 312

Führerprinzip, 181, 193

Full Metal Jacket (Kubrick), 40

Furtwängler, Wilhelm, 171

Futurists, 168–69

Gallica, 363

gaming. *See* computer games.

Garcia Marquez, Gabriel, 37

Gareis, Carl, 107
GATT, 236, 264, 275, 279, 291, 300, 301
Gay-Lussac, Joseph, 98
Geiger, Christophe, 416n25
geistiges Eigentum, 107, 129, 246
General Agreement on Tariffs and Trade. *See* GATT
genetically modified organisms, 302
genius, 15, 68, 131, 172, 173, 373
Gephardt, Richard, 46, 48
Germania 3: Gespenster am toten Mann (Müller), 348
Germanic law, 172, 176, 193
German national anthem, 185
Gershwin, George and Ira, 5; heirs of, 39
Getz, Stan, 271
ghostwriters, 30, 232
Giannini, Amedeo, 449n9
Gierke, Otto von, 108–9, 459n229
Gilbert and Sullivan, 113, 226
Ginsburg, Jane, 49, 233, 333, 334, 427n29, 435n112
Ginsburg, Ruth Bader, 251, 290
globalization, 21; of intellectual property regulation, 24, 379
God, 56, 88
Goebbels, Joseph, 170, 171, 174, 184, 186
Goethe, Johann Wolfgang von, 5, 36, 118, 123, 124, 125, 246, 375
Goldbaum, Wenzel, 187
Goldman, Bo, 238
Goldsmith, Kenneth, 271
Goldstein, Paul, 416n34
Gone with the Wind (Mitchell), 134
goodwill, 8
Google, 287, 293, 295, 343, 364, 369, 381, 382; Google Books project, 214, 310, 329, 345, 359–65, 368, 376; Google Books settlement, 363, 367–68; in France, 368–69
Gospels of Matthew, Mark, Luke, and John, 41
Gounod, Charles, 371
Gowers Report, UK (2006), 441n63
Goya, Francisco, 272
graduated response to infringement, France, 354, 356
graffiti, 150
graphic arts, 90
Grateful Dead, 322, 377
Gray v. Russell, 133
Great Dictator (Chaplin), 40

Great Expectations (Dickens), 7
Great Ormond Street Hospital for Children, 23
Green Party, 306, 351, 356; ideology of, 165, 342
Greenberg, Clement, 33
Gregory Committee, UK (1952), 225, 232
Grieg, Edvard, 46
Grieg Fund, 46
Griffith, D. W., 39
Grimm brothers, 41, 243, 275
Grokster. See *MGM Studios v. Grokster*
Grolier's, 376
group work, 328
Grub Street, 323
Guatemala, 23, 242
Guattari, Félix, 340
Gucci, 18
guilds, 59
Guillou, Jan, 344
Guinan, James L., 485n130
Guino, Richard, 270
Guizot, François, 117
Gürtner, Franz, 185
Gutenberg, Johannes, 263, 320, 361
Guttenberg, Karl-Theodor zu, 338
Gyles v. Wilcox, 91

Habermas, Jürgen, 343
hackers, 12, 21, 318, 335, 336, 387
HADOPI law, France, 356–57
Hajek, Otto Herbert, 34
Hale, Mrs. Herbert Dudley, 148
Hamilton, Ian, 220
Hamish Hamilton, 39
Hammett, Dashiell, 374
Hardinge, Lord, 221
Hardwicke, Lord, 91
Hardy, Thomas, 31
Hargrave, Francis, 87
Hargreaves Report, UK (2011), 309, 337
harm. *See* damage(s)
Harper, publishers, 118, 436n132
Harvard University, 374, 376
Hatch, Orrin, 238, 254
Hausmusik, 125, 186
Hawthorne, Nathaniel, 231, 374
Hegel, Georg W. F., 191; and property, 404
Hegemann, Helene, 338
Heidelberg Appeal (2009), 343, 347
Heine, Heinrich, 7, 184
heirs. *See* descendants

Helprin, Mark, 271, 376, 377
Hemingway, Ernest, 38
Hemingway, Sean, 38
Henriade (Voltaire), 87
Henry of Navarre, 87
Herbert, Victor, 139
Héricourt, Louis d', 58, 60
Hess, Gabriel, 216
Hesse, Grand Duchy of, 80
high culture, 16
high tech industries. *See* Silicon Valley
hip-hop, 327
History of England (Macaulay), 117
History of France (Guizot), 117
Hitler, Adolf, 170, 173, 174, 178, 179, 202, 209, 452n59
HIV drugs, 274
hive mind, 324, 329
Hoffmann, Willy, 143, 175–76, 179, 180, 182, 185, 189, 193
Hogarth, William, 86
Holland, 2, 23, 202, 242, 276, 302, 314, 326, 347, 393
Hollande, François, 502n178
Hollywood, 11, 12, 32, 37, 49, 50, 201, 215, 217, 226, 230, 236, 237, 238, 239, 243, 248, 254, 261, 264, 278, 294, 299, 374, 388, 390; and France, 353; and intellectual property campaigns, 293, 373; as smaller than university world, 408
Holmes, Oliver Wendell, 403
Holst, Gustav, 41
Holy Roman Empire, 400
home electronics manufacturers, 292
Home Recording Rights Coalition, 293
Homer, 270, 326, 329
homestyle exception, TRIPs, 252, 301, 310
honor, 32, 145, 165, 167, 173, 177, 203, 234; in digital age, 272; Nazi view of, 176–77, 183
Horkheimer, Max, 343
Horst Wessel song, 185
Hotten, John Camden, 121
House of Commons, 86
House of Lords, 67, 68, 221, 232, 233, 234
House of Representatives, US, 120, 250
Hubbard, Gardiner, 114
Hubbard, L. Ron, 220
Hughes, Charles Evans, 250
Hughes, Howard, 468n171
Hugo, Jean, 43
Hugo, Marguerite, 43

Hugo, Pierre, 43
Hugo, Victor, 5, 35, 36, 43–44, 75, 123, 141, 154, 243, 347, 351
human rights, authors rights as, 44, 166
Humboldt University, Berlin, 505n253
Hume, David, 402
Hungary, 338
Hunterian Art Gallery, Glasgow, 445n148
Huston, John, 1, 45, 48
Huysmans, J. K., 375
hypertext, 377

IBM, 236
Ibsen, Henrik, 375
idea/expression distinction, 86–87, 90, 106, 284; blurring of, 126, 132, 134, 348
ideas, ownership of, 86; rights to, 126
immigrants, 114; German, 118
immoral works, 89
impressions of books. *See* editions
inalienability of rights, 127, 145, 152, 180, 193, 202, 205, 234
incidental use, 312–13
India, 117, 155, 275, 277, 301
industrial designs, 279
Information Infrastructure Taskforce, 280
Information Society Directive, EU, 2001, 130, 138, 307, 309, 310, 311, 312, 314, 339; and fair use, 347; implementation in France, 350, 364
infringement, 27, 139
inheritance, 29, 101–2, 111, 151; law, 100–101
injuria, 107
integrated circuit layouts, 279
integrity right, 17, 29, 32–34, 43, 73, 78, 91, 149–51; in Berne, 168; and compulsory licensing, 139; under fascism, 165, 174; in France, 96–97, 104, 105, 206; in Germany, 108–9, 157, 172, 180, 189, 209; and globalization, 272; and postmodernism, 271–72; in UK, 227, 228, 234; US, 228
Intel, 295
intellectual property: assignable, 58, 60, 61; campaigns in defense of, 293; economic role, 18, 232, 235, 275–76, 278–29, 300–302; enforcement of, 19; as expression of personality, 87, 128–29; in Germany, 107; globalization of, 264, 273–78; importing and exporting of, 161, 231, 235, 238, 274, 275, 278, 291, 393–94, 406; as primary form of property, 58–59; trade in, 273–80

Intellectual Property Protection Act, US (2006), 300
intellectual property rights, 21, 63–64, 242, 394
interactive works, 272, 273
interest groups and copyright, 51
international copyright, in US, 114–17, 119, 120–22, 124, 125, 160, 162, 231
International Film Congress (1935), 186
International Literary and Artistic Association, 144
International Literary Congress, Paris (1878), 35, 43, 84, 95, 123; and Berne Union, 154
international organizations and copyright, 392–93
International Sanitary Conferences, 155
International Telegraph Union, 155
internauts. *See* born-digital generation
internet, 21, 266, 267, 273, 282, 321, 343, 357, 358
internet industries. *See* Silicon Valley
internet providers, liability, 281, 282, 286, 308
interoperability, 286, 354
interpreters, 30, 32, 40, 44, 46
intertextuality, 270
inventions, 60, 63
inventors, 131, 192
iPod, 354
Iran, 296
Iron Curtain, 359
Iron Curtain, The (film), 1
Irving, Washington, 120, 231, 324, 371, 374
It Takes Two (film), 348
Italian Society of Authors and Publishers, 247
Italy, 29, 32, 35, 165, 202, 242, 277
Ives, Charles, 374

Jacksonian politics, 115, 321
James, Henry, 215
Jamin, Maxime, 206
Japan, 19, 276, 280, 300
Jaszi, Peter, 299
Jaws (Spielberg), 135
Jeanneney, Jean-Noël, 363, 365
Jefferson, Thomas, 64, 69, 245, 359, 400, 403; and property, 71
Jerrold, Douglas, 90
Jews: and modernism, 169; under Nazism, 174, 188, 214–15
Joan of Arc, 36
Johnson, Samuel, 73

journalists, 138, 158, 194, 208, 233, 237, 257, 285, 323
journals. *See* periodicals
Joyce, James, 39, 256, 270
Joyce, Stephen, 39, 259, 272
JSTOR, 331, 388
Judiciary Committee: of the House of Representatives, 285; of the Senate, 378
jukeboxes, 139, 238
July Monarchy, France, 64, 83, 87, 97, 98, 101, 109, 129, 164, 205, 242, 245, 255, 298, 324, 387
Jünger, Ernst, 169
juvenilia, 99, 105, 149
Juvisy, France, 150

Kafka, Franz, 31, 375
Kant, Immanuel, 77–78, 103, 106, 108, 129, 144, 145, 199, 383
Karjala, Denis, 242, 381
Kastenmeier, Robert, 235
Kästner, Erich, 348
Keats, John, 230
Kehr, Ludwig Christian, 321
Keidan, Jonathan, 39
Kelly, Kevin, 329, 364, 376
Kennedy, Ted, 252
Kentucky, 161
Kilroe, Edwin P., 231
kings of Cultureburg, 33
Kipling, Rudyard, 37
Kiss, 377
KKK, 40
Klimt, Gustav, 477n339
Klippenberger, Martin, 34
Klopstock, Friedrich, 375
know-how, 18
Koch-Mehrin, Silvana, 498n106
Kohl, Helmut, 498n106
Kohl, Herb, 255
Kohler, Josef, 107–8, 128, 129, 141, 146, 459n229
Koons, Jeff, 137, 371
Kopsch, Julius, 143, 175–76, 179, 180, 193, 322
Kostabi, Mark 271
Kramer, Wilhelm August, 106–7, 324, 479n17
Kubrick, Stanley, 40

La Fontaine, Jean de, 58, 61
labor theory of property, 53, 55, 58
Laboulaye, Edouard, 81
Lacordaire, Jean-Baptiste, 147
Lagauche, Serge, 337

laissez-faire, 110, 356
Lakanal, Joseph, 59, 102, 255
Lake Poets, 89
Lamartine, Alphonse de, 98–103, 122, 140, 151, 162, 165, 243, 245, 247, 255, 375, 396
Lamennais, Hugues-Félicité, 35
Lammer, Norbert, 498n106
Landelle, Guillaume de la, 95
land reform, England, 1925, 400
land. *See* real estate
Landseer, Charles, 227
Landseer, Edwin, 227
Lang, Jack, 502n178
Lanier, Jaron, 376
Larkin, Philip, 31, 375
Latin, 89, 157
Lavenas, 149
Lavergne, Léonce de, 122
law and economics approach to copyright, 288–91, 333
law of nature, 69
Law on Musical Performance Rights, Germany (1933), 186
Law on Peasant Estates, Germany (1933), 182–83
Law on the Digitization of Out-of-Print Works, France (2012), 35, 369
Law on the Rights of Descendants, France (14 July 1866), 105, 144
law professors, 45, 299, 319, 327, 332–33; in Europe, 339–40, 346–47
Lea, Henry Charles, 71
League of Nations, 393
Leahy, Patrick, 252
leasing of digital works, 268
Le Chapelier, Isaac, 59, 62, 75, 205, 353
Leclerc, bookseller, 60
Lecocq, Charles, 151
lectures, 137–38, 208, 258
Leeds Music Corporation, 37
left-wing parties and copyright, 201, 306, 319, 342–44, 349–57, 373, 378, 391–92, 396, 398
legal profession. *See* law professors
Léger, Fernand, 40
Leggett, William, 321
Legrand, Marc-Antoine, 75
Lehman, Bruce, 280, 299
Lemerre, Alphonse, 148
Lepore, Jill, 388
Lessig, Lawrence, 23, 387, 475n313
Lessing, Gotthard, 375, 430n96

letters, 86, 127, 133
Leverkusen, West Germany, 34
Levi, Carlo, 375
Levi, Leone, 51
Levi, Primo, 375
Levine, Sherrie, 328
Lewis, C. S., 375
Lewis, Jerry, 237
Lewis, Wyndham, 169
Lherbette, Armand Jacques, 99
Liaisons dangereuses, Les (Vadim), 42
libel, 37, 166, 226
liberals, 306
libertarianism, US, 378
Librarian/Library of Congress, 219, 239, 285–86, 310, 362
librarians, 219, 231, 280, 318, 340
libraries, 97, 136, 252, 267, 285, 286, 292, 297, 305, 310–11, 312; budgets of, 311, 366; collective intelligence of, 329; digitizing, 361–63, 368; and e-books, 268; lending, 437n140; as publishers, 361; universal, 382
library deposit of works, 159, 258
Licensing Act, UK (1662), 66
Lieber, Francis, 133
Liechtenstein, 381
Lieder, 5, 158
Life of Johnson (Boswell), 38
Light That Failed, The (Kipling), 37
"Lili Marleen," 164
Linda, Solomon, 481n55
Linguet, Simon, 61, 96
Lion King (Disney), 275
Liquid Feedback, 342
Lisbon Agenda, EU, 302
Liszt, Franz, 41
literacy, 113, 117
literary property. *See* intellectual property
literature, US, 119–20
Little Mermaid statue, 6
Locke, John, 55–56, 66, 204, 399; and ideas of property, 66, 76, 146, 217, 384, 402
logic of networks, 295, 300, 360
London, 2, 39, 55, 118, 119
Longfellow, Henry Wadsworth, 231, 374
Louisiana, 401
Lowell, James Russell, 120, 374
lower middle classes and Nazis, 183–84
Lower Saxony, 338
Lucania, Italy, 375
Lucas, George, 237

Luftmenschen, 25
Luftwaffe, 40
Luther, Martin, 88
luxury brands, 302
Lyon, 55

Macaulay, Thomas Babington, 52, 110, 112, 114, 117, 125, 160, 162, 242, 245, 351, 357–58, 392, 396
MacCarthy, Patrick, 39
Macleod, Henry Dunning, 8
Macmillan, Alexander, 85
Mahler, Gustav, 36
Maillard, Georges, 144
Mainz, Germany, 47
Mallet, Louis, 111, 322
Malskat, Lothar, 270
Manet, Édouard, 41, 270
Mansfield, 1st Earl of, Lord Chief Justice, 91, 92
Mansfield, Katherine, 31
manufacturing clause, US copyright, 122, 160–61, 213–15, 219, 231
manuscripts, 55, 149, 221, 230
Manzoni, Alessandro, 35
Marinetti, Filippo, 169
Marino Faliero, Doge of Venice (Byron), 90
Marion, Simon, 56
market, and works, 44, 47, 52, 169, 211, 318, 407
Martin, David, 359
Marwitz, Bruno, 193
Marx, Karl, 320
Marxism/Marxists, 172, 201, 343
mash-ups, 305, 327
Masson. See *B. Gaudichot, dit Michel Masson, c. Gaudichot fils*
materialism, of modernity, 169, 174, 210
Mathews, Cornelius, 373
Matignon Agreements, 194
Matisse, Henri, 102
Mattel Corporation, 272
Matthew Effect, 360
Maugham, Robert, 133
Max Planck Institute for Intellectual Property and Competition Law, Munich, 346
Max und Moritz (Busch), 172
McGill, Meredith, 435n103
McGraw-Hill, 365
meaning of works, 270, 272
media, mass, 169–70, 194, 197, 201, 323, 344. See also content industries

medleys. See potpourris, musical
Mein Kampf (Hitler), 173
Méligny, Marthe de, 102
melody, 139, 184–85, 212
Memories of My Melancholy Whores (Garcia Marquez), 37
Menken, Alan, 476n326
Metallica, 377, 392
Metamorphoses (Ovid), 31
Metzger, Gustav, 34, 271
Mexico, 23, 242
MGM Studios v. Grokster, 269, 294
Miami, 2
Michael of Greece, Prince, 2, 25, 44
Mickey Mouse, 248, 302
microfilming, 214, 361
micropayments, 266
Microsoft Corporation, 478n1
Middleton, George, 187
Midwest, US, 116
military and copyright, 392
Mill, John Stuart, 402
Millar v. Taylor, 35, 63, 67, 85, 91
Millet, Jean-François, 255
Mills, E. C., 215
Ministry of Interior: France, 375; Germany, 178, 244
Ministry of Justice, Germany, 177, 179, 180, 182, 184, 187, 188, 189, 209, 223
Ministry of Popular Enlightenment and Propaganda, Germany, 178
Misérables, Les (Hugo), 6, 43, 243, 347
Mitchell, Margaret, 134
Mitterand, François, 222, 375
Mitterand, Frédéric, 501n160, 503n213
modernism, 168
modernist art, 171, 450n29
Molière, 46, 75
Molinari, Gustave de, 124
Mona Lisa, 32, 41, 179
Monde, Le, 332
Monet, Claude, 221, 249
monopolies, publishing, 62, 63, 65, 66, 69, 70, 73, 83, 110–11, 115; in France, 75
monopoly, copyright as, 136, 252, 330
Montaigne, Michel de, 270
Moore, William Harrison, 167
moral rights, 9, 10, 11, 15–16, 20, 28–40; as based on nature, 128; collectivist view of, 169, 190–91, 193; different approaches to, 145–46; in digital age, 314–16, 319; early use

of term, 100, 146, 157; in EU, 315, 347; as extending property rights, 146; and fascism, 164–65, 168–69, 197–98; as form of property, 33; in France, 83, 147, 370; in Germany, 124, 147, 156–57, 209–10; origins of, 103; perpetual, 37, 41, 127, 146, 174, 205–6; and postmodernism, 270–71, 273–74; as progressive, 47; and public interest, 51; in UK, 24, 200, 225–35, 241; in US, 200, 225–30, 235–41; in US states, 235–36; as waivable, 232

Morillot, André, 29, 105–6, 128, 147
Morrill, Justin, 114
Morse, Samuel, 120
mortality statistics, 69
Motion Picture Association, 231, 243, 335, 374
Motion Picture Producers and Distributors of America, 216, 232
Motown, 201, 230
movies. *See* film
Mozart, Wolfgang Amadeus, 4, 32, 46, 271
MP3, 323, 336
Müller, Heiner, 348
Müller, Wilhelm, 5
multimedia, 306
Munich, 34
murals. *See* frescos
Murdoch, Rupert, 296, 366
Muret, Marc Antoine de, 56
Musée du Luxembourg, 272
music, 127; adaptation of, 230; Baroque, 49; in film, 223; in Nazi Germany, 184–85; popular, 184, 212, 232, 469n194
musical performances, 139, 156, 158
music boxes, 141–44, 156
music industry, 293, 294, 295–96. *See also* content industry; music publishers
Music of Changes (Cage), 271
music publishers, 141–44
Music Publishers' Association, UK, 243
music scores, 128, 311
Musikalisches Würfelspiel (Mozart), 271
Mussolini, Benito, 163, 164, 165, 396

Naples, 124
Napoleon I, 245, 404
Napoleon III, 141, 246, 320
Napoleonic Code, 6, 83, 94, 105, 150, 194, 401, 404, 405; and property, 98, 100–101, 206, 260, 396
Napoleonic era, 96
Napster, 294

Narrenschiff, Das (Brant), 88
Nashville, 2, 201, 230, 278
National Assembly, France, 59, 195, 353, 357, 370
National Association of Broadcasters, 214
National Cable Television Association, 236
National Convention, France, 59, 255
National Film Preservation Act, 1988, US, 48, 239
National Liberals, Germany, 123, 125
National Library of Medicine, 298
National Literary Fund, France, 43
National Public Radio, 337
National Security Administration, 335
National Socialist Lawyers' Federation, 179–81, 188
natural rights, 10, 11, 16, 20, 23, 28, 45, 53, 56, 58, 75, 81, 95, 109, 127, 219–20; as basis of copyright, 63, 64, 65, 69, 72–73, 288; and fair use, 137; in France, 128, 204–5; in Germany, 76, 79, 128, 130, 197; as property, 398–99; and publishers, 53, 57; and slavery, 116; to works, 84, 94, 144, 146, 258, 259, 347, 381, 384; to works, argument reverses, 103, 205; to works in UK, 110–11; to works in US, 119
Nature (periodical), 331
Nazis, 18, 39, 42; aesthetics of, 170–71; and big business, 178, 459n226; and compulsory licensing, 143–44, 175–76, 181, 186, 191; and copyright duration, 125, 163, 183–84; and copyright reform, 183; and copyright tradition, 164; and moral rights, 170–77; party, 178; Party Congress of (1934), 171. *See also* fascism
Nazism. *See* fascism
Nelson, Ted, 377
neoconservatism, 289, 344
Neustetel, Leopold Joseph, 107, 322
New Deal, 176
New Republic (periodical), 33
New World (periodical), 118
New York, 44, 235, 401
New Yorker, 377
New York Public Library, 362
New York Times, 376
news reporting, 137–38, 156; in France, 208, 312–13; in Germany, 158, 313
newspapers, US, 115, 240, 295
Newsweek, 237
New Zealand, 166, 182
Nicaragua, 242

Nicolai, Friedrich, 80
Nietzsche, Friedrich, 38
Night of 4 August 1789, France, 75
Night of the Long Knives, Germany (1934), 178
Nike, 18
Nobel Prize, 328, 365, 485n127
No-Copyright Party, US, 341
Nolde, Emil, 170
noninfringing uses, 294
non-literal copying, 134
nonrivalrous property, 64, 265
Nord, Philip, 459n212
Norman Conquest, 399
North American Free Trade Agreement, 291, 301
Norway, 46, 169, 182, 194
Norwegian Academy of Music, 46
Nuit de sérail, La (Prince Michael of Greece), 2
Nuremberg Laws, Germany (1935), 215

Obama administration, 296, 487n162
Old Regime, France, 56, 59, 73–75, 255, 392, 396
Olivennes, Denis, 355
Olson, Theodore, 474n287, 476n332
Oman, Ralph, 278
"On the Illegality of Unauthorized Editions" (Kant), 77
One Flew Over the Cuckoo's Nest (Forman), 238
open access, 12, 46, 149, 319, 329, 391; in Germany, 124, 158, 197, 347
open access activists, 28, 264, 292, 296, 334–35, 388
open access debate: in France, 350–59, 370; in Germany, 358; start of in Europe, 339, 345–46
open access movement, 297–300, 334–36, 358
opera, 187, 228
Operation Payback, 335
originality, 28, 131, 371
orphan works, 300, 368, 369
Ottoman Empire, 112
Out of Africa (Pollack), 2
Ovid, 31
ownership, family, 102
Oxford University, 23, 68, 376; library of, 362
Ozawa, Seiji, 36

Paine, Thomas, 227, 402
painters, 75, 92, 108, 157, 320
paintings, 127, 128, 396
Palo Alto, 278
Pamela (Richardson), 38
paracopyright, 283
Pardessus, Jean-Marie, 149
Paris, 2, 38, 44, 87
Parlement of Paris, 56
Parley, Peter, 231
Parliament, UK, 66, 68, 60, 93, 110, 243, 321
parody, 138, 208, 299, 309, 327
Parsifal (Wagner), 42, 47, 174
passing off, 167
pastiche. See parody
patchwriting, 327
Patent Committee, US Senate, 231
patent law, Germany (1936), 181, 191–92, 196
Patent Law, US (1790), 113
patents, 8, 18, 19, 63, 69, 70, 86, 87, 99, 110, 132, 139, 276, 279; and developing nations, 274; in Germany, 163; in UK, 276; in US, 113, 379–80
paternity. See attribution
patronage, 54, 58, 318, 325, 407–08
Patterson, James, 271
Paul, Christian, 351, 354, 356
Paulus, Heinrich, 31
Peasant Revolt, England (1381), 89
pedophilia, 377
Peer Gynt suites (Grieg), 46
penal sanctions. See criminalizing infringement
Penn, William, 400
Pennsylvania, 8
penny press, 51, 323
Pension Reform, Germany (1957), 209
performance rights, 90, 127
performers, 30, 32, 40, 377, 389
performing arts, 32
periodicals, 93, 118, 156, 194, 199, 215, 217, 221, 234, 237; science, 296, 347, 366, 388
personal computers, 293
personal connection, author to work, 59–62, 100, 103
personal rights, 35, 37, 72, 77, 152, 176
personal rights to works, 84, 172; in Anglophone world, 226
personality, 8, 29; authorial, 36, 45
personality rights, 11, 20, 104, 107, 108–9, 128, 145, 259; under Nazis, 181

Peter Pan (Barrie), 23
Peters, Mary-Beth, 299
Peters, Richard, 71
petitions, on copyright, 110, 117, 121
Pfeiffer, Pauline, 38
Pfister, Laurent, 426n20
Pfizer, 236
pharmaceuticals, 18, 265, 274, 275, 276, 359, 380
Philadelphia, 116, 133
Philippines, 275
Philips Corporation, 276
phonographs, 141–44, 170, 184, 323
photocopiers/copying, 292, 293, 298
photographers, 237
photography, 84, 93, 127, 128, 132, 137, 156, 234, 323
Piaf, Edith, 247
Picasso, Pablo, 39, 270
Pinkerton's, 374
Piola Caselli, Eduardo, 166, 167, 168, 170, 190, 191, 193
PIPA, 296, 345, 358
piracy, 19, 76, 273–74, 275–76, 321; digital, 265; as growing economic problem, 236; as political issue, 331; in US, 83, 113–14, 321, 299
Pirate Bay, 332, 341, 392
pirate editions, 57, 79, 85, 88, 92, 107; in UK, 121; in US, 118, 123, 231
pirate parties, 12, 21, 51, 319, 340–45, 388
Pirate Party: Berlin, 341–44; Sweden, 328, 336, 341, 344–45, 392
pirates, commercial, 330, 331; ideologically motivated, 331–32, 336
Pittsburgh, 40
Place, Vanessa, 271
plagiarism, 78, 132, 272, 327, 328, 338
Plaisant, Marcel, 195
Planets, The (Holst), 41
plant varieties, 279, 302
Playboy, 237
player pianos, 141–44, 291
playwrights, 74, 75, 90
Plunderphonics, 327
Pluquet, François-André, 61, 63, 87
Pocahontas (Disney), 275
Poe, Edgar Allen, 231, 374
poet laureate, 89
poetry, 137, 158, 216, 267
poets, 5, 157, 212, 407
Poland, 36, 165, 169, 202, 242, 359
political culture, American, 71

Pollack, Sydney, 2, 49, 237
Ponta, Victor, 498n106
Pontedera, Italy, 2
Pope v. Curl, 86
Pope, Alexander, 86
Popular Front government, France, 25, 141, 169, 194, 204
populism and copyright, 49, 397
Porgy and Bess (Gershwin), 5, 39
pornography, 189, 377
Porsche, 164
portable property, 7
Portalis, Joseph-Marie, 87
Porter, Vincent, 469n200
portraits, 108, 148, 150, 157, 218, 234
Portugal, 23, 165, 169, 242, 247, 360
Posner, Richard, 338
postal system, US, 115, 240
posthumous rights, 167
posthumous works, 101, 180, 181, 211
postmodernism, 269–72, 323, 371, 389
postmortem authors' rights, 203
post-Romanticism, 273, 327, 328
potpourris, musical, 184–85
Pound, Ezra, 28, 169, 270
Praga, Marco, 42
pragmatism, 371
Prelude (Wordsworth), 255
Preminger, Otto, 5
Prenzlauer Berg, 344
preservation codes, 41
Preston, William, 118
Prince, 377
print runs, 117, 119
printing, invention of, 54
privacy rights, 108, 145, 165, 226, 227, 234, 381; digital, 335
private copying, 138, 139, 144, 208, 292; in digital age, 268–69, 309; in France, 351, 352
privileges, for inventions, 60
privileges, publishing, 20, 30, 53, 54, 55, 56, 62, 65, 69, 80, 104, 205; in France, 74, 97; in Germany, 76
Privy Council, 28, 140, 160
prizes, 325
propaganda, 186, 193
property: American views of, 71; capitalist, 101; taxes, 4
property, conventional, 3–4, 6, 7, 23, 53, 56, 58, 62–63, 68, 76, 393; compared to intellectual, 62, 107, 128, 152, 242, 253, 260, 282, 398;

property, conventional (*cont.*)
  contradictions of, 82–83, 95, 146; history of, 398–405
property, intangible, immaterial, or incorpo-real, 7–8, 18, 56, 85–88; in France, 152; in Germany, 107, 129; in UK, 128
property rights, 20, 28, 76, 129, 242; and moral rights, 146
Protect Intellectual Property Act. *See* PIPA
protectionism, 115, 118, 119–20, 160, 230
Proudhon, Pierre-Joseph, 101, 122, 125, 241, 332, 394, 396
Proust, Marcel, 246
Prussia, 36
Prussian Academy of Science, 124, 246
pseudonym, 31, 210
public access. *See* open access
public domain, 9, 10, 14–16, 21, 30, 34, 43, 44, 54, 57, 65, 72, 147; as communist concept, 124, 438n173; and compulsory licensing, 139; in France, 75, 122, 123; in Germany, 184; inevitable growth of, 390–91; in US, 162, 252; works removed from, 256
Public Domain Enhancement Acts, US, 259
public domain works, 216
public health, 274
public interest in works, 30, 50, 51, 71, 95, 111; under Clinton administration, 280
public schools, 162
Publication of Lectures Act, UK (1835), 258
publication right, 79
publicity, rights of, 227
publishers: authorized, 57; dissertation, Germany, 366–67; European, 363, 365–66, 388; in France, 311, 321, 368, 392; in Germany, 125, 184, 247, 274, 310; Kant's view of, 77; pirate, 54, 62, 110, 264, 297; provincial, 55, 321; scientific, 296; in Scotland, 55; in Switzer-land, 55; in UK, 51, 85, 110, 111, 117, 119, 140, 233, 274, 323, 392; in US, 115–18, 136, 238, 295, 322, 390; in US South, 117. *See also* booksellers
Pucelle d'Orleans, La (Voltaire), 36
Punch, 116
Putnam, George Haven, 119, 253
Putnam, George Palmer, 118, 119

Qing Dynasty, 321
quotation, 138

Rabaté, Jean-Michel, 311
Rabelais, François, 46

racial community and copyright, under Nazis, 173–75 177, 179, 181, 183, 184, 190, 193
Racine, Jean, 36, 75, 97, 255, 270
radio, 169, 170, 172, 175, 182, 184, 186, 201, 215, 252, 277, 323
railway, 8
Ralite, Jack, 364
rap music, 327
rapprochement between authors' rights and copyright, 224, 260, 303
ratchet effect and copyright, 156
Ray, Nicholas, 40
Raynal, Guillaume Thomas, 227
Ready-mades, 34, 271
real estate, 4, 7, 58, 146, 393, 399–401; expropri-ation of, 7, 402
Rebel without a Cause (Ray), 40
reception theory, 324
recording industry, 21, 379, 391, 408
Recording Industry Association of America, 335, 355
Recreation of First Public Demonstration of Auto-Destructive Art (Metzger), 34
Redmond, Washington, 278
Reds (Beatty), 48
Reichskulturkammer, 170, 181, 209
Reichsmusikkammer, 174, 185
Reichsparsifalkommissar, 42
Reichstag, German, 118, 156, 157, 279
Reinbothe, Jörg, 306
remix culture, 328
remixology, 327
Renaissance, 130, 327
Renault, editor, 149
Renoir, Pierre-Auguste, 270
Renouard, Augustin-Charles, 122, 133, 147
rental rights, 301; to musical scores, 267, 269
rent regulation, 6, 33
repenting. *See* withdrawal
reprint publishers. *See* publishers, US; pub-lishers, pirate
reprinting of books, 111, 113, 321
reproduction right, art, 92, 128, 157
republication of books, 80
repurchase of artworks, 33
reputation, 32, 33, 73, 104, 105, 108, 118, 145, 149–50, 167, 203, 234, 237; in digital age, 272; and Nazis, 176, 180
resale right. See *droit de suite*
reservation of rights, 146
respect. *See* integrity
restoration of artwork, 32

reverse engineering, 286, 292
Richardson, Samuel, 38
Richter, Hans, 47
"Ride of the Valkyries" (Wagner), 39
Riefenstahl, Leni, 186
Rigamonti, Cyrill P., 469n197
right of first publication, 227, 228
right of respect. *See* integrity right
rights, human, 6, 17
rights owners, 15
right to be forgotten, 381
right-wing parties and copyright, 201, 349, 353–54, 378, 396
Rimbaud, Arthur, 38, 207
Rimbaud, Isabelle, 38
Rite of Spring (Stravinsky), 37
RKO Pictures, 26
Roberts, George, 131
Robinson, James, 134
Rodgers, Richard, 255; and Hammerstein, 41
Rogers, Ginger, 237
Romains, Jules, 441n64
Romania, 165, 338
Roman law, 56, 76, 77, 85, 107, 172, 193; Nazi view of, 176, 453n77; and property, 399–400, 403–4
Romantic artists, 8, 163, 179, 199, 237, 314, 326, 328, 377; and authorship, 37, 370
Romanticism, 15, 49, 94, 101, 103, 130–32, 168, 201; in digital era, 269–70, 271
Roman traditions, 169
Rome, 56, 164, 165, 168
Roosevelt, Franklin D., 176, 214
Root, Jesse, 401
Rostropovich, Mstislav, 40
Rothschild family, 124
Rouen, 133
Royal Copyright Commission, UK (1878), 5, 36, 84, 93, 111–12, 226, 322; and compulsory licensing, 140
Royal Copyright Commission, UK (1909), 140, 226, 245, 253
royalties, 27, 51, 111, 126, 138, 139, 143, 160, 195, 246, 325; in digital age, 266, 307; for fair use, 212, 311; paid in US, 113, 117–18
Ruffini, Francesco, 193
Running Man, The (Schwarzenegger), 135
Ruscha, Ed, 240
Ruskin, John, 51
Russia, 37, 112
Ruth Hall (Fern), 229

Sachs, Nelly, 36, 421n117
Sade, Marquis de, 38
Safe Harbor Agreement (2000), 508n320
Safe harbor provisions, DMCA, 286–87, 294, 308
Sainte-Beuve, Charles Augustin, 31
Saint-Exupéry, Antoine de, 246
sales right, 79
Salinger, J. D., 220
Salvandy, Narcisse-Achille de, 324
Salzburg, Austria, 2
sampling, 271, 327
Sand, George, 31
Sarkozy, Nicolas, 303, 337, 338, 355, 370
satellite broadcasts, 307
Savigny, Friedrich, 76, 423n150
Saxo Grammaticus, 270
Sayers, Dorothy, 375
Scandinavian nations, and copyright, 155, 203, 302, 314, 326, 393
scanning, 307
Scarlatti, Domenico, 48
Schäffle, Albert, 123
Schavan, Annette, 338
Schelling, Friedrich, 31, 270
Schiller, Friedrich, 118, 123, 243, 246
Schlager, 184
Schmitt, Pál, 498n106
Schoenberg, Randol, 477n339
Schöne Müllerin, Die (Müller), 5
school anthologies, 137
Schopenhauer, Arthur, 184
Schubert, Franz, 5, 185
Schwarzenegger, Arnold, 135
schweigsame Frau, Die (Strauss), 174
Scientology, 220
Scott, Walter, 37, 89, 111, 118, 119, 321
scriptwriters, 222, 223
sculpture, 127, 396
Sculpture Act, UK (1798), 93, 217
search engines, 360
Second Circuit Court of Appeals, 286
Second Republic, France, 98
Second Treatise on Government (Locke), 55, 57
Second World War, 35, 125, 145, 200, 236, 370
Sédaine, Michel-Jean, 255
Seine Tribunal, 151
semiconductor chip, 18
Senate: France, 353, 356, 370; US, 120, 255
Seneca, 56
servitudes, 146

Shakespeare, William, 37, 46, 85, 270, 275
Shaw, George Bernard, 27, 143
sheet music, 141, 291, 320, 379, 409
Sherman, Roger, 119
Shields, David, 328
Shostakovich, Dimitri, 1, 40
Siku Quanshu, 321
Silicon Valley, 12, 230, 264, 287, 291–97, 317, 336, 344, 379, 394; business model in, 295; economic importance of, 293
Siméon, Joseph-Balthazar, 97
Simmons, Gene, 377
Simon, Jules, 438n173
Simon, Paul, 252
Singapore, 236, 277
'68 generation, 343–44
slavery, 25, 45, 116–17, 402, 436n117
Smith, Adam, 332, 402, 477n340
Smith, David, 33
Smith, Logan Pearsall, 162, 387
Smith, Sydney, 231
Smithee, Allen, 32
Smythe, Sydney, Lord Chief Baron, 92
Snow White (Disney), 274
Snow, Michael, 40
Social Democratic Party, Germany, 34, 397
socialism and intellectual property, 64
socialist nations, 325
socialists, 18, 76, 98, 222, 306; in France, 350, 373, 397. *See also* left-wing parties
socially bound law: Nazi idea of 175, 193, 195, 197, 246; in West Germany, 208–9, 213
social movements, 340
social networks, 297
social utility, 11
social values, embodied in copyright, 46
Société des Gens de Lettres, 42–43
society as the author, 42
software, 18, 28, 137, 200, 211, 233–34, 236, 249; patented, 276; pirated, 275; TRIPs, 279; rental right to, 268, 279
software industry: France, 224; US, 297
Song of Norway (Wright and Forrest), 46
Sonny Bono Copyright Extension Act, US (1998), 248, 252, 254, 259, 298, 341
Sony Corporation, 269, 292, 294
SOPA, 296, 345, 358
Sophocles, 41
Sorrows of Young Werther, The (Goethe), 36, 377
sound recordings, 48, 128, 132, 139, 141–44,

156, 215, 224, 320, 391, 409; rental of, 268, 279
Sousa, John Philip, 142, 143, 184, 327, 409
South, US, 116–17, 135, 161
Southern District Court, NY, 365, 367
Southey, Robert, 89
South Korea, 236, 276, 277
Soviets, 168, 171, 172, 190, 194, 196
SPADEM, 312
Spain, 202, 247, 360
Spann, Othmar, 324
Spears, Britney, 331
specific performance, 148
Spectator, 63
Spencer, Herbert, 118
Spielberg, Steven, 49, 237
Spitzweg, Carl, 179
spouses, 35
Springer, 296, 366
St. Petersburg, 47
Stagma, 186
Star Wars (Lucas), 237
state: and moral rights, 207, 211; and works, 35, 41–42, 165, 181, 191, 193, 195
state copyright acts, US, 65, 69
State Department, US, 232
Stationers' Company, London, 55, 66, 111, 284
Statue of Liberty, 81
statute, as basis for rights, 20, 53–54, 56, 62, 63, 64, 65, 68, 70–72, 81, 95, 220, 258; in France, 74, 98
Statute of Anne, 1710, 22, 65, 66, 67, 68, 69, 70, 88, 89, 91, 92, 132, 244, 258, 284; and public domain, 65, 75; and translations, 133
statutory copyright, 65
statutory damages, 330
statutory licensing. *See* compulsory licensing
Steamboat Round the Bend (Ford), 226
Steinmeier, Frank-Walter, 498n106
stenographers, 321
Stevens, Wallace, 374
Stewart, Jimmy, 237
Stichting Bescherming Rechten Entertainment Industrie Nederland, 335
Stieglitz, Alfred, 34
Stockholm, 36
Stop Online Piracy Act. *See* SOPA
Story, Joseph, 133, 371
Stowe, Harriet Beecher, 121, 132, 134
Strasbourg effect, 381
Strauss, Johann, 46